The Epistles of Clement
Works by and Attributed to Clement of Rome
This Edition Edited by Anthony Uyl

Woodstock, Ontario, 2017

The Epistles of Clement
Works by and Attributed to Clement of Rome (?-99)
Originally Edited by Philip Schaff (1819-1893)
This Edition Edited by Anthony Uyl
Originally Printed in: Ante-Nicene Fathers I & VIII: Originally Printed in 1885

The text of The Epistles of Clement is all in the Public Domain. This edition is published by Devoted Publishing a division of 2165467 Ontario Inc.

**What kind of philosophies do you have?
Let us know!**

Contact us at: devotedpub@hotmail.com
Visit our shop on Facebook: @DevotedPublishing

Published in Woodstock, Ontario, Canada 2017

For bulk educational rates, please contact us at the above email address.

ISBN: 978-1-77356-031-1

Table of Contents

Introductory Note to the First Epistle of Clement to the Corinthians [a.d. 30-100.] 34

The First Epistle of Clement to the Corinthians [1] 36

    Chapter I - The salutation. Praise of the Corinthians before the breaking forth of schism among them 36

    Chapter II - Praise of the Corinthians continued 36

    Chapter III - The sad state of the Corinthian church after sedition arose in it from envy and emulation 36

    Chapter IV - Many evils have already flowed from this source in ancient times 37

    Chapter V - No less evils have arisen from the same source in the most recent times. The martyrdom of Peter and Paul 37

    Chapter VI - Continuation. Several other martyrs 37

    Chapter VII - An exhortation to repentance 38

    Chapter VIII - Continuation respecting repentance 38

    Chapter IX - Examples of the saints 38

    Chapter X - Continuation of the above 38

    Chapter XI - Continuation. Lot 39

    Chapter XII - The rewards of faith and hospitality. Rahab 39

    Chapter XIII - An exhortation to humility 39

    Chapter XIV - We should obey God rather than the authors of sedition 39

    Chapter XV - We must adhere to those who cultivate peace, not to those who merely pretend to do so 40

    Chapter XVI - Christ as an example of humility 40

    Chapter XVII - The saints as examples of humility 40

    Chapter XVIII - David as an example of humility 41

    Chapter XIX - Imitating these examples, let us seek after peace 41

    Chapter XX - The peace and harmony of the universe 41

    Chapter XXI - Let us obey God, and not the authors of sedition 42

    Chapter XXII - These exhortations are confirmed by the Christian faith, which proclaims the misery of sinful conduct 42

    Chapter XXIII - Be humble, and believe that Christ will come again 42

    Chapter XXIV - God continually shows us in nature that there will be a resurrection 43

    Chapter XXV - The phoenix an emblem of our resurrection 43

    Chapter XXVI - We shall rise again, then, as the Scripture also testifies 43

    Chapter XXVII - In the hope of the resurrection, let us cleave to the omnipotent and omniscient God 43

    Chapter XXVIII - God sees all things: therefore let us avoid transgression 44

    Chapter XXIX - Let us also draw near to God in purity of heart 44

    Chapter XXX - Let us do those things that please God, and flee from those He hates, that we may be blessed 44

    Chapter XXXI - Let us see by what means we may obtain the divine blessing 44

    Chapter XXXII - We are justified not by our own works, but by faith 45

    Chapter XXXIII - But let us not give up the practice of good works and love. God Himself is an example to us of good works 45

Chapter XXXIV - Great is the reward of good works with God. Joined together in harmony, let us implore that reward from Him 45

Chapter XXXV - Immense is this reward. How shall we obtain it? 46

Chapter XXXVI - All blessings are given to us through Christ 46

Chapter XXXVII - Christ is our leader, and we His soldiers 46

Chapter XXXVIII - Let the members of the Church submit themselves, and no one exalt himself above another 47

Chapter XXXIX - There is no reason for self-conceit 47

Chapter XL - Let us preserve in the Church the order appointed by God 47

Chapter XLI - Continuation of the same subject 47

Chapter XLII - The order of ministers in the Church 48

Chapter XLIII - Moses of old stilled the contention which arose concerning the priestly dignity 48

Chapter XLIV - The ordinances of the apostles, that there might be no contention respecting the priestly office 48

Chapter XLV - It is the part of the wicked to vex the righteous 49

Chapter XLVI - Let us cleave to the righteous: your strife is pernicious 49

Chapter XLVII - Your recent discord is worse than the former which took place in the times of Paul 49

Chapter XLVIII - Let us return to the practice of brotherly love 50

Chapter XLIX - The praise of love 50

Chapter L - Let us pray to be thought worthy of love 50

Chapter LI - Let the partakers in strife acknowledge their sins 50

Chapter LII - Such a confession is pleasing to God 51

Chapter LIII - The love of Moses towards his people 51

Chapter LIV - He who is full of love will incur every loss, that peace may be restored to the Church. 51

Chapter LV - Examples of such love 51

Chapter LVI - Let us admonish and correct one another 52

Chapter LVII - Let the authors of sedition submit themselves 52

Chapter LVIII - Blessings sought for all that call upon God 52

Chapter LIX - The Corinthians are exhorted speedily to send back word that peace has been restored. The benediction 53

    Footnotes: 53

Two Epistles Concerning Virginity 59

  Introductory Notice to Two Epistles Concerning Virginity 59

    Footnotes: 60

The First Epistle of the Blessed Clement, the Disciple of Peter the Apostle 61

  Chapter I - The Salutation 61

  Chapter II - For True Virginity Perfect Virtue is Necessary 61

  Chapter III - True Virgins Prove Themselves Such by Self-Denial, as Does the True Believer by Good Works 61

  Chapter IV - Continuation of the Remarks on Self-Denial; Object and Reward of True Virgins 62

Chapter V - The Irksomeness and the Enemies of Virginity..62

Chapter VI - Divinity of Virginity...63

Chapter VII - The True Virgin..63

Chapter VIII - Virgins, by the Laying Aside of All Carnal Affection, are Imitators of God...............63

Chapter IX - Continuation of the Subject of Mortification; Dignity of Persons Consecrated to God..64

Chapter X - Denunciation of Dangerous and Scandalous Association with Maidens.......................64

Chapter XI - Perniciousness of Idleness; Warning Against the Empty Longing to Be Teachers; Advice About Teaching and the Use of Divine Gifts 65

Chapter XII - Rules for Visits, Exorcisms, and How People are to Assist the Sick, and to Walk in All Things Without Offence. 65

Chapter XIII - What Priests Should Be and Should Not Be..66

Footnotes: 67

The Second Epistle of the Same Clement..71

Chapter I - He Describes the Circumspectness of His Intercourse with the Other Sex, and Tells How in His Journeys He Acts at Places Where There are Brethren Only..71

Chapter II - His Behaviour in Places Where There Were Christians of Both Sexes 71

Chapter III - Rules for the Conduct of Celibate Brethren in Places Where There are Only Married Christians 72

Chapter IV - Conduct of the Holy Man Where There are Women Only..72

Chapter V - Where There is Only One Woman, the Father Does Not Make a Stay; How Carefully Stumbling-Blocks Must Be Avoided 72

Chapter VI - How Christians Should Behave Themselves Among Heathens 73

Chapter VII - Uses of Considering Admonitory Examples, as Well as Instructive Patterns 74

Chapter VIII - Joseph and Potiphar's Wife; Of What Kind Love to Females Ought to Be 74

Chapter IX - Samson's Admonitory Fall...74

Chapter X - David's Sin, So Admonitory to Us Weak Men..74

Chapter XI - Admonitory History of the Incestuous Children of David 75

Chapter XII - Solomon's Infatuation Through Women...75

Chapter XIII - The History of Susanna Teaches Circumspection with the Eyes and in Society 75

Chapter XIV - Examples of Circumspect Behaviour from the Old Testament 76

Chapter XV - The Example of Jesus; How We May Allow Ourselves to Be Served by Women 76

Chapter XVI - Exhortation to Union and to Obedience; Conclusion...77

Footnotes: 77

Pseudo-Clementine Literature 78

Introductory Notice to the Pseudo-Clementine Literature 79

Footnotes: 80

Recognitions of Clement 81

Introductory Notice to The Recognitions of Clement 81

Footnotes: 82

Rufinus, Presbyter of Aquileia; His Preface to Clement's Book of Recognitions 83

Footnotes: 84

Book I...85

The Epistles of Clement

Chapter I - Clement's Early History; Doubts ... 85

Chapter II - His Distress ... 85

Chapter III - His Dissatisfaction with the Schools of the Philosophers ... 85

Chapter IV - His Increasing Disquiet ... 86

Chapter V - His Design to Test the Immortality of the Soul ... 86

Chapter VI - Hears of Christ ... 86

Chapter VII - Arrival of Barnabas at Rome ... 87

Chapter VIII - His Preaching ... 87

Chapter IX - Clement's Interposition on Behalf of Barnabas ... 88

Chapter X - Intercourse with Barnabas ... 88

Chapter XI - Departure of Barnabas ... 88

Chapter XII - Clement's Arrival at Caesarea, and Introduction to Peter ... 89

Chapter XIII - His Cordial Reception by Peter ... 89

Chapter XIV - His Account of Himself ... 89

Chapter XV - Peter's First Instruction ... 90

Chapter XVI - Instruction Continued: the True Prophet ... 90

Chapter XVII - Peter Requests Him to Be His Attendant ... 90

Chapter XVIII - His Profiting by Peter's Instruction ... 91

Chapter XIX - Peter's Satisfaction ... 91

Chapter XX - Postponement of Discussion with Simon Magus ... 91

Chapter XXI - Advantage of the Delay ... 92

Chapter XXII - Repetition of Instructions ... 92

Chapter XXIII - Repetition Continued ... 93

Chapter XXIV - Repetition Continued ... 93

Chapter XXV - Repetition Continued ... 93

Chapter XXVI - Friendship of God; How Secured ... 94

Chapter XXVII - Account of the Creation ... 94

Chapter XXVIII - Account of the Creation Continued ... 95

Chapter XXIX - The Giants: the Flood ... 95

Chapter XXX - Noah's Sons ... 95

Chapter XXXI - World After the Flood ... 96

Chapter XXXII - Abraham ... 96

Chapter XXXIII - Abraham: His Posterity ... 96

Chapter XXXIV - The Israelites in Egypt ... 96

Chapter XXXV - The Exodus ... 97

Chapter XXXVI - Allowance of Sacrifice for a Time ... 97

Chapter XXXVII - The Holy Place ... 97

Chapter XXXVIII - Sins of the Israelites ... 98

Chapter XXXIX - Baptism Instituted in Place of Sacrifices ... 98

Chapter XL - Advent of the True Prophet ... 98

Chapter XLI - Rejection of the True Prophet ... 98

Chapter XLII - Call of the Gentiles 99

Chapter XLIII - Success of the Gospel 99

Chapter XLIV - Challenge by Caiaphas 99

Chapter XLV - The True Prophet: Why Called the Christ 100

Chapter XLVI - Anointing 100

Chapter XLVII - Adam Anointed a Prophet 100

Chapter XLVIII - The True Prophet, a Priest 101

Chapter XLIX - Two Comings of Christ 101

Chapter L - His Rejection by the Jews 101

Chapter LI - The Only Saviour 101

Chapter LII - The Saints Before Christ's Coming 102

Chapter LIII - Animosity of the Jews 102

Chapter LIV - Jewish Sects 102

Chapter LV - Public Discussion 103

Chapter LVI - Sadducees Refuted 103

Chapter LVII - Samaritan Refuted 103

Chapter LVIII - Scribes Refuted 104

Chapter LIX - Pharisees Refuted 104

Chapter LX - Disciples of John Refuted 104

Chapter LXI - Caiaphas Answered 105

Chapter LXII - Foolishness of Preaching 105

Chapter LXIII - Appeal to the Jews 105

Chapter LXIV - Temple to Be Destroyed 105

Chapter LXV - Tumult Stilled by Gamaliel 106

Chapter LXVI - Discussion Resumed 106

Chapter LXVII - Speech of Gamaliel 106

Chapter LXVIII - The Rule of Faith 107

Chapter LXIX - Two Comings of Christ 107

Chapter LXX - Tumult Raised by Saul 107

Chapter LXXI - Flight to Jericho 108

Chapter LXXII - Peter Sent to Caesarea 108

Chapter LXXIII - Welcomed by Zacchaeus 108

Chapter LXXIV - Simon Magus Challenges Peter 108

   Footnotes: 109

Book II 112

   Chapter I - Power of Habit 112

   Chapter II - Curtailment of Sleep 112

   Chapter III - Need of Caution 113

   Chapter IV - Prudence in Dealing with Opponents 113

   Chapter V - Simon Magus, a Formidable Antagonist 113

   Chapter VI - Simon Magus: His Wickedness 113

- Chapter VII - Simon Magus: His History 114
- Chapter VIII - Simon Magus: His History 114
- Chapter IX - Simon Magus: His Profession 114
- Chapter X - Simon Magus: His Deception 115
- Chapter XI - Simon Magus, at the Head of the Sect of Dositheus 115
- Chapter XII - Simon Magus and Luna 115
- Chapter XIII - Simon Magus: Secret of His Magic 116
- Chapter XIV - Simon Magus, Professes to Be God 116
- Chapter XV - Simon Magus, Professed to Have Made a Boy of Air 117
- Chapter XVI - Simon Magus: Hopelessness of His Case 117
- Chapter XVII - Men Enemies to God 117
- Chapter XVIII - Responsibility of Men 118
- Chapter XIX - Disputation Begun 118
- Chapter XX - The Kingdom of God and His Righteousness 119
- Chapter XXI - Righteousness the Way to the Kingdom 119
- Chapter XXII - Righteousness; What It is 119
- Chapter XXIII - Simon Refuses Peace 120
- Chapter XXIV - Peter's Explanation 120
- Chapter XXV - Principles on Which the Discussion Should Be Conducted ... 120
- Chapter XXVI - Simon's Interruption 121
- Chapter XXVII - Questions and Answers 121
- Chapter XXVIII - Consistency of Christ's Teaching 121
- Chapter XXIX - Peace and Strife 122
- Chapter XXX - Peace to the Sons of Peace 122
- Chapter XXXI - Peace and War 122
- Chapter XXXII - Simon's Challenge 123
- Chapter XXXIII - Authority 123
- Chapter XXXIV - Order of Proof 123
- Chapter XXXV - How Error Cannot Stand with Truth 124
- Chapter XXXVI - Altercation 124
- Chapter XXXVII - Simon's Subtlety 124
- Chapter XXXVIII - Simon's Creed 125
- Chapter XXXIX - Argument for Polytheism 125
- Chapter XL - Peter's Answer 126
- Chapter XLI - The Answer, Continued 126
- Chapter XLII - Guardian Angels 126
- Chapter XLIII - No God But Jehovah 127
- Chapter XLIV - The Serpent, the Author of Polytheism 127
- Chapter XLV - Polytheism Inexcusable 127
- Chapter XLVI - Christ Acknowledged the God of the Jews 128
- Chapter XLVII - Simon's Cavil 128

Chapter XLVIII - Peter's Answer 128

Chapter XLIX - The Supreme Light 128

Chapter L - Simon's Presumption 129

Chapter LI - The Sixth Sense 129

Chapter LII - Reductio Ad Absurdu 129

Chapter LIII - Simon's Blasphemy 130

Chapter LIV - How Simon Learned from the Law What the Law Does Not Teach 130

Chapter LV - Simon's Objections Turned Against Himself 131

Chapter LVI - No God Above the Creator 131

Chapter LVII - Simon's Inconsistency 131

Chapter LVIII - Simon's God Unjust 132

Chapter LIX - The Creator Our Father 132

Chapter LX - The Creator the Supreme God 133

Chapter LXI - Imagination 133

Chapter LXII - Peter's Experience of Imagination 133

Chapter LXIII - Peter's Reverie 134

Chapter LXIV - Andrew's Rebuke 134

Chapter LXV - Fallacy of Imagination 134

Chapter LXVI - Existence and Conception 135

Chapter LXVII - The Law Teaches of Immensity 135

Chapter LXVIII - The Visible and the Invisible Heaven 135

Chapter LXIX - Faith and Reason 136

Chapter LXX - Adjournment 136

Chapter LXXI - Separation from the Unclean 136

Chapter LXXII - The Remedy 136

    Footnotes; 137

Book III [1] 140

Chapter I - Pearls Before Swine 140

Chapter XII [3] - Second Day's Discussion 140

Chapter XIII - Simon a Seducer 140

Chapter XIV - Simon Claims the Fulfilment of Peter's Promise 141

Chapter XV - Simon's Arrogance 141

Chapter XVI - Existence of Evil 142

Chapter XVII - Not Admitted by All 142

Chapter XVIII - Manner of Conducting the Discussion 142

Chapter XIX - Desire of Instruction 143

Chapter XX - Common Principles 143

Chapter XXI - Freedom of the Will 143

Chapter XXII - Responsibility 144

Chapter XXIII - Origin of Evil 144

Chapter XXIV - God the Author of Good, Not of Evil 145

Chapter XXV - "Who Hath Resisted His Will?" ... 145

Chapter XXVI - No Goodness Without Liberty ... 145

Chapter XXVII - The Visible Heaven ... 146

Chapter XXVIII - Why to Be Dissolved ... 146

Chapter XXIX - Corruptible and Temporary Things Made by the Incorruptible and Eternal ... 146

Chapter XXXI - Diligence in Study ... 147

Chapter XXXII - Peter's Private Instruction ... 147

Chapter XXXIII - Learners and Cavillers ... 148

Chapter XXXIV - Against Order is Against Reason ... 148

Chapter XXXV - Learning Before Teaching ... 148

Chapter XXXVI - Self-Evidence of the Truth ... 149

Chapter XXXVII - God Righteous as Well as Good ... 149

Chapter XXXVIII - God's Justice Shown at the Day of Judgment ... 150

Chapter XXXIX - Immortality of the Soul ... 150

Chapter XL - Proved by the Success of the Wicked in This Life ... 150

Chapter XLI - Cavils of Simon ... 150

Chapter XLII - "Full of All Subtlety and All Mischief." ... 151

Chapter XLIII - Simon's Subterfuges ... 152

Chapter XLIV - Sight or Hearing? ... 152

Chapter XLV - A Home-Thrust ... 152

Chapter XLVI - Simon's Rage ... 153

Chapter XLVII - Simon's Vaunt ... 153

Chapter XLVIII - Attempts to Create a Disturbance ... 153

Chapter XLIX - Simon's Retreat ... 154

Chapter L - Peter's Benediction ... 154

Chapter LI - Peter's Accessibility ... 154

Chapter LII - False Signs and Miracles ... 155

Chapter LIII - Self-Love the Foundation of Goodness ... 155

Chapter LIV - God to Be Supremely Loved ... 155

Chapter LV - Ten Commandments Corresponding to the Plagues of Egypt ... 156

Chapter LVI - Simon Resisted Peter, as the Magicians Moses ... 156

Chapter LVII - Miracles of the Magicians ... 156

Chapter LVIII - Truth Veiled with Love ... 157

Chapter LIX - Good and Evil in Pairs ... 157

Chapter LX - Uselessness of Pretended Miracles ... 157

Chapter LXI - Ten Pairs ... 158

Chapter LXII - The Christian Life ... 158

Chapter LXIII - A Deserter from Simon's Camp ... 158

Chapter LXIV - Declaration of Simon's Wickedness ... 159

Chapter LXV - Peter Resolves to Follow Simon ... 159

Chapter LXVI - Zacchaeus Made Bishop of Caesarea; Presbyters and Deacons Ordained ... 160

Chapter LXVII - Invitation to Baptism..160

Chapter LXVIII - Twelve Sent Before Him...160

Chapter LXIX - Arrangements Approved by All the Brethren..............................161

Chapter LXX - Departure of the Twelve..161

Chapter LXXI - Peter Prepares the Caesareans for His Departure.......................161

Chapter LXXII - More Than Ten Thousand Baptized...162

Chapter LXXIII - Tidings of Simon...162

Chapter LXXIV - Farewell to Caesarea...162

Chapter LXXV - Contents of Clement's Despatches to James..............................162

    Footnotes:..163

Book IV...165

    Chapter I - Halt at Dora..165

    Chapter II - Reception in the House of Maro..165

    Chapter III - Simon's Flight..165

    Chapter IV - The Harvest Plenteous..166

    Chapter V - Moses and Christ..166

    Chapter VI - A Congregation...166

    Chapter VII - The Sick Healed...167

    Chapter VIII - Providence Vindicated...167

    Chapter IX - State of Innocence a State of Enjoyment...................................167

    Chapter X - Sin the Cause of Suffering..168

    Chapter XI - Suffering Salutary..168

    Chapter XII - Translation of Enoch..168

    Chapter XIII - Origin of Idolatry..168

    Chapter XIV - God Both Good and Righteous..169

    Chapter XV - How Demons Get Power Over Men..169

    Chapter XVI - Why They Wish to Possess Men..169

    Chapter XVII - The Gospel Gives Power Over Demons.................................169

    Chapter XVIII - This Power in Proportion to Faith...170

    Chapter XIX - Demons Incite to Idolatry...170

    Chapter XX - Folly of Idolatry..170

    Chapter XXI - Heathen Oracles..170

    Chapter XXII - Why They Sometimes Come True..171

    Chapter XXIII - Evil Not in Substance...171

    Chapter XXIV - Why God Permits Evil...171

    Chapter XXV - Evil Beings Turned to Good Account....................................172

    Chapter XXVI - Evil Angels Seducers...172

    Chapter XXVII - Ham the First Magician...172

    Chapter XXVIII - Tower of Babel..172

    Chapter XXIX - Fire-Worship of the Persians...173

    Chapter XXX - Hero-Worship..173

Chapter XXXI - Idolatry Led to All Immorality 173

Chapter XXXII - Invitation 174

Chapter XXXIII - The Weakest Christian More Powerful Than the Strongest Demon 174

Chapter XXXIV - Temptation of Christ 174

Chapter XXXV - False Apostles 175

Chapter XXXVI - The Garments Unspotted 175

Chapter XXXVII - The Congregation Dismissed 175

    Footnotes: 175

Book V 178

Chapter I - Peter's Salutation 178

Chapter II - Suffering the Effect of Sin 178

Chapter III - Faith and Unbelief 178

Chapter IV - Ignorance the Mother of Evils 178

Chapter V - Advantages of Knowledge 179

Chapter VI - Free-Will 179

Chapter VII - Responsibility of Knowledge 179

Chapter VIII - Desires of the Flesh to Be Subdued 180

Chapter IX - The Two Kingdoms 180

Chapter X - Jesus the True Prophet 180

Chapter XI - The Expectation of the Gentiles 180

Chapter XII - Call of the Gentiles 181

Chapter XIII - Invitation of the Gentiles 181

Chapter XIV - Idols Unprofitable 181

Chapter XV - Folly of Idolatry 182

Chapter XVI - God Alone a Fit Object of Worship 182

Chapter XVII - Suggestions of the Old Serpent 182

Chapter XVIII - His First Suggestion 183

Chapter XIX - His Second Suggestion 183

Chapter XX - Egyptian Idolatry 184

Chapter XXI - Egyptian Idolatry More Reasonable Than Others 184

Chapter XXII - Second Suggestion Continued 184

Chapter XXIII - Third Suggestion 185

Chapter XXIV - Fourth Suggestion 185

Chapter XXV - Fifth Suggestion 185

Chapter XXVI - Sixth Suggestion 186

Chapter XXVII - Creatures Take Vengeance on Sinners 186

Chapter XXVIII - Eternity of Punishments 187

Chapter XXIX - God's Care of Human Things 187

Chapter XXX - Religion of Fathers to Be Abandoned 187

Chapter XXXI - Paganism, Its Enormities 188

Chapter XXXII - True Religion Calls to Sobriety and Modesty 188

Chapter XXXIII - Origin of Impiety 188
Chapter XXXIV - Who are Worshippers of God? 189
Chapter XXXV - Judgment to Come 189
Chapter XXXVI - Conclusion of Discourse 189
    Footnotes: 190

Book VI 191
    Chapter I - Diligence in Study 191
    Chapter II - Much to Be Done in a Little Time 191
    Chapter III - Righteous Anger 191
    Chapter IV - Not Peace, But a Sword 192
    Chapter V - How the Fight Begins 192
    Chapter VI - God to Be Loved More Than Parents 192
    Chapter VII - The Earth Made for Men 193
    Chapter VIII - Necessity of Baptism 193
    Chapter IX - Use of Baptism 193
    Chapter X - Necessity of Good Works 194
    Chapter XI - Inward and Outward Cleansing 194
    Chapter XII - Importance of Chastity 194
    Chapter XIII - Superiority of Christian Morality 195
    Chapter XIV - Knowledge Enhances Responsibility 195
    Chapter XV - Bishops, Presbyters, Deacons, and Widows Ordained at Tripolis 195
    Footnotes: 196

Book VII 197
    Chapter I - Journey from Tripolis 197
    Chapter II - Disciples Divided into Two Bands 197
    Chapter III - Order of March 197
    Chapter IV - Clement's Joy at Remaining with Peter 198
    Chapter V - Clement's Affection for Peter 198
    Chapter VI - Peter's Simplicity of Life 198
    Chapter VII - Peter's Humility 199
    Chapter VIII - Clement's Family History 199
    Chapter IX - Disappearance of His Mother and Brothers 199
    Chapter X - Disappearance of His Father 199
    Chapter XI - Different Effects of Suffering on Heathens and Christians 200
    Chapter XII - Excursion to Aradus 200
    Chapter XIII - The Beggar Woman 200
    Chapter XIV - The Woman's Grief 200
    Chapter XV - The Woman's Story 201
    Chapter XVI - The Woman's Story Continued 201
    Chapter XVII - The Woman's Story Continued 201
    Chapter XVIII - The Woman's Story Continued 202

The Epistles of Clement

Chapter XIX - Peter's Reflections on the Story 202

Chapter XX - Peter's Statement to the Woman 202

Chapter XXI - A Discovery 202

Chapter XXII - A Happy Meeting 203

Chapter XXIII - A Miracle 203

Chapter XXIV - Departure from Aradus 203

Chapter XXV - Journeyings 204

Chapter XXVI - Recapitulation 204

Chapter XXVII - Recapitulation Continued 204

Chapter XXVIII - More Recognitions 205

Chapter XXIX - "Nothing Common or Unclean." 205

Chapter XXX - "Who Can Forbid Water?" 205

Chapter XXXI - Too Much Joy 206

Chapter XXXII - "He Bringeth Them Unto Their Desired Haven." 206

Chapter XXXIII - Another Wreck Prevented 206

Chapter XXXIV - Baptism Must Be Preceded by Fasting 207

Chapter XXXV - Desiring the Salvation of Others 207

Chapter XXXVI - The Sons' Pleading 207

Chapter XXXVII - Peter Inexorable 208

Chapter XXXVIII - Reward of Chastity 208

   Footnotes: 209

Book VIII 210

Chapter I - The Old Workman 210

Chapter II - Genesis 210

Chapter III - A Friendly Conference 210

Chapter IV - The Question Stated 211

Chapter V - Freedom of Discussion Allowed 211

Chapter VI - The Other Side of the Question Stated 212

Chapter VII - The Way Cleared 212

Chapter VIII - Instincts 212

Chapter IX - Simple and Compound 213

Chapter X - Creation Implies Providence 213

Chapter XI - General or Special Providence 214

Chapter XII - Prayer Inconsistent with Genesis 214

Chapter XIII - A Creator Necessary 214

Chapter XIV - Mode of Creation 215

Chapter XV - Theories of Creation 215

Chapter XVI - The World Made of Nothing by a Creator 215

Chapter XVII - Doctrine of Atoms Untenable 216

Chapter XVIII - The Concourse of Atoms Could Not Make the World 216

Chapter XIX - More Difficulties of the Atomic Theory 216

Chapter XX - Plato's Testimony	217
Chapter XXI - Mechanical Theory	217
Chapter XXII - Motions of the Stars	217
Chapter XXIII - Providence in Earthly Things	218
Chapter XXIV - Rivers and Seas	218
Chapter XXV - Plants and Animals	218
Chapter XXVI - Germination of Seeds	219
Chapter XXVII - Power of Water	219
Chapter XXVIII - The Human Body	219
Chapter XXIX - Symmetry of the Body	220
Chapter XXX - Breath and Blood	220
Chapter XXXI - The Intestines	220
Chapter XXXII - Generation	220
Chapter XXXIII - Correspondences in Creation	221
Chapter XXXIV - Time of Making the World	221
Chapter XXXV - A Contest of Hospitality	221
Chapter XXXVI - Arrangements for To-Morrow	222
Chapter XXXVII - "The Form of Sound Words, Which Ye Have Heard of Me."	222
Chapter XXXVIII - The Chief Man's House	222
Chapter XXXIX - Recapitulation of Yesterday's Argument	223
Chapter XL - Genesis	223
Chapter XLI - The Rainbow	223
Chapter XLII - Types and Forms	224
Chapter XLIII - Things Apparently Useless and Vile Made by God	224
Chapter XLIV - Ordinate and Inordinate	225
Chapter XLV - Motions of the Sun and Moon	225
Chapter XLVI - Sun and Moon Ministers Both of Good and Evil	225
Chapter XLVII - Chastisements on the Righteous and the Wicked	226
Chapter XLVIII - Chastisements for Sins	226
Chapter XLIX - God's Precepts Despised	226
Chapter L - The Flood	227
Chapter LI - Evils Brought in by Sin	227
Chapter LII - "No Rose Without Its Thorn."	227
Chapter LIII - Everything Has Its Corresponding Contrary	228
Chapter LIV - An Illustration	228
Chapter LV - The Two Kingdoms	229
Chapter LVI - Origin of Evil	229
Chapter LVII - The Old Man Unconvinced	229
Chapter LVIII - Sitting in Judgment Upon God	230
Chapter LIX - The True Prophet	230
Chapter LX - His Deliverances Not to Be Questioned	230

The Epistles of Clement

- Chapter LXI - Ignorance of the Philosophers 231
- Chapter LXII - End of the Conference 231
  - Footnotes: 231

Book IX 233
- Chapter I - An Explanation 233
- Chapter II - Preliminaries 233
- Chapter III - Beginning of the Discussion 234
- Chapter IV - Why the Evil Prince Was Made 234
- Chapter V - Necessity of Inequality 234
- Chapter VI - Arrangements of the World for the Exercise of Virtue 234
- Chapter VII - The Old and the New Birth 235
- Chapter VIII - Uses of Evils 235
- Chapter IX - "Conceived in Sin." 236
- Chapter X - Tow Smeared with Pitch 236
- Chapter XI - Fear 236
- Chapter XII - Astrologers 237
- Chapter XIII - Retribution Here or Hereafter 237
- Chapter XIV - Knowledge Deadens Lusts 237
- Chapter XV - Fear of Men and of God 238
- Chapter XVI - Imperfect Conviction 238
- Chapter XVII - Astrological Lore [9] 238
- Chapter XVIII - The Reply 239
- Chapter XIX - Refutation of Astrology 239
- Chapter XX - Brahmans 239
- Chapter XXI - Districts of Heaven 239
- Chapter XXII - Customs of the Gelones 240
- Chapter XXIII - Manners of the Susidae 240
- Chapter XXIV - Different Customs of Different Countries 240
- Chapter XXV - Not Genesis, But Free-Will 241
- Chapter XXVI - Climates 241
- Chapter XXVII - Doctrine of "Climates" Untenable 241
- Chapter XXVIII - Jewish Customs 241
- Chapter XXIX - The Gospel More Powerful Than "Genesis." 242
- Chapter XXX - "Genesis" Inconsistent with God's Justice 242
- Chapter XXXI - Value of Knowledge 242
- Chapter XXXII - Stubborn Facts 243
- Chapter XXXIII - An Approaching Recognition 243
- Chapter XXXIV - The Other Side of the Story 243
- Chapter XXXV - Revelations 244
- Chapter XXXVI - New Revelations 244
- Chapter XXXVII - Another Recognition 244

Chapter XXXVIII - "Angels Unawares." 245
   Footnotes: 245
Book X 247
   Chapter I - Probation 247
   Chapter II - A Difficulty 247
   Chapter III - A Suggestion 248
   Chapter IV - Free Inquiry 248
   Chapter V - Good and Evil 248
   Chapter VI - Peter's Authority 249
   Chapter VII - Clement's Argument 249
   Chapter VIII - Admitted Evils 249
   Chapter IX - Existence of Evil on Astrological Principles 250
   Chapter X - How to Make Progress 250
   Chapter XI - Test of Astrology 251
   Chapter XII - Astrology Baffled by Free-Will 251
   Chapter XIII - People Admitted 251
   Chapter XIV - No Man Has Universal Knowledge 252
   Chapter XV - Clement's Disclosure 252
   Chapter XVI - "Would that All God's People Were Prophets." 252
   Chapter XVII - Gentile Cosmogony 253
   Chapter XVIII - Family of Saturn 253
   Chapter XIX - Their Destinies 253
   Chapter XX - Doings of Jupiter 254
   Chapter XXI - A Black Catalogue 254
   Chapter XXII - Vile Transformation of Jupiter 255
   Chapter XXIII - Why a God? 255
   Chapter XXIV - Folly of Polytheism 255
   Chapter XXV - Dead Men Deified 256
   Chapter XXVI - Metamorphoses 256
   Chapter XXVII - Inconsistency of Polytheists 256
   Chapter XXVIII - Buttresses of Gentilism 256
   Chapter XXIX - Allegories 257
   Chapter XXX - Cosmogony of Orpheus 257
   Chapter XXXI - Hesiod's Cosmogony 257
   Chapter XXXII - Allegorical Interpretation 258
   Chapter XXXIII - Allegory of Jupiter, Etc. 258
   Chapter XXXIV - Other Allegories 258
   Chapter XXXV - Uselessness of These Allegories 259
   Chapter XXXVI - The Allegories an Afterthought 259
   Chapter XXXVII - Like Gods, Like Worshippers 259
   Chapter XXXVIII - Writings of the Poets 259

Chapter XXXIX - All for the Best ... 260

Chapter XL - Further Information Sought ... 260

Chapter XLI - Explanation of Mythology ... 260

Chapter XLII - Interpretation of Scripture ... 261

Chapter XLIII - A Word of Exhortation ... 261

Chapter XLIV - Earnestness ... 261

Chapter XLV - All Ought to Repent ... 262

Chapter XLVI - The Sure Word of Prophecy ... 262

Chapter XLVII - "A Faithful Saying, and Worthy of All Acceptation." ... 262

Chapter XLVIII - Errors of the Philosophers ... 263

Chapter XLIX - God's Long-Suffering ... 263

Chapter L - Philosophers Not Benefactors of Men ... 263

Chapter LI - Christ the True Prophet ... 264

Chapter LII - Appion and Anubion ... 264

Chapter LIII - A Transformation ... 264

Chapter LIV - Excitement in Antioch ... 265

Chapter LV - A Stratagem ... 265

Chapter LVI - Simon's Design in the Transformation ... 265

Chapter LVII - Great Grief ... 266

Chapter LVIII - How It All Happened ... 266

Chapter LIX - A Scene of Mourning ... 266

Chapter LX - A Counterplot ... 267

Chapter LXI - A Mine Dug ... 267

Chapter LXII - A Case of Conscience ... 267

Chapter LXIII - A Pious Fraud ... 268

Chapter LXIV - A Competition in Lying ... 268

Chapter LXV - Success of the Plot ... 268

Chapter LXVI - Truth Told by Lying Lips ... 269

Chapter LXVII - Faustinianus is Himself Again ... 269

Chapter LXVIII - Peter's Entry into Antioch ... 269

Chapter LXIX - Peter's Thanksgiving ... 270

Chapter LXX - Miracles ... 270

Chapter LXXI - Success ... 270

Chapter LXXII - Happy Ending ... 270

Footnotes: ... 271

Introductory Notice to The Clementine Homilies ... 273

Footnote: ... 273

Epistle of Peter to James ... 274

Chapter I - Doctrine of Reserve ... 274

Chapter II - Misrepresentation of Peter's Doctrine ... 274

Chapter III - Initiation ... 275

Chapter IV - An Adjuration Concerning the Receivers of the Book 275
Chapter V - The Adjuration Accepted 276
   Footnotes: 276

Epistle of Clement to James 277
   Chapter I - Peter's Martyrdom 277
   Chapter II - Ordination of Clement 277
   Chapter III - Nolo Episcopari 277
   Chapter IV - The Recompense of the Reward 278
   Chapter V - A Charge 278
   Chapter VI - The Duty of a Bishop 278
   Chapter VII - Duties of Presbyters 279
   Chapter VIII - "Do Good Unto All?" 279
   Chapter IX - "Let Brotherly Love Continue." 279
   Chapter X - "Whatsoever Things are Honest." 279
   Chapter XI - Doubts to Be Satisfied 280
   Chapter XII - Duties of Deacons 280
   Chapter XIII - Duties of Catechists 280
   Chapter XIV - The Vessel of the Church 280
   Chapter XV - Incidents of the Voyage 281
   Chapter XVI - The Bishop's Labours and Reward 281
   Chapter XVII - The People's Duties 281
   Chapter XVIII - "As a Heathen Man and a Publican." 281
   Chapter XIX - Installation of Clement 282
   Chapter XX - Clement's Obedience 282
      Footnotes: 282

The Clementine Homilies 283
Homily I 283
   Chapter I - Boyish Questionings 283
   Chapter II - Good Out of Evil 283
   Chapter III - Perplexity 283
   Chapter IV - More Perplexity 284
   Chapter V - A Resolution 284
   Chapter VI - Tidings from Judaea 284
   Chapter VII - The Gospel in Rome 285
   Chapter VIII - Departure from Rome 285
   Chapter IX - Preaching of Barnabas 285
   Chapter X - Cavils of the Philosophers 286
   Chapter XI - Clement's Zeal 286
   Chapter XII - Clement's Rebuke of the People 287
   Chapter XIII - Clement Instructed by Barnabas 287
   Chapter XIV - Departure of Barnabas 287

Chapter XV - Introduction to Peter 288

Chapter XVI - Peter's Salutation 288

Chapter XVII - Questions Propounded 288

Chapter XVIII - Causes of Ignorance 289

Chapter XIX - The True Prophet 289

Chapter XX - Peter's Satisfaction with Clement 289

Chapter XXI - Unalterable Conviction 290

Chapter XXII - Thanksgiving 290

    Footnotes: 290

Homily II 292

Chapter I - Peter's Attendants 292

Chapter II - A Sound Mind in a Sound Body 292

Chapter III - Forewarned is Forearmed 292

Chapter IV - A Request 292

Chapter V - Excellence of the Knowledge of the True Prophet 293

Chapter VI - The True Prophet 293

Chapter VII - Unaided Quest of Truth Profitless 293

Chapter VIII - Test of Truth 294

Chapter IX - "The Weak Things of the World." 294

Chapter X - Test of the Prophet 294

Chapter XI - Ignorance, Knowledge, Foreknowledge 294

Chapter XII - Doctrine of the True Prophet 294

Chapter XIII - Future Rewards and Punishments 295

Chapter XIV - Righteousness and Unrighteousness 295

Chapter XV - Pairs 295

Chapter XVI - Man's Ways Opposite to God's 295

Chapter XVII - First the Worse, Then the Better 296

Chapter XVIII - Mistake About Simon Magus 296

Chapter XIX - Justa, a Proselyte 296

Chapter XX - Divorced for the Faith 296

Chapter XXI - Justa's Adopted Sons, Associates with Simon 297

Chapter XXII - Doctrines of Simon 297

Chapter XXIII - Simon a Disciple of the Baptist 297

Chapter XXIV - Electioneering Stratagems 297

Chapter XXV - Simon's Deceit 298

Chapter XXVI - His Wickedness 298

Chapter XXVII - His Promises 298

Chapter XXVIII - Fruitless Counsel 299

Chapter XXIX - Immortality of the Soul 299

Chapter XXX - An Argument 299

Chapter XXXI - A Dilemma 300

Chapter XXXII - Simon's Prodigies 300

Chapter XXXIII - Doctrine of Pairs 300

Chapter XXXIV - Useless and Philanthropic Miracles 301

Chapter XXXV - Discussion Postponed 301

Chapter XXXVI - All for the Best 301

Chapter XXXVII - Spies in the Enemy's Camp 301

Chapter XXXVIII - Corruption of the Law 302

Chapter XXXIX - Tactics 302

Chapter XL - Preliminary Instruction 302

Chapter XLI - Asking for Information, Not Contradiction 302

Chapter XLII - Right Notions of God Essential to Holiness 303

Chapter XLIII - A Priori Argument on the Divine Attributes 303

Chapter XLIV - The Same Continued 303

Chapter XLV - How God is to Be Thought of 304

Chapter XLVI - Judgment to Come 304

Chapter XLVII - A Pertinent Question 304

Chapter XLVIII - A Particular Case 304

Chapter XLIX - Reductio a.d. Absurdum 305

Chapter L - A Satisfactory Answer 305

Chapter LI - Weigh in the Balance 305

Chapter LII - Sins of the Saints Denied 305

Chapter LIII - Close of the Conference 306

   Footnotes: 306

Homily III 308

   Chapter I - The Morning of the Discussion 308

   Chapter II - Simon's Design 308

   Chapter III - His Object 308

   Chapter IV - Snares Laid for the Gentiles 308

   Chapter V - Use of Errors 309

   Chapter VI - Purgatory and Hell 309

   Chapter VII - What is Impiety? 309

   Chapter VIII - Wiles of the Devil 309

   Chapter IX - Uncertainty of the Scriptures 310

   Chapter X - Simon's Intention 310

   Chapter XI - Distinction Between Prediction and Prophecy 310

   Chapter XII - The Same 310

   Chapter XIII - Prophetic Knowledge Constant 311

   Chapter XIV - Prophetic Spirit Constant 311

   Chapter XV - Christ's Prophecies 311

   Chapter XVI - Doctrine of Conjunction 311

   Chapter XVII - Whether Adam Had the Spirit 311

- Chapter XVIII - Adam Not Ignorant ... 312
- Chapter XIX - Reign of Christ ... 312
- Chapter XX - Christ the Only Prophet Has Appeared in Different Ages ... 312
- Chapter XXI - The Eating of the Forbidden Fruit Denied ... 313
- Chapter XXII - Male and Female ... 313
- Chapter XXIII - Two Kinds of Prophecy ... 313
- Chapter XXIV - The Prophetess a Misleader ... 313
- Chapter XXV - Cain's Name and Nature ... 313
- Chapter XXVI - Abel's Name and Nature ... 314
- Chapter XXVII - The Prophet and the Prophetess ... 314
- Chapter XXVIII - Spiritual Adultery ... 314
- Chapter XXIX - The Signal Given ... 314
- Chapter XXX - Apostolic Salutation ... 315
- Chapter XXXI - Faith in God ... 315
- Chapter XXXII - Invitation ... 315
- Chapter XXXIII - Works of Creation ... 315
- Chapter XXXIV - Extent of Creation ... 315
- Chapter XXXV - "These are a Part of His Ways." ... 316
- Chapter XXXVI - Dominion Over the Creatures ... 316
- Chapter XXXVII - "Whom to Know is Life Eternal." ... 316
- Chapter XXXVIII - Simon's Challenge ... 316
- Chapter XXXIX - Defects Ascribed to God ... 317
- Chapter XL - Peter's Answer ... 317
- Chapter XLI - "Status Quaestionis." ... 317
- Chapter XLII - Was Adam Blind? ... 318
- Chapter XLIII - God's Foreknowledge ... 318
- Chapter XLIV - God's Decrees ... 318
- Chapter XLV - Sacrifices ... 319
- Chapter XLVI - Disparagements of God ... 319
- Chapter XLVII - Foreknowledge of Moses ... 319
- Chapter XLVIII - Test of Truth ... 319
- Chapter XLIX - The True Prophet ... 320
- Chapter L - His Teaching Concerning the Scriptures ... 320
- Chapter LI - His Teaching Concerning the Law ... 320
- Chapter LII - Other Sayings of Christ ... 320
- Chapter LIII - Other Sayings of Christ ... 320
- Chapter LIV - Other Sayings ... 321
- Chapter LV - Teaching of Christ ... 321
- Chapter LVI - Teaching of Christ ... 321
- Chapter LVII - Teaching of Christ ... 321
- Chapter LVIII - Flight of Simon ... 321

Chapter LIX - Peter's Resolution to Follow 321

Chapter LX - Successor to Be Appointed 322

Chapter LXI - Monarchy 322

Chapter LXII - Obedience Leads to Peace 322

Chapter LXIII - Zacchaeus Appointed 322

Chapter LXIV - The Bishopric 323

Chapter LXV - Nolo Episcopar 323

Chapter LXVI - Danger of Disobedience 323

Chapter LXVII - Duties of Church Office-Bearers 323

Chapter LXVIII - "Marriage Always Honourable." 324

Chapter LXIX - "Not Forsaking the Assembling of Yourselves Together." 324

Chapter LXX - "Hear the Bishop." 324

Chapter LXXI - Various Duties of Christians 324

Chapter LXXII - Ordination 325

Chapter LXXIII - Baptisms 325

   Footnotes: 325

Homily IV 328

   Chapter I - Bernice's Hospitality 328

   Chapter II - Simon's Practices 328

   Chapter III - Object of the Mission 328

   Chapter IV - Simon's Doings 328

   Chapter V - Discretion the Better Part of Valour 329

   Chapter VI - Simon's Departure 329

   Chapter VII - Appion's Salutation 329

   Chapter VIII - A Challenge 329

   Chapter IX - Unworthy Ends of Philosophers 330

   Chapter X - A Cool Retreat 330

   Chapter XI - Truth and Custom 330

   Chapter XII - Genesis 330

   Chapter XIII - Destiny 331

   Chapter XIV - "Doctrine According to Godliness." 331

   Chapter XV - Wickedness of the Gods 331

   Chapter XVI - Wickedness of Jupiter 331

   Chapter XVII - "Their Makers are Like Unto Them." 332

   Chapter XVIII - Second Nature 332

   Chapter XIX - "Where Ignorance is Bliss." 332

   Chapter XX - False Theories of Philosophers 332

   Chapter XXI - Evils of Adultery 333

   Chapter XXII - A More Excellent Way 333

   Chapter XXIII - "Whither Shall I Go from Thy Presence?" 333

   Chapter XXIV - Allegory 334

Chapter XXV - An Engagement for To-Morrow ... 334
   Footnotes: ... 334

Homily V ... 336
   Chapter I - Appion Does Not Appear ... 336
   Chapter II - Clement's Previous Knowledge of Appion ... 336
   Chapter III - Clement's Trick ... 336
   Chapter IV - Appion's Undertaking ... 337
   Chapter V - Theory of Magic ... 337
   Chapter VI - Scruples ... 337
   Chapter VII - A Distinction with a Difference ... 337
   Chapter VIII - Flattery or Magic ... 338
   Chapter IX - A Love-Letter ... 338
   Chapter X - The Lover to the Beloved One ... 338
   Chapter XI - "All Uncleanness with Greediness." ... 339
   Chapter XII - Jupiter's Amours ... 339
   Chapter XIII - Jupiter's Amours Continued ... 339
   Chapter XIV - Jupiter's Undisguised Amours ... 340
   Chapter XV - Unnatural Lusts ... 340
   Chapter XVI - Praise of Unchastity ... 340
   Chapter XVII - The Constellations ... 340
   Chapter XVIII - The Philosophers Advocates of Adultery ... 341
   Chapter XIX - Close of the Love-Letter ... 341
   Chapter XX - The Use Made of It ... 341
   Chapter XXI - Answer to Appion's Letter ... 341
   Chapter XXII - Lying Fables ... 342
   Chapter XXIII - The Gods No Gods ... 342
   Chapter XXIV - If a Principle Be Good, Carry It Out ... 342
   Chapter XXV - Better to Marry Than to Burn ... 343
   Chapter XXVI - Close of the Answer ... 343
   Chapter XXVII - A Reason for Hatred ... 343
   Chapter XXVIII - The Hoax Confessed ... 343
   Chapter XXIX - Appion's Resentment ... 343
   Chapter XXX - A Discussion Promised ... 344
   Footnotes: ... 344

Homily VI ... 345
   Chapter I - Clement Meets Appion ... 345
   Chapter II - The Myths are Not to Be Taken Literally ... 345
   Chapter III - Appion Proceeds to Interpret the Myths ... 346
   Chapter IV - Origin of Chaos ... 346
   Chapter V - Kronos and Rhea Explained ... 346
   Chapter VI - Phanes and Pluto ... 347

- Chapter VII - Poseidon, Zeus, and Metis ... 347
- Chapter VIII - Pallas and Hera ... 347
- Chapter IX - Artemis ... 347
- Chapter X - All Such Stories are Allegorical ... 348
- Chapter XI - Clement Has Heard All This Before ... 348
- Chapter XII - Epitome of Appion's Explanation ... 348
- Chapter XIII - Kronos and Aphrodite ... 348
- Chapter XIV - Peleus and Thetis, Prometheus, Achilles, and Polyxena ... 349
- Chapter XV - The Judgment of Paris ... 349
- Chapter XVI - Hercules ... 349
- Chapter XVII - They are Blameworthy Who Invented Such Stories ... 349
- Chapter XVIII - The Same ... 350
- Chapter XIX - None of These Allegories are Consistent ... 350
- Chapter XX - These Gods Were Really Wicked Magicians ... 350
- Chapter XXI - Their Graves are Still to Be Seen ... 351
- Chapter XXII - Their Contemporaries, Therefore, Did Not Look on Them as Gods ... 351
- Chapter XXIII - The Egyptians Pay Divine Honours to a Man ... 351
- Chapter XXIV - What is Not God ... 351
- Chapter XXV - The Universe is the Product of Mind ... 352
- Chapter XXVI - Peter Arrives from Caesarea ... 352
  - Footnotes: ... 352

Homily VII ... 354
- Chapter I - Peter Addresses the People ... 354
- Chapter II - Reason of Simon's Power ... 354
- Chapter III - The Remedy ... 354
- Chapter IV - The Golden Rule ... 355
- Chapter V - Peter Departs for Sidon ... 355
- Chapter VI - Peter in Sidon ... 355
- Chapter VII - The Two Paths ... 355
- Chapter VIII - The Service of God's Appointment ... 356
- Chapter IX - Simon Attacks Peter ... 356
- Chapter X - Simon is Driven Away ... 356
- Chapter XI - The Way of Salvation ... 356
- Chapter XII - Peter Goes to Byblus and Tripolis ... 357
  - Footnotes: ... 357

Homily VIII ... 358
- Chapter I - Peter's Arrival at Tripolis ... 358
- Chapter II - Peter's Thoughtfulness ... 358
- Chapter III - A Conversation Interrupted ... 358
- Chapter IV - Many Called ... 359
- Chapter V - Faith the Gift of God ... 359

- Chapter VI - Concealment and Revelation 359
- Chapter VII - Moses and Christ 359
- Chapter VIII - A Large Congregation 360
- Chapter IX - "Vindicate the Ways of God to Men." 360
- Chapter X - The Original Law 360
- Chapter XI - Cause of the Fall of Man 360
- Chapter XII - Metamorphoses of the Angels 361
- Chapter XIII - The Fall of the Angels 361
- Chapter XIV - Their Discoveries 361
- Chapter XV - The Giants 361
- Chapter XVI - Cannibalism 362
- Chapter XVII - The Flood 362
- Chapter XVIII - The Law to the Survivors 362
- Chapter XIX - The Law to the Giants or Demons 362
- Chapter XX - Willing Captives 363
- Chapter XXI - Temptation of Christ 363
- Chapter XXII - The Marriage Supper 363
- Chapter XXIII - The Assembly Dismissed 363
- Chapter XXIV - The Sick Healed 364
  - Footnotes: 364

Homily IX 365
- Chapter I - Peter's Discourse Resumed 365
- Chapter II - Monarchy and Polyarchy 365
- Chapter III - Family of Noe 365
- Chapter IV - Zoroaster 365
- Chapter V - Hero-Worship 366
- Chapter VI - Fire-Worship 366
- Chapter VII - Sacrificial Orgies 366
- Chapter VIII - The Best Merchandise 366
- Chapter IX - How Demons Get Power Over Men 367
- Chapter X - How They are to Be Expelled 367
- Chapter XI - Unbelief the Demon's Stronghold 367
- Chapter XII - Theory of Disease 367
- Chapter XIII - Deceits of the Demons 368
- Chapter XIV - More Tricks 368
- Chapter XV - Test of Idols 368
- Chapter XVI - Powers of the Demons 369
- Chapter XVII - Reasons Why Their Deceits are Not Detected 369
- Chapter XVIII - Props of the System 369
- Chapter XIX - Privileges of the Baptized 370
- Chapter XX - "Not Almost, But Altogether Such as I Am." 370

- Chapter XXI - The Demons Subject to the Believer ... 370
- Chapter XXII - "Rather Rejoice." ... 370
- Chapter XXIII - The Sick Healed ... 371
  - Footnotes: ... 371

Homily X ... 372
- Chapter I - The Third Day in Tripolis ... 372
- Chapter II - Ignorance and Error ... 372
- Chapter III - Man the Lord of All ... 372
- Chapter IV - Faith and Duty ... 372
- Chapter V - The Fear of God ... 373
- Chapter VI - Restoration of the Divine Image ... 373
- Chapter VII - Unprofitableness of Idols ... 373
- Chapter VIII - No Gods Which are Made with Hands ... 373
- Chapter IX - "Eyes Have They, But They See Not." ... 374
- Chapter X - Idolatry a Delusion of the Serpent ... 374
- Chapter XI - Why the Serpent Tempts to Sin ... 374
- Chapter XII - Ignorantia Neminem Excusa ... 374
- Chapter XIII - Condemnation of the Ignorant ... 375
- Chapter XIV - Polytheistic Illustration ... 375
- Chapter XV - Its Inconclusiveness ... 375
- Chapter XVI - Gods of the Egyptians ... 375
- Chapter XVII - The Egyptians' Defence of Their System ... 376
- Chapter XVIII - Answer to the Egyptians ... 376
- Chapter XIX - God's Peculiar Attribute ... 376
- Chapter XX - Neither the World Nor Any of Its Parts Can Be God ... 377
- Chapter XXI - Idols Not Animated by the Divine Spirit ... 377
- Chapter XXII - Confutation of Idol-Worship ... 377
- Chapter XXIII - Folly of Idolatry ... 377
- Chapter XXIV - Impotence of Idols ... 378
- Chapter XXV - Servants Become Masters ... 378
- Chapter XXVI - The Sick Healed ... 378
  - Footnotes: ... 378

Homily XI ... 379
- Chapter I - Morning Exercises ... 379
- Chapter II - "Giving All Diligence." ... 379
- Chapter III - "Behold What Indignation." ... 379
- Chapter IV - The Golden Rule ... 379
- Chapter V - Forasmuch as Ye Did It Unto One of These ... 380
- Chapter VI - Why God Suffers Objects of Idolatry to Subsist ... 380
- Chapter VII - "Let Both Grow Together Till the Harvest." ... 380
- Chapter VIII - Liberty and Necessity ... 381

Chapter IX - God a Jealous God 381
Chapter X - The Creatures Avenge God's Cause 381
Chapter XI - Immortality of the Soul 382
Chapter XII - Idols Unprofitable 382
Chapter XIII - Arguments in Favour of Idolatry Answered 382
Chapter XIV - Heathen Orgies 383
Chapter XV - Heathen Worshippers Under the Power of the Demon 383
Chapter XVI - All Things Work for Good to Them that Love God 383
Chapter XVII - Speaking the Truth in Love 384
Chapter XVIII - Charming of the Serpent 384
Chapter XIX - Not Peace, But a Sword 384
Chapter XX - What If It Be Already Kindled? 384
Chapter XXI - "If I Be a Father, Where is My Fear?" 385
Chapter XXII - "The Gods that Have Not Made the Heavens." 385
Chapter XXIII - "To Whom Much is Given." 385
Chapter XXIV - "Born of Water." 386
Chapter XXV - Good Works to Be Well Done 386
Chapter XXVI - Baptism 386
Chapter XXVII - All Need Baptism 386
Chapter XXVIII - Purification 387
Chapter XXIX - Outward and Inward Purity 387
Chapter XXX - "Whatsoever Things are Pure." 387
Chapter XXXI - "What Do Ye More Than Others?" 387
Chapter XXXII - "To Whom Much is Given." 388
Chapter XXXIII - The Queen of the South and the Men of Nineveh 388
Chapter XXXIV - Peter's Daily Work 388
Chapter XXXV - "Beware of False Prophets." 388
Chapter XXXVI - Farewell to Tripolis 389
   Footnotes: 389
Homily XII 390
Chapter I - Two Bands 390
Chapter II - Love of Preachers and Their Converts 390
Chapter III - Submission 390
Chapter IV - Clement's Joy 391
Chapter V - Clement's Office of Service 391
Chapter VI - Peter's Frugality 391
Chapter VII - "Not to Be Ministered Unto, But to Minister." 392
Chapter VIII - Family History 392
Chapter IX - The Lost Ones 392
Chapter X - The Seeker Lost 392
Chapter XI - The Afflictions of the Righteous 393

Chapter XII - A Pleasure Trip 393
Chapter XIII - A Woman of a Sorrowful Spirit 393
Chapter XIV - Balm in Gilead 393
Chapter XV - The Woman's Story 394
Chapter XVI - The Shipwreck 394
Chapter XVII - The Fruitless Search 394
Chapter XVIII - Trouble Upon Trouble 395
Chapter XIX - Evasions 395
Chapter XX - Peter's Account of the Matter 395
Chapter XXI - A Disclosure 395
Chapter XXII - The Lost Found 396
Chapter XXIII - Reward of Hospitality 396
Chapter XXIV - All Well Arranged 396
Chapter XXV - Philanthropy and Friendship 397
Chapter XXVI - What is Philanthropy 397
Chapter XXVII - Who Can Judge 398
Chapter XXVIII - Difficulty of Judging 398
Chapter XXIX - Sufferings of the Good 398
Chapter XXX - Offences Must Come 398
Chapter XXXI - "Howbeit, They Meant It Not." 399
Chapter XXXII - The Golden Rule 399
Chapter XXXIII - Fear and Love 399
   Footnotes: 400
Homily XIII 401
Chapter I - Journey to Laodicea 401
Chapter II - Peter Relates to Nicetas and Aquila the History of Clement and His Family 401
Chapter III - Recognition of Nicetas and Aquila 401
Chapter IV - The Mother Must Not Take Food with Her Son 402
Chapter V - Mattidia Wishes to Be Baptized 402
Chapter VI - The Sons Reveal Themselves to the Mother 402
Chapter VII - Nicetas Tells What Befell Him 403
Chapter VIII - Nicetas Like to Be Deceived by Simon Magus 403
Chapter IX - The Mother Begs Baptism for Herself and Her Hostess 403
Chapter X - Mattidia Values Baptism Aright 404
Chapter XI - Mattidia Has Unintentionally Fasted One Day 404
Chapter XII - The Difficulty Solved 404
Chapter XIII - Peter on Chastity 405
Chapter XIV - Peter's Speech Continued 405
Chapter XV - Peter's Speech Continued 405
Chapter XVI - Peter's Speech Continued 405
Chapter XVII - Peter's Speech Continued 406

Chapter XVIII - Peter's Speech Continued ... 406

Chapter XIX - Peter's Speech Ended ... 406

Chapter XX - Peter Addresses Mattidia ... 407

Chapter XXI - The Same Subject Continued ... 407

   Footnotes: ... 407

Homily XIV ... 409

Chapter I - Mattidia is Baptized in the Sea ... 409

Chapter II - The Reason of Peter's Lateness ... 409

Chapter III - The Old Man Does Not Believe in God or Providence ... 409

Chapter IV - Peter's Arguments Against Genesis ... 410

Chapter V - Practical Refutation of Genesis ... 410

Chapter VI - The Old Man Opposes His Personal Experience to the Argument of Peter ... 411

Chapter VII - The Old Man Tells His Story ... 411

Chapter VIII - The Old Man Gives Information in Regard to Faustus the Father of Clement ... 411

Chapter IX - Faustus Himself Appears ... 412

Chapter X - Faustus Explains His Narrative to Peter ... 412

Chapter XI - Discussion on Genesis ... 412

Chapter XII - Clement Undertakes the Discussion ... 413

   Footnotes: ... 413

Homily XV ... 415

Chapter I - Peter Wishes to Convert Faustus ... 415

Chapter II - Reason for Listening to Peter's Arguments ... 415

Chapter III - Obstacles to Faith ... 415

Chapter IV - Providence Seen in the Events of the Life of Faustus and His Family ... 416

Chapter V - Difference Between the True Religion and Philosophy ... 416

Chapter VI - The Love of Man ... 416

Chapter VII - The Explanation of a Parable; The Present and the Future Life ... 417

Chapter VIII - The Present and the Future ... 417

Chapter IX - Possessions are Transgressions ... 418

Chapter X - Poverty Not Necessarily Righteous ... 418

Chapter XI - Exposition of the True Religion Promised ... 419

   Footnotes: ... 419

Homily XVI ... 421

Chapter I - Simon Wishes to Discuss with Peter the Unity of God ... 421

Chapter II - The Same Subject Continued ... 421

Chapter III - The Mode of the Discussion ... 421

Chapter IV - The Prejudices of Faustus Rather on the Side of Simon Than on that of Peter ... 422

Chapter V - Peter Commences the Discussion ... 422

Chapter VI - Simon Appeals to the Old Testament to Prove that There are Many Gods ... 423

Chapter VII - Peter Appeals to the Old Testament to Prove the Unity of God ... 423

Chapter VIII - Simon and Peter Continue the Discussion ... 424

Chapter IX - Simon Tries to Show that the Scriptures Contradict Themselves..................424

Chapter X - Peter's Explanation of the Apparent Contradictions of Scripture 424

Chapter XI - Gen. I. 26 Appealed to by Simon..425

Chapter XII - Peter's Explanation of the Passage...425

Chapter XIII - The Contradictions of the Scriptures Intended to Try Those Who Read Them 425

Chapter XIV - Other Beings Called Gods 426

Chapter XV - Christ Not God, But the Son of God 426

Chapter XVI - The Unbegotten and the Begotten Necessarily Different from Each Other..............426

Chapter XVII - The Nature of God...427

Chapter XVIII - The Name of God...427

Chapter XIX - The Shape of God in Man...427

Chapter XX - The Character of God...427

Chapter XXI - Simon Promises to Appeal to the Teaching of Christ. Peter Dismisses the Multitudes 428

    Footnotes: 428

Homily XVII 431

    Chapter I - Simon Comes to Peter 431

    Chapter II - Simon's Speech Against Peter 431

    Chapter III - Simon's Accusation of Peter 431

    Chapter IV - It is Asserted that Christ's Teaching is Different from Peter's....................432

    Chapter V - Jesus Inconsistent in His Teaching...432

    Chapter VI - Peter Goes Out to Answer Simon 433

    Chapter VII - Man in the Shape of God..433

    Chapter VIII - God's Figure...433

    Chapter IX - God the Centre or Heart of the Universe 434

    Chapter X - The Nature and Shape of God 434

    Chapter XI - The Fear of God..435

    Chapter XII - The Fear and Love of God..435

    Chapter XIII - The Evidence of the Senses Contrasted with that from Supernatural Vision............435

    Chapter XIV - The Evidence of the Senses More Trustworthy Than that of Supernatural Vision....436

    Chapter XV - The Evidence from Dreams Discussed...436

    Chapter XVI - None But Evil Demons Appear to the Impious...437

    Chapter XVII - The Impious See True Dreams and Visions...437

    Chapter XVIII - The Nature of Revelation 437

    Chapter XIX - Opposition to Peter Unreasonable..438

    Chapter XX - Another Subject for Discussion Proposed 438

    Footnotes: 439

Homily XVIII..441

    Chapter I - Simon Maintains that the Framer of the World is Not the Highest God 441

    Chapter II - Definition of Goodness and Justice 441

    Chapter III - God Both Good and Just...442

Chapter IV - The Unrevealed God 442

Chapter V - Peter Doubts Simon's Honesty 443

Chapter VI - The Nature of Revelation 443

Chapter VII - Simon Confesses His Ignorance 444

Chapter VIII - The Work of Revelation Belongs to the Son Alone 444

Chapter IX - How Simon Bears His Exposure 445

Chapter X - Peter's Reply to Simon 445

Chapter XI - Simon Professes to Utter His Real Sentiments 445

Chapter XII - Simon's Opinions Expounded by Peter 446

Chapter XIII - Peter's Explanation of the Passage 446

Chapter XIV - Simon Refuted 446

Chapter XV - Matthew XI. 25 Discussed 447

Chapter XVI - These Things Hidden Justly from the Wise 447

Chapter XVII - The Way to the Kingdom Not Concealed from the Israelites 447

Chapter XVIII - Isaiah I. 3 Explained 448

Chapter XIX - Misconception of God in the Old Testament 448

Chapter XX - Some Parts of the Old Testament Written to Try Us 448

Chapter XXI - Simon's Astonishment at Peter's Treatment of the Scriptures 448

Chapter XXII - Peter Worships One God 449

Chapter XXIII - Simon Retires 449

   Footnotes: 450

Homily XIX 452

Chapter I - Simon Undertakes to Prove that the Creator of the World is Not Blameless 452

Chapter II - The Existence of the Devil Affirmed 452

Chapter III - Peter Refuses to Discuss Certain Questions in Regard to the Devil 453

Chapter IV - Suppositions in Regard to the Devil's Origin 453

Chapter V - God Not Deserving of Blame in Permitting the Existence of the Devil 454

Chapter VI - Peter Accuses Simon of Being Worse Than the Devil 454

Chapter VII - Peter Suspects Simon of Not Believing Even in a God 455

Chapter VIII - Peter Undertakes to Discuss the Devil's Origin 455

Chapter IX - Theories in Regard to the Origin of the Devil 455

Chapter X - The Absolute God Entirely Incomprehensible by Man 456

Chapter XI - The Application of the Attributes of Man to God 456

Chapter XII - God Produced the Wicked One, But Not Evil 457

Chapter XIII - God the Maker of the Devil 457

Chapter XIV - Is Matter Eternal? 457

Chapter XV - Sin the Cause of Evil 458

Chapter XVI - Why the Wicked One is Entrusted with Power 458

Chapter XVII - The Devil Has Not Equal Power with God 459

Chapter XVIII - Is the Devil a Relation? 459

Chapter XIX - Some Actions Really Wicked 460

Chapter XX - Pain and Death the Result of Sin 460

Chapter XXI - The Uses of Lust, Anger, Grief 461

Chapter XXII - Sins of Ignorance 461

Chapter XXIII - The Inequalities of Lot in Human Life 462

Chapter XXIV - Simon Rebuked by Faustus 462

Chapter XXV - Simon Retires 463

    Footnotes: 463

Homily XX 466

Chapter I - Peter is Willing to Gratify Sophonias 466

Chapter II - The Two Ages 466

Chapter III - The Work of the Good One and of the Evil One 466

Chapter IV - Men Sin Through Ignorance 467

Chapter V - Sophonias Maintains that God Cannot Produce What is Unlike Himself 467

Chapter VI - God's Power of Changing Himself 468

Chapter VII - The Objection Answered, that One Cannot Change Himself 468

Chapter VIII - The Origin of the Good One Different from that of the Evil One 469

Chapter IX - Why the Wicked One is Appointed Over the Wicked by the Righteous God 469

Chapter X - Why Some Believe, and Others Do Not 470

Chapter XI - Arrival of Appion and Annubion 470

Chapter XII - Faustus Appears to His Friends with the Face of Simon 470

Chapter XIII - The Flight of Simon 471

Chapter XIV - The Change in the Form of Faustus Caused by Simon 471

Chapter XV - The Repentance of Faustus 472

Chapter XVI - Why Simon Gave to Faustus His Own Shape 472

Chapter XVII - Annubion's Services to Faustus 472

Chapter XVIII - Peter Promises to Restore to Faustus His Own Shape 473

Chapter XIX - Peter's Instructions to Faustus 473

Chapter XX - Faustus, His Wife, and Sons, Prepare to Go to Antioch 473

Chapter XXI - Appion and Athenodorus Return in Quest of Faustus 474

Chapter XXII - Appion and Athenodorus Return to Simon 474

Chapter XXIII - Peter Goes to Antioch 475

    Footnotes: 475

Introductory Note to the First Epistle of Clement to the Corinthians [a.d. 30-100.]

Clement was probably a Gentile and a Roman. He seems to have been at Philippi with St. Paul (a.d. 57) when that first-born of the Western churches was passing through great trials of faith. There, with holy women and others, he ministered to the apostle and to the saints. As this city was a Roman colony, we need not inquire how a Roman happened to be there. He was possibly in some public service, and it is not improbable that he had visited Corinth in those days. From the apostle, and his companion, St. Luke, he had no doubt learned the use of the Septuagint, in which his knowledge of the Greek tongue soon rendered him an adept. His copy of that version, however, does not always agree with the Received Text, as the reader will perceive.

A co-presbyter with Linus and Cletus, he succeeded them in the government of the Roman Church. I have reluctantly adopted the opinion that his Epistle was written near the close of his life, and not just after the persecution of Nero. It is not improbable that Linus and Cletus both perished in that fiery trial, and that Clement's immediate succession to their work and place occasions the chronological difficulties of the period. After the death of the apostles, for the Roman imprisonment and martyrdom of St. Peter seem historical, Clement was the natural representative of St. Paul, and even of his companion, the "apostle of the circumcision;" and naturally he wrote the Epistle in the name of the local church, when brethren looked to them for advice. St. John, no doubt, was still surviving at Patmos or in Ephesus; but the Philippians, whose intercourse with Rome is attested by the visit of Epaphroditus, looked naturally to the surviving friends of their great founder; nor was the aged apostle in the East equally accessible. All roads pointed towards the Imperial City, and started from its Milliarium Aureum. But, though Clement doubtless wrote the letter, he conceals his own name, and puts forth the brethren, who seem to have met in council, and sent a brotherly delegation (Chap. lix.). The entire absence of the spirit of Diotrephes (3 John 9), and the close accordance of the Epistle, in humility and meekness, with that of St. Peter (1 Pet. v. 1-5), are noteworthy features. The whole will be found animated with the loving and faithful spirit of St. Paul's dear Philippians, among whom the writer had learned the Gospel.

Clement fell asleep, probably soon after he despatched his letter. It is the legacy of one who reflects the apostolic age in all the beauty and evangelical truth which were the first-fruits of the Spirit's presence with the Church. He shares with others the aureole of glory attributed by St. Paul (Phil. iv. 3), "His name is in the Book of Life."

The plan of this publication does not permit the restoration, in this volume, of the recently discovered portions of his work. It is the purpose of the editor to present this, however, with other recently discovered relics of primitive antiquity, in a supplementary volume, should the undertaking meet with sufficient encouragement. The so-called second Epistle of Clement is now known to be the work of another, and has been relegated to another place in this series.

The following is the Introductory Notice of the original editors and translators, Drs. Roberts and Donaldson:--

The first Epistle, bearing the name of Clement, has been preserved to us in a single manuscript only. Though very frequently referred to by ancient Christian writers, it remained unknown to the scholars of Western Europe until happily discovered in the Alexandrian manuscript. This ms. of the Sacred Scriptures (known and generally referred to as Codex A) was presented in 1628 by Cyril, Patriarch of Constantinople, to Charles I., and is now preserved in the British Museum. Subjoined to the books of the New Testament contained in it, there are two writings described as the Epistles of one Clement. Of these, that now before us is the first. It is tolerably perfect, but there are many slight lacunæ, or gaps, in the ms., and one whole leaf is supposed to have been lost towards the close. These lacunæ, however, so numerous in some chapters, do not generally extend beyond a word or syllable, and can for the most part be easily supplied.

Who the Clement was to whom these writings are ascribed, cannot with absolute certainty be determined. The general opinion is, that he is the same as the person of that name referred to by St. Paul (Phil. iv. 3). The writings themselves contain no statement as to their author. The first, and by far the longer of them, simply purports to have been written in the name of the Church at Rome to the Church at Corinth. But in the catalogue of contents prefixed to the ms. they are both plainly attributed to one

Clement; and the judgment of most scholars is, that, in regard to the first Epistle at least, this statement is correct, and that it is to be regarded as an authentic production of the friend and fellow-worker of St. Paul. This belief may be traced to an early period in the history of the Church. It is found in the writings of Eusebius (Hist. Eccl., iii. 15), of Origen (Comm. in Joan., i. 29), and others. The internal evidence also tends to support this opinion. The doctrine, style, and manner of thought are all in accordance with it; so that, although, as has been said, positive certainty cannot be reached on the subject, we may with great probability conclude that we have in this Epistle a composition of that Clement who is known to us from Scripture as having been an associate of the great apostle.

The date of this Epistle has been the subject of considerable controversy. It is clear from the writing itself that it was composed soon after some persecution (chap. i.) which the Roman Church had endured; and the only question is, whether we are to fix upon the persecution under Nero or Domitian. If the former, the date will be about the year 68; if the latter, we must place it towards the close of the first century or the beginning of the second. We possess no external aid to the settlement of this question. The lists of early Roman bishops are in hopeless confusion, some making Clement the immediate successor of St. Peter, others placing Linus, and others still Linus and Anacletus, between him and the apostle. The internal evidence, again, leaves the matter doubtful, though it has been strongly pressed on both sides. The probability seems, on the whole, to be in favour of the Domitian period, so that the Epistle may be dated about a.d. 97.

This Epistle was held in very great esteem by the early Church. The account given of it by Eusebius (Hist. Eccl., iii. 16) is as follows: "There is one acknowledged Epistle of this Clement (whom he has just identified with the friend of St. Paul), great and admirable, which he wrote in the name of the Church of Rome to the Church at Corinth, sedition having then arisen in the latter Church. We are aware that this Epistle has been publicly read in very many churches both in old times, and also in our own day." The Epistle before us thus appears to have been read in numerous churches, as being almost on a level with the canonical writings. And its place in the Alexandrian ms., immediately after the inspired books, is in harmony with the position thus assigned it in the primitive Church. There does indeed appear a great difference between it and the inspired writings in many respects, such as the fanciful use sometimes made of Old-Testament statements, the fabulous stories which are accepted by its author, and the general diffuseness and feebleness of style by which it is distinguished. But the high tone of evangelical truth which pervades it, the simple and earnest appeals which it makes to the heart and conscience, and the anxiety which its writer so constantly shows to promote the best interests of the Church of Christ, still impart an undying charm to this precious relic of later apostolic times.

[N.B.--A sufficient guide to the recent literature of the Clementine mss. and discoveries may be found in The Princeton Review, 1877, p. 325, also in Bishop Wordsworth's succinct but learned Church History to the Council of Nicæa, p. 84. The invaluable edition of the Patres Apostolici, by Jacobson (Oxford, 1840), with a critical text and rich prolegomena and annotations, cannot be dispensed with by any Patristic inquirer. A. C. C.]

The First Epistle of Clement to the Corinthians [1]

Chapter I - The salutation. Praise of the Corinthians before the breaking forth of schism among them

The Church of God which sojourns at Rome, to the Church of God sojourning at Corinth, to them that are called and sanctified by the will of God, through our Lord Jesus Christ: Grace unto you, and peace, from Almighty God through Jesus Christ, be multiplied.

Owing, dear brethren, to the sudden and successive calamitous events which have happened to ourselves, we feel that we have been somewhat tardy in turning our attention to the points respecting which you consulted us; [2] and especially to that shameful and detestable sedition, utterly abhorrent to the elect of God, which a few rash and self-confident persons have kindled to such a pitch of frenzy, that your venerable and illustrious name, worthy to be universally loved, has suffered grievous injury. [3] For who ever dwelt even for a short time among you, and did not find your faith to be as fruitful of virtue as it was firmly established? [4] Who did not admire the sobriety and moderation of your godliness in Christ? Who did not proclaim the magnificence of your habitual hospitality? And who did not rejoice over your perfect and well-grounded knowledge? For ye did all things without respect of persons, and walked in the commandments of God, being obedient to those who had the rule over you, and giving all fitting honour to the presbyters among you. Ye enjoined young men to be of a sober and serious mind; ye instructed your wives to do all things with a blameless, becoming, and pure conscience, loving their husbands as in duty bound; and ye taught them that, living in the rule of obedience, they should manage their household affairs becomingly, and be in every respect marked by discretion.

Chapter II - Praise of the Corinthians continued

Moreover, ye were all distinguished by humility, and were in no respect puffed up with pride, but yielded obedience rather than extorted it, [5] and were more willing to give than to receive. [6] Content with the provision which God had made for you, and carefully attending to His words, ye were inwardly filled [7] with His doctrine, and His sufferings were before your eyes. Thus a profound and abundant peace was given to you all, and ye had an insatiable desire for doing good, while a full outpouring of the Holy Spirit was upon you all. Full of holy designs, ye did, with true earnestness of mind and a godly confidence, stretch forth your hands to God Almighty, beseeching Him to be merciful unto you, if ye had been guilty of any involuntary transgression. Day and night ye were anxious for the whole brotherhood, [8] that the number of God's elect might be saved with mercy and a good conscience. [9] Ye were sincere and uncorrupted, and forgetful of injuries between one another. Every kind of faction and schism was abominable in your sight. Ye mourned over the transgressions of your neighbours: their deficiencies you deemed your own. Ye never grudged any act of kindness, being "ready to every good work." [10] Adorned by a thoroughly virtuous and religious life, ye did all things in the fear of God. The commandments and ordinances of the Lord were written upon the tablets of your hearts. [11]

Chapter III - The sad state of the Corinthian church after sedition arose in it from envy and emulation

Every kind of honour and happiness [12] was bestowed upon you, and then was fulfilled that which is written, "My beloved did eat and drink, and was enlarged and became fat, and kicked." [13] Hence flowed emulation and envy, strife and sedition, persecution and disorder, war and captivity. So the worthless rose up against the honoured, those of no reputation against such as were renowned, the foolish against the wise, the young against those advanced in years. For this reason righteousness and peace are now far departed from you, inasmuch as every one abandons the fear of God, and is become blind in His faith, [14] neither walks in the ordinances of His appointment, nor acts a part becoming a Christian, [15] but walks after his own wicked lusts, resuming the practice of an unrighteous and ungodly envy, by which death itself entered into the world. [16]

Chapter IV - Many evils have already flowed from this source in ancient times

For thus it is written: "And it came to pass after certain days, that Cain brought of the fruits of the earth a sacrifice unto God; and Abel also brought of the firstlings of his sheep, and of the fat thereof. And God had respect to Abel and to his offerings, but Cain and his sacrifices He did not regard. And Cain was deeply grieved, and his countenance fell. And God said to Cain, Why art thou grieved, and why is thy countenance fallen? If thou offerest rightly, but dost not divide rightly, hast thou not sinned? Be at peace: thine offering returns to thyself, and thou shalt again possess it. And Cain said to Abel his brother, Let us go into the field. And it came to pass, while they were in the field, that Cain rose up against Abel his brother, and slew him." [17] Ye see, brethren, how envy and jealousy led to the murder of a brother. Through envy, also, our father Jacob fled from the face of Esau his brother. [18] Envy made Joseph be persecuted unto death, and to come into bondage. [19] Envy compelled Moses to flee from the face of Pharaoh king of Egypt, when he heard these words from his fellow-countryman, "Who made thee a judge or a ruler over us? wilt thou kill me, as thou didst kill the Egyptian yesterday?" [20] On account of envy, Aaron and Miriam had to make their abode without the camp. [21] Envy brought down Dathan and Abiram alive to Hades, through the sedition which they excited against God's servant Moses. [22] Through envy, David underwent the hatred not only of foreigners, but was also persecuted by Saul king of Israel. [23]

Chapter V - No less evils have arisen from the same source in the most recent times. The martyrdom of Peter and Paul

But not to dwell upon ancient examples, let us come to the most recent spiritual heroes. [24] Let us take the noble examples furnished in our own generation. Through envy and jealousy, the greatest and most righteous pillars [of the Church] have been persecuted and put to death. [25] Let us set before our eyes the illustrious [26] apostles. Peter, through unrighteous envy, endured not one or two, but numerous labours and when he had at length suffered martyrdom, departed to the place of glory due to him. Owing to envy, Paul also obtained the reward of patient endurance, after being seven times thrown into captivity, [27] compelled [28] to flee, and stoned. After preaching both in the east and west, he gained the illustrious reputation due to his faith, having taught righteousness to the whole world, and come to the extreme limit of the west, [29] and suffered martyrdom under the prefects. [30] Thus was he removed from the world, and went into the holy place, having proved himself a striking example of patience.

Chapter VI - Continuation. Several other martyrs

To these men who spent their lives in the practice of holiness, there is to be added a great multitude of the elect, who, having through envy endured many indignities and tortures, furnished us with a most excellent example. Through envy, those women, the Danaids [31] and Dircæ, being persecuted, after they had suffered terrible and unspeakable torments, finished the course of their faith with stedfastness, [32] and though weak in body, received a noble reward. Envy has alienated wives from their husbands, and changed that saying of our father Adam, "This is now bone of my bones, and flesh of my flesh." [33] Envy and strife have overthrown great cities and rooted up mighty nations.

Chapter VII - An exhortation to repentance

These things, beloved, we write unto you, not merely to admonish you of your duty, but also to remind ourselves. For we are struggling on the same arena, and the same conflict is assigned to both of us. Wherefore let us give up vain and fruitless cares, and approach to the glorious and venerable rule of our holy calling. Let us attend to what is good, pleasing, and acceptable in the sight of Him who formed us. Let us look stedfastly to the blood of Christ, and see how precious that blood is to God, [34] which, having been shed for our salvation, has set the grace of repentance before the whole world. Let us turn to every age that has passed, and learn that, from generation to generation, the Lord has granted a place of repentance to all such as would be converted unto Him. Noah preached repentance, and as many as listened to him were saved. [35] Jonah proclaimed destruction to the Ninevites; [36] but they, repenting of their sins, propitiated God by prayer, and obtained salvation, although they were aliens [to the covenant] of God.

Chapter VIII - Continuation respecting repentance

The ministers of the grace of God have, by the Holy Spirit, spoken of repentance; and the Lord of all things has himself declared with an oath regarding it, "As I live, saith the Lord, I desire not the death of the sinner, but rather his repentance;" [37] adding, moreover, this gracious declaration, "Repent, O house of Israel, of your iniquity. [38] Say to the children of My people, Though your sins reach from earth to heaven, and though they be redder [39] than scarlet, and blacker than sackcloth, yet if ye turn to Me with your whole heart, and say, Father! I will listen to you, as to a holy [40] people." And in another place He speaks thus: "Wash you, and become clean; put away the wickedness of your souls from before mine eyes; cease from your evil ways, and learn to do well; seek out judgment, deliver the oppressed, judge the fatherless, and see that justice is done to the widow; and come, and let us reason together. He declares, Though your sins be like crimson, I will make them white as snow; though they be like scarlet, I will whiten them like wool. And if ye be willing and obey Me, ye shall eat the good of the land; but if ye refuse, and will not hearken unto Me, the sword shall devour you, for the mouth of the Lord hath spoken these things." [41] Desiring, therefore, that all His beloved should be partakers of repentance, He has, by His almighty will, established [these declarations].

Chapter IX - Examples of the saints

Wherefore, let us yield obedience to His excellent and glorious will; and imploring His mercy and loving-kindness, while we forsake all fruitless labours, [42] and strife, and envy, which leads to death, let us turn and have recourse to His compassions. Let us stedfastly contemplate those who have perfectly ministered to His excellent glory. Let us take (for instance) Enoch, who, being found righteous in obedience, was translated, and death was never known to happen to him. [43] Noah, being found faithful, preached regeneration to the world through his ministry; and the Lord saved by him the animals which, with one accord, entered into the ark.

Chapter X - Continuation of the above

Abraham, styled "the friend," [44] was found faithful, inasmuch as he rendered obedience to the words of God. He, in the exercise of obedience, went out from his own country, and from his kindred, and from his father's house, in order that, by forsaking a small territory, and a weak family, and an insignificant house, he might inherit the promises of God. For God said to him, "Get thee out from thy country, and from thy kindred, and from thy father's house, into the land which I shall show thee. And I will make thee a great nation, and will bless thee, and make thy name great, and thou shall be blessed. And I will bless them that bless thee, and curse them that curse thee; and in thee shall all the families of the earth be blessed." [45] And again, on his departing from Lot, God said to him. "Lift up thine eyes, and look from the place where thou now art, northward, and southward, and eastward, and westward; for all the land which thou seest, to thee will I give it, and to thy seed for ever. And I will make thy seed as the dust of the earth, [so that] if a man can number the dust of the earth, then shall thy seed also be numbered." [46] And again [the Scripture] saith, "God brought forth Abram, and spake unto him, Look up now to heaven, and count the stars if thou be able to number them; so shall thy seed be. And Abram believed God, and it was counted to him for righteousness." [47] On account of his faith and hospitality, a son was given him in his old age; and in the exercise of obedience, he offered him as a sacrifice to God on one of the mountains which He showed him. [48]

Chapter XI - Continuation. Lot

On account of his hospitality and godliness, Lot was saved out of Sodom when all the country round was punished by means of fire and brimstone, the Lord thus making it manifest that He does not forsake those that hope in Him, but gives up such as depart from Him to punishment and torture. [49] For Lot's wife, who went forth with him, being of a different mind from himself and not continuing in agreement with him [as to the command which had been given them], was made an example of, so as to be a pillar of salt unto this day. [50] This was done that all might know that those who are of a double mind, and who distrust the power of God, bring down judgment on themselves [51] and become a sign to all succeeding generations.

Chapter XII - The rewards of faith and hospitality. Rahab

On account of her faith and hospitality, Rahab the harlot was saved. For when spies were sent by Joshua, the son of Nun, to Jericho, the king of the country ascertained that they were come to spy out their land, and sent men to seize them, in order that, when taken, they might be put to death. But the hospitable Rahab receiving them, concealed them on the roof of her house under some stalks of flax. And when the men sent by the king arrived and said "There came men unto thee who are to spy out our land; bring them forth, for so the king commands," she answered them, "The two men whom ye seek came unto me, but quickly departed again and are gone," thus not discovering the spies to them. Then she said to the men, "I know assuredly that the Lord your God hath given you this city, for the fear and dread of you have fallen on its inhabitants. When therefore ye shall have taken it, keep ye me and the house of my father in safety." And they said to her, "It shall be as thou hast spoken to us. As soon, therefore, as thou knowest that we are at hand, thou shalt gather all thy family under thy roof, and they shall be preserved, but all that are found outside of thy dwelling shall perish." [52] Moreover, they gave her a sign to this effect, that she should hang forth from her house a scarlet thread. And thus they made it manifest that redemption should flow through the blood of the Lord to all them that believe and hope in God. [53] Ye see, beloved, that there was not only faith, but prophecy, in this woman.

Chapter XIII - An exhortation to humility

Let us therefore, brethren, be of humble mind, laying aside all haughtiness, and pride, and foolishness, and angry feelings; and let us act according to that which is written (for the Holy Spirit saith, "Let not the wise man glory in his wisdom, neither let the mighty man glory in his might, neither let the rich man glory in his riches; but let him that glorieth glory in the Lord, in diligently seeking Him, and doing judgment and righteousness" [54]), being especially mindful of the words of the Lord Jesus which He spake, teaching us meekness and long-suffering. For thus He spoke: "Be ye merciful, that ye may obtain mercy; forgive, that it may be forgiven to you; as ye do, so shall it be done unto you; as ye judge, so shall ye be judged; as ye are kind, so shall kindness be shown to you; with what measure ye mete, with the same it shall be measured to you." [55] By this precept and by these rules let us establish ourselves, that we walk with all humility in obedience to His holy words. For the holy word saith, "On whom shall I look, but on him that is meek and peaceable, and that trembleth at My words?" [56]

Chapter XIV - We should obey God rather than the authors of sedition

It is right and holy therefore, men and brethren, rather to obey God than to follow those who, through pride and sedition, have become the leaders of a detestable emulation. For we shall incur no slight injury, but rather great danger, if we rashly yield ourselves to the inclinations of men who aim at exciting strife and tumults, so as to draw us away from what is good. Let us be kind one to another after the pattern of the tender mercy and benignity of our Creator. For it is written, "The kind-hearted shall inhabit the land, and the guiltless shall be left upon it, but transgressors shall be destroyed from off the face of it." [57] And again [the Scripture] saith, "I saw the ungodly highly exalted, and lifted up like the cedars of Lebanon: I passed by, and, behold, he was not; and I diligently sought his place, and could not find it. Preserve innocence, and look on equity: for there shall be a remnant to the peaceful man." [58]

Chapter XV - We must adhere to those who cultivate peace, not to those who merely pretend to do so

Let us cleave, therefore, to those who cultivate peace with godliness, and not to those who hypocritically profess to desire it. For [the Scripture] saith in a certain place, "This people honoureth Me with their lips, but their heart is far from Me." [59] And again: "They bless with their mouth, but curse with their heart." [60] And again it saith, "They loved Him with their mouth, and lied to Him with their tongue; but their heart was not right with Him, neither were they faithful in His covenant." [61] "Let the deceitful lips become silent," [62] [and "let the Lord destroy all the lying lips, [63] and the boastful tongue of those who have said, Let us magnify our tongue; our lips are our own; who is lord over us? For the oppression of the poor, and for the sighing of the needy, will I now arise, saith the Lord: I will place him in safety; I will deal confidently with him." [64]

Chapter XVI - Christ as an example of humility

For Christ is of those who are humble-minded, and not of those who exalt themselves over His flock. Our Lord Jesus Christ, the Sceptre of the majesty of God, did not come in the pomp of pride or arrogance, although He might have done so, but in a lowly condition, as the Holy Spirit had declared regarding Him. For He says, "Lord, who hath believed our report, and to whom is the arm of the Lord revealed? We have declared [our message] in His presence: He is, as it were, a child, and like a root in thirsty ground; He has no form nor glory, yea, we saw Him, and He had no form nor comeliness; but His form was without eminence, yea, deficient in comparison with the [ordinary] form of men. He is a man exposed to stripes and suffering, and acquainted with the endurance of grief: for His countenance was turned away; He was despised, and not esteemed. He bears our iniquities, and is in sorrow for our sakes; yet we supposed that [on His own account] He was exposed to labour, and stripes, and affliction. But He was wounded for our transgressions, and bruised for our iniquities. The chastisement of our peace was upon Him, and by His stripes we were healed. All we, like sheep, have gone astray; [every] man has wandered in his own way; and the Lord has delivered Him up for our sins, while He in the midst of His sufferings openeth not His mouth. He was brought as a sheep to the slaughter, and as a lamb before her shearer is dumb, so He openeth not His mouth. In His humiliation His judgment was taken away; who shall declare His generation? for His life is taken from the earth. For the transgressions of my people was He brought down to death. And I will give the wicked for His sepulchre, and the rich for His death, [65] because He did no iniquity, neither was guile found in His mouth. And the Lord is pleased to purify Him by stripes. [66] If ye make [67] an offering for sin, your soul shall see a long-lived seed. And the Lord is pleased to relieve Him of the affliction of His soul, to show Him light, and to form Him with understanding, [68] to justify the Just One who ministereth well to many; and He Himself shall carry their sins. On this account He shall inherit many, and shall divide the spoil of the strong; because His soul was delivered to death, and He was reckoned among the transgressors, and He bare the sins of many, and for their sins was He delivered." [69] And again He saith, "I am a worm, and no man; a reproach of men, and despised of the people. All that see Me have derided Me; they have spoken with their lips; they have wagged their head, [saying] He hoped in God, let Him deliver Him, let Him save Him, since He delighteth in Him." [70] Ye see, beloved, what is the example which has been given us; for if the Lord thus humbled Himself, what shall we do who have through Him come under the yoke of His grace?

Chapter XVII - The saints as examples of humility

Let us be imitators also of those who in goat-skins and sheep-skins [71] went about proclaiming the coming of Christ; I mean Elijah, Elisha, and Ezekiel among the prophets, with those others to whom a like testimony is borne [in Scripture]. Abraham was specially honoured, and was called the friend of God; yet he, earnestly regarding the glory of God, humbly declared, "I am but dust and ashes." [72] Moreover, it is thus written of Job, "Job was a righteous man, and blameless, truthful, God-fearing, and one that kept himself from all evil." [73] But bringing an accusation against himself, he said, "No man is free from defilement, even if his life be but of one day." [74] Moses was called faithful in all God's house; [75] and through his instrumentality, God punished Egypt [76] with plagues and tortures. Yet he, though thus greatly honoured, did not adopt lofty language, but said, when the divine oracle came to him out of the bush, "Who am I, that Thou sendest me? I am a man of a feeble voice and a slow tongue." [77] And again he said, "I am but as the smoke of a pot." [78]

Chapter XVIII - David as an example of humility

But what shall we say concerning David, to whom such testimony was borne, and of whom [79] God said, "I have found a man after Mine own heart, David the son of Jesse; and in everlasting mercy have I anointed him?" [80] Yet this very man saith to God, "Have mercy on me, O Lord, according to Thy great mercy; and according to the multitude of Thy compassions, blot out my transgression. Wash me still more from mine iniquity, and cleanse me from my sin. For I acknowledge my iniquity, and my sin is ever before me. Against Thee only have I sinned, and done that which was evil in Thy sight; that Thou mayest be justified in Thy sayings, and mayest overcome when Thou [81] art judged. For, behold, I was conceived in transgressions, and in my sins did my mother conceive me. For, behold, Thou hast loved truth; the secret and hidden things of wisdom hast Thou shown me. Thou shalt sprinkle me with hyssop, and I shall be cleansed; Thou shalt wash me, and I shall be whiter than snow. Thou shalt make me to hear joy and gladness; my bones, which have been humbled, shall exult. Turn away Thy face from my sins, and blot out all mine iniquities. Create in me a clean heart, O God, and renew a right spirit within me. [82] Cast me not away from Thy presence, and take not Thy Holy Spirit from me. Restore to me the joy of Thy salvation, and establish me by Thy governing Spirit. I will teach transgressors Thy ways, and the ungodly shall be converted unto Thee. Deliver me from blood-guiltiness, [83] O God, the God of my salvation: my tongue shall exult in Thy righteousness. O Lord, Thou shalt open my mouth, and my lips shall show forth Thy praise. For if Thou hadst desired sacrifice, I would have given it; Thou wilt not delight in burnt-offerings. The sacrifice [acceptable] to God is a bruised spirit; a broken and a contrite heart God will not despise." [84]

Chapter XIX - Imitating these examples, let us seek after peace

Thus the humility and godly submission of so great and illustrious men have rendered not only us, but also all the generations before us, better; even as many as have received His oracles in fear and truth. Wherefore, having so many great and glorious examples set before us, let us turn again to the practice of that peace which from the beginning was the mark set before us; [85] and let us look stedfastly to the Father and Creator of the universe, and cleave to His mighty and surpassingly great gifts and benefactions of peace. Let us contemplate Him with our understanding, and look with the eyes of our soul to His long-suffering will. Let us reflect how free from wrath He is towards all His creation.

Chapter XX - The peace and harmony of the universe

The heavens, revolving under His government, are subject to Him in peace. Day and night run the course appointed by Him, in no wise hindering each other. The sun and moon, with the companies of the stars, roll on in harmony according to His command, within their prescribed limits, and without any deviation. The fruitful earth, according to His will, brings forth food in abundance, at the proper seasons, for man and beast and all the living beings upon it, never hesitating, nor changing any of the ordinances which He has fixed. The unsearchable places of abysses, and the indescribable arrangements of the lower world, are restrained by the same laws. The vast unmeasurable sea, gathered together by His working into various basins, [86] never passes beyond the bounds placed around it, but does as He has commanded. For He said, "Thus far shalt thou come, and thy waves shall be broken within thee." [87] The ocean, impassable to man, and the worlds beyond it, are regulated by the same enactments of the Lord. The seasons of spring, summer, autumn, and winter, peacefully give place to one another. The winds in their several quarters [88] fulfill, at the proper time, their service without hindrance. The ever-flowing fountains, formed both for enjoyment and health, furnish without fail their breasts for the life of men. The very smallest of living beings meet together in peace and concord. All these the great Creator and Lord of all has appointed to exist in peace and harmony; while He does good to all, but most abundantly to us who have fled for refuge to His compassions through Jesus Christ our Lord, to whom be glory and majesty for ever and ever. Amen.

Chapter XXI - Let us obey God, and not the authors of sedition

Take heed, beloved, lest His many kindnesses lead to the condemnation of us all. [For thus it must be] unless we walk worthy of Him, and with one mind do those things which are good and well-pleasing in His sight. For [the Scripture] saith in a certain place, "The Spirit of the Lord is a candle searching the secret parts of the belly." [89] Let us reflect how near He is, and that none of the thoughts or reasonings in which we engage are hid from Him. It is right, therefore, that we should not leave the post which His will has assigned us. Let us rather offend those men who are foolish, and inconsiderate, and lifted up, and who glory in the pride of their speech, than [offend] God. Let us reverence the Lord Jesus Christ, whose blood was given for us; let us esteem those who have the rule over us; [90] let us honour the aged [91] among us; let us train up the young men in the fear of God; let us direct our wives to that which is good. Let them exhibit the lovely habit of purity [in all their conduct]; let them show forth the sincere disposition of meekness; let them make manifest the command which they have of their tongue, by their manner [92] of speaking; let them display their love, not by preferring [93] one to another, but by showing equal affection to all that piously fear God. Let your children be partakers of true Christian training; let them learn of how great avail humility is with God--how much the spirit of pure affection can prevail with Him--how excellent and great His fear is, and how it saves all those who walk in [94] it with a pure mind. For He is a Searcher of the thoughts and desires [of the heart]: His breath is in us; and when He pleases, He will take it away.

Chapter XXII - These exhortations are confirmed by the Christian faith, which proclaims the misery of sinful conduct

Now the faith which is in Christ confirms all these [admonitions]. For He Himself by the Holy Ghost thus addresses us: "Come, ye children, hearken unto Me; I will teach you the fear of the Lord. What man is he that desireth life, and loveth to see good days? Keep thy tongue from evil, and thy lips from speaking guile. Depart from evil, and do good; seek peace, and pursue it. The eyes of the Lord are upon the righteous, and His ears are [open] unto their prayers. The face of the Lord is against them that do evil, to cut off the remembrance of them from the earth. The righteous cried, and the Lord heard him, and delivered him out of all his troubles." [95] "Many are the stripes [appointed for] the wicked; but mercy shall compass those about who hope in the Lord." [96]

Chapter XXIII - Be humble, and believe that Christ will come again

The all-merciful and beneficent Father has bowels [of compassion] towards those that fear Him, and kindly and lovingly bestows His favours upon those who come to Him with a simple mind. Wherefore let us not be double-minded; neither let our soul be lifted [97] up on account of His exceedingly great and glorious gifts. Far from us be that which is written, "Wretched are they who are of a double mind, and of a doubting heart; who say, These things we have heard even in the times of our fathers; but, behold, we have grown old, and none of them has happened unto us." [98] Ye foolish ones! compare yourselves to a tree: take [for instance] the vine. First of all, it sheds its leaves, then it buds, next it puts forth leaves, and then it flowers; after that comes the sour grape, and then follows the ripened fruit. Ye perceive how in a little time the fruit of a tree comes to maturity. Of a truth, soon and suddenly shall His will be accomplished, as the Scripture also bears witness, saying, "Speedily will He come, and will not tarry;" [99] and, "The Lord shall suddenly come to His temple, even the Holy One, for whom ye look." [100]

Chapter XXIV - God continually shows us in nature that there will be a resurrection

Let us consider, beloved, how the Lord continually proves to us that there shall be a future resurrection, of which He has rendered the Lord Jesus Christ the first-fruits [101] by raising Him from the dead. Let us contemplate, beloved, the resurrection which is at all times taking place. Day and night declare to us a resurrection. The night sinks to sleep, and the day arises; the day [again] departs, and the night comes on. Let us behold the fruits [of the earth], how the sowing of grain takes place. The sower [102] goes forth, and casts it into the ground; and the seed being thus scattered, though dry and naked when it fell upon the earth, is gradually dissolved. Then out of its dissolution the mighty power of the providence of the Lord raises it up again, and from one seed many arise and bring forth fruit.

Chapter XXV - The phoenix an emblem of our resurrection

Let us consider that wonderful sign [of the resurrection] which takes place in Eastern lands, that is, in Arabia and the countries round about. There is a certain bird which is called a phoenix. This is the only one of its kind, and lives five hundred years. And when the time of its dissolution draws near that it must die, it builds itself a nest of frankincense, and myrrh, and other spices, into which, when the time is fulfilled, it enters and dies. But as the flesh decays a certain kind of worm is produced, which, being nourished by the juices of the dead bird, brings forth feathers. Then, when it has acquired strength, it takes up that nest in which are the bones of its parent, and bearing these it passes from the land of Arabia into Egypt, to the city called Heliopolis. And, in open day, flying in the sight of all men, it places them on the altar of the sun, and having done this, hastens back to its former abode. The priests then inspect the registers of the dates, and find that it has returned exactly as the five hundredth year was completed. [103]

Chapter XXVI - We shall rise again, then, as the Scripture also testifies

Do we then deem it any great and wonderful thing for the Maker of all things to raise up again those that have piously served Him in the assurance of a good faith, when even by a bird He shows us the mightiness of His power to fulfil His promise? [104] For [the Scripture] saith in a certain place, "Thou shalt raise me up, and I shall confess unto Thee;" [105] and again, "I laid me down, and slept; I awaked, because Thou art with me;" [106] and again, Job says, "Thou shalt raise up this flesh of mine, which has suffered all these things." [107]

Chapter XXVII - In the hope of the resurrection, let us cleave to the omnipotent and omniscient God

Having then this hope, let our souls be bound to Him who is faithful in His promises, and just in His judgments. He who has commanded us not to lie, shall much more Himself not lie; for nothing is impossible with God, except to lie. [108] Let His faith therefore be stirred up again within us, and let us consider that all things are nigh unto Him. By the word of His might [109] He established all things, and by His word He can overthrow them. "Who shall say unto Him, What hast thou done? or, Who shall resist the power of His strength?" [110] When and as He pleases He will do all things, and none of the things determined by Him shall pass away. [111] All things are open before Him, and nothing can be hidden from His counsel. "The heavens [112] declare the glory of God, and the firmament showeth His handy-work. Day unto day uttereth speech, and night unto night showeth knowledge. And there are no words or speeches of which the voices are not heard." [113]

Chapter XXVIII - God sees all things: therefore let us avoid transgression

Since then all things are seen and heard [by God], let us fear Him, and forsake those wicked works which proceed from evil desires; [114] so that, through His mercy, we may be protected from the judgments to come. For whither can any of us flee from His mighty hand? Or what world will receive any of those who run away from Him? For the Scripture saith in a certain place, "Whither shall I go, and where shall I be hid from Thy presence? If I ascend into heaven, Thou art there; if I go away even to the uttermost parts of the earth, there is Thy right hand; if I make my bed in the abyss, there is Thy Spirit."[115] Whither, then, shall any one go, or where shall he escape from Him who comprehends all things?

Chapter XXIX - Let us also draw near to God in purity of heart

Let us then draw near to Him with holiness of spirit, lifting up pure and undefiled hands unto Him, loving our gracious and merciful Father, who has made us partakers in the blessings of His elect. [116] For thus it is written, "When the Most High divided the nations, when He scattered [117] the sons of Adam, He fixed the bounds of the nations according to the number of the angels of God. His people Jacob became the portion of the Lord, and Israel the lot of His inheritance." [118] And in another place [the Scripture] saith, "Behold, the Lord taketh unto Himself a nation out of the midst of the nations, as a man takes the first-fruits of his threshing-floor; and from that nation shall come forth the Most Holy."[119]

Chapter XXX - Let us do those things that please God, and flee from those He hates, that we may be blessed

Seeing, therefore, that we are the portion of the Holy One, let us do all those things which pertain to holiness, avoiding all evil-speaking, all abominable and impure embraces, together with all drunkenness, seeking after change, [120] all abominable lusts, detestable adultery, and execrable pride. "For God," saith [the Scripture], "resisteth the proud, but giveth grace to the humble." [121] Let us cleave, then, to those to whom grace has been given by God. Let us clothe ourselves with concord and humility, ever exercising self-control, standing far off from all whispering and evil-speaking, being justified by our works, and not our words. For [the Scripture] saith, "He that speaketh much, shall also hear much in answer. And does he that is ready in speech deem himself righteous? Blessed is he that is born of woman, who liveth but a short time: be not given to much speaking." [122] Let our praise be in God, and not of ourselves; for God hateth those that commend themselves. Let testimony to our good deeds be borne by others, as it was in the case of our righteous forefathers. Boldness, and arrogance, and audacity belong to those that are accursed of God; but moderation, humility, and meekness to such as are blessed by Him.

Chapter XXXI - Let us see by what means we may obtain the divine blessing

Let us cleave then to His blessing, and consider what are the means [123] of possessing it. Let us think [124] over the things which have taken place from the beginning. For what reason was our father Abraham blessed? was it not because he wrought righteousness and truth through faith? [125] Isaac, with perfect confidence, as if knowing what was to happen, [126] cheerfully yielded himself as a sacrifice. [127] Jacob, through reason [128] of his brother, went forth with humility from his own land, and came to Laban and served him; and there was given to him the sceptre of the twelve tribes of Israel.

Chapter XXXII - We are justified not by our own works, but by faith

Whosoever will candidly consider each particular, will recognise the greatness of the gifts which were given by him. [129] For from him [130] have sprung the priests and all the Levites who minister at the altar of God. From him also [was descended] our Lord Jesus Christ according to the flesh. [131] From him [arose] kings, princes, and rulers of the race of Judah. Nor are his other tribes in small glory, inasmuch as God had promised, "Thy seed shall be as the stars of heaven." [132] All these, therefore, were highly honoured, and made great, not for their own sake, or for their own works, or for the righteousness which they wrought, but through the operation of His will. And we, too, being called by His will in Christ Jesus, are not justified by ourselves, nor by our own wisdom, or understanding, or godliness, or works which we have wrought in holiness of heart; but by that faith through which, from the beginning, Almighty God has justified all men; to whom be glory for ever and ever. Amen.

Chapter XXXIII - But let us not give up the practice of good works and love. God Himself is an example to us of good works

What shall we do, then, brethren? Shall we become slothful in well-doing, and cease from the practice of love? God forbid that any such course should be followed by us! But rather let us hasten with all energy and readiness of mind to perform every good work. For the Creator and Lord of all Himself rejoices in His works. For by His infinitely great power He established the heavens, and by His incomprehensible wisdom He adorned them. He also divided the earth from the water which surrounds it, and fixed it upon the immoveable foundation of His own will. The animals also which are upon it He commanded by His own word [133] into existence. So likewise, when He had formed the sea, and the living creatures which are in it, He enclosed them [within their proper bounds] by His own power. Above all, [134] with His holy and undefiled hands He formed man, the most excellent [of His creatures], and truly great through the understanding given him-- the express likeness of His own image. For thus says God: "Let us make man in Our image, and after Our likeness. So God made man; male and female He created them." [135] Having thus finished all these things, He approved them, and blessed them, and said, "Increase and multiply." [136] We see, [137] then, how all righteous men have been adorned with good works, and how the Lord Himself, adorning Himself with His works, rejoiced. Having therefore such an example, let us without delay accede to His will, and let us work the work of righteousness with our whole strength.

Chapter XXXIV - Great is the reward of good works with God. Joined together in harmony, let us implore that reward from Him

The good servant [138] receives the bread of his labour with confidence; the lazy and slothful cannot look his employer in the face. It is requisite, therefore, that we be prompt in the practice of well-doing; for of Him are all things. And thus He forewarns us: "Behold, the Lord [cometh], and His reward is before His face, to render to every man according to his work." [139] He exhorts us, therefore, with our whole heart to attend to this, [140] that we be not lazy or slothful in any good work. Let our boasting and our confidence be in Him. Let us submit ourselves to His will. Let us consider the whole multitude of His angels, how they stand ever ready to minister to His will. For the Scripture saith, "Ten thousand times ten thousand stood around Him, and thousands of thousands ministered unto Him, [141] and cried, Holy, holy, holy, [is] the Lord of Sabaoth; the whole creation is full of His glory." [142] And let us therefore, conscientiously gathering together in harmony, cry to Him earnestly, as with one mouth, that we may be made partakers of His great and glorious promises. For [the Scripture] saith, "Eye hath not seen, nor ear heard, neither have entered into the heart of man, the things which He hath prepared for them that wait for Him." [143]

Chapter XXXV - Immense is this reward. How shall we obtain it?

How blessed and wonderful, beloved, are the gifts of God! Life in immortality, splendour in righteousness, truth in perfect confidence, [144] faith in assurance, self-control in holiness! And all these fall under the cognizance of our understandings [now]; what then shall those things be which are prepared for such as wait for Him? The Creator and Father of all worlds, [145] the Most Holy, alone knows their amount and their beauty. Let us therefore earnestly strive to be found in the number of those that wait for Him, in order that we may share in His promised gifts. But how, beloved, shall this be done? If our understanding be fixed by faith towards God; if we earnestly seek the things which are pleasing and acceptable to Him; if we do the things which are in harmony with His blameless will; and if we follow the way of truth, casting away from us all unrighteousness and iniquity, along with all covetousness, strife, evil practices, deceit, whispering, and evil-speaking, all hatred of God, pride and haughtiness, vainglory and ambition. [146] For they that do such things are hateful to God; and not only they that do them, but also those that take pleasure in them that do them. [147] For the Scripture saith, "But to the sinner God said, Wherefore dost thou declare my statutes, and take my covenant into thy mouth, seeing thou hatest instruction, and castest my words behind thee? When thou sawest a thief, thou consentedst with [148] him, and didst make thy portion with adulterers. Thy mouth has abounded with wickedness, and thy tongue contrived [149] deceit. Thou sittest, and speakest against thy brother; thou slanderest [150] thine own mother's son. These things thou hast done, and I kept silence; thou thoughtest, wicked one, that I should be like to thyself. But I will reprove thee, and set thyself before thee. Consider now these things, ye that forget God, lest He tear you in pieces, like a lion, and there be none to deliver. The sacrifice of praise will glorify Me, and a way is there by which I will show him the salvation of God." [151]

Chapter XXXVI - All blessings are given to us through Christ

This is the way, beloved, in which we find our Saviour, [152] even Jesus Christ, the High Priest of all our offerings, the defender and helper of our infirmity. By Him we look up to the heights of heaven. By Him we behold, as in a glass, His immaculate and most excellent visage. By Him are the eyes of our hearts opened. By Him our foolish and darkened understanding blossoms [153] up anew towards His marvellous light. By Him the Lord has willed that we should taste of immortal knowledge, [154] "who, being the brightness of His majesty, is by so much greater than the angels, as He hath by inheritance obtained a more excellent name than they." [155] For it is thus written, "Who maketh His angels spirits, and His ministers a flame of fire." [156] But concerning His Son [157] the Lord spoke thus: "Thou art my Son, to-day have I begotten Thee. Ask of Me, and I will give Thee the heathen for Thine inheritance, and the uttermost parts of the earth for Thy possession." [158] And again He saith to Him, "Sit Thou at My right hand, until I make Thine enemies Thy footstool." [159] But who are His enemies? All the wicked, and those who set themselves to oppose the will of God. [160]

Chapter XXXVII - Christ is our leader, and we His soldiers

Let us then, men and brethren, with all energy act the part of soldiers, in accordance with His holy commandments. Let us consider those who serve under our generals, with what order, obedience, and submissiveness they perform the things which are commanded them. All are not prefects, nor commanders of a thousand, nor of a hundred, nor of fifty, nor the like, but each one in his own rank performs the things commanded by the king and the generals. The great cannot subsist without the small, nor the small without the great. There is a kind of mixture in all things, and thence arises mutual advantage. [161] Let us take our body for an example. [162] The head is nothing without the feet, and the feet are nothing without the head; yea, the very smallest members of our body are necessary and useful to the whole body. But all work [163] harmoniously together, and are under one common rule[164] for the preservation of the whole body.

Chapter XXXVIII - Let the members of the Church submit themselves, and no one exalt himself above another

Let our whole body, then, be preserved in Christ Jesus; and let every one be subject to his neighbour, according to the special gift [165] bestowed upon him. Let the strong not despise the weak, and let the weak show respect unto the strong. Let the rich man provide for the wants of the poor; and let the poor man bless God, because He hath given him one by whom his need may be supplied. Let the wise man display his wisdom, not by [mere] words, but through good deeds. Let the humble not bear testimony to himself, but leave witness to be borne to him by another. [166] Let him that is pure in the flesh not grow proud [167] of it, and boast, knowing that it was another who bestowed on him the gift of continence. Let us consider, then, brethren, of what matter we were made,--who and what manner of beings we came into the world, as it were out of a sepulchre, and from utter darkness. [168] He who made us and fashioned us, having prepared His bountiful gifts for us before we were born, introduced us into His world. Since, therefore, we receive all these things from Him, we ought for everything to give Him thanks; to whom be glory for ever and ever. Amen.

Chapter XXXIX - There is no reason for self-conceit

Foolish and inconsiderate men, who have neither wisdom [169] nor instruction, mock and deride us, being eager to exalt themselves in their own conceits. For what can a mortal man do? or what strength is there in one made out of the dust? For it is written, "There was no shape before mine eyes, only I heard a sound, [170] and a voice [saying], What then? Shall a man be pure before the Lord? or shall such an one be [counted] blameless in his deeds, seeing He does not confide in His servants, and has charged [171] even His angels with perversity? The heaven is not clean in His sight: how much less they that dwell in houses of clay, of which also we ourselves were made! He smote them as a moth; and from morning even until evening they endure not. Because they could furnish no assistance to themselves, they perished. He breathed upon them, and they died, because they had no wisdom. But call now, if any one will answer thee, or if thou wilt look to any of the holy angels; for wrath destroys the foolish man, and envy killeth him that is in error. I have seen the foolish taking root, but their habitation was presently consumed. Let their sons be far from safety; let them be despised [172] before the gates of those less than themselves, and there shall be none to deliver. For what was prepared for them, the righteous shall eat; and they shall not be delivered from evil." [173]

Chapter XL - Let us preserve in the Church the order appointed by God

These things therefore being manifest to us, and since we look into the depths of the divine knowledge, it behoves us to do all things in [their proper] order, which the Lord has commanded us to perform at stated times. [174] He has enjoined offerings [to be presented] and service to be performed [to Him], and that not thoughtlessly or irregularly, but at the appointed times and hours. Where and by whom He desires these things to be done, He Himself has fixed by His own supreme will, in order that all things being piously done according to His good pleasure, may be acceptable unto Him. [175] Those, therefore, who present their offerings at the appointed times, are accepted and blessed; for inasmuch as they follow the laws of the Lord, they sin not. For his own peculiar services are assigned to the high priest, and their own proper place is prescribed to the priests, and their own special ministrations devolve on the Levites. The layman is bound by the laws that pertain to laymen.

Chapter XLI - Continuation of the same subject

Let every one of you, brethren, give thanks to God in his own order, living in all good conscience, with becoming gravity, and not going beyond the rule of the ministry prescribed to him. Not in every place, brethren, are the daily sacrifices offered, or the peace-offerings, or the sin-offerings and the trespass-offerings, but in Jerusalem only. And even there they are not offered in any place, but only at the altar before the temple, that which is offered being first carefully examined by the high priest and the ministers already mentioned. Those, therefore, who do anything beyond that which is agreeable to His will, are punished with death. Ye see, [176] brethren, that the greater the knowledge that has been vouchsafed to us, the greater also is the danger to which we are exposed.

Chapter XLII - The order of ministers in the Church

The apostles have preached the Gospel to us from [177] the Lord Jesus Christ; Jesus Christ [has done so] from [178] God. Christ therefore was sent forth by God, and the apostles by Christ. Both these appointments, [179] then, were made in an orderly way, according to the will of God. Having therefore received their orders, and being fully assured by the resurrection of our Lord Jesus Christ, and established [180] in the word of God, with full assurance of the Holy Ghost, they went forth proclaiming that the kingdom of God was at hand. And thus preaching through countries and cities, they appointed the first-fruits [of their labours], having first proved them by the Spirit, [181] to be bishops and deacons of those who should afterwards believe. Nor was this any new thing, since indeed many ages before it was written concerning bishops and deacons. For thus saith the Scripture in a certain place, "I will appoint their bishops [182] in righteousness, and their deacons [183] in faith." [184]

Chapter XLIII - Moses of old stilled the contention which arose concerning the priestly dignity

And what wonder is it if those in Christ who were entrusted with such a duty by God, appointed those [ministers] before mentioned, when the blessed Moses also, "a faithful servant in all his house,"[185] noted down in the sacred books all the injunctions which were given him, and when the other prophets also followed him, bearing witness with one consent to the ordinances which he had appointed? For, when rivalry arose concerning the priesthood, and the tribes were contending among themselves as to which of them should be adorned with that glorious title, he commanded the twelve princes of the tribes to bring him their rods, each one being inscribed with the name [186] of the tribe. And he took them and bound them [together], and sealed them with the rings of the princes of the tribes, and laid them up in the tabernacle of witness on the table of God. And having shut the doors of the tabernacle, he sealed the keys, as he had done the rods, and said to them, Men and brethren, the tribe whose rod shall blossom has God chosen to fulfil the office of the priesthood, and to minister unto Him. And when the morning was come, he assembled all Israel, six hundred thousand men, and showed the seals to the princes of the tribes, and opened the tabernacle of witness, and brought forth the rods. And the rod of Aaron was found not only to have blossomed, but to bear fruit upon it. [187] What think ye, beloved? Did not Moses know beforehand that this would happen? Undoubtedly he knew; but he acted thus, that there might be no sedition in Israel, and that the name of the true and only God might be glorified; to whom be glory for ever and ever. Amen.

Chapter XLIV - The ordinances of the apostles, that there might be no contention respecting the priestly office

Our apostles also knew, through our Lord Jesus Christ, and there would be strife on account of the office [188] of the episcopate. For this reason, therefore, inasmuch as they had obtained a perfect foreknowledge of this, they appointed those [ministers] already mentioned, and afterwards gave instructions, [189] that when these should fall asleep, other approved men should succeed them in their ministry. We are of opinion, therefore, that those appointed by them, [190] or afterwards by other eminent men, with the consent of the whole Church, and who have blamelessly served the flock of Christ in a humble, peaceable, and disinterested spirit, and have for a long time possessed the good opinion of all, cannot be justly dismissed from the ministry. For our sin will not be small, if we eject from the episcopate [191] those who have blamelessly and holily fulfilled its duties. [192] Blessed are those presbyters who, having finished their course before now, have obtained a fruitful and perfect departure [from this world]; for they have no fear lest any one deprive them of the place now appointed them. But we see that ye have removed some men of excellent behaviour from the ministry, which they fulfilled blamelessly and with honour.

Chapter XLV - It is the part of the wicked to vex the righteous

Ye are fond of contention, brethren, and full of zeal about things which do not pertain to salvation. Look carefully into the Scriptures, which are the true utterances of the Holy Spirit. Observe [193] that nothing of an unjust or counterfeit character is written in them. There [194] you will not find that the righteous were cast off by men who themselves were holy. The righteous were indeed persecuted, but only by the wicked. They were cast into prison, but only by the unholy; they were stoned, but only by transgressors; they were slain, but only by the accursed, and such as had conceived an unrighteous envy against them. Exposed to such sufferings, they endured them gloriously. For what shall we say, brethren? Was Daniel [195] cast into the den of lions by such as feared God? Were Ananias, and Azarias, and Mishael shut up in a furnace [196] of fire by those who observed [197] the great and glorious worship of the Most High? Far from us be such a thought! Who, then, were they that did such things? The hateful, and those full of all wickedness, were roused to such a pitch of fury, that they inflicted torture on those who served God with a holy and blameless purpose [of heart], not knowing that the Most High is the Defender and Protector of all such as with a pure conscience venerate [198] His all-excellent name; to whom be glory for ever and ever. Amen. But they who with confidence endured [these things] are now heirs of glory and honour, and have been exalted and made illustrious[199] by God in their memorial for ever and ever. Amen.

Chapter XLVI - Let us cleave to the righteous: your strife is pernicious

Such examples, therefore, brethren, it is right that we should follow; [200] since it is written, "Cleave to the holy, for those that cleave to them shall [themselves] be made holy." [201] And again, in another place, [the Scripture] saith, "With a harmless man thou shalt prove [202] thyself harmless, and with an elect man thou shalt be elect, and with a perverse man thou shalt show [203] thyself perverse."[204] Let us cleave, therefore, to the innocent and righteous, since these are the elect of God. Why are there strifes, and tumults, and divisions, and schisms, and wars [205] among you? Have we not [all] one God and one Christ? Is there not one Spirit of grace poured out upon us? And have we not one calling in Christ? [206] Why do we divide and tear to pieces the members of Christ, and raise up strife against our own body, and have reached such a height of madness as to forget that "we are members one of another?" [207] Remember the words of our Lord Jesus Christ, how [208] He said, "Woe to that man [by whom [209] offences come]! It were better for him that he had never been born, than that he should cast a stumbling-block before one of my elect. Yea, it were better for him that a millstone should be hung about [his neck], and he should be sunk in the depths of the sea, than that he should cast a stumbling-block before one of my little ones." [210] Your schism has subverted [the faith of] many, has discouraged many, has given rise to doubt in many, and has caused grief to us all. And still your sedition continueth.

Chapter XLVII - Your recent discord is worse than the former which took place in the times of Paul

Take up the epistle of the blessed Apostle Paul. What did he write to you at the time when the Gospel first began to be preached? [211] Truly, under the inspiration [212] of the Spirit, he wrote to you concerning himself, and Cephas, and Apollos, [213] because even then parties [214] had been formed among you. But that inclination for one above another entailed less guilt upon you, inasmuch as your partialities were then shown towards apostles, already of high reputation, and towards a man whom they had approved. But now reflect who those are that have perverted you, and lessened the renown of your far-famed brotherly love. It is disgraceful, beloved, yea, highly disgraceful, and unworthy of your Christian profession, [215] that such a thing should be heard of as that the most stedfast and ancient Church of the Corinthians should, on account of one or two persons, engage in sedition against its presbyters. And this rumour has reached not only us, but those also who are unconnected [216] with us; so that,

The Epistles of Clement

through your infatuation, the name of the Lord is blasphemed, while danger is also brought upon yourselves.

Chapter XLVIII - Let us return to the practice of brotherly love

Let us therefore, with all haste, put an end [217] to this [state of things]; and let us fall down before the Lord, and beseech Him with tears, that He would mercifully [218] be reconciled to us, and restore us to our former seemly and holy practice of brotherly love. For [such conduct] is the gate of righteousness, which is set open for the attainment of life, as it is written, "Open to me the gates of righteousness; I will go in by them, and will praise the Lord: this is the gate of the Lord: the righteous shall enter in by it." [219] Although, therefore, many gates have been set open, yet this gate of righteousness is that gate in Christ by which blessed are all they that have entered in and have directed their way in holiness and righteousness, doing all things without disorder. Let a man be faithful: let him be powerful in the utterance of knowledge; let him be wise in judging of words; let him be pure in all his deeds; yet the more he seems to be superior to others [in these respects], the more humble-minded ought he to be, and to seek the common good of all, and not merely his own advantage.

Chapter XLIX - The praise of love

Let him who has love in Christ keep the commandments of Christ. Who can describe the [blessed] bond of the love of God? What man is able to tell the excellence of its beauty, as it ought to be told? The height to which love exalts is unspeakable. Love unites us to God. Love covers a multitude of sins.[220] Love beareth all things, is long-suffering in all things. [221] There is nothing base, nothing arrogant in love. Love admits of no schisms: love gives rise to no seditions: love does all things in harmony. By love have all the elect of God been made perfect; without love nothing is well-pleasing to God. In love has the Lord taken us to Himself. On account of the Love he bore us, Jesus Christ our Lord gave His blood for us by the will of God; His flesh for our flesh, and His soul for our souls. [222]

Chapter L - Let us pray to be thought worthy of love

Ye see, beloved, how great and wonderful a thing is love, and that there is no declaring its perfection. Who is fit to be found in it, except such as God has vouchsafed to render so? Let us pray, therefore, and implore of His mercy, that we may live blameless in love, free from all human partialities for one above another. All the generations from Adam even unto this day have passed away; but those who, through the grace of God, have been made perfect in love, now possess a place among the godly, and shall be made manifest at the revelation [223] of the kingdom of Christ. For it is written, "Enter into thy secret chambers for a little time, until my wrath and fury pass away; and I will remember a propitious [224] day, and will raise you up out of your graves." [225] Blessed are we, beloved, if we keep the commandments of God in the harmony of love; that so through love our sins may be forgiven us. For it is written, "Blessed are they whose transgressions are forgiven, and whose sins are covered. Blessed is the man whose sin the Lord will not impute to him, and in whose mouth there is no guile."[226] This blessedness cometh upon those who have been chosen by God through Jesus Christ our Lord; to whom be glory for ever and ever. Amen.

Chapter LI - Let the partakers in strife acknowledge their sins

Let us therefore implore forgiveness for all those transgressions which through any [suggestion] of the adversary we have committed. And those who have been the leaders of sedition and disagreement ought to have respect [227] to the common hope. For such as live in fear and love would rather that they themselves than their neighbours should be involved in suffering. And they prefer to bear blame themselves, rather than that the concord which has been well and piously [228] handed down to us should suffer. For it is better that a man should acknowledge his transgressions than that he should harden his heart, as the hearts of those were hardened who stirred up sedition against Moses the servant of God, and whose condemnation was made manifest [unto all]. For they went down alive into Hades, and death swallowed them up. [229] Pharaoh with his army and all the princes of Egypt, and the chariots with their riders, were sunk in the depths of the Red Sea, and perished, [230] for no other reason than that their foolish hearts were hardened, after so many signs and wonders had been wrought in the land of Egypt by Moses the servant of God.

Chapter LII - Such a confession is pleasing to God

The Lord, brethren, stands in need of nothing; and He desires nothing of any one, except that confession be made to Him. For, says the elect David, "I will confess unto the Lord; and that will please Him more than a young bullock that hath horns and hoofs. Let the poor see it, and be glad." [231] And again he saith, "Offer [232] unto God the sacrifice of praise, and pay thy vows unto the Most High. And call upon Me in the day of thy trouble: I will deliver thee, and thou shalt glorify Me." [233] For "the sacrifice of God is a broken spirit." [234]

Chapter LIII - The love of Moses towards his people

Ye understand, beloved, ye understand well the Sacred Scriptures, and ye have looked very earnestly into the oracles of God. Call then these things to your remembrance. When Moses went up into the mount, and abode there, with fasting and humiliation, forty days and forty nights, the Lord said unto him, "Moses, Moses, get thee down quickly from hence; for thy people whom thou didst bring out of the land of Egypt have committed iniquity. They have speedily departed from the way in which I commanded them to walk, and have made to themselves molten images." [235] And the Lord said unto him, "I have spoken to thee once and again, saying, I have seen this people, and, behold, it is a stiff-necked people: let Me destroy them, and blot out their name from under heaven; and I will make thee a great and wonderful nation, and one much more numerous than this." [236] But Moses said, "Far be it from Thee, Lord: pardon the sin of this people; else blot me also out of the book of the living." [237] O marvellous [238] love! O insuperable perfection! The servant speaks freely to his Lord, and asks forgiveness for the people, or begs that he himself might perish [239] along with them.

Chapter LIV - He who is full of love will incur every loss, that peace may be restored to the Church.

Who then among you is noble-minded? who compassionate? who full of love? Let him declare, "If on my account sedition and disagreement and schisms have arisen, I will depart, I will go away whithersoever ye desire, and I will do whatever the majority [240] commands; only let the flock of Christ live on terms of peace with the presbyters set over it." He that acts thus shall procure to himself great glory in the Lord; and every place will welcome [241] him. For "the earth is the Lord's, and the fulness thereof." [242] These things they who live a godly life, that is never to be repented of, both have done and always will do.

Chapter LV - Examples of such love

To bring forward some examples from among the heathen: Many kings and princes, in times of pestilence, when they had been instructed by an oracle, have given themselves up to death, in order that by their own blood they might deliver their fellow-citizens [from destruction]. Many have gone forth from their own cities, that so sedition might be brought to an end within them. We know many among ourselves who have given themselves up to bonds, in order that they might ransom others. Many, too, have surrendered themselves to slavery, that with the price [243] which they received for themselves, they might provide food for others. Many women also, being strengthened by the grace of God, have performed numerous manly exploits. The blessed Judith, when her city was besieged, asked of the elders permission to go forth into the camp of the strangers; and, exposing herself to danger, she went out for the love which she bare to her country and people then besieged; and the Lord delivered Holofernes into the hands of a woman. [244] Esther also, being perfect in faith, exposed herself to no less danger, in order to deliver the twelve tribes of Israel from impending destruction. For with fasting and humiliation she entreated the everlasting God, who seeth all things; and He, perceiving the humility of her spirit, delivered the people for whose sake she had encountered peril. [245].

Chapter LVI - Let us admonish and correct one another

Let us then also pray for those who have fallen into any sin, that meekness and humility may be given to them, so that they may submit, not unto us, but to the will of God. For in this way they shall secure a fruitful and perfect remembrance from us, with sympathy for them, both in our prayers to God, and our mention of them to the saints. [246] Let us receive correction, beloved, on account of which no one should feel displeased. Those exhortations by which we admonish one another are both good [in themselves] and highly profitable, for they tend to unite [247] us to the will of God. For thus saith the holy Word: "The Lord hath severely chastened me, yet hath not given me over to death." [248] "For whom the Lord loveth He chasteneth, and scourgeth every son whom He receiveth." [249] "The righteous," saith it, "shall chasten me in mercy, and reprove me; but let not the oil of sinners make fat my head." [250] And again he saith, "Blessed is the man whom the Lord reproveth, and reject not thou the warning of the Almighty. For He causes sorrow, and again restores [to gladness]; He woundeth, and His hands make whole. He shall deliver thee in six troubles, yea, in the seventh no evil shall touch thee. In famine He shall rescue thee from death, and in war He shall free thee from the power [251] of the sword. From the scourge of the tongue will He hide thee, and thou shalt not fear when evil cometh. Thou shalt laugh at the unrighteous and the wicked, and shalt not be afraid of the beasts of the field. For the wild beasts shall be at peace with thee: then shalt thou know that thy house shall be in peace, and the habitation of thy tabernacle shall not fail. [252] Thou shall know also that thy seed shall be great, and thy children like the grass of the field. And thou shall come to the grave like ripened corn which is reaped in its season, or like a heap of the threshing-floor which is gathered together at the proper time."[253] Ye see, beloved, that protection is afforded to those that are chastened of the Lord; for since God is good, He corrects us, that we may be admonished by His holy chastisement.

Chapter LVII - Let the authors of sedition submit themselves

Ye therefore, who laid the foundation of this sedition, submit yourselves to the presbyters, and receive correction so as to repent, bending the knees of your hearts. Learn to be subject, laying aside the proud and arrogant self-confidence of your tongue. For it is better for you that ye should occupy [254] a humble but honourable place in the flock of Christ, than that, being highly exalted, ye should be cast out from the hope of His people. [255] For thus speaketh all-virtuous Wisdom: [256] "Behold, I will bring forth to you the words of My Spirit, and I will teach you My speech. Since I called, and ye did not hear; I held forth My words, and ye regarded not, but set at naught My counsels, and yielded not at My reproofs; therefore I too will laugh at your destruction; yea, I will rejoice when ruin cometh upon you, and when sudden confusion overtakes you, when overturning presents itself like a tempest, or when tribulation and oppression fall upon you. For it shall come to pass, that when ye call upon Me, I will not hear you; the wicked shall seek Me, and they shall not find Me. For they hated wisdom, and did not choose the fear of the Lord; nor would they listen to My counsels, but despised My reproofs. Wherefore they shall eat the fruits of their own way, and they shall be filled with their own ungodliness." ... [257]

Chapter LVIII - Blessings sought for all that call upon God

May God, who seeth all things, and who is the Ruler of all spirits and the Lord of all flesh--who chose our Lord Jesus Christ and us through Him to be a peculiar [258] people--grant to every soul that calleth upon His glorious and holy Name, faith, fear, peace, patience, long-suffering, self-control, purity, and sobriety, to the well-pleasing of His Name, through our High Priest and Protector, Jesus Christ, by whom be to Him glory, and majesty, and power, and honour, both now and for evermore. Amen.

Chapter LIX - The Corinthians are exhorted speedily to send back word that peace has been restored. The benediction

Send back speedily to us in peace and with joy these our messengers to you: Claudius Ephebus and Valerius Bito, with Fortunatus: that they may the sooner announce to us the peace and harmony we so earnestly desire and long for [among you], and that we may the more quickly rejoice over the good order re-established among you. The grace of our Lord Jesus Christ be with you, and with all everywhere that are the called of God through Him, by whom be to Him glory, honour, power, majesty, and eternal dominion, [259] from everlasting to everlasting. [260] Amen. [261]

Footnotes:

1. In the only known ms. of this Epistle, the title is thus given at the close.
2. [Note the fact that the Corinthians asked this of their brethren, the personal friends of their apostle St. Paul. Clement's own name does not appear in this Epistle.]
3. Literally, "is greatly blasphemed."
4. Literally, "did not prove your all-virtuous and firm faith."
5. Eph. v. 21; 1 Pet. v. 5.
6. Acts xx. 35.
7. Literally, "ye embraced it in your bowels." [Concerning the complaints of Photius (ninth century) against Clement, see Bull's Defensio Fidei Nicænæ, Works, vol. v. p. 132.]
8. 1 Pet. ii. 17.
9. So, in the ms., but many have suspected that the text is here corrupt. Perhaps the best emendation is that which substitutes sunaistheseos, "compassion," for suneideseos, "conscience."
10. Tit. iii. 1.
11. Prov. vii. 3.
12. Literally, "enlargement"
13. Deut. xxxii. 15.
14. It seems necessary to refer autou to God, in opposition to the translation given by Abp. Wake and others.
15. Literally, "Christ;" comp. 2 Cor. i. 21, Eph. iv. 20.
16. Wisdom ii. 24.
17. Gen. iv. 3-8. The writer here, as always, follows the reading of the Septuagint, which in this passage both alters and adds to the Hebrew text. We have given the rendering approved by the best critics; but some prefer to translate, as in our English version, "unto thee shall be his desire, and thou shalt rule over him." See, for an ancient explanation of the passage, Irenæus, Adv. Hær., iv. 18, 3.
18. Gen. xxvii. 41, etc.
19. Gen. xxxvii.
20. Ex. ii. 14.
21. Num. xii. 14, 15. [In our copies of the Septuagint this is not affirmed of Aaron.]
22. Num. xvi. 33.
23. 1 Kings xviii. 8, etc.
24. Literally, "those who have been athletes."
25. Some fill up the lacuna here found in the ms. so as to read, "have come to a grievous death."
26. Literally, "good." [The martyrdom of St. Peter is all that is thus connected with his arrival in Rome. His numerous labours were restricted to the Circumcision.]
27. Seven imprisonments of St. Paul are not referred to in Scripture.
28. Archbishop Wake here reads "scourged." We have followed the most recent critics in filling up the numerous lacunæ in this chapter.
29. Some think Rome, others Spain, and others even Britain, to be here referred to. [See note at end.]
30. That is, under Tigellinus and Sabinus, in the last year of the Emperor Nero; but some think Helius and Polycletus are referred to; and others, both here and in the preceding sentence, regard the words as denoting simply the witness borne by Peter and Paul to the truth of the gospel before the rulers of the earth.

31. Some suppose these to have been the names of two eminent female martyrs under Nero; others regard the clause as an interpolation. [Many ingenious conjectures might be cited; but see Jacobson's valuable note, Patres Apostol., vol. i. p. 30.]
32. Literally, "have reached to the stedfast course of faith."
33. Gen. ii. 23.
34. Some insert "Father."
35. Gen. vii.; 1 Pet. iii. 20; 2 Pet. ii. 5.
36. Jon. iii.
37. Ezek. xxxiii. 11.
38. Ezek. xviii. 30.
39. Comp. Isa. i. 18.
40. These words are not found in Scripture, though they are quoted again by Clem. Alex. (Pædag., i. 10) as from Ezekiel.
41. Isa. i. 16-20.
42. Some read mataiologian, "vain talk."
43. Gen. v. 24; Heb. xi. 5. Literally, "and his death was not found."
44. Isa. xli. 8; 2 Chron. xx. 7; Judith viii. 19; Jas. ii. 23.
45. Gen. xii. 1-3.
46. Gen. xiii. 14-16.
47. Gen. xv. 5, 6; Rom. iv. 3.
48. Gen. xxi. 22; Heb. xi. 17.
49. Gen. xix.; comp. 2 Pet. ii. 6-9.
50. So Joseph., Antiq., i. 11, 4; Irenæus, Adv. Hær., iv. 31.
51. Literally, "become a judgment and sign."
52. Josh. ii.; Heb. xi. 31.
53. Others of the Fathers adopt the same allegorical interpretation, e.g., Justin Mar., Dial. c. Tryph., n. 111; Irenæus, Adv. Hær., iv. 20. [The whole matter of symbolism under the law must be more thoroughly studied if we would account for such strong language as is here applied to a poetical or rhetorical figure.]
54. Jer. ix. 23, 24; 1 Cor. i. 31; 2 Cor. x. 17.
55. Comp. Matt. vi. 12-15, Matt. vii. 2; Luke vi. 36-38.
56. Isa. lxvi. 2.
57. Prov. ii. 21, 22.
58. Ps. xxxvii. 35-37. "Remnant" probably refers either to the memory or posterity of the righteous.
59. Isa. xxix. 13; Matt. xv. 8; Mark vii. 6.
60. Ps. lxii. 4.
61. Ps. lxxviii. 36, 37.
62. Ps. xxxi. 18.
63. These words within brackets are not found in the ms., but have been inserted from the Septuagint by most editors.
64. Ps. xii. 3-5.
65. The Latin of Cotelerius, adopted by Hefele and Dressel, translates this clause as follows: "I will set free the wicked on account of His sepulchre, and the rich on account of His death."
66. The reading of the ms. is tes pleges, "purify, or free, Him from stripes." We have adopted the emendation of Junius.
67. Wotton reads, "If He make."
68. Or, "fill Him with understanding," if plesai should be read instead of plasai, as Grabe suggests.
69. Isa. liii. The reader will observe how often the text of the Septuagint, here quoted, differs from the Hebrew as represented by our authorized English version.
70. Ps. xxii. 6-8.
71. Heb. xi. 37.
72. Gen. xviii. 27.
73. Job i. 1.
74. Job xiv. 4, 5. [Septuagint.]
75. Num. xii. 7; Heb. iii. 2.
76. Some fill up the lacuna which here occurs in the ms. by "Israel."
77. Ex. iii. 11, Ex. iv. 10.
78. This is not found in Scripture. [They were probably in Clement's version. Comp. Ps. cxix. 83.]
79. Or, as some render, "to whom."
80. Ps. lxxxix. 21.
81. Or, "when Thou judgest."

82. Literally, "in my inwards."
83. Literally, "bloods."
84. Ps. li. 1-17.
85. Literally, "Becoming partakers of many great and glorious deeds, let us return to the aim of peace delivered to us from the beginning." Comp. Heb. xii. 1.
86. Or, "collections."
87. Job xxxviii. 11.
88. Or, "stations."
89. Prov. xx. 27.
90. Comp. Heb. xiii. 17; 1 Thess. v. 12, 13.
91. Or, "the presbyters."
92. Some read, "by their silence."
93. Comp. 1 Tim. v. 21.
94. Some translate, "who turn to Him."
95. Ps. xxxiv. 11-17.
96. Ps. xxxii. 10.
97. Or, as some render, "neither let us have any doubt of."
98. Some regard these words as taken from an apocryphal book, others as derived from a fusion of Jas. i. 8 and 2 Pet. iii. 3, 4.
99. Hab. ii. 3; Heb. x. 37.
100. Mal. iii. 1.
101. Comp. 1 Cor. xv. 20; Col. i. 18.
102. Comp. Luke viii. 5.
103. This fable respecting the phoenix is mentioned by Herodotus (ii. 73) and by Pliny (Nat. Hist., x. 2) and is used as above by Tertullian (De Resurr., §13) and by others of the Fathers.
104. Literally, "the mightiness of His promise."
105. Ps. xxviii. 7, or some apocryphal book.
106. Comp. Ps. iii. 6.
107. Job xix. 25, 26.
108. Comp. Tit. i. 2; Heb. vi. 18.
109. Or, "majesty."
110. Wisdom xii. 12, Wisdom xi. 22.
111. Comp. Matt. xxiv. 35.
112. Literally, "If the heavens," etc.
113. Ps. xix. 1-3.
114. Literally, "abominable lusts of evil deeds."
115. Ps. cxxxix. 7-10
116. Literally "has made us to Himself a part of election."
117. Literally, "sowed abroad."
118. Deut. xxxii. 8, 9.
119. Formed apparently from Num. xviii. 27 and 2 Chron. xxxi. 14. Literally, the closing words are, "the holy of holies."
120. Some translate, "youthful lusts."
121. Prov. iii. 34; Jas. iv. 6; 1 Pet. v. 5.
122. Job xi. 2, 3. The translation is doubtful. [But see Septuagint.]
Footnotes:
123. Literally, "what are the ways of His blessing."
124. Literally, "unroll."
125. Comp. Jas. ii. 21.
126. Some translate, "knowing what was to come."
127. Gen. xxii.
128. So Jacobson: Wotton reads, "fleeing from his brother."
129. The meaning is here very doubtful. Some translate, "the gifts which were given to Jacob by Him," i.e., God.
130. MS. auton, referring to the gifts: we have followed the emendation autou, adopted by most editors. Some refer the word to God, and not Jacob.
131. Comp. Rom. ix. 5.
132. Gen. xxii. 17, Gen. xxviii. 4.
133. Or, "commandment."
134. Or, "in addition to all."
135. Gen. i. 26, 27.
136. Gen. i. 28.

137. Or, "let us consider."
138. Or, "labourer."
139. Isa. xl. 10, Isa. lxii. 11; Rev. xxii. 12.
140. The text here seems to be corrupt. Some translate, "He warns us with all His heart to this end, that," etc.
141. Dan. vii. 10.
142. Isa. vi. 3.
143. 1 Cor. ii. 9.
144. Some translate, "in liberty."
145. Or, "of the ages."
146. The reading is doubtful: some have aphiloxenian, "want of a hospitable spirit." [So Jacobson.]
147. Rom. i. 32.
148. Literally, "didst run with."
149. Literally, "didst weave."
150. Or, "layest a snare for."
151. Ps. l. 16-23. The reader will observe how the Septuagint followed by Clement differs from the Hebrew.
152. Literally, "that which saves us."
153. Or, "rejoices to behold."
154. Or, "knowledge of immortality."
155. Heb. i. 3, 4.
156. Ps. civ. 4; Heb. i. 7.
157. Some render, "to the Son."
158. Ps. ii. 7, 8; Heb. i. 5.
159. Ps. cx. 1; Heb. i. 13.
160. Some read, "who oppose their own will to that of God."
161. Literally, "in these there is use."
162. 1 Cor. xii. 12, etc.
163. Literally, "all breathe together."
164. Literally, "use one subjection."
165. Literally, "according as he has been placed in his charism."
166. Comp. Prov. xxvii. 2.
167. The ms. is here slightly torn, and we are left to conjecture.
168. Comp. Ps. cxxxix. 15.
169. Literally, "and silly and uninstructed."
170. Literally, "a breath."
171. Or, "has perceived."
172. Some render, "they perished at the gates."
173. Job iv. 16-18, Job xv. 15, Job iv. 19-21, Job v. 1-5.
174. Some join kata kairous tetagmenous, "at stated times." to the next sentence. [1 Cor. xvi. 1, 2.]
175. Literally, "to His will." [Comp. Rom. xv. 15, 16, Greek.]
176. Or, "consider." [This chapter has been cited to prove the earlier date for this Epistle. But the reference to Jerusalem may be an ideal present.]
177. Or, "by the command of."
178. Or, "by the command of."
179. Literally, "both things were done."
180. Or, "confirmed by."
181. Or, "having tested them in spirit."
182. Or, "overseers."
183. Or, "servants."
184. Isa. lx. 17, Sept.; but the text is here altered by Clement. The LXX. have "I will give thy rulers in peace, and thy overseers in righteousness."
185. Num. xii. 7; Heb. iii. 5.
186. Literally, "every tribe being written according to its name."
187. See Num. xvii.
188. Literally, "on account of the title of the oversight." Some understand this to mean, "in regard to the dignity of the episcopate;" and others simply, "on account of the oversight."
189. The meaning of this passage is much controverted. Some render, "left a list of other approved persons;" while others translate the unusual word epinome, which causes the difficulty, by "testamentary direction," and many others deem the text corrupt. We have given what seems the simplest version of the text as it stands. [Comp. the versions of Wake, Chevallier, and others.]

190. i.e., the apostles.
191. Or, "oversight."
192. Literally, "presented the offerings."
193. Or, "Ye perceive."
194. Or, "For."
195. Dan. vi. 16.
196. Dan. iii. 20.
197. Literally, "worshipped."
198. Literally, "serve."
199. Or, "lifted up."
200. Literally, "To such examples it is right that we should cleave."
201. Not found in Scripture.
202. Literally, "be."
203. Or, "thou wilt overthrow."
204. Ps. xviii. 25, 26.
205. Or, "war." Comp. Jas. iv. 1.
206. Comp. Eph. iv. 4-6.
207. Rom. xii. 5.
208. This clause is wanting in the text.
209. This clause is wanting in the text.
210. Comp. Matt. xviii. 6, Matt. xxvi. 24; Mark ix. 42; Luke xvii. 2.
211. Literally, "in the beginning of the Gospel." [Comp. Phil. iv. 15.]
212. Or, "spiritually."
213. 1 Cor. iii. 13, etc.
214. Or, "inclinations for one above another."
215. Literally, "of conduct in Christ."
216. Or, "aliens from us," i.e., the Gentiles.
217. Literally "remove."
218. Literally, "becoming merciful."
219. Ps. cxviii. 19, 20.
220. Jas. v. 20; 1 Pet. iv. 8.
221. Comp. 1 Cor. xiii. 4, etc.
222. [Comp. Irenæus, v. 1; also Mathetes, Ep. to Diognetus, cap. ix.]
223. Literally, "visitation."
224. Or, "good."
225. Isa. xxvi. 20.
226. Ps. xxxii. 1, 2.
227. Or, "look to."
228. Or, "righteously."
229. Num. xvi.
230. Ex. xiv.
231. Ps. lxix. 31, 32.
232. Or, "sacrifice."
233. Ps. l. 14, 15.
234. Ps. li. 17.
235. Ex. xxxii. 7, etc.; Deut. ix. 12, etc.
236. Ex. xxxii. 9, etc.
237. Ex. xxxii. 32.
238. Or, "mighty."
239. Literally, "be wiped out."
240. Literally, "the multitude." [Clement here puts words into the mouth of the Corinthian presbyters. It has been strangely quoted to strengthen a conjecture that he had humbly preferred Linus and Cletus when first called to preside.]
241. Or, "receive."
242. Ps. xxiv. 1; 1 Cor. x. 26, 28.
243. Literally, "and having received their prices, fed others." [Comp. Rom. xvi. 3, 4, and Phil. ii. 30.]
244. Judith viii. 30.
245. Esth. vii., viii.
246. Literally, "there shall be to them a fruitful and perfect remembrance, with compassions both towards God and the saints."
247. Or, "they unite."

The Epistles of Clement

248. Ps. cxviii. 18.
249. Prov. iii. 12; Heb. xii. 6.
250. Ps. cxli. 5.
251. Literally, "hand."
252. Literally, "err" or "sin."
253. Job v. 17-26.
254. Literally, "to be found small and esteemed."
255. Literally, "His hope." [It has been conjectured that elpidos should be epaulidos, and the reading, "out of the fold of his people." See Chevallier.]
256. Prov. i. 23-31. [Often cited by this name in primitive writers.]
257. Junius (Pat. Young), who examined the ms. before it was bound into its present form, stated that a whole leaf was here lost. The next letters that occur are ipon, which have been supposed to indicate eipon or elipon. Doubtless some passages quoted by the ancients from the Epistle of Clement, and not now found in it, occurred in the portion which has thus been lost.
258. Comp. Tit. ii. 14.
259. Literally, "an eternal throne."
260. Literally, "From the ages to the ages of ages."
261. [Note St. Clement's frequent doxologies.] [N.B.--The language of Clement concerning the Western progress of St. Paul (cap. v.) is our earliest postscript to his Scripture biography. It is sufficient to refer the reader to the great works of Conybeare and Howson, and of Mr. Lewin, on the Life and Epistles of St. Paul. See more especially the valuable note of Lewin (vol. ii. p. 294) which takes notice of the opinion of some learned men, that the great Apostle of the Gentiles preached the Gospel in Britain. The whole subject of St. Paul's relations with British Christians is treated by Williams, in his Antiquities of the Cymry, with learning and in an attractive manner. But the reader will find more ready to his hand, perhaps, the interesting note of Mr. Lewin, on Claudia and Pudens (2 Tim. iv. 21), in his Life and Epistles of St. Paul, vol. ii. p. 392. See also Paley's Horæ Paulinæ, p. 40. London, 1820.]

Two Epistles Concerning Virginity

Attributed to Clement of Rome.
[Translated by the Rev. B. P. Pratten.]

Introductory Notice to Two Epistles Concerning Virginity

By Professor M. B. Riddle, D.D.

Among the "Pseudo-Clementina" the Two Epistles concerning Virginity must properly be placed.

The evidence against the genuineness seems conclusive; yet, with the exception of the homily usually styled the Second Epistle of Clement, [1] no spurious writings attributed to the great Roman Father can be assigned an earlier date than these two letters.

Uhlhorn, in view of the reference to the sub-introductae, thinks they were written shortly before the time of Cyprian; [2] and this seems very probable.

Jerome was acquainted with the writings (Ad Jovinum, i. 12), and possibly Epiphanius (Haer., xxx. 15).

Hence we may safely allow an early date.

Yet these evidences of age tell against the genuineness.

1. Early works of this character would not have disappeared from notice to such an extent, had they been authenticated as writings of Clement.

Supporting, as they do, the ascetic tendency prevalent in the Western Church at and after the date when they are first noticed by Christian writers, they would have been carefully preserved and frequently cited, had they been genuine.

The name of the great Roman Father would have been so weighty, that the advocates of celibacy would have kept the documents in greater prominence.

The silence of Eusebius respecting the letters is an important fact in this discussion.

2. A second argument against the genuineness is derived from the ascetic tone itself.

Such pronounced statements are not, we must firmly hold, to be found in the Christian literature of the sub-apostolic age.

This historical argument is further sustained by other indications in the epistles.

They point to a stage of ecclesiastical development which belongs to a much later period than that of Clement.

3. The use of Scripture in these letters seems to be conclusive against the Clementine authorship.

A comparison with the citations in the genuine Epistle of Clement shows that these writings make much greater use of the Pauline (particularly the Pastoral) Epistles; that the Old Testament is less frequently cited, and that the mode of handling proof-texts is that of a later age.

4. The judgment of the most candid patristic scholars is against the genuineness.

Of Protestants, Wetstein stands alone in supporting the Clementine authorship; and his position is readily explained by the fact that he discovered the Syriac version which restored the writings to modern scholars (see below).

The genuineness is defended by Villecourt and Beelen (see below), also by Moehler, Champagny, and Brueck.

But such experts as Mansi, Hefele, Alzog, and Funk, among Roman Catholics, unite with Protestant scholars in assigning a later date, and consequently in denying the Clementine authorship.

Translator's Introductory Notice.

While the great mass of early Christian literature bearing the name of Clement of Rome is undoubtedly spurious, the case is somewhat different with regard to the two following epistles.

Not only have Roman Catholic writers maintained their genuineness with great ingenuity and learning, but Wetstein, who first edited them, argued powerfully for their being received as the authentic productions of Clement; and even Neander has admitted that they may possibly have been written by that friend and fellow-labourer of the apostles.

The Epistles of Clement

Their literary history in modern times is somewhat curious.

Wetstein unexpectedly discovered them appended to a copy of the Syriac Peschito version of the New Testament furnished to him by Sir James Porter, then British ambassador at Constantinople.

He soon afterwards (1752) published them in Syriac, accompanied by a Latin version of his own, with Prolegomena, in which he upheld their genuineness.

This speedily called forth two works, one by Lardner (1753), and a second by Venema (1754), in both of which their authenticity was disputed.

To these writings Wetstein himself, and, after his death, Gallandius, published rejoinders; but the question remained as far from positive settlement as ever, and continues sub-judice even at the present day

It is generally admitted (and, of course, asserted by those that maintain their truly Clementine origin) that Greek was the original language of these epistles.

Many have argued that they contain plain references to the sub-introductae spoken of in the literature of the third century, and that therefore they were probably composed in the Oriental Church about that period.

These epistles have been very carefully edited in recent times by the Roman Catholic scholars Villecourt (1853) and Beelen (1856).

Both have argued strenuously for the genuineness of the letters, but it may be doubted if they have succeeded in repelling all the objections of Lardner and Venema.

Beelen's work is a highly scholarly production, and his Prolegomena are marked by great fulness and perspicuity.

A German translation of these epistles was published by Zingerle (1821).

They are now for the first time translated into the English language.

The translation is made from the text of Beelen.

The division into chapters is due to Wetstein.

Footnotes:

1. See vol. vii. pp. 6-3.
2. Against this class Cyprian stoutly contended.
Comp. Cyprian, Ante-Nicene Fathers, vol. v. pp. 357, 358, 54-59.

The First Epistle of the Blessed Clement, the Disciple of Peter the Apostle.

Chapter I - The Salutation

To all those who love and cherish their life which is in Christ through God the Father, and obey the truth of God in hope of eternal life; to those who bear affection towards their brethren and towards their neighbours in the love of God; to the blessed brother virgins, [1] who devote themselves to preserve virginity "for the sake of the kingdom of heaven;" [2] and to the holy sister virgins:
the peace which is in God. [3]

Chapter II - For True Virginity Perfect Virtue is Necessary

Of all virgins of either sex who have truly resolved to preserve virginity for the sake of the kingdom of heaven--of each and every one of them it is required that he be worthy of the kingdom of heaven in every thing.

For not by eloquence [4] or renown, [5] by station [6] and descent, or by beauty or strength, or by length of life, [7] is the kingdom of heaven obtained; but it is obtained by the power of faith, when a man exhibits the works of faith.

For whosoever is truly righteous, his works testify concerning his faith, that he is truly a believer, with a faith which is great, a faith which is perfect, a faith which is in God, a faith which shines in good works, that the Father of all may be glorified through Christ.

Now, those who are truly virgins for the sake of God give heed to Him who hath said, "Let not righteousness and faith fail thee; bind them on thy neck, and thou shalt find favour for thyself; and devise thou good things before God and before men." [8]"The paths," therefore, "of the righteous shine as the light, and the light of them advances until the day is perfect." [9]For the beams of their light illumine the whole creation even now by good works, as those who are truly "the light of the world,"[10] giving light to "those who sit in darkness," [11] that they may arise and go forth from the darkness by the light of the good works of the fear of God, "that they may see our good works and glorify our Father who is in heaven." [12]For it is required of the man of God, that in all his words and works he be perfect, and that in his life he be adorned with all exemplary and well-ordered behaviour,[13] and do all his deeds in righteousness, as a man of God.

Chapter III - True Virgins Prove Themselves Such by Self-Denial, as Does the True Believer by Good Works

For virgins are a beautiful pattern to believers, and to those who shall believe.

The name alone, indeed, without works, does not introduce into the kingdom of heaven; but, if a man be truly a believer, such an one can be saved.

For, if a person be only called a believer in name, whilst he is not such in works, he cannot possibly be a believer.

"Let no one," therefore, "lead you astray with the empty words of error." [14]For, merely because a person is called a virgin, if he be destitute of works excellent and comely, and suitable to virginity, he cannot possibly be saved.

For our Lord called such virginity as that "foolish," as He said in the Gospel; [15] and because it had neither oil nor light, it was left outside of the kingdom of heaven, and was shut out from the joy of the bridegroom, and was reckoned with His enemies.

For such persons as these "have the appearance only of the fear of God, but the power of it they deny." [16]For they "think with themselves that they are something, whilst they are nothing, and are deceived.

But let every one constantly try [17] his works," [18] and know himself; for empty worship does he offer, whosoever he be that makes profession of virginity and sanctity, "and denies its power."

For virginity of such a kind is impure, and disowned by all good works.

For "every tree whatsoever is known from its fruits." [19]"See that thou understand [20] what I say: God will give thee understanding." [21]For whosoever engages before God to preserve sanctity must be girded with all the holy power of God. And, if with true fear [22] he crucify his body, he for the sake of the fear of God excuses himself from that word in which the Scripture [23] has said:

"Be fruitful, and multiply," [24] and shuns all the display, and care, and sensuality, [25] and fascination of this world, and its revelries and its drunkenness, and all its luxury and ease, and withdraws from the entire life of [26] this world, and from its snares, and nets, and hindrances; and, whilst thou walkest [27] upon the earth, be zealous that thy work and thy business be in heaven.

Chapter IV - Continuation of the Remarks on Self-Denial; Object and Reward of True Virgins

For he who covets for himself these things so great and excellent, withdraws and severs himself on this account from all the world, that he may go and live a life divine and heavenly, like the holy angels, in work pure and holy, and "in the holiness [28] of the Spirit of God," [29] and that he may serve God Almighty through Jesus Christ for the sake of the kingdom of heaven.

On this account he severs himself from all the appetites of the body.

And not only does he excuse himself from this command, "Be fruitful, and multiply," but he longs for the "hope promised" and prepared "and laid up in heaven" [30] by God, who has declared with His mouth, and He does not lie, that it is "better than sons and daughters," [31] and that He will give to virgins a notable place in the house of God, which is something "better than sons and daughters," and better than the place of those who have passed a wedded life in sanctity, and whose "bed has not been defiled." [32] For God will give to virgins the kingdom of heaven, as to the holy angels, by reason of this great and noble profession.

Chapter V - The Irksomeness and the Enemies of Virginity

Thou desirest, then, to be a virgin?

Knowest thou what hardship and irksomeness there is in true virginity--that which stands constantly at all seasons before God, and does not withdraw from His service, and "is anxious how it may please its Lord with a holy body, and with its spirit?" [33]Knowest thou what great glory pertains to virginity, and is it for this that thou dost set thyself to practise it?

Dost thou really know and understand what it is thou art eager to do?

Art thou acquainted with the noble task of holy virginity?

Dost thou know how, like a man, to enter "lawfully" upon [34] this contest and "strive," [35] that, in the might of the Holy Spirit, [36] thou choosest this for thyself, that thou mayest be crowned with a crown of light, and that they may lead thee about in triumph through "the Jerusalem above"? [37]If so be, then, that thou longest for all these things, conquer the body; conquer the appetites of the flesh; conquer the world in the Spirit of God; conquer these vain things of time, which pass away and grow old, and decay, and come to an end; conquer the dragon; [38] conquer the lion; [39] conquer the serpent;[40] conquer Satan;-- through Jesus Christ, who doth strengthen thee by the hearing of His words and the divine Eucharist. [41]"Take up thy cross and follow" [42] Him who makes thee clean, Jesus Christ thy Lord.

Strive to run straight forward and boldly, not with fear, but with courage, relying on the promise of thy Lord, that thou shalt obtain the victor-crown [43] of thy "calling on high" [44] through Jesus Christ.

For whosoever walks perfect in faith, and not fearing, doth in very deed receive the crown of virginity, which is great in its toil and great in its reward.

Dost thou understand and know how honourable a thing is sanctity? [45]Dost thou understand how great and exalted and excellent is the glory of virginity? [46]

Chapter VI - Divinity of Virginity

The womb of a holy virgin [47] carried our Lord Jesus Christ, the Son of God; and the body which our Lord wore, and in which He carried on the conflict in this world, He put on from a holy virgin.

From this, therefore, understand the greatness and dignity of virginity.

Dost thou wish to be a Christian?

Imitate Christ in everything.

John, the ambassador, he who came before our Lord, he "than whom there was not a greater among those born of women," [48] the holy messenger of our Lord, was a virgin.

Imitate, therefore, the ambassador of our Lord, and be his follower [49] in every thing.

That John, again, who "reclined on the bosom of our Lord, and whom He greatly loved," [50] --he, too, was a holy person. [51] For it was not without reason that our Lord loved him.

Paul, also, and Barnabas, and Timothy, with all the others, "whose names are written in the book of life," [52] --these, I say, all cherished and loved sanctity, [53] and ran in the contest, and finished their course without blemish, as imitators of Christ, and as sons of the living God.

Moreover, also, Elijah and Elisha, and many other holy men, we find to have lived a holy [54] and spotless life.

If, therefore, thou desirest to be like these, imitate them with all thy power.

For the Scripture has said, "The elders who are among you, honour; and, seeing their manner of life and conduct, imitate their faith." [55] And again it saith, "Imitate me, my brethren, as I imitate Christ." [56]

Chapter VII - The True Virgin

Those, therefore, who imitate Christ, imitate Him earnestly.

For those who have "put on Christ" [57] in truth, express His likeness in their thoughts, and in their whole life, and in all their behaviour:

in word, and in deeds, and in patience, and in fortitude, and in knowledge, and in chastity, and in long-suffering, and in a pure heart, and in faith, and in hope, and in full and perfect love towards God. No virgin, therefore, unless they be in everything as Christ, and as those "who are Christs," [58] can be saved.

For every virgin who is in God is holy in her body and in her spirit, and is constant in the service of her Lord, not turning away from it any whither, but waiting upon Him always in purity and holiness in the Spirit of God, being "solicitous how she may please her Lord," [59] by living purely and without stain, and solicitous to be pleasing before Him in every thing.

She who is such does not withdraw from our Lord, but in spirit is ever with her Lord:

as it is written, "Be ye holy, as I am holy, saith the Lord." [60]

Chapter VIII - Virgins, by the Laying Aside of All Carnal Affection, are Imitators of God

For, if a man be only in name called holy, he is not holy; but he must be holy in everything:

in his body and in his spirit.

And those who are virgins rejoice at all times in becoming like God and His Christ, and are imitators of them.

For in those that are such there is not "the mind [61] of the flesh."

In those who are truly believers, and "in whom the Spirit of Christ dwells" [62] --in them "the mind of the flesh" cannot be:

which is fornication, uncleanness, wantonness; idolatry, [63] sorcery; enmity, jealousy, rivalry, wrath, disputes, dissensions, ill-will; drunkenness, revelry; buffoonery, foolish talking, boisterous laughter; backbiting, insinuations; bitterness, rage; clamour, abuse, insolence of speech; malice, inventing of evil, falsehood; talkativeness, [64] babbling; [65] threatenings, gnashing of teeth, readiness to accuse, [66] jarring, [67] disdainings, blows; perversions of the right, [68] laxness in judgment; haughtiness, arrogance, ostentation, pompousness, boasting of family, of beauty, of position, of wealth, of an arm of flesh; [69] quarrelsomeness, injustice, [70] eagerness for victory; hatred, anger, envy, perfidy, retaliation; [71] debauchery, gluttony, "overreaching (which is idolatry)," [72] "the love of money (which is the root of all evils);" [73] love of display, vainglory, love of rule, assumption, pride (which is called death, and which "God fights against"). [74] Every man with whom are these and such like things--every such man is of the flesh.

For, "he that is born of the flesh is flesh; and he that is of the earth speaketh of the earth," [75] and his thoughts are of the earth.

And "the mind of the flesh is enmity towards God.

For it does not submit itself to the law of God; for it cannot do so," [76] because it is in the flesh, "in which dwells no good," [77] because the Spirit of God is not in it.

For this cause justly does the Scripture say regarding such a generation as this:

"My Spirit shall not dwell in men for ever, because they are flesh." [78] "Whosoever, therefore, has not the Spirit of God in him, is none of His:" [79] as it is written, "The Spirit of God departed from Saul, and an evil spirit troubled him, which was sent upon him from God." [80]

Chapter IX - Continuation of the Subject of Mortification; Dignity of Persons Consecrated to God

He in whomsoever the Spirit of God is, is in accord with the will of the Spirit of God; and, because he is in accord with the Spirit of God, therefore does he mortify the deeds of the body and live unto God, "treading down and subjugating the body and keeping it under; so that, while preaching to others," he may be a beautiful example and pattern to believers, and may spend his life in works which are worthy of the Holy Spirit, so that he may "not be cast away," [81] but may be approved before God and before men.

For in "the man who is of God," [82] with him I say there is nothing of the mind of the flesh; and especially in virgins of either sex; but the fruits of all of them are "the fruits of the Spirit" [83] and of life, and they are truly the city of God, and the houses and temples in which God abides and dwells, and among which He walks, as in the holy city of heaven.

For in this "do ye appear to the world as lights, in that ye give heed to the Word of life," [84] and thus ye are in truth the praise, and the boast, and the crown of rejoicing, and the delight of good servants in our Lord Jesus Christ.

For all who see you will "acknowledge that ye are the seed which the Lord hath blessed;" [85] in very deed a seed honourable and holy, and "a priestly kingdom, a holy people, the people of the inheritance," [86] the heirs of the promises of God; of things which do not decay, nor wither; of "that which eye hath not seen, and ear hath not heard, and which hath not come up into the heart of man; of that which God hath prepared for those who love Him and keep His commandments." [87]

Chapter X - Denunciation of Dangerous and Scandalous Association with Maidens

Now, we are persuaded of you, my brethren, that your thoughts are occupied about those things which are requisite for your salvation. [88] But we speak thus [89] in consequence of the evil rumours and reports concerning shameless men, who, under pretext of the fear of God, have their dwelling with maidens, and so, expose themselves to danger, and walk with them along the road and in solitary places[90] alone--a course which is full of dangers, and full of stumbling-blocks and snares and pitfalls; nor is it in any respect right for Christians and those who fear God so to conduct themselves.

Others, too, eat and drink with them at entertainments allowing themselves in loose behaviour and much uncleanness--such as ought not to be among believers, and especially among those who have chosen for themselves a life of holiness. [91] Others, again, meet together for vain and trifling conversation and merriment, and that they may speak evil of one another; and they hunt up tales against one another, and are idle: persons with whom we do not allow you even to eat bread.

Then, others gad about among the houses of virgin brethren or sisters, on pretence of visiting them, or reading the Scriptures to them, or exorcising them.

Forasmuch as they are idle and do no work, they pry into those things which ought not to be inquired into, and by means of plausible words make merchandise of the name of Christ.

These are men from whom the divine apostle kept aloof, because of the multitude of their evil deeds; as it is written:

"Thorns sprout in the hands of the idle;" [92] and, "The ways of the idle are full of thorns." [93]

Chapter XI - Perniciousness of Idleness; Warning Against the Empty Longing to Be Teachers; Advice About Teaching and the Use of Divine Gifts

Such are the ways of all those who do not work, but go hunting for tales, and think to themselves that this is profitable and right. [94]

For such persons are like those idle and prating widows "who go wandering about [95] among houses" [96] with their prating, and hunt for idle tales, and carry them from house to house with much exaggeration, without fear of God.

And besides all this, barefaced men as they are, [97] under pretence of teaching, they set forth a variety of doctrines.

And would that they taught the doctrines of truth!

But it is this which is so disquieting, that they understand not what they mean, and assert that which is not true:

because they wish to be teachers, and to display themselves as skilful in speaking; because they traffic in iniquity in the name of Christ--which it is not right for the servants of God to do.

And they hearken not to that which the Scripture has said:

"Let not many be teachers among you, my brethren, and be not all of you prophets." [98] For "he who does not transgress in word is a perfect man, able to keep down and subjugate his whole body." [99] And, "If a man speak, let him speak in the words [100] of God." [101] And, "If there is in thee understanding, give an answer to thy brother but if not, put thy hand on thy mouth." [102] For, "at one time it is proper to keep silence, and at another thee to speak." [103] And again it says "When a man speaks in season, it is honourable [104] to him." [105] And again it says:

"Let your speech be seasoned with grace.

For it is required of a man to know how to give an answer to every one in season." [106] For "he that utters whatsoever comes to his mouth, that man produces strife; and he that utters a superfluity of words increases vexation; and he that is hasty with his lips falls into evil.

For because of the unruliness of the tongue cometh anger; but the perfect man keeps watch over his tongue, and loves his soul's life." [107] For these are they "who by good words and fair speeches lead astray the hearts of the simple, and, while offering them blessings, lead them astray." [108] Let us, therefore, fear the judgment which awaits teachers.

For a severe judgment will those teachers receive "who teach, but do not," [109] and those who take upon them the name of Christ falsely, and say:

We teach the truth, and yet go wandering about idly, and exalt themselves, and make their boast" in the mind of the flesh." [110] These, moreover, are like "the blind man who leads the blind man, and they both fall into the ditch." [111] And they will receive judgment, because in their talkativeness and their frivolous teaching they teach natural [112] wisdom and the "frivolous error of the plausible words of the wisdom of men," [113] "according to the will of the prince of the dominion of the air, and of the spirit which works in those men who will not obey, according to the training of this world, and not according to the doctrine of Christ." [114] But if thou hast received "the word of knowledge, or the word of instruction, or of prophecy," [115] blessed be God, "who helps every man without grudging--that God who gives to every man and does not upbraid him." [116] With the gift, therefore, which thou hast received from our Lord, serve thy spiritual brethren, the prophets who know that the words which thou speakest are those of our Lord; and declare the gift which thou hast received in the Church for the edification of the brethren in Christ (for good and excellent are those things which help the men of God), if so be that they are truly with thee. [117]

Chapter XII - Rules for Visits, Exorcisms, and How People are to Assist the Sick, and to Walk in All Things Without Offence.

Moreover, also, this is comely and useful, that a man "visit orphans and widows," [118] and especially those poor persons who have many children.

These things are, without controversy, required of the servants of God, and comely and suitable for them.

This also, again, is suitable and right and comely for those who are brethren in Christ, that they should visit those who are harassed by evil spirits, and pray and pronounce adjurations [119] over them, intelligently, offering such prayer as is acceptable before God; not with a multitude of fine words, [120] well prepared and arranged, so that they may appear to men eloquent and of a good memory.

Such men are "like a sounding pipe, or a tinkling cymbal;" [121] and they bring no help to those over whom they make their adjurations; but they speak with terrible words, and affright people, but do not act with true faith, according to the teaching of our Lord, who hath said:

"This kind goeth not out but by fasting and prayer," [122] offered unceasingly and with earnest mind. And let them holily ask and beg of God, with cheerfulness and all circumspection and purity, without hatred and without malice.

In this way let us approach a brother or a sister who is sick, and visit them in a way that is right, without guile, and without covetousness, and without noise, and without talkativeness, and without such behaviour as is alien from the fear of God, and without haughtiness, but with the meek and lowly spirit of Christ.

Let them, therefore, with fasting and with prayer make their adjurations, and not with the elegant and well-arranged and fitly-ordered words of learning, but as men who have received the gift of healing from God, confidently, to the glory of God.

By [123] your fastings and prayers and perpetual watching, together with your other good works, mortify the works of the flesh by the power of the Holy Spirit.

He who acts thus "is a temple of the Holy Spirit of God." [124] Let this man cast out demons, and God will help him.

For it is good that a man help those that are sick.

Our Lord hath said:

"Cast out demons," at the same time commanding many other acts of healing; and, "Freely ye have received, freely give." [125] For such persons as these a goodly recompense is laid up by God, because they serve their brethren with the gifts which have been given them by the Lord.

This is also comely and helpful to the servants of God, because they act according to the injunctions of our Lord, who hath said:

"I was sick, and ye visited Me, and so on." [126]

And this is comely and right and just, that we visit our neighbours for the sake of God with all seemliness of manner and purity of behaviour; as the Apostle hath said:

"Who is sick, and I am not sick? who is offended, and I am not offended?" [127] But all these things are spoken in reference to the love with which a man should love his neighbour.

And in these things let us occupy ourselves, [128] without giving offence, and let us not do anything with partiality or for the shaming of others, but let us love the poor as the servants of God, and especially let us visit them.

For this is comely before God and before men, that we should remember the poor, and be lovers of the brethren and of strangers, for the sake of God and for the sake of those who believe in God, as we have learnt from the law and from the prophets, and from our Lord Jesus Christ, concerning the love of the brotherhood and the love of strangers:

for ye know the words which have been spoken concerning the love of the brotherhood and the love of strangers; [129] powerfully are the words spoken to all those who do them.

Chapter XIII - What Priests Should Be and Should Not Be

Beloved brethren! that a man should build up and establish the brethren on the faith in one God, this also is manifest and well-known.

This too, again, is comely, that a man should not be envious of his neighbour.

And moreover, again, it is suitable and comely that all those who work the works of the Lord should work the works of the Lord in the fear of God.

Thus is it required of them to conduct themselves.

That "the harvest is great, but the workmen are few," this also is well-known and manifest.

Let us, therefore, "ask of the Lord of the harvest" that He would send forth workmen into the harvest; [130] such workmen as "shall skilfully dispense the word of truth;" workmen "who shall not be ashamed;" [131] faithful workmen; workmen who shall be "the light of the world;" [132] workmen who "work not for the food that perisheth, but for that food which abideth unto life eternal;" [133] workmen who shall be such as the apostles; workmen who imitate the Father, and the Son, and the Holy Spirit; who are concerned for the salvation of men; not "hireling" [134] workmen; not workmen to whom the fear of God and righteousness appear to be gain; not workmen who "serve their belly;" not workmen who "with fair speeches and pleasant words mislead the hearts of the innocent;" [135] not workmen who imitate the children of light, while they are not light but darkness--"men whose end is destruction;"[136] not workmen who practise iniquity and wickedness and fraud; not "crafty workmen;"[137] not workmen "drunken" and "faithless;" [138] nor workmen who traffic in Christ;[139] not misleaders; not "lovers of money; not malevolent." [140]

Let us, therefore, contemplate and imitate the faithful who have conducted themselves well in the Lord, as is becoming and suitable to our calling and profession.

Thus let us do service before God in justice and righteousness, and without blemish, "occupying ourselves with things good and comely before God and also before men." [141] For this is comely, that God be glorified in us in all things.

Here endeth the first Epistle of Clement.

Footnotes:

1. In later Greek parthenos was used of both sexes (comp. Rev. xiv. 4).
The Syriac original employs both a masculine and a feminine form. This will not always be indicated in the following translation.
2. Matt. xix. 12.
3. Or "to the holy virgins who are in God: peace."
So Zingerle, and probably Wetstein.
4. Zing., not so well, takes this to mean, "by the confession of the mouth" (durch das muendliche Bekenntniss), comparing Matt. vii. 21.
5. Lit. "by word or by name."
6. The Greek word schema, here adopted in the Syriac, is sometimes thus used.--Beelen.
7. Lit. "much time."
8. Prov. iii. 3, 4 (LXX.).
9. Lit. "fixed." Prov. iv. 18.
10. Matt. v. 14.
11. Isa. ix. 2; Matt. iv. 16.
12. Matt. v. 16; 1 Pet. ii. 12.
13. Probably referring to 1 Cor. xiv. 40.--Beelen.
14. Eph. v. 6.
15. Matt. xxv. 2.
16. Tim. iii. 5.
17. Lit. "let every one be trying."
18. Gal. vi. 3, 4.
19. Matt. xii. 33. [More probably Luke vi. 44.--R.]
20. Or "consider."
There is no play on words in the passage quoted (2 Tim. ii. 7), nor perhaps was this intended in the Syriac.
21. 2 Tim. ii. 7.
22. Lit. "true in fear of God."
The reading is probably faulty.--Beelen.
23. The ellipsis is usually to be thus filled up in these epistles. [In similar cases which follow, italics will not be used.--R.]
24. Gen. i. 28.
25. Or "the sensual pleasures."
26. Or "from all intercourse with."
27. Either something is here omitted by the transcriber, or Clement has varied the form of expression.--Beelen.
28. "Sanctification."--Beelen. [So A.V. The R.V. correctly renders hagiasmos, "sanctification," in every instance.--R.]
29. 2 Thess. ii. 13.
30. Col. i. 5.
31. Isa. lvi. 4, 5.
32. Heb. xiii. 4.

The Epistles of Clement

33. 1 Cor. vii. 34.
34. Lit. "descend to."
35. 2 Tim. ii. 5.
36. The words, "in the might of the Holy Spirit," appear to obscure the sense.--Beelen.
37. Gal. iv. 26.
38. Rev. xii. 7.
39. 1 Pet. v. 8.
40. 2 Cor. xi. 3.
41. Lit. "the Eucharist of the Godhead."
This is an evidence of later date than the sub-apostolic age.--R.]
42. Matt. xvi. 24.
43. Lit. "crown of victory."
44. Phil. iii. 14.
45. i.e. continency. [The use of the terms "sanctity," "holy," etc., in the limited sense of "continency," "chaste," etc., is strong evidence of the later origin.--R]
46. The last two sentences properly belong to chap. vi.
47. Or "the Holy Virgin."
48. Matt. xi. 11.
49. Lit. "lover," or "friend."
50. John xxi. 20.
51. i.e., a virgin.
52. Phil. iv. 3.
53. i.e., virginity.
54. i.e., celibate, or chaste.
55. Heb. xiii. 7.
56. 1 Cor. xi. 1.
57. Rom. xiii. 14.
58. Gal. v. 24.
59. 1 Cor. vii. 32.
60. 1 Pet. i. 15 (cf. Lev. xi. 44).
61. Rom. viii. 6 (phronema).
62. Rom. viii. 9.
63. Lit. "the worship of idols." The single word *** sometimes used to express "idolatry" (as in Eph. Syr., opp. tom. i. p. 116), is not found in these epistles.
64. Lit. "much talking."
65. Lit. "empty words."
66. The word thus rendered is not in the lexicons, but is well illustrated by Isa. xxix. 21 ("that make a man an offender"), where the Hiphil of cht' is used, corresponding to the Aphel of the same root, from which the present word is derived.
67. The word is used in the Peschito of 1 Tim. vi. 5, to express diaparatribai ("incessant quarrellings," Alf.); [R.V., "wranglings."--R.].
68. Ex. Conject. Beelen.
The word is not in the lexicons.
69. Or "power."
70. Lit. "folly;" but so used in 2 Cor. xii. 13.
71. Or "returning of evils."
72. Col. iii. 5.
73. 1 Tim. vi. 10.
74. 1 Pet. v. 5; Jas. iv. 6.
75. John iii. 6, 31.
76. Rom. viii. 7.
77. Rom. vii. 18.
78. Gen. vi. 3. [This is an example of the vicious method of interpretation, not yet extirpated, which carries Paul's distinctive use of the term "flesh" back to the Pentateuch, where no ethical sense is necessarily implied.--R.]
79. Rom. vii. 9. [The Apostle speaks of "the Spirit of Christ."--R.]
80. 1 Sam. xvi. 14.
81. 1 Cor. ix. 27.
82. 1 Tim. vi. 11.
83. Gal. v. 22.
84. Phil. ii. 15, 16.
85. Isa. lxi. 9.

86. 1 Pet. ii. 9.
87. 1 Cor. ii. 9.
88. Or "life."
89. The words which follow, "concerning those things which we speak," appear not to be genuine.--Beelen.
90. Beelen supposes a hen dia duoin: "along the lonely road."
91. i.e., virginity.
92. Prov. xxvi. 9.
93. Prov. xv. 19 (LXX.).
94. Lit. "profit and righteousness."
95. Lit. "go about and wander."
96. 1 Tim. v. 13.
97. Lit, "in their barefacedness."
98. 1 Cor. xii. 29. [But compare Jas. iii. 1: "Be not many teachers" (R.V.), which precedes the next citation.--R.]
99. Jas. iii. 2.
100. Lit. "speech."
101. 1 Pet. iv. 11.
102. Ecclus. v. 14.
103. Eccl. iii. 7.
104. Lit. "beautiful."
105. Prov. xxv. 11.
106. Lit. "in his place." Col. iv. 6.
107. Lit. "his soul for life." Prov. xviii. 6; xiii. 3; xxi. 23.
108. Rom. xvi. 17-19.
109. Matt. xxiii. 3.
110. Col. ii. 18.
111. Matt. xv. 14.
112. As 1 Cor. xv. 44 (psuchikos).--See Jas. iii. 15 [also 1 Cor. ii. 13, 14.--R.].
113. See Col. ii. 8.
114. Eph. ii. 2; Col. ii. 8.
115. 1 Cor. xii. 8-10.
116. Jas. i. 5.
117. An obscure clause, which Beelen supposes to be due to the misapprehension of the Syrian translator.

Perhaps the difficulty will be met if we read "gifts," as do Wets. and Zing., by a change in the pointing.
118. Jas. i. 27.
119. Or "exorcisms."
120. Lit. "elegant and numerous words."
121. 1 Cor. xiii. 1.
122. Matt. xvii. 21. [Or Mark ix. 29; the verse in Matthew is of doubtful genuineness.--R.]
123. Or "in."
124. 1 Cor. vi. 19.
125. Matt. x. 8.
126. Lit. "and things similar to these," Matt. xxv. 36.
127. 2 Cor. xi. 29.
128. Lit. "let us be."
129. Beelen here omits, as spurious, the words, "because this same thing is pleasant and agreeable to you: because ye are all taught of God."
130. Matt. ix. 37, 38.
131. Lit. "without shame," 2 Tim. ii. 15.
132. Matt. v. 14.
133. John vi. 27.
134. John x. 12, 13.
135. Rom. xvi. 18.
136. Phil. iii. 9.
137. 2 Cor. xi. 13.
138. See Matt. xxiv. 45-51.
139. [Comp. the term christemporos "Christ-monger," "Christ-trafficker," in Teaching, chap. xii. 5, vol. vii. p. 381.--R.]
140. 1 Tim. iii. 3; Tit. i. 7.

141. Rom. xii. 17.

The Second Epistle of the Same Clement

Chapter I - He Describes the Circumspectness of His Intercourse with the Other Sex, and Tells How in His Journeys He Acts at Places Where There are Brethren Only

I would, moreover, have you know, my brethren, of what sort is our conduct in Christ, as well as that of all our brethren, in the various places in which we are.

And if so be that you approve it, do ye also conduct yourselves in like manner in the Lord.

Now we, if God help us, conduct ourselves thus:

with maidens we do not dwell, nor have we anything in common with them; with maidens we do not eat, nor drink; and, where a maiden sleeps, we do not sleep; neither do women wash our feet, nor anoint us; and on no account do we sleep where a maiden sleeps who is unmarried or has taken the vow:[1] even though she be in some other place if she be alone, we do not pass the night there.[2] Moreover, if it chance that the time for rest overtake us in a place, whether in the country, or in a village, or in a town, or in a hamlet, [3] or wheresoever we happen to be, and there are found brethren in that place, we turn in to one who is a brother, and call together there all the brethren, and speak to them words of encouragement and exhortation. [4] And those among us who are gifted in speaking will speak such words as are earnest, and serious, and chaste, in the fear of God, and exhort them to please God in everything, and abound and go forward in good works, and "be free from [5] anxious care in everything," [6] as is fit and right for the people of God.

Chapter II - His Behaviour in Places Where There Were Christians of Both Sexes

And if, moreover, it chance that we are distant from our homes and from our neighbours, and the day decline and the eventide overtake us, and the brethren press us, through love of the brotherhood and by reason of their affection for strangers, to stay with them, so that we may watch with them, and they may hear the holy word of God and do it, and be fed with the words of the Lord, so that they may be mindful of them, and they set before us bread and water and that which God provides, and we be willing and consent to stay through the night with them; if there be there a holy man, [7] with him we turn in and lodge, and that same brother will provide and prepare whatever is necessary for us; and he himself waits upon us, and he himself washes our feet for us and anoints us with ointment, and he himself gets ready a bed for us, that we may sleep in reliance on God.

All these things will that consecrated brother, who is in the place in which we tarry, do in his own person.

He will himself serve the brethren, and each one of the brethren who are in the same place will join with him in rendering all those services [8] which are requisite for the brethren.

But with us may no female, whether young maiden or married woman, be there at that time; [9] nor she that is aged, [10] nor she that has taken the vow; not even a maid-servant, whether Christian or heathen; but there shall only be men with men.

And, if we see it to be requisite to stand and pray for the sake of the women, and to speak words of exhortation and edification, we call together the brethren and all the holy sisters and maidens, and likewise all the other women who are there, inviting them with all modesty and becoming behaviour to come and feast on the truth. [11] And those among us who are skilled in speaking speak to them, and exhort them in those words which God has given us.

And then we pray, and salute [12] one another, the men the men.

But the women and the maidens will wrap their hands in their garments; and we also, with circumspection and with all purity, our eyes looking upwards, shall wrap our right hand in our garments; and then they will come and give us the salutation on our right hand wrapped in our garments.

Then we go where God permits us.

Chapter III - Rules for the Conduct of Celibate Brethren in Places Where There are Only Married Christians

And if again we chance to come into a place where there is no consecrated brother, but all are married, all those who are there will receive the brother who comes to them, and minister to him, and care for his wants [13] in everything, assiduously, with good-will.

And the brother shall be ministered to by them in the way that is suitable.

And the brother will say to the married persons who are in that place:

We holy men do not eat or drink with women, nor are we waited on by women or by maidens, nor do women wash our feet for us, nor do women anoint us, nor do women prepare our bed for us, nor do we sleep where women sleep, so that we may be without reproach in everything, lest any one should be offended or stumble at us.

And, whilst we observe all these things, "we are without offence to every man." [14] As persons, therefore, "who know the fear of the Lord, we persuade men, and to God we are made manifest." [15]

Chapter IV - Conduct of the Holy Man Where There are Women Only

But if we chance to come into a place where there are no Christian men, but all the believers are women and maidens, [16] and they press us to pass the night there in that place, we call them all together to some suitable place, [17] and ask them how they do; and according to that which we learn from them, and what we see to be their state of mind, we address them in a suitable manner, as men fearing God.

And when they have all assembled and come together, and we see that they are in peace, [18] we address to them words of exhortation in the fear of God, and read the Scripture to them, with purity and in the concise [19] and weighty words of the fear of God.

We do everything as for their edification.

And as to those who are married, we speak to them in the Lord in a manner suited to them.

And if, moreover, the day decline and the eventide draw on, we select, in order to pass the night there, a woman who is aged and the most exemplary [20] of them all; and we speak to her to give us a place all to ourselves, where no woman enters, nor maiden.

And this old woman herself will bring us a lamp, and whatever is requisite for us she will herself bring us.

From love to the brethren, she will bring whatever is requisite for the service of stranger brethren.

And she herself, when the time for sleep is come, will depart and go to her house in peace.

Chapter V - Where There is Only One Woman, the Father Does Not Make a Stay; How Carefully Stumbling-Blocks Must Be Avoided

But if, moreover, we chance upon a place, and find there one believing woman only, and no other person be there but she only, we do not stop there, nor pray there, nor read the Scriptures there, but we flee as from before the face of a serpent, and as from before the face of sin. Not that we disdain the believing woman--far be it from us to be so minded towards our brethren in Christ!--but, because she is alone, we are afraid lest any one should make insinuations against us in words of falsehood.

For the hearts of men are firmly set [21] on evil.

And, that we may not give a pretext to those who desire to get a pretext against us and to speak evil of us, and that we may not be a stumbling-block to any one, on this account we cut off the pretext of those who desire to get a pretext against us; on this account we must be "on our guard that we be to no one a stumbling-block, neither to the Jews, nor to the Gentiles, nor yet to the Church of God; and we must not seek that which is profitable to ourselves only, but that which is for the profit of many, so that they may be saved." [22] For this does not profit us, that another stumble because of us.

Let us, therefore, be studiously on our guard at all times, that we do not smite our brethren and give them to drink of a disquieting conscience through our being to them a stumbling-block.

For "if for the sake of meat our brother be made sad, or shocked, or made weak, or caused to stumble, we are not walking in the love of God.

For the sake of meat thou causest him to perish for whose sake Christ died." [23] For, in "thus sinning against your brethren and wounding their sickly consciences, ye sin against Christ Himself.

For, if for the sake of meat my brother is made to stumble," let us who are believers say, "Never will we eat flesh, that we may not make our brother to stumble." [24] These things, moreover, does ever one who truly loves God, who truly takes up his cross, and puts on Christ, and loves his neighbour; the man who watches over himself that he be not a stumbling-block to any one, that no one be caused to stumble because of him and die because he is constantly with maidens and lives in the same house with them--a thing which is not right--to the overthrow of those who see and hear.

Evil conduct like this is fraught with stumbling and peril, and is akin [25] to death.

But blessed is that man who is circumspect and fearful in everything for the sake of purity!

Chapter VI - How Christians Should Behave Themselves Among Heathens

If, moreover, it chance that we go to a place in which there are no Christians, and it be important for us to stay there a few days, let us be "wise as serpents, and harmless as doves;" [26] and let us "not be as the foolish, but as the wise," [27] in all the self-restraint of the fear of God, that God may be glorified in everything through our Lord Jesus Christ, through our chaste and holy behaviour.

For, "whether we eat, or drink, or do anything else, let us do it as for the glory of God." [28] Let "all those who see us acknowledge that we are a blessed seed," [29] "sons of the living God," [30] in everything--in all our words in shamefastness, in purity, in humility, forasmuch as we do not copy the heathen in anything, nor are as believers like other men, but in everything are estranged from the wicked.

And we "do not cast that which is holy before dogs, nor pearls before swine;" [31] but with all possible self-restraint, and with all discretion, and with all fear of God, and with earnestness of mind we praise God.

For we do not minister where heathens are drinking and blaspheming in their feasts with words of impurity, because of their wickedness. [32] Therefore do we not sing psalms to the heathens, nor do we read to them the Scriptures, that we may not be like common singers, either those who play on the lyre,[33] or those who sing with the voice, or like soothsayers, as many are, who follow these practices and do these things, that they may sate themselves with a paltry mouthful of bread, and who, for the sake of a sorry cup of wine, go about "singing the songs of the Lord in the strange land" [34] of the heathen, and doing what is not right.

Do not so, my brethren; we beseech you, my brethren, let not these deeds be done among you; but put away those who choose thus to behave themselves with infamy and disgrace.

It is not proper, my brethren, that these things should be so.

But we beseech you, brethren in righteousness, that these things be so done with you as with us, as for a pattern of believers, and of those who shall believe.

Let us be of the flock of Christ, in all righteousness, and in all holy and unblemished conduct, behaving ourselves with uprightness and sanctity, as is right for believers, and observing those things which are praiseworthy, and pure, and holy, and honourable, and noble; and do ye promote [35] all those things which are profitable.

For ye are "our joy, and our crown," and our hope, and our life, "if so be that ye stand in the Lord."[36] So be it! [37]

Chapter VII - Uses of Considering Admonitory Examples, as Well as Instructive Patterns

Let us consider, therefore, my brethren, and see how all the righteous fathers conducted themselves during the whole time of their sojourn in this life, and let us search and examine from the law down to the New Testament.

For this is both becoming and profitable, that we should know how many men there have been, and who they were, that have perished through women; and who and how many have been the women that have perished through men, by reason of the constancy with which they have associated with one another.

And further, also, for the same reason, I will show how many have been the men, and who they were, that lived all their lifetime, and continued even to the close, with one another in the performance of chaste works without blemish.

And it is manifest and well-known that this is so. [38]

Chapter VIII - Joseph and Potiphar's Wife; Of What Kind Love to Females Ought to Be

There is Joseph, faithful, and intelligent, and wise, and who feared God in everything.

Did not a woman conceive an excessive passion for the beauty of this chaste and upright man?

And, when he would not yield and consent to gratify her passionate desire, [39] she cast the righteous man into every kind of distress and torment, to within a little of death, [40] by bearing false witness.

But God delivered him from all the evils that came upon him through this wretched woman.

Ye see, my brethren, what distresses the constant sight of the person of the Egyptian woman brought upon the righteous man.

Therefore, let us not be constantly with women, nor with maidens.

For this is not profitable for those who truly wish to "gird up their loins." [41] For it is required that we love the sisters in all purity and chasteness, and with all curbing of thought, in the fear of God, not associating constantly with them, nor finding access to them at every hour.

Chapter IX - Samson's Admonitory Fall

Hast thou not heard concerning Samson the Nazarite, "with whom was the Spirit of God," [42] the man of great strength?

This man, who was a Nazarite, and consecrated to God, and who was gifted with strength and might, a woman brought to ruin with her wretched body, and with her vile passion.

Art thou, perchance, such a man as he?

Know thyself, and know the measure of thy strength. [43]"The married woman catcheth precious souls." [44]Therefore, we do not allow any man whatsoever to sit with a married woman; much less to live in the same house with a maiden who has taken the vow, or to sleep where she sleeps, or to be constantly with her.

For this is to be hated and abominated by those who fear God.

Chapter X - David's Sin, So Admonitory to Us Weak Men

Does not the case of David instruct thee, whom God "found a man after His heart," [45] one faithful, faultless, pious, true?

This same man saw the beauty of a woman--I mean of Bathsheba--when he saw her as she was cleansing herself and washing unclothed.

This woman the holy man saw, and was thoroughly [46] captivated with desire by the sight of her.[47]See, then, what evils he committed because of a woman, and how this righteous man sinned, and gave command that the husband of this woman should be killed in battle.

Ye have seen what wicked schemes he laid and executed, and how, because of his passion for a woman, he perpetrated a murder--he, David, who was called "the anointed of the Lord." [48]Be admonished, O man:

for, if such men as these have been brought to ruin through women, what is thy righteousness, or what art thou among the holy, that thou consortest with women and with maidens day and night, with much silliness, without fear of God?

Not thus, my brethren, not thus let us conduct ourselves; but let us be mindful of that word which is spoken concerning a woman:

"Her hands lay snares, and her heart spreadeth nets; but the just shall escape from her, whilst the wicked falleth into her hands." [49]Therefore let us, who are consecrated, [50] be careful not to live in the same house with females who have taken the vow.

For such conduct as this is not becoming nor right for the servants of God.

Chapter XI - Admonitory History of the Incestuous Children of David

Hast thou not read concerning Amnon and Tamar, the children of David? This Amnon conceived a passion for his sister, and humbled her, and did not spare her, because he longed for her with a shameful passion; and he proved wicked and profligate because of his constant intercourse with her, without the fear of God, and he "wrought uncleanness in Israel." [51]Therefore, it is not proper for us, nor right for us, to associate with sisters, indulging in laughter and looseness; but we ought to behave towards them with all chasteness and purity, and in the fear of the Lord.

Chapter XII - Solomon's Infatuation Through Women

Hast thou not read the history of Solomon, the son of David, the man to whom God gave wisdom, and knowledge, and largeness of mind, [52] and riches, and much glory, beyond all men?

Yet this same man, through women, came to ruin, [53] and departed from the Lord.

Chapter XIII - The History of Susanna Teaches Circumspection with the Eyes and in Society

Hast thou not read, and dost thou not know, concerning those elders who were in the days of Susanna, who, because they were constantly with women, and looking upon the beauty which was another's, [54] fell into the depths of wantonness, and were not able to keep themselves in a chaste mind, [55] but were overcome by a depraved disposition, and came suddenly [56] upon the blessed Susanna to corrupt her.

But she did not consent to their foul passion, but cried unto God, and God saved her out of the hands of the bad old men.

Does it not, therefore, behove us to tremble and be afraid, forasmuch as these old men, judges and elders of the people of God, fell from their dignity because of a woman?

For they did not keep in mind that which is said:

"Look thou not on the beauty which is another's;" and, "The beauty of woman has destroyed many;" [57] and "With a married woman do not sit;" [58] and that, again, in which it says:

"Is there any one that puts fire in his bosom, and does not burn his clothes;" [59] or, "Does a man walk on fire, and his feet are not scorched?

So whosoever goeth in to another man's wife is not pure from evil, and whosoever comes near to her shall not escape." [60]And again it says:

"Thou shalt not long after the beauty a woman, lest she take thee captive with her eyelids;" [61] and, "Thou shalt not look upon a maiden, lest thou perish through desire of her;" [62] and, "With a woman that sings beautifully thou shalt not constantly be;" [63] and, "Let him that thinketh he standeth take heed lest he fall." [64]

Chapter XIV - Examples of Circumspect Behaviour from the Old Testament

But see what it says also concerning those holy men, the prophets, and concerning the apostles of our Lord.

Let us see whether any one of these holy men was constantly with maidens, or with young married women, or with such widows as the divine apostle declines to receive. Let us consider, in the fear of God, the manner of life of these holy men.

Lo! we find it written concerning Moses and Aaron, that they acted and lived in the company of[65] men, who themselves also followed a course of conduct like theirs.

And thus did Joshua also, the son of Nun.

Woman was there none with them; but they by themselves used holily to minister before God, men with men.

And not only so; but they taught the people, that, whensoever the host moved, every tribe should move on apart, and the women with the women apart, and that they should go into the rear behind the host, and the men also apart by their tribes.

And, according to the command of the Lord, so did they set out, like a wise people, that there might be no disorder on account of the women when the host moved.

With beautiful and well-ordered arrangements did they march without stumbling.

For lo! the Scriptures bear testimony to my words:

"When the children of Israel had crossed over the Sea of Suth, Moses and the children of Israel sang the praises of the Lord, and said:

We will praise the Lord, because He is exceedingly to be praised." [66] And, after that Moses had finished [67] singing praises, then Miriam, the sister of Moses and Aaron, took a timbrel in her hands, and all the women went out after her, and sang praises with her, women with women apart, and men with men apart.

Then again, we find that Elisha and Gehazi and the sons of the prophets lived together in the fear of God, and that they had no females living with them.

Micah too, and all the prophets likewise, we find to have lived in this manner in the fear of the Lord.

Chapter XV - The Example of Jesus; How We May Allow Ourselves to Be Served by Women

And, not to extend our discourse to too great length, what shall we say concerning our Lord Jesus Christ?

Our Lord Himself was constantly with His twelve disciples when He had come forth to the world.

And not only so; but also, when He was sending them out, He sent them out two and two together, men with men; but women were not sent with them, and neither in the highway nor in the house did they associate with women or with maidens:

and thus they pleased God in everything.

Also, when our Lord Jesus Christ Himself was talking with the woman of Samaria by the well alone, "His disciples came" and found Him talking with her, "and wondered that Jesus was standing and talking with a woman." [68]

Is He not a rule, such as may not be set aside, an example, and a pattern to all the tribes of men?

And not only so; but also, when our Lord was risen from the place of the dead, and Mary came to the place of sepulture, she ran and fell at the feet of our Lord and worshipped Him, and would have taken hold of Him.

But He said to her:

"Touch Me not; for I am not yet ascended to My Father." [69] Is it not, then, matter for astonishment, that, while our Lord did not allow Mary, the blessed woman, to touch His feet, yet thou livest with them, and art waited on by women and maidens, and sleepest where they sleep, and women wash thy feet for thee, and anoint thee!

Alas for this culpable state of mind!

Alas for this state of mind which is destitute of fear!

Alas for this affrontery and folly, which is without fear of God!

Dost thou not judge thine own self?

Dost thou not examine thine own self?

Dost thou not know thine own self and the measure of thy strength?

These things, moreover, are trustworthy, and these things are true and right; and these are rules immutable for those who behave themselves uprightly in our Lord.

Many holy women, again, ministered to holy men of their substance, as the Shunammite woman ministered to Elisha; but she did not live with him, but the prophet lived in a house apart.

And, when her son died, she wanted to throw herself at the feet of the prophet; but his attendant would not allow her, but restrained her.

But Elisha said to his servant:

"Let her alone, because her soul is distressed." [70]From these things, then, we ought to understand their manner of life.

To Jesus Christ our Lord women ministered of their substance:

but they did not live with him; but chastely, and holily, and unblameably they behaved before the Lord, and finished their course, and received the crown in [71] our Lord God Almighty.

Chapter XVI - Exhortation to Union and to Obedience; Conclusion

Therefore, we beseech you, our brethren in our Lord, that these things be observed with you, as with us, and that we may be of the same mind, that we may be one in you and ye may be one in us, and that in everything we may be of one soul and one heart in our Lord.

Whosoever knoweth the Lord heareth us; and every one who is not of God heareth not us.

He who desires truly to keep sanctity heareth us; and the virgin who truly desires to keep virginity heareth us; but she who does not truly desire to keep virginity doth not hear us.

Finally, farewell in our Lord, and rejoice in the Lord, all ye saints.

Peace and joy be with you from God the Father through Jesus Christ our Lord.

So be it.

Here endeth the Second Epistle of Clement, the disciple of Peter.

His prayer be with us!

So be it.

Footnotes:

1. Lit. "or is a daughter of the covenant."
2. Beelen's rendering, "we do not even pass the night," seems not to be favoured either by the arrangement or the context.
3. Lit "dwelling-place."
4. Or "consolation."
So paraklesis in the N.T. has both senses.
5. Lit. "without."
6. Phil. iv. 6.
7. i.e., one who has taken the vow of celibacy.
8. Lit. "will with him minister all those things."
9. [The minuteness of all these precepts is of itself suspicious. The "simplicity" of the earlier age had evidently passed when these prohibitions were penned.--R.]
10. ***,
Beelen's conjecture for ***, "rich."
Zingerle proposes ***, "about to be married."
11. Lit. "come to the delight of the truth."
12. Lit. "ask of the peace of."
13. Lit. "for that which in his;" or "for what belongs to him."
14. 2 Cor. vi. 3.
15. 2 Cor. v. 11.
16. Lit. "all of them are believing women and maidens."
17. Lit. "some place on the right side."
The Syrian translator has probably mistaken the meaning of eis hena topon dexion, where dexion may be compared with dexter in Hor., Sat., ii. 1, 18.--Beelen.
18. Probably meaning, "when we have inquired of their welfare."
19. Lit. "compressed."
20. Lit. "chaste," or "modest."
21. Or "are set and fixed."
22. 1 Cor. x. 32, 33.

The Epistles of Clement

23. Rom. xiv. 15.
[The Apostle's noble and consistent counsel to the "strong" brethren at Rome is in sharp contrast with the use here made of it.
Only one of the "weak" brethren could have written this epistle.--R.]
24. 1 Cor. viii. 12, 13.
25. Lit. "near."
26. Matt. x. 16.
27. Eph. v. 15.
28. 1 Cor. x. 31.
29. Isa. lxi. 9.
30. Phil. ii. 15.
31. Matt. vii. 6.
32. Beelen joins "because of their wickedness" with the words that follow.
33. Or "cithara."
34. Ps. cxxxvii. 4.
35. Or "set on foot."
36. Phil. iv. 1.
37. Or "Amen."
38. Wetstein and Zingerle join on this sentence to the next, by a change of the construction.
39. Lit. "her passion and her desire."
40. Lit. "even to death."
41. Luke xii. 35.
42. Judges xiii. 25.
43. Lit. "know thy measure."
44. Prov. vi. 26.
45. 1 Sam. xvi. 13; Ps. lxxxix. 20, seqq.; Acts xiii. 22.
46. Lit. "verily."
47. "By the pleasure derived from the sight of her."--Beelen.
48. Ps. xviii. 50; 2 Sam. xix. 21.
49. Eccl. vii. 26.
50. Lit. "holy."
51. Gen. xxxiv. 7.
52. Lit. "heart."
53. Or "perished."
54. Susanna having a husband, Joachim.
55. Lit. "a mind of chasteness."
56. Lit. "rose."
57. Ecclus. ix. 8, 9.
58. Ecclus. ix. 12.
59. Prov. vi. 27.
60. Prov. vi. 28, 29.
61. Prov. vi. 25.
62. Ecclus. ix. 5.
63. Ecclus. ix. 4.
64. 1 Cor. x. 12.
65. Lit. "their conduct and living was with."
66. Exod. xv. 1.
67. Lit. "ceased from."
68. John iv. 27.
69. John xx. 17.
70. 2 Kings iv. 27.
71. Beelen suggests the reading "from," or to render the present text "by."

Pseudo-Clementine Literature

Introductory Notice to the Pseudo-Clementine Literature

By Professor M. B. Riddle, D.D.

The name "Pseudo-Clementine Literature" (or, more briefly, "Clementina") is applied to a series of writings, closely resembling each other, purporting to emanate from the great Roman Father.

But, as Dr. Schaff remarks, in this literature he is evidently confounded with "Flavius Clement, kinsman of the Emperor Domitian." [1] These writings are three in number:

(1) the Recognitions, of which only the Latin translation of Rufinus has been preserved; [2] (2) the Homilies, twenty in number, of which a complete collection has been known since 1853; (3) the Epitome, "an uninteresting extract from the Homilies, to which are added extracts from the letter of Clement to James, from the Martyrium of Clement by Simeon Metaphrastes, etc." [3] Other writings may be classed with these; but they are of the same general character, except that most of them show the influence of a later age, adapting the material more closely to the orthodox doctrine.

The Recognitions and the Homilies appear in the pages which follow. The former are given a prior position, as in the Edinburgh series.

It probably cannot be proven that these represent the earlier form of this theological romance; but the Homilies, "in any case, present the more doctrinally developed and historically important form of the other treatises, which are essentially similar." [4] They are therefore with propriety placed after the Recognitions, which do not seem to have been based upon them, but upon some earlier document. [5]

The critical discussion of the Clementina has been keen, but has not reached its end.

It necessarily involves other questions, about which there is still great difference of opinion.

A few results seem to be established:--

(1) The entire literature is of Jewish-Christian, or Ebionitic, origin.

The position accorded to "James, the Lord's brother," in all the writings, is a clear indication of this; so is the silence respecting the Apostle Paul.

The doctrinal statements, "though not perfectly homogeneous" (Uhlhorn), are Judaistic, even when mixed with Gnostic speculation of heathen origin.

This tendency is, perhaps, not so clearly marked in the Recognitions as in the Homilies; but both partake largely of the same general character.

More particularly, the literature has been connected with the Ebionite sect called the Elkesaites; and some regard the Homilies as containing a further development of their system. [6] This is not definitely established, but finds some support in the resemblance between the baptismal forms, as given by Hippolytus in the case of the Elkesaites, [7] and those indicated in the Recognitions and Homilies, especially the latter. [8]

(2) The entire literature belongs to the class of fictitious writing "with a purpose."

The Germans properly term the Homilies a "Tendenz-Romance."

The many "lives of Christ" written in our day to insinuate some other view of our Lord's person than that given in the canonical Gospels, furnish abundant examples of the class.

The Tuebingen school, finding here a real specimen of the influence of party feeling upon quasi-historical literature, naturally pressed the Clementina in support of their theory of the origin of the Gospels.

(3) The discussion leaves it quite probable, though not yet certain, that all the works are "independent elaborations--perhaps at first hand, perhaps at second or third--of some older tract not now extant." [9] Some of the opinions held respecting the relations of the two principal works are given by the Edinburgh translator in his Introductory Notice.

It is only necessary here to indicate the progress of the modern discussion.

Neander, as early as 1818, gave some prominence to the doctrinal view of the Homilies.

He was followed by Baur, who found in these writings, as indicated above, support for his theory of the origin of historical Christianity.

It is to be noted, however, that the heterogeneous mixture of Ebionism and Gnosticism in the doctrinal views proved perplexing to the leader of the Tuebingen school.

Schliemann [10] took ground against Baur, collecting much material, and carefully investigating the question. Both authors give the priority to the Homilies.

While Baur went too far in one direction, Schliemann, perhaps, failed to recognise fully the basis of truth in the position of the former.

The next important step in the discussion was made by Hilgenfeld, [11] whose views are briefly given in the Notice which follows.

Hilgenfeld assigned the priority to the Recognitions, though he traced all the literature to an earlier work.

Uhlhorn [12] at first attempted to prove that the Recognitions were a revision of the Homilies.

Further contributions were made by Lehmann [13] and Lipsius. [14] The former discovered in the Recognitions two distinct parts by different authors (i.-iii., iv.-ix.), tracing all the literature to the Kerygma of Peter.

The latter finds the basis of the whole in the Acta Petri, which show a strong anti-Pauline tendency.

Influenced by these investigations, Uhlhorn modified his views. Lechler, [15] while not positive in his convictions, makes the following prudent statement:

"An older work lies at the basis both of the Homilies and Recognitions, bearing the title, Kerygmen des Petrus. [16] To this document sometimes the Homilies, sometimes the Recognitions, correspond more faithfully; its historical contents are more correctly seen from the Recognitions, its doctrinal contents from the Homilies."

Other views, some of them quite fanciful, have been presented.

The prevalent opinion necessarily leaves us in ignorance of the authors of this literature.

The date of composition, or editing, cannot be definitely fixed.

In their present form the several works may be as old as the first half of the third century, and the common basis may be placed in the latter half of the second century.

How far the anti-Pauline tendency is carried, is a matter of dispute. Baur and many others think Simon is meant to represent Paul; [17] but this is difficult to believe, though we must admit the disposition to ignore the Apostle to the Gentiles.

As to the literary merit of these productions the reader must judge.

For convenience in comparison of the two works, the following table has been prepared, based on the order of the Recognitions.

The correspondences are not exact, and the reader is referred to the footnotes for fuller details.

Footnotes:

1. History of the Christian Church, vol. ii. p. 436, new edition.
2. See the Introductory Note of the Edinburgh translator.
3. Uhlhorn, article Clementines, Schaff-Herzog, i. p. 497.

A second Epitome has been published by Dressel; see Introductory Notice to Homilies.

4. Lechler, Apostolic and Post-Apostolic Times, ii. p. 268, Edinburgh translation, 1886, from 3rd edition.
5. Uhlhorn; see infra.
6. Comp. Uhlhorn, p. 392; Schaff, History, ii. p. 436; Lechler, ii. p. 288.

See Schaff-Herzog, i. art. Elkesaites.

7. See Hippolytus, Refutation of all Heresies, book ix. 8-12, Ante-Nicene Fathers, vol. v. pp. 131-134.

The forms occur in chap. 10, pp. 132, 133.

8. See Recognitions, i. 45-48; Homilies, Epistle of Peter to James, 4, Homily XIV. 1.
9. This is the last opinion of Uhlhorn (Herzog, Real-Encykl., 1877, art. Clementinen; comp. Schaff-Herzog, i. p. 498).

This author had previously defended the priority of the Homilies (Die Homilien und Rekognitionen des Clemens Romanus, Goettingen, 1854; comp. Herzog, edition of 1854, art. Clementinen).

10. Die Clementinen nebst den verwandten Schriften, und der Ebionitismus, Hamburg, 1844.
11. Die Clementinischen Rekognitionen und Homilien, nach ihrem Ursprung und Inhalt dargestellt, Jena, 1848.
12. See supra, note 3.

Uhlhorn found the nucleus of the literature in Homilies, xvi.-xix.

13. Die Clementinischen Schriften, Gotha, 1869.
14. Die Quellen der roemischen Petrussage, Kiel, 1872.
15. Apostolic and Post-Apostolic Times, vol. ii. p. 270.
16. So Hilgenfeld, Lehmann, Uhlhorn.
17. See especially Homilies, xvii. 19.

Here there is "probably only an incidental sneer at Paul" (Schaff, History, ii. p. 438).

Recognitions of Clement

Introductory Notice to The Recognitions of Clement

[By the Translator, Rev. Thomas Smith, D.D.]

The Recognitions of Clement is a kind of philosophical and theological romance.

The writer of the work seems to have had no intention of presenting his statements as facts; but, choosing the disciples of Christ and their followers as his principal characters, he has put into their mouths the most important of his beliefs, and woven the whole together by a thread of fictitious narrative.

The Recognitions is one of a series; the other members of which that have come down to us are the Clementine Homilies and two Epitomes. [1]

The authorship, the date, and the doctrinal character of these books have been subjects of keen discussion in modern times.

Especial prominence has been given to them by the Tuebingen school.

Hilgenfeld says:

"There is scarcely a single writing which is of so great importance for the history of Christianity in its first stage, and which has already given such brilliant disclosures at the hands of the most renowned critics in regard to the earliest history of the Christian Church, as the writings ascribed to the Roman Clement, the Recognitions and Homilies." [2] The importance thus attached to these strange and curious documents by one school of theologians, has compelled men of all shades of belief to investigate the subject; but after all their investigations, a great variety of opinion still prevails on almost every point connected with these books.

We leave our readers to judge for themselves in regard to the doctrinal statements, and confine ourselves to a notice of some of the opinions in regard to the authorship and date of the Recognitions.[3]

The first question that suggests itself in regard to the Recognitions is, whether the Recognitions or the Homilies are the earliest form of the book, and what relation do they bear to each other?

Some maintain that they are both the productions of the same author, and that the one is a later and altered edition of the other; and they find some confirmation of this in the preface of Rufinus.

Others think that both books are expansions of another work which formed the basis.

And others maintain that the one book is a rifacimento of the other by a different hand.

Of this third party, some, like Cave, Whiston, Rosenmueller, Stauedlin, Hilgenfeld, and many others, believe that the Recognitions was the earliest [4] of the two forms; while others, as Clericus, Moehler, Luecke, Schliemann, and Uhlhorn, give priority to the Clementines.

Hilgenfeld supposes that the original writing was the Kerugma Petrou, which still remains in the work; that besides this there are three parts,--one directed against Basilides, the second the Travels of Peter (periodoi) and the third the Recognitions.

There are also, he believes, many interpolated passages of a much later date than any of these parts. [5]

No conclusion has been reached in regard to the author.

Some have believed that it is a genuine work of Clement.

Whiston maintained that it was written by some of his hearers and companions.

Others have attributed the work to Bardesanes.

But most acknowledge that there is no possibility of discovering who was the author.

Various opinions exist as to the date of the book.

It has been attributed to the first, second, third, and fourth centuries, and some have assigned even a later date.

If we were to base our arguments on the work as it stands, the date assigned would be somewhere in the first half of the third century.

A passage from the Recognitions is quoted by Origen [6] in his Commentary on Genesis, written in

231; and mention is made in the work of the extension of the Roman franchise to all nations under the dominion of Rome,--an event which took place in the region of Caracalla, a.d. 211.

The Recognitions also contains a large extract from the work De Fato, ascribed to Bardesanes, but really written by a scholar of his.

Some have thought that Bardesanes or his scholar borrowed from the Recognitions; but more recently the opinion has prevailed, that the passage was not originally in the Recognitions, but was inserted in the Recognitions towards the middle of the third century, or even later. [7]

Those who believe the work made up of various documents assign various dates to these documents.

Hilgenfeld, for instance, believes that the Kerugma Petrou was written before the time of Trojan, and the Travels of Peter about the time of his reign.

Nothing is known of the place in which the Recognitions was written. Some, as Schliemann, have supposed Rome, some Asia Minor, and recently Uhlhorn has tried to trace it to Eastern Syria. [8]

The Greek of the Recognitions is lost.

The work has come down to us in the form of a translation by Rufinus of Aquileia (d. 410 a.d.).

In his letter to Gaudentius, Rufinus states that he omitted some portions difficult of comprehension, but that in regard to the other parts he had translated with care, and an endeavour to be exact even in rendering the phraseology.

The best editions of the Recognitions are those by Cotelerius, often reprinted, and by Gersdorf, Lipsiae, 1838; but the text is not in a satisfactory condition.

Footnotes:

1. [See supra, p. 69, and Introductory Notice to Homilies.--R.]

2. Die Clementinischen Rekognitionen und Homilien, nach ihrem Ursprung und Inhalt dargestellt, von Dr. Adolf Hilgenfeld, Jena, 1848, p. 1.

[Despite the morbid taste of this school for heretical writings, and the now proven incorrectness of the "tendency-theory," due credit must be given to Baur and his followers for awakening a better critical discernment among the students of ecclesiastical history.

Hilgenfeld's judgments, in the higher and lower criticism also, are frequently very incorrect; but he has done much to further a correct estimate of the Clementina.

See Introductory Notice, supra.--R.]

3. [The title, which varies in different manuscripts, is derived from the "narrating, in the last books, of the re-union of the scattered members of the Clementine family, who all at last find themselves together in Christianity, and are baptized by Peter" (Schaff, History).--R.]

4. See Schliemann, Die Clementinen, Hamburg, 1844, p. 295.

5. [See a brief account of the discussion supra, p, 70.--R.]

6. Philocalia, cap. 22.

7. See Merx, Bardesanes von Edessa, Halle, 1863, p. 113.

8. Die Homilien und Rekognitionen des Clemens Romanus, nach ihrem Ursprung und Inhalt dargestellt, von Gerhard Uhlhorn, Goettingen, 1854, p. 429.

[Schaff thinks "the Homilies probably originated in East Syria, the Recognitions in Rome."

But Rufinus gives no intimation of the Roman origin of the Greek work he translated.

Still, the apparently more orthodox character of the Recognitions suggests an editor from the Western Church.--R.]

Rufinus, Presbyter of Aquileia; His Preface to Clement's Book of Recognitions

To Bishop Gaudentius.

To thee, indeed, O Gaudentius, thou choice glory of our doctors, belongs such vigour of mind, yea, such grace of the Spirit, that whatever you say even in the course of your daily preaching, whatever you deliver in the church, ought to be preserved in books, and handed down to posterity for their instruction.

But we, whom slenderness of wit renders less ready, and now old age renders slow and inactive, though after many delays, yet at length present to you the work which once the virgin Sylvia of venerable memory enjoined upon us, that we should render Clement into our language, and you afterwards by hereditary right demanded of us; and thus we contribute to the use and profit of our people, no small spoil, as I think, taken from the libraries of the Greeks, so that we may feed with foreign nourishment those whom we cannot with our own.

For foreign things usually seem both more pleasant, and sometimes also more profitable.

In short, almost everything is foreign that brings healing to our bodies, that opposes diseases, and neutralizes poisons.

For Judaea sends us Lacryma balsami, Crete Coma dictamni, Arabia her flower of spices, India reaps her crop of spikenard; which, although they reach us in a somewhat more broken condition than when they leave their native fields, yet retain entire the sweetness of their odour and their healing virtue.

Receive therefore, my soul, [1] Clement returning to you; receive him now in a Roman dress.

And wonder not if haply the florid countenance of eloquence appear less in him than usual.

It matters not, provided the sense tastes the same.

Therefore we transport foreign merchandise into our country with much labour.

And I know not with how grateful countenances my countrymen welcome me, bringing to them the rich spoils of Greece, and unlocking hidden treasures of wisdom with the key of our language.

But may God grant your prayers, that no unlucky eye nor any livid aspect may meet us, lest, by an extreme kind of prodigy, while those from whom he is taken do not envy, yet those upon whom he is bestowed should repine.

Truly it is right to point out the plan of our translation to you, who have read these works also in Greek, lest haply in some parts you may think the order of translation not kept.

I suppose you are aware that there are two editions in Greek of this work of Clement,--the 'Anagnoseis , that is, Recognitions; and that there are two collections of books, differing in some points, but in many containing the same narrative.

In short, the last part of this work, in which is the relation concerning the transformation of Simon, is contained in one of the collections, but is not at all in the other. [2]There are also in both collections some dissertations concerning the Unbegotten God and the Begotten, and on some other subjects, which, to say nothing more, are beyond our comprehension. [3]These, therefore, as being beyond our powers, I have chosen to reserve for others, rather than to produce in an imperfect state.

But in the rest, we have given our endeavour, so far as we could, not to vary either from the sentiments or even from the language and modes of expression; and this, although it renders the style of the narrative less ornate, yet it makes it more faithful.

The epistle in which the same Clement, writing to James the Lord's brother, informs him of the death of Peter, and that he had left him his successor in his chair and teaching, and in which also the whole subject of church order is treated, I have not prefixed to this work, both because it is of later date, and because I have already translated and published it. [4] But I do not think it out of place to explain here what in that letter will perhaps seem to some to be inconsistent.

For some ask, Since Linus and Cletus were bishops in the city of Rome before this Clement, how could Clement himself, writing to James, say that the chair of teaching was handed over to him by Peter? [5]Now of this we have heard this explanation, that Linus and Cletus were indeed bishops in the city of Rome before Clement, but during the lifetime of Peter: that is, that they undertook the care of the episcopate, and that he fulfilled the office of apostleship; as is found also to have been the case at Caesarea, where, when he himself was present, he yet had Zacchaeus, ordained by himself, as bishop.

And in this way both statements will appear to be true, both that these bishops are reckoned before

Clement, and yet that Clement received the teacher's seat on the death of Peter.

But now let us see how Clement, writing to James the Lord's brother, begins his narrative.

Footnotes:

1. Var. readings:
"magnanimous one," "my lord," "my friend."

2. [The reference is probably to the transformation of the father of Clement into the appearance of Simon Magus.

This is narrated in both the Recognitions (book x. 53, etc.) and in the Homilies (xx. 12, etc.), though the latter book closes without any statement of the restoration.

It would seem unlikely, then, that Rufinus refers to the Homilies as the "other" collection.

The recovery of the closing portion of that work has given us its account of the transformation.--R.]

3. [How far Rufinus has omitted portions which occurred in Greek cannot be known.

It is quite probable that the apparent heresy of some passages, rather than their incomprehensibility, led him to omit them. This may be urged in favour of the priority of the Homilies, but is not conclusive.--R.]

4. [There is no good reason for doubting that Rufinus refers to the extant epistle prefixed to the Homilies, and forming, with "the Epistle of Peter to James," which precedes it, a preface and fictitious authentication of that collection.--R.]

5. [The language of Rufinus confirms that of Irenaeus, Eusebius, and Jerome, as to the episcopal succession at Rome (assuming that Cletus and Anacletus, named by Irenaeus, is identical with Cletus).

For other variations, see Church Histories and Encyclopaedias (under Clemens Romanus).

The current opinion at Rome in the beginning of the fifth century is evident from this passage.

Comp. Ante-Nicene Fathers, vol. i. pp. 1, 2.--R.]

Book I

Chapter I - Clement's Early History; Doubts

I Clement, who was born in the city of Rome, [1] was from my earliest age a lover of chastity; while the bent of my mind held me bound as with chains of anxiety and sorrow.

For a thought that was in me--whence originating, I cannot tell--constantly led me to think of my condition of mortality, and to discuss such questions as these: Whether there be for me any life after death, or whether I am to be wholly annihilated:

whether I did not exist before I was born, and whether there shall be no remembrance of this life after death, and so the boundlessness of time shall consign all things to oblivion and silence; so that not only we shall cease to be, but there shall be no remembrance that we have ever been.

This also I revolved in my mind: when the world was made, or what was before it was made, or whether it has existed from eternity.

For it seemed certain, that if it had been made, it must be doomed to dissolution; and if it be dissolved, what is to be afterwards?--unless, perhaps, all things shall be buried in oblivion and silence, or something shall be, which the mind of man cannot now conceive.

Chapter II - His Distress

While I was continually revolving in my mind these and such like questions, suggested I know not how, I was pining away wonderfully through excess of grief; and, what was worse, if at any time I thought to cast aside such cares, as being of little use, the waves of anxiety rose all the higher upon me.

For I had in me that most excellent companion, who would not suffer me to rest--the desire of immortality: for, as the subsequent issue showed, and the grace of Almighty God directed, this bent of mind led me to the quest of truth, and the acknowledgment of the true light; and hence it came to pass, that ere long I pitied those whom formerly in my ignorance I believed to be happy.

Chapter III - His Dissatisfaction with the Schools of the Philosophers

Having therefore such a bent of mind from my earliest years, the desire of learning something led me to frequent the schools of the philosophers.

There I saw that nought else was done, save that doctrines were asserted and controverted without end, contests were waged, and the arts of syllogisms and the subtleties of conclusions were discussed.

If at any time the doctrine of the immortality of the soul prevailed, I was thankful; if at any time it was impugned, I went away sorrowful.

Still, neither doctrine had the power of truth over my heart.

This only I understood, that opinions and definitions of things were accounted true or false, not in accordance with their nature and the truth of the arguments, but in proportion to the talents of those who supported them.

And I was all the more tortured in the bottom of my heart, because I was neither able to lay hold of any of those things which were spoken as firmly established, nor was I able to lay aside the desire of inquiry; but the more I endeavoured to neglect and despise them, so much the more eagerly, as I have said, did a desire of this sort, creeping in upon me secretly as with a kind of pleasure, take possession of my heart and mind.

Chapter IV - His Increasing Disquiet

Being therefore straitened in the discovery of things, I said to myself, Why do we labour in vain, since the end of things is manifest? For if after death I shall be no more, my present torture is useless; but if there is to be for me a life after death, let us keep for that life the excitements that belong to it, lest perhaps some sadder things befall me than those which I now suffer, unless I shall have lived piously and soberly; and, according to the opinions of some of the philosophers, I be consigned to the stream of dark-rolling Phlegethon, or to Tartarus, like Sisyphus and Tityus, and to eternal punishment in the infernal regions, like Ixion and Tantalus.

And again I would answer to myself:

But these things are fables; or if it be so, since the matter is in doubt, it is better to live piously.

But again I would ponder with myself, How should I restrain myself from the lust of sin, while uncertain as to the reward of righteousness?--and all the more when I have no certainty what righteousness is, or what is pleasing to God; and when I cannot ascertain whether the soul be immortal, and be such that it has anything to hope for; nor do I know what the future is certainly to be.

Yet still I cannot rest from thoughts of this sort.

Chapter V - His Design to Test the Immortality of the Soul

What, then, shall I do?

This shall I do.

I shall proceed to Egypt, and there I shall cultivate the friendship of the hierophants or prophets, who preside at the shrines.

Then I shall win over a magician by money, and entreat him, by what they call the necromantic art, to bring me a soul from the infernal regions, as if I were desirous of consulting it about some business.

But this shall be my consultation, whether the soul be immortal.

Now, the proof that the soul is immortal will be put past doubt, not from what it says, or from what I hear, but from what I see:

for seeing it with my eyes, I shall ever after hold the surest conviction of its immortality; and no fallacy of words or uncertainty of hearing shall ever be able to disturb the persuasion produced by sight.

However, I related this project to a certain philosopher with whom I was intimate, who counselled me not to venture upon it; "for," said he, "if the soul should not obey the call of the magician, you henceforth will live more hopelessly, as thinking that there is nothing after death, and also as having tried things unlawful.

If, however, you seem to see anything, what religion or what piety can arise to you from things unlawful and impious?

For they say that transactions of this sort are hateful to the Divinity, and that God sets Himself in opposition to those who trouble souls after their release from the body."

When I heard this, I was indeed staggered in my purpose; yet I could not in any way either lay aside my longing, or cast off the distressing thought.

Chapter VI - Hears of Christ

Not to make a long story of it, whilst I was tossed upon these billows of my thought, a certain report, which took its rise in the regions of the East in the reign of Tiberius Caesar, gradually reached us; and gaining strength as it passed through every place, like some good message sent from God, it was filling the whole world, and suffered not the divine will to be concealed in silence.

For it was spread over all places, announcing that there was a certain person in Judaea, who, beginning in the springtime, [2] was preaching the kingdom of God to the Jews, and saying that those should receive it who should observe the ordinances of His commandments and His doctrine.

And that His speech might be believed to be worthy of credit, and full of the Divinity, He was said to perform many mighty works, and wonderful signs and prodigies by His mere word; so that, as one having power from God, He made the deaf to hear, and the blind to see, and the lame to stand erect, and expelled every infirmity and all demons from men; yea, that He even raised dead persons who were brought to Him; that He cured lepers also, looking at them from a distance; and that there was absolutely nothing which seemed impossible to Him.

These and such like things were confirmed in process of time, not now by frequent rumours, but by the plain statements of persons coming from those quarters; and day by day the truth of the matter was further disclosed.

Chapter VII - Arrival of Barnabas at Rome

At length meetings began to be held in various places in the city, and this subject to be discussed in conversation, and to be a matter of wonder who this might be who had appeared, and what message He had brought from God to men; until, about the same year, a certain man, standing in a most crowded place in the city, made proclamation to the people, saying:

"Hear me, O ye citizens of Rome.

The Son of God is now in the regions of Judaea, promising eternal life to every one who will hear Him, but upon condition that he shall regulate his actions according to the will of Him by whom He hath been sent, even of God the Father.

Wherefore turn ye from evil things to good, from things temporal to things eternal.

Acknowledge that there is one God, ruler of heaven and earth, in whose righteous sight ye unrighteous inhabit His world.

But if ye be converted, and act according to His will, then, coming to the world to come, and being made immortal, ye shall enjoy His unspeakable blessings and rewards." [3]Now, the man who spoke these things to the people was from the regions of the East, by nation a Hebrew, by name Barnabas, who said that he himself was one of His disciples, and that he was sent for this end, that he should declare these things to those who would hear them. [4]When I heard these things, I began, with the rest of the multitude, to follow him, and to hear what he had to say.

Truly I perceived that there was nothing of dialectic artifice in the man, but that he expounded with simplicity, and without any craft of speech, such things as he had heard from the Son of God, or had seen.

For he did not confirm his assertions by the force of arguments, but produced, from the people who stood round about him, many witnesses of the sayings and marvels which he related.

Chapter VIII - His Preaching

Now, inasmuch as the people began to assent willingly to the things which were sincerely spoken, and to embrace his simple discourse, those who thought themselves learned or philosophic began to laugh at the man, and to flout him, and to throw out for him the grappling-hooks of syllogisms, like strong arms.

But he, unterrified, regarding their subtleties as mere ravings, did not even judge them worthy of an answer, but boldly pursued the subject which he had set before him.

At length, some one having proposed this question to him as he was speaking, Why a gnat has been so formed, that though it is a small creature, and has six feet, yet it has got wings in addition; whereas an elephant, though it is an immense animal, and has no wings, yet has only four feet; he, paying no attention to the question, went on with his discourse, which had been interrupted by the unseasonable challenge, only adding this admonition at every interruption:

"We have it in charge to declare to you the words and the wondrous works of Him who hath sent us, and to confirm the truth of what we speak, not by artfully devised arguments, but by witnesses produced from amongst yourselves.

For I recognise many standing in the midst of you whom I remember to have heard along with us the things which we have heard, and to have seen what we have seen.

But be it in your option to receive or to spurn the tidings which we bring to you.

For we cannot keep back what we know to be for your advantage, because, if we be silent, woe is to us; but to you, if you receive not what we speak, destruction.

I could indeed very easily answer your foolish challenges, if you asked for the sake of learning truth,--I mean as to the difference of a gnat and an elephant; but now it were absurd to speak to you of these creatures, when the very Creator and Framer of all things is unknown by you."

The Epistles of Clement

Chapter IX - Clement's Interposition on Behalf of Barnabas

When he had thus spoken, all, as with one consent, with rude voice raised a shout of derision, to put him to shame, and to silence him, crying out that he was a barbarian and a madman.

When I saw matters going on in this way, being filled, I know not whence, with a certain zeal, and inflamed with religious enthusiasm, I could not keep silence, but cried out with all boldness, "Most righteously does Almighty God hide His will from you, whom He foresaw to be unworthy of the knowledge of Himself, as is manifest to those who are really wise, from what you are now doing.

For when you see that preachers of the will of God have come amongst you, because their speech makes no show of knowledge of the grammatical art, but in simple and unpolished language they set before you the divine commands, so that all who hear may be able to follow and to understand the things that are spoken, you deride the ministers and messengers of your salvation, not knowing that it is the condemnation of you who think yourselves skilful and eloquent, that rustic and barbarous men have the knowledge of the truth; whereas, when it has come to you, it is not even received as a guest, while, if your intemperance and lust did not oppose, it ought to have been a citizen and a native.

Thus you are convicted of not being friends of truth and philosophers, but followers of boasting and vain speakers.

Ye think that truth dwells not in simple, but in ingenious and subtle words, and produce countless thousands of words which are not to be rated at the worth of one word.

What, then, do ye think will become of you, all ye crowd of Greeks, if there is to be, as he says, a judgment of God?

But now give over laughing at this man to your own destruction, and let any one of you who pleases answer me; for, indeed, by your barking you annoy the ears even of those who desire to be saved, and by your clamour you turn aside to the fall of infidelity the minds that are prepared for faith.

What pardon can there be for you who deride and do violence to the messenger of the truth when he offers to you the knowledge of God? whereas, even if he brought you nothing of truth, yet, even for the kindness of his intentions towards you, you ought to receive with gratitude and welcome."

Chapter X - Intercourse with Barnabas

While I was urging these and similar arguments, a great excitement was stirred up amongst the bystanders, some being moved with pity as towards a stranger, and approving my speech as in accordance with that feeling; others, petulant and stolid, rousing the anger of their undisciplined minds as much against me as against Barnabas.

But as the day was declining to evening, I laid hold of Barnabas by the right hand, and led him away, although reluctantly, to my house; and there I made him remain, lest perchance any one of the rude rabble should lay hands upon him.

While we were thus placed in contact for a few days, I gladly heard him discoursing the word of truth; yet he hastened his departure, saying that he must by all means celebrate at Judaea a festal day of his religion which was approaching, and that there he should remain in future with his countrymen and his brethren, evidently indicating that he was horrified at the wrong that had been done to him.

Chapter XI - Departure of Barnabas

At length I said to him, "Only expound to me the doctrine of that man who you say has appeared, and I will arrange your sayings in my language, and will preach the kingdom and righteousness of Almighty God; and after that, if you wish it, I shall even sail along with you, for I am extremely desirous to see Judaea, and perhaps I shall remain with you always."

To this he answered, "If indeed you wish to see our country, and to learn those things which you desire, set sail with me even now; or, if there be anything that detains you now, I shall leave with you directions to my dwelling, so that when you please to come you may easily find me; for tomorrow I shall set out on my journey."

When I saw him determined, I went down with him to the harbour, and carefully took from him the directions which he gave me to find his dwelling.

I told him that, but for the necessity of getting some money which was due to me, I should not at all delay, but that I should speedily follow him.

Having told him this, I commended him to the kindness of those who had charge of the ship, and returned sad; for I was possessed of the memory of the intercourse which I had had with an excellent guest and a choice friend.

Chapter XII - Clement's Arrival at Caesarea, and Introduction to Peter

Having then stopped for a few days, and having in some measure finished the business of collecting what was owing to me (for I neglected many things through my desire of hastening, that I might not be hindered from my purpose), I set sail direct for Judaea, and after fifteen days landed at Caesarea Stratonis, which is the largest city in Palestine. [5]When I had landed, and was seeking for an inn, I learned from the conversation of the people, that one Peter, a most approved disciple of Him who appeared in Judaea, and showed many signs and miracles divinely performed among men, was going to hold a discussion of words and questions the next day with one Simon, a Samaritan. Having heard this, I asked to be shown his lodging; and having found it, and standing before the door, I informed the doorkeeper who I was, and whence I came; and, behold, Barnabas coming out, as soon as he saw me rushed into my arms, weeping for joy, and, seizing me by the hand, led me in to Peter.

Having pointed him out to me at a distance, "This," said he, "is Peter, of whom I spoke, to you as the greatest in the wisdom of God, and to whom also I have spoken constantly of you. Enter, therefore, as one well known to him.

For he is well acquainted with all the good that is in thee, and has carefully made himself aware of your religious purpose, whence also he is greatly desirous to see you.

Therefore I present you to him to-day as a great gift."

At the same time, presenting me, he said, "This, O Peter, is Clement."

Chapter XIII - His Cordial Reception by Peter

But Peter most kindly, when he heard my name, immediately ran to me and kissed me.

Then, having made me sit down, he said, "Thou didst well to receive as thy guest Barnabas, preacher of the truth, nothing fearing the rage of the insane people.

Thou shalt be blessed.

For as you have deemed an ambassador of the truth worthy of all honour, so the truth herself shall receive thee a wanderer and a stranger, and shall enroll thee a citizen of her own city; and then there shall be great joy to thee, because, imparting a small favour, thou shalt be written heir of eternal blessings.

Now, therefore, do not trouble yourself to explain your mind to me; for Barnabas has with faithful speech informed me of all things about you and your dispositions, almost daily and without ceasing, recalling the memory of your good qualities.

And to point out to you shortly, as to a friend already of one mind with us, what is your best course; if there is nothing to hinder you, come along with us, and hear the word of the truth, which we are going to speak in every place until we come even to the city of Rome; and now, if you wish anything, speak."

Chapter XIV - His Account of Himself

Having detailed to him what purpose I had conceived from the beginning, and how I had been distracted with vain inquiries, and all those things which at first I intimated to thee, my lord James, so that I need not repeat the same things now, I willingly agreed to travel with him; "for that," said I, "is just what I was most eagerly desirous of.

But first I should wish the scheme of truth to be expounded to me, that I may know whether the soul is mortal or immortal; and if immortal, whether it shall be brought into judgment for those things which it does here. Further, I desire to know what that righteousness is, which is pleasing to God; then, further, whether the world was created, and why it was created, and whether it is to be dissolved, and whether it is to be renovated and made better, or whether after this there shall be no world at all; and, not to mention everything, I should wish to be told what is the case with respect to these and such like things."

To this Peter answered, "I shall briefly impart to you the knowledge of these things, O Clement: therefore listen."

Chapter XV - Peter's First Instruction

Causes of Ignorance.
"The will and counsel of God has for many reasons been concealed from men; first, indeed, through bad instruction, wicked associations, evil habits, unprofitable conversation, and unrighteous presumptions.

On account of all these, I say, first error, then contempt, then infidelity and malice, covetousness also, and vain boasting, and other such like evils, have filled the whole house of this world, like some enormous smoke, and preventing those who dwell in it from seeing its Founder aright, and from perceiving what things are pleasing to Him. What, then, is fitting for those who are within, excepting with a cry brought forth from their inmost hearts to invoke His aid, who alone is not shut up in the smoke-filled house, that He would approach and open the door of the house, so that the smoke may be dissipated which is within, and the light of the sun which shines without may be admitted."

Chapter XVI - Instruction Continued: the True Prophet

"He, therefore, whose aid is needed for the house filled with the darkness of ignorance and the smoke of vices, is He, we say, who is called the true Prophet, who alone can enlighten the souls of men, so that with their eyes they may plainly see the way of safety.

For otherwise it is impossible to get knowledge of divine and eternal things, unless one learns of that true Prophet; because, as you yourself stated a little ago, the belief of things, and the opinions of causes, are estimated in proportion to the talents of their advocates: hence, also, one and the same cause is now thought just, now unjust; and what now seemed true, anon becomes false on the assertion of another.

For this reason, the credit of religion and piety demanded the presence of the true Prophet, that He Himself might tell us respecting each particular, how the truth stands, and might teach us how we are to believe concerning each. [6]And therefore, before all else, the credentials of the prophet himself must be examined with all care; and when you have once ascertained that he is a prophet, it behoves you thenceforth to believe him in everything, and not further to discuss the particulars which he teaches, but to hold the things which he speaks as certain and sacred; which things, although they seem to be received by faith, yet are believed on the ground of the probation previously instituted.

For when once at the outset the truth of the prophet is established on examination, the rest is to be heard and held on the ground of the faith by which it is already established that he is a teacher of truth.

And as it is certain that all things which pertain to divine knowledge ought to be held according to the rule of truth, so it is beyond doubt that from none but Himself alone can it be known what is true."

Chapter XVII - Peter Requests Him to Be His Attendant

Having thus spoken, he set forth to me so openly and so clearly who that Prophet was, and how He might be found, that I seemed to have before my eyes, and to handle with my hand, the proofs which he produced concerning the prophetic truth; and I was struck with intense astonishment, how no one sees, though placed before his eyes, those things which all are seeking for.

Whence, by his command, reducing into order what he had spoken to me, I compiled a book concerning the true Prophet, and sent it to you from Caesarea by his command.

For he said that he had received a command from you to send you every year an account of his sayings and doings. [7]Meantime, at the beginning of his discourse which he delivered to me the first day, when he had instructed me very fully concerning the true Prophet, and very many things besides, he added also this:

"See," said he, "for the future, and be present at the discussions which whenever any necessity arises, I shall hold with those who contradict; against whom, when I dispute, even if I shall seem to be worsted, I shall not be afraid of your being led to doubt of those things which I have stated to you; because, even if I shall seem to be beaten, yet those things shall not therefore seem to be uncertain which the true Prophet has delivered to us.

Yet I hope that we shall not be overcome in disputations either, if only our hearers are reasonable, and friends of truth, who can discern the force and bearing of words, and recognise what discourse comes from the sophistical art, not containing truth, but an image of truth; and what that is, which, uttered simply and without craft, depends for all its power not on show and ornament, but on truth and reason."

Chapter XVIII - His Profiting by Peter's Instruction

To this I answered:
"I give thanks to God Almighty, because I have been instructed as I wished and desired.

At all events, you may depend upon me so far, that I can never come to doubt of those things which I have learned of you; so that even if you yourself should at any time wish to transfer my faith from the true Prophet, you should not be able, because I have drunk in with all my heart what you have spoken. And that you may not think that I am promising you a great thing when I say that I cannot be moved away from this faith, it is with me a certainty, that whoever has received this account of the true Prophet, can never afterwards so much as doubt of its truth.

And therefore I am confident with respect to this heaven-taught doctrine, in which all the art of malice is overborne.

For in opposition to this prophecy neither any art can stand, nor the subtleties of sophisms and syllogism; but every one who hears of the true Prophet must of necessity long immediately for the truth itself, nor will he afterwards, under pretext of seeking the truth, endure diverse errors.

Wherefore, O my lord Peter, be not further anxious about me, as if I were one who does not know what he has received, and how great a gift has been conferred on him.

Be assured that you have conferred a favour on one who knows and understands its value:

nor can I be easily deceived on that account, because I seem to have gotten quickly what I long desired; for it may be that one who desires gets quickly, while another does not even slowly attain the things which he desires."

Chapter XIX - Peter's Satisfaction

Then Peter, when he heard me speak thus, said:
"I give thanks to my God, both for your salvation and for my own peace; for I am greatly delighted to see that you have understood what is the greatness of the prophetic virtue, and because, as you say, not even I myself, if I should wish it (which God forbid!), should be able to turn you away to another faith.

Now henceforth begin to be with us, and to-morrow be present at our discussions, for I am to have a contest with Simon the magician."

When he had thus spoken, he retired to take food along with his friends; but he ordered me to eat by myself; [8] and after the meal, when he had sung praise to God and given thanks, he rendered to me an account of this proceeding, and added, "May the Lord grant to thee to be made like to us in all things, that, receiving baptism, thou mayest be able to meet with us at the same table."

Having thus spoken, he ordered me to go to rest, for by this time both fatigue and the time of the day called to sleep.

Chapter XX - Postponement of Discussion with Simon Magus

Early next morning Zacchaeus [9] came in to us, and after salutation, said to Peter:
"Simon puts off the discussion till the eleventh day of the present month, which is seven days hence, for he says that then he will have more leisure for the contest.

But to me it seems that his putting off is also advantageous to us, so that more may come together, who may be either hearers or judges of our disputation.

However, if it seem proper to you, let us occupy the interval in discussing among ourselves the things which, we suppose, may come into the controversy; so that each of us, knowing what things are to be proposed, and what answers are to be given, may consider with himself if they are all right, or if an adversary shall be able to find anything to object, or to set aside the things which we bring against him.

But if the things which are to be spoken by us are manifestly impregnable on every side, we shall have confidence in entering upon the examination.

And indeed, this is my opinion, that first of all it ought to be inquired what is the origin of all things, or what is the immediate [10] thing which may be called the cause of all things which are:

then, with respect to all things that exist, whether they have been made, and by whom, through whom, and for whom; whether they have received their subsistence from one, or from two, or from many; and whether they have been taken and fashioned from none previously subsisting, or from some:

then, whether there is any virtue in the highest things, or in the lower; whether there is anything which is better than all, or anything that is inferior to all; whether there are any motions, or none; whether those things which are seen were always, and shall be always; whether they have come into existence without a creator, and shall pass away without a destroyer.

If, I say, the discussion begin with these things, I think that the things which shall be inquired into, being discussed with diligent examination, will be easily ascertained.

And when these are ascertained, the knowledge of those that follow will be easily found.

I have stated my opinion; be pleased to intimate what you think of the matter. [11] "

Chapter XXI - Advantage of the Delay

To this Peter answered:

"Tell Simon in the meantime to do as he pleases, and to rest assured that, Divine Providence granting, he shall always find us ready."

Then Zacchaeus went out to intimate to Simon what he had been told.

But Peter, looking at us, and perceiving that I was saddened by the putting off of the contest, said:

"He who believes that the world is administered by the providence of the Most High God, ought not, O Clement, my friend, to take it amiss, in whatever way particular things happen, being assured that the righteousness of God guides to a favourable and fitting issue even those things which seem superfluous or contrary in any business, and especially towards those who worship Him more intimately; and therefore he who is assured of these things, as I have said, if anything occur contrary to his expectation, he knows how to drive away grief from his mind on that account, holding it unquestionable in his better judgment, that, by the government of the good God, even what seems contrary may be turned to good.

Wherefore, O Clement, even now let not this delay of the magician Simon sadden you:

for I believe that it has been done by the providence of God, for your advantage; that I may be able, in this interval of seven days, to expound to you the method of our faith without any distraction, and the order continuously, according to the tradition of the true Prophet, who alone knows the past as it was, the present as it is, and the future as it shall be:

which things were indeed plainly spoken by Him, but are not plainly written; so much so, that when they are read, they cannot be understood without an expounder, on account of the sin which has grown up with men, as I said before.

Therefore I shall explain all things to you, that in those things which are written you may clearly perceive what is the mind of the Lawgiver."

Chapter XXII - Repetition of Instructions

When he had said this, he began to expound to me point by point of those chapters of the law which seemed to be in question, from the beginning of the creation even to that point of time at which I came to him at Caesarea, telling me that the delay of Simon had contributed to my learning all things in order.

"At other times," said he, "we shall discourse more fully on individual points of which we have now spoken shortly, according as the occasion of our conversation shall bring them before us; so that, according to my promise, you may gain a full and perfect knowledge of all.

Since, then, by this delay we have to-day on our hands, I wish to repeat to you again what has been spoken, that it may be the better recalled to your memory."

Then he began in this way to refresh my recollection of what he had said:

"Do you remember, O friend Clement, the account I gave you of the eternal age, that knows no end?"

Then said I, "Never, O Peter, shall I retain anything, if I can lose or forget that."

Chapter XXIII - Repetition Continued

Then Peter, having heard my answer with pleasure, said:
"I congratulate you because you have answered thus, not because you speak of these things easily, but because you profess that you remember them; for the most sublime truths are best honoured by means of silence. Yet, for the credit of those things which you remember concerning things not to be spoken, [12] tell me what you retain of those things which we spoke of in the second place, which can easily be spoken out, that, perceiving your tenacity of memory, I may the more readily point out to you, and freely open, the things of which I wish to speak." Then I, when I perceived that he rejoiced in the good memory of his hearers, said:

"Not only am I mindful of your definition, but also of that preface which was prefixed to the definition; and of almost all things that you have expounded, I retain the sense complete, though not all the words; because the things that you have spoken have been made, as it were, native to my soul, and inborn.

For you have held out a most sweet cup to me in my excessive thirst.

And that you may not suppose that I am occupying you with words, being unmindful of things, I shall now call to mind the things which were spoken, in which the order of your discussion greatly helps me; for the way in which the things that you said followed by consequence upon one another, and were arranged in a balanced manner, makes them easily recalled to memory by the lines of their order.

For the order of sayings is useful for remembering them:

for when you begin to follow them point by point in succession, when anything is wanting, immediately the sense seeks for it; and when it has found it, retains it, or at all events, if it cannot discover it, there will be no reluctance to ask it of the master.

But not to delay in granting what you demand of me, I shall shortly rehearse what you delivered to me concerning the definition of truth."

Chapter XXIV - Repetition Continued

"There always was, there is now, and there ever shall be, that by which the first Will begotten from eternity consists; and from the first Will proceeds a second Will.

After these came the world; and from the world came time:

from this, the multitude of men; from the multitude the election of the beloved, from whose oneness of mind the peaceful kingdom of God is constructed.

But the rest, which ought to follow these, you promised to tell me at another time.

After this, when you had explained about the creation of the world, you intimated the decree of God, "which He, of His own good pleasure, announced in the presence of all the first angels," and which He ordained as an eternal law to all; and how He established two kingdoms,--I mean that of the present time and that of the future,--and appointed times to each, and decreed that a day of judgment should be expected, which He determined, in which a severance is to be made of things and of souls:

so that the wicked indeed shall be consigned to eternal fire for their sins; but those who have lived according to the will of God the Creator, having received a blessing for their good works, effulgent with brightest light, introduced into an eternal abode, and abiding in incorruption, shall receive eternal gifts of ineffable blessings."

Chapter XXV - Repetition Continued

While I was going on thus, Peter, enraptured with joy, and anxious for me as if I had been his son, lest perhaps I should fail in recollection of the rest, and be put to shame on account of those who were present, said:

"It is enough, O Clement; for you have stated these things more clearly than I myself explained them."

Then said I, "Liberal learning has conferred upon me the power of orderly narration, and of stating those things clearly for which there is occasion.

And if we use learning in asserting the errors of antiquity, we ruin ourselves by gracefulness and smoothness of speech; but if we apply learning and grace of speech to the assertion of the truth, I think that not a little advantage is thereby gained.

Be that as it may, my lord Peter, you can but imagine with what thankfulness I am transported for all the rest of your instruction indeed, but especially for the statement of that doctrine which you gave:

There is one God, whose work the world is, and who, because He is in all respects righteous, shall render to every one according to his deeds.

And after that you added:

For the assertion of this dogma countless thousands of words will be brought forward; but in those to whom is granted knowledge of the true Prophet, all this forest of words is cut down.

And on this account, since you have delivered to me a discourse concerning the true Prophet, you have strengthened me with all confidence of your assertions."

And then, having perceived that the sum of all religion and piety consists in this, I immediately replied:

"You have proceeded most excellently, O Peter:

wherefore, in future, expound unhesitatingly, as to one who already knows what are the foundations of faith and piety, the traditions of the true Prophet, who alone, as has been clearly proved, is to be believed.

But that exposition which requires assertions and arguments, reserve for the unbelievers, to whom you have not yet judged it proper to commit the indubitable faith of prophetic grace."

When I had said this, I added:

"You promised that you would give at the proper time two things:

first this exposition, at once simple and entirely free from error; and then an exposition of each individual point as it may be evolved in the course of the various questions which shall be raised.

And after this you expounded the sequence of things in order from the beginning of the world, even to the present time; and if you please, I can repeat the whole from memory."

Chapter XXVI - Friendship of God; How Secured

To this Peter answered:

"I am exceedingly delighted, O Clement, that I commit my words to so safe a heart; for to be mindful of the things that are spoken is an indication of having in readiness the faith of works.

But he from whom the wicked demon steals away the words of salvation, and snatches them away from his memory, cannot be saved, even though he wish it; for he loses the way by which life is reached. Wherefore let us the rather repeat what has been spoken, and confirm it in your heart, that is, in what manner or by whom the world was made, that we may proceed to the friendship of the Creator.

But His friendship is secured by living well, and by obeying His will; which will is the law of all that live.

We shall therefore unfold these things briefly to you, in order that they may be the more surely remembered.

Chapter XXVII - Account of the Creation

"In the beginning, [13] when God had made the heaven and the earth, [14] as one house, the shadow which was cast by the mundane bodies involved in darkness those things which were enclosed in it.

But when the will of God had introduced light, that darkness which had been caused by the shadows of bodies was straightway dispelled:

then at length light is appointed for the day, darkness for the night.

And now the water which was within the world, in the middle space of that first heaven and earth, congealed as if with frost, and solid as crystal, is distended, and the middle spaces of the heaven and earth are separated as by a firmament of this sort; and that firmament the Creator called heaven, so called by the name of that previously made:

and so He divided into two portions that fabric of the universe, although it was but one house.

The reason of the division was this, that the upper portion might afford a dwelling-place to angels, and the lower to men. After this, the place of the sea and the chaos which had been made received that portion of the water which remained below, by order of the eternal Will; and these flowing down to the sunk and hollow places, the dry land appeared; and the gatherings of the waters were made seas.

And after this the earth, which had appeared, produced various species of herbs and shrubs.

It gave forth fountains also, and rivers, not only in the plains, but on the mountains.

And so all things were prepared, that men who were to dwell in it might have it in their power to use all these things according to their will, that is, either for good or evil."

Chapter XXVIII - Account of the Creation Continued

"After this He adorns that visible heaven with stars.

He places in it also the sun and the moon, that the day might enjoy the light of the one, the night that of the other; and that at the same time they might be for an indication of things past, present, and future.

For they were made for signs of seasons and of days, which, although they are seen indeed by all, are understood only by the learned and intelligent.

And when, after this, He had ordered living creatures to be produced from the earth and the waters, He made Paradise, which also He named a place of delights.

But after all these things He made man, on whose account He had prepared all things, whose internal species [15] is older, and for whose sake all things that are were made, given up to his service, and assigned to the uses of his habitation."

Chapter XXIX - The Giants: the Flood

"All things therefore being completed which are in heaven, and in earth, and in the waters, and the human race also having multiplied, in the eighth generation, righteous men, who had lived the life of angels, being allured by the beauty of women, fell into promiscuous and illicit connections with these;[16] and thenceforth acting in all things without discretion, and disorderly, they changed the state of human affairs and the divinely prescribed order of life, so that either by persuasion or force they compelled all men to sin against God their Creator.

In the ninth generation are born the giants, so called from of old, [17] not dragon-footed, as the fables of the Greeks relate, but men of immense bodies, whose bones, of enormous size, are still shown in some places for confirmation.

But against these the righteous providence of God brought a flood upon the world, that the earth might be purified from their pollution, and every place might be turned into a sea by the destruction of the wicked.

Yet there was then found one righteous man, by name Noah, who, being delivered in an ark with his three sons and their wives, became the colonizer of the world after the subsiding of the waters, with those animals and seeds which he had shut up with him."

Chapter XXX - Noah's Sons

"In the twelfth generation, when God had blessed men, and they had begun to multiply, [18] they received a commandment that they should not taste blood, for on account of this also the deluge had been sent. In the thirteenth generation, when the second of Noah's three sons had done an injury to his father, and had been cursed by him, he brought the condition of slavery upon his posterity.

His elder brother meantime obtained the lot of a dwelling-place in the middle region of the world, in which is the country of Judaea; the younger obtained the eastern quarter, and he the western.

In the fourteenth generation one of the cursed progeny first erected an altar to demons, for the purpose of magical arts, and offered there bloody sacrifices.

In the fifteenth generation, for the first time, men set up an idol and worshipped it. Until that time the Hebrew language, which had been given by God to men, bore sole sway.

In the sixteenth generation the sons of men migrated from the east, and, coming to the lands that had been assigned to their fathers, each one marked the place of his own allotment by his own name.

In the seventeenth generation Nimrod I. reigned in Babylonia, and built a city, and thence migrated to the Persians, and taught them to worship fire." [19]

Chapter XXXI - World After the Flood

"In the eighteenth generation walled cities were built, armies were organized and armed, judges and laws were sanctioned, temples were built, and the princes of nations were adored as gods.

In the nineteenth generation the descendants of him who had been cursed after the flood, going beyond their proper bounds which they had obtained by lot in the western regions, drove into the eastern lands those who had obtained the middle portion of the world, and pursued them as far as Persia, while themselves violently took possession of the country from which they expelled them.

In the twentieth generation a son for the first time died before his father, [20] on account of an incestuous crime."

Chapter XXXII - Abraham

"In the twenty-first generation there was a certain wise man, of the race of those who were expelled, of the family of Noah's eldest son, by name Abraham, from whom our Hebrew nation is derived. [21]When the whole world was again overspread with errors, and when for the hideousness of its crimes destruction was ready for it, this time not by water, but fire, and when already the scourge was hanging over the whole earth, beginning with Sodom, this man, by reason of his friendship with God, who was well pleased with him, obtained from God that the whole world should not equally perish.

From the first this same man, being an astrologer, was able, from the account and order of the stars, to recognise the Creator, while all others were in error, and understood that all things are regulated by His providence.

Whence also an angel, [22] standing by him in a vision, instructed him more fully concerning those things which he was beginning to perceive.

He showed him also what belonged to his race and posterity, and promised him that those districts should be restored rather than given to them.

Chapter XXXIII - Abraham: His Posterity

"Therefore Abraham, when he was desirous to learn the causes of things, and was intently pondering upon what had been told him, the true Prophet appeared to him, who alone knows the hearts and purpose of men, and disclosed to him all things which he desired.

He taught him the knowledge of the Divinity; intimated the origin of the world, and likewise its end; showed him the immortality of the soul, and the manner of life which was pleasing to God; declared also the resurrection of the dead, the future judgment, the reward of the good, the punishment of the evil,--all to be regulated by righteous judgment:

and having given him all this information plainly and sufficiently, He departed again to the invisible abodes.

But while Abraham was still in ignorance, as we said to you before, two sons were born to him, of whom the one was called Ismael, and the other Heliesdros.

From the one are descended the barbarous nations, from the other the people of the Persians, some of whom have adopted the manner of living and the institutions of their neighbours, the Brachmans. Others settled in Arabia, of whose posterity some also have spread into Egypt.

From them some of the Indians and of the Egyptians have learned to be circumcised, and to be of purer observance than others, although in process of time most of them have turned to impiety what was the proof and sign of purity."

Chapter XXXIV - The Israelites in Egypt

"Nevertheless, as he had got these two sons during the time while he still lived in ignorance of things, having received the knowledge of God, he asked of the Righteous One that he might merit to have offspring by Sarah, who was his lawful wife, though she was barren. She obtained a son. whom he named Isaac, from whom came Jacob, and from him the twelve patriarchs, and from these twelve seventy-two.

These, when famine befell came into Egypt with all their family; and in the course of four hundred years, being multiplied by the blessing and promise of God, they were afflicted by the Egyptians.

And when they were afflicted the true Prophet appeared to Moses, [23] and struck the Egyptians with ten plagues, when they refused to let the Hebrew people depart from them, and return to their native land; and he brought the people of God out of Egypt.

But those of the Egyptians who survived the plagues, being infected with the animosity of their king, pursued after the Hebrews.

And when they had overtaken them at the sea-shore, and thought to destroy and exterminate them all, Moses, pouring out prayer to God, divided the sea into two parts, so that the water was held on the right hand and on the left as if it had been frozen, and the people of God passed as over a dry road; but the Egyptians who were pursuing them, rashly entering, were drowned.

For when the last of the Hebrews came out, the last of the Egyptians went down into the sea; and straightway the waters of the sea, which by his command were held bound as with frost, were loosed by his command who had bound them, and recovering their natural freedom, inflicted punishment on the wicked nation.

Chapter XXXV - The Exodus

"After this, Moses, by the command of God, whose providence is over all, led out the people of the Hebrews into the wilderness; and, leaving the shortest road which leads from Egypt to Judaea, he led the people through long windings of the wilderness, that, by the discipline of forty years, the novelty of a changed manner of life might root out the evils which had clung to them by a long-continued familiarity with the customs of the Egyptians.

Meantime they came to Mount Sinai, and thence the law was given to them with voices and sights from heaven, written in ten precepts, of which the first and greatest was that they should worship God Himself alone, and not make to themselves any appearance or form [24] to worship.

But when Moses had gone up to the mount, and was staying there forty days, the people, although they had seen Egypt struck with the ten plagues, and the sea parted and passed over by them on foot, manna also given to them from heaven for bread, and drink supplied to them out of the rock that followed [25] them, which kind of food was turned into whatever taste any one desired; and although, being placed under the torrid region of heaven, they were shaded by a cloud in the day-time, that they might not be scorched by the heat, and by night were enlightened by a pillar of fire, lest the horror of darkness should be added to the wasteness of the wilderness;--those very people, I say, when Moses stayed in the mount, made and worshipped a golden calf's head, after the fashion of Apis, whom they had seen worshipped in Egypt; and after so many and so great marvels which they had seen, were unable to cleanse and wash out from themselves the defilements of old habit.

On this account, leaving the short road which leads from Egypt to Judaea, Moses conducted them by an immense circuit of the desert, if haply he might be able, as we mentioned before, to shake off the evils of old habit by the change of a new education."

Chapter XXXVI - Allowance of Sacrifice for a Time

"When meantime Moses, that faithful and wise steward, perceived that the vice of sacrificing to idols had been deeply ingrained into the people from their association with the Egyptians, and that the root of this evil could not be extracted from them, he allowed them indeed to sacrifice, but permitted it to be done only to God, that by any means he might cut off one half of the deeply ingrained evil, leaving the other half to be corrected by another, and at a future time; by Him, namely, concerning whom he said himself, A prophet shall the Lord your God raise unto you, whom ye shall hear even as myself, according to all things which He shall say to you.

Whosoever shall not hear that prophet, his soul shall be cut off from his people. [26]

Chapter XXXVII - The Holy Place

"In addition to these things, he also appointed a place in which alone it should be lawful to them to sacrifice to God. [27] And all this was arranged with this view, that when the fitting time should come, and they should learn by means of the Prophet that God desires mercy and not sacrifice, [28] they might see Him who should teach them that the place chosen of God, in which it was suitable that victims should be offered to God, is his Wisdom; and that on the other hand they might hear that this place, which seemed chosen for a time, often harassed as it had been by hostile invasions and plunderings, was at last to be wholly destroyed. [29] And in order to impress this upon them, even before the coming of the true Prophet, who was to reject at once the sacrifices and the place, it was often plundered by enemies and burnt with fire, and the people carried into captivity among foreign nations, and then brought back when they betook themselves to the mercy of God; that by these things they might be taught that a people who offer sacrifices are driven away and delivered up into the hands of the enemy, but they who do mercy and righteousness are without sacrifices freed from captivity, and restored to their native land.

But it fell out that very few understood this; for the greater number, though they could perceive and observe these things, yet were held by the irrational opinion of the vulgar:

for right opinion with liberty is the prerogative of a few."

Chapter XXXVIII - Sins of the Israelites

"Moses, [30] then, having arranged these things, and having set over the people one Auses to bring them to the land of their fathers, himself by the command of the living God went up to a certain mountain, and there died.

Yet such was the manner of his death, that till this day no one has found his burial-place.

When, therefore, the people reached their fathers' land, by the providence of God, at their first onset the inhabitants of wicked races are routed, and they enter upon their paternal inheritance, which was distributed among them by lot. For some time thereafter they were ruled not by kings, but judges, and remained in a somewhat peaceful condition.

But when they sought for themselves tyrants rather than kings, then also with regal ambition they erected a temple in the place which had been appointed to them for prayer; and thus, through a succession of wicked kings, the people fell away to greater and still greater impiety."

Chapter XXXIX - Baptism Instituted in Place of Sacrifices

"But when the time began to draw near that what was wanting in the Mosaic institutions should be supplied, as we have said, and that the Prophet should appear, of whom he had foretold that He should warn them by the mercy of God to cease from sacrificing; lest haply they might suppose that on the cessation of sacrifice there was no remission of sins for them, He instituted baptism by water amongst them, in which they might be absolved from all their sins on the invocation of His name, and for the future, following a perfect life, might abide in immortality, being purified not by the blood of beasts, but by the purification of the Wisdom of God.

Subsequently also an evident proof of this great mystery is supplied in the fact, that every one who, believing in this Prophet who had been foretold by Moses, is baptized in His name, shall be kept unhurt from the destruction of war which impends over the unbelieving nation, and the place itself; but that those who do not believe shall be made exiles from their place and kingdom, that even against their will they may understand and obey the will of God."

Chapter XL - Advent of the True Prophet

"These things therefore having been fore-arranged, He who was expected comes, bringing signs and miracles as His credentials by which He should be made manifest.

But not even so did the people believe, though they had been trained during so many ages to the belief of these things.

And not only did they not believe, but they added blasphemy to unbelief, saying that He was a gluttonous man and a belly-slave, and that He was actuated by a demon, [31] even He who had come for their salvation.

To such an extent does wickedness prevail by the agency of evil ones; so that, but for the Wisdom of God assisting those who love the truth, almost all would have been involved in impious delusion. Therefore He chose us twelve, [32] the first who believed in Him, whom He named apostles; and afterwards other seventy-two most approved disciples, [33] that, at least in this way recognising the pattern of Moses, [34] the multitude might believe that this is He of whom Moses foretold, the Prophet that was to come." [35]

Chapter XLI - Rejection of the True Prophet

"But some one perhaps may say that it is possible for any one to imitate a number; but what shall we say of the signs and miracles which He wrought?

For Moses had wrought miracles and cures in Egypt.

He also of whom he foretold that He should rise up a prophet like unto himself, though He cured every sickness and infirmity among the people, wrought innumerable miracles, and preached eternal life, was hurried by wicked men to the cross; which deed was, however, by His power turned to good.

In short, while He was suffering, all the world suffered with Him; for the sun was darkened, the mountains were torn asunder, the graves were opened, the veil of the temple was rent, [36] as in lamentation for the destruction impending over the place.

And yet, though all the world was moved, they themselves are not even now moved to the consideration of these so great things."

Chapter XLII - Call of the Gentiles

"But inasmuch as it was necessary that the Gentiles should be called into the room of those who remained unbelieving, [37] so that the number might be filled up which had been shown to Abraham, [38] the preaching of the blessed kingdom of God is sent into all the world.

On this account worldly spirits are disturbed, who always oppose those who are in quest of liberty, and who make use of the engines of error to destroy God's building; while those who press on to the glory of safety and liberty, being rendered braver by their resistance to these spirits, and by the toil of great struggles against them, attain the crown of safety not without the palm of victory.

Meantime, when He had suffered, and darkness had overwhelmed the world from the sixth even to the ninth hour, [39] as soon as the sun shone out again, and things were returned to their usual course, even wicked men returned to themselves and their former practices, their fear having abated.

For some of them, watching the place with all care, when they could not prevent His rising again, said that He was a magician; others pretended that he was stolen away." [40]

Chapter XLIII - Success of the Gospel

"Nevertheless, the truth everywhere prevailed; for, in proof that these things were done by divine power, we who had been very few became in the course of a few days, by the help of God, far more than they.

So that the priests at one time were afraid, lest haply, by the providence of God, to their confusion, the whole of the people should come over to our faith.

Therefore they often sent to us, and asked us to discourse to them concerning Jesus, whether He were the Prophet whom Moses foretold, who is the eternal Christ. [41]For on this point only does there seem to be any difference between us who believe in Jesus, and the unbelieving Jews.

But while they often made such requests to us, and we sought for a fitting opportunity, a week of years was completed from the passion of the Lord, the Church of the Lord which was constituted in Jerusalem was most plentifully multiplied and grew, being governed with most righteous ordinances by James, who was ordained bishop in it by the Lord."

Chapter XLIV - Challenge by Caiaphas

"But when we twelve apostles, on the day of the passover, had come together with an immense multitude, and entered into the church of the brethren, each one of us, at the request of James, [42] stated briefly, in the hearing of the people, what we had done in every place. [43]While this was going on, Caiaphas, the high priest, sent priests to us, and asked us to come to him, that either we should prove to him that Jesus is the eternal Christ, or he to us that He is not, and that so all the people should agree upon the one faith or the other; and this he frequently entreated us to do.

But we often put it off, always seeking for a more convenient time."

Then I, Clement, answered to this:

"I think that this very question, whether He is the Christ, is of great importance for the establishment of the faith; otherwise the high priest would not so frequently ask that he might either learn or teach concerning the Christ."

Then Peter:

"You have answered rightly, O Clement; for as no one can see without eyes, nor hear without ears, nor smell without nostrils, nor taste without a tongue, nor handle anything without hands, so it is impossible, without the true Prophet, to know what is pleasing to God."

And I answered: "I have already learned from your instruction that this true prophet is the Christ;

but I should wish to learn what the Christ means, or why He is so called, that a matter of so great importance may not be vague and uncertain to me."

Chapter XLV - The True Prophet: Why Called the Christ

Then Peter began to instruct me in this manner: [44]"When God had made the world, as Lord of the universe, He appointed chiefs over the several creatures, over the trees even, and the mountains, and the fountains, and the rivers, and all things which He had made, as we have told you; for it were too long to mention them one by one.

He set, therefore, an angel as chief over the angels, a spirit over the spirits, a star over the stars, a demon over the demons, a bird over the birds, a beast over the beasts, a serpent over the serpents, a fish over the fishes, a man over men, who is Christ Jesus.

But He is called Christ by a certain excellent rite of religion; for as there are certain names common to kings, as Arsaces among the Persians, Caesar among the Romans, Pharaoh among the Egyptians, so among the Jews a king is called Christ.

And the reason of this appellation is this: Although indeed He was the Son of God, and the beginning of all things, He became man; Him first God anointed with oil which was taken from the wood of the tree of life:

from that anointing therefore He is called Christ.

Thence, moreover, He Himself also, according to the appointment of His Father, anoints with similar oil every one of the pious when they come to His kingdom, for their refreshment after their labours, as having got over the difficulties of the way; so that their light may shine, and being filled with the Holy Spirit, they may be endowed with immortality. [45]But it occurs to me that I have sufficiently explained to you the whole nature of that branch from which that ointment is taken."

Chapter XLVI - Anointing

"But now also I shall, by a very short representation, recall you to the recollection of all these things.

In the present life, Aaron, the first high priest, [46] was anointed with a composition of chrism, which was made after the pattern of that spiritual ointment of which we have spoken before.

He was prince of the people, and as a king received first-fruits and tribute from the people, man by man; and having undertaken the office of judging the people, he judged of things clean and things unclean.

But if any one else was anointed with the same ointment, as deriving virtue from it, he became either king, or prophet, or priest.

If, then, this temporal grace, compounded by men, had such efficacy, consider now how potent was that ointment extracted by God from a branch of the tree of life, when that which was made by men could confer so excellent dignities among men.

For what in the present age is more glorious than a prophet, more illustrious than a priest, more exalted than a king?"

Chapter XLVII - Adam Anointed a Prophet

To this, I replied:

"I remember, Peter, that you told me of the first man that he was a prophet; but you did not say that he was anointed. If then there be no prophet without anointing, how could the first man be a prophet, since he was not anointed?"

Then Peter, smiling, said: "If the first man prophesied, it is certain that he was also anointed. For although he who has recorded the law in his pages is silent as to his anointing, yet he has evidently left us to understand these things.

For as, if he had said that he was anointed, it would not be doubted that he was also a prophet, although it were not written in the law; so, since it is certain that he was a prophet, it is in like manner certain that he was also anointed, because without anointing he could not be a prophet.

But you should rather have said, If the chrism was compounded by Aaron, by the perfumer's art, how could the first man be anointed before Aaron's time, the arts of composition not yet having been discovered?"

Then I answered, "Do not misunderstand me, Peter; for I do not speak of that compounded ointment and temporal oil, but of that simple and eternal ointment, which you told me was made by God, after whose likeness you say that that other was compounded by men."

Chapter XLVIII - The True Prophet, a Priest

Then Peter answered, with an appearance of indignation:

"What! do you suppose, Clement, that all of us can know all things before the time? But not to be drawn aside now from our proposed discourse, we shall at another time, when your progress is more manifest, explain these things more distinctly.

"Then, however, a priest or a prophet, being anointed with the compounded ointment, putting fire to the altar of God, was held illustrious in all the world.

But after Aaron, who was a priest, another is taken out of the waters.

I do not speak of Moses, but of Him who, in the waters of baptism, was called by God His Son. [47] For it is Jesus who has put out, by the grace of baptism, that fire which the priest kindled for sins; for, from the time when He appeared, the chrism has ceased, by which the priesthood or the prophetic or the kingly office was conferred."

Chapter XLIX - Two Comings of Christ

"His coming, therefore, was predicted by Moses, who delivered the law of God to men; but by another also before him, as I have already informed you.

He therefore intimated that He should come, humble indeed in His first coming, but glorious in His second.

And the first, indeed, has been already accomplished; since He has come and taught, and He, the Judge of all, has been judged and slain.

But at His second coming He shall come to judge, and shall indeed condemn the wicked, but shall take the pious into a share and association with Himself in His kingdom.

Now the faith of His second coming depends upon His first. For the prophets--especially Jacob and Moses--spoke of the first, but some also of the second.

But the excellency of prophecy is chiefly shown in this, that the prophets spoke not of things to come, according to the sequence of things; otherwise they might seem merely as wise men to have conjectured what the sequence of things pointed out."

Chapter L - His Rejection by the Jews

"But what I say is this:

It was to be expected that Christ should be received by the Jews, to whom He came, and that they should believe on Him who was expected for the salvation of the people, according to the traditions of the fathers; but that the Gentiles should be averse to Him, since neither promise nor announcement concerning Him had been made to them, and indeed he had never been made known to them even by name.

Yet the prophets, contrary to the order and sequence of things, said that He should be the expectation of the Gentiles, and not of the Jews. [48] And so it happened.

For when He came, he was not at all acknowledged by those who seemed to expect Him, in consequence of the tradition of their ancestors; whereas those who had heard nothing at all of Him, both believe that He has come, and hope that he is to come.

And thus in all things prophecy appears faithful, which said that He was the expectation of the Gentiles.

The Jews, therefore, have erred concerning the first coming of the Lord; and on this point only there is disagreement betwixt us and them.

For they themselves know and expect that Christ shall come; but that he has come already in humility--even he who is called Jesus--they do not know.

And this is a great confirmation of His coming, that all do not believe on Him."

Chapter LI - The Only Saviour

"Him, therefore, has God appointed in the end of the world; because it was impossible that the evils of men could be removed by any other, provided that the nature of the human race were to remain entire, i.e., the liberty of the will being preserved.

This condition, therefore, being preserved inviolate, He came to invite to His kingdom all righteous ones, and those who have been desirous to please Him.

For these He has prepared unspeakable good things, and the heavenly city Jerusalem, which shall shine above the brightness of the sun, for the habitation of the saints.

But the unrighteous, and the wicked and those who have despised God, and have devoted the life given them to diverse wickednesses, and have given to the practice of evil the time which was given them for the work of righteousness He shall hand over to fitting and condign vengeance.

But the rest of the things which shall then be done, it is neither in the power of angels nor of men to tell or to describe.

This only it is enough for us to know, that God shall confer upon the good an eternal possession of good things."

Chapter LII - The Saints Before Christ's Coming

When he had thus spoken, I answered:
"If those shall enjoy the kingdom of Christ, whom His coming shall find righteous, shall then those be wholly deprived of the kingdom who have died before His coming?"

Then Peter says:
"You compel me, O Clement, to touch upon things that are unspeakable.

But so far as it is allowed to declare them, I shall not shrink from doing so.

Know then that Christ, who was from the beginning, and always, was ever present with the pious, though secretly, through all their generations:

especially with those who waited for Him, to whom He frequently appeared.

But the time was not yet that there should be a resurrection of the bodies that were dissolved; but this seemed rather to be their reward from God, that whoever should be found righteous, should remain longer in the body; or, at least, as is clearly related in the writings of the law concerning a certain righteous man, that God translated him. [49]In like manner others were dealt with, who pleased His will, that, being translated to Paradise, they should be kept for the kingdom.

But as to those who have not been able completely to fulfil the rule of righteousness, but have had some remnants of evil in their flesh, their bodies are indeed dissolved, but their souls are kept in good and blessed abodes, that at the resurrection of the dead, when they shall recover their own bodies, purified even by the dissolution, they may obtain an eternal inheritance in proportion to their good deeds.

And therefore blessed are all those who shall attain to the kingdom of Christ; for not only shall they escape the pains of hell, but shall also remain incorruptible, and shall be the first to see God the Father, and shall obtain the rank of honour among the first in the presence of God."

Chapter LIII - Animosity of the Jews

"Wherefore there is not the least doubt concerning Christ; and all the unbelieving Jews are stirred up with boundless rage against us, fearing lest haply He against whom they have sinned should be He.

And their fear grows all the greater, because they know that, as soon as they fixed Him on the cross, the whole world showed sympathy with Him; and that His body, although they guarded it with strict care, could nowhere be found; and that innumerable multitudes are attaching themselves to His faith.

Whence they, together with the high priest Caiaphas, were compelled to send to us again and again, that an inquiry might be instituted concerning the truth of His name.

And when they were constantly entreating that they might either learn or teach concerning Jesus, whether He were the Christ, it seemed good to us to go up into the temple, and in the presence of all the people to bear witness concerning Him, and at the same time to charge the Jews with many foolish things which they were doing.

For the people was now divided into many parties, ever since the days of John the Baptist."

Chapter LIV - Jewish Sects

"For when the rising of Christ was at hand for the abolition of sacrifices, and for the bestowal of the grace of baptism, the enemy, understanding from the predictions that the time was at hand, wrought various schisms among the people, that, if haply it might be possible to abolish the former sin, [50] the latter fault might be incorrigible.

The first schism, therefore, was that of those who were called Sadducees, which took their rise almost in the time of John. These, as more righteous than others, began to separate themselves from the assembly of the people, and to deny the resurrection of the dead, [51] and to assert that by an argument of infidelity, saying that it was unworthy that God should be worshipped, as it were, under the promise of a reward.

The first author of this opinion was Dositheus; [52] the second was Simon.

Another schism is that of the Samaritans; for they deny the resurrection of the dead, and assert that God is not to be worshipped in Jerusalem, but on Mount Gerizim.

They indeed rightly, from the predictions of Moses, expect the one true Prophet; but by the wickedness of Dositheus they were hindered from believing that Jesus is He whom they were expecting.

The scribes also, and Pharisees, are led away into another schism; but these, being baptized by John, and holding the word of truth received from the tradition of Moses as the key of the kingdom of heaven, have hid it from the hearing of the people. [53] Yea, some even of the disciples of John, who seemed to be great ones, have separated themselves from the people, and proclaimed their own master as the Christ.

But all these schisms have been prepared, that by means of them the faith of Christ and baptism might be hindered."

Chapter LV - Public Discussion

"However, as we were proceeding to say, when the high priest had often sent priests to ask us that we might discourse with one another concerning Jesus; when it seemed a fit opportunity, and it pleased all the Church, we went up to the temple, and, standing on the steps together with our faithful brethren, the people kept perfect silence; and first the high priest began to exhort the people that they should hear patiently and quietly, and at the same time witness and judge of those things that were to be spoken.

Then, in the next place, exalting with many praises the rite or sacrifice which had been bestowed by God upon the human race for the remission of sins, he found fault with the baptism of our Jesus, as having been recently brought in in opposition to the sacrifices.

But Matthew, [54] meeting his propositions, showed clearly, that whosoever shall not obtain the baptism of Jesus shall not only be deprived of the kingdom of heaven, but shall not be without peril at the resurrection of the dead, even though he be fortified by the prerogative of a good life and an upright disposition.

Having made these and such like statements, Matthew stopped."

Chapter LVI - Sadducees Refuted

"But the party of the Sadducees, who deny the resurrection of the dead, were in a rage, so that one of them cried out from amongst the people, saying that those greatly err who think that the dead ever arise.

In opposition to him, Andrew, my brother, answering, declared that it is not an error, but the surest matter of faith, that the dead rise, in accordance with the teaching of Him of whom Moses foretold that He should come the true Prophet.

Or if,' says he, you do not think that this is He whom Moses foretold, let this first be inquired into, so that when this is clearly proved to be He, there may be no further doubt concerning the things which He taught.'

These, and many such like things, Andrew proclaimed, and then stopped."

Chapter LVII - Samaritan Refuted

"But a certain Samaritan, speaking against the people and against God, and asserting that neither are the dead to rise, nor is that worship of God to be maintained which is in Jerusalem, but that Mount Gerizim is to be reverenced, added also this in opposition to us, that our Jesus was not He whom Moses foretold as a Prophet to come into the world. Against him, and another who supported him in what he said, James and John, the sons of Zebedee, strove vigorously; and although they had a command not to enter into their cities, [55] nor to bring the word of preaching to them, yet, lest their discourse, unless it were confined, should hurt the faith of others, they replied so prudently and so powerfully, that they put them to perpetual silence.

For James made an oration concerning the resurrection of the dead, with the approbation of all the people; while John showed that if they would abandon the error of Mount Gerizim, they should consequently acknowledge that Jesus was indeed He who, according to the prophecy of Moses, was expected to come; since, indeed, as Moses wrought signs and miracles, so also did Jesus.

And there is no doubt but that the likeness of the signs proves Him to be that prophet of whom he said that He should come, like himself.'

Having declared these things, and more to the same effect, they ceased."

Chapter LVIII - Scribes Refuted

"And, behold, one of the scribes, shouting out from the midst of the people, says:

The signs and miracles which your Jesus wrought, he wrought not as a prophet, but as a magician.'

Him Philip eagerly encounters, showing that by this argument he accused Moses also.

For when Moses wrought signs and miracles in Egypt, in like manner as Jesus also did in Judaea, it cannot be doubted that what was said of Jesus might as well be said of Moses.

Having made these and such like protestations, Philip was silent."

Chapter LIX - Pharisees Refuted

"Then a certain Pharisee, hearing this, chid Philip because he put Jesus on a level with Moses.

To whom Bartholomew, answering, boldly declared that we do not only say that Jesus was equal to Moses, but that He was greater than he, because Moses was indeed a prophet, as Jesus was also, but that Moses was not the Christ, as Jesus was, and therefore He is doubtless greater who is both a prophet and the Christ, than he who is only a prophet.

After following out this train of argument, he stopped.

After him James the son of Alphaeus gave an address to the people, with the view of showing that we are not to believe on Jesus on the ground that the prophets foretold concerning Him, but rather that we are to believe the prophets, that they were really prophets, because the Christ bears testimony to them; for it is the presence and coming of Christ that show that they are truly prophets:

for testimony must be borne by the superior to his inferiors, not by the inferiors to their superior.

After these and many similar statements, James also was silent.

After him Lebbaeus began vehemently to charge it upon the people that they did not believe in Jesus, who had done them so much good by teaching them the things that are of God, by comforting the afflicted, healing the sick, relieving the poor; yet for all these benefits their return had been hatred and death.

When he had declared these and many more such things to the people, he ceased."

Chapter LX - Disciples of John Refuted

"And, behold, one of the disciples of John asserted that John was the Christ, and not Jesus, inasmuch as Jesus Himself declared that John was greater than all men and all prophets. [56]If, then,' said he, he be greater than all, he must be held to be greater than Moses, and than Jesus himself.

But if he be the greatest of all, then must he be the Christ.'

To this Simon the Canaanite, answering, asserted that John was indeed greater than all the prophets, and all who are born of women, yet that he is not greater than the Son of man.

Accordingly Jesus is also the Christ, whereas John is only a prophet:

and there is as much difference between him and Jesus, as between the forerunner and Him whose forerunner he is; or as between Him who gives the law, and him who keeps the law.

Having made these and similar statements, the Canaanite also was silent.

After him Barnabas, [57] who also is called Matthias, who was substituted as an apostle in the place of Judas, began to exhort the people that they should not regard Jesus with hatred, nor speak evil of Him.

For it were far more proper, even for one who might be in ignorance or in doubt concerning Jesus, to love than to hate Him.

For God has affixed a reward to love, a penalty to hatred.

For the very fact,' said he, that He assumed a Jewish body, and was born among the Jews, how has not this incited us all to love Him?'

When he had spoken this, and more to the same effect, he stopped."

Chapter LXI - Caiaphas Answered

"Then Caiaphas attempted to impugn the doctrine of Jesus, saying that He spoke vain things, for He said that the poor are blessed; [58] and promised earthly rewards; and placed the chief gift in an earthly inheritance; and promised that those who maintain righteousness shall be satisfied with meat and drink; and many things of this sort He is charged with teaching.

Thomas, in reply, proves that his accusation is frivolous; showing that the prophets, in whom Caiaphas believes, taught these things much more, and did not show in what manner these things are to be, or how they are to be understood; whereas Jesus pointed out how they are to be taken.

And when he had spoken these things, and others of like kind, Thomas also held his peace."

Chapter LXII - Foolishness of Preaching

"Therefore Caiaphas, again looking at me, and sometimes in the way of warning and sometimes in that of accusation, said that I ought for the future to refrain from preaching Christ Jesus, lest I should do it to my own destruction, and lest, being deceived myself, I should also deceive others.

Then, moreover, he charged me with presumption, because, though I was unlearned, a fisherman, and a rustic, I dared to assume the office of a teacher.

As he spoke these things, and many more of like kind, I said in reply, that I incurred less danger, if, as he said, this Jesus were not the Christ, because I received Him as a teacher of the law; but that he was in terrible danger if this be the very Christ, as assuredly He is:

for I believe in Him who has appeared; but for whom else, who has never appeared, does he reserve his faith?

But if I, an unlearned and uneducated man, as you say, a fisherman and a rustic, have more understanding than wise elders, this, said I, ought the more to strike terror into you.

For if I disputed with any learning, and won over you wise and learned men, it would appear that I had acquired this power by long learning, and not by the grace of divine power; but now, when, as I have said, we unskilled men convince and overcome you wise men, who that has any sense does not perceive that this is not a work of human subtlety, but of divine will and gift?"

Chapter LXIII - Appeal to the Jews

"Thus we argued and bore witness; and we who were unlearned men and fishermen, taught the priests concerning the one only God of heaven; the Sadducees, concerning the resurrection of the dead; the Samaritans, concerning the sacredness of Jerusalem (not that we entered into their cities, but disputed with them in public); the scribes and Pharisees, concerning the kingdom of heaven; the disciples of John, that they should not suffer John to be a stumbling-block to them; and all the people, that Jesus is the eternal Christ.

At last, however, I warned them, that before we should go forth to the Gentiles, to preach to them the knowledge of God the Father, they should themselves be reconciled to God, receiving His Son; for I showed them that in no way else could they be saved, unless through the grace of the Holy Spirit they hasted to be washed with the baptism of threefold invocation, and received the Eucharist of Christ the Lord, whom alone they ought to believe concerning those things which He taught, that so they might merit to attain eternal salvation; but that otherwise it was utterly impossible for them to be reconciled to God, even if they should kindle a thousand altars and a thousand high altars to Him."

Chapter LXIV - Temple to Be Destroyed

"For we,' said I, have ascertained beyond doubt that God is much rather displeased with the sacrifices which you offer, the time of sacrifices having now passed away; and because ye will not acknowledge that the time for offering victims is now past, therefore the temple shall be destroyed, and the abomination of desolation [59] shall stand in the holy place; and then the Gospel shall be preached to the Gentiles for a testimony against you, that your unbelief may be judged by their faith.

For the whole world at different times suffers under divers maladies, either spreading generally over all, or affecting specially. Therefore it needs a physician to visit it for its salvation.

We therefore bear witness to you, and declare to you what has been hidden from every one of you. It is for you to consider what is for your advantage.'"

Chapter LXV - Tumult Stilled by Gamaliel

"When I had thus spoken, the whole multitude of the priests were in a rage, because I had foretold to them the overthrow of the temple. Which when Gamaliel, a chief of the people, saw--who was secretly our brother in the faith, but by our advice remained among them--because they were greatly enraged and moved with intense fury against us, he stood up, and said, [60] Be quiet for a little, O men of Israel, for ye do not perceive the trial which hangs over you.

Wherefore refrain from these men; and if what they are engaged in be of human counsel, it will soon come to an end; but if it be from God, why will you sin without cause, and prevail nothing? For who can overpower the will of God?

Now therefore, since the day is declining towards evening, I shall myself dispute with these men to-morrow, in this same place, in your hearing, so that I may openly oppose and clearly confute every error.'

By this speech of his their fury was to some extent checked, especially in the hope that next day we should be publicly convicted of error; and so he dismissed the people peacefully."

Chapter LXVI - Discussion Resumed

"Now when we had come to our James, while we detailed to him all that had been said and done, we supped, and remained with him, spending the whole night in supplication to Almighty God, that the discourse of the approaching disputation might show the unquestionable truth of our faith.

Therefore, on the following day, James the bishop went up to the temple with us, and with the whole church.

There we found a great multitude, who had been waiting for us from the middle of the night. Therefore we took our stand in the same place as before, in order that, standing on an elevation, we might be seen by all the people.

Then, when profound silence was obtained, Gamaliel, who, as we have said, was of our faith, but who by a dispensation remained amongst them, that if at any time they should attempt anything unjust or wicked against us, he might either check them by skillfully adopted counsel, or might warn us, that we might either be on our guard or might turn it aside;--he therefore, as if acting against us, first of all looking to James the bishop, addressed him in this manner:--

Chapter LXVII - Speech of Gamaliel

"If I, Gamaliel, deem it no reproach either to my learning or to my old age to learn something from babes and unlearned ones, if haply there be anything which it is for profit or for safety to acquire (for he who lives reasonably knows that nothing is more precious than the soul), ought not this to be the object of love and desire to all, to learn what they do not know, and to teach what they have learned?

For it is most certain that neither friendship, nor kindred, nor lofty power, ought to be more precious to men than truth.

Therefore you, O brethren, if ye know anything more, shrink not from laying it before the people of God who are present, and also before your brethren; while the whole people shall willingly and in perfect quietness hear what you say.

For why should not the people do this, when they see even me equally with themselves willing to learn from you, if haply God has revealed something further to you?

But if you in anything are deficient, be not ye ashamed in like manner to be taught by us, that God may fill up whatever is wanting on either side.

But if any fear now agitates you on account of some of our people whose minds are prejudiced against you, and if through fear of their violence you dare not openly speak your sentiments, in order that I may deliver you from this fear, I openly swear to you by Almighty God, who liveth for ever, that I will suffer no one to lay hands upon you.

Since, then, you have all this people witnesses of this my oath, and you hold the covenant of our sacrament as a fitting pledge, let each one of you, without any hesitation, declare what he has learned; and let us, brethren, listen eagerly and in silence.'"

Chapter LXVIII - The Rule of Faith

"These sayings of Gamaliel did not much please Caiaphas; and holding him in suspicion, as it seemed, he began to insinuate himself cunningly into the discussions:
for, smiling at what Gamaliel had said, the chief of the priests asked of James, the chief of the bishops, [61] that the discourse concerning Christ should not be drawn but from the Scriptures; that we may know,' said he, whether Jesus be the very Christ or no.'
Then said James, We must first inquire from what Scriptures we are especially to derive our discussion.'
Then he, with difficulty, at length overcome by reason, answered, that it must be derived from the law; and afterwards he made mention also of the prophets."

Chapter LXIX - Two Comings of Christ

"To him our James began to show, that whatsoever things the prophets say they have taken from the law, and what they have spoken is in accordance with the law.
He also made some statements respecting the books of the Kings, in what way, and when, and by whom they were written, and how they ought to be used.
And when he had discussed most fully concerning the law, and had, by a most clear exposition, brought into light whatever things are in it concerning Christ, he showed by most abundant proofs that Jesus is the Christ, and that in Him are fulfilled all the prophecies which related to His humble advent.
For he showed that two advents of Him are foretold:
one in humiliation, which He has accomplished; the other in glory, which is hoped for to be accomplished, when He shall come to give the kingdom to those who believe in Him, and who observe all things which He has commanded.
And when he had plainly taught the people concerning these things, he added this also:
That unless a man be baptized in water, in the name of the threefold blessedness, as the true Prophet taught, he can neither receive remission of sins nor enter into the kingdom of heaven; and he declared that this is the prescription of the unbegotten God.
To which he added this also:
Do not think that we speak of two unbegotten Gods, or that one is divided into two, or that the same is made male and female.
But we speak of the only-begotten Son of God, not sprung from another source, but ineffably self-originated; and in like manner we speak of the Paraclete.' [62] But when he had spoken some things also concerning baptism, through seven successive days he persuaded all the people and the high priest that they should hasten straightway to receive baptism."

Chapter LXX - Tumult Raised by Saul

"And when matters were at that point that they should come and be baptized, some one of our enemies, [63] entering the temple with a few men, began to cry out, and to say, What mean ye, O men of Israel?
Why are you so easily hurried on?
Why are ye led headlong by most miserable men, who are deceived by Simon, a magician?'
While he was thus speaking, and adding more to the same effect, and while James the bishop was refuting him, he began to excite the people and to raise a tumult, so that the people might not be able to hear what was said. Therefore he began to drive all into confusion with shouting, and to undo what had been arranged with much labour, and at the same time to reproach the priests, and to enrage them with revilings and abuse, and, like a madman, to excite every one to murder, saying, What do ye?
Why do ye hesitate?
Oh sluggish and inert, why do we not lay hands upon them, and pull all these fellows to pieces?'
When he had said this, he first, seizing a strong brand from the altar, set the example of smiting.
Then others also, seeing him, were carried away with like readiness.
Then ensued a tumult on either side, of the beating and the beaten.
Much blood is shed; there is a confused flight, in the midst of which that enemy attacked James, and threw him headlong from the top of the steps; and supposing him to be dead, he cared not to inflict further violence upon him."

Chapter LXXI - Flight to Jericho

"But our friends lifted him up, for they were both more numerous and more powerful than the others; but, from their fear of God, they rather suffered themselves to be killed by an inferior force, than they would kill others.

But when the evening came the priests shut up the temple, and we returned to the house of James, and spent the night there in prayer.

Then before daylight we went down to Jericho, to the number of 5000 men.

Then after three days one of the brethren came to us from Gamaliel, whom we mentioned before, bringing to us secret tidings that that enemy had received a commission from Caiaphas, the chief priest, that he should arrest all who believed in Jesus, and should go to Damascus with his letters, and that there also, employing the help of the unbelievers, he should make havoc among the faithful; and that he was hastening to Damascus chiefly on this account, because he believed that Peter had fled thither. [64] And about thirty days thereafter he stopped on his way while passing through Jericho going to Damascus. At that time we were absent, having gone out to the sepulchres of two brethren which were whitened of themselves every year, by which miracle the fury of many against us was restrained, because they saw that our brethren were had in remembrance before God."

Chapter LXXII - Peter Sent to Caesarea

"While, therefore, we abode in Jericho, and gave ourselves to prayer and fasting, James the bishop sent for me, and sent me here to Caesarea, saying that Zacchaeus had written to him from Caesarea, that one Simon, a Samaritan magician, was subverting many of our people, asserting that he was one Stans,[65] --that is, in other words, the Christ, and the great power of the high God, which is superior to the Creator of the world; at the same time that he showed many miracles, and made some doubt, and others fall away to him.

He informed me of all things that had been ascertained respecting this man from those who had formerly been either his associates or his disciples, and had afterwards been converted to Zacchaeus.

Many therefore there are, O Peter,' said James, for whose safety's sake it behoves you to go and to refute the magician, and to teach the word of truth.

Therefore make no delay; nor let it grieve you that you set out alone, knowing that God by Jesus will go with you, and will help you, and that soon, by His grace, you will have many associates and sympathizers.

Now be sure that you send me in writing every year an account of your sayings and doings, and especially at the end of every seven years.'

With these expressions he dismissed me, and in six days I arrived at Caesarea." [66]

Chapter LXXIII - Welcomed by Zacchaeus

"When I entered the city, our most beloved brother Zacchaeus met me; and embracing me, brought me to this lodging, in which he himself stayed, inquiring of me concerning each of the brethren, especially concerning our honourable brother James.

And when I told him that he was still lame on one foot, on his immediately asking the cause of this, I related to him all that I have now detailed to you, how we had been called by the priests and Caiaphas the high priest to the temple, and how James the archbishop, standing on the top of the steps, had for seven successive days shown the whole people from the Scriptures of the Lord that Jesus is the Christ; and how, when all were acquiescing that they should be baptized by him in the name of Jesus, an enemy did all those things which I have already mentioned, and which I need not repeat."

Chapter LXXIV - Simon Magus Challenges Peter

"When Zacchaeus had heard these things, he told me in return of the doings of Simon; and in the meantime Simon himself--how he heard of my arrival I do not know--sent a message to me, saying, Let us dispute to-morrow in the hearing of the people.'

To which I answered, Be it so, as it pleaseth you.'

And this promise of mine was known over the whole city, so that even you, who arrived on that very day, learned that I was to hold a discussion with Simon on the following day, and having found out my abode, according to the directions which you had received from Barnabas, came to me.

Clement of Rome

But I so rejoiced at your coming, that my mind, moved I know not how, hastened to expound all things quickly to you, yet especially that which is the main point in our faith, concerning the true Prophet, which alone, I doubt not, is a sufficient foundation for the whole of our doctrine.

Then, in the next place, I unfolded to you the more secret meaning of the written law, through its several heads, which there was occasion to unfold; neither did I conceal from you the good things of the traditions.

But what remains, beginning from tomorrow, you shall hear from day to day in connection with the questions which will be raised in the discussion with Simon, until by God's favour we reach that city of Rome to which we believe that our journey is to be directed."

I then declared that I owed him all thanks for what he had told me, and promised that I would most readily do all that he commanded.

Then, having taken food, he ordered me to rest, and he also betook himself to rest."

Footnotes:

1. [The first six chapters closely resemble the corresponding chapters of Homily I. The variations are no greater than might readily appear in a version.--R.]
2. V. R. in the time of Tiberius Caesar.
3. [In Homily I. a warning of future punishment is added.--R.]
4. [The narrative in the Homilies is fuller; the preacher at Rome is not named; Clement attempts to go to Judaea, is driven to Alexandria, and meets Barnabas there; the occurrences here given in chaps. 8-11 are placed in Alexandria, whence Clement goes, after the departure of Barnabas, to Caesarea where he meets Peter (comp. chap. 12).--R.]
5. [The two accounts of the meeting with Peter at Caesarea are closely parallel.--R.]
6. [This discourse is given somewhat more fully here than in the Homilies.--R.]
7. [Comp. Homily I. 20, where there is a curious inconsistency. Both accounts seem to insert this to tally with the fictitious relation to James, and both may be used to support the theory of a common documentary basis.--R.]
8. [In the Homilies this is not expressed, but implied. The whole passage suggests a separatism quite contrary to Pauline precept. Compare the more detailed statement of separatism in book ii. 70, 72, vii. 29; Homily XIII. 4.--R.]
9. [Identified in the Homilies with the publican of Jericho. Fifteen others are named in Homily II. 1; some of them are introduced in Recognitions, ii. 1.--R.]
10. Here we follow a marginal reading.
11. [This chapter has no direct parallel in the Homilies. While there is a general resemblance in the remainder of book i. to Homily II., much of the matter is peculiar, or at least introduced in a connection different from that of the Homilies.--R.]
12. That is, that I may be sure that you remember these things.
13. [Hilgenfeld regards chaps. 27-72 as part of the Jewish-Christian document called Kerygma Petri, of which an outline is given in book iii. 75. This he thinks was of Roman origin. Certainly these chapters bear many marks of an earlier origin than most of the pseudo-Clementine literature. Much of the matter is not found elsewhere in this literature: the tone of the discourse is much superior; the instruction represented as given to Clement, is quite well adapted to his needs as a heathen inquirer; the views presented are not so extravagant as much that occurs in the Homilies; the attempt to adjust the statements to the New-Testament narrative is skilfully made, and there is not lacking a great vraisemblance. It may not be improper to add, that the impressions first given in regard to this passage were made upon the writer of this note quite independently of Hilgenfeld's theory; some of them committed to writing without a thought of maintaining that theory.--R.]
14. Gen. i. 1.
15. That is, his soul, according to the doctrine of the pre-existence of souls.
16. Gen. vi. 2. [Compare with this chapter Homily VIII. 12-17, where there are many more fanciful details.--R]
17. The writer here translates the words of the Septuagint, of hoi gigantes hoi ap' aionos hoi anthropoi hoi onomastoi, illi qui a seculo nominantur. We have given the translation of our authorized version. It is likely, however, that the writer believed the name to imply that they lived to a great age, as is maintained by Diodorus quoted by Suicer on the word, or he may have traced the word to ge.
18. Gen. ix. 1.
19. [With this chapter compare Homily IX. 3-7.--R.]
20. Gen. xi. 28.

The Epistles of Clement

21. [This orderly and consistent explanation of the Old-Testament economy (chaps. 32-39) is peculiar to the Recognitions.--R.]
22. Gen xv., xxii.
23. Exod. iii.
24. That is, picture or statue.
25. Comp. 1 Cor. x. 4.
26. Deut. xvii. 15; Acts iii. 22, 23.
27. Deut. xii. 11; 2 Chron. vii. 12.
28. Hos. vi. 6; Matt. ix. 13; xii. 7.
29. Matt. xxiv. 2; Luke xix. 44.
30. Deut. xxxi.-xxxiv.
31. Matt. ix.; John vii.
32. Matt. x.
33. Luke x.
34. Num. xi. 16.
35. Deut. xviii. 15.
36. Matt. xxvii. 45, 51, 52.
37. [Chaps. 42, 43, show little of the Ebionitic tendency, except in the attempt to reduce the difference between Jews and Christians to the single point of belief in the Messiahship of Jesus.--R]
38. Gen. xv.; Acts xiii.
39. Matt. xxvii. 45.
40. Matt. xxviii. 13.
41. John xii. 34.
42. [Evidently "the Lord's brother."
Comp. chap. 68.--R.]
43. This account of occurrences in Jerusalem (chaps. 45-70) is probably meant to supplement Acts v. and viii.
The date tallies with the stoning of Stephen, to which there is no allusion.
The whole bears abundant marks of "manipulation" of the New-Testament record.--R.]
44. [The discourse of chaps. 45-52 is interesting from its christological consistency.
The doctrine, while showing Ebionitic origin, is closer to the Catholic view than that of the Homilies.--R.]
45. [The references to oil in chaps. 45-48, particularly the connection of anointing with baptism, have been regarded, since the discovery of the full text of Hippolytus, as showing traces of relationship to the system of the Elkesaites.
See Introductory Notice.
In the forms given by Hippolytus (see Ante-Nicene Fathers, v. pp. 132, 133) the oil is represented as one of "seven witnesses" to be adjured by the subject of baptism.--R.]
46. Exod. xxix.; Lev. viii.
47. Matt. iii. 17.
48. Gen. xlix. 10.
49. Gen. v. 24.
50. That is, the sin of sacrifice.
51. Matt. xxii. 23.
52. [Comp. book ii. 8-11 and Homily II. 24.
The writer here confuses the later Dositheus with an earlier teacher, whose disciple Zadok was the founder of the sect of the Sadduccees.--R.]
53. Luke xi. 52.
54. [Here we encounter that favourite notion of apocryphal writers, that each Apostle must he represented as contributing his portion to the statement and defence of the faith.--R.]
55. Matt. x. 5.
56. Matt. xi. 9, 11.
57. We should doubtless read "Barsabas."
58. Matt. v. 3; Luke vi. 20.
59. Dan. ix. 27; Matt. xxiv. 15.
60. Acts v. 35-39.
61. [This title is consistent with the position accorded to James the Lord's brother in the entire pseudo-Clementine literature.--R.]
62. [This sentence seems to have been framed to accord with the Catholic doctrine.--R.]
63. A marginal note in one of the manuscripts states that this enemy was Saul.
[This is confirmed by chap. 71.--R.]
64. Acts xxii. 5.

[There is an evident attempt to cast a slur upon the apostle Paul, but the suppression of the name is significant.--R.]

65. [Comp. book ii. 7 and Homily II. 22, 24.--R.]

66. [The visit of Peter to Caesarea narrated in Acts x. was for a very different purpose. It is probable that the author of the Recognitions connected the persecution by Saul and the sorceries of Simon because of the similar juxtaposition in Acts viii.--R.]

Book II

Chapter I - Power of Habit

When the day dawned which had been fixed for the discussion with Simon, Peter, rising at the first cock-crowing, aroused us also:

for we were sleeping in the same apartment, thirteen of us in all; [1] of whom, next to Peter, Zacchaeus was first, then Sophonius, Joseph and Michaeas, Eliesdrus, Phineas, Lazarus, and Elisaeus:

after these I (Clement) and Nicodemus; then Niceta and Aquila, who had formerly been disciples of Simon, and were converted to the faith of Christ under the teaching of Zacchaeus.

Of the women there was no one present.

As the evening light [2] was still lasting, we all sat down; and Peter, seeing that we were awake, and that we were giving attention to him, having saluted us, immediately began to speak, as follows:--

"I confess, brethren, that I wonder at the power of human nature, which I see to be fit and suited to every call upon it.

This, however, it occurs to me to say of what I have found by experience, that when the middle of the night is passed, I awake of my own accord, and sleep does not come to me again.

This happens to me for this reason, that I have formed the habit of recalling to memory the words of my Lord, which I heard from Himself; and for the longing I have towards them, I constrain my mind and my thoughts to be roused, that, awaking to them, and recalling and arranging them one by one, I may retain them in my memory.

From this, therefore, whilst I desire to cherish the sayings of the Lord with all delight in my heart, the habit of waking has come upon me, even if there be nothing that I wish to think of.

Thus, in some unaccountable way, when any custom is established, the old custom is changed, provided indeed you do not force it above measure, but as far as the measure of nature admits.

For it is not possible to be altogether without sleep; otherwise night would not have been made for rest."

Chapter II - Curtailment of Sleep

Then I, when I heard this, said:

"You have very well said, O Peter; for one custom is superseded by another.

For when I was at sea, I was at first distressed, and all my system was disordered, so that I felt as if I had been beaten, and could not bear the tossing and tumult of the sea; but after a few days, when I had got accustomed to it, I began to bear it tolerably, so that I was glad to take food immediately in the morning along with the sailors, whereas before it was not my custom to eat anything before the seventh hour.

Now, therefore, simply from the custom which I then acquired, hunger reminds me about that time at which I used to eat with the sailors; which, however, I hope to get rid of, when once another custom shall have been formed.

I believe, therefore, that you also have acquired the habit of wakefulness, as you state; and you have wished at a fitting time to explain this to us, that we also may not grudge to throw off and dispense with some portion of our sleep, that we may be able to take in the precepts of the living doctrine.

For when the food is digested, and the mind is under the influence of the silence of night, those things which are seasonably taught abide in it."

Chapter III - Need of Caution

Then Peter, being pleased to hear that I understood the purport of his preface, that he had delivered it for our advantage; and commending me, doubtless for the purpose of encouraging, and stimulating me, began to deliver the following discourse: [3]"It seems to me to be seasonable and necessary to have some discussion relating to those things that are near at hand; that is, concerning Simon.

For I should wish to know of what character and of what conduct he is.

Wherefore, if any one of you has any knowledge of him, let him not fail to inform me; for it is of consequence to know these things beforehand.

For if we have it in charge, that when we enter into a city we should first learn who in it is worthy,[4] that we may eat with him, how much more is it proper for us to ascertain who or what sort of man he is to whom the words of immortality are to be committed!

For we ought to be careful, yea, extremely careful, that we cast not our pearls before swine. [5]

Chapter IV - Prudence in Dealing with Opponents

"But for other reasons also it is of importance that I should have some knowledge of this man.

For if I know that in those things concerning which it cannot be doubted that they are good, he is faultless and irreproachable,--that is to say, if he is sober, merciful, upright, gentle, and humane, which no one doubts to be good qualities,--then it will seem to be fitting, that upon him who possesses these good virtues, that which is lacking of faith and knowledge should be conferred; and so his life, which is in other respects worthy of approbation, should be amended in those points in which it shall appear to be imperfect.

But if he remains wrapped up and polluted in those sins which are manifestly such, it does not become me to speak to him at all of the more secret and sacred things of divine knowledge, but rather to protest and confront him, that he cease from sin, and cleanse his actions from vice.

But if he insinuate himself, and lead us on to speak what he, while he acts improperly, ought not to hear, it will be our part to parry him cautiously.

For not to answer him at all does not seem proper, for the sake of the hearers, lest haply they may think that we decline the contest through want of ability to answer him, and so their faith may be injured through their misunderstanding of our purpose."

Chapter V - Simon Magus, a Formidable Antagonist

When Peter had thus spoken to us, Niceta asks permission to say something to him; [6] and Peter having granted permission, he says: "With your pardon, I beseech you, my lord Peter, to hear me, who am very anxious for thee, and who am afraid lest, in the contest which you have in hand with Simon, you should seem to be overmatched.

For it very frequently happens that he who defends the truth does not gain the victory, since the hearers are either prejudiced, or have no great interest in the better cause.

But over and above all this, Simon himself is a most vehement orator, trained in the dialectic art, and in the meshes of syllogisms; and what is worse than all, he is greatly skilled in the magic art.

And therefore I fear, lest haply, being so strongly fortified on every side, he shall be thought to be defending the truth, whilst he is alleging falsehoods, in the presence of those who do not know him.

For neither should we ourselves have been able to escape from him, and to be converted to the Lord, had it not been that, while we were his assistants, and the sharers of his errors, we had ascertained that he was a deceiver and a magician."

Chapter VI - Simon Magus: His Wickedness

When Niceta had thus spoken, Aquila also, asking that he might be permitted to speak, proceeded in manner following:

"Receive, I entreat thee, most excellent Peter, the assurance of my love towards thee; for indeed I also am extremely anxious on thy account.

And do not blame us in this, for indeed to be concerned for any one cometh of affection; whereas to be indifferent is no less than hatred.

But I call God to witness that I feel for thee, not as knowing thee to be weaker in debate,--for indeed I was never present at any dispute in which thou wert engaged,--but because I well know the impieties of this man, I think of thy reputation, and at the same time the souls of the hearers, and above all, the interests of the truth itself.

For this magician is vehement towards all things that he wishes, and wicked above measure. For in all things we know him well, since from boyhood we have been assistants and ministers of his wickedness; and had not the love of God rescued us from him, we should even now be engaged in the same evil deeds with him.

But a certain inborn love towards God rendered his wickedness hateful to us, and the worship of God attractive to us. Whence I think also that it was the work of Divine Providence, that we, being first made his associates, should take knowledge in what manner or by what art he effects the prodigies which he seems to work.

For who is there that would not be astonished at the wonderful things which he does?

Who would not think that he was a god come down from heaven for the salvation of men?

For myself, I confess, if I had not known him intimately, and had taken part in his doings, I would easily have been carried away with him.

Whence it was no great thing for us to be separated from his society, knowing as we did that he depends upon magic arts and wicked devices.

But if thou also thyself wish to know all about him--who, what, and whence he is, and how he contrives what he does--then listen."

Chapter VII - Simon Magus: His History

"This Simon's father was Antonius, and his mother Rachel.

By nation he is a Samaritan, from a village of the Gettones; by profession a magician yet exceedingly well trained in the Greek literature; desirous of glory, and boasting above all the human race, so that he wishes himself to be believed to be an exalted power, which is above God the Creator, and to be thought to be the Christ, and to be called the Standing One.

And he uses this name as implying that he can never be dissolved, asserting that his flesh is so compacted by the power of his divinity, that it can endure to eternity.

Hence, therefore, he is called the Standing One, as though he cannot fall by any corruption."

Chapter VIII - Simon Magus: His History

"For after that John the Baptist was killed, as you yourself also know, when Dositheus had broached his heresy, [7] with thirty other chief disciples, and one woman, who was called Luna [8] --whence also these thirty appear to have been appointed with reference to the number of the days, according to the course of the moon--this Simon ambitious of evil glory, as we have said, goes to Dositheus, and pretending friendship, entreats him, that if any one of those thirty should die, he should straightway substitute him in room of the dead:

for it was contrary to their rule either to exceed the fixed number, or to admit any one who was unknown, or not yet proved; whence also the rest, desiring to become worthy of the place and number, are eager in every way to please, according to the institutions of their sect each one of those who aspire after admittance into the number, hoping that he may be deemed worthy to be put into the place of the deceased, when, as we have said, any one dies.

Therefore Dositheus, being greatly urged by this man, introduced Simon when a vacancy occurred among the number."

Chapter IX - Simon Magus: His Profession

"But not long after he fell in love with that woman whom they call Luna; and he confided all things to us as his friends:

how he was a magician, and how he loved Luna, and how, being desirous of glory, he was unwilling to enjoy her ingloriously, but that he was waiting patiently till he could enjoy her honourably; yet so if we also would conspire with him towards the accomplishment of his desires.

And he promised that, as a reward of this service, he would cause us to be invested with the highest honours, and we should be believed by men to be gods; Only, however, on condition,' says he, that you confer the chief place upon me, Simon, who by magic art am able to show many signs and prodigies, by means of which either my glory or our sect may be established.

For I am able to render myself invisible to those who wish to lay hold of me, and again to be visible when I am willing to be seen. ⁹If I wish to flee, I can dig through the mountains, and pass through rocks as if they were clay.

If I should throw myself headlong from a lofty mountain, I should be borne unhurt to the earth, as if I were held up; when bound, I can loose myself, and bind those who had bound me; being shut up in prison, I can make the barriers open of their own accord; I can render statues animated, so that those who see suppose that they are men.

I can make new trees suddenly spring up, and produce sprouts at once.

I can throw myself into the fire, and not be burnt; I can change my countenance, so that I cannot be recognised; but I can show people that I have two faces.

I shall change myself into a sheep or a goat; I shall make a beard to grow upon little boys; I shall ascend by flight into the air; I shall exhibit abundance of gold, and shall make and unmake kings.

I shall be worshipped as God; I shall have divine honours publicly assigned to me, so that an image of me shall be set up, and I shall be worshipped and adored as God.

And what need of more words?

Whatever I wish, that I shall be able to do.

For already I have achieved many things by way of experiment.

In short,' says he, once when my mother Rachel ordered me to go to the field to reap, and I saw a sickle lying, I ordered it to go and reap; and it reaped ten times more than the others.

Lately, I produced many new sprouts from the earth, and made them bear leaves and produce fruit in a moment; and the nearest mountain I successfully bored through."'

Chapter X - Simon Magus: His Deception

"But when he spoke thus of the production of sprouts and the perforation of the mountain, I was confounded on this account, because he wished to deceive even us, in whom he seemed to place confidence; for we knew that those things had been from the days of our fathers, which he represented as having been done by himself lately.

We then, although we heard these atrocities from him, and worse than these, yet we followed up his crimes, and suffered others to be deceived by him, telling also many lies on his behalf; and this before he did any of the things which he had promised, so that while as yet he had done nothing, he was by some thought to be God."

Chapter XI - Simon Magus, at the Head of the Sect of Dositheus

"Meantime, at the outset, as soon as he was reckoned among the thirty disciples of Dositheus, he began to depreciate Dositheus himself, saying that he did not teach purely or perfectly, and that this was the result not of ill intention, but of ignorance.

But Dositheus, when he perceived that Simon was depreciating him, fearing lest his reputation among men might be obscured (for he himself was supposed to be the Standing One), moved with rage, when they met as usual at the school, seized a rod, and began to beat Simon; but suddenly the rod seemed to pass through his body, as if it had been smoke.

On which Dositheus, being astonished, says to him, Tell me if thou art the Standing One, that I may adore thee.'

And when Simon answered that he was, then Dositheus, perceiving that he himself was not the Standing One, fell down and worshipped him, and gave up his own place as chief to Simon, ordering all the rank of thirty men to obey him; himself taking the inferior place which Simon formerly occupied.

Not long after this he died."

Chapter XII - Simon Magus and Luna

"Therefore, after the death of Dositheus Simon took Luna to himself; and with her he still goes about, as you see, deceiving multitudes, and asserting that he himself is a certain power which is above God the Creator, while Luna, who is with him, has been brought down from the higher heavens, and that she is Wisdom, the mother of all things, for whom, says he, the Greeks and barbarians contending, were able in some measure to see an image of her; but of herself, as she is, as the dweller with the first and only God, they were wholly ignorant. Propounding these and other things of the same sort, he has deceived many.

But I ought also to state this, which I remember that I myself saw.

Once, when this Luna of his was in a certain tower, a great multitude had assembled to see her, and were standing around the tower on all sides; but she was seen by all the people to lean forward, and to look out through all the windows of that tower. [10]Many other wonderful things he did and does; so that men, being astonished at them, think that he himself is the great God."

Chapter XIII - Simon Magus: Secret of His Magic

"Now when Niceta and I once asked him to explain to us how these things could be effected by magic art, and what was the nature of that thing, Simon began thus to explain it to us as his associates.

I have,' said he, made the soul of a boy, unsullied and violently slain, and invoked by unutterable adjurations, to assist me; and by it all is done that I command.'

But,' said I, is it possible for a soul to do these things?'

He answered:

I would have you know this, that the soul of man holds the next place after God, when once it is set free from the darkness of his body.

And immediately it acquires prescience: wherefore it is invoked for necromancy.'

Then I answered:

Why, then, do not the souls of persons who are slain take vengeance on their slayers?'

Do you not remember,' said he, that I told you, that when it goes out of the body it acquires knowledge of the future?'

I remember,' said I.

Well, then,' said he, as soon as it goes out of the body, it immediately knows that there is a judgment to come, and that every one shall suffer punishment for those evils that he hath done; and therefore they are unwilling to take vengeance on their slayers, because they themselves are enduring torments for their own evil deeds which they had done here, and they know that severer punishments await them in the judgment.

Moreover, they are not permitted by the angels who preside over them to go out, or to do anything.'

Then,' I replied, if the angels do not permit them to come hither, or to do what they please, how can the souls obey the magician who invokes them?'

It is not,' said he, that they grant indulgence to the souls that are willing to come:

but when the presiding angels are adjured by one greater than themselves, they have the excuse of our violence who adjure them, to permit the souls which we invoke to go out:

for they do not sin who suffer violence, but we who impose necessity upon them.'

Thereupon Niceta, not able longer to refrain, hastily answered, as indeed I also was about to do, only I wished first to get information from him on several points; but, as I said, Niceta, anticipating me, said:

And do you not fear the day of judgment, who do violence to angels, and invoke souls, and deceive men, and bargain for divine honour to yourself from men?

And how do you persuade us that there shall be no judgment, as some of the Jews confess, and that souls are not immortal, as many suppose, though you see them with your very eyes, and receive from them assurance of the divine judgment?'"

Chapter XIV - Simon Magus, Professes to Be God

"At those sayings of his Simon grew pale; but after a little, recollecting himself, he thus answered: Do not think that I am a man of your race.

I am neither magician, nor lover of Luna, nor son of Antonius.

For before my mother Rachel and he came together, she, still a virgin, conceived me, while it was in my power to be either small or great, and to appear as a man among men. [11]Therefore I have chosen you first as my friends, for the purpose of trying you, that I may place you first in my heavenly and unspeakable places when I shall have proved you.

Therefore I have pretended to be a man, that I might more clearly ascertain if you cherish entire affection towards me.' But when I heard that, judging him indeed to be a wretch, yet wondering at his impudence; and blushing for him, and at the same time fearing lest he should attempt some evil against us, I beckoned to Niceta to feign for a little along with me, and said to him:

Be not angry with us, corruptible men, O thou incorruptible God, but rather accept our affection, and our mind willing to know who God is; for we did not till now know who thou art, nor did we perceive that thou art he whom we were seeking.'"

Chapter XV - Simon Magus, Professed to Have Made a Boy of Air

"As we spoke these and such like words with looks suited to the occasion, this most vain fellow believed that we were deceived; and being thereby the more elated, he added also this:
I shall now be propitious to you, for the affection which you bear towards me as God; for you loved me while you did not know me, and were seeking me in ignorance.
But I would not have you doubt that this is truly to be God, when one is able to become small or great as he pleases; for I am able to appear to man in whatever manner I please.
Now, then, I shall begin to unfold to you what is true.
Once on a time, I, by my power, turning air into water, and water again into blood, and solidifying it into flesh, formed a new human creature--a boy--and produced a much nobler work than God the Creator.
For He created a man from the earth, but I from air--a far more difficult matter; and again I unmade him and restored him to air, but not until I had placed his picture and image in my bed-chamber, as a proof and memorial of my work.'
Then we understood that he spake concerning that boy, whose soul, after he had been slain by violence, he made use of for those services which he required."

Chapter XVI - Simon Magus: Hopelessness of His Case

But Peter, hearing these things, said with tears: [12]"Greatly do I wonder at the infinite patience of God, and, on the other hand, at the audacity of human rashness in some.
For what further reason can be found to persuade Simon that God judges the unrighteous, since he persuades himself that he employs the obedience of souls for the service of his crimes?
But, in truth, he is deluded by demons.
Yet, although he is sure by these very things that souls are immortal, and are judged for the deeds which they have done, and although he thinks that he really sees those things which we believe by faith; though, as I said, he is deluded by demons, yet he thinks that he sees the very substance of the soul.
How shall such a man, I say, be brought to confess either that he acts wickedly while he occupies such an evil position, or that he is to be judged for those things which he hath done, who, knowing the judgment of God, despises it, and shows himself an enemy to God, and dares commit such horrid things?
Wherefore it is certain, my brethren, that some oppose the truth and religion of God, not because it appears to them that reason can by no means stand with faith, but because they are either involved in excess of wickedness, or prevented by their own evils, or elated by the swelling of their heart, so that they do not even believe those things which they think that they see with their own eyes."

Chapter XVII - Men Enemies to God

"But, inasmuch as inborn affection towards God the Creator seemed to suffice for salvation to those who loved Him, the enemy studies to pervert this affection in men, and to render them hostile and ungrateful to their Creator.
For I call heaven and earth to witness, that if God permitted the enemy to rage as much as he desires, all men should have perished long ere now; but for His mercy's sake God doth not suffer him.
But if men would turn their affection towards God, all would doubtless be saved, even if for some faults they might seem to be corrected for righteousness.
But now the most of men have been made enemies of God, whose hearts the wicked one has entered, and has turned aside towards himself the affection which God the Creator had implanted in them, that they might have it towards Him.
But of the rest, who seemed for a time to be watchful, the enemy, appearing in a phantasy of glory and splendour, and promising them certain great and mighty things, has caused their mind and heart to wander away from God; yet it is for some just reason that he is permitted to accomplish these things."

Chapter XVIII - Responsibility of Men

"To this Aquila answered:

"How, then, are men in fault, if the wicked one, transforming himself into the brightness of light, [13] promises to men greater things than the Creator Himself does?"

Then Peter answered:

"I think," says he "that nothing is more unjust than this; and now listen while I tell you how unjust it is.

If your son, whom you have trained and nourished with all care, and brought to man's estate, should be ungrateful to you, and should leave you and go to another, whom perhaps he may have seen to be richer, and should show to him the honour which he owed to you, and, through hope of greater profit, should deny his birth, and refuse you your paternal rights, would this seem to you right or wicked?"

Then Aquila answered:

"It is manifest to all that it would be wicked."

Then Peter said:

"If you say that this would be wicked among men, how much more so is it in the case of God, who, above all men, is worthy of honour from men; whose benefits we not only enjoy, but by whose means and power it is that we began to be when we were not, and whom, if we please, we shall obtain from Him to be for ever in blessedness!

In order, therefore, that the unfaithful may be distinguished from the faithful, and the pious from the impious, it has been permitted to the wicked one to use those arts by which the affections of every one towards the true Father may be proved.

But if there were in truth some strange God, were it right to leave our own God, who created us, and who is our Father and our Maker, and to pass over to another?"

"God forbid!" said Aquila.

Then said Peter:

"How, then, shall we say that the wicked one is the cause of our sin, when this is done by permission of God, that those may be proved and condemned in the day of judgment, who, allured by greater promises, have abandoned their duty towards their true Father and Creator; while those who have kept the faith and the love of their own Father, even with poverty, if so it has befallen, and with tribulation, may enjoy heavenly gifts and immortal dignities in His kingdom.

But we shall expound these things more carefully at another time.

Meantime I desire to know what Simon did after this."

Chapter XIX - Disputation Begun

And Niceta answered:

"When he perceived that we had found him out, having spoken to one another concerning his crimes, we left him, and came to Zacchaeus, telling him those same things which we have now told to you.

But he, receiving us most kindly, and instructing us concerning the faith of our Lord Jesus Christ, enrolled us in the number of the faithful."

When Niceta had done speaking, Zacchaeus, who had gone out a little before, entered, saying, "It is time, O Peter, that you proceed to the disputation; for a great crowd, collected in the court of the house, is awaiting you, in the midst of whom stands Simon, supported by many attendants."

Then Peter, when he heard this, ordering me to withdraw for the sake of prayer (for I had not yet been washed from the sins which I had committed in ignorance), said to the rest, "Brethren, let us pray that God, for His unspeakable mercy through His Christ, would help me going out on behalf of the salvation of men who have been created by Him."

Having said this, and having prayed, he went forth to the court of the house, in which a great multitude of people were assembled; and when he saw them all looking intently on him in profound silence, and Simon the magician standing in the midst of them like a standard-bearer, he began in manner following. [14]

Chapter XX - The Kingdom of God and His Righteousness

"Peace be to all of you who are prepared to give your right hands to truth: [15]for whosoever are obedient to it seem indeed themselves to confer some favour upon God; whereas they do themselves obtain from Him the gift of His greatest bounty, walking in His paths of righteousness.

Wherefore the first duty of all is to inquire into the righteousness of God and His kingdom; [16] His righteousness, that we may be taught to act rightly; His kingdom, that we may know what is the reward appointed for labour and patience; in which kingdom there is indeed a bestowal of eternal good things upon the good, but upon those who have acted contrary to the will of God, a worthy infliction of penalties in proportion to the doings of every one.

It becomes you, therefore, whilst you are here,--that is, whilst you are in the present life,--to ascertain the will of God, while there is opportunity also of doing it.

For if any one, before he amends his doings, wishes to investigate concerning things which he cannot discover, such investigation will be foolish and ineffectual.

For the time is short, and the judgment of God shall be occupied with deeds, not questions. Therefore before all things let us inquire into this, what or in what manner we must act that we may merit to obtain eternal life.

Chapter XXI - Righteousness the Way to the Kingdom

"For if we occupy the short time of this life with vain and useless questions, we shall without doubt go into the presence of God empty and void of good works, when, as I have said, our works shall be brought into judgment.

For everything has its own time and place.

This is the place, this the time of works; the world to come, that of recompenses. That we may not therefore be entangled, by changing the order of places and times, let us inquire, in the first place, what is the righteousness of God; so that, like persons going to set out on a journey, we may be filled with good works as with abundant provision, so that we may be able to come to the kingdom of God, as to a very great city.

For to those who think aright, God is manifest even by the operations of the world which He hath made, using the evidence of His creation; [17] and therefore, since there ought to be no doubt about God, we have now to inquire only about His righteousness and His kingdom.

But if our mind suggest to us to make any inquiry concerning secret and hidden things before we inquire into the works of righteousness, we ought to render to ourselves a reason, because if acting well we shall merit to obtain salvation:then, going to God chaste and clean, we shall be filled with the Holy Spirit, and shall know all things that are secret and hidden, without any cavilling of questions; whereas now, even if any one should spend the whole of his life in inquiring into these things, he not only shall not be able to find them, but shall involve himself in greater errors, because he did not first enter through the way of righteousness, and strive to reach the haven of life."

Chapter XXII - Righteousness; What It is

"And therefore I advise that His righteousness be first inquired into, that, pursuing our journey through it, and placed in the way of truth, we may be able to find the true Prophet, running not with swiftness of foot, but with goodness of works, and that, enjoying His guidance, we may be under no danger of mistaking the way.

For if under His guidance we shall merit to enter that city to which we desire to come, all things concerning which we now inquire we shall see with our eyes, being made, as it were, heirs of all things.

Understand, therefore, that the way is this course of our life; the travellers are those who do good works; the gate is the true Prophet, of whom we speak; the city is the kingdom in which dwells the Almighty Father, whom only those can see who are of pure heart. [18]Let us not then think the labour of this journey hard, because at the end of it there shall be rest.

For the true Prophet Himself also from the beginning of the world, through the course of time, hastens to rest.

For He is present with us at all times; and if at any time it is necessary, He appears and corrects us, that He may bring to eternal life those who obey Him.

Therefore this is my judgment, as also it is the pleasure of the true Prophet, that inquiry should first be made concerning righteousness, by those especially who profess that they know God.

If therefore any one has anything to propose which he thinks better, let him speak; and when he has spoken, let him hear, but with patience and quietness:

for in order to this at the first, by way of salutation, I prayed for peace to you all."

Chapter XXIII - Simon Refuses Peace

To this Simon answered: [19]"We have no need of your peace; for if there be peace and concord, we shall not be able to make any advance towards the discovery of truth.

For robbers and debauchees have peace among themselves, and every wickedness agrees with itself; and if we have met with this view, that for the sake of peace we should give assent to all that is said, we shall confer no benefit upon the hearers; but, on the contrary, we shall impose upon them, and shall depart friends.

Wherefore, do not invoke peace, but rather battle, which is the mother of peace; and if you can, exterminate errors.

And do not seek for friendship obtained by unfair admissions; for this I would have you know, above all, that when two fight with each other, then there will be peace when one has been defeated and has fallen. And therefore fight as best you can, and do not expect peace without war, which is impossible; or if it can be attained, show us how."

Chapter XXIV - Peter's Explanation

To this Peter answered:

"Hear with all attention, O men, what we say. Let us suppose that this world is a great plain, and that from two states, whose kings are at variance with each other, two generals were sent to fight:

and suppose the general of the good king gave this counsel, that both armies should without bloodshed submit to the authority of the better king, whereby all should be safe without danger; but that the opposite general should say, No, but we must fight; that not he who is worthy, but who is stronger, may reign, with those who shall escape;--which, I ask you, would you rather choose?

I doubt not but that you would give your hands to the better king, with the safety of all.

And I do not now wish, as Simon says that I do, that assent should be given, for the sake of peace, to those things that are spoken amiss but that truth be sought for with quietness and order.

Chapter XXV - Principles on Which the Discussion Should Be Conducted

"For some, in the contest of disputations, when they perceive that their error is confuted, immediately begin, for the sake of making good their retreat, to create a disturbance, and to stir up strifes, that it may not be manifest to all that they are defeated; and therefore I frequently entreat that the investigation of the matter in dispute may be conducted with all patience and quietness, so that if perchance anything seem to be not rightly spoken, it may be allowed to go back over it, and explain it more distinctly.

For sometimes a thing may be spoken in one way and heard in another, while it is either advanced too obscurely, or not attended to with sufficient care; and on this account I desire that our conversation should be conducted patiently, so that neither should the one snatch it away from the other, nor should the unseasonable speech of one contradicting interrupt the speech of the other; and that we should not cherish the desire of finding fault, but that we should be allowed, as I have said, to go over again what has not been clearly enough spoken, that by fairest examination the knowledge of the truth may become clearer.

For we ought to know, that if any one is conquered by the truth, it is not he that is conquered, but the ignorance which is in him, which is the worst of all demons; so that he who can drive it out receives the palm of salvation.

For it is our purpose to benefit the hearers, not that we may conquer badly, but that we may be well conquered for the acknowledgment of the truth.

For if our speech be actuated by the desire of seeking the truth, even although we shall speak anything imperfectly through human frailty, God in His unspeakable goodness will fill up secretly in the understandings of the hearers those things that are lacking.

For He is righteous; and according to the purpose of every one, He enables some to find easily what they seek, while to others He renders even that obscure which is before their eyes.

Since, then, the way of God is the way of peace, let us with peace seek the things which are God's.

If any one has anything to advance in answer to this, let him do so; but if there is no one who wishes to answer, I shall begin to speak, and I myself shall bring forward what another may object to me, and shall refute it."

Chapter XXVI - Simon's Interruption

When therefore Peter had begun to continue his discourse, Simon, interrupting his speech, said: "Why do you hasten to speak whatever you please?

I understand your tricks.

You wish to bring forward those matters whose explanation you have well studied, that you may appear to the ignorant crowd to be speaking well; but I shall not allow you this subterfuge.

Now therefore, since you promise, as a brave man, to answer to all that any one chooses to bring forward, be pleased to answer me in the first place."

Then Peter said:

"I am ready, only provided that our discussion may be with peace."

Then Simon said:

"Do not you see, O simpleton, that in pleading for peace you act in opposition to your Master, and that what you propose is not suitable to him who promises that he will overthrow ignorance?

Or, if you are right in asking peace from the audience, then your Master was wrong in saying, I have not come to send peace on earth, but a sword.' [20] For either you say well, and he not well; or else, if your Master said well, then you not at all well:

for you do not understand that your statement is contrary to his, whose disciple you profess yourself to be."

Chapter XXVII - Questions and Answers

Then Peter:

"Neither He who sent me did amiss in sending a sword upon the earth, nor do I act contrary to Him in asking peace of the hearers.

But you both unskilfully and rashly find fault with what you do not understand:

for you have heard that the Master came not to send peace on earth; but that He also said, Blessed are the peace-makers, for they shall be called the very sons of God,' [21] you have not heard.

Wherefore my sentiments are not different from those of the Master when I recommend peace, to the keepers of which He assigned blessedness."

Then Simon said:

"In your desire to answer for your Master, O Peter, you have brought a much more serious charge against him, if he himself came not to make peace, yet enjoined upon others to keep it.

Where, then, is the consistency of that other saying of his, it is enough for the disciple that he be as his master?'" [22]

Chapter XXVIII - Consistency of Christ's Teaching

To this Peter answered:

"Our Master, who was the true Prophet, and ever mindful of Himself, neither contradicted Himself, nor enjoined upon us anything different from what Himself practised.

For whereas He said, I am not come to send peace on earth, but a sword; and henceforth you shall see father separated from son, son from father, husband from wife and wife from husband, mother from daughter and daughter from mother, brother from brother, father-in-law from daughter-in-law, friend from friend,' all these contain the doctrine of peace; and I will tell you how.

At the beginning of His preaching, as wishing to invite and lead all to salvation, and induce them to bear patiently labours and trials, He blessed the poor, and promised that they should obtain the kingdom of heaven for their endurance of poverty, in order that under the influence of such a hope they might bear with equanimity the weight of poverty, despising covetousness; for covetousness is one, and the greatest, of most pernicious sins.

But He promised also that the hungry and the thirsty should be satisfied with the eternal blessings of righteousness, in order that they might bear poverty patiently, and not be led by it to undertake any unrighteous work.

In like manner, also, He said that the pure in heart are blessed, and that thereby they should see God, in order that every one desiring so great a good might keep himself from evil and polluted thoughts."

Chapter XXIX - Peace and Strife

"Thus, therefore, our Master, inviting His disciples to patience, impressed upon them that the blessing of peace was also to be preserved with the labour of patience.

But, on the other hand, He mourned over those who lived in riches and luxury, who bestowed nothing upon the poor; proving that they must render an account, because they did not pity their neighbours, even when they were in poverty, whom they ought to love as themselves.

And by such sayings as these He brought some indeed to obey Him, but others He rendered hostile.

The believers therefore, and the obedient, He charges to have peace among themselves. and says to them, Blessed are the peacemakers, for they shall be called the very sons of God.' [23]But to those who not only did not believe, but set themselves in opposition to His doctrine, He proclaims the war of the word and of confutation, and says that henceforth ye shall see son separated from father, and husband from wife, and daughter from mother, and brother from brother, and daughter-in-law from mother-in-law, and a man's foes shall be they of his own house.' [24]For in every house, when there begins to be a difference betwixt believer and unbeliever, there is necessarily a contest:

the unbelievers, on the one hand, fighting against the faith; and the believers on the other, confuting the old error and the vices of sins in them."

Chapter XXX - Peace to the Sons of Peace

"In like manner, also, during the last period of His teaching, He wages war against the scribes and Pharisees, charging them with evil deeds and unsound doctrine, and with hiding the key of knowledge which they had handed down to them from Moses, by which the gate of the heavenly kingdom might be opened. [25]But when our Master sent us forth to preach, He commanded us, that into whatsoever city or house we should enter, we should say, Peace be to this house.'

And if,' said He, a son of peace be there, your peace shall come upon him; but if there be not, your peace shall return to you.'

Also that, going out from that house or city, we should shake off upon them the very dust which adhered to our feet.

But it shall be more tolerable for the land of Sodom and Gomorrah in the day of judgment than for that city or house.' [26] This indeed He commanded to be done at length, if first the word of truth be preached in the city or house, whereby they who receive the faith of the truth may become sons of peace and sons of God; and those who will not receive it may be convicted as enemies of peace and of God."

Chapter XXXI - Peace and War

"Thus, therefore, we, observing the commands of our Master, first offer peace to our hearers, that the way of salvation may be known without any tumult.

But if any one do not receive the words of peace, nor acquiesce in the truth, we know how to direct against him the war of the word, and to rebuke him sharply by confuting his ignorance and charging home upon him his sins.

Therefore of necessity we offer peace, that if any one is a son of peace, our peace may come upon him; but from him who makes himself an enemy of peace, our peace shall return to ourselves.

We do not therefore, as you say, propose peace by agreement with the wicked, for indeed we should straightway have given you the right hand; but only in order that, through our discussing quietly and patiently, it might be more easily ascertained by the hearers which is the true speech.

But if you differ and disagree with yourself, how shall you stand?

He must of necessity fall who is divided in himself; for every kingdom divided against itself shall not stand.' [27]If you have aught to say to this, say on."

Chapter XXXII - Simon's Challenge

Then said Simon:
"I am astonished at your folly.
For you so propound the words of your Master, as if it were held to be certain concerning him that he is a prophet; while I can very easily prove that he often contradicted himself.
In short, I shall refute you from those words which you have yourself brought forward.
For you say, that he said that every kingdom or every city divided in itself shall not stand; and elsewhere you say, that he said that he would send a sword, that he might separate those who are in one house, so that son shall be divided from father, daughter from mother, brother from brother; so that if there be five in one house, three shall be divided against two, and two against three. [28]If, then, everything that is divided falls, he who makes divisions furnishes causes of falling; and if he is such, assuredly he is wicked.
Answer this if you can."

Chapter XXXIII - Authority

Then Peter:
"Do not rashly take exception, O Simon, against the things which you do not understand.
In the first place, I shall answer your assertion, that I set forth the words of my Master, and from them resolve matters about which there is still doubt.
Our Lord, when He sent us apostles to preach, enjoined us to teach all nations [29] the things which were committed to us.
We cannot therefore speak those things as they were spoken by Himself.
For our commission is not to speak, but to teach those things, and from them to show how every one of them rests upon truth.
Nor, again, are we permitted to speak anything of our own.
For we are sent; and of necessity he who is sent delivers the message as he has been ordered, and sets forth the will of the sender.
For if I should speak anything different from what He who sent me enjoined me, I should be a false apostle, not saying what I am commanded to say, but what seems good to myself.
Whoever does this, evidently wishes to show himself to be better than he is by whom he is sent, and without doubt is a traitor.
If, on the contrary, he keeps by the things that he is commanded, and brings forward most clear assertions of them, it will appear that he is accomplishing the work of an apostle; and it is by striving to fulfil this that I displease you. Blame me not, therefore, because I bring forward the words of Him who sent me.
But if there is aught in them that is not fairly spoken, you have liberty to confute me; but this can in no wise be done, for He is a prophet, and cannot be contrary to Himself.
But if you do not think that He is a prophet, let this be first inquired into."

Chapter XXXIV - Order of Proof

Then said Simon:
"I have no need to learn this from you, but how these things agree with one another.
For if he shall be shown to be inconsistent, he shall be proved at the same time not to be a prophet."
Then says Peter:
"But if I first show Him to be a prophet, it will follow that what seems to be inconsistency is not such.
For no one can be proved to be a prophet merely by consistency, because it is possible for many to attain this; but if consistency does not make a prophet, much more inconsistency does not.
Because, therefore, there are many things which to some seem inconsistent, which yet have consistency in them on a more profound investigation; as also other things which seem to have consistency, but which, being more carefully discussed, are found to be inconsistent; for this reason I do not think there is any better way to judge of these things than to ascertain in the first instance whether He be a prophet who has spoken those things which appear to be inconsistent.
For it is evident that, if He be found a prophet, those things which seem to be contradictory must have consistency, but are misunderstood.

Concerning these things, therefore, proofs will be properly demanded.

For we apostles are sent to expound the sayings and affirm the judgments of Him who has sent us; but we are not commissioned to say anything of our own, but to unfold the truth, as I have said, of His words."

Chapter XXXV - How Error Cannot Stand with Truth

Then Simon said:

"Instruct us, therefore, how it can be consistent that he who causes divisions, which divisions cause those who are divided to fall, can either seem to be good, or to have come for the salvation of men."

Then Peter said:

"I will tell you how our Master said that every kingdom and every house divided against itself cannot stand; and whereas He Himself did this, see how it makes for salvation.

By the word of truth He certainly divides the kingdom of the world, which is founded in error, and every home in it, that error may fall, and truth may reign.

But if it happen to any house, that error, being introduced by any one, divides the truth, then, where error has gained a footing, it is certain that truth cannot stand." Then Simon said:

"But it is uncertain whether your master divides error or truth."

Then Peter:

"That belongs to another question; but if you are agreed that everything which is divided falls, it remains that I show, if only you will hear in peace, that our Jesus has divided and dispelled error by teaching truth."

Chapter XXXVI - Altercation

Then said Simon:

"Do not repeat again and again your talk of peace, but expound briefly what it is that you think or believe."

Peter answered:

"Why are you afraid of hearing frequently of peace? for do you not know that peace is the perfection of law?

For wars and disputes spring from sins; and where there is no sin, there is peace of soul; but where there is peace, truth is found in disputations, righteousness in works."

Then Simon:

"You seem to me not to be able to profess what you think."

Then Peter:

"I shall speak, but according to my own judgment, not under constraint of your tricks.

For I desire that what is salutary and profitable be brought to the knowledge of all and therefore I shall not delay to state it as briefly as possible. There is one God; and He is the creator of the world, a righteous judge, rendering to every one at some time or other according to his deeds. [30]But now for the assertion of these things I know that countless thousands of words can be called forth."

Chapter XXXVII - Simon's Subtlety

Then Simon said:

"I admire, indeed, the quickness of your wit, yet I do not embrace the error of your faith.

For you have wisely foreseen that you may be contradicted; and you have even politely confessed, that for the assertion of these things countless thousands of words will be called forth, for no one agrees with the profession of your faith.

In short, as to there being one God, and the world being His work, who can receive this doctrine?

Neither, I think, any one of the Pagans, even if he be an unlearned man, and certainly no one of the philosophers; but not even the rudest and most wretched of the Jews, nor I myself, who am well acquainted with their law."

Then Peter said:

"Put aside the opinions of those who are not here, and tell us face to face what is your own."

Then Simon said:

"I can state what I really think; but this consideration makes me reluctant to do so, that if I say what is neither acceptable to you, nor seems right to this unskilled rabble, you indeed, as confounded, will straightway shut your ears, that they may not be polluted with blasphemy, forsooth, and will take to flight because you cannot find an answer; while the unreasoning populace will assent to you, and embrace you as one teaching those things which are commonly received among them; and will curse me, as professing things new and unheard of, and instilling my error into the minds of others."

Chapter XXXVIII - Simon's Creed

Then Peter:
"Are not you making use of long preambles, as you accused us of doing, because you have no truth to bring forward?

For if you have, begin without circumlocution, if you have so much confidence. And if, indeed, what you say be displeasing to any one of the hearers, he will withdraw; and those who remain shall be compelled by your assertion to approve what is true.

Begin, therefore, to expound what seemeth to you to be right."
Then Simon said:
"I say that there are many gods; but that there is one incomprehensible and unknown to all, and that He is the God of all these gods."

Then Peter answered:
"This God whom you assert to be incomprehensible and unknown to all, can you prove His existence from the Scriptures of the Jews, [31] which are held to be of authority, or from some others of which we are all ignorant, or from the Greek authors, or from your own writings? Certainly you are at liberty to speak from whatever writings you please, yet so that you first show that they are prophetic; for so their authority will be held without question."

Chapter XXXIX - Argument for Polytheism

Then Simon said:
"I shall make use of assertions from the law of the Jews only.

For it is manifest to all who take interest in religion, that this law is of universal authority, yet that every one receives the understanding of this law according to his own judgment.

For it has so been written by Him who created the world, that the faith of things is made to depend upon it.

Whence, whether any one wishes to bring forward truth, or any one to bring forward falsehood, no assertion will be received without this law.

Inasmuch, therefore, as my knowledge is most fully in accordance with the law, I rightly declared that there are many gods, of whom one is more eminent than the rest, and incomprehensible, even He who is God of gods.

But that there are many gods, the law itself informs me.

For, in the first place, it says this in the passage where one in the figure of a serpent speaks to Eve, the first woman, On the day ye eat of the tree of the knowledge of good and evil, ye shall be as gods,' [32] that is, as those who made man; and after they have tasted of the tree, God Himself testifies, saying to the rest of the gods, Behold, Adam is become as one of us;' [33] thus, therefore, it is manifest that there were many gods engaged in the making of man.

Also, whereas at the first God said to the other gods, Let us make man after our image and likeness;' [34] also His saying, Let us drive him out;' [35] and again, Come, let us go down, and confound their language;' [36] all these things indicate that there are many gods.

But this also is written, Thou shalt not curse the gods, nor curse the chief of thy people;' [37] and again this writing, God alone led them, and there was no strange god with them,' [38] shows that there are many gods.

There are also many other testimonies which might be adduced from the law, not only obscure, but plain, by which it is taught that there are many gods. [39]One of these was chosen by lot, that he might be the god of the Jews.

But it is not of him that I speak, but of that God who is also his God, whom even the Jews themselves did not know.

For he is not their God, but the God of those who know him."

Chapter XL - Peter's Answer

When Peter had heard this, he answered:
"Fear nothing, Simon:
for, behold, we have neither shut our ears, nor fled; but we answer with words of truth to those things which you have spoken falsely, asserting this first, that there is one God, even the God of the Jews, who is the only God, the Creator of heaven and earth, who is also the God of all those whom you call gods.
If, then, I shall show you that none is superior to Him, but that He Himself is above all, you will confess that your error is above all." [40]Then Simon said:
"Why, indeed, though I should be unwilling to confess it, would not the hearers who stand by charge me with unwillingness to profess the things that are true?"

Chapter XLI - The Answer, Continued

"Listen, then," says Peter, "that you may know, first of all, that even if there are many gods, as you say, they are subject to the God of the Jews, to whom no one is equal, than whom no one can be greater; for it is written that the prophet Moses thus spoke to the Jews:
The Lord your God is the God of gods, and the Lord of lords, the great God.' [41]Thus, although there are many that are called gods, yet He who is the God of the Jews is alone called the God of gods.
For not every one that is called God is necessarily God.
Indeed, even Moses is called a god to Pharaoh, [42] and it is certain that he was a man; and judges were called gods, and it is evident that they were mortal.
The idols also of the Gentiles are called gods, and we all know that they are not; but this has been inflicted as a punishment on the wicked, that because they would not acknowledge the true God, they should regard as God whatever form or image should occur to them.
Because they refused to receive the knowledge of the One who, as I said, is God of all, therefore it is permitted to them to have as gods those who can do nothing for their worshippers.
For what can either dead images or living creatures confer upon men, since the power of all things is with One?

Chapter XLII - Guardian Angels

"Therefore the name God is applied in three ways: [43]either because he to whom it is given is truly God, or because he is the servant of him who is truly; and for the honour of the sender, that his authority may be full, he that is sent is called by the name of him who sends, as is often done in respect of angels:
for when they appear to a man, if he is a wise and intelligent man, he asks the name of him who appears to him, that he may acknowledge at once the honour of the sent, and the authority of the sender.
For every nation has an angel, to whom God has committed the government of that nation; and when one of these appears, although he be thought and called God by those over whom he presides, yet, being asked, he does not give such testimony to himself.
For the Most High God, who alone holds the power of all things, has divided all the nations of the earth into seventy-two parts, and over these He hath appointed angels as princes.
But to the one among the archangels who is greatest, was committed the government of those who, before all others, received the worship and knowledge of the Most High God.
But holy men also, as we have said, are made gods to the wicked, as having received the power of life and death over them, as we mentioned above with respect to Moses and the judges. Wherefore it is also written concerning them, Thou shalt not curse the gods, and thou shalt not curse the prince of thy people.' [44]Thus the princes of the several nations are called gods.
But Christ is God of princes, who is Judge of all.
Therefore neither angels, nor men, nor any creature, can be truly gods, forasmuch as they are placed under authority, being created and changeable:
angels, for they were not, and are; men, for they are mortal; and every creature, for it is capable of dissolution, if only He dissolve it who made it.
And therefore He alone is the true God, who not only Himself lives, but also bestows life upon others, which He can also take away when it pleaseth Him.

Chapter XLIII - No God But Jehovah

"Wherefore the Scripture exclaims in name of the God of the Jews, saying, Behold, behold, seeing that I am God, and there is none else besides me, I will kill, and I will make alive; I will smite, and I will heal; and there is none who can deliver out of my hands.' [45] See therefore how, by some ineffable virtue, the Scripture, opposing the future errors of those who should affirm that either in heaven or on earth there is any other god besides Him who is the God of the Jews, decides thus:

The Lord your God is one God, in heaven above, and in the earth beneath; and besides Him there is none else.' [46] How, then, hast thou dared to say that there is any other God besides Him who is the God of the Jews?

And again the Scripture says, Behold, to the Lord thy God belong the heaven, and the heaven of heavens, the earth, and all things that are in them:

nevertheless I have chosen your fathers, that I might love them, and you after them.' [47] Thus that judgment is supported by the Scripture on every side, that He who created the world is the true and only God.

Chapter XLIV - The Serpent, the Author of Polytheism

"But even if there be others, as we have said, who are called gods, they are under the power of the God of the Jews; for thus saith the Scripture to the Jews, The Lord our God, He is God of gods, and Lord of lords.' [48] Him alone the Scripture also commands to be worshipped, saying, Thou shalt worship the Lord thy God, and Him only shalt thou serve;' [49] and, Hear, O Israel:

the Lord thy God is one God.' [50]

Yea, also the saints, filled with the Spirit of God, and bedewed with the drops of His mercy, cried out, saying, Who is like unto Thee among the gods? O Lord, who is like unto Thee?' [51] And again, Who is God, but the Lord; and who is God, but our Lord?' [52] Therefore Moses, when he saw that the people were advancing, by degrees initiated them in the understanding of the monarchy and the faith of one God, as he says in the following words:

Thou shalt not make mention of the names of other gods;' [53] doubtless remembering with what penalty the serpent was visited, which had first named gods. [54] For it is condemned to feed upon dust, and is judged worthy of such food, for this cause, that it first of all introduced the name of gods into the world.

But if you also wish to introduce many gods, see that you partake not the serpent's doom.

Chapter XLV - Polytheism Inexcusable

"For be sure of this, that you shall not have us participators in this attempt; nor will we suffer ourselves to be deceived by you.

For it will not serve us for an excuse in the judgment, if we say that you deceived us; because neither could it excuse the first woman, that she had unhappily believed the serpent; but she was condemned to death, because she believed badly.

For this cause therefore, Moses, also commending the faith of one God to the people, says, Take heed to thyself, that thou be not seduced from the Lord thy God.' [55] Observe that he makes use of the same word which the first woman also made use of in excusing herself, saying that she was seduced; but it profited her nothing.

But over and above all this, even if some true prophet should arise, who should perform signs and miracles, but should wish to persuade us to worship other gods besides the God of the Jews, we should never be able to believe him.

For so the divine law has taught us, handing down a secret injunction more purely by means of tradition, for thus it saith:

If there arise among you a prophet, or one dreaming a dream, and give you signs or wonders, and these signs or wonders come to pass, and he say to you, Let us go and worship strange gods, whom ye know not; ye shall not hear the words of that prophet, nor the dream of that dreamer, because proving he hath proved you, that he may see if ye love the Lord your God.' [56]

Chapter XLVI - Christ Acknowledged the God of the Jews

"Wherefore also our Lord, who wrought signs and wonders, preached the God of the Jews; and therefore we are right in believing what He preached.

But as for you, even if you were really a prophet, and performed signs and wonders, as you promise to do, if you were to announce other gods besides Him who is the true God, it would be manifest that you were raised up as a trial to the people of God; and therefore you can by no means be believed.

For He alone is the true God, who is the God of the Jews; and for this reason our Lord Jesus Christ did not teach them that they must inquire after God, for Him they knew well already, but that they must seek His kingdom and righteousness, [57] which the scribes and Pharisees, having received the key of knowledge, had not shut in, but shut out. [58]For if they had been ignorant of the true God, surely He would never have left the knowledge of this thing, which was the chief of all, and blamed them for small and little things, as for enlarging their fringes, and claiming the uppermost rooms in feasts, and praying standing in the highways, and such like things; which assuredly, in comparison of this great charge, ignorance of God, seem to be small and insignificant matters."

Chapter XLVII - Simon's Cavil

To this Simon replied: [59]"From the words of your master I shall refute you, because even he introduces to all men a certain God who was known.

For although both Adam knew the God who was his creator, and the maker of the world; and Enoch knew him, inasmuch as he was translated by him; and Noah, since he was ordered by him to construct the ark; and although Abraham, and Isaac, and Jacob, and Moses, and all, even every people and all nations, know the maker of the world, and confess him to be a God, yet your Jesus, who appeared long after the patriarchs, says:

No one knows the Son, but the Father; neither knoweth any one the Father, but the Son, and he to whom the Son has been pleased to reveal Him.' [60]Thus, therefore, even your Jesus confesses that there is another God, incomprehensible and unknown to all."

Chapter XLVIII - Peter's Answer

Then Peter says:
"You do not perceive that you are making statements in opposition to yourself.

For if our Jesus also knows Him whom ye call the unknown God, then He is not known by you alone.

Yea, if our Jesus knows Him, then Moses also, who prophesied that Jesus should come, assuredly could not himself be ignorant of Him.

For he was a prophet; and he who prophesied of the Son doubtless knew the Father. For if it is in the option of the Son to reveal the Father to whom He will, then the Son, who has been with the Father from the beginning, and through all generations, as He revealed the Father to Moses, so also to the other prophets; but if this be so, it is evident that the Father has not been unknown to any of them.

But how could the Father be revealed to you, who do not believe in the Son, since the Father is known to none except him to whom the Son is pleased to reveal Him?

But the Son reveals the Father to those who honour the Son as they honour the Father." [61]

Chapter XLIX - The Supreme Light

Then Simon said:
"Remember that you said that God has a son, which is doing Him wrong; for how can He have a son, unless He is subject to passions, like men or animals?

But on these points there is not time now to show your profound folly, for I hasten to make a statement concerning the immensity of the supreme light; and so now listen.

My opinion is, that there is a certain power of immense and ineffable light, whose greatness may be held to be incomprehensible, of which power even the maker of the world is ignorant, and Moses the lawgiver, and Jesus your master." [62]

Chapter L - Simon's Presumption

Then Peter: [63]"Does it not seem to you to be madness, that any one should take upon himself to assert that there is another God than the God of all; and should say that he supposes there is a certain power, and should presume to affirm this to others, before he himself is sure of what he says?

Is any one so rash as to believe your words, of which he sees that you are yourself doubtful, and to admit that there is a certain power unknown to God the Creator, and to Moses, and the prophets, and the law, and even to Jesus our Master, which power is so good, that it will not make itself known to any but to one only, and that one such an one as thou!

Then, further, if that is a new power, why does it not confer upon us some new sense, in addition to those five which we possess, that by that new sense, bestowed upon us by it, we may be able to receive and understand itself which is new?

Or if it cannot bestow such a sense upon us, how has it bestowed it upon you? Or if it has revealed itself to you, why not also to us?

But if you of yourself understand things which not even the prophets were able to perceive or understand, come, tell us what each one of us is thinking now; for if there is such a spirit in you that you know those things which are above the heavens, which are unknown to all, and incomprehensible by all, much more easily do you know the thoughts of men upon the earth.

But if you cannot know the thoughts of us who are standing here, how can you say that you know those things which, you assert, are known to none?"

Chapter LI - The Sixth Sense

"But believe me, that you could never know what light is unless you had received both vision and understanding from light itself; so also in other things.

Hence, having received understanding, you are framing in imagination something greater and more sublime, as if dreaming, but deriving all your hints from those five senses, to whose Giver you are unthankful.

But be sure of this, that until you find some new sense which is beyond those five which we all enjoy, you cannot assert the existence of a new God."

Then Simon answered:

"Since all things that exist are in accordance with those five senses, that power which is more excellent than all cannot add anything new."

Then Peter said: "It is false; for there is also a sixth sense, namely that of foreknowledge: for those five senses are capable of knowledge, but the sixth is that of foreknowledge: and this the prophets possessed.

How, then, can you know a God who is unknown to all, who do not know the prophetic sense, which is that of prescience?"

Then Simon began to say:

"This power of which I speak, incomprehensible and more excellent than all, ay, even than that God who made the world, neither any of the angels has known, nor of the demons, nor of the Jews, nay, nor any creature which subsists by means of God the creator.

How, then, could that creator's law teach me that which the creator himself did not know, since neither did the law itself know it, that it might teach it?"

Chapter LII - Reductio Ad Absurdu

Then Peter said:

"I wonder how you have been able to learn more from the law than the law was able to know or to teach; and how you say that you adduce proofs from the law of those things which you are pleased to assert, when you declare that neither the law, nor He who gave the law--that is, the Creator of the world--knows those things of which you speak!

But this also I wonder at, how you, who alone know these things, should be standing here now with us all, circumscribed by the limits of this small court."

Then Simon, seeing Peter and all the people laughing, said:

"Do you laugh, Peter, while so great and lofty matters are under discussion?"

Then said Peter:

"Be not enraged, Simon, for we are doing no more than keeping our promise:
for we are neither shutting our ears, as you said, nor did we take to flight as soon as we heard you

propound your unutterable things; but we have not even stirred from the place.

For indeed you do not even propound things that have any resemblance to truth, which might to a certain extent frighten us.

Yet, at all events, disclose to us the meaning of this saying, how from the law you have learned of a God whom the law itself does not know, and of whom He who gave the law is ignorant." Then Simon said:

"If you have done laughing, I shall prove it by clear assertions."

Then Peter said:

"Assuredly I shall give over, that I may learn from you how you have learned from the law what neither the law nor the God of the law Himself knows."

Chapter LIII - Simon's Blasphemy

Then says Simon:

"Listen:

it is manifest to all, and ascertained in a manner of which no account can be given, [64] that there is one God, who is better than all, from whom all that is took its beginning; whence also of necessity, all things that are after him are subject to him, as the chief and most excellent of all.

When, therefore, I had ascertained that the God who created the world, according to what the law teaches, is in many respects weak, whereas weakness is utterly incompatible with a perfect God, and I saw that he is not perfect, I necessarily concluded that there is another God who is perfect. [65] For this God, as I have said, according to what the writing of the law teaches, is shown to be weak in many things.

In the first place, because the man whom he formed was not able to remain such as he had intended him to be; and because he cannot be good who gave a law to the first man, that he should eat of all the trees of paradise, but that he should not touch the tree of knowledge; and if he should eat of it, he should die.

For why should he forbid him to eat, and to know what is good and what evil, that, knowing, he might shun the evil and choose the good?

But this he did not permit; and because he did eat in violation of the commandment, and discovered what is good, and learned for the sake of honour to cover his nakedness (for he perceived it to be unseemly to stand naked before his Creator), he condemns to death him who had learned to do honour to God, and curses the serpent who had shown him these things.

But truly, if man was to be injured by this means, why did he place the cause of injury in paradise at all?

But if that which he placed in paradise was good, it is not the part of one that is good to restrain another from good."

Chapter LIV - How Simon Learned from the Law What the Law Does Not Teach

"Thus then, since he who made man and the world is, according to what the law relates, imperfect, we are given to understand, without doubt, that there is another who is perfect.

For it is of necessity that there be one most excellent of all, on whose account also every creature keeps its rank.

Whence also I, knowing that it is every way necessary that there be some one more benignant and more powerful than that imperfect God who gave the law, understanding what is perfect from comparison of the imperfect, understood even from the Scripture that God who is not mentioned there.

And in this way I was able, O Peter, to learn from the law what the law did not know.

But even if the law had not given indications from which it might be gathered that the God who made the world is imperfect, it was still possible for me to infer from those evils which are done in this world, and are not corrected, either that its creator is powerless, if he cannot correct what is done amiss; or else, if he does not wish to remove the evils, that he is himself evil; but if he neither can nor will, that he is neither powerful nor good.

And from this it cannot but be concluded that there is another God more excellent and more powerful than all.

If you have aught to say to this, say on."

Chapter LV - Simon's Objections Turned Against Himself

Peter answered:

"O Simon, they are wont to conceive such absurdities against God who do not read the law with the instruction of masters, but account themselves teachers, and think that they can understand the law, though he has not explained it to them who has learned of the Master. ⁶⁶Nevertheless now, that we also may seem to follow the book of the law according to your apprehension of it; inasmuch as you say that the creator of the world is shown to be both impotent and evil, how is it that you do not see that that power of yours, which you say is superior to all, fails and lies under the very same charges? For the very same thing may be said of it, that it is either powerless, since it does not correct those things which here are done amiss; or if it can and will not, it is evil; or if it neither can nor will, then it is both impotent and imperfect.

Whence that new power of yours is not only found liable to a similar charge, but even to a worse one, if, in addition to all these things, it is believed to be, when it is not. For He who created the world, His existence is manifest by His very operation in creating the world, as you yourself also confess.

But this power which you say that you alone know, affords no indication of itself, by which we might perceive, at least, that it is, and subsists."

Chapter LVI - No God Above the Creator

"What kind of conduct, then, would it be that we should forsake God, in whose world we live and enjoy all things necessary for life, and follow I know not whom, from whom we not only obtain no good, but cannot even know that he exists?

Nor truly does he exist.

For whether you call him light, and brighter than that light which we see, you borrow that very name from the Creator of the world; or whether you say that he is a substance above all, you derive from Him the idea with enlargement of speech. ⁶⁷Whether you make mention of mind, or goodness, or life, or whatever else, you borrow the words from Him.

Since, then, you have nothing new concerning that power you speak of, not only as regards understanding, but even in respect of naming him, how do you introduce a new God, for whom you cannot even find a new name?

For not only is the Creator of the world called a Power, but even the ministers of His glory, and all the heavenly host.

Do you not then think it better that we should follow our Creator God, as a Father who trains us and endows us as He knows how?

But if, as you say, there be some God more benignant than all, it is certain that he will not be angry with us; or if he be angry, he is evil.

For if our God is angry and punishes, He is not evil, but righteous, for He corrects and amends His own sons. But he who has no concern with us, if he shall punish us, how should he be good?

Inflicting punishments upon us because we have not been drawn by vain imaginations to forsake our own Father and follow him, how can you assert that he is so good, when he cannot be regarded as even just?"

Chapter LVII - Simon's Inconsistency

Then Simon:

"Do you so far err, Peter, as not to know that our souls were made by that good God, the most excellent of all, but they have been brought down as captives into this world?"

To this Peter answered:

"Then he is not unknown by all, as you said a little while ago; and yet how did the good God permit his souls to be taken captive, if he be a power over all?"

Then Simon said:

"He sent God the creator to make the world; and he, when he had made it, gave out that himself was God."

Then Peter said:

"Then he is not, as you said, unknown to Him who made the world; nor are souls ignorant of him, if indeed they were stolen away from him.

To whom, then, can he be unknown, if both the Creator of the world know him, as having been sent by him; and all souls know him, as having been violently withdrawn from him?

Then, further, I wish you would tell us whether he who sent the creator of the world did not know that he would not keep faith?

For if he did not know it, then he was not prescient; while if he foreknew it, and suffered it, he is himself guilty of this deed, since he did not prevent it; but if he could not, then he is not omnipotent.

But if, knowing it as good, he did not prohibit it, he is found to be better, who presumed to do that which he who sent him did not know to be good."

Chapter LVIII - Simon's God Unjust

Then Simon said:

"He receives those who will come to him, and does them good."

Peter answered:

"But there is nothing new in this; for He whom you acknowledge to be the Creator of the world also does so." Then Simon:

"But the good God bestows salvation if he is only acknowledged; but the creator of the world demands also that the law be fulfilled."

Then said Peter:

"He saves adulterers and men-slayers, if they know him; but good, and sober, and merciful persons, if they do not know him, in consequence of their having no information concerning him, he does not save!

Great and good truly is he whom you proclaim, who is not so much the saviour of the evil, as he is one who shows no mercy to the good."

Then Simon:

"It is truly very difficult for man to know him, as long as he is in the flesh; for blacker than all darkness, and heavier than all clay, is this body with which the soul is surrounded."

Then says Peter:

"That good God of yours demands things which are difficult; but He who is truly God seeks easier things.

Let him then, since he is so good, leave us with our Father and Creator; and when once we depart from the body, and leave that darkness that you speak of, we shall more easily know Him; and then the soul shall better understand that God is its Creator, and shall remain with Him, and shall no more be harassed with diverse imaginations; nor shall wish to betake itself to another power, which is known to none but Simon only, and which is of such goodness that no one can come to it, unless he be first guilty of impiety towards his own father!

I know not how this power can be called either good or just, which no one can please except by acting impiously towards him by whom he was made!"

Chapter LIX - The Creator Our Father

Then Simon:

"It is not impious for the sake of greater profit and advantage to flee to him who is of richer glory."

Then Peter:

"If, as you say, it is not impious to flee to a stranger, it is at all events much more pious to remain with our own father, even if he be poor.

But if you do not think it impious to leave our father, and flee to another, as being better than he; and you do not believe that our Creator will take this amiss; much more the good God will not be angry, because, when we were strangers to him, we have not fled to him, but have remained with our own Creator.

Yea, I think he will rather commend us the more for this, that we have kept faith with God our Creator; for he will consider that, if we had been his creatures, we should never have been seduced by the allurements of any other to forsake him.

For if any one, allured by richer promises, shall leave his own father and betake himself to a stranger, it may be that he will leave him in his turn, and go to another who shall promise him greater things, and this the rather because he is not his son, since he could leave even him who by nature was his father."

Then Simon said:

"But what if souls are from him, and do not know him, and he is truly their father?"

Chapter LX - The Creator the Supreme God

Then Peter said:

"You represent him as weak enough.

For if, as you say, he is more powerful than all, it can never be believed the weaker wrenched the spoils from the stronger. [68]Or if God the Creator was able by violence to bring down souls into this world, how can it be that, when they are separated from the body and freed from the bonds of captivity, the good God shall call them to the sufferance of punishment, on the ground that they, either through his remissness or weakness, were dragged away to this place, and were involved in the body, as in the darkness of ignorance?

You seem to me not to know what a father and a God is:

but I could tell you both whence souls are, and when and how they were made; but it is not permitted to me now to disclose these things to you, who are in such error in respect of the knowledge of God."

Then said Simon:

"A time will come when you shall be sorry that you did not understand me speaking of the ineffable power."

Then said Peter:

"Give us then, as I have often said, as being yourself a new God, or as having yourself come down from him, some new sense, by means of which we may know that new God of whom you speak; for those five senses, which God our Creator has given us, keep faith to their own Creator, and do not perceive that there is any other God, for so their nature necessitates them."

Chapter LXI - Imagination

To this Simon answered:

"Apply your mind to those things which I am going to say, and cause it, walking in peaceable paths, to attain to those things which I shall demonstrate.

Listen now, therefore.

Did you never in thought reach forth your mind into regions or islands situated far away, and remain so fixed in them, that you could not even see the people that were before you, or know where yourself were sitting, by reason of the delightfulness of those things on which you were gazing?"

And Peter said:

"It is true, Simon, this has often occurred to me."

Then Simon said:

"In this way now reach forth your sense into heaven, yea above the heaven, and behold that there must be some place beyond the world, or outside the world, in which there is neither heaven nor earth, and where no shadow of these things produces darkness; and consequently, since there are neither bodies in it, nor darkness occasioned by bodies, there must of necessity be immense light; and consider of what sort that light must be, which is never succeeded by darkness.

For if the light of this sun fills this whole world, how great do you suppose that bodiless and infinite light to be?

So great, doubtless, that this light of the sun would seem to be darkness and not light, in comparison."

Chapter LXII - Peter's Experience of Imagination

When Simon thus spoke, Peter answered: [69]"Now listen patiently concerning both these matters, that is, concerning the example of stretching out the senses, and concerning the immensity of light.

I know that I myself, O Simon, have sometimes in thought extended my sense, as you say, into regions and islands situated afar off, and have seen them with my mind not less than if it had been with my eyes.

When I was at Capernaum, occupied in the taking of fishes, and sat upon a rock, holding in my hand a hook attached to a line, and fitted for deceiving the fishes, I was so absorbed that I did not feel a fish adhering to it while my mind eagerly ran through my beloved Jerusalem, to which I had frequently gone up, waking, for the sake of offerings and prayers.

But I was accustomed also to admire this Caesarea, hearing of it from others, and to long to see it; and I seemed to myself to see it, although I had never been in it; and I thought of it what was suitable to be thought of a great city, its gates, walls, baths, streets, lanes, markets, and the like, in accordance with

The Epistles of Clement

what I had seen in other cities; and to such an extent was I delighted with the intentness of such inspection, that, as you said, I neither saw one who was present and standing by me, nor knew where myself was sitting."

Then said Simon:
"Now you say well."

Chapter LXIII - Peter's Reverie

Then Peter:
"In short, when I did not perceive, through the occupation of my mind, that I had caught a very large fish which was attached to the hook, and that although it was dragging the hook-line from my hand, my brother Andrew, who was sitting by me, seeing me in a reverie and almost ready to fall, thrusting his elbow into my side as if he would awaken me from sleep, said:
Do you not see, Peter, what a large fish you have caught?
Are you out of your senses, that you are thus in a stupor of astonishment?
Tell me, What is the matter with you?'
But I was angry with him for a little, because he had withdrawn me from the delight of those things which I was contemplating; then I answered that I was not suffering from any malady, but that I was mentally gazing on the beloved Jerusalem, and at the same time on Caesarea; and that, while I was indeed with him in the body, in my mind I was wholly carried away thither.
But he, I know not whence inspired, uttered a hidden and secret word of truth."

Chapter LXIV - Andrew's Rebuke

"Give over,' says he, O Peter.
What is it that you are doing?
For those who are beginning to be possessed with a demon, or to be disturbed in their minds, begin in this way.
They are first carried away by fancies to some pleasant and delightful things, then they are poured out in vain and fond motions towards things which have no existence.
Now this happens from a certain disease of mind, by reason of which they see not the things which are, but long to bring to their sight those which are not.
But thus it happens also to those who are suffering phrenzy, and seem to themselves to see many images, because their soul, being torn and withdrawn from its place by excess of cold or of heat, suffers a failure of its natural service.
But those also who are in distress through thirst, when they fall asleep, seem to themselves to see rivers and fountains, and to drink; but this befalls them through being distressed by the dryness of the unmoistened body. Wherefore it is certain that this occurs through some ailment either of the soul or body.'

Chapter LXV - Fallacy of Imagination

"In short, that you may receive the faith of the matter; concerning Jerusalem, which I had often seen, I told my brother what places and what gatherings of people I had seemed to myself to see.
But also concerning Caesarea, which I had never seen, I nevertheless contended that it was such as I had conceived it in my mind and thought.
But when I came hither, and saw nothing at all like to those things which I had seen in phantasy, I blamed myself, and observed distinctly, that I had assigned to it gates, and walls, and buildings from others which I had seen, taking the likeness in reality from others.
Nor indeed can any one imagine anything new, and of which no form has ever existed. For even if any one should fashion from his imagination bulls with five heads, he only forms them with five heads out of those which he has seen with one head.
And you therefore, now, if truly you seem to yourself to perceive anything with your thought, and to look above the heavens, there is no doubt but that you imagine them from those things which you see, placed as you are upon the earth.
But if you think that there is easy access for your mind above the heavens, and that you are able to conceive the things that are there, and to apprehend knowledge of that immense light, I think that for him who can comprehend these things, it were easier to throw his sense, which knows how to ascend thither, into the heart and breast of some one of us who stand by, and to tell what thoughts he is

cherishing in his breast.

If therefore you can declare the thoughts of the heart of any one of us, who is not pre-engaged in your favour, we shall perhaps be able to believe you, that you are able to know those things that are above the heavens, although these are much loftier."

Chapter LXVI - Existence and Conception

To this Simon replied: [70]"O thou who hast woven a web of many frivolities, listen now.

It is impossible that anything which comes into a man's thoughts should not also subsist in truth and reality. For things that do not subsist, have no appearances; [71] but things that have no appearances, cannot present themselves to our thoughts." Then said Peter:

"If everything that can come into our thoughts has a subsistence, then, with respect to that place of immensity which you say is outside the world, if one thinks in his heart that it is light, and another that it is darkness, how can one and the same place be both light and darkness, according to their different thoughts concerning it?"

Then said Simon:

"Let pass for the present what I have said; and tell us what you suppose to be above the heavens."

Chapter LXVII - The Law Teaches of Immensity

Then said Peter:

"If you believed concerning the true fountain of light, I could instruct you what and of what sort is that which is immense, and should render, not a vain fancy, but a consistent and necessary account of the truth, and should make use, not of sophistical assertions, but testimonies of the law and nature, that you might know that the law especially contains what we ought to believe in regard to immensity.

But if the doctrine of immensity is not unknown to the law, then assuredly, nought else can be unknown to it; and therefore it is a false supposition of yours, that there is anything of which the law is not cognisant.

Much more shall nothing be unknown to Him who gave the law.

Yet I cannot speak anything to you of immensity and of those things which are without limit, unless first you either accept our account of those heavens which are bounded by a certain limit, or else propound your own account of them.

But if you cannot understand concerning those which are comprehended within fixed boundaries, much more can you neither know nor learn anything concerning those which are without limit."

Chapter LXVIII - The Visible and the Invisible Heaven

To this Simon answered:

"It seems to me to be better to believe simply that God is, and that that heaven which we see is the only heaven in the whole universe."

But Peter said:

"Not so; but it is proper to confess one God who truly is; but that there are heavens, which were made by Him, as also the law says, of which one is the higher, in which also is contained the visible firmament; and that that higher heaven is perpetual and eternal, with those who dwell in it; but that this visible heaven is to be dissolved and to pass away at the end of the world, in order that that heaven which is older and higher may appear after the judgment to the holy and the worthy."

To this Simon answered:

"That these things are so, as you say, may appear to those who believe them; but to him who seeks for reasons of these things, it is impossible that they can be produced from the law, and especially concerning the immensity of light."

The Epistles of Clement

Chapter LXIX - Faith and Reason

Then Peter:

"Do not think that we say that these things are only to be received by faith, but also that they are to be asserted by reason. For indeed it is not safe to commit these things to bare faith without reason, since assuredly truth cannot be without reason.

And therefore he who has received these things fortified by reason, can never lose them; whereas he who receives them without proofs, by an assent to a simple statement of them, can neither keep them safely, nor is certain if they are true; because he who easily believes, also easily yields. But he who has sought reason for those things which he has believed and received, as though bound by chains of reason itself, can never be torn away or separated from those things which he hath believed.

And therefore, according as any one is more anxious in demanding a reason, by so much will he be the firmer in preserving his faith."

Chapter LXX - Adjournment

To this Simon replied:

"It is a great thing which you promise, that the eternity of boundless light can be shown from the law."

And when Peter said, "I shall show it whenever you please," Simon answered: "Since now it is a late hour, I shall stand by you and oppose you to-morrow; and if you can prove that this world was created, and that souls are immortal, you shall have me to assist you in your preaching."

When he had said thus, he departed, and was followed by a third part of all the people who had come with him, who were about one thousand men.

But the rest with bended knees prostrated themselves before Peter; and he, invoking upon them the name of God, cured some who had demons, healed others who were sick, and so dismissed the people rejoicing, commanding them to come early the next day.

But Peter, when the crowds had withdrawn, commanded the table to be spread on the ground, in the open air, in the court where the disputation had been held, and sat down together with those eleven; but I dined reclining with some others who also had made a beginning of hearing the word of God, and were greatly beloved.

Chapter LXXI - Separation from the Unclean

But Peter, most benignantly regarding me, lest haply that separation might cause me sorrow, says to me:

"It is not from pride, O Clement, that I do not eat with those who have not yet been purified; but I fear lest perhaps I should injure myself, and do no good to them. [72] For this I would have you know for certain, that every one who has at any time worshipped idols, and has adored those whom the pagans call gods, or has eaten of the things sacrificed to them, is not without an unclean spirit; for he has become a guest of demons, and has been partaker with that demon of which he has formed the image in his mind, either through fear or love. [73] And by these means he is not free from an unclean spirit, and therefore needs the purification of baptism, that the unclean spirit may go out of him, which has made its abode in the inmost affections of his soul, and what is worse, gives no indication that it lurks within, for fear it should be exposed and expelled."

Chapter LXXII - The Remedy

"For these unclean spirits love to dwell in the bodies of men, that they may fulfil their own desires by their service, and, inclining the motions of their souls to those things which they themselves desire, may compel them to obey their own lusts, that they may become wholly vessels of demons. [74] One of whom is this Simon, who is seized with such disease, and cannot now be healed, because he is sick in his will and purpose.

Nor does the demon dwell in him against his will; and therefore, if any one would drive it out of him, since it is inseparable from himself, and, so to speak, has now become his very soul, he should seem rather to kill him, and to incur the guilt of manslaughter.

Let no one of you therefore be saddened at being separated from eating with us, for every one ought to observe that it is for just so long a time as he pleases.

Clement of Rome

For he who wishes soon to be baptized is separated but for a little time, but he for a longer who wishes to be baptized later.

Every one therefore has it in his own power to demand a shorter or a longer time for his repentance; and therefore it lies with you, when you wish it, to come to our table; and not with us, who are not permitted to take food with any one who has not been baptized.

It is rather you, therefore, who hinder us from eating with you, if you interpose delays in the way of your purification, and defer your baptism."

Having said thus, and having blessed, he took food.

And afterwards, when he had given thanks to God, he went into the house and went to bed; and we all did the like, for it was now night.

Footnotes:

1. [With this list compare that in iii. 68, where four others are added (or substituted), and some importance given to the number twelve.

See also Homily II. 1.

The variety and correspondence point to the use of a common basis.--R.]

2. That is, the lamp which had been lighted in the evening.

3. [In the Homilies the discourse before the discussion with Simon is much fuller.--R.]

4. Matt. x. 11.

5. Matt. vii. 6.

6. [The statements of Niceta and Aquila are introduced in the Homilies before the postponement of the discussion with Simon.

There is a remarkable variety in the minor details respecting Simon as given in the two narratives.--R.]

7. [Comp. i. 54.

In Homily II. 23 Simon is said to be a follower of John the Baptist, one of the thirty chief men: so Dositheus.

Here Dositheus is represented as the head of a separate sect; so in i. 54.--R.]

8. [Called "Helena" in the Homilies, and identified apparently with Helen, the cause of the Trojan War.--R.]

9. [The statements made in the Recognitions respecting the claims of Simon are more extravagant and blasphemous than those occurring in the Homilies.

Comp. the latter, ii, 26-32.--R.]

10. The meaning seems to be, that she was seen at all the windows at once.--Tr.

11. [This parody of the miraculous conception is not found in the Homilies.--R.]

12. [In Homily II. 37-53 the discourse of Peter is quite different and far less worthy.

In Homily III. 1-28 a similar discourse is given, just before the discussion with Simon, abounding in statements that suggest erroneous views of Scripture, and indicate a Gnostic origin.--R.]

13. 2 Cor. xi. 14.

14. [Three discussions with Simon Magus are detailed in the pseudo-Clementine literature,--one in the Recognitions, ii. 20-iii. 48; two in the Homilies, iii. 30-58 and xvi.-xix.

The differences between these are quite remarkable. I.

External Differences.--That in the Recognitions is assigned to Caesarea and is represented as lasting three days, details of each day's discussion being given.

The earlier one in the Homilies is given the same place and time, but it is very brief.

The details of the first day alone are mentioned; and it resembles that in the Recognitions less than does the later one.

This is represented as taking place at Laodicea, and as occupying four days.

The account is the longest of the three.

In its historical setting this discussion has no parallel in the Recognitions.

Faustus, the father of Clement, is made the umpire; and this discussion before him takes the place of the discussions with him which occupy so large a part of Recognitions, viii.-x. II.

Internal Differences.--Of course there are many thoughts common to the discussions; but the treatment is so varied as to form one of the most perplexing points in the literary problem.

All are somewhat irregular in arrangement, hence an analysis is difficult. The discussion in the Recognitions seems to be more ethical and philosophical than those in the Homilies; the latter contain more theosophical views.

Both of them emphasize the falsehoods of Scripture and abound more in sophistries and verbal sword-play.

In the Recognitions against Simon's polytheism and theory of an unknown God, Peter opposes the righteousness of God, emphasizing the freedom of the will, discussing the existence and origin of evil, reverting to the righteousness of God as proving the immortality of the soul.

The defeat of Simon is narrated in a peculiar way. The Caesarean discussion in the Homilies is very briefly narrated.

After the preliminary parley, Simon attacks the God of the Scriptures attributing defects to Him.

Peter's reply, while explaining many passages correctly, is largely taken up with a statement of the view of the Scripture peculiar to the Homilies.

This is really the weapon with which Simon is defeated.

The discussion, therefore, presents few points of resemblance to that in the Recognitions. The Laodicean discussion in the Homilies, covering four days, is of a higher character than the preceding.

It is not strictly parallel to that in the Recognitions. The opening argument is concerning polytheism.

To Peter's monotheism Simon opposes the contradictions of Scripture:

these Peter explains, including some christological statements which lead to a declaration of the nature, name and character of God.

On the second day, after some personal discussion, Simon asserts that Christ's teaching differs from that of Peter; the argument reverts to the shape and figure of God. The evidence of the senses is urged against fancied revelations, which are attributed to demons.

On the third day the question of God the Framer of the world is introduced, and His moral character.

Peter explains the nature of revelation, with some sharp personal thrusts at Simon, but soon reverts to the usual explanation of Scripture. On the fourth day the existence of the evil one becomes the prominent topic: the existence of sin is pressed; and the discussion closes with a justification of the inequalities of human life, and an expression of judgment against Simon by Faustus. Throughout these portions footnotes have been added, to indicate the correspondences of thought in the several accounts--R.]

15. [This opening sentence occurs in the Homilies, but in other parts the discourses differ.

This is far more dignified and consistent than that in the Homilies, which at once introduces a claim to authority as messenger of the Prophet.--R.]

16. Matt. vi. 33.
17. Rom. i. 20.
18. Matt. v. 8.
19. [In Homily III. 38, 39, Simon is represented as at once attacking the Apostle and his monotheism; the arguments are, in the main, those given in chap. 39 of this book.

Chaps. 23-36 are without a direct parallel in the Homilies.--R.]

20. Matt. x. 34.
21. Matt. v. 9.
22. Matt. x. 25.
23. Matt. v. 9.
24. Matt. x. 35, 36; Luke xii. 53.
25. Matt. xxiii.; Luke xi.
26. Matt. x. 12-15; Luke x. 5, 6.
27. Matt. xii. 25.
28. Luke xii. 51-53.
29. Matt. xxviii. 19, 20.
30. [The discussion in the Homilies is represented as virtually beginning with this statement of the Apostle; comp. Homily III. 37. The arguments here, however, are given with greater detail.--R.]
31. [In both the Recognitions and the Homilies the contest turns upon the monotheistic teaching of the Old Testament and the supreme Deity of Jehovah.

This is rightly regarded as an evidence of Ebionitic origin. But Gnostic elements enter again and again.--R.]

32. Gen. iii. 5.
33. Gen. iii. 22.
34. Gen. i. 26.
35. Gen. iii. 22.
36. Gen. xi. 7.
37. Exod. xxii. 28.
38. Deut. xxxii. 12.
39. [Compare Homily XVI. 6.--R.]
40. [The reply of Peter here is of a higher character than that given in the Homilies (see iii. 40, etc.).

Indeed, the report of the entire discussion in the Recognitions shows a superior conception of the Apostle.--R.]

41. Deut. x. 17.

42. Exod. vii. 1.
43. [This remarkable chapter is peculiar to the Recognitions. The angelology seems to be Ebionitic, rather than Gnostic.--R.]
44. Exod. xxii. 28.
45. Deut. xxxii. 39.
46. Deut. iv. 39.
47. Deut x. 14, 15.
48. Deut. x. 17.
49. Deut. vi. 13, x. 20.
50. Deut. vi. 4.
51. Ps. lxxxvi. 8; lxxi. 19.
52. Ps. xviii. 31.
53. Josh. xxiii. 7, in Sept.
54. Gen. iii.
[The same thought occurs in Homily X. 10, 11 --R.]
55. Deut. viii. 11.
56. Deut. xiii. 1-3.
57. Matt. vi. 33.
58. Luke xi. 52.
59. [Compare Homily XVII. 4.--R.]
60. Matt. xi. 27.
[Comp. Luke x. 22. This objection is given in Homilies XVII. 4, XVIII. 4.--R.]
61. John v. 23.
62. This chapter presents the topic which is made the main point in a subsequent discussion with Simon; see Homily XVIII.--R.]
63. [With chaps. 50, 51, comp. Homily XVII. 13, etc.--R.]
64. We render by a periphrasis the expression ineffabili quadam ratione compertum.
The meaning seems to be, that the belief of the existence and unity of God is not the result of reasoning, but of intuition or instinct.
65. [The argument of Simon here differs from that represented in Homilies XVII., XVIII.
There Simon asserts that the Framer of the world is not the highest God, because He is not both just and good. Comp. also book iii. 37, 38.--R.]
66. [The attitude of the Apostle Peter toward the Old Testament is differently represented in the Homilies, where false views are admitted to exist in the Scriptures. Comp. Homilies II. 38, 40, 41, 51, III. 4, 5, etc.--R.]
67. That is, you take the idea of substance from the God of the Jews, and only enlarge it by the addition of the words above all.
68. Luke xi. 22.
69. [This story (chaps. 62-65) is peculiar to the Recognitions. In Homily XVII. 14-19 there is an argument against the trustworthiness of supernatural visions, which is supposed to be anti-Pauline in its aim.--R.]
70. [The remaining chapters of this book hare no exact parallel in the Homilies.--R.]
71. That is, have no visible or sensible species, according to the Platonic theory of perception.
72. [Comp. book i. 19, vii. 29; Homilies I. 22, XIII. 4.--R.]
73. 1 Cor. x. 20.
74. On the demonology of this work see book iv. 15-19; comp. Homily IX. 8-22.--R.]

Book III [1]

Chapter I - Pearls Before Swine

Meantime Peter, rising at the crowing of the cock, and wishing to rouse us, found us awake, the evening light still burning; and when, according to custom, he had saluted us, and we had all sat down, he thus began.

"Nothing is more difficult, my brethren, than to reason concerning the truth in the presence of a mixed multitude of people. For that which is may not be spoken to all as it is, on account of those who hear wickedly and treacherously; yet it is not proper to deceive, on account of those who desire to hear the truth sincerely. What, then, shall he do who has to address a mixed multitude?

Shall he conceal what is true?

How, then, shall he instruct those who are worthy?

But if he set forth pure truth to those who do not desire to obtain salvation, he does injury to Him by whom he has been sent, and from whom he has received commandment not to throw the pearls of His words before swine and dogs, [2] who, striving against them with arguments and sophisms, roll them in the mud of carnal understanding, and by their barkings and base answers break and weary the preachers of God's word.

Wherefore I also, for the most part, by using a certain circumlocution, endeavour to avoid publishing the chief knowledge concerning the Supreme Divinity to unworthy ears."

Then, beginning from the Father, and the Son, and the Holy Spirit, he briefly and plainly expounded to us, so that all of us hearing him wondered that men have forsaken the truth, and have turned themselves to vanity.

Chapter XII [3] - Second Day's Discussion

But when the day had dawned, some one came in and said:

"There is a very great multitude waiting in the court, and in the midst of them stands Simon, endeavouring to preoccupy the ears of the people with most wicked persuasions."

Then Peter, immediately going out, stood in the place where he had disputed the day before, and all the people turning to him with joy, gave heed to him.

But when Simon perceived that the people rejoiced at the sight of Peter, and were moved to love him, he said in confusion:

"I wonder at the folly of men, who call me a magician, and love Peter; whereas, having knowledge of me of old, they ought to love me rather.

And therefore from this sign those who have sense may understand that Peter may rather seem to be the magician, since affection is not borne to me, to whom it is almost due from acquaintance, but is abundantly expended upon him, to whom it is not due by any familiarity." [4]

Chapter XIII - Simon a Seducer

While Simon was talking on in this style, Peter, having saluted the people in his usual way, thus answered:

"O Simon, his own conscience is sufficient for every one to confute him; but if you wonder at this, that those who are acquainted with you not only do not love you but even hate you, learn the reason from me.

Since you are a seducer you profess to proclaim the truth; and on this account you had many friends who had a desire to learn the truth.

But when they saw in you things contrary to what you professed, they being, as I said, lovers of truth, began not only not to love you, but even to hate you.

But yet they did not immediately forsake you, because you still promised that you could show them what is true.

As long, therefore, as no one was present who could show them, they bore with you; but since the hope of better instruction has dawned upon them, they despise you, and seek to know what they understand to be better.

And you indeed, acting by nefarious arts, thought at first that you should escape detection.

But you are detected.

For you are driven into a corner, and, contrary to your expectation, you are made notorious, not only as being ignorant of the truth, but as being unwilling to hear it from those who know it.

For if you had been willing to hear, that saying would have been exemplified in you, of Him who said that there is nothing hidden which shall not be known, nor covered which shall not be disclosed.'"[5]

Chapter XIV - Simon Claims the Fulfilment of Peter's Promise

While Peter spoke these words, and others to the same effect, Simon answered:

"I will not have you detain me with long speeches, Peter; I claim from you what you promised yesterday.

You then said that you could show that the law teaches concerning the immensity of the eternal light, and that there are only two heavens, and these created, and that the higher is the abode of that light, in which the ineffable Father dwells alone for ever; but that after the pattern of that heaven is made this visible heaven, which you asserted is to pass away.

You said, therefore, that the Father of all is one, because there cannot be two infinites; else neither of them would be infinite, because in that in which the one subsists, he makes a limit of the subsistence of the other.

Since then you not only promised this, but are able to show it from the law, leave off other matters and set about this."

Then Peter said:

"If I were asked to speak of these things only on your account, who come only for the purpose of contradicting, you should never hear a single discourse from me; but seeing it is necessary that the husbandman, wishing to sow good ground, should sow some seeds, either in stony places, or places that are to be trodden of men, or in places filled with brambles and briers (as our Master also set forth, indicating by these the diversities of the purposes of several souls),[6] I shall not delay."

Chapter XV - Simon's Arrogance

Then said Simon:

"You seem to me to be angry; but if it be so, it is not necessary to enter into the conflict."

Then Peter:

"I see that you perceive that you are to be convicted, and you wish politely to escape from the contest; for what have you seen to have made me angry against you, a man desiring to deceive so great a multitude, and when you have nothing to say, pretending moderation, who also command, forsooth, by your authority that the controversy shall be conducted as you please, and not as order demands?"

Then Simon:

"I shall enforce myself to bear patiently your unskilfulness, that I may show that you indeed wish to seduce the people, but that I teach the truth.

But now I refrain from a discussion concerning that boundless light.

Answer me, therefore, what I ask of you.

Since God, as you say, made all things, whence comes evil?"[7]

Then said Peter:

"To put questions in this way is not the part of an opponent, but of a learner.

If therefore you wish to learn, confess it; and I shall first teach you how you ought to learn, and when you have learned to listen, then straightway I shall begin to teach you.

But if you do not wish to learn, as though you knew all things, I shall first set forth the faith which I preach, and do you also set forth what you think to be true; and when the profession of each of us has been disclosed, let our hearers judge whose discourse is supported by truth."

To this Simon answered:

"This is a good joke:

behold a fellow who offers to teach me!

Nevertheless I shall suffer you, and bear with your ignorance and your arrogance.

I confess, then, I do wish to learn; let us see how you can teach me."

Chapter XVI - Existence of Evil

Then Peter said:
"If you truly wish to learn, then first learn this, how unskilfully you have framed your question; for you say, Since God has created all things, whence is evil?
But before you asked this, three sorts of questions should have had the precedence:
First, Whether there be evil?
Secondly, What evil is?
Thirdly, To whom it is, and whence?"
To this Simon answered:
"Oh thou most unskilful and unlearned, is there any man who does not confess that there is evil in this life?
Whence I also, thinking that you had even the common sense of all men, asked, whence evil is; not as wishing to learn, since I know all things, least of all from you, who know nothing, but that I might show you to be ignorant of all things.
And that you may not suppose that it is because I am angry that I speak somewhat sternly, know that I am moved with compassion for those who are present, whom you are attempting to deceive."
Then Peter said:
"The more wicked are you, if you can do such wrong, not being angry; but smoke must rise where there is fire.
Nevertheless I shall tell you, lest I should seem to take you up with words, so as not to answer to those things which you have spoken disorderly.
You say that all confess the existence of evil, which is verily false; for, first of all, the whole Hebrew nation deny its existence."

Chapter XVII - Not Admitted by All

Then Simon, interrupting his discourse, said:
"They do rightly who say that there is no evil."
Then Peter answered:
"We do not propose to speak of this now, but only to state the fact that the existence of evil is not universally admitted.
But the second question that you should have asked is, What is evil?--a substance, an accident, or an act?
And many other things of the same sort.
And after that, towards what, or how it is, or to whom it is evil,--whether to God, or to angels, or to men, to the righteous or the wicked, to all or to some, to one's self or to no one?
And then you should inquire, Whence it is?--whether from God, or from nothing; whether it has always been, or has had its beginning in time; whether it is useful or useless? and many other things which a proposition of this sort demands."
To this Simon answered:
"Pardon me; I was in error concerning the first question; but suppose that I now ask first, whether evil is or not?"

Chapter XVIII - Manner of Conducting the Discussion

Then Peter said:
"In what way do you put the question; as wishing to learn, or to teach or for the sake of raising the question?
If indeed as wishing to learn, I have something to teach you first, that coming by consequence and the right order of doctrine, you may understand from yourself what evil is.
But if you put the question as an instructor, I have no need to be taught by you, for I have a Master from whom I have learned all things.
But if you ask merely for the sake of raising a question and disputing, let each of us first set forth his opinion, and so let the matter be debated.

For it is not reasonable that you should ask as one wishing to learn, and contradict as one teaching, so that after my answer it should be in your discretion to say whether I have spoken well or ill.

Wherefore you cannot stand in the place of a gainsayer and be judge of what we say.

And therefore, as I said, if a discussion is to be held, let each of us state his sentiments; and while we are placed in conflict, these religious hearers will be just judges."

Chapter XIX - Desire of Instruction

Then Simon said:
"Does it not seem to you to be absurd that an unskilled people should sit in judgment upon our sayings?"

Then Peter:
"It is not so; for what perhaps is less clear to one, can be investigated by many, for oftentimes even a popular rumour has the aspect of a prophecy.

But in addition to all this, all these people stand here constrained by the love of God, and by a desire to know the truth, and therefore all these are to be regarded as one, by reason of their affection being one and the same towards the truth; as, on the other hand, two are many and diverse, if they disagree with each other.

But if you wish to receive an indication how all these people who stand before us are as one man, consider from their very silence and quietness how with all patience, as you see, they do honour to the truth of God, even before they learn it, for they have not yet learned the greater observance which they owe to it.

Wherefore I hope, through the mercy of God, that He will accept the religious purpose of their mind towards Him, and will give the palm of victory to him who preaches the truth, that He may make manifest to them the herald of truth."

Chapter XX - Common Principles

Then Simon:
"On what subject do you wish the discussion to be held? Tell me, that I also may define what I think, and so the inquiry may begin."

And Peter answered:
"If indeed, you will do as I think right, I would have it done according to the precept of my Master, who first of all commanded the Hebrew nation, whom He knew to have knowledge of God, and that it is He who made the world, not that they should inquire about Him whom they knew, but that, knowing Him, they should investigate His will and His righteousness; because it is placed in men's power that, searching into these things, they may find, and do, and observe those things concerning which they are to be judged. Therefore He commanded us to inquire, not whence evil cometh, as you asked just now, but to seek the righteousness of the good God, and His kingdom; and all these things, says He, shall be added to you." [8] Then Simon said:

"Since these things are commanded to Hebrews, as having a right knowledge of God, and being of opinion that every one has it in his power to do these things concerning which he is to be judged,--but my opinion differs from theirs,--where do you wish me to begin?"

Chapter XXI - Freedom of the Will

Then said Peter:
"I advise that the first inquiry be, whether it be in our power to know whence we are to be judged."
But Simon said:
"Not so; but concerning God, about whom all who are present are desirous to hear."
Then Peter:
"You admit, then, that something is in the power of the will:
only confess this, if it is so, and let us inquire, as you say, concerning God."
To this Simon answered:
"By no means." Then Peter said:
"If, then, nothing is in our power, it is useless for us to inquire anything concerning God, since it is not in the power of those who seek to find; hence I said well, that this should be the first inquiry, whether anything is in the power of the will." [9] Then said Simon:
"We cannot even understand this that you say, if there is anything in the power of the will."

The Epistles of Clement

But Peter, seeing that he was turning to contention, and, through fear of being overcome, was confounding all things as being in general uncertain, answered:

"How then do you know that it is not in the power of man to know anything, since this very thing at least you know?"

Chapter XXII - Responsibility

Then Simon said:

"I know not whether I know even this; for every one, according as it is decreed to him by fate, either does, or understands, or suffers."

Then Peter said:

"See, my brethren, into what absurdities Simon has fallen, who before my coming was teaching that men have it in their power to be wise and to do what they will, but now, driven into a corner by the force of my arguments, he denies that man has any power either of perceiving or of acting; and yet he presumes to profess himself to be a teacher!

But tell me how then God judges according to truth every one for his doings, if men have it not in their own power to do anything?

If this opinion be held, all things are torn up by the roots; vain will be the desire of following after goodness; yea, even in vain do the judges of the world administer laws and punish those who do amiss, for they had it not in their power not to sin; vain also will be the laws of nations which assign penalties to evil deeds.

Miserable also will those be who laboriously keep righteousness; but blessed those who, living in pleasure, exercise tyranny, living in luxury and wickedness.

According to this, therefore, there can be neither righteousness, nor goodness, nor any virtue, nor, as you would have it, any God.

But, O Simon, I know why you have spoken thus:

truly because you wished to avoid inquiry, lest you should be openly confuted; and therefore you say that it is not in the power of man to perceive or to discern anything.

But if this had really been your opinion, you would not surely, before my coming, have professed yourself before the people to be a teacher.

I say, therefore, that man is under his own control."

Then said Simon:

"What is the meaning of being under his own control? Tell us."

To this Peter:

"If nothing can be learned, why do you wish to hear?"

And Simon said:

"You have nothing to answer to this."

Chapter XXIII - Origin of Evil

Then said Peter:

"I shall speak, not as under compulsion from you, but at the request of the hearers.

The power of choice is the sense of the soul, possessing a quality by which it can be inclined towards what acts it wills."

Then Simon, applauding Peter for what he had spoken, said:

"Truly you have expounded it magnificently and incomparably, for it is my duty to bear testimony to your speaking well.

Now if you will explain to me this which I now ask you, in all things else I shall submit to you. What I wish to learn, then, is this:

if what God wishes to be, is; and what He does not wish to be, is not. Answer me this."

Then Peter:

"If you do not know that you are asking an absurd and incompetent question, I shall pardon you and explain; but if you are aware that you are asking inconsequently, you do not well."

Then Simon said:

"I swear by the Supreme Divinity, whatsoever that may be, which judges and punishes those who sin, that I know not what I have said inconsequently, or what absurdity there is in my words, that is, in those that I have just uttered."

Chapter XXIV - God the Author of Good, Not of Evil

To this Peter answered:
"Since, then, you confess that you are ignorant, now learn.
Your question demanded our deliverance on two matters that are contrary to one another.
For every motion is divided into two parts, so that a certain part is moved by necessity, and another by will; and those things which are moved by necessity are always in motion, those which are moved by will, not always.
For example, the sun's motion is performed by necessity to complete its appointed circuit, and every state and service of heaven depends upon necessary motions.
But man directs the voluntary motions of his own actions.
And thus there are some things which have been created for this end, that in their services they should be subject to necessity, and should be unable to do aught else than what has been assigned to them; and when they have accomplished this service, the Creator of all things, who thus arranged them according to His will, preserves them. But there are other things, in which there is a power of will, and which have a free choice of doing what they will.
These, as I have said, do not remain always in that order in which they were created: but according as their will leads them, and the judgment of their mind inclines them, they effect either good or evil; and therefore He hath proposed rewards to those who do well, and penalties to those who do evil. [10]

Chapter XXV - "Who Hath Resisted His Will?"

You say, therefore, if God wishes anything to be, it is; and if He do not wish it, it is not.
But if I were to answer that what He wishes is, and what He wishes not is not, you would say that then He wishes the evil things to be which are done in the world, since everything that He wishes is, and everything that He wishes not is not.
But if I had answered that it is not so that what God wishes is, and what He wishes not is not, then you would retort upon me that God must then be powerless, if He cannot do what He wills; and you would be all the more petulant, as thinking that you had got a victory, though had said nothing to the point.
Therefore you are ignorant, O Simon, yea very ignorant, how the will of God acts in each individual case.
For some things, as we have said, He has so willed to be, that they cannot be otherwise than as they are ordained by Him; and to these He has assigned neither rewards nor punishments; but those which He has willed to be so that they have it in their power to do what they will, He has assigned to them according to their actions and their wills, to earn either rewards or punishments.
Since, therefore, as I have informed you, all things that are moved are divided into two parts, according to the distinction that I formerly stated, everything that God wills is, and everything that He wills not is not.

Chapter XXVI - No Goodness Without Liberty

To this Simon answered:
"Was not He able to make us all such that we should be good, and that we should not have it in our power to be otherwise?"
Peter answered:
"This also is an absurd question.
For if He had made us of an unchangeable nature and incapable of being moved away from good, we should not be really good, because we could not be aught else; and it would not be of our purpose that we were good; and what we did would not be ours, but of the necessity of our nature. [11]But how can that be called good which is not done of purpose? And on this account the world required long periods, until the number of souls which were predestined to fill it should be completed, and then that visible heaven should be folded up like a scroll, and that which is higher should appear, and the souls of the blessed, being restored to their bodies, should be ushered into light; but the souls of the wicked, for their impure actions being surrounded with fiery spirit, should be plunged into the abyss of unquenchable fire, to endure punishments through eternity.
Now that these things are so, the true Prophet. has testified to us; concerning whom, if you wish to

know that He is a prophet, I shall instruct you by innumerable declarations.

For of those things which were spoken by Him, even now everything that He said is being fulfilled; and those things which He spoke with respect to the future are believed to be about to be fulfilled, for faith is given to the future from those things which have already come to pass."

Chapter XXVII - The Visible Heaven

Why Made.

But Simon, perceiving that Peter was clearly assigning a reason from the head of prophecy, from which the whole question is settled, declined that the discourse should take this turn; and thus answered: "Give me an answer to the questions that I put, and tell me, if that visible heaven is, as you say, to be dissolved, why was it made at first?"

Peter answered:

"It was made for the sake of this present life of men, that there might be some sort of interposition and separation, lest any unworthy one might see the habitation of the celestials and the abode of God Himself, which are prepared in order to be seen by those only who are of pure heart. [12]But now, that is in the time of the conflict, it has pleased Him that those things be invisible, which are destined as a reward to the conquerors."

Then Simon said:

"If the Creator is good, and the world is good, how shall He who is good ever destroy that which is good?

But if He shall destroy that which is good, how shall He Himself be thought to be good?

But if He shall dissolve and destroy it as evil, how shall He not appear to be evil, who has made that which is evil?"

Chapter XXVIII - Why to Be Dissolved

To this Peter replied:

"Since we have promised not to run away from your blasphemies, we endure them patiently, for you shall yourself render an account for the things that you speak.

Listen now, therefore.

If indeed that heaven which is visible and transient had been made for its own sake, there would have been some reason in what you say, that it ought not to be dissolved.

But if it was made not for its own sake, but for the sake of something else, it must of necessity be dissolved, that that for which it seems to have been made may appear.

As I might say, by way of illustration, however fairly and carefully the shell of the egg may seem to have been formed, it is yet necessary that it be broken and opened, that the chick may issue from it, and that may appear for which the form of the whole egg seems to have been moulded.

So also, therefore, it is necessary that the condition of this world pass away, that that sublimer condition of the heavenly kingdom may shine forth."

Chapter XXIX - Corruptible and Temporary Things Made by the Incorruptible and Eternal

Then Simon:

"It does not seem to me that the heaven, which has been made by God, can be dissolved.

For things made by the Eternal One are eternal, while things made by a corruptible one are temporary and decaying."

Then Peter:

"It is not so.

Indeed corruptible and temporary things of all sorts are made by mortal creatures; but the Eternal does not always make things corruptible, nor always incorruptible; but according to the will of God the Creator, so will be the things which He creates.

For the power of God is not subject to law, but His will is law to His creatures."

Then Simon answered:

"I call you back to the first question.

You said now that God is visible to no one; but when that heaven shall be dissolved, and that superior condition of the heavenly kingdom shall shine forth, then those who are pure in heart [13] shall see God; which statement is contrary to the law, for there it is written that God said, None shall see my face and live.'" [14]

Chapter XXX - How the Pure in Heart See God

Then Peter answered:
"To those who do not read the law according to the tradition of Moses, my speech appears to be contrary to it; but I will show you how it is not contradictory.
God is seen by the mind, not by the body; by the spirit, not by the flesh.
Whence also angels, who are spirits, see God; and therefore men, as long as they are men, cannot see Him.
But after the resurrection of the dead, when they shall have been made like the angels, [15] they shall be able to see God.
And thus my statement is not contrary to the law; neither is that which our Master said, Blessed are they of a pure heart, for they shall see God.' [16]For He showed that a time shall come in which of men shall be made angels, who in the spirit of their mind shall see God." After these and many similar sayings, Simon began to assert with many oaths, saying:
"Concerning one thing only render me a reason, whether the soul is immortal, and I shall submit to your will in all things. But let it be to-morrow, for to-day it is late."
When therefore Peter began to speak, Simon went out, and with him a very few of his associates; and that for shame.
But all the rest, turning to Peter, on bended knees prostrated themselves before him; and some of those who were afflicted with diverse sicknesses, or invaded by demons, were healed by the prayer of Peter, and departed rejoicing, as having obtained at once the doctrine of the true God, and also His mercy. When therefore the crowds had withdrawn, and only we his attendants remained with him, we sat down on couches placed on the ground, each one recognising his accustomed place, and having taken food, and given thanks to God, we went to sleep.

Chapter XXXI - Diligence in Study

But on the following day, Peter, as usual, rising before dawn, found us already awake and ready to listen; and thus began:
"I entreat you, my brethren and fellow-servants, that if any of you is not able to wake, he should not torment himself through respect to my presence, because sudden change is difficult; but if for a long time one gradually accustoms himself, that will not be distressing which comes of use. For we had not all the same training; although in course of time we shall be able to be moulded into one habit, for they say that custom holds the place of a second nature.
But I call God to witness that I am not offended, if any one is not able to wake; but rather by this, if, when any one sleeps all through the night, he does not in the course of the day fulfil that which he omitted in the night.
For it is necessary to give heed intently and unceasingly, to the study of doctrine, that our mind may be filled with the thought of God only: because in the mind which is filled with the thought of God, no place will be given to the wicked one."

Chapter XXXII - Peter's Private Instruction

When Peter spoke thus to us, every one of us eagerly assured him, that ere now we were awake, being satisfied with short sleep, but that we were afraid to arouse him, because it did not become the disciples to command the master; "and yet even this, O Peter, we had almost ventured to take upon ourselves, because our hearts, agitated with longing for your words, drove sleep wholly from our eyes.
But again our affection towards you opposed it, and did not suffer us violently to rouse you." Then Peter said:
"Since therefore you assert that you are willingly awake through desire of hearing, I wish to repeat to you more carefully, and to explain in their order, the things that were spoken yesterday without arrangement.
And this I propose to do throughout these daily disputations, that by night, when privacy of time and place is afforded, I shall unfold in correct order, and by a straight line of explanation, anything that in the controversy has not been stated with sufficient fulness."
And then he began to point out to us how the yesterday's discussion ought to have been conducted, and how it could not be so conducted on account of the contentiousness or the unskilfulness of his

opponent; and how therefore he only made use of assertion, and only overthrew what was said by his adversary, but did not expound his own doctrines either completely or distinctly.

Then repeating the several matters to us, he discussed them in regular order and with full reason.

Chapter XXXIII - Learners and Cavillers

But when the day began to be light, after prayer he went out to the crowds and stood in his accustomed place, for the discussion; and seeing Simon standing in the middle of the crowd, he saluted the people in his usual way, and said to them:

"I confess that I am grieved with respect to some men, who come to us in this way that they may learn something, but when we begin to teach them, they profess that they themselves are masters, and while indeed they ask questions as ignorant persons, they contradict as knowing ones.

But perhaps some one will say, that he who puts a question, puts it indeed in order that he may learn, but when that which he hears does not seem to him to be right, it is necessary that he should answer, and that seems to be contradiction which is not contradiction, but further inquiry.

Chapter XXXIV - Against Order is Against Reason

"Let such a one then hear this:
The teaching of all doctrine has a certain order, and there are some things which must be delivered first, others in the second place, and others in the third, and so all in their order; and if these things be delivered in their order, they become plain; but if they be brought forward out of order, they will seem to be spoken against reason.

And therefore order is to be observed above all things, if we seek for the purpose of finding what we seek.

For he who enters rightly upon the road, will observe the second place in due order, and from the second will more easily find the third; and the further he proceeds, so much the more will the way of knowledge become open to him, even until he arrive at the city of truth, whither he is bound, and which he desires to reach.

But he who is unskilful, and knows not the way of inquiry, as a traveller in a foreign country, ignorant and wandering, if he will not employ a native of the country as a guide,--undoubtedly when he has strayed from the way of truth, shall remain outside the gates of life, and so, involved in the darkness of black night, shall walk through the paths of perdition.

Inasmuch therefore, as, if those things which are to be sought, be sought in an orderly manner, they can most easily be found, but the unskilful man is ignorant of the order of inquiry, it is right that the ignorant man should yield to the knowing one, and first learn the order of inquiry, that so at length he may find the method of asking and answering."

Chapter XXXV - Learning Before Teaching

To this Simon replied:
"Then truth is not the property of all, but of those only who know the art of disputation, which is absurd; for it cannot be, since He is equally the God of all, that all should not be equally able to know His will."

Then Peter:
"All were made equal by Him, and to all He has given equally to be receptive of truth.

But that none of those who are born, are born with education, but education is subsequent to birth, no one can doubt.

Since, therefore, the birth of men holds equity in this respect, that all are equally capable of receiving discipline, the difference is not in nature, but in education.

Who does not know that the things which any one learns, he was ignorant of before he learned them?"

Then Simon said "You say truly."

Then Peter said, "If then in those arts which are in common use, one first learns and then teaches, how much more ought those who profess to be the educators of souls, first to learn, and so to teach, that they may not expose themselves to ridicule, if they promise to afford knowledge to others, when they themselves are unskilful?"

Then Simon:
"This is true in respect of those arts which are in common use; but in the word of knowledge, as

soon as any one has heard, he has learned."

Chapter XXXVI - Self-Evidence of the Truth

Then said Peter:
"If indeed one hear in an orderly and regular manner he is able to know what is true; but he who refuses to submit to the rule of a reformed life and a pure conversation, which truly is the proper result of knowledge of the truth, will not confess that he knows what he does know.

For this is exactly what we see in the case of some who, abandoning the trades which they learned in their youth, betake themselves to other performances, and by way of excusing their own sloth, begin to find fault with the trade as unprofitable."

Then Simon:
"Ought all who hear to believe that whatever they hear is true?"

Then Peter:
"Whoever hears an orderly statement of the truth, cannot by any means gainsay it, but knows that what is spoken is true, provided he also willingly submit to the rules of life.

But those who, when they hear, are unwilling to betake themselves to good works, are prevented by the desire of doing evil from acquiescing in those things which they judge to be right.

Hence it is manifest that it is in the power of the hearers to choose which of the two they prefer.

But if all who hear were to obey, it would be rather a necessity of nature, leading all in one way.

For as no one can be persuaded to become shorter or taller, because the force of nature does not permit it; so also, if either all were converted to the truth by a word, or all were not converted, it would be the force of nature which compelled all in the one case, and none at all in the other, to be converted."

Chapter XXXVII - God Righteous as Well as Good

Then said Simon:
"Inform us, therefore, what he who desires to know the truth must first learn."

Then Peter:
"Before all things it must be inquired what it is possible for man to find out.

For of necessity the judgment of God turns upon this, if a man was able to do good and did it not.

And therefore men must inquire whether they have it in their power by seeking to find what is good, and to do it when they have found it; for this is that for which they are to be judged.

But more than this there is no occasion for any one but a prophet to know: for what is the need for men to know how the world was made?

This, indeed, would be necessary to be learned if we had to enter upon a similar construction.

But now it is sufficient for us, in order to the worship of God, to know that He made the world; but how He made it is no subject of inquiry for us, because, as I have said, it is not incumbent upon us to acquire the knowledge of that art, as though we were about to make something similar.

But neither are we to be judged for this, why we have not learned how the world was made, but only for that, if we be without knowledge of its Creator.

For we shall know that the Creator of the world is the righteous and good God, if we seek Him in the paths of righteousness.

For if we only know regarding Him that He is good, such knowledge is not sufficient for salvation.

For in the present life not only the worthy, but also the unworthy, enjoy His goodness and His benefits.

But if we believe Him to be not only good, but also righteous, and if, according to what we believe concerning God, we observe righteousness in the whole course of our life, we shall enjoy His goodness for ever.

In a word, to the Hebrews, whose opinion concerning God was that He is only good, our Master said that they should seek also His righteousness; [17] that is, that they should know that He is good indeed in this present time, that all may live in His goodness, but that He shall be righteous at the day of judgment, to bestow eternal rewards upon the worthy, from which the unworthy shall be excluded.

Chapter XXXVIII - God's Justice Shown at the Day of Judgment

Then Simon:
"How can one and the same being be both good and righteous?" [18]Peter answered:
"Because without righteousness, goodness would be unrighteousness; for it is the part of a good God to bestow His sunshine and rain equally on the just and the unjust; [19] but this would seem to be unjust, if He treated the good and the bad always with equal fortune, and were it not that He does it for the sake of the fruits, which all may equally enjoy who are born in this world. But as the rain given by God equally nourishes the corn and the tares, but at the time of harvest the crops are gathered into the barn, but the chaff or the tares are burnt in the fire, [20] so in the day of judgment, when the righteous shall be introduced into the kingdom of heaven, and the unrighteous shall be cast out, then also the justice of God shall be shown.

For if He remained for ever alike to the evil and the good, this would not only not be good, but even unrighteous and unjust; that the righteous and the unrighteous should be held by Him in one order of desert."

Chapter XXXIX - Immortality of the Soul

Then said Simon:
"The one point on which I should wish to be satisfied is, whether the soul is immortal; for I cannot take up the burden of righteousness unless I know first concerning the immortality of the soul; for indeed if it is not immortal, the profession of your preaching cannot stand."
Then said Peter:
"Let us first inquire whether God is just; for if this were ascertained, the perfect order of religion would straight-way be established."
Then Simon:
"With all your boasting of your knowledge of the order of discussion, you seem to me now to have answered contrary to order; for when I ask you to show whether the soul is immortal, you say that we must first inquire whether God is just."
Then said Peter:
"That is perfectly right and regular."
Simon:
"I should wish to learn how."

Chapter XL - Proved by the Success of the Wicked in This Life

"Listen, then," said Peter:
"Some men who are blasphemers against God, and who spend their whole life in injustice and pleasure die in their own bed and obtain honourable burial; while others who worship God, and maintain their life frugally with all honesty and sobriety, die in deserted places for their observance of righteousness, so that they are not even thought worthy of burial.

Where, then, is the justice of God, if there be no immortal soul to suffer punishment in the future for impious deeds, or enjoy rewards for piety and rectitude?"
Then Simon said:
"It is this indeed that makes me incredulous, because many well-doers perish miserably, and again many evil-doers finish long lives in happiness." [21]

Chapter XLI - Cavils of Simon

Then said Peter:
"This very thing which draws you into incredulity, affords to us a certain conviction that there shall be a judgment.

For since it is certain that God is just, it is a necessary consequence that there is another world, in which every one receiving according to his deserts, shall prove the justice of God.

But if all men were now receiving according to their deserts, we should truly seem to be deceivers when we say that there is a judgment to come; and therefore this very fact, that in the present life a return is not made to every one according to his deeds, affords, to those who know that God is just, an indubitable proof that there shall be a judgment."

Then said Simon:

"Why, then, am I not persuaded of it?"

Peter:

"Because you have not heard the true Prophet saying, Seek first His righteousness, and all these things shall be added to you.' [22]"Then said Simon: "Pardon me if I am unwilling to seek righteousness, before I know if the soul is immortal."

Then Peter:

"You also pardon me this one thing, because I cannot do otherwise than the Prophet of truth has instructed me."

Then said Simon:

"It is certain that you cannot assert that the soul is immortal, and therefore you cavil, knowing that if it be proved to be mortal, the whole profession of that religion which you are attempting to propagate will be plucked up by the roots. And therefore, indeed, I commend your prudence, while I do not approve your persuasiveness; for you persuade many to embrace your religion, and to submit to the restraint of pleasure, in hope of future good things; to whom it happens that they lose the enjoyment of things present, and are deceived with hopes of things future.

For as soon as they die, their soul shall at the same time be extinguished."

Chapter XLII - "Full of All Subtlety and All Mischief."

But Peter, when he heard him speak thus, grinding his teeth, and rubbing his forehead with his hand, and sighing with profound grief, said: [23]"Armed with the cunning of the old serpent, you stand forth to deceive souls; and therefore, as the serpent is more subtile than any other beast, you profess that you are a teacher from the beginning.

And again, like the serpent you wished to introduce many gods; but now, being confuted in that, you assert that there is no God at all.

For by occasion of I know not what unknown God, you denied that the Creator of the world is God, but asserted that He is either an evil being, or that He has many equals, or, as we have said, that He is not God at all.

And when you had been overcome in this position, you now assert that the soul is mortal, so that men may not live righteously and uprightly in hope of things to come.

For if there be no hope for the future, why should not mercy be given up, and men indulge in luxury and pleasures, from which it is manifest that all unrighteousness springs?

And while you introduce so impious a doctrine into the miserable life of men, you call yourself pious, and me impious, because, under the hope of future good things, I will not suffer men to take up arms and fight against one another, plunder and subvert everything, and attempt whatsoever lust may dictate.

And what will be the condition of that life which you would introduce, that men will attack and be attacked, be enraged and disturbed, and live always in fear?

For those who do evil to others must expect like evil to themselves.

Do you see that you are a leader of disturbance and not of peace, of iniquity and not of equity?

But I feigned anger, not because I could not prove that the soul is immortal, but because I pity the souls which you are endeavouring to deceive.

I shall speak, therefore, but not as compelled by you; for I know how I should speak; and you will be the only one who wants not so much persuasion as admonition on this subject.

But those who are really ignorant of this, I shall instruct as is suitable."

Chapter XLIII - Simon's Subterfuges

Then says Simon:
"If you are angry, I shall neither ask you any questions, nor do I wish to hear you."
Then Peter:
"If you are now seeking a pretext for escaping, you have full liberty, and need not use any special pretext.
For all have heard you speaking all amiss, and have perceived that you can prove nothing, but that you only asked questions for the sake of contradiction; which any one can do.
For what difficulty is there in replying, after the clearest proofs have been adduced, You have said nothing to the purpose?'
But that you may know that I am able to prove to you in a single sentence that the soul is immortal, I shall ask you with respect to a point which all know; answer me, and I shall prove to you in one sentence that it is immortal."
Then Simon, who had thought that he had got, from the anger of Peter, a pretext for departing, stopped on account of the remarkable promise that was made to him, and said:
"Ask me then, and I shall answer you what all know, that I may hear in a single sentence, as you have promised, how the soul is immortal."

Chapter XLIV - Sight or Hearing?

Then Peter:
"I shall speak so that it may be proved to you before all the rest.
Answer me, therefore, which of the two can better persuade an incredulous man, seeing or hearing?"
Then Simon said:
"Seeing." Then Peter:
"Why then do you wish to learn from me by words, what is proved to you by the thing itself and by sight?"
Then Simon:
"I know not what you mean."
Then Peter:
"If you do not know, go now to your house, and entering the inner bed-chamber you will see an image placed, containing the figure of a murdered boy clothed in purple; ask him, and he will inform you either by hearing or seeing.
For what need is there to hear from him if the soul is immortal, when you see it standing before you?
For if it were not in being, it assuredly could not be seen.
But if you know not what image I speak of, let us straightway go to your house, with ten other men, of those who are here present." [24]

Chapter XLV - A Home-Thrust

But Simon hearing this, and being smitten by his conscience, changed colour and became bloodless; for he was afraid, if he denied it, that his house would be searched, or that Peter in his indignation would betray him more openly, and so all would learn what he was.
Thus he answered:
"I beseech thee, Peter, by that good God who is in thee, to overcome the wickedness that is in me.
Receive me to repentance, and you shall have me as an assistant in your preaching.
For now I have learned in very deed that you are a prophet of the true God, and therefore you alone know the secret and hidden things of men." [25] Then said Peter:
"You see, brethren, Simon seeking repentance; in a little while you shall see him returning again to his infidelity.
For, thinking that I am a prophet, forasmuch as I have disclosed his wickedness, which he supposed to be secret and hidden, he has promised that he will repent.
But it is not lawful for me to lie, nor must I deceive, whether this infidel be saved or not saved.
For I call heaven and earth to witness, that I spoke not by a prophetic spirit what I said, and what I intimated, as far as was possible, to the listening crowds; but I learned from some who once were his associates in his works, but have now been converted to our faith, what things he did in secret.

Therefore I spoke what I knew, not what I foreknew."

Chapter XLVI - Simon's Rage

But when Simon heard this, he assailed Peter with curses and reproaches, saying:
"Oh most wicked and most deceitful of men, to whom fortune, not truth, hath given the victory.

But I sought repentance not for defect of knowledge, but in order that you, thinking that by repentance I should become your disciple, might entrust to me all the secrets of your profession, and so at length, knowing them all, I might confute you.

But as you cunningly understood for what reason I had pretended penitence, and acquiesced as if you did not understand my stratagem, that you might first expose me in presence of the people as unskilful, then foreseeing that being thus exposed to the people, I must of necessity be indignant, and confess that I was not truly penitent, you anticipated me, that you might say, that I should, after my penitence, again return to my infidelity, that you might seem to have conquered on all sides, both if I continued in the penitence which I had professed, and if I did not continue; and so you should be believed to be wise, because you had foreseen these things, while I should seem to be deceived, because I did not foresee your trick.

But you foreseeing mine, have used subtlety and circumvented me.

But, as I said, your victory is the result of fortune, not of truth:

yet I know why I did not foresee this; because I stood by you and spoke with you in my goodness, and bore patiently with you.

But now I shall show you the power of my divinity, so that you shall quickly fall down and worship me."

Chapter XLVII - Simon's Vaunt

"I am the first power, who am always, and without beginning. [26] But having entered the womb of Rachel, I was born of her as a man, that I might be visible to men.

I have flown through the air; I have been mixed with fire, and been made one body with it; I have made statues to move; I have animated lifeless things; I have made stones bread; I have flown from mountain to mountain; I have moved from place to place, upheld by angels' hands, and have lighted on the earth.

Not only have I done these things; but even now I am able to do them, that by facts I may prove to all, that I am the Son of God, enduring to eternity, and that I can make those who believe on me endure in like manner for ever.

But your words are all vain; nor can you perform any real works such as I have now mentioned, as he also who sent you is a magician, who yet could not deliver himself from the suffering of the cross."

Chapter XLVIII - Attempts to Create a Disturbance

To this speech of Simon, Peter answered:
"Do not meddle with the things that belong to others; for that you are a magician, you have confessed and made manifest by the very deeds that you have done; but our Master, who is the Son of God and of man, is manifestly good; and that he is truly the Son of God has been told, and shall be told to those to whom it is fitting.

But if you will not confess that you are a magician, let us go, with all this multitude, to your house, and then it will be evident who is a magician."

While Peter was speaking thus, Simon began to assail him with blasphemies and curses, that he might make a riot, and excite all so that he could not be refuted, and that Peter, withdrawing on account of his blasphemy, might seem to be overcome.

But he stood fast, and began to charge him more vehemently.

The Epistles of Clement
Chapter XLIX - Simon's Retreat

Then the people in indignation cast Simon from the court, and drove him forth from the gate of the house; and only one person followed him when he was driven out. [27]Then silence being obtained, Peter began to address the people in this manner:

"You ought, brethren, to bear with wicked men patiently; knowing that although God could cut them off, yet He suffers them to remain even till the day appointed, in which judgment shall pass upon all.

Why then should not we bear with those whom God suffers?

Why should not we bear with fortitude the wrongs that they do to us, when He who is almighty does not take vengeance on them, that both His own goodness and the impiety of the wicked may be known?

But if the wicked one had not found Simon to be his minister, he would doubtless have found another:

for it is of necessity that in this life offences come, but woe to that man by whom they come;[128] and therefore Simon is rather to be mourned over, because he has become a choice vessel for the wicked one, which undoubtedly would not have happened had he not received power over him for his former sins.

For why should I further say that he once believed in our Jesus, and was persuaded that souls are immortal? [29]Although in this he is deluded by demons, yet he has persuaded himself that he has the soul of a murdered boy ministering to him in whatever he pleases to employ it in; in which truly, as I have said, he is deluded by demons, and therefore I spoke to him according to his own ideas:

for he has learned from the Jews, that judgment and vengeance are to be brought forth against those who set themselves against the true faith, and do not repent.

But here are men to whom, as being perfect in crimes, the wicked one appears, that he may deceive them, so that they may never be turned to repentance.

Chapter L - Peter's Benediction

"You therefore who are turned to the Lord by repentance, bend to Him your knees."

When he had said this, all the multitude bent their knees to God; and Peter, looking towards heaven, prayed for them with tears that God, for His goodness, would deign to receive those betaking themselves to Him.

And after he had prayed and had instructed them to meet early the next day, he dismissed the multitude.

Then according to custom, having taken food, we went to sleep.

Chapter LI - Peter's Accessibility

Peter, therefore, rising at the usual hour of the night, found us waking; and when, saluting us, in his usual manner, he had taken his seat, first of all Niceta, said:

"If you will permit me, my lord Peter, I have something to ask of you."

Then Peter said:

"I permit not only you, but all, and not only now, but always, that every one confess what moves him, and the part in his mind that is pained, in order that he may obtain healing.

For things which are covered with silence, and are not made known to us, are cured with difficulty, like maladies of long standing; and therefore, since the medicine of seasonable and necessary discourse cannot easily be applied to those who keep silence, every one ought to declare in what respect his mind is feeble through ignorance.

But to him who keeps silence, it belongs to God alone to give a remedy.

We indeed also can do it, but by the lapse of a long time.

For it is necessary than the discourse of doctrine, proceeding in order from the beginning, and meeting each single question, should disclose all things, and resolve and reach to all things, even to that which every one required in his mind; but that, as I have said, can only be done in the course of a long time. Now, then, ask what you please."

Chapter LII - False Signs and Miracles

Then Niceta said:
"I give you abundant thanks, O most clement Peter; but this is what I desire to learn, how Simon, who is the enemy of God, is able to do such and so great things?
For indeed he told no lie in his declaration of what he has done."
To this the blessed Peter thus answered:
"God, who is one and true, has resolved to prepare good and faithful friends for His first begotten; but knowing that none can be good, unless they have in their power that perception by which they may become good, that they may be of their own intent what they choose to be,--and otherwise they could not be truly good, if they were kept in goodness not by purpose, but by necessity,--has given to every one the power of his own will, that he may be what he wishes to be.
And again, foreseeing that that power of will would make some choose good things and others evil, and so that the human race would necessarily be divided into two classes, He has permitted each class to choose both a place and a king, whom they would.
For the good King rejoices in the good, and the wicked one in the evil.
And although I have expounded those things more fully to you, O Clement, in that treatise in which I discoursed on predestination and the end, yet it is fitting that I should now make clear to Niceta also, as he asks me, what is the reason than Simon, whose thoughts are against God, is able to do so great marvels.

Chapter LIII - Self-Love the Foundation of Goodness

"First of all, then, he is evil, in the judgment of God, who will not inquire what is advantageous to himself.
For how can any one love another, if he does not love himself?
Or to whom will that man not be an enemy, who cannot be a friend to himself?
In order, therefore, that there might be a distinction between those who choose good and those who choose evil, God has concealed that which is profitable to men, i.e., the possession of the kingdom of heaven, and has laid it up and hidden it as a secret treasure, so that no one can easily attain it by his own power or knowledge.
Yet He has brought the report of it, under various names and opinions, through successive generations, to the hearing of all:
so that whosoever should be lovers of good, hearing it, might inquire and discover what is profitable and salutary to them; but that they should ask it, not from themselves, but from Him who has hidden it, and should pray that access and the way of knowledge might be given to them:
which way is opened to those only who love it above all the good things of this world; and on no other condition can any one even understand it, however wise he may seem; but that those who neglect to inquire what is profitable and salutary to themselves, as self-haters and self-enemies, should be deprived of its good things, as lovers of evil things.

Chapter LIV - God to Be Supremely Loved

"It behoves, therefore, the good to love that way above all things, that is, above riches, glory, rest, parents, relatives, friends, and everything in the world.
But he who perfectly loves this possession of the kingdom of heaven, will undoubtedly cast away all practice of evil habit, negligence, sloth, malice, anger, and such like.
For if you prefer any of these to it, as loving the vices of your own lust more than God, you shall not attain to the possession of the heavenly kingdom; for truly it is foolish to love anything more than God.
For whether they be parents, they die; or relatives, they do not continue; or friends, they change.
But God alone is eternal, and abideth unchangeable.
He, therefore, who will not seek after that which is profitable to himself, is evil, to such an extent that his wickedness exceeds the very prince of impiety.
For he abuses the goodness of God to the purpose of his own wickedness, and pleases himself; but the other neglects the good things of his own salvation, that by his own destruction he may please the evil one."

Chapter LV - Ten Commandments Corresponding to the Plagues of Egypt

"On account of those, therefore, who by neglect of their own salvation please the evil one, and those who by study of their own profit seek to please the good One, ten things have been prescribed as a test to this present age, according to the number of the ten plagues which were brought upon Egypt.

For when Moses, according to the commandment of God, demanded of Pharaoh that he should let the people go, and in token of his heavenly commission showed signs, his rod being thrown upon the ground was turned into a serpent. [30]And when Pharaoh could not by these means be brought to consent, as having freedom of will, again the magicians seemed to do similar signs, by permission of God, that the purpose of the king might be proved from the freedom of his will, whether he would rather believe the signs wrought by Moses, who was sent by God, or those which the magicians rather seemed to work than actually wrought.

For truly he ought to have understood from their very name that they were not workers of truth, because they were not called messengers of God, but magicians, as the tradition also intimates.

Moreover, they seemed to maintain the contest up to a certain point, and afterwards they confessed of themselves, and yielded to their superior. [31]Therefore the last plague is inflicted, [32] the destruction of the first-born, and then Moses is commanded to consecrate the people by the sprinkling of blood; and so, gifts being presented, with much entreaty he is asked to depart with the people.

Chapter LVI - Simon Resisted Peter, as the Magicians Moses

"In a similar transaction I see that I am even now engaged.

For as then, when Moses exhorted the king to believe God, the magicians opposed him by a pretended exhibition of similar signs, and so kept back the unbelievers from salvation; so also now, when I have come forth to teach all nations to believe in the true God, Simon the magician resists me, acting in opposition to me, as they also did in opposition to Moses; in order that whosoever they be from among the nations that do not use sound judgment, they may be made manifest; but that those may be saved who rightly distinguish signs from signs." While Peter thus spoke, Niceta answered:

"I beseech you that you would permit me to state whatever occurs to my mind."

Then Peter, being delighted with the eagerness of his disciples, said:

"Speak what you will."

Chapter LVII - Miracles of the Magicians

Then said Niceta:

"In what respect did the Egyptians sin in not believing Moses, since the magicians wrought like signs, even although they were done rather in appearance than in truth?

For if I had been there then, should I not have thought, from the fact that the magicians did like things to those which Moses did, either that Moses was a magician, or that the magicians wrought their signs by divine commission?

For I should not have thought it likely that the same things could be effected by magicians, even in appearance, which he who was sent by God performed.

And now, in what respect do they sin who believe Simon, since they see him do so great marvels?

Or is it not marvellous to fly through the air, to be so mixed with fire as to become one body with it, to make statues walk, brazen dogs bark, and other such like things, which assuredly are sufficiently wonderful to those who know not how to distinguish?

Yea, he has also been seen to make bread of stones.

But if he sins who believes those who do signs, how shall it appear that he also does not sin who has believed our Lord for His signs and works of power?"

Chapter LVIII - Truth Veiled with Love

Then said Peter:
"I take it well that you bring the truth to the rule, and do not suffer hindrances of faith to lurk in your soul.
For thus you can easily obtain the remedy.
Do you remember that I said, that the worst of all things is when any one neglects to learn what is for his good?"
Niceta answered:
"I remember."
Then Peter:
"And again, that God has veiled His truth, that He may disclose it to those who faithfully follow Him?"
"Neither," said Niceta, "have I forgotten this."
Then said Peter:
"What think you then?
That God has buried His truth deep in the earth, and has heaped mountains upon it, that it may be found by those only who are able to dig down into the depths? It is not so; but as He has surrounded the mountains and the earth with the expanse of heaven, so hath He veiled the truth with the curtain of His own love, that he alone may be able to reach it, who has first knocked at the gate of divine love.

Chapter LIX - Good and Evil in Pairs

"For, as I was beginning to say, [33] God has appointed for this world certain pairs; and he who comes first of the pairs is of evil, he who comes second, of good.
And in this is given to every man an occasion of right judgment, whether he is simple or prudent.
For if he is simple, and believes him who comes first, though moved thereto by signs and prodigies, he must of necessity, for the same reason, believe him who comes second; for he will be persuaded by signs and prodigies, as he was before.
When he believes this second one, he will learn from him that he ought not to believe the first, who comes of evil; and so the error of the former is corrected by the emendation of the latter. But if he will not receive the second, because he has believed the first, he will deservedly be condemned as unjust; for unjust it is, that when he believed the first on account of his signs, he will not believe the second, though he bring the same, or even greater signs. But if he has not believed the first, it follows that he may be moved to believe the second.
For his mind has not become so completely inactive but that it may be roused by the redoubling of marvels.
But if he is prudent, he can make distinction of the signs.
And if indeed he has believed in the first, he will be moved to the second by the increase in the miracles, and by comparison he will apprehend which are better; although clear tests of miracles are recognised by all learned men, as we have shown in the regular order of our discussion.
But if any one, as being whole and not needing a physician, is not moved to the first, he will be drawn to the second by the very continuance of the thing, and will make a distinction of signs and marvels after this fashion;--he who is of the evil one, the signs that he works do good to no one; but those which the good man worketh are profitable to men."

Chapter LX - Uselessness of Pretended Miracles

"For tell me, I pray you, what is the use of showing statues walking, dogs of brass or stone barking, mountains dancing, of flying through the air, and such like things, which you say that Simon did?
But those signs which are of the good One, are directed to the advantage of men, as are those which were done by our Lord, who gave sight to the blind and hearing to the deaf, raised up the feeble and the lame, drove away sicknesses and demons, raised the dead, and did other like things, as you see also that I do.
Those signs, therefore, which make for the benefit of men, and confer some good upon them, the wicked one cannot do, excepting only at the end of the world.
For then it shall be permitted him to mix up with his signs some good ones, as the expelling of demons or the healing of diseases; by this means going beyond his bounds, and being divided against

The Epistles of Clement

himself, and fighting against himself, he shall be destroyed.

And therefore the Lord has foretold, that in the last times there shall be such temptation, that, if it be possible, the very elect shall be deceived; that is to say, that by the marks of signs being confused, even those must be disturbed who seem to be expert in discovering spirits and distinguishing miracles.

Chapter LXI - Ten Pairs

"The ten pairs [34] of which we have spoken have therefore been assigned to this world from the beginning of time.

Cain and Abel were one pair.

The second was the giants and Noah; the third, Pharaoh and Abraham; the fourth, the Philistines and Isaac; the fifth, Esau and Jacob; the sixth, the magicians and Moses the lawgiver; the seventh, the tempter and the Son of man; the eighth, Simon and I, Peter; the ninth, all nations, and he who shall be sent to sow the word among the nations; the tenth, Antichrist and Christ.

Concerning these pairs we shall give you fuller information at another time."

When Peter spoke thus, Aquila said:

"Truly there is need of constant teaching, that one may learn what is true about everything."

Chapter LXII - The Christian Life

But Peter said:

"Who is he that is earnest toward instruction, and that studiously inquires into every particular, except him who loves his own soul to salvation, and renounces all the affairs of this world, that he may have leisure to attend to the word of God only?

Such is he whom alone the true Prophet deems wise, even he who sells all that he has and buys the one true pearl, [35] who understands what is the difference between temporal things and eternal, small and great, men and God.

For he understands what is the eternal hope in presence of the true and good God.

But who is he that loves God, save him who knows His wisdom?

And how can any one obtain knowledge of God's wisdom, unless he be constant in hearing His word?

Whence it comes, that he conceives a love for Him, and venerates Him with worthy honour, pouring out hymns and prayers to Him, and most pleasantly resting in these, accounteth it his greatest damage if at any time he speak or do aught else even for a moment of time; because, in reality, the soul which is filled with the love of God can neither look upon anything except what pertains to God, nor, by reason of love of Him, can be satisfied with meditating upon those things which it knows to be pleasing to Him.

But those who have not conceived affection for Him, nor bear His love lighted up in their mind, are as it were placed in darkness and cannot see light; and therefore, even before they begin to learn anything of God, they immediately faint as though worn out by labour; and filled with weariness, they are straightway hurried by their own peculiar habits to those words with which they are pleased. For it is wearisome and annoying to such persons to hear anything about God; and that for the reason I have stated, because their mind has received no sweetness of divine love."

Chapter LXIII - A Deserter from Simon's Camp

While Peter was thus speaking, the day dawned; and, behold, one of the disciples of Simon came, crying out: [36]"I beseech thee, O Peter, receive me, a wretch, who have been deceived by Simon the magician, to whom I gave heed as to a heavenly God, by reason of those miracles which I saw him perform.

But when I heard your discourses, I began to think him a man, and indeed a wicked man; nevertheless, when he went out from this I alone followed him, for I had not yet clearly perceived his impieties.

But when he saw me following him, he called me blessed, and led me to his house; and about the middle of the night he said to me, I shall make you better than all men, if you will remain with me even till the end.'

When I had promised him this, he demanded of me an oath of perseverance; and having got this, he placed upon my shoulders some of his polluted and accursed secret things, that I might carry them, and ordered me to follow him.

But when we came to the sea, he went aboard a boat which happened to be there, and took from my neck what he had ordered me to carry.

And as he came out a little after, bringing nothing with him, he must have thrown it into the sea.

Then he asked me to go with him, saying that he was going to Rome, and that there he would please the people so much, that he should be reckoned a god, and publicly gifted with divine honours.

Then,' said he, if you wish to return hither, I shall send you back, loaded with all riches, and upheld by various services.'

When I heard this, and saw nothing in him in accordance with this profession, but perceived that he was a magician and a deceiver, I answered:

Pardon me, I pray you; for I have a pain in my feet, and therefore I am not able to leave Caesarea. Besides, I have a wife and little children, whom I cannot leave by any means.'

When he heard this, he charged me with sloth, and set out towards Dora, saying, You will be sorry, when you hear what glory I shall get in the city of Rome.'

And after this he set out for Rome, as he said; but I hastily returned hither, entreating you to receive me to penitence, because I have been deceived by him."

Chapter LXIV - Declaration of Simon's Wickedness

When he who had returned from Simon had thus spoken, Peter ordered him to sit down in the court.

And he himself going forth, and seeing immense crowds, far more than on the previous days, stood in his usual place; and pointing out him who had come, began to discourse as follows:

"This man whom I point out to you, brethren, has just come to me, telling me of the wicked practices of Simon, and how he has thrown the implements of his wickedness into the sea, not induced to do so by repentance, but being afraid lest, being detected, he should be subjected to the public laws.

And he asked this man, as he tells me, to remain with him, promising him immense gifts; and when he could not persuade him to do so, he left him, reproaching him for sluggishness, and set out for Rome."

When Peter had intimated this to the crowd, the man himself who had returned from Simon stood up, and began to state to the people everything relating to Simon's crimes.

And when they were shocked by the things which they heard that Simon had done by his magical acts, Peter said: [37]

Chapter LXV - Peter Resolves to Follow Simon

"Be not, my brethren, distressed by those things that have been done, but give heed to the future: for what is passed is ended; but the things which threaten are dangerous to those who shall fall in with them.

For offences shall never be wanting in this world, [38] so long as the enemy is permitted to act according to his will; in order that the prudent and those who understood his wiles may be conquerors in the contests which he raises against them; but that those who neglect to learn the things that pertain to the salvation of their souls, may be taken by him with merited deceptions.

Since, therefore, as you have heard, Simon has gone forth to preoccupy the ears of the Gentiles who are called to salvation, it is necessary that I also follow upon his track, so that whatever disputations he raises may be corrected by us. But inasmuch as it is right that greater anxiety should be felt concerning you who are already received within the walls of life,--for if that which has been actually acquired perish, a positive loss is sustained; while with respect to that which has not yet been acquired, if it can be got, there is so much gain; but if not, the only loss is that there is no gain;--in order, therefore, that you may be more and more confirmed in the truth, and the nations who are called to salvation may in no way be prevented by the wickedness of Simon, I have thought good to ordain Zacchaeus as pastor over you, [39] and to remain with you myself for three months; and so to go to the Gentiles, lest through our delaying longer, and the crimes of Simon stalking in every direction, they should become incurable."

The Epistles of Clement

Chapter LXVI - Zacchaeus Made Bishop of Caesarea; Presbyters and Deacons Ordained

At this announcement all the people wept, hearing that he was going to leave them; and Peter, sympathizing with them, himself also shed tears; and looking up to heaven, he said:

"To Thee, O God, who hast made heaven and earth, and all things that are in them, we pour out the prayer of supplication, that Thou wouldest comfort those who have recourse to Thee in their tribulation.

For by reason of the affection that they have towards Thee, they do love me who have declared to them Thy truth.

Wherefore guard them with the right hand of Thy compassion; for neither Zacchaeus nor any other man can be a sufficient guardian to them."

When he had said this, and more to the same effect, he laid his hands upon Zacchaeus, and prayed that he might blamelessly discharge the duty of his bishopric.

Then he ordained twelve presbyters and four deacons, and said:

"I have ordained you this Zacchaeus as a bishop, knowing that he has the fear of God, and is expert in the Scriptures. You ought therefore to honour him as holding the place of Christ, obeying him for your salvation, and knowing that whatever honour and whatever injury is done to him, redounds to Christ, and from Christ to God.

Hear him therefore with all attention, and receive from him the doctrine of the faith; and from the presbyters the monitions of life; and from the deacons the order of discipline.

Have a religious care of widows; vigorously assist orphans; take pity on the poor; teach the young modesty;--and in a word, sustain one another as circumstances shall demand; worship God, who created heaven and earth; believe in Christ; love one another; be compassionate to all; and fulfil charity not only in word, but in act and deed."

Chapter LXVII - Invitation to Baptism

When he had given them these and such like precepts, he made proclamation to the people, saying:

"Since I have resolved to stay three months with you, if any one desires it, let him be baptized; that, stripped of his former evils, he may for the future, in consequence of his own conduct, become heir of heavenly blessings, as a reward for his good actions.

Whosoever will, then, let him come to Zacchaeus and give his name to him, and let him hear from him the mysteries of the kingdom of heaven.

Let him attend to frequent fastings, and approve himself in all things, that at the end of these three months he may be baptized on the day of the festival.

But every one of you shall be baptized in ever flowing waters, the name of the Trine Beatitude being invoked over him; he being first anointed with oil sanctified by prayer, that so at length, being consecrated by these things, he may attain a perception of holy things." [40]

Chapter LXVIII - Twelve Sent Before Him

And when he had spoken at length on the subject of baptism, he dismissed the crowd, and betook himself to his usual place of abode; and there, while the twelve stood around him (viz. Zacchaeus and Sophonias, Joseph and Michaeus, Eleazar and Phineas, Lazarus and Eliseus, I Clement and Nicodemus, Niceta and Aquila), he addressed us to the following effect:

"Let us, my brethren, consider what is right; for it is our duty to bring some help to the nations, which are called to salvation.

You have yourselves heard that Simon has set out, wishing to anticipate our journey.

Him we should have followed step by step, that wheresoever he tries to subvert any, we might immediately confute him.

But since it appears to me to be unjust to forsake those who have been already converted to God, and to bestow our care upon those who are still afar off, I think it right that I should remain three months with those in this city who have been turned to the faith, and should strengthen them; and yet that we should not neglect those who are still far off, lest haply, if they be long infected with the power of pernicious doctrine, it be more difficult to recover them. Therefore I wish (only, however, if you also think it right), that for Zacchaeus, whom we have now ordained bishop, Benjamin the son of Saba be substituted; and for Clement (whom I have resolved to have always by me, because, coming from the

Gentiles, he has a great desire to hear the word of God) there be substituted Ananias the son of Safra; and for Niceta and Aquila, who have been but lately converted to the faith of Christ, Rubelus the brother of Zacchaeus, and Zacharias the builder.

I wish, therefore, to complete the number of twelve by substituting these four for the other four, that Simon may feel that I in them am always with him." [41]

Chapter LXIX - Arrangements Approved by All the Brethren

Having therefore separated me, Clement, and Niceta and Aquila, he said to those twelve:

"I wish you the day after to-morrow to proceed to the Gentiles, and to follow in the footsteps of Simon, that you may inform me of all his proceedings.

You will also inquire diligently the sentiments of every one, and announce to them that I shall come to them without delay; and, in short, in all places instruct the Gentiles to expect my coming."

When he had spoken these things, and others to the same effect, he said:

"You also, my brethren, if you have anything to say to these things, say on, lest haply it be not right which seems good to me alone."

Then all, with one voice applauding him, said:

"We ask you rather to arrange everything according to your own judgment, and to order what seems good to yourself; for this we think to be the perfect work of piety, if we fulfil what you command."

Chapter LXX - Departure of the Twelve

Therefore, on the day appointed, when they had ranged themselves before Peter, they said:

"Do not think, O Peter, that it is a small grief to us that we are to be deprived of the privilege of hearing you for three months; but since it is good for us to do what you order, we shall most readily obey.

We shall always retain in our hearts the remembrance of your face; and so we set out actively, as you have commanded us."

Then he, having poured out a prayer to the Lord for them, dismissed them. And when those twelve who had been sent forward had gone, Peter entered, according to custom, and stood in the place of disputation. And a multitude of people had come together, even a larger number than usual; and all with tears gazed upon him, by reason of what they had heard from him the day before, that he was about to go forth on account of Simon.

Then, seeing them weeping, he himself also was similarly affected, although he endeavoured to conceal and to restrain his tears.

But the trembling of his voice, and the interruption of his discourse, betrayed that he was distressed by similar emotion.

Chapter LXXI - Peter Prepares the Caesareans for His Departure

However, rubbing his forehead with his hand, he said:

"Be of good courage, my brethren, and comfort your sorrowful hearts by means of counsel, referring all things to God, whose will alone is to be fulfilled and to be preferred in all things.

For let us suppose for a moment, that by reason of the affection that we have towards you, we should act against His will, and remain with you, is He not able, by sending death upon me, to appoint to me a longer separation from you? And therefore it is better for us to carry out this shorter separation with His will, as those to whom it is prescribed to obey God in all things.

Hence you also ought to obey Him with like submission, inasmuch as you love me from no other reason than on account of your love of Him.

As friends of God, therefore, acquiesce in His will; but also judge yourselves what is right.

Would it not have seemed wicked, if, when Simon was deceiving you, I had been detained by the brethren in Jerusalem, and had not come to you, and that although you had Zacchaeus among you, a good and eloquent man?

So now also consider that it would be wicked, if, when Simon has gone forth to assail the Gentiles, who are wholly without a defender, I should be detained by you, and should not follow him.

Wherefore let us see to it, that we do not, by an unreasonable affection, accomplish the will of the wicked one."

Chapter LXXII - More Than Ten Thousand Baptized

"Meantime I shall remain with you three months, as I promised.

Be ye constant in hearing the word; and at the end of that time, if any are able and willing to follow us, they may do so, if duty will admit of it.

And when I say if duty will admit I mean that no one by his departure must sadden any one who ought not to be saddened, as by leaving parents who ought not to be left, or a faithful wife, or any other person to whom he is bound to afford comfort for God's sake." Meantime, disputing and teaching day by day, he filled up the time appointed with the labour of teaching; and when the festival day arrived, upwards of ten thousand were baptized.

Chapter LXXIII - Tidings of Simon

But in those days a letter was received from the brethren who had gone before, in which were detailed the crimes of Simon, how going from city to city he was deceiving multitudes, and everywhere maligning Peter, so that, when he should come, no one might afford him a hearing.

For he asserted that Peter was a magician, a godless man, injurious, cunning, ignorant, and professing impossible things.

"For," says he, "he asserts that the dead shall rise again, which is impossible.

But if any one attempts to confute him, he is cut off by secret snares by him, through means of his attendants.

Wherefore, I also," says he, "when I had vanquished him and triumphed over him, fled for fear of his snares, lest he should destroy me by incantations, or compass my death by plots."

They intimated also that he mainly stayed at Tripolis. [42]

Chapter LXXIV - Farewell to Caesarea

Peter therefore ordered the letter to be read to the people; and after the reading of it, he addressed them and gave them full instructions about everything, but especially that they should obey Zacchaeus, whom he had ordained bishop over them.

Also he commended the presbyters and the deacons to the people, and not less the people to them.

And then, announcing that he should spend the winter at Tripolis, he said:

"I commend you to the grace of God, being about to depart to-morrow, with God's will.

But during the whole three months which he spent at Caesarea, for the sake of instruction, whatever he discoursed of in the presence of the people in the day-time, he explained more fully and perfectly in the night, in private to us, as more faithful and completely approved by him.

And at the same time he commanded me, because he understood that I carefully stored in my memory what I heard, to commit to writing whatever seemed worthy of record, and to send it to you, my lord James, as also I did, in obedience to his command."

Chapter LXXV - Contents of Clement's Despatches to James

The first book, [43] therefore, of those that I formerly sent to you, contains an account of the true Prophet, and of the peculiarity of the understanding of the law, according to what the tradition of Moses teacheth.

The second contains an account of the beginning, and whether there be one beginning or many, and that the law of the Hebrews knows what immensity is.

The third, concerning God, and those things that have been ordained by Him.

The fourth, that though there are many that are called gods, there is but one true God, according to the testimonies of the Scriptures.

The fifth, that there are two heavens, one of which is that visible firmament which shall pass away, but the other is eternal and invisible.

The sixth, concerning good and evil; and that all things are subjected to good by the Father; and why, and how, and whence evil is, and that it co-operates with good, but not with a good purpose; and what are the signs of good, and what those of evil; and what is the difference between duality and conjunction.

The seventh, what are the things which the twelve apostles treated of in the presence of the people in the temple.

The eighth, concerning the words of the Lord which seem to be contradictory, but are not; and what is the explanation of them.

The ninth, that the law which has been given by God is righteous and perfect, and that it alone can make pure.

The tenth, concerning the carnal birth of men, and concerning the generation which is by baptism; and what is the succession of carnal seed in man; and what is the account of his soul, and how the freedom of the will is in it, which, seeing it is not unbegotten, but made, could not be immoveable from good.

Concerning these several subjects, therefore, whatever Peter discoursed at Caesarea, according to his command, as I have said, I have sent you written in ten volumes. [44]But on the next day, as had been determined, we set out from Caesarea with some faithful men, who had resolved to accompany Peter.

Footnotes:

1. [The larger part of book iii. has no direct parallel in the Homilies, though, of course, many of the views presented are given in the latter under different circumstances.--R.]
2. Matt. vii. 6.
3. Chaps ii.-xii. are wanting in the mss. of best authority; and it seems to us indisputable that they form no part of the original work. For this reason, and because we have found them utterly untranslatable, we have omitted them.
4. [Comp. Homily XVII. 2 for a similar accusation made by Simon.--R.]
5. Matt. x. 26.
6. Luke viii. 5.
[Comp. Matt. xiii. 3, etc.; Mark iv. 3, etc.--R.]
7. [In Homily XIX. the discussion with Simon is respecting the existence of the evil one. Here the treatment is apparently of a higher philosophical character.--R.]
8. Matt. vi. 33.
9. [Comp. Homilies XI. 8, XIX. 15.
But in the Recognitions this topic is more frequently treated.
See chap. 26, and elsewhere.--R.]
10. [Comp. Homily XIX. 12.
The argument here is far more philosophical.--R.]
11. [Comp. Homily XIX. 15.--R.]
12. Matt. v. 8.
13. Matt. v. 8.
14. Ex. xxxiii. 20.
15. Matt. xxii. 30.
16. Matt. v. 8.
17. Matt. vi. 33.
18. [Comp. Homilies XVII. 4, etc., XVIII. 1.
The objection is of Gnostic origin.--R.]
19. Matt. v. 45.
20. Matt. iii. 12.
21. [Comp. Homily XIX. 23.--R.]
22. Matt. vi. 33.
23. [The concluding portion of this discussion (chaps. 42-48) is peculiar alike in its argument and its colloquies.--R.]
24. [Comp. book ii. 15 and Homily II. 26.--R.]
25. Evidently parodied from Acts viii. 18-24.
This incident is peculiar to the Recognitions.--R.]
26. [Compare with this chapter book ii. 9, 14; Homily II. 32.--R.]
27. [This account of the close of the discussion is peculiar to the Recognitions.--R.]
28. Matt. xviii. 7.
29. Acts viii. 13.
30. Ex. vii., viii.
31. Ex. viii. 19.
32. Ex. xii.

33. [The substance of chaps. 59, 60, occurs in Homily II. 33, 34, just before the postponement of the discussion with Simon.--R.]

34. [On the doctrine of pairs compare Homily II. 15, etc., 33; III. 23.--R.]

35. Matt. xiii. 46.

36. [This incident is narrated only in the Recognitions.--R.]

37. [With the remainder of the book compare Homily III. 58-73.
The resemblance is general rather than particular.--R.]

38. Matt. xviii. 7; Luke xvii. 1.

39. [In the Homilies full details are given respecting the choice of Zacchaeus (who is identified with the publican in Luke xix.), his unwillingness to serve; precepts are also added concerning Church officers.--R.]

40. This may be translated, "that he may partake of holy things." Cotelerius supposes the words "holy things" to mean the body and blood of Christ.

41. [Compare with this chapter the lists in book ii. 1 and in Homily II. 1.
The special significance attached to the number twelve is peculiar to this passage.--R.]

42. [In Homily III. 58 Simon is represented as doing great miracles at Tyre.
Peter follows him there, but finds that he has gone.
The long discussions with him are assigned to Laodicea.
See Homilies, xvi., etc.--R.]

43. Cotelerius remarks that these ten books previously sent to James (if they ever existed) ought to be distinguished from the ten books of the Recognitions, which were addressed to the same James, but written after those now mentioned.

44. [This chapter furnishes some positive evidence that the Recognitions are based upon an earlier work.
The topics here named do not correspond with those of the Homilies, except in the most general way.
Hence this passage does not favour the theory that the author of the Recognitions had the Homilies before him when he wrote.
Even in xvi.-xix. of the later work, which Uhlhorn regarded as the nucleus of the entire literature, the resemblances are slight.
As already intimated (see Introductory Notice, p. 71), Uhlhorn has abandoned this theory. On the other hand the chapter bears marks of being the conclusion to a complete document.
It can therefore be urged in support of the new view of Lehmann (Die Clementinischen Schriften, Gotha, 1869), that the Recognitions are made up of two parts (books i.-iii., iv.-x.) by two different authors, both parts being based on earlier documents.
This chapter is regarded by Hilgenfeld as containing a general outline of the Kerygma Petri, a Jewish-Christian document of Roman origin.
In i. 27-72 he finds a remnant of this document incorporated in the Recognitions.--R.]

Book IV

Chapter I - Halt at Dora

Having set out from Caesarea on the way to Tripolis, we made our first stoppage at a small town called Dora, because it was not far distant; and almost all those who had believed through the preaching of Peter could scarcely bear to be separated from him, but walked along with us, again and again gazing upon him, again and again embracing him, again and again conversing with him, until we came to the inn.

On the following day we came to Ptolemais, where we stayed ten days; and when a considerable number had received the word of God, we signified to some of them who seemed particularly attentive, and wished to detain us longer for the sake of instruction, that they might, if so disposed, follow us to Tripolis.

We acted in the same way at Tyre, and Sidon, and Berytus, and announced to those who desired to hear further discourses, that we were to spend the winter at Tripolis.[1] Therefore, as all those who were anxious followed Peter from each city, we were a great multitude of elect ones when we entered into Tripolis. On our arrival, the brethren who had been sent before met us before the gates of the city; and taking us under their charge, conducted us to the various lodgings which they had prepared.

Then there arose a commotion in the city, and a great assemblage of persons desirous to see Peter.[2]

Chapter II - Reception in the House of Maro

And when we had come to the house of Maro, in which preparation had been made for Peter, he turned to the crowd, and told them that he would address them the day after to-morrow.

Therefore the brethren who had been sent before assigned lodgings to all who had come with us. Then, when Peter had entered into the house of Maro, and was asked to partake of food, he answered that he would by no means do so, until he had ascertained whether all those that had accompanied him were provided with lodgings.

Then he learned from the brethren who had been sent before, that the citizens had received them not only hospitably, but with all kindness, by reason of their love towards Peter; so much so, that several were disappointed because there were no guests for them; for that all had made such preparations, that even if many more had come, there would still have been a deficiency of guests for the hosts, not of hosts for the guests.

Chapter III - Simon's Flight

Thereupon Peter was greatly delighted, and praised the brethren, and blessed them, and requested them to remain with him.

Then, when he had bathed in the sea, and had taken food, he went to sleep in the evening; and rising, as usual, at cock-crow, while the evening light was still burning, he found us all awake.

Now there were in all sixteen of us, viz. Peter and I, Clement, Niceta and Aquila, and those twelve who had preceded us.[3] Saluting us, then, as was his wont, Peter said: "Since we are not taken up with others to-day, let us be taken up with ourselves.

I shall tell you what took place at Caesarea after your departure, and you shall tell us of the doings of Simon here."

And while the conversation was going on on these subjects, at daybreak some of the members of the family came in and told Peter that Simon, when he heard of Peter's arrival, departed in the night, on the way to Syria. They also stated that the crowds thought that the day which he had said was to intervene was a very long time for their affection, and that they were standing in impatience before the gate, conversing among themselves about those things which they wished to hear, and that they hoped that they should by all means see him before the time appointed; and that as the day became lighter the multitudes were increasing, and that they were trusting confidently, whatever they might be presuming upon, that they should hear a discourse from him.

"Now then," said they, "instruct us to tell them what seems good to you; for it is absurd that so great a multitude should have come together, and should depart with sadness, through no answer being returned to them.

For they will not consider that it is they that have not waited for the appointed day but rather they will think that you are slighting them."

Chapter IV - The Harvest Plenteous

Then Peter, filled with admiration, said: [4]"You see, brethren, how every word of the Lord spoken prophetically is fulfilled.

For I remember that He said, The harvest indeed is plenteous, but the labourers are few; ask therefore the Lord of the harvest, that He would send out labourers into His harvest.' [5]Behold, therefore, the things which are foretold in a mystery are fulfilled.

But whereas He said also, Many shall come from the east and the west, from the north and the south, and shall recline in the bosom of Abraham, and Isaac, and Jacob;' [6] this also is, as you see, in like manner fulfilled. Wherefore I entreat you, my fellow-servants and helpers, that you would learn diligently the order of preaching, and the ways of absolutions, that ye may be able to save the souls of men, which by the secret power of God acknowledge whom they ought to love, even before they are taught.

For you see that these men, like good servants, long for him whom they expect to announce to them the coming of their Lord, that they may be able to fulfil His will when they have learned it.

The desire, therefore, of hearing the word of God, and inquiring into His will, they have from God; and this is the beginning of the gift of God, which is given to the Gentiles, that by this they may be able to receive the doctrine of truth.

Chapter V - Moses and Christ

"For so also it was given to the people of the Hebrews from the beginning, that they should love Moses, and believe his word; whence also it is written:

The people believed God, and Moses His servant.' [7]What, therefore, was of peculiar gift from God toward the nation of the Hebrews, we see now to be given also to those who are called from among the Gentiles to the faith.

But the method of works is put into the power and will of every one, and this is their own; but to have an affection towards a teacher of truth, this is a gift of the heavenly Father.

But salvation is in this, that you do His will of whom you have conceived a love and affection through the gift of God; lest that saying of His be addressed to you which He spoke, Why call ye me Lord, Lord, and do not what I say?' [8]It is therefore the peculiar gift bestowed by God upon the Hebrews, that they believe Moses; and the peculiar gift bestowed upon the Gentiles is that they love Jesus.

For this also the Master intimated, when He said, I will confess to Thee, O Father, Lord of heaven and earth, because Thou hast concealed these things from the wise and prudent, and hast revealed them to babes.' [9]By which it is certainly declared, that the people of the Hebrews, who were instructed out of the law, did not know Him; but the people of the Gentiles have acknowledged Jesus, and venerate Him; on which account also they shall be saved, not only acknowledging Him, but also doing His will.

But he who is of the Gentiles, and who has it of God to believe Moses, ought also to have it of his own purpose to love Jesus also.

And again, the Hebrew, who has it of God to believe Moses, ought to have it also of his own purpose to believe in Jesus; so that each of them, having in himself something of the divine gift, and something of his own exertion, may be perfect by both.

For concerning such an one our Lord spoke, as of a rich man, Who brings forth from his treasures things new and old.' [10]

Chapter VI - A Congregation

"But enough has been said of these things for time presses, and the religious devotion of the people invites us to address them."

And when he had thus spoken, he asked where there was a suitable place for discussion.

And Maro said:

"I have a very spacious hall [11] which can hold more than five hundred men, and there is also a garden within the house; or if it please you to be in some public place, all would prefer it, for there is nobody who does not desire at least to see your face."

Then Peter said:

"Show me the hall, or the garden."

And when he had seen the hall, he went in to see the garden also; and suddenly the whole multitude, as if some one had called them, rushed into the house, and thence broke through into the garden, where Peter was already standing, selecting a fit place for discussion.

Chapter VII - The Sick Healed

But when he saw that the crowds had, like the waters of a great river, poured over the narrow passage, he mounted upon a pillar which happened to stand near the wall of the garden, and first saluted the people in a religious manner.

But some of those who were present, and who had been for a long time distressed by demons, threw themselves on the ground, while the unclean spirits entreated that they might be allowed but for one day to remain in the bodies that they had taken possession of.

But Peter rebuked them, and commanded them to depart; and they went out without delay.

After these, others who had been afflicted with long-standing sicknesses asked Peter that they might receive healing; and he promised that he would entreat the Lord for them as soon as his discourse of instruction was completed.

But as soon as he promised, they were freed from their sicknesses; [12] and he ordered them to sit down apart, with those who had been freed from the demons, as after the fatigue of labour.

Meantime, while this was going on, a vast multitude assembled, attracted not only by the desire of hearing Peter, but also by the report of the cures which had been accomplished.

But Peter, beckoning with his hand to the people to be still, and settling the crowds in tranquillity, began to address them as follows:--

Chapter VIII - Providence Vindicated

"It seems to me necessary, at the outset of a discourse concerning the true worship of God, first of all to instruct those who have not as yet acquired any knowledge of the subject, that throughout the divine providence must be maintained to be without blame, by which the world is ruled and governed.

Moreover, the reason of the present undertaking, and the occasion offered by those whom the power of God has healed, suggest this subject for a beginning, viz. to show that for good reason very many persons are possessed of demons, that so the justice of God may appear.

For ignorance will be found to be the mother of almost all evils.

But now let us come to the reason.

Chapter IX - State of Innocence a State of Enjoyment

"When God had made man after His own image and likeness, He grafted into His work a certain breathing and odour of His divinity, that so men, being made partakers of His Only-begotten, might through Him be also friends of God and sons of adoption.

Whence also He Himself, as the true Prophet, knowing with what actions the Father is pleased, instructed them in what way they might obtain that privilege.

At that time, therefore, there was among men only one worship of God--a pure mind and an uncorrupted spirit.

And for this reason every creature kept an inviolable covenant with the human race.

For by reason of their reverence of the Creator, no sickness, or bodily disorder, or corruption of food, had power over them; whence it came to pass, that a life of a thousand years did not fall into the frailty of old age.

Chapter X - Sin the Cause of Suffering

"But when men, leading a life void of distress, began to think that the continuance of good things was granted them not by the divine bounty, but by the chance of things, and to accept as a debt of nature, not as a gift of God's goodness, their enjoyment without any exertion of the delights of the divine complaisance,--men, being led by these things into contrary and impious thoughts, came at last, at the instigation of idleness, to think that the life of gods was theirs by nature, without any labours or merits on their part.

Hence they go from bad to worse, to believe that neither is the world governed by the providence of God, nor is there any place for virtues, since they knew that they themselves possessed the fulness of ease and delights, without the assignment of any works previously, and without any labours were treated as the friends of God.

Chapter XI - Suffering Salutary

"By the most righteous judgment of God, therefore, labours and afflictions are assigned as a remedy to men languishing in the vanity of such thoughts.

And when labour and tribulations came upon them, they were excluded from the place of delights and amenity.

Also the earth began to produce nothing to them without labour; and then men's thoughts being turned in them, they were warned to seek the aid of their Creator, and by prayers and vows to ask for the divine protection.

And thus it came to pass, that the worship of God, which they had neglected by reason of their prosperity, they recovered through their adversity; and their thoughts towards God, which indulgence had perverted, affliction corrected.

So therefore the divine providence, seeing that this was more profitable to man, removed from them the ways of benignity and abundance, as being hurtful, and introduced the way of vexation and tribulation. [13]

Chapter XII - Translation of Enoch

"But [14] that He might show that these things were done on account of the ungrateful, He translated to immortality a certain one of the first race of men, because He saw that he was not unmindful of His grace, and because he hoped to call on the name of God; [15] while the rest, who were so ungrateful that they could not be amended and corrected even by labours and tribulations, were condemned to a terrible death.

Yet amongst them also He found a certain one, who was righteous with his house, [16] whom He preserved, having enjoined him to build an ark, in which he and those who were commanded to go with him might escape, when all things should be destroyed by a deluge:

in order that, the wicked being cut off by the overflow of waters, the world might receive a purification; and he who had been preserved for the continuance of the race, being purified by water, might anew repair the world.

Chapter XIII - Origin of Idolatry

"But when all these things were done, men turned again to impiety; [17] and on this account a law was given by God to instruct them in the manner of living.

But in process of time, the worship of God and righteousness were corrupted by the unbelieving and the wicked, as we shall show more fully by and by.

Moreover, perverse and erratic religions were introduced, to which the greater part of men gave themselves up, by occasion of holidays and solemnities, instituting drinkings and banquets, following pipes, and flutes, and harps, and diverse kinds of musical instruments, and indulging themselves in all kinds of drunkenness and luxury.

Hence every kind of error took rise; hence they invented groves and altars, fillets and victims, and after drunkenness they were agitated as if with mad emotions.

By this means power was given to the demons to enter into minds of this sort, so that they seemed to lead insane dances and to rave like Bacchanalians; hence were invented the gnashing of teeth, and bellowing from the depth of their bowels; hence a terrible countenance and a fierce aspect in men, so that he whom drunkenness had subverted and a demon had instigated, was believed by the deceived and the erring to be filled with the Deity.

Chapter XIV - God Both Good and Righteous

"Hence, since so many false and erratic religions have been introduced into the world, [18] we have been sent, as good merchants, bringing unto you the worship of the true God, handed down from the fathers, and preserved; as the seeds of which we scatter these words amongst you, and place it in your choice to choose what seems to you to be right. For if you receive those things which we bring you, you shall not only be able yourselves to escape the incursions of the demon, but also to drive them away from others; and at the same time you shall obtain the rewards of eternal good things.

But those who shall refuse to receive those things which are spoken by us, shall be subject in the present life to diverse demons and disorders of sicknesses, and their souls after their departure from the body shall be tormented for ever.

For God is not only good, but also just; for if He were always good, and never just to render to every one according to his deeds, goodness would be found to be injustice.

For it were injustice if the impious and the pious were treated by Him alike.

Chapter XV - How Demons Get Power Over Men

"Therefore demons, as we have just said, when once they have been able, by means of opportunities afforded them, to convey themselves through base and evil actions into the bodies of men, if they remain in them a long time through their own negligence, because they do not seek after what is profitable to their souls, they necessarily compel them for the future to fulfil the desires of the demons who dwell in them.

But what is worst of all, at the end of the world, when that demon shall be consigned to eternal fire, of necessity the soul also which obeyed him, shall with him be tortured in eternal fires, together with its body which it hath polluted.

Chapter XVI - Why They Wish to Possess Men

"Now that the demons are desirous of occupying the bodies of men, this is the reason.

They are spirits having their purpose turned to wickedness.

Therefore by immoderate eating and drinking, and lust, they urge men on to sin, but only those who entertain the purpose of sinning, who, while they seem simply desirous of satisfying the necessary cravings of nature, give opportunity to the demons to enter into them, because through excess they do not maintain moderation.

For as long as the measure of nature is kept, and legitimate moderation is preserved, the mercy of God does not give them liberty to enter into men.

But when either the mind falls into impiety, or the body is filled with immoderate meat or drink, then, as if invited by the will and purpose of those who thus neglect themselves, they receive power as against those who have broken the law imposed by God.

Chapter XVII - The Gospel Gives Power Over Demons

"You see, then, how important is the acknowledgment of God, and the observance of the divine religion, which not only protects those who believe from the assaults of the demon, but also gives them command over those who rule over others.

And therefore it is necessary for you, who are of the Gentiles, to betake yourselves to God, and to keep yourselves from all uncleanness, that the demons may be expelled, and God may dwell in you.

And at the same time, by prayers, commit yourselves to God, and call for His aid against the impudence of the demons; for whatever things ye ask, believing, ye shall receive.' [19]

But even the demons themselves, in proportion as they see faith grow in a man, in that proportion they depart from him, residing only in that part in which something of infidelity still remains; but from those who believe with full faith, they depart without any delay.

For when a soul has come to the faith of God, it obtains the virtue of heavenly water, by which it extinguishes the demon like a spark of fire.

Chapter XVIII - This Power in Proportion to Faith

"There is therefore a measure of faith, which, if it be perfect, drives the demon perfectly from the soul; but if it has any defect, something on the part of the demon still remains in the portion of infidelity; and it is the greatest difficulty for the soul to understand when or how, whether fully or less fully, the demon has been expelled from it. For if he remains in any quarter, when he gets an opportunity, he suggests thoughts to men's hearts; and they, not knowing whence they come, believe the suggestions of the demons, as if they were the perceptions of their own souls.

Thus they suggest to some to follow pleasure by occasion of bodily necessity; they excuse the passionateness of others by excess of gall; they colour over the madness of others by the vehemence of melancholy; and even extenuate the folly of some as the result of abundance of phlegm.

But even if this were so, still none of these could be hurtful to the body, except from the excess of meats and drinks; because, when these are taken in excessive quantities, their abundance, which the natural warmth is not sufficient to digest, curdles into a sort of poison, and it, flowing through the bowels and all the veins like a common sewer, renders the motions of the body unhealthy and base.

Wherefore moderation is to be attained in all things, that neither may place be given to demons, nor the soul, being possessed by them, be delivered along with them to be tormented in eternal fires.

Chapter XIX - Demons Incite to Idolatry

"There is also another error of the demons, which they suggest to the senses of men, that they should think that those things which they suffer, they suffer from such as are called gods, in order that thereby, offering sacrifices and gifts, as if to propitiate them, they may strengthen the worship of false religion, and avoid us who are interested in their salvation, that they may be freed from error; but this they do, as I have said, not knowing that these things are suggested to them by demons, for fear they should be saved.

It is therefore in the power of every one, since man has been made possessed of free-will, whether he shall hear us to life, or the demons to destruction.

Also to some, the demons, appearing visibly under various figures, sometimes throw out threats, sometimes promise relief from sufferings, that they may instil into those whom they deceive the opinion of their being gods, and that it may not be known that they are demons.

But they are not concealed from us, who know the mysteries of the creation, and for what reason it is permitted to the demons to do those things in the present world; how it is allowed them to transform themselves into what figures they please, and to suggest evil thoughts, and to convey themselves, by means of meats and of drink consecrated to them, into the minds or bodies of those who partake of it, and to concoct vain dreams to further the worship of some idol.

Chapter XX - Folly of Idolatry

"And yet who can be found so senseless as to be persuaded to worship an idol, whether it be made of gold or of any other metal?

To whom is it not manifest that the metal is just that which the artificer pleased? How then can the divinity be thought to be in that which would not be at all unless the artificer had pleased?

Or how can they hope that future things should be declared to them by that in which there is no perception of present things?

For although they should divine something, they should not straightway be held to be gods; for divination is one thing, divinity is another.

For the Pythons also seem to divine, yet they are not gods; and, in short, they are driven out of men by Christians.

And how can that be God which is put to flight by a man?

But perhaps you will say, What as to their effecting cures, and their showing how one can be cured?

On this principle, physicians ought also to be worshipped as gods, for they cure many; and in proportion as any one is more skilful, the more he will cure.

Chapter XXI - Heathen Oracles

"Whence it is evident that they since they are demoniac spirits, know some things both more quickly and more perfectly than men; for they are not retarded in their learning by the heaviness of a body.

And therefore they, as being spirits, know without delay and without difficulty what physicians attain after a long time and by much labour.

It is not wonderful, therefore, if they know somewhat more than men do; but this is to be observed, that what they know they do not employ for the salvation of souls, but for the deception of them, that by means of it they may indoctrinate them in the worship of false religion.

But God, that the error of so great deception might not be concealed, and that He Himself might not seem to be a cause of error in permitting them so great licence to deceive men by divinations, and cures, and dreams, has of His mercy furnished men with a remedy, and has made the distinction of falsehood and truth patent to those who desire to know.

This, therefore, is that distinction:

what is spoken by the true God, whether by prophets or by diverse visions, is always true; but what is foretold by demons is not always true.

It is therefore an evident sign that those things are not spoken by the true God, in which at any time there is falsehood; for in truth there is never falsehood.

But in the case of those who speak falsehoods, there may occasionally be a slight mixture of truth, to give as it were seasoning to the falsehoods.

Chapter XXII - Why They Sometimes Come True

"But if any one say, What is the use of this, that they should be permitted even sometimes to speak truth, and thereby so much error be introduced amongst men? let him take this for answer:

If they had never been allowed to speak any truth, then they would not foretell anything at all; while if they did not foretell, they would not be known to be demons.

But if demons were not known to be in this world, the cause of our struggle and contest would be concealed from us, and we should suffer openly what was done in secret, that is, if the power were granted to them of only acting against us, and not of speaking. But now, since they sometimes speak truth, and sometimes falsehood, we ought to acknowledge, as I have said, that their responses are of demons, and not of God, with whom there is never falsehood.

Chapter XXIII - Evil Not in Substance

"But if any one, proceeding more curiously, inquire:

What then was the use of God's making these evil things, which should have so great a tendency to subvert the minds of men? [20]To one proposing such a question, we answer that we must first of all inquire whether there is any evil in substance.

And although it would be sufficient to say to him that it is not suitable that the creature judge the Creator, but that to judge the work of another belongs to him who is either of equal skill or equal power; yet, to come directly to the point, we say absolutely that there is no evil in substance.

But if this be so, then the Creator of substance is vainly blamed.

Chapter XXIV - Why God Permits Evil

"But you will meet me by saying, Even if it has come to this through freedom of will, was the Creator ignorant that those whom He created would fall away into evil?

He ought therefore not to have created those who, He foresaw, would deviate from the path of righteousness. Now we tell those who ask such questions, that the purpose of assertions of the sort made by us is to show why the wickedness of those who as yet were not, did not prevail over the goodness of the Creator. [21]For if, wishing to fill up the number and measure of His creation, He had been afraid of the wickedness of those who were to be, and like one who could find no other way of remedy and cure, except only this, that He should refrain from His purpose of creating, lest the wickedness of those who were to be should be ascribed to Him; what else would this show but unworthy suffering and unseemly feebleness on the part of the Creator, who should so fear the actings of those who as yet were not, that He refrained from His purposed creation?

Chapter XXV - Evil Beings Turned to Good Account

"But, setting aside these things, let us consider this earnestly, that God the Creator of the universe, foreseeing the future differences of His creation, foresaw and provided diverse ranks and different offices to each of His creatures, according to the peculiar movements which were produced from freedom of will; so that while all men are of one substance in respect of the method of creation, there should yet be diversity in ranks and offices, according to the peculiar movements of minds, to be produced from liberty of will.

Therefore He foresaw that there would be faults in His creatures; and the method of His justice demanded that punishment should follow faults, for the sake of amendment.

It behoved, therefore, that there should be ministers of punishment, and yet that freedom of will should draw them into that order.

Moreover, those also must have enemies to conquer, who had undertaken the contests for the heavenly rewards.

Thus, therefore, neither are those things destitute of utility which are thought to be evil, since the conquered unwillingly acquire eternal rewards for those by whom they are conquered.

But let this suffice on these points, for in process of time even more secret things shall be disclosed.

Chapter XXVI - Evil Angels Seducers

"Now therefore, since you do not yet understand how great darkness of ignorance surrounds you, meantime I wish to explain to you whence the worship of idols began in this world.

And by idols, I mean those lifeless images which you worship, whether made of wood, or earthenware, or stone, or brass, or any other metals: of these the beginning was in this wise.

Certain angels, having left the course of their proper order, began to favour the vices of men, [22] and in some measure to lend unworthy aid to their lust, in order that by these means they might indulge their own pleasures the more; and then, that they might not seem to be inclined of their own accord to unworthy services, taught men that demons could, by certain arts--that is, by magical invocations--be made to obey men; and so, as from a furnace and workshop of wickedness, they filled the whole world with the smoke of impiety, the light of piety being withdrawn.

Chapter XXVII - Ham the First Magician

"For these and some other causes, a flood was brought upon the world, [23] as we have said already, and shall say again; and all who were upon the earth were destroyed, except the family of Noah, who survived, with his three sons and their wives.

One of these, by name Ham, unhappily discovered the magical act, and handed down the instruction of it to one of his sons, who was called Mesraim, from whom the race of the Egyptians and Babylonians and Persians are descended.

Him the nations who then existed called Zoroaster, [24] admiring him as the first author of the magic art; under whose name also many books on this subject exist.

He therefore, being much and frequently intent upon the stars, and wishing to be esteemed a god among them, began to draw forth, as it were, certain sparks from the stars, and to show them to men, in order that the rude and ignorant might be astonished, as with a miracle; and desiring to increase this estimation of him, he attempted these things again and again, until he was set on fire, and consumed by the demon himself, whom he accosted with too great importunity.

Chapter XXVIII - Tower of Babel

"But the foolish men who were then, whereas they ought to have abandoned the opinion which they had conceived of him, inasmuch as they had seen it confuted by his mortal punishment, extolled him the more. For raising a sepulchre to his honour, they went so far as to adore him as a friend of God, and one who had been removed to heaven in a chariot of lightning, and to worship him as if he were a living star.

Hence also his name was called Zoroaster after his death--that is, living star--by those who, after one generation, had been taught to speak the Greek language.

In fine, by this example, even now many worship those who have been struck with lightning, honouring them with sepulchres, and worshipping them as friends of God.

But this man was born in the fourteenth generation, and died in the fifteenth, in which the tower was built, and the languages of men were divided into many.

Chapter XXIX - Fire-Worship of the Persians

"First among whom is named a certain king Nimrod, the magic art having been handed down to him as by a flash, whom the Greeks, also called Ninus, and from whom the city of Nineveh took its name.

Thus, therefore, diverse and erratic superstitions took their beginning from the magic art.

For, because it was difficult to draw away the human race from the love of God, and attach them to deaf and lifeless images, the magicians made use of higher efforts, that men might be turned to erratic worship, by signs among the stars, and motions brought down as it were from heaven, and by the will of God.

And those who had been first deceived, collecting the ashes of Zoroaster,--who, as we have said, was burnt up by the indignation of the demon, to whom he had been too troublesome,--brought them to the Persians, that they might be preserved by them with perpetual watching, as divine fire fallen from heaven, and might be worshipped as a heavenly God.

Chapter XXX - Hero-Worship

"By a like example, other men in other places built temples, set up statues, instituted mysteries and ceremonies and sacrifices, to those whom they had admired, either for some arts or for virtue, or at least had held in very great affection; and rejoiced, by means of all things belonging to gods, to hand down their fame to posterity; and that especially, because, as we have already said, they seemed to be supported by some phantasies of magic art, so that by invocation of demons something seemed to be done and moved by them towards the deception of men.

To these they add also certain solemnities, and drunken banquets, in which men might with all freedom indulge; and demons, conveyed into them in the chariot of repletion, might be mixed with their very bowels, and holding a place there, might bind the acts and thoughts of men to their own will.

Such errors, then, having been introduced from the beginning, and having been aided by lust and drunkenness, in which carnal men chiefly delight, the religion of God, which consisted in continence and sobriety, began to become rare amongst men, and to be well-nigh abolished.

Chapter XXXI - Idolatry Led to All Immorality

"For whereas at first, men worshipping a righteous and all-seeing God, neither dared sin nor do injury to their neighbours, being persuaded that God sees the actions and movements of every one; when religious worship was directed to lifeless images, concerning which they were certain that they were incapable of hearing, or sight, or motion, they began to sin licentiously, and to go forward to every crime, because they had no fear of suffering anything at the hands of those whom they worshipped as gods.

Hence the madness of wars burst out; hence plunderings, rapines, captivities, and liberty reduced to slavery; each one, as he could, satisfied his lust and his covetousness, although no power can satisfy covetousness.

For as fire, the more fuel it gets, is the more extensively kindled and strengthened, so also the madness of covetousness is made greater and more vehement by means of those things which it acquires.

Chapter XXXII - Invitation

"Wherefore begin now with better understanding to resist yourselves in those things which you do not rightly desire; [25] if so be that you can in any way repair and restore in yourselves that purity of religion and innocence of life which at first were bestowed upon man by God, that thereby also the hope of immortal blessings may be restored to you.

And give thanks to the bountiful Father of all, by Him whom He has constituted King of peace, and the treasury of unspeakable honours, that even at the present time your sins may be washed away with the water of the fountain, or river, or even sea:

the threefold name of blessedness being called over you, that by it not only evil spirits may be driven out, if any dwell in you, but also that, when you have forsaken your sins, and have with entire faith and entire purity of mind believed in God, you may drive out wicked spirits and demons from others also, and may be able to set others free from sufferings and sicknesses.

For the demons themselves know and acknowledge those who have given themselves up to God, and sometimes they are driven out by the mere presence of such, as you saw a little while ago, how, when we had only addressed to you the word of salutation, straightway the demons, on account of their respect for our religion, began to cry out, and could not bear our presence even for a little.

Chapter XXXIII - The Weakest Christian More Powerful Than the Strongest Demon

"Is it, then, that we are of another and a superior nature, and that therefore the demons are afraid of us?

Nay, we are of one and the same nature with you, but we differ in religion.

But if you will also be like us, we do not grudge it, but rather we exhort you, and wish you to be assured, that when the same faith and religion and innocence of life shall be in you that is in us, you will have equal and the same power and virtue against demons, through God rewarding your faith.

For as he who has soldiers under him, although he may be inferior, and they superior to him in strength, yet says to this one, Go, and he goeth; and to another, Come, and he cometh; and to another, Do this, and he doeth it;' [26] and this he is able to do, not by his own power, but by the fear of Caesar; so every faithful one commands the demons, although they seem to be much stronger than men, and that not by means of his own power, but by means of the power of God, who has put them in subjection.

For even that which we have just spoken of, that Caesar is held in awe by all soldiers, and in every camp, and in his whole kingdom, though he is but one man, and perhaps feeble in respect of bodily strength, this is not effected but by the power of God, who inspires all with fear, that they may be subject to one.

Chapter XXXIV - Temptation of Christ

"This we would have you know assuredly, that a demon has no power against a man, unless one voluntarily submit himself to his desires. [27] Whence even that one who is the prince of wickedness, approached Him who, as we have said, is appointed of God King of peace, tempting Him, and began to promise Him all the glory of the world; because he knew that when he had offered this to others, for the sake of deceiving them, they had worshipped him.

Therefore, impious as he was, and unmindful of himself, which indeed is the special peculiarity of wickedness, he presumed that he should be worshipped by Him by whom he knew that he was to be destroyed.

Therefore our Lord, confirming the worship of one God, answered him:

It is written, Thou shalt worship the Lord thy God, and Him only shalt thou serve.' [28] And he, terrified by this answer, and fearing lest the true religion of the one and true God should be restored, hastened straightway to send forth into this world false prophets, and false apostles, and false teachers, who should speak indeed in the name of Christ, but should accomplish the will of the demon.

Chapter XXXV - False Apostles

"Wherefore observe the greatest caution, that you believe no teacher, unless he bring from Jerusalem the testimonial of James the Lord's brother, or of whosoever may come after him. [29]For no one, unless he has gone up thither, and there has been approved as a fit and faithful teacher for preaching the word of Christ,--unless, I say, he brings a testimonial thence, is by any means to be received.

But let neither prophet nor apostle be looked for by you at this time, besides us.

For there is one true Prophet, whose words we twelve apostles preach; for He is the accepted year of God, having us apostles as His twelve months.

But for what reason the world itself was made, or what diversities have occurred in it, and why our Lord, coming for its restoration, has chosen and sent us twelve apostles, shall be explained more at length at another time.

Meantime He has commanded us to go forth to preach, and to invite you to the supper of the heavenly King, which the Father hath prepared for the marriage of His Son, and that we should give you wedding garments, that is, the grace of baptism; [30] which whosoever obtains, as a spotless robe with which he is to enter to the supper of the King, ought to beware that it be not in any part of it stained with sin, and so he be rejected as unworthy and reprobate.

Chapter XXXVI - The Garments Unspotted

"But the ways in which this garment may be spotted are these:

If any one withdraw from God the Father and Creator of all, receiving another teacher besides Christ, who alone is the faithful and true Prophet, and who has sent us twelve apostles to preach the word; if any one think otherwise than worthily of the substance of the Godhead, which excels all things;--these are the things which even fatally pollute the garment of baptism.

But the things which pollute it in actions are these:

murders, adulteries, hatreds, avarice, evil ambition.

And the things which pollute at once the soul and the body are these:

to partake of the table of demons, that is, to taste things sacrificed, or blood, or a carcase which is strangled, [31] and if there be aught else which has been offered to demons.

Be this therefore the first step to you of three; which step brings forth thirty commands, and the second sixty, and the third a hundred, [32] as we shall expound more fully to you at another time."

Chapter XXXVII - The Congregation Dismissed

When he had thus spoken, and had charged them to come to the same place in good time on the following day, he dismissed the crowds; and when they were unwilling to depart, Peter said to them:

"Do me this favour on account of the fatigue of yesterday's journey; and now go away, and meet in good time to-morrow."

And so they departed with joy.

But Peter, commanding me to withdraw a little for the purpose of prayer, [33] afterwards ordered the couches to be spread in the part of the garden which was covered with shade; and every one, according to custom, recognising the place of his own rank, we took food.

Then, as there was still some portion of the day left, he conversed with us concerning the Lord's miracles; and when evening was come, he entered his bed-chamber and went to sleep.

Footnotes:

1. [In books iv.-vi. the scene is laid at Tripolis.

The same city is the locality to which Homilies VIII.-XI. are assigned.

The intervening portion (Homilies IV.-VII.) gives the details of the journey here alluded to, telling of various discourses at Tyre.

Some of the matter of these discourses occurs in the Recognitions, but under different circumstances.

The heathen disputants are not the same. The parallelisms of the portions assigned to Tripolis are as follows:

book iv. has its counterpart in Homily VIII. and in much of Homily IX.; book v. has a parallel in Homily X. and it, parts of XI.; book vi. in its general outline resembles Homily XI. The discourses of the Apostle as given in the Recognitions are more orderly and logical than those in the Homilies.

The Epistles of Clement

The views presented differ somewhat, in accordance with the general character of the two works.

Much of the matter in the Recognitions occurs in a different order in the Homilies, but the internal evidence seems to point to the priority of the former.

Both might be different manipulations of a common documentary source, but that theory is not necessarily applicable to these portions of the literature.--R.]

2. ["Maroones," Homily VIII. 1.--R.]
3. [Comp. Homily VIII. 3.--R.]
4. [With chaps. 4-11 compare Homily VIII. 4-11.
The correspondence is quite close.--R.]
5. Matt. ix. 37, 38.
6. Luke xiii. 29; Matt. viii. 11.
7. Ex. xiv. 31.
8. Luke vi. 46.
9. Matt. xi. 25.
[Luke x. 21; comp. Homily XVIII. 15-17.--R.]
10. Matt. xiii. 52.
11. AEdes, in the singular, probably a temple.
12. [In Homilies VIII. 8, 24, IX. 24, the healing takes place after the discourses.--R.]
13. [In Homily VIII. 12-16 there is inserted a curious account of the fall of man and angels, and of a race of giants.--R.]
14. [Chap. 12 has no exact parallel in the Homilies, but Homily VIII. 17 resembles it.--R.]
15. There seems to be here a mixing up of the translation of Enoch with the statement that in the days of Enos men began to call on the name of the Lord; Gen. iv. 26.
16. Gen. vi. 9.
17. [There is a similar chapter in Homily IX. 7, but in a discourse on the following day.--R.]
18. [With chaps. 14-22 compare Homily IX. 8-18.
The general outline is the same, and the resemblances quite close in the larger part of both passages.--R.]
19. Matt. xxi. 22.
20. [Chaps. 23-26 have no exact parallel in the Homilies; comp. book iii. 16-26.
The questions of the origin of evil and of free-will are more fully treated in the Recognitions.--R.]
21. There is considerable variety of reading in this sentence, and the precise meaning is somewhat obscure.

The general sense, however, is sufficiently evident, that if God had refrained from creating those who He foresaw, would fall into evil, this would have been to subject His goodness to their evil.

22. [Comp. Homily VIII. 13.--R.]
23. [With chaps. 27-31 compare Homily IX. 3-7.
The resemblances are quite close.
See also book i. 30, 31.--R.]
24. [With chaps. 27-31 compare Homily IX. 3-7.
The resemblances are quite close.
See also book i. 30, 31.--R.]
25. [To chaps. 32, 33, a close parallel is found in Homily IX. 19-21.--R.]
26. Matt. viii. 9.
[Luke vii. 8.--R.]
27. [The close of this discourse, chaps. 34-37, resembles that of the first at Tripolis, in Homily VIII. 21, 24.
As already indicated, much of Homily IX. finds a parallel in this book.--R.]
28. Matt. iv. 10.
[Luke iv. 8.--R.]
29. [This is peculiar in this connection.
There is, at least, a suggestion of anti-Pauline spirit in its teaching.--R.]
30. [Matt. xxii. 2-14.]
31. [In Homily VII. 8 a similar injunction is given, at Sidon.
The language in both places recalls Acts xv. 20 and 1 Cor. x. 21.
But most of the chapter is peculiar to the Recognitions.--R.]
32. Matt. xiii. 23.
[Comp. Mark iv. 8, 20, where the order of the numbers corresponds with that of the Recognitions.
The interpretation is a fanciful one, indicating not only Judaistic legalism, but the notion of esoteric teaching.
The passage shows Ebionitic tendencies.--R.]
33. Clement, being not yet baptized, is represented as not permitted to join with the disciples, even

in prayer.

[Comp. i. 19, ii. 70-72. This separation is indicated in the Homilies, but more emphasis is placed upon it in the Recognitions.--R.]

Book V

Chapter I - Peter's Salutation

But on the following day, [1] Peter rising a little earlier than usual, found us asleep; and when he saw it, he gave orders that silence should be kept for him, as though he himself wished to sleep longer, that we might not be disturbed in our rest.

But when we rose refreshed with sleep, we found him, having finished his prayer, waiting for us in his bed-chamber.

And as it was already dawn, he addressed us shortly, saluting us according to his custom, and forthwith proceeded to the usual place for the purpose of teaching; and when he saw that many had assembled there, having invoked peace upon them according to the first religious form, he began to speak as follows:--

Chapter II - Suffering the Effect of Sin

"God, the Creator of all, at the beginning made man after His own image, and gave him dominion over the earth and sea, and over the air; as the true Prophet has told us, and as the very reason of things instructs us: for man alone is rational, and it is fitting that reason should rule over the irrational.

At first, therefore, while he was still righteous, he was superior to all disorders and all frailty; but when he sinned, as we taught you yesterday, and became the servant of sin, he became at the same time liable to frailty.

This therefore is written, that men may know that, as by impiety they have been made liable to suffer, so by piety they may be made free from suffering; and not only free from suffering, but by even a little faith in God be able to cure the sufferings of others.

For thus the true Prophet promised us, saying, Verily I say to you, that if ye have faith as a grain of mustard seed, ye shall say to this mountain, Remove hence, and it shall remove.' [2] Of this saving you have yourselves also had proofs; for you saw yesterday how at our presence the demons removed and were put to flight, with those sufferings which they had brought upon men.

Chapter III - Faith and Unbelief

"Whereas therefore some men suffer, and others cure those who suffer, it is necessary to know the cause at once of the suffering and the cure; and this is proved to be nought else than unbelief on the part of the sufferers, and faith on the part of those who cure them.

For unbelief, while it does not believe that there is to be a judgment by God, affords licence to sin, and sin makes men liable to sufferings; but faith, believing that there is to be a judgment of God, restrains men from sin; and those who do not sin are not only free from demons and sufferings, but can also put to flight the demons and sufferings of others.

Chapter IV - Ignorance the Mother of Evils

"From [3] all these things, therefore, it is concluded that all evil springs from ignorance; and ignorance herself, the mother of all evils, is sprung from carelessness and sloth, and is nourished, and increased, and rooted in the senses of men by negligence; and if any one teach that she is to be put to flight, she is with difficulty and indignantly torn away, as from an ancient and hereditary abode.

And therefore we must labour for a little, that we may search out the presumptions of ignorance, and cut them off by means of knowledge, especially in those who are preoccupied with some erroneous opinions, by means of which ignorance is the more firmly rooted in them, as under the appearance of a certain kind of knowledge; for nothing is worse than for one to believe that he knows what he is ignorant of, and to maintain that to be true which is false.

This is as if a drunk man should think himself to be sober, and should act indeed in all respects as a drunk man, and yet think himself to be sober, and should wish to be called so by others.

Thus, therefore, are those also who do not know what is true, yet hold some appearance of knowledge, and do many evil things as if they were good, and hasten destruction as if it were to salvation.

Chapter V - Advantages of Knowledge

"Wherefore we must, above all things, hasten to the knowledge of the truth, that, as with a light kindled thereat, we may be able to dispel the darkness of errors:

for ignorance, as we have said, is a great evil; but because it has no substance, it is easily dispelled by those who are in earnest.

For ignorance is nothing else than not knowing what is good for us; once know this, and ignorance perishes.

Therefore the knowledge of truth ought to be eagerly sought after; and no one can confer it except the true Prophet.

For this is the gate of life to those who will enter, and the road of good works to those going to the city of salvation.

Chapter VI - Free-Will

"Whether any one, truly hearing the word of of the true Prophet; is willing or unwilling to receive it, and to embrace His burden, that is, the precepts of life, he has either in his power, for we are free in will. [4]For if it were so, that those who hear had it not in their power to do otherwise than they had heard, there were some power of nature in virtue of which it were not free to him to pass over to another opinion.

Or if, again, no one of the hearers could at all receive it, this also were a power of nature which should compel the doing of some one thing, and should leave no place for the other course.

But now, since it is free for the mind to turn its judgment to which side it pleases, and to choose the way which it approves, it is clearly manifest that there is in men a liberty of choice.

Chapter VII - Responsibility of Knowledge

"Therefore, before any one hears what is good for him, it is certain that he is ignorant; and being ignorant, he wishes and desires to do what is not good for him; wherefore he is not judged for that.

But when once he has heard the causes of his error, and has received the method of truth, then, if he remain in those errors with which he had been long ago preoccupied, he shall rightly be called into judgment, to suffer punishment, because he has spent in the sport of errors that portion of life which was given him to be spent in living well.

But he who, hearing those things, willingly receives them, and is thankful that the teaching of good things has been brought to him, inquires more eagerly, and does not cease to learn, until he ascertains whether there be truly another world, in which rewards are prepared for the good. And when he is assured of this, he gives thanks to God because He has shown him the light of truth; and for the future directs his actions in all good works, for which he is assured that there is a reward prepared in the world to come; while he constantly wonders and is astonished at the errors of other men, and that no one sees the truth which is placed before his eyes.

Yet he himself, rejoicing in the riches of wisdom which he hath found, desires insatiably to enjoy them, and is delighted with the practice of good works; hastening to attain, with a clean heart and a pure conscience, the world to come, when he shall be able even to see God, the king of all.

Chapter VIII - Desires of the Flesh to Be Subdued

"But the sole cause of our wanting and being deprived of all these things is ignorance.

For while men do not know how much good there is in knowledge, they do not suffer the evil of ignorance to be removed from them; for they know not how great a difference is involved in the change of one of these things for the other.

Wherefore I counsel every learner willingly to lend his ear to the word of God, and to hear with love of the truth what we say, that his mind, receiving the best seed, may bring forth joyful fruits by good deeds.

For if, while I teach the things which pertain to salvation, any one refuses to receive them, and strives to resist them with a mind occupied by evil opinions, he shall have the cause of his perishing, not from us, but from himself.

For it is his duty to examine with just judgment the things which we say, and to understand that we speak the words of truth, that, knowing how things are, and directing his life in good actions, he may be found a partaker of the kingdom of heaven, subjecting to himself the desires of the flesh, and becoming lord of them, that so at length he himself also may become the pleasant possession of the Ruler of all.

Chapter IX - The Two Kingdoms

"For he who persists in evil, and is the servant of evil, cannot be made a portion of good so long as he persists in evil, because from the beginning, as we have said, God instituted two kingdoms, and has given to each man the power of becoming a portion of that kingdom to which he shall yield himself to obey.

And since it is decreed by God that no one man can be a servant of both kingdoms, therefore endeavour with all earnestness to betake yourselves to the covenant and laws of the good King.

Wherefore also the true Prophet, when He was present with us, and saw some rich men negligent with respect to the worship of God, thus unfolded the truth of this matter:

No one,' said He, can serve two masters; ye cannot serve God and mammon;' [5] calling riches, in the language of His country, mammon.

Chapter X - Jesus the True Prophet

"He therefore is the true Prophet, who appeared to us, as you have heard, in Judaea, who, standing in public places, by a simple command made the blind see, the deaf hear, cast out demons, restored health to the sick, and life to the dead; and since nothing was impossible to Him, He even perceived the thoughts of men, which is possible for none but God only.

He proclaimed the kingdom of God; and we believed Him as a true Prophet in all that He spoke, deriving the confirmation of our faith not only from His words, but also from His works; and also because the sayings of the law, which many generations before had set forth His coming, were fulfilled in Him; and the figures of the doings of Moses, and of the patriarch Jacob before him, bore in all respects a type of Him.

It is evident also that the time of His advent, that is, the very time at which He came, was foretold by them; and, above all, it was contained in the sacred writings, that He was to be waited for by the Gentiles.

And all these things were equally fulfilled in Him.

Chapter XI - The Expectation of the Gentiles

"But that which a prophet of the Jews foretold, that He was to be waited for by the Gentiles, [6] confirms above measure the faith of truth in Him.

For if he had said that He was to be waited for by the Jews, he would not have seemed to prophesy anything extraordinary, that He whose coming had been promised for the salvation of the world should be the object of hope to the people of the same tribe with Himself, and to His own nation:

for that this would take place, would seem rather to be a matter of natural inference than one requiring the grandeur of a prophetic utterance.

But now, whereas the prophets say that all that hope which is set forth concerning the salvation of the world, and the newness of the kingdom which is to be established by Christ, and all things which are declared concerning Him are to be transferred to the Gentiles; the grandeur of the prophetic office is confirmed, not according to the sequence of things, but by an incredible fulfilment of the prophecy.

For the Jews from the beginning had understood by a most certain tradition that this man should at some time come, by whom all things should be restored; and daily meditating and looking out for His coming, when they saw Him amongst them, and accomplishing the signs and miracles, as had been written of Him, being blinded with envy, they could not recognise Him when present, in the hope of whom they rejoiced while He was absent; yet the few of us who were chosen by Him understood it.

Chapter XII - Call of the Gentiles

"But this happened by the providence of God, that the knowledge of this good One should be handed over to the Gentiles, and those who had never heard of Him, nor had learned from the prophets, should acknowledge Him, while those who had acknowledged Him in their daily meditations should not know Him.

For, behold, by you who are now present, and desire to hear the doctrine of His faith, and to know what, and how, and of what sort is His coming, the prophetic truth is fulfilled.

For this is what the prophets foretold, that He is to be sought for by you, who never heard of Him.[7] And, therefore, seeing that the prophetic sayings are fulfilled even in yourselves, you rightly believe in Him alone, you rightly wait for Him, you rightly inquire concerning Him, that you not only may wait for Him, but also believing, you may obtain the inheritance of His kingdom; according to what Himself said, that every one is made the servant of him to whom he yields subjection. [8]

Chapter XIII - Invitation of the Gentiles

"Wherefore awake, and take to yourselves our Lord and God, even that Lord who is Lord both of heaven and earth, and conform yourselves to His image and likeness, as the true Prophet Himself teaches, saying, Be ye merciful, as also your heavenly Father is merciful, who makes His sun to rise upon the good and the evil, and rains upon the just and the unjust.' [9]Imitate Him, therefore, and fear Him, as the commandment is given to men, Thou shalt worship the Lord thy God, and Him only shalt thou serve.' [10]For it is profitable to you to serve this Lord alone, that through Him knowing the one God, ye may be freed from the many whom ye vainly feared.

For he who fears not God the Creator of all, but fears those whom he himself with his own hands hath made, what does he do but make himself subject to a vain and senseless fear, and render himself more vile and abject than those very things, the fear of which he has conceived in his mind?

But rather, by the goodness of Him who inviteth you, return to your former nobleness, and by good deeds show that you bear the image of your Creator, that by contemplation of His likeness ye may be believed to be even His sons.

Chapter XIV - Idols Unprofitable

"Begin, [11] therefore, to cast out of your minds the vain ideas of idols, and your useless and empty fears, that at the same time you may also escape the condition of unrighteous bondage.

For those have become your lords, who could not even have been profitable servants to you.

For how should lifeless images seem fit even to serve you, when they can neither hear, nor see, nor feel anything?

Yea, even the material of which they are made, whether it be gold or silver, or even brass or wood, though it might have profited you for necessary uses, you have rendered wholly inefficient and useless by fashioning gods out of it.

We therefore declare to you the true worship of God, and at the same time warn and exhort the worshippers, that by good deeds they imitate Him whom they worship, and hasten to return to His image and likeness, as we said before.

The Epistles of Clement

Chapter XV - Folly of Idolatry

"But I should like if those who worship idols would tell me if they wish to become like those whom they worship?

Does any one of you wish to see in such sort as they see? or to hear after the manner of their hearing? or to have such understanding as they have?

Far be this from any of my hearers!

For this were rather to be thought a curse and a reproach to a man, who bears in himself the image of God, although he has lost the likeness.

What sort of gods, then, are they to be reckoned, the imitation of whom would be execrable to their worshippers, and to have whose likeness would be a reproach?

What then?

Melt your useless images, and make useful vessels.

Melt the unserviceable and inactive metal, and make implements fit for the use of men.

But, says one, human laws do not allow us. [12]He says well; for it is human laws, and not their own power, that prevents it. What kind of gods, then, are those which are defended by human laws, and not by their own energies?

And so also they are preserved from thieves by watch-dogs and the protection of bolts, at least if they be of silver, or gold, or even of brass; for those that are of stone and earthenware are protected by their own worthlessness, for no one will steal a stone or a crockery god.

Hence those seem to be the more miserable whose more precious metal exposes them to the greater danger.

Since, then, they can be stolen, since they must be guarded by men, since they can be melted, and weighed out, and forged with hammers, ought men possessed of understanding to hold them as gods?

Chapter XVI - God Alone a Fit Object of Worship

"Oh! into what wretched plight the understanding of men has fallen! For if it is reckoned the greatest folly to fear the dead, what shall we judge of those who fear something that is worse than the dead are? For those images are not even to be reckoned among the number of the dead, because they were never alive.

Even the sepulchres of the dead are preferable to them, since, although they are now dead, yet they once had life; but those whom you worship never possessed even such base life as is in all, the life of frogs and owls.

But why say more about them, since it is enough to say to him who adores them:

Do you not see that he whom you adore sees not, hear that he whom you adore hears not, and understand that he understands not?--for he is the work of man's hand, and necessarily is void of understanding.

You therefore worship a god without sense, whereas every one who has sense believes that not even those things are to be worshipped which have been made by God and have sense, [13] such as the sun, moon, and stars, and all things that are in heaven and upon earth.

For they think it reasonable, that not those things which have been made for the service of the world, but the Creator of those things themselves, and of the whole world, should be worshipped.

For even these things rejoice when He is adored and worshipped, and do not take it well that the honour of the Creator should be bestowed on the creature.

For the worship of God alone is acceptable to them, who alone is uncreated, and all things also are His creatures.

For as it belongs to him who alone is uncreated to be God, so everything that has been created is not truly God.

Chapter XVII - Suggestions of the Old Serpent

"Above all, therefore, you ought to understand the deception of the old serpent [14] and his cunning suggestions, who deceives you as it were by prudence, and as by a sort of reason creeps through your senses; and beginning at the head, he glides through your inner marrow, accounting the deceiving of you a great gain.

Therefore he insinuates into your minds opinions of gods of whatsoever kinds, only that he may withdraw you from the faith of one God knowing that your sin is his comfort. For he, for his wickedness, was condemned from the beginning to eat dust, for that he caused to be again resolved into dust him who had been taken from the dust, even till the time when your souls shall be restored, being brought through the fire; as we shall instruct you more fully at another time.

From him, therefore, proceed all the errors and doubts, by which you are driven from the faith and belief of one God.

Chapter XVIII - His First Suggestion

"And first of all he suggests to men's thoughts not to hear the words of truth, by which they might put to flight the ignorance of those things which are evils.

And this he does, as by the presentation of another knowledge, making a show of that opinion which very many hold, to think that they shall not be held guilty if they have been in ignorance, and that they shall not be called to account for what they have not heard; and thereby he persuades them to turn aside from hearing the word.

But I tell you, in opposition to this, that ignorance is in itself a most deadly poison, which is sufficient to ruin the soul without any aid from without.

And therefore there is no one who is ignorant who shall escape through his ignorance, but it is certain that he shall perish.

For the power of sin naturally destroys the sinner.

But since the judgment shall be according to reason, the cause and origin of ignorance shall be inquired into, as well as of every sin.

For he who is unwilling to know how he may attain to life, and prefers to be in ignorance lest he thereby be made guilty, from this very fact is judged as if he knew and had knowledge.

For he knew what it was that he was unwilling to hear; and the cunning obtained by the artifice of the serpent will avail him nothing for an excuse, for he will have to do with Him to whom the heart is open.

But that you may know that ignorance of itself brings destruction, I assure you that when the soul departs from the body, if it leave it in ignorance of Him by whom it was created, and from whom in this world it obtained all things that were necessary for its uses, it is driven forth from the light of His kingdom as ungrateful and unfaithful.

Chapter XIX - His Second Suggestion

"Again, the wicked serpent suggests another opinion to men, which many of you are in the habit of bringing forward,--that there is, as we say, one God, who is Lord of all; but these also, they say, are gods.

For as there is one Caesar, and he has under him many judges,--for example, prefects, consuls, tribunes, and other officers,--in like manner we think, that while there is one God greater than all, yet still that these gods are ordained in this world, after the likeness of those officers of whom we have spoken, subject indeed to that greater God, yet ruling us and the things that are in this world.

In answer to this, I shall show you how, in those very things which you propose for deception, you are confuted by the reasons of truth.

You say that God occupies the place of Caesar, and those who are called gods represent His judges and officers.

Hold then, as you have adduced it, by the example of Caesar; and know that, as one of Caesar's judges or administrators, as prefects, proconsuls, generals, or tribunes, may lawfully take the name of Caesar,--or else both he who should take it and those who should confer it should be destroyed together,--so also in this case you ought to observe, that if any one give the name of God to any but Himself, and he accept it, they shall partake one and the same destruction, by a much more terrible fate than the servants of Caesar.

For he who offends against Caesar shall undergo temporal destruction; but he who offends against Him who is the sole and true God, shall suffer eternal punishment, and that deservedly, as having injured by a wrongful condition the name which is unique. [15]

Chapter XX - Egyptian Idolatry

"Although this word God is not the name of God, but meantime that word is employed by men as His name; and therefore, as I have said, when it is used reproachfully, the reproach is referred to the injury of the true name.

In short, the ancient Egyptians, who thought that they had discovered the theory of the heavenly revolutions and the nature of the stars, nevertheless, through the demon's blocking up their senses, subjected the incommunicable name to all kinds of indignity.

For some taught that their ox, which is called Apis, ought to be worshipped; others taught that the he-goat, others that cats, the ibis, a fish also, a serpent, onions, drains, crepitus ventris, ought to be regarded as deities, and innumerable other things, which I am ashamed even to mention."

Chapter XXI - Egyptian Idolatry More Reasonable Than Others

When Peter was speaking thus, all we who heard him laughed.
Then said Peter:
"You laugh at the absurdities of others, because through long custom you do not see your own.

For indeed it is not without reason that you laugh at the folly of the Egyptians, who worship dumb animals, while they themselves are rational.

But I will tell you how they also laugh at you; for they say, We worship living animals, though mortal; but you worship and adore things which never were alive at all.

They add this also, that they are figures and allegories of certain powers by whose help the race of men is governed.

Taking refuge in this for shame, they fabricate these and similar excuses, and so endeavour to screen their error.

But this is not the time to answer the Egyptians, and leaving the care of those who are present to heal the disease of the absent.

For it is a certain indication that you are held to be free from sickness of this sort, since you do not grieve over it as your own, but laugh at it as that of others.

Chapter XXII - Second Suggestion Continued

"But let us come back to you, whose opinion it is that God should be regarded as Caesar, and the gods as the ministers and deputies of Caesar.

Follow me attentively, and I shall presently show you the lurking-places of the serpent, which lie in the crooked windings of this argument.

It ought to be regarded by all as certain and beyond doubt, that no creature can be on a level with God, because He was made by none, but Himself made all things; nor indeed can any one be found so irrational, as to suppose that the thing made can be compared with the maker.

If therefore the human mind, not only by reason, but even by a sort of natural instinct, rightly holds this opinion, that that is called God to which nothing can be compared or equalled, but which exceeds all and excels all; how can it be supposed that that name which is believed to be above all, is rightly given to those whom you think to be employed for the service and comfort of human life?

But we shall add this also.
This world was undoubtedly made, and is corruptible, as we shall show more fully by and by; meantime it is admitted both that it has been made and that it is corruptible.

If therefore the world cannot be called God, and rightly so, because it is corruptible, how shall parts of the world take the name of God?

For inasmuch as the whole world cannot be God, much more its parts cannot.

Therefore, if we come back to the example of Caesar, you will see how far you are in error.

It is not lawful for any one, though a man of the same nature with him, to be compared with Caesar:

do you think, then, that any one ought to be compared with God, who excels all in this respect, that He was made by none, but Himself made all things?

But, indeed, you dare not give the name of Caesar to any other, because he immediately punishes one who offends against him; you dare give that of God to others, because He delays the punishment of offenders against Him, in order to their repentance.

Chapter XXIII - Third Suggestion

"Through the mouths of others also that serpent is wont to speak in this wise:
We adore visible images in honour of the invisible God. [16]Now this is most certainly false.
For if you really wished to worship the image of God, you would do good to man, and so worship the true image of God in him.
For the image of God is in every man, though His likeness is not in all, but where the soul is benign and the mind pure.
If, therefore, you wish truly to honour the image of God, we declare to you what is true, that you should do good to and pay honour and reverence to man, who is made in the image of God; that you minister food to the hungry, drink to the thirsty, clothing to the naked, hospitality to the stranger, and necessary things to the prisoner; and that is what will be regarded as truly bestowed upon God.
And so far do these things go to the honour of God's image, that he who does not these things is regarded as casting reproach upon the divine image.
What, then, is that honour of God which consists in running from one stone or wooden figure to another, in venerating empty and lifeless figures as deities, and despising men in whom the image of God is of a truth?
Yea, rather be assured, that whoever commits murder or adultery, or anything that causes suffering or injury to men, in all these the image of God is violated.
For to injure men is a great impiety towards God.
Whenever, therefore, you do to another what you would not have another do to you, you defile the image of God with undeserved distresses.
Understand, therefore, that that is the suggestion of the serpent lurking within you, which persuades you that you may seem to be pious when you worship insensible things, and may not seem impious when you injure sensible and rational beings.

Chapter XXIV - Fourth Suggestion

"But to these things the serpent answers us with another mouth, and says:
If God did not wish these things to be, then they should not be.
I am not telling you how it is that many contrary things are permitted to be in this world for the probation of every one's mind. But this is what is suitable to be said in the meantime:
If, according to you, everything that was to be worshipped ought not to have been, there would have been almost nothing in this world.
For what is there that you have left without worshipping it?
The sun, the moon, the stars, the water, the earth, mountains, trees, stones, men; there is no one of these that ye have not worshipped.
According to your saying, therefore, none of these ought to have been made by God, that you might not have anything that you could worship!
Yea, He ought not even to have made men themselves to be the worshippers!
But this is the very thing which that serpent which lurks within you desires:
for he spares none of you; he would have no one of you escape from destruction.
But it shall not be so.
For I tell you, that not that which is worshipped is in fault, but he who worships.
For with God is righteous judgment; and He judges in one way the sufferer, and in another way the doer, of wrong.

Chapter XXV - Fifth Suggestion

"But you say:
Then those who adore what ought not to be adored, should be immediately destroyed by God, to prevent others doing the like.
But are you wiser than God, that you should offer Him counsel? [17]He knows what to do.
For with all who are placed in ignorance He exercises patience, because He is merciful and gracious; and He foresees that many of the ungodly become godly, and that even some of those who worship impure statues and polluted images have been converted to God, and forsaking their sins and doing good works, attain to salvation.
But it is said:
We ought never to have come even to the thought of doing these things.

You do not know what freedom of will is, and you forget that he is good who is so by his own intention; but, he who is retained in goodness by necessity cannot be called good, because it is not of himself that he is so.

Because, therefore, there is in every one liberty to choose good or evil, he either acquires rewards, or brings destruction on himself.

Nay it is said, God brings to our minds whatsoever we think.

What mean ye, O men?

Ye blaspheme. For if He brings all our thoughts into our minds, then it is He that suggests to us thoughts of adultery, and covetousness, and blasphemy, and every kind of effeminacy.

Cease, I entreat of you, these blasphemies, and understand what is the honour worthy of God.

And say not, as some of you are wont to say, that God needs not honour from men.

Indeed, He truly is in need of none; but you ought to know that the honour which you bestow upon God is profitable to yourselves.

For what is so execrable, as for a man not to render thanks to his Creator?

Chapter XXVI - Sixth Suggestion

"But it is said:

We do better, who give thanks both to Himself, and to all with Him.

In this you do not understand that there is the ruin of your salvation.

For it is as if a sick man should call in for his cure at once a physician and poisoners; since these could indeed injure him, but not cure him; and the true physician would refuse to mix his remedies with their poisons, lest either the man's destruction should be ascribed to the good, or his recovery, to the injurious.

But you say:

Is God then indignant or envious, if, when He benefits us, our thanks be rendered to others?

Even if He be not indignant, at all events He does not wish to be the author of error, that by means of His work credit should be given to a vain idol.

And what is so impious, so ungrateful, as to obtain a benefit from God, and to render thanks to blocks of wood and stone?

Wherefore arise, and understand your salvation.

For God is in need of no one, nor does He require anything, nor is He hurt by anything; but we are either helped or hurt, in that we are grateful or ungrateful.

For what does God gain from our praises, or what does He lose by our blasphemies?

Only this we must remember, that God brings into proximity and friendship with Himself the soul that renders thanks to Him.

But the wicked demon possesses the ungrateful soul.

Chapter XXVII - Creatures Take Vengeance on Sinners

"But this also I would have you know, that upon such souls God does not take vengeance directly, but His whole creation rises up and inflicts punishments upon the impious; and although in the present world the goodness of God bestows the light of the world and the services of the earth alike upon the pious and the impious, yet not without grief does the sun afford his light, and the other elements perform their service, to the impious.

And, in short, sometimes even in opposition to the goodness of the Creator, the elements are wearied out by the crimes of the wicked; and thence it is that either the fruit of the earth is blighted, or the composition of the air is vitiated, or the heat of the sun is increased beyond measure, or there is an excessive amount of rain or of cold.

Thence pestilence, and famine, and death in various forms stalk forth, for the creature hastens to take vengeance on the wicked; yet the goodness of God restrains it, and bridles its indignation against the wicked, and compels it to be obedient to His mercy, rather than to be inflamed by the sins and the crimes of men. For the patience of God waiteth for the conversion of men, as long as they are in this body.

Chapter XXVIII - Eternity of Punishments

"But if any persist in impiety till the end of life, then as soon as the soul, which is immortal, departs, it shall pay the penalty of its persistence in impiety.

For even the souls of the impious are immortal, though perhaps they themselves would wish them to end with their bodies.

But it is not so; for they endure without end the torments of eternal fire, and to their destruction they have not the quality of mortality.

But perhaps you will say to me, You terrify us, O Peter.

And how shall we speak to you the things which are in reality?

Can we declare to you the truth by keeping silence?

We cannot state the things which are, otherwise than as they are.

But if we were silent, we should make ourselves the cause of the ignorance that is ruinous to you, and should satisfy the serpent that lurks within you, and blocks up your senses, who cunningly suggests these things to you, that he may make you always the enemies of God.

But we are sent for this end, that we may betray his disguises to you; and melting your enmities, may reconcile you to God, that you may be converted to Him, and may please Him by good works.

For man is at enmity with God, and is in an unreasonable and impious state of mind and wicked disposition towards Him, especially when he thinks that he knows something, and is in ignorance.

But when you lay aside these, and begin to be pleased and displeased with the same things which please and displease God, and to will what God willeth then ye shall truly be called His friends.

Chapter XXIX - God's Care of Human Things

"But perhaps some of you will say, God has no care of human things; and if we cannot even attain to the knowledge of Him, how shall we attain to His friendship?

That God does concern Himself with the affairs of men, His government of the world bears witness:

for the sun daily waits upon it, the showers minister to it; the fountains, rivers, winds, and all elements, attend upon it; and the more these things become known to men, the more do they indicate God's care over men. For unless by the power of the Most High, the more powerful would never minister to the inferior; and by this God is shown to have not only a care over men, but some great affection, since He has deputed such noble elements to their service.

But that men may also attain to the friendship of God, is proved to us by the example of those to whose prayers He has been so favourable, that He has withheld the heaven from rain when they wished, and has again opened it when they prayed. [18]

And many other things He has bestowed upon those who does His will, which could not be bestowed but upon His friends.

But you will say, What harm is done to God if these things also are worshipped by us?

If any one of you should pay to another the honour that is due to his father, from whom he has received innumerable benefits, and should reverence a stranger and foreigner as his father, should you not think that he was undutiful towards his father, and most deserving to be disinherited?

Chapter XXX - Religion of Fathers to Be Abandoned

"Others say, It is wicked if we do not worship those idols which have come down to us from our fathers, and prove false to the religion bequeathed to us by our ancestors.

On this principle, if any one's father was a robber or a base fellow, he ought not to change the manner of life handed down to him by his fathers, nor to be recalled from his father's errors to a better way; and it is reckoned impious if one do not sin with his parents, or does not persist in impiety with them. Others say, We ought not to be troublesome to God, and to be always burdening Him with complaints of our miseries, or with the exigencies of our petitions.

How foolish and witless an answer!

Do you think it is troublesome to God if you thank Him for His benefits, while you do not think it troublesome to Him if, for His gifts, you render thanks to stocks and stones?

And how comes it, that when rain is withheld in a long drought, we all turn our eyes to heaven, and entreat the gift of rain from God Almighty, and all of us with our little ones pour out prayers on

God and entreat His compassion?

But truly ungrateful souls, when they obtain the blessing, quickly forget: for as soon as they have gathered in their harvest or their vintage, straightway they offer the first-fruits to deaf and dumb images, and pay vows in temples or groves for those things which God has bestowed upon them, and then offer sacrifices to demons; and having received a favour, deny the bestower of the favour. [19]

Chapter XXXI - Paganism, Its Enormities

"But some say, These things are instituted for the sake of joy, and for refreshing our minds; and they have been devised for this end, that the human mind may be relaxed for a little from cares and sorrows.

See now what a charge you yourselves bring upon the things which you practise. If these things have been invented for the purpose of lightening sorrow and affording enjoyment, how is it that the invocations of demons are performed in groves and woods?

What is the meaning of the insane whirlings, and the slashing of limbs, and the cutting off of members? How is it that mad rage is produced in them?

How is insanity produced?

How is it that women are driven violently, raging with dishevelled hair?

Whence the shrieking and gnashing of teeth?

Whence the bellowing of the heart and the bowels, and all those things which, whether they are pretended or are contrived by the ministration of demons, are exhibited to the terror of the foolish and ignorant?

Are these things done for the sake of lightening the mind, or rather for the sake of oppressing it?

Do ye not yet perceive nor understand, that these are the counsels of the serpent lurking within you, which draws you away from the apprehension of truth by irrational suggestions of errors, that he may hold you as slaves and servants of lust and concupiscence and every disgraceful thing?

Chapter XXXII - True Religion Calls to Sobriety and Modesty

"But I protest to you with the clear voice of preaching, that, on the contrary, the religion of God calls you to sobriety and modesty; orders you to refrain from effeminacy and madness, and by patience and gentleness to prevent the inroads of anger; to be content with your own possessions, and with the virtue of frugality; not even when driven by poverty to plunder the goods of others, but in all things to observe justice; to withdraw yourselves wholly from the idol sacrifices:

for by these things you invite demons to you, and of your own accord give them the power of entering into you; and so you admit that which is the cause either of madness or of unlawful love.

Chapter XXXIII - Origin of Impiety

"Hence is the origin of all impiety; hence murders, adulteries, thefts; and a nursery is formed of all evils and wickednesses, while you indulge in profane libations and odours, and give to wicked spirits an opportunity of ruling and obtaining some sort of authority over you. For when they invade your senses, what do they else than work the things which belong to lust and injustice and cruelty, and compel you to be obedient to all things that are pleasing to them?

God, indeed, permits you to suffer this at their hands by a certain righteous judgment, that from the very disgrace of your doings and your feelings you may understand how unworthy it is to be subject to demons and not to God.

Hence also, by the friendship of demons, men are brought to disgraceful and base deeds; hence, men proceed even to the destruction of life, either through the fire of lust, or through the madness of anger through excess of grief, so that, as is well [20] known, some have even laid violent hands upon themselves.

And this, as we have said, by a just sentence of God they are not prevented from doing, that they may both understand to whom they have yielded themselves in subjection, and know whom they have forsaken.

Chapter XXXIV - Who are Worshippers of God?

"But some one will say, These passions sometimes befall even those who worship God. It is not true.

For we say, that he is a worshipper of God, who does the will of God, and observes the precepts of His law. For in God's estimation he is not a Jew who is called a Jew among men (nor is he a Gentile that is called a Gentile), but he who, believing in God, fulfils His law and does His will, though he be not circumcised. [21]He is the true worshipper of God, who not only is himself free from passions, but also sets others free from them; though they be so heavy that they are like mountains, he removes them by means of the faith with which he believes in God.

Yea, by faith he truly removes mountains with their trees, if it be necessary. [22]But he who seems to worship God, but is neither fortified by a full faith, nor by obedience to the commandments, but is a sinner, has given a place in himself, by reason of his sins, to passions, which are appointed of God for the punishment of those who sin, that they may exact from them the deserts of their sins by means of punishments inflicted, and may bring them purified to the general judgment of all, provided always that their faith do not fail them in their chastisement.

For the chastisement of unbelievers in the present life is a judgment, by which they begin to be separated from future blessings; but the chastisement of those who worship God, while it is inflicted upon them for sins into which they have fallen, exacts from them the due of what they have done, that, preventing the judgment, they may pay the debt of their sin in the present life, and be freed, at least in half, from the eternal punishments which are there prepared.

Chapter XXXV - Judgment to Come

"But he does not receive these things as true who does not believe that there is to be a judgment of God, and therefore, being bound by the pleasures of the present life, is shut out from eternal good things; and therefore we do not neglect to proclaim to you what we know to be necessary for your salvation, and to show you what is the true worship of God, that, believing in God, you may be able, by means of good works, to be heirs with us of the world to come.

But if you are not yet convinced that what we say is true, meantime, in the first instance, you ought not to take it amiss and to be hostile to us because we announce to you the things which we consider to be good, and because we do not grudge to bestow also upon you that which we believe brings salvation to ourselves, labouring, as I have said, with all eagerness, that we may have you as fellow-heirs of the blessings which we believe are to befall ourselves.

But whether those things which we declare to you are certainly true, you shall not be able to know otherwise than by rendering obedience to the things which are commanded, that you may be taught by the issue of things, and the most certain end of blessedness.

Chapter XXXVI - Conclusion of Discourse

"And, therefore, although the serpent lurking within you occupies your senses with a thousand arts of corruption, and throws in your way a thousand obstacles, by which he may turn you away from the hearing of saving instruction, all the more ought you to resist him, and despising his suggestions, to come together the more frequently to hear the word and receive instruction from us, because nobody can learn anything who is not taught." [23]

And when he had done speaking, he ordered those to be brought to him who were oppressed by sickness or demons, and laid his hands upon them with prayer; and so he dismissed the crowds, charging them to resort to the hearing of the word during the days that he was to remain there. Therefore, when the crowds had departed, Peter washed his body in the waters which ran through the garden, with as many of the others as chose to do so; and then ordered the couches to be spread on the ground under a very shady tree, and directed us to recline according to the order established at Caesarea.

And thus, having taken food and given thanks to God after the manner of the Hebrews, as there was yet some portion of the day remaining, he ordered us to question him on any matters that we pleased.

And although we were with him twenty in all, he explained to every one whatever he pleased to ask of him; the particulars of which I set down in books and sent to you some time ago.

And when evening came we entered with him into the lodging, and went to sleep, each one in his own place.

Footnotes:

1. [Book v. has a partial parallel in Homily X., which is assigned to the second day at Tripolis. The matter here is more extensive. Chaps. 1, 2, show some resemblance to Homily X. 3-6.--R.]
2. Matt. xvii. 20.
3. [Chaps. 4, 5, resemble somewhat Homily X. 2, which contains a preliminary discourse of the Apostle to his followers.--R.]
4. [Here again the doctrine of free-will is pressed, the Homilies containing no parallel. Chaps. 6-13 have no corresponding passage in Homily X.--R.]
5. Matt. vi. 24.
6. Gen. xlix. 10.
[This detailed statement of the call of the Gentiles is peculiar to the Recognitions; comp. i. 42. Such passages seem to indicate a tendency less anti-Pauline than that of the Homilies, yet the christology and soteriology are Ebionitic.--R.]
7. Isa. lxv. 1.
8. John viii. 34.
9. Luke vi. 36; Matt. v. 45.
10. Deut. vi. 13; Matt. iv. 10.
11. [The parallel with Homily X. recurs at this chapter, and continues for several chapters.--R.]
12. [This, with the more specific statement of Homily X. 8, points to an early date.--R.]
13. It was a very prevalent opinion among the ancient philosophers, that the heavenly bodies have some kind of life and intelligence.
14. [Comp. book ii. 45. In Homily X. 10, etc., the influence of the serpent is spoken of, but the discourse here is much fuller. There is, however, a general agreement in outline between chaps. 17-22 here and Homily X. 10-21.--R.]
15. The writer means, that insult is offered to that name which belongs to God alone by giving it to others, and thus placing it in a position which is unjust to it.
16. [To chaps. 23-36 a parallel is afforded by Homily XI. 4-18.--R.]
17. Rom. xi. 34.
18. 1 Kings xvii.; xviii.; Jas. v. 17, 18.
19. Literally, "change the bestower of it for another."
20. The original has here, "as is often known;" that is, as people know from many instances having occurred within their own knowledge.
21. Rom. ii. 28; Rev. ii. 9.
22. Matt. xvii. 20; Luke xvii. 6.
23. [The latter half of this discourse, as already indicated (see note on chap. 23), finds a parallel in Homily XI. 4-18, which forms the first half of that discourse.--R.]

Book VI

Chapter I - Diligence in Study

But as soon as day began to advance the dawn upon the retiring darkness, Peter having gone into the garden to pray, and returning thence and coming to us, by way of excuse for awaking and coming to us a little later than usual, said this: [1]"Now that the spring-time has lengthened the day, of course the night is shorter; if, therefore, one desires to occupy some portion of the night in study, he must not keep the same hours [2] for waking at all seasons, but should spend the same length of time in sleeping, whether the night be longer or shorter, and be exceedingly careful that he do not cut off from the period which he is wont to have for study, and so add to his sleep and lessen his time of keeping awake.

And this also is to be observed, lest haply if sleep be interrupted while the food is still undigested, the undigested mass lead the mind, and by the exhalation of crude spirits render the inner sense confused and disturbed.

It is right, therefore, that that part also be cherished with sufficient rest, so that, those things being sufficiently accomplished which are due to it, the body may be able in other things to render due service to the mind."

Chapter II - Much to Be Done in a Little Time

When he had said this, as very many had already assembled in the accustomed place of the garden to hear him, Peter went forth; and having saluted the crowds in his usual manner, began to speak as follows: [3]"Since, indeed, as land neglected by the cultivator necessarily produces thorns and thistles, so your sense, by long neglect, has produced a plentiful crop of noxious opinions of things and dogmas of false science; there is need now of much care in cultivating the field of your mind, that the word of truth, which is the true and diligent husbandman of the heart, may cultivate it with continual instructions.

It is therefore your part to render obedience to it, and to lop off superfluous occupations and anxieties, lest a noxious growth choke the good seed of the word.

For it may be that a short and earnest diligence may repair a long time's neglect; for the time of every one's life is uncertain, and therefore we must hasten to salvation, lest haply sudden death seize upon him who delays.

Chapter III - Righteous Anger

"And all the more eagerly must we strive on this account, that while there is time, the collected vices of evil custom may be cut off.

And this you shall not be able to do otherwise, than by being angry with yourselves on account of your profitless and base doings.

For this is righteous and necessary anger, by which every one is indignant with himself, and accuses himself for those things in which he has erred and done amiss; and by this indignation a certain fire is kindled in us, which, applied as it were to a barren field, consumes and burns up the roots of vile pleasure, and renders the soil of the heart more fertile for the good seed of the word of God.

And I think that you have sufficiently worthy causes of anger, from which that most righteous fire may be kindled, if you consider into what errors the evil of ignorance has drawn you, and how it has caused you to fall and rush headlong into sin, from what good things it has withdrawn you, and into what evils it has driven you, and, what is of more importance than all the rest, how it has made you liable to eternal punishments in the world to come.

Is not the fire of most righteous indignation kindled within you for all these things, now that the light of truth has shone upon you; and does not the flame of that anger which is pleasing to God rise within you, that every sprout may be burnt up and destroyed from the root, if haply any shoot of evil concupiscence has budded within you?

Chapter IV - Not Peace, But a Sword

Hence, also, He who hath sent us, when He had come, [4] and had seen that all the world had fallen into wickedness, did not forthwith give peace to him who is in error, lest He should confirm him in evil; but set the knowledge of truth in opposition to the ruins of ignorance of it, that, if haply men would repent and look upon the light of truth, they might rightly grieve that they had been deceived and drawn away into the precipices of error, and might kindle the fire of salutary anger against the ignorance that had deceived them.

On this account, therefore, He said, I have come to send fire on the earth; and how I wish that it were kindled!' [5]There is therefore a certain fight, which is to be fought by us in this life; for the word of truth and knowledge necessarily separates men from error and ignorance, as we have often seen putrified and dead flesh in the body separated by the cutting knife from its connection with the living members.

Such is the effect produced by knowledge of the truth.

For it is necessary that, for the sake of salvation, the son, for example, who has received the word of truth, be separated from his unbelieving parents; or again, that the father be separated from his son, or the daughter from her mother.

And in this manner the battle of knowledge and ignorance, of truth and error, arises between believing and unbelieving kinsmen and relations.

And therefore He who has sent us said again, I am not come to send peace on earth, but a sword.'[6]

Chapter V - How the Fight Begins

"But if any one say, How does it seem right for men to be separated from their parents? I will tell you how.

Because, if they remained with them in error, they would do no good to them, and they would themselves perish with them.

It is therefore right, and very right, that he who will be saved be separated from him who will not.

But observe this also, that this separation does not come from those who understand aright; for they wish to be with their relatives, and to do them good, and to teach them better things.

But it is the vice peculiar to ignorance, that it will not bear to have near it the light of truth, which confutes it; and therefore that separation originates with them.

For those who receive the knowledge of the truth, because it is full of goodness, desire, if it be possible, to share it with all, as given by the good God; yea, even with those who hate and persecute them:

for they know that ignorance is the cause of their sin.

Wherefore, in short, the Master Himself, when He was being led to the cross by those who knew Him not, prayed the Father for His murderers, and said, Father, forgive their sin, for they know not what they do!' [7]The disciples also, in imitation of the Master, even when themselves were suffering, in like manner prayed for their murderers. [8]But if we are taught to pray even for our murderers and persecutors, how ought we not to bear the persecutions of parents and relations, and to pray for their conversion?

Chapter VI - God to Be Loved More Than Parents

"Then let us consider carefully, in the next place, what reason we have for loving our parents.

For this cause, it is said, we love them, because they seem to be the authors of our life.

But our parents are not authors of our life, but means of it.

For they do not bestow life, but afford the means of our entering into this life; while the one and sole author of life is God.

If, therefore we would love the Author of our life, let us know that it is He that is to be loved.

But then it is said, We cannot know Him; but them we know, and hold in affection. Be it so:

you cannot know what God is, but you can very easily know what God is not.

For how can any man fail to know that wood, or stone, or brass, or other such matter, is not God?

But if you will not give your mind to consider the things which you might easily apprehend, it is certain that you are hindered in the knowledge of God, not by impossibility, but by indolence; for if you had wished it, even from these useless images you might have been set on the way of understanding.

Chapter VII - The Earth Made for Men

"For it is certain that these images are made with iron tools; but iron is wrought by fire, which fire is extinguished by water.

But water is moved by spirit; and spirit has its beginning from God.

For thus saith the prophet Moses:

In the beginning God made the heaven and the earth.

But the earth was invisible, and unarranged; and darkness was over the deep:

and the Spirit of God was upon the waters.' [9] Which Spirit, like the Creator's hand, by command of God separated light from darkness; and after that invisible heaven produced this visible one, that He might make the higher places a habitation for angels, and the lower for men.

For your sake, therefore, by command of God, the water which was upon the face of the earth withdrew, that the earth might produce fruits for you; and into the earth also He inserted veins of moisture, that fountains and rivers might flow forth from it for you.

For your sake it was commanded to bring forth living creatures, and all things which could serve for your use and pleasure. Is it not for you that the winds blow, that the earth, conceiving by them, may bring forth fruits?

Is it not for you that the showers fall, and the seasons change?

Is it not for you that the sun rises and sets, and the moon undergoes her changes?

For you the sea offers its service, that all things may be subject to you, ungrateful as you are. For all these things shall there not be a righteous punishment of vengeance, because beyond all else you are ignorant of the bestower of all these things, whom you ought to acknowledge and reverence above all?

Chapter VIII - Necessity of Baptism

"But now I lead you to understanding by the same paths.

For you see that all things are produced from waters.

But water was made at first by the Only-begotten; and the Almighty God is the head of the Only-begotten, by whom we come to the Father in such order as we have stated above.

But when you have come to the Father you will learn that this is His will, that you be born anew by means of waters, which were first created. [10] For he who is regenerated by water, having filled up the measure of good works, is made heir of Him by whom he has been regenerated in incorruption.

Wherefore, with prepared minds, approach as sons to a father, that your sins may be washed away, and it may be proved before God that ignorance was their sole cause.

For if, after the learning of these things, you remain in unbelief, the cause of your destruction will be imputed to yourselves, and not to ignorance.

And do you suppose that you can have hope towards God, even if you cultivate all piety and all righteousness, but do not receive baptism.

Yea rather, he will be worthy of greater punishment, who does good works not well; for merit accrues to men from good works, but only if they be done as God commands.

Now God has ordered every one who worships Him to be sealed by baptism; but if you refuse, and obey your own will rather than God's, you are doubtless contrary and hostile to His will.

Chapter IX - Use of Baptism

"But you will perhaps say, What does the baptism of water contribute towards the worship of God?

In the first place, because that which hath pleased God is fulfilled.

In the second place, because, when you are regenerated and born again of water and of God, the frailty of your former birth, which you have through men, is cut off, and so at length you shall be able to attain salvation; but otherwise it is impossible. For thus hath the true prophet testified to us with an oath:

Verily I say to you, That unless a man is born again of water, he shall not enter into the kingdom of heaven.' [11] Therefore make haste; for there is in these waters a certain power of mercy which was borne upon them at the beginning, and acknowledges those who are baptized under the name of the threefold sacrament, and rescues them from future punishments, presenting as a gift to God the souls that are consecrated by baptism.

Betake yourselves therefore to these waters, for they alone can quench the violence of the future fire; and he who delays to approach to them, it is evident that the idol of unbelief remains in him, and by it he is prevented from hastening to the waters which confer salvation.

For whether you be righteous or unrighteous, baptism is necessary for you in every respect:

for the righteous, that perfection may be accomplished in him, and he may be born again to God; for the unrighteous, that pardon may be vouchsafed him of the sins which he has committed in ignorance.

Therefore all should hasten to be born again to God without delay, because the end of every one's life is uncertain.

Chapter X - Necessity of Good Works

"But when you have been regenerated by water, show by good works the likeness in you of that Father who hath begotten you.

Now you know God, honour Him as a father; and His honour is, that you live according to His will.

And His will is, that you so live as to know nothing of murder or adultery, to flee from hatred and covetousness, to put away anger, pride, and boasting, to abhor envy, and to count all such things entirely unsuitable to you.

There is truly a certain peculiar observance of our religion, which is not so much imposed upon men, as it is sought out by every worshipper of God by reason of its purity. By reason of chastity, I say, of which there are many kinds, but first, that every one be careful that he come not near a menstruous woman;' for this the law of God regards as detestable.

But though the law had given no admonition concerning these things, should we willingly, like beetles, roll ourselves in filth?

For we ought to have something more than the animals, as reasonable men, and capable of heavenly senses, whose chief study it ought to be to guard the conscience from every defilement of the heart.

Chapter XI - Inward and Outward Cleansing

"Moreover, it is good, and tends to purity, also to wash the body with water.

I call it good, not as if it were that prime good of the purifying of the mind, but because this of the washing of the body is the sequel of that good.

For so also our Master rebuked some of the Pharisees and scribes, who seemed to be better than others, and separated from the people, calling them hypocrites, because they purified only those things which were seen of men, but left defiled and sordid their hearts, which God alone sees.

To some therefore of them--not to all--He said, Woe to you, scribes and Pharisees, hypocrites! because ye cleanse the outside of the cup and platter, but the inside is full of pollution.

O blind Pharisees, first make clean what is within, and what is without shall be clean also.' [12]For truly, if the mind be purified by the light of knowledge, when once it is clean and clear, then it necessarily takes care of that which is without a man, that is, his flesh, that it also may be purified.

But when that which is without, the cleansing of the flesh, is neglected, it is certain that there is no care taken of the purity of the mind and the cleanness of the heart.

Thus therefore it comes to pass, that he who is clean inwardly is without doubt cleansed outwardly also, but not always that he who is clean outwardly is also cleansed inwardly--to wit, when he does these things that he may please men.

Chapter XII - Importance of Chastity

"But this kind of chastity is also to be observed, that sexual intercourse must not take place heedlessly and for the sake of mere pleasure, but for the sake of begetting children. [13]And since this observance is found even amongst some of the lower animals, it were a shame if it be not observed by men, reasonable, and worshipping God.

But there is this further reason why chastity should be observed by those who hold the true worship of God, in those forms of it of which we have spoken, and others of like sort, that it is observed strictly even amongst those who are still held by the devil in error, for even amongst them there is in some degree the observance of chastity.

What then?

Will you not observe, now that you are reformed, what you observed when you were in error?

Chapter XIII - Superiority of Christian Morality

"But perhaps some one of you will say, Must we then observe all things which we did while we worshipped idols?

Not all.

But whatever things were done well, these you ought to observe even now; because, if anything is rightly done by those who are in error, it is certain that that is derived from the truth; whereas, if anything is not rightly done in the true religion, that is, without doubt, borrowed from error.

For good is good, though it be done by those who are in error; and evil is evil, though it be done by those who follow the truth.

Or shall we be so foolish, that if we see a worshipper of idols to be sober, we shall refuse to be sober, lest we should seem to do the same things which he does who worships idols?

It is not so.

But let this be our study, that if those who err do not commit murder, we should not even be angry; if they do not commit adultery, we should not even covet another's wife; if they love their neighbours, we should love even our enemies; if they lend to those who have the means of paying, we should give to those from whom we do not hope to receive anything.

And in all things, we who hope for the inheritance of the eternal world ought to excel those who know only the present world; knowing that if their works, when compared with our works, be found like and equal in the day of judgment, there will be confusion to us, because we are found equal in our works to those who are condemned on account of ignorance, and had no hope of the world to come.

Chapter XIV - Knowledge Enhances Responsibility

"And truly confusion is our worthy portion, if we have done no more than those who are inferior to us in knowledge.

But if it be confusion to us, to be found equal to them in works, what shall become of us if the examination that is to take place find us inferior and worse than them?

Hear, therefore, how our true Prophet has taught us concerning these things; for, with respect to those who neglect to hear the words of wisdom, He speaks thus:

The queen of the south shall rise in judgment with this generation, and shall condemn it, because she came from the ends of the earth to hear the wisdom of Solomon; and, behold, a greater than Solomon is here, and they hear Him not.' [14]But with respect to those who refused to repent of their evil deeds, He spoke thus:

The men of Nineve shall rise in the judgment with this generation, and shall condemn it; for they repented at the preaching of Jonas; and, behold, a greater than Jonas is here.' [15]You see, therefore, how He condemned those who were instructed out of the law, by adducing the example of those who came from Gentile ignorance, and showing that the former were not even equal to those who seemed to live in error.

From all these things, then, the statement that He propounded is proved, that chastity, which is observed to a certain extent even by those who live in error, should be held much more purely and strictly, in all its forms, as we showed above, by us who follow the truth; and the rather because with us eternal rewards are assigned to its observance."

Chapter XV - Bishops, Presbyters, Deacons, and Widows Ordained at Tripolis

When he had said these things, and others to the same effect, he dismissed the crowds; and having, according to his custom, supped with his friends, he went to sleep.

And while in this manner he was teaching the word of God for three whole months, and converting multitudes to the faith, at the last he ordered me to fast; and after the fast he conferred on me the baptism of ever-flowing water, in the fountains which adjoin the sea. [16]And when, for the grace of regeneration divinely conferred upon me, we had joyfully kept holiday with our brethren, Peter ordered those who had been appointed to go before him, to proceed to Antioch, and there to wait three months more.

And they having gone, he himself led down to the fountains, which, I have said, are near the sea, those who had fully received the faith of the Lord, and baptized them; and celebrating [17] the Eucharist with them, he appointed, as bishop over them, Maro, who had entertained him in his house, and who

The Epistles of Clement

was now perfect in all things; and with him he ordained twelve presbyters and deacons at the same time.

He also instituted the order of widows, and arranged all the services of the Church; and charged them all to obey Maro their bishop in all things that he should command them.

And thus all things being suitably arranged, when the three months were fulfilled, we bade farewell to those who were at Tripolis, and set out for Antioch.

Footnotes:

1. [Comp. book iii. 31.
To this there is no parallel in the Homilies.--R.]
2. It will be remembered that the hours were variable periods, and began to be reckoned from sunrise.
3. [To chaps. 2, 3, there is a parallel in the corresponding chapters of Homily XI.
Then follows a long passage similar to that in book v. 23-36.--R.]
4. [The remaining chapters of this book (4-14) correspond with Homily XI. 19-33.
The discourse here is somewhat fuller, but the order of topics is the same throughout.--R.]
5. Luke xii. 49.
6. Matt. x. 34.
7. Luke xxiii. 34.
8. Acts vii. 60.
9. Gen. i. 1, 2.
10. [There is no exact parallel to these statements in the corresponding chapter of the Homilies (xi. 26).--R.]
11. John iii. 5.
[This passage is cited, with additions, in Homily XI. 26.--R.]
12. Matt. xxiii. 25, 26.
13. [This chapter is more specific in its statements than Homily XI. 30, to which it has a general resemblance.--R.]
14. Matt. xii. 42; Luke xi. 31.
15. Matt. xii. 41; Luke xi. 32.
16. [Comp. Homily XI. 35, 36, which, however, contain additional matter.--R.]
17. Literally, "breaking the Eucharist."

Book VII

Chapter I - Journey from Tripolis

At length leaving Tripolis, [1] a city of Phoenicia, we made our first halt at Ortosias, not far from Tripolis; and there we remained the next day also, because almost all those that had believed in the Lord, unable to part from Peter, followed him thus far.

Thence we came to Antharadus.

But because there were many in our company, Peter said to Niceta and Aquila:

"As there are immense crowds of brethren with as, and we bring upon ourselves no little envy as we enter into every city, it seems to me that we must take means, without doing so unpleasing a thing as to prevent their following us, to secure that the wicked one shall not stir up envy against us on account of any display!

I wish, therefore, that you, Niceta and Aquila, would go before us with them, so that you may lead the multitude divided into two sections, that we may enter every city of the Gentiles travelling apart, rather than in one assemblage.

Chapter II - Disciples Divided into Two Bands

"But I know that you think it sad to be separated from me for the space of at least two days. Believe me, that in whatever degree you love me, my affection towards you is tenfold greater.

But if, by reason of our mutual affection, we will not do the things that are right and honourable, such love will appear to be unreasonable.

And therefore, without bating a little of our love, let us attend to those things which seem useful and necessary; especially since not a day can pass in which you may not be present at my discussions.

For I purpose to pass through the most noted cities of the provinces one by one, as you also know, and to reside three months in each for the sake of teaching. Now, therefore, go before me to Laodicea, which is the nearest city, and I shall follow you after two or three days, so far as I purpose. But you shall wait for me at the inn nearest to the gate of the city; and thence again, when we have spent a few days there, you shall go before me to more distant cities.

And this I wish you to do at every city, for the sake of avoiding envy as much as in us lies, and also that the brethren who are with us, finding lodgings prepared in the several cities by your foresight, may not seem to be vagabonds."

Chapter III - Order of March

When Peter thus spoke, they of course acquiesced, saying:

"It does not greatly sadden us to do this, because we are ordered by you, who have been chosen by the foresight of Christ to do and to counsel well in all things; but also because, while it is a heavy loss not to see our lord Peter for one, or it may be two days, yet it is not intolerable.

And we think of our twelve brethren who go before us, and who are deprived of the advantage of hearing and seeing you for a whole month out of the three that you stay in every city.

Therefore we shall not delay doing as you order, because you order all things aright."

And thus saying, they went forward, having received instructions that they should speak to the brethren who journeyed with them outside the city, and request them not to enter the cities in a crowd and with tumult, but apart, and divided.

Chapter IV - Clement's Joy at Remaining with Peter

But when they were gone, I Clement rejoiced greatly because he had kept me with himself, and I said to him:

"I give thanks to God that you have not sent me forward with the others, for I should have died through sadness."

Then said Peter:

"And what will happen if necessity shall demand that you be sent anywhere for the purpose of teaching? Would you die if you were separated from me for a good purpose?

Would you not put a restraint upon yourself, to bear patiently what necessity has laid upon you?

Or do you not know that friends are always together, and are joined in memory, though they be separated bodily; as, on the other hand, some persons are near to one another in body, but are separate in mind?"

Chapter V - Clement's Affection for Peter

Then I answered:

"Think not, my lord, that I suffer these things unreasonably; but there is a certain cause and reason of this affection of mine towards you.

For I have you alone as the object of all my affections, instead of father and mother, and brethren; but above all this, is the fact that you alone are the cause of my salvation and knowledge of the truth.

And also this I do not count of least moment, that my youthful age is subject to the snares of lusts; and I am afraid to be without you, by whose sole presence all effeminacy, however irrational it be, is put to shame; although I trust, by the mercy of God, that even my mind, from what it has conceived through your instruction, shall be unable to receive aught else into its thoughts. Besides, I remember your saying at Caesarea, If any one wishes to accompany me, without violating dutifulness, let him accompany me.' And by this you meant that he should not make any one sad, to whom he ought according to God's appointment to cleave; for example, that he should not leave a faithful wife, or parents, or the like.

Now from these I am entirely free, and so I am fit for following you; and I wish you would grant me that I might perform to you the service of a servant."

Chapter VI - Peter's Simplicity of Life

Then Peter, laughing, said:

"And do you not think, Clement, that very necessity must make you my servant?

For who else can spread my sheets, and arrange my beautiful coverlets?

Who will be at hand to keep my rings, and prepare my robes, which I must be constantly changing?

Who shall superintend my cooks, and provide various and choice meats to be prepared by most recondite and various art; and all those things which are procured at enormous expense, and are brought together for men of delicate up-bringing, yea rather, for their appetite, as for some enormous beast?

But perhaps, although you live with me, you do not know my manner of life.

I live on bread alone, with olives, and seldom even with pot-herbs; and my dress is what you see, a tunic with a pallium:

and having these, I require nothing more.

This is sufficient for me, because my mind does not regard things present, but things eternal, and therefore no present and visible thing delights me. Whence I embrace and admire indeed your good mind towards me; and I commend you the more, because, though you have been accustomed to so great abundance, you have been able so soon to abandon it, and to accommodate yourself to this life of ours, which makes use of necessary things alone.

For we--that is, I and my brother Andrew--have grown up from our childhood not only orphans, but also extremely poor, and through necessity have become used to labour, whence now also we easily bear the fatigues of our journeyings.

But rather, if you would consent and allow it, I, who am a working man, could more easily discharge the duty of a servant to you."

Chapter VII - Peter's Humility

But I trembled when I heard this, and my tears immediately gushed forth, because so great a man, who is worth more than the whole world, had addressed such a proposal to me.

Then he, when he saw me weeping, inquired the reason; and I answered him:

"How have I so sinned against you, that you should distress me with such a proposal?"

Then Peter: "If it is evil that I said I should serve you, you were first in fault in saying the same thing to me."

Then said I:

"The cases are not alike:

for it becomes me to do this to you; but it is grievous that you, who are sent as the herald of the Most High God to save the souls of men, should say it to me."

Then said Peter:

"I should agree with you, were it not that our Lord, who came for the salvation of the whole world, and who was nobler than any creature, submitted to be a servant, that He might persuade us not to be ashamed to perform the ministry of servants to our brethren."

Then said I:

"It were foolishness in me to suppose that I can prevail with you; nevertheless I give thanks to the providence of God, because I have merited to have you instead of parents."

Chapter VIII - Clement's Family History

Then said Peter:

"Is there then no one of your family surviving?"

I answered:

"There are indeed many powerful men, coming of the stock of Caesar; for Caesar himself gave a wife to my father, as being his relative, and educated along with him, and of a suitably noble family. By her my father had twin sons, born before me, not very like one another, as my father told me; for I never knew them.

But indeed I have not a distinct recollection even of my mother; but I cherish the remembrance of her face, as if I had seen it in a dream.

My mother's name was Matthidia, my father's Faustinianus:

my brothers', Faustinus and Faustus. [2]Now, when I was barely five years old, my mother saw a vision--so I learned from my father--by which she was warned that, unless she speedily left the city with her twin sons, and was absent for ten years, she and her children should perish by a miserable fate.

Chapter IX - Disappearance of His Mother and Brothers

"Then my father, who tenderly loved his sons, put them on board a ship with their mother, and sent them to Athens to be educated, with slaves and maid-servants, and a sufficient supply of money; retaining me only to be a comfort to him, and thankful for this, that the vision had not commanded me also to go with my mother.

And at the end of a year my father sent men to Athens with money for them, desiring also to know how they did; but those who were sent never returned.

Again, in the third year, my sorrowful father sent other men with money, who returned in the fourth year, and related that they had seen neither my mother nor my brothers, that they had never reached Athens, and that no trace had been found of any one of those who had been with them.

Chapter X - Disappearance of His Father

"My father hearing this, and confounded with excessive sorrow, not knowing whither to go or where to seek, went down with me to the harbour, and began to ask of the sailors whether any of them had seen or heard of the bodies of a mother and two little children being cast ashore anywhere, four years ago; when one told one story and another another, but nothing definite was disclosed to us searching in this boundless sea.

Yet my father, by reason of the great affection which he bore to his wife and children, was fed with vain hopes, until he thought of placing me under guardians and leaving me at Rome, as I was now twelve years old, and himself going in quest of them.

Therefore he went down to the harbour weeping, and going on board a ship, took his departure; and from that time till now I have never received any letters from him, nor do I know whether he is alive or dead.

But I rather suspect that he also has perished, either through a broken heart or by shipwreck; for twenty years have now elapsed since then, and no tidings of him have ever reached me."

Chapter XI - Different Effects of Suffering on Heathens and Christians

Peter, hearing this, shed tears of sympathy, and said to his friends who were present:
"If any man who is a worshipper of God had endured what this man's father has endured, immediately men would assign his religion as the cause of his calamities; but when these things happen to miserable Gentiles, they charge their misfortunes upon fate.

I call them miserable, because they are both vexed with errors here, and are deprived of future hope; whereas, when the worshippers of God suffer these things, their patient endurance of them contributes to their cleansing from sin."

Chapter XII - Excursion to Aradus

After this, one of those present began to ask Peter, that early next day we should go to a neighbouring island called Aradus, which was not more than six furlongs off, to see a certain wonderful work that was in it, viz. vine-wood [3] columns of immense size.

To this Peter assented, as he was very complaisant; but he charged us that, when we left the ship, we should not rush all together to see it:
"for," said he, "I do not wish you to be noticed by the crowd."

When therefore, next day, we reached the island by ship in the course of an hour, forthwith we hastened to the place where the wonderful columns were. They were placed in a certain temple, in which there were very magnificent works of Phidias, on which every one of us gazed earnestly.

Chapter XIII - The Beggar Woman

But when Peter had admired only the columns, being no wise ravished with the grace of the painting, he went out, and saw before the gates a poor woman asking alms of those who went in; and looking earnestly at her, he said:
"Tell me, O woman, what member of your body is wanting, that you subject yourself to the indignity of asking alms, and do not rather gain your bread by labouring with your hands which God has given you."

But she, sighing, said:
"Would that I had hands which could be moved; but now only the appearance of hands has been preserved, for they are lifeless, and have been rendered feeble and without feeling by my knawing of them."

Then Peter said:
"What has been the cause of your inflicting so great an injury upon yourself?"

"Want of courage," said she, "and nought else; for if I had had any bravery in me, I could either have thrown myself from a precipice, or cast myself into the depths of the sea, and so ended my griefs."

Chapter XIV - The Woman's Grief

Then Peter said:
"Do you think, O woman, that those who destroy themselves are set free from torments, and not rather that the souls of those who lay violent hands upon themselves are subjected to greater punishments?"

Then said she:
"I wish I were sure that souls live in the infernal regions, for I would gladly embrace the suffering of the penalty of suicide, only that I might see my darling children, if it were but for an hour."

Then Peter:
"What thing is it so great, that effects you with so heavy sadness? I should like to know.

For if you informed me of the cause, I might be able both to show you clearly, O woman, that souls do live in the infernal regions; and instead of the precipice or the deep sea, I might give you some remedy, that you may be able to end your life without torment."

Chapter XV - The Woman's Story

Then the woman, hearing this welcome promise, began to say:
"It is neither easy of belief, nor do I think it necessary to tell, what is my extraction, or what is my country.

It is enough only to explain the cause of my grief, why I have rendered my hands powerless by gnawing them.

Being born of noble parents, and having become the wife of a suitably powerful man, I had two twin sons, and after them one other. But my husband's brother was vehemently enflamed with unlawful love towards me; and as I valued chastity above all things, and would neither consent to so great wickedness, nor wished to disclose to my husband the baseness of his brother, I considered whether in any way I could escape unpolluted, and yet not set brother against brother, and so bring the whole race of a noble family into disgrace.

I made up my mind, therefore, to leave my country with my two twins, until the incestuous love should subside, which the sight of me was fostering and inflaming; and I thought that our other son should remain to comfort his father to some extent.

Chapter XVI - The Woman's Story Continued

"Now in order to carry out this plan, I pretended that I had had a dream, in which some deity stood by me in a vision, and told me that I should immediately depart from the city with my twins, and should be absent until he should command me to return; and that, if I did not do so, I should perish with all my children.

And so it was done.

For as soon as I told the dream to my husband, he was terrified; and sending with me my twin sons, and also slaves and maid-servants, and giving me plenty of money, he ordered me to sail to Athens, where I might educate my sons, and that I should stay there until he who commanded me to depart should give me leave to return.

While I was sailing along with my sons, I was shipwrecked in the night by the violence of the winds, and, wretch that I am, was driven to this place; and when all had perished, a powerful wave caught me, and cast me upon a rock.

And while I sat there with this only hope, that haply I might be able to find my sons, I did not throw myself into the deep, although then my soul, disturbed and drunk with grief, had both the courage and the power to do it.

Chapter XVII - The Woman's Story Continued

"But when the day dawned, and I with shouting and howling was looking around, if I could even see the corpses of my unhappy sons anywhere washed ashore, some of those who saw me were moved with compassion, and searched, first over the sea, and then also along the shores, if they could find either of my children.

But when neither of them was anywhere found, the women of the place, taking pity on me, began to comfort me, every one telling her own griefs, that I might take consolation from the likeness of their calamities to my own.

But this saddened me all the more; for my disposition was not such that I could regard the misfortunes of others as comforts to me.

And when many desired to receive me hospitably, a certain poor woman who dwells here constrained me to enter into her hut, saying that she had had a husband who was a sailor, and that he had died at sea while a young man, and that, although many afterwards asked her in marriage, she preferred widowhood through love of her husband.

Therefore,' said she, we shall share whatever we can gain by the labour of our hands.'

Chapter XVIII - The Woman's Story Continued

"And, not to detain you with a long and profitless story, I willingly dwelt with her on account of the faithful affection which she retained for her husband.

But not long after, my hands (unhappy woman that I was!), long torn with gnawing, became powerless, and she who had taken me in fell into palsy, and now lies at home in her bed; also the affection of those women who had formerly pitied me grew cold.

We are both helpless.

I, as you see, sit begging; and when I get anything, one meal serves two wretches.

Behold, now you have heard enough of my affairs; why do you delay the fulfilment of your promise, to give me a remedy, by which both of us may end our miserable life without torment?"

Chapter XIX - Peter's Reflections on the Story

While she was speaking, Peter, being distracted with much thought, stood like one thunder-struck; and I Clement coming up, said:

"I have been seeking you everywhere, and now what are we to do?"

But he commanded me to go before him to the ship, and there to wait for him; and because he must not be gainsayed, I did as he commanded me.

But he, as he afterwards told me the whole, being struck with a sort of suspicion, asked of the woman her family, and her country, and the names of her sons; "and straightway," he said, "if you tell me these things, I shall give you the remedy."

But she, like one suffering violence, because she would not confess these things, and yet was desirous of the remedy, feigned one thing after another, saying that she was an Ephesian, and her husband a Sicilian, and giving false names to her sons.

Then Peter, supposing that she had answered truly, said: "Alas! O woman, I thought that some great joy should spring up to us to-day; for I suspected that you were a certain woman, concerning whom I lately learned certain like things."

But she adjured him, saying: "I entreat you to tell me what they are, that I may know if amongst women there be one more unfortunate than myself."

Chapter XX - Peter's Statement to the Woman

Then Peter, incapable of deception, and moved with compassion, began to say:

"There is a certain young man among those who follow me for the sake of religion and sect, a Roman citizen, who told me that he had a father and two twin brothers, of whom not one is left to him.

My mother,' he said, as I learned from my father, saw a vision, that she should depart from the Roman city for a time with her twin sons, else they should perish by a dreadful death; and when she had departed, she was nevermore seen.'

And afterwards his father set out to search for his wife and sons, and was also lost."

Chapter XXI - A Discovery

When Peter had thus spoken, the woman, struck with astonishment, fainted.

Then Peter began to hold her up, and to comfort her, and to ask what was the matter, or what she suffered.

But she at length, with difficulty recovering her breath, and nerving herself up to the greatness of the joy which she hoped for, and at the same time wiping her face, said:

"Is he here, the youth of whom you speak?"

But Peter, when he understood the matter, said:

"Tell me first, or else you shall not see him."

Then she said:

"I am the mother of the youth."

Then says Peter:

"What is his name?"

And she answered:

"Clement."

Then said Peter:

"It is himself; and he it was that spoke with me a little while ago, and whom I ordered to go before me to the ship."

Then she fell down at Peter's feet and began to entreat him that he would hasten to the ship.

Then Peter said:

"Yes, if you will promise me that you will do as I say."

Then she said:

"I will do anything; only show me my only son, for I think that in him I shall see my twins also."

Then Peter said:

"When you have seen him, dissemble for a little time, until we leave the island."

"I will do so," she said.

Chapter XXII - A Happy Meeting

Then Peter, holding her hand, led her to the ship.

And when I saw him giving his hand to the woman, I began to laugh; yet, approaching to do him honour, I tried to substitute my hand for his, and to support the woman.

But as soon as I touched her hand, she uttered a loud scream, and rushed into my embrace, and began to devour me with a mother's kisses.

But I, being ignorant of the whole matter, pushed her off as a mad woman; and at the same time, though with reverence, I was somewhat angry with Peter.

Chapter XXIII - A Miracle

But he said:

"Cease:

what mean you, O Clement, my son?

Do not push away your mother."

But I, as soon as I heard these words, immediately bathed in tears, fell upon my mother, who had fallen down, and began to kiss her.

For as soon as I heard, by degrees I recalled her countenance to my memory; and the longer I gazed, the more familiar it grew to me.

Mean time a great multitude assembled, hearing that the woman who used to sit and beg was recognised by her son, who was a good man. [4]And when we wished to sail hastily away from the island, my mother said to me:

"My darling son, it is right that I should bid farewell to the woman who took me in; for she is poor, and paralytic, and bedridden."

When Peter and all who were present heard this, they admired the goodness and prudence of the woman; and immediately Peter ordered some to go and to bring the woman in her bed as she lay.

And when she had been brought, and placed in the midst of the crowd, Peter said, in the presence of all:

"If I am a preacher of truth, for confirming the faith of all those who stand by, that they may know and believe that there is one God, who made heaven and earth, in the name of Jesus Christ, His Son, let this woman rise."

And as soon as he had said this, she arose whole, and fell down at Peter's feet; and greeting her friend and acquaintance with kisses asked of her was the meaning of it all.

But she shortly related to her the whole proceeding of the Recognition, [5] so that the crowds standing around wondered.

Chapter XXIV - Departure from Aradus

Then Peter, so far as he could, and as time permitted, addressed the crowds on the faith of God, and the ordinances of religion; and then added, that if any one wished to know more accurately about these things, he should come to Antioch, "where," said he, "we have resolved to stay three months, and to teach fully the things which pertain to salvation.

For if," said he, "men leave their country and their parents for commercial or military purposes, and do not fear to undertake long voyages, why should it be thought burdensome or difficult to leave home for three months for the sake of eternal life?"

When he had said these things, and more to the same purpose, I presented a thousand drachmas to the woman who had entertained my mother, and who had recovered her health by means of Peter, and in the presence of all committed her to the charge of a certain good man, the chief person in that town, who promised that he would gladly do what we demanded of him.

I also distributed a little money among some others, and among those women who were said formerly to have comforted my mother in her miseries, to whom I also expressed my thanks.

And after this we sailed, along with my mother, to Antaradus.

Chapter XXV - Journeyings

And when we had come to our lodging, [6] my mother began to ask of me what had become of my father; and I told her that he had gone to seek her, and never returned.

But she, hearing this, only sighed; for her great joy on my account lightened her other sorrows.

And the next day she journeyed with us, sitting with Peter's wife; and we came to Balaneae, where we stayed three days, and then went on to Pathos, and afterwards to Gabala; and so we arrived at Laodicea, where Niceta and Aquila met us before the gates, and kissing us, conducted us to a lodging.

But Peter, seeing that it was a large and splendid city, said that it was worthy that we should stay in it ten days, or even longer. Then Niceta and Aquila asked of me who was this unknown woman; and I answered:

"It is my mother, whom God has given back to me by means of my lord Peter."

Chapter XXVI - Recapitulation

And when I had said this, Peter began to relate the whole matter to them in order, [7] and said, "When we had come to Aradus, [8] and I had ordered you to go on before us, the same day after you had gone, Clement was led in the course of conversation to tell me of his extraction and his family, and how he had been deprived of his parents, and had had twin brothers older than himself, and that, as his father told him, his mother once saw a vision, by which she was ordered to depart from the city of Rome with her twin sons, else she and they should suddenly perish.

And when she had told his father the dream, he, loving his sons with tender affection, and afraid of any evil befalling them, put his wife and sons on board a ship with all necessaries, and sent them to Athens to be educated.

Afterwards he sent once and again persons to inquire after them, but nowhere found even a trace of them.

At last the father himself went on the search, and until now he is nowhere to be found.

When Clement had given me this narrative, there came one to us, asking us to go to the neighbouring island of Aradus, to see vine-wood columns of wonderful size.

I consented; and when we came to the place, all the rest went into the interior of the temple; but I--for what reason I know not--had no mind to go farther.

Chapter XXVII - Recapitulation Continued

"But while I was waiting outside for them, I began to notice this woman, and to wonder in what part of her body she was disabled, that she did not seek her living by the labour of her hands, but submitted to the shame of beggary.

I therefore asked of her the reason of it. She confessed that she was sprung of a noble race, and was married to a no less noble husband, whose brother,' said she, being inflamed by unlawful love towards me, desired to defile his brother's bed.

This I abhorring, and yet not daring to tell my husband of so great wickedness, lest I should stir up war between the brothers, and bring disgrace upon the family, judged it better to depart from my country with my two twin sons, leaving the younger boy to be a comfort to his father.

And that this might be done with an honourable appearance, I thought good to feign a dream, and to tell my husband that there stood by me in a vision a certain deity, who told me to set out from the city immediately with my two twins, and remain until he should instruct me to return.'

She told me that her husband, when he heard this, believed her, and sent her to Athens, with the twin children to be educated there; but that they were driven by a terrible tempest upon that island, where, when the ship had gone to pieces, she was lifted by a wave upon a rock, and delayed killing herself only for this, until,' said she, I could embrace at least the dead limbs of my unfortunate sons, and commit them to burial.

But when the day dawned, and crowds had assembled, they took pity upon me, and threw a garment over me. But I, miserable, entreated them with many tears, to search if they could find anywhere the bodies of my unfortunate sons.

And I, tearing all my body with my teeth, with wailing and howlings cried out constantly, Unhappy woman that I am, where is my Faustus? where my Faustinus?'"

Chapter XXVIII - More Recognitions

And when Peter said this, [9] Niceta and Aquila suddenly started up, and being astonished, began to be greatly agitated, saying:

"O Lord, Thou Ruler and God of all, are these things true, or are we in a dream?"

Then Peter said:

"Unless we be mad, these things are true." But they, after a short pause, and wiping their faces, said:

"We are Faustinus and Faustus;

and even at the first, when you began this narrative, we immediately fell into a suspicion that the matters that you spoke of might perhaps relate to us; yet again considering that many like things happen in men's lives, we kept silence, although our hearts were struck by some hope.

Therefore we waited for the end of your story, that, if it were entirely manifest that it related to us, we might then confess it."

And when they had thus spoken, they went in weeping to our mother.

And when they found her asleep, and wished to embrace her, Peter prevented them, saying:

"Permit me first to prepare your mother's mind, lest haply by the great and sudden joy she lose her reason, and her understanding be disturbed, especially as she is now stupefied with sleep."

Chapter XXIX - "Nothing Common or Unclean."

Therefore, when our mother had risen from her sleep, Peter began to address her, saying:

"I wish you to know, O woman, an observance of our religion.

We worship one God, who made the world, and we keep His law, in which He commands us first of all to worship Him, and to reverence His name, to honour our parents, and to preserve chastity and uprightness.

But this also we observe, not to have a common table with Gentiles, unless when they believe, and on the reception of the truth are baptized, and consecrated by a certain threefold invocation of the blessed name; and then we eat with them. [10] Otherwise, even if it were a father or a mother, or wife, or sons, or brothers, we cannot have a common table with them.

Since, therefore, we do this for the special cause of religion, let it not seem hard to you that your son cannot eat with you, until you have the same judgment of the faith that he has."

Chapter XXX - "Who Can Forbid Water?"

Then she, when she heard this, said:

"And what hinders me to be baptized to-day?

For even before I saw you I was wholly alienated from those whom they call gods because they were not able to do anything for me, although I frequently, and almost daily, sacrificed to them.

And as to chastity, what shall I say, when neither in former times did pleasures deceive me, nor afterwards did poverty compel me to sin?

But I think you know well enough how great was my love of chastity, when I pretended that dream that I might escape the snares of unhallowed love, and that I might go abroad with my two twins, and when I left this my son Clement alone to be a comfort to his father.

For if two were scarcely enough for me, how much more it would have saddened their father, if he had had none at all?

For he was wretched through his great affection towards our sons, so that even the authority of the dream could scarce prevail upon him to give up to me Faustinus and Faustus, the brothers of this Clement, and that himself should be content with Clement alone."

The Epistles of Clement

Chapter XXXI - Too Much Joy

While she was yet speaking, my brothers could contain themselves no longer, but rushed into their mother's embrace with many tears, and kissed her.

But she said:

"What is the meaning of this?"

"Then said Peter:

"Be not disturbed, O woman; be firm.

These are your sons Faustinus and Faustus, whom you supposed to have perished in the deep; but how they are alive, and how they escaped in that horrible night, and how the one of them is called Niceta and the other Aquila, they will be able to explain to you themselves, and we also shall hear it along with you."

When Peter had said this, our mother fainted, being overcome with excess of joy; and after some time, being restored and come to herself, she said: "I beseech you, darling sons, tell me what has befallen you since that dismal and cruel night."

Chapter XXXII - "He Bringeth Them Unto Their Desired Haven."

Then Niceta began to say:

"On that night, O mother, when the ship was broken up, and we were being tossed upon the sea, supported on a fragment of the wreck, certain men, whose business it was to rob by sea, found us, and placed us in their boat, and overcoming the power of the waves by rowing, by various stretches brought us to Caesarea Stratonis.

There they starved us, and beat us, and terrified us, that we might not disclose the truth; and having changed our names, they sold us to a certain widow, a very honourable women, named Justa.

She, having bought us, treated us as sons, so that she carefully educated us in Greek literature and liberal arts.

And when we grew up, we also attended to philosophic studies, that we might be able to confute the Gentiles, by supporting the doctrines of the divine religion by philosophic disputations.

Chapter XXXIII - Another Wreck Prevented

"But we adhered, for friendship's sake and boyish companionship, to one Simon, a magician, who was educated along with us, so that we were almost deceived by him.

For there is mention made in our religion of a certain Prophet, whose coming was hoped for by all who observe that religion, through whom immortal and happy life is promised to be given to those who believe in Him.

Now we thought that this Simon was he. But these things shall be explained to you, O mother, at a more convenient season.

Meanwhile, when we were almost deceived by Simon, a certain colleague of my lord Peter, Zacchaeus by name, warned us that we should not be duped by the magician, but presented us to Peter on his arrival, that by him we might be taught the things which were sound and perfect.

And this we hope will happen to you also, even as God has vouchsafed it to us, that we may be able to eat and have a common table with you.

Thus therefore it was, O mother, that you believed that we were drowned in the sea, while we were stolen by pirates."

Chapter XXXIV - Baptism Must Be Preceded by Fasting

When Niceta had spoken thus, our mother fell down at Peter's feet, entreating and beseeching him that both herself and her hostess might be baptized without delay; "that," said she, "I may not even for a single day suffer the loss of the company and society of my sons."

In like manner, we her sons also entreated Peter.

But he said:

"What! Do you think that I alone am unpitiful, and that I do not wish you to enjoy your mother's society at meals?

But she must fast at least one day first, and so be baptized; and this because I have heard from her a certain declaration, by which her faith has been made manifest to me, and which has given evidence of her belief; otherwise she must have been instructed and taught many days before she could have been baptized."

Chapter XXXV - Desiring the Salvation of Others

Then said I:

"I pray you, my lord Peter, tell us what is that declaration which you say afforded you evidence of her faith?"

Then Peter:

"It is her asking that her hostess, whose kindnesses she wishes to requite, may be baptized along with her.

Now she would not ask that this grace be bestowed upon her whom she loves, unless she believed that there is some great boon in baptism.

Whence, also, I find fault with very many, who, when they are themselves baptized and believe, yet do nothing worthy of faith with those whom they love, such as wives, or children, or friends, whom they do not exhort to that which they themselves have attained, as they would do if indeed they believed that eternal life is thereby bestowed.

In short, if they see them to be sick, or to be subject to any danger bodily, they grieve and mourn, because they are sure that in this destruction threatens them.

So, then, if they were sure of this, that the punishment of eternal fire awaits those who do not worship God, when would they cease warning and exhorting?

Or, if they refused, how would they not mourn and bewail them, being sure that eternal torments awaited them?

Now, therefore, we shall send for that woman at once, and see if she loves the faith of our religion; and as we find, so shall we act.

But since your mother has judged so faithfully concerning baptism, let her fast only one day before baptism."

Chapter XXXVI - The Sons' Pleading

But she declared with an oath, in presence of my lord Peter's wife, that from the time she recognised her son, she had been unable to take any food from excess of joy, excepting only that yesterday she drank a cup of water.

Peter's wife also bore witness, saying that it was even so.

Then Aquila said:

"What, then, hinders her being baptized?"

Then Peter, smiling, said:

"But this is not the fast of baptism, for it was not done in order to baptism."

Then Niceta said:

"But perhaps God, wishing that our mother, on our recognition, should not be separated even for one day from participation of our table, pre-ordained this fasting.

For as in her ignorance she preserved her chastity, that it might profit her in order to the grace of baptism; so she fasted before she knew the reason of fasting, that it might profit her in order to baptism, and that immediately, from the beginning of our acquaintance, she might enjoy communion of the table with us."

Chapter XXXVII - Peter Inexorable

Then said Peter: [11]"Let not the wicked one prevail against us, taking occasion from a mother's love; but let you, and me with you, fast this day along with her, and to-morrow she shall be baptized: for it is not right that the precepts of truth be relaxed and weakened in favour of any person or friendship.

Let us not shrink, then, from suffering along with her, for it is a sin to transgress any commandment.

But let us teach our bodily senses, which are without us, to be in subjection to our inner senses; and not compel our inner senses, which savour the things that be of God, to follow the outer senses, which savour the things that be of the flesh.

For to this end also the Lord commanded, saying:

Whosoever shall look upon a woman to lust after her, hath committed adultery with her already in his heart.'

And to this He added:

If thy right eye offend thee, pluck it out, and cast it from thee:

for it is profitable for thee that one of thy members perish, rather than thy whole body be cast into hell-fire.' [12]He does not say, has offended thee, that you should then cast away the cause of sin after you have sinned; but if it offend you, that is, that before you sin you should cut off the cause of the sin that provokes and irritates you.

But let none of you think, brethren, that the Lord commended the cutting off of the members.

His meaning is, that the purpose should be cut off, not the members, and the causes which allure to sin, in order that our thought, borne up on the chariot of sight, may push towards the love of God, supported by the bodily senses; [13] and not give loose reins to the eyes of the flesh as to wanton horses, eager to turn their running outside the way of the commandments, but may subject the bodily sight to the judgment of the mind, and not suffer those eyes of ours, which God intended to be viewers and witnesses of His work, to become panders of evil desire. And therefore let the bodily senses as well as the internal thought be subject to the law of God, and let them serve His will, whose work they acknowledge themselves to be."

Chapter XXXVIII - Reward of Chastity

Therefore, as the order and reason of the mystery demanded, on the following day she was baptized in the sea, [14] and returning to the lodging, was initiated in all the mysteries of religion in their order.

And we her sons, Niceta and Aquila, and I Clement, were present.

And after this we dined with her, and glorified God with her, thankfully acknowledging the zeal and teaching of Peter, who showed us, by the example of our mother, that the good of chastity is not lost with God; [15] "as, on the other hand," said he, "unchastity does not escape punishment, though it may not be punished immediately, but slowly.

But so well pleasing," said he, "is chastity to God, that it confers some grace in the present life even upon those who are in error; for future blessedness is laid up for those only who preserve chastity and righteousness by the grace of baptism.

In short, that which has befallen your mother is an example of this, for all this welfare has been restored to her in reward of her chastity, for the guarding and preserving of which continence alone is not sufficient; but when any one perceives that snares and deceptions are being prepared, he must straightway flee as from the violence of fire or the attack of a mad dog, and not trust that he can easily frustrate snares of this kind by philosophizing or by humouring them; but, as I have said, he must flee and withdraw to a distance, as your mother also did through her true and entire love of chastity.

And on this account she has been preserved to you, and you to her; and in addition, she has been endowed with the knowledge of eternal life."

When he had said this, and much more to the same effect, the evening having come, we went to sleep.

Footnotes:

1. [The narrative of book vii. is given in Homilies XII., XIII.; chap. 38 including some details of Homily XIV. 1.

The variations in the narrative portions are unimportant:
but the Homilies contain longer discourses of the Apostle.

Chaps 1-24 here correspond quite exactly with Homily XII. 1-24; the topics of the respective chapters being the same, and the variations mainly in forms of expression.--R.]

2. [Comp. Homily XII. 8, where the names given are:
Mattidia, Faustus (father); Faustinus and Faustinianus, the twin sons.
With these names some connect the German legend of Faust; see Schaff, History, ii. 442.--R.]

3. Various reading, "glass."

4. Perhaps, "a man in good position."

5. [This is the title-word of the book, as is evident.
Hence the italics here, and not in Homily XII. 23.--R.]

6. [At this point a discourse of the Apostle on "philanthropy" is inserted in the Homilies (xii. 25-33).

Homily XIII. 1 corresponds with this chapter.--R.]

7. [This account is fuller than that in Homily XIII. 2.--R.]

8. There is a confusion in the text between Aradus and Antaradus. [Aradus is the name of the Island, Antaradus that of the neighbouring city.--R.]

9. [With chaps. 28-36 the narrative in Homily XIII. 3-11 corresponds quite closely.--R.]

10. [Comp. Homily XIII. 4.--R.]

11. [In Homily XIII. 12 the Apostle is represented as thus deferring the baptism; but a longer discourse on chastity (chaps. 13-21) is given, assigned to the evening of that day.--R.]

12. Matt. v. 28, 29.

13. Here a marginal reading is followed.
The reading of the text is:
"In order that our thought, borne on the chariot of contemplation, may hasten on, invisible to the bodily senses, towards the love of God."
But the translation of aspectus by "contemplation" is doubtful.

14. [The baptism is narrated in Homily XIV. 1.--R.]

15. [In Homily XIII. 20, 21, a longer discourse, to the same effect, is recorded; but it is addressed to the mother the evening before her baptism.--R.]

Book VIII

Chapter I - The Old Workman

Now the next morning Peter took my brothers and me with him, and we went down to the harbour to bathe in the sea, and thereafter we retired to a certain secret place for prayer.

But a certain poor old man, a workman, as he appeared by his dress, began to observe us eagerly, without our seeing him, that he might see what we were doing in secret. [1]And when he saw us praying, he waited till we came out, and then saluted us, and said:

"If you do not take it amiss, and regard me as an inquisitive and importunate person, I should wish to converse with you; for I take pity on you, and would not have you err under the appearance of truth, and be afraid of things that have no existence; or if you think that there is any truth in them, then declare it to me. If, therefore, you take it patiently, I can in a few words instruct you in what is right; but if it be unpleasant to you, I shall go on, and do my business."

To him Peter answered:

"Speak what you think good, and we will gladly hear, whether it be true or false; for you are to be welcomed, because, like a father anxious on behalf of his children, you wish to put us in possession of what you regard as good."

Chapter II - Genesis

Then the old man proceeded to say:

"I saw you bathe in the sea, and afterwards retire into a secret place; wherefore observing, without your noticing me, what you were doing, I saw you praying.

Therefore, pitying your error, I waited till you came out, that I might speak to you, and instruct you not to err in an observance of this sort; because there is neither any God, nor any worship, neither is there any providence in the world, but all things are done by fortuitous chance and genesis, as I have discovered most clearly for myself, being accomplished beyond others in the discipline of learning.[2]Do not err, therefore:

for whether you pray, or whether you do not pray, whatever your genesis contains, that shall befall you."

Then I Clement was affected, I know not how, in my heart, recollecting many things in him that seemed familiar to me; for some one says well, that that which is sprung from any one, although it may be long absent, yet a spark of relationship is never extinguished. [3]Therefore I began to ask of him who and whence he was, and how descended.

But he, not wishing to answer these questions, said:

"What has that to do with what I have told you?

But first, if you please, let us converse of those matters which we have propounded; and afterwards, if circumstances require, we can disclose to one another, as friends to friends, our names, and families, and country, and other things connected with these."

Yet we all admired the eloquence of the man, and the gravity of his manners, and the calmness of his speech.

Chapter III - A Friendly Conference

But Peter, walking along leisurely while conversing, was looking out for a suitable place for a conference.

And when he saw a quiet recess near the harbour, he made us sit down; and so he himself first began. Nor did he hold the old man in any contempt, nor did he look down upon him because his dress was poor and mean.

He said, therefore:

"Since you seem to me to be a learned man, and a compassionate, inasmuch as you have come to us, and wish that to be known to us which you consider to be good, we also wish to expound to you what things we believe to be good and right; and if you do not think them true, you will take in good part our good intentions towards you, as we do yours towards us." While Peter was thus speaking, a great multitude assembled.

Then said the old man:

"Perhaps the presence of a multitude disconcerts you." Peter replied:

"Not at all, except only on this account, that I am afraid lest haply, when the truth is made manifest in the course of our discussion, you be ashamed in presence of the multitude to yield and assent to the things which you may have understood to be spoken truly."

To this the old man answered:

"I am not such a fool in my old age, that, understanding what is true, I should deny it for the favour of the rabble."

Chapter IV - The Question Stated

Then Peter began to say:

"Those who speak the word of truth, and who enlighten the souls of men, seem to me to be like the rays of the sun, which, when once they have come forth and appeared to the world, can no longer be concealed or hidden, while they are not so much seen by men, as they afford sight to all.

Therefore it was well said by One to the heralds of the truth, Ye are the light of the world, and a city set upon a hill cannot be hid; neither do men light a candle and put it under a bushel, but upon a candlestick, that it may enlighten all who are in the house.'[4]"

Then said the old man:

"He said well, whoever he is.

But let one of you state what, according to his opinion, ought to be followed, that we may direct our speech to a definite aim.

For, in order to find the truth, it is not sufficient to overthrow the things that are spoken on the other side, but also that one should himself bring forward what he who is on the other side may oppose.

Therefore, in order that both parties may be on an equal footing, it seems to me to be right that each of us should first enunciate what opinion he holds.

And, if you please, I shall begin first.

I say, then, that the world is not governed according to the providence of God, because we see that many things in it are done unjustly and disorderly; but I say that it is genesis that does and regulates all things."

Chapter V - Freedom of Discussion Allowed

When Peter was about to reply to this, Niceta, anticipating him, said: [5]"Would my lord Peter allow me to answer to this; and let it not be thought forward that I, a young man, should have an encounter with an old man, but rather let me converse as a son with a father."

Then said the old man:

"Not only do I wish, my son, that you should set forth your opinions; but also if any one of your associates, if any one even of the bystanders, thinks that he knows anything, let him unhesitatingly state it:

we shall gladly hear it; for it is by the contribution of many that the things that are unknown are more easily found out."

Then Niceta therefore answered:

"Do not deem me to have done rashly, my father, because I have interrupted the speech of my lord Peter; but rather I meant to honour him by doing this.

For he is a man of God, full of all knowledge, who is not ignorant even of Greek learning, because he is filled with the Spirit of God, to whom nothing is unknown.

But because it is suitable to him to speak of heavenly things, I shall answer concerning those things which pertain to the babbling of the Greeks.

But after we have disputed in the Grecian manner, and we have come to that point where no issue appears, then he himself, as filled with the knowledge of God, shall openly and clearly disclose to us the truth on all matters, so that not we only, but also all who are around us as hearers, shall learn the way of truth.

And therefore now let him sit as umpire; and when either of us shall yield, then let him, taking up the matter, give an unquestionable judgment."

Chapter VI - The Other Side of the Question Stated

When Niceta had thus spoken, those who had assembled conversed among themselves:
"Is this that Peter of whom we heard, the most approved disciple of Him who appeared in Judaea, and wrought many signs and miracles?"

And they stood gazing upon him with great fear and veneration, as conferring upon the Lord the honour of His good servant.

Which when Peter observed, he said to them:
"Let us hear with all attention, holding an impartial judgment of what shall be said by each; and after their encounter we also shall add what may seem necessary."

And when Peter had said this, the crowds rejoiced.

Then Niceta began to speak as follows:
"You have laid down, my father, that the world is not governed by the providence of God, but that all things are subject to genesis, whether the things which relate to the dispositions, or those which relate to the doings of every one.

This I could answer immediately; but because it is right to observe order, we also lay down what we hold, as you yourself requested should be done. I say that the world is governed by the providence of God, at least in those things which need His government.

For He it is alone who holds all things in His hand, who also made the world; the just God, who shall at some time render to every one according to his deeds.

Now, then, you have our position; go on as you please, either overthrowing mine or establishing your own, that I may meet your statements.

Or if you wish me to speak first, I shall not hesitate."

Chapter VII - The Way Cleared

Then the old man answered:
"Whether it pleases you, my son, to speak first, or whether you prefer that I should speak, makes no difference, especially with those who discuss in a friendly spirit.

However, speak you first, and I will gladly hear; and I wish you may be able even to follow out those things that are to be spoken by me, and to put in opposition to them those things that are contrary to them, and from the comparison of both to show the truth."

Niceta answered:
"If you wish it, I can even state your side of the argument, and then answer it." Then the old man:
"Show me first how you can know what I have not yet spoken, and so I shall believe that you can follow out my side of the argument."

Then Niceta:
"Your sect is manifest, even by the proposition which you have laid down, to those who are skilled in doctrines of this sort; and its consequence is certain.

And because I am not ignorant what are the propositions of the philosophers, I know what follows from those things which you have propounded; especially because I have frequented the schools of Epicurus in preference to the other philosophers.

But my brother Aquila has attended more to the Pyrrhonists, and our other brother to the Platonists and Aristotelians; therefore you have to do with learned hearers." [6]Then said the old man:
"You have well and logically informed us how you perceived the things that follow from the statements which have been enunciated. But I professed something more than the tenet of Epicurus; for I introduced the genesis, and asserted that it is the cause of all the doings of men."

Chapter VIII - Instincts

When the old man had said this, I Clement said to him:
"Hear, my father:
if my brother Niceta bring you to acknowledge that the world is not governed without the providence of God, I shall be able to answer you in that part which remains concerning the genesis; for I am well acquainted with this doctrine."

And when I had thus spoken, my brother Aquila said:
"What is the use of our calling him father, when we are commanded to call no man father upon

earth?" [7]Then, looking to the old man, he said, "Do not take it amiss, my father, that I have found fault with my brother for calling you father, for we have a precept not to call any one by that name."

When Aquila said that, all the assembly of the bystanders, as well as the old man and Peter, laughed.

And when Aquila asked the reason of their all laughing, I said to him:

"Because you yourself do the very thing which you find fault with in another; for you called the old man father."

But he denied it, saying:

"I am not aware that I called him father." Meantime Peter was moved with certain suspicions,[8] as he told us afterwards; and looking to Niceta, he said, "Go on with what you have proposed."

Chapter IX - Simple and Compound

Then Niceta began as follows: [9]"Everything that is, is either simple or compound.

That which is simple is without number, division, colour, difference, roughness, smoothness, weight, lightness, quality, quantity, and therefore without end.

But that which is compound is either compounded of two, or of three, or even of four elements, or at all events of several; and things which are compounded can also of necessity be divided."

The old man, hearing this, said:

"You speak most excellently and learnedly, my son."

Then Niceta went on: "Therefore that which is simple, and which is without any of those things by which that which subsists can be dissolved, is without doubt incomprehensible and infinite, knowing neither beginning nor end, and therefore is one and alone, and subsisting without an author.

But that which is compound is subject to number, and diversity, and division,--is necessarily compounded by some author, and is a diversity collected into one species.

That which is infinite is therefore, in respect of goodness, a Father; in respect of power, a Creator.

Nor can the power of creating cease in the Infinite, nor the goodness be quiescent; but He is impelled by goodness to change existing things, and by power to arrange and strengthen them.

Therefore some things, as we have said, are changed, and composed of two or three, some of four, others of more elements.

But since our inquiry at present is concerning the method of the world and its substance, which, it is agreed, is compounded of four elements, to which all those ten differences belong which we have mentioned above, let us begin at these lower steps, and come to the higher.

For a way is afforded us to intellectual and invisible things from those which we see and handle; as is contained in arithmetical instructions, where, when inquiry is made concerning divine things, we rise from the lower to the higher numbers; but when the method respecting present and visible things is expounded, the order is directed from the higher to the lower numbers. Is it not so?"

Chapter X - Creation Implies Providence

Then the old man said:

"You are following it out exceedingly well." Then Niceta:

"Now, then, we must inquire concerning the method of the world; of which the first inquiry is divided into two parts.

For it is asked whether it has been made or not?

And if it has not been made, itself must be that Unbegotten from which all things are.

But if it has been made, concerning this again the question is divided into two parts, whether it was made by itself, or by another.

And if indeed it was made by itself, then without doubt providence is excluded.

If providence is not admitted, in vain is the mind incited to virtue, in vain justice is maintained, if there be no one to render to the just man according to his merits.

But even the soul itself will not appear to be immortal, if there be no dispensation of providence to receive it after its escape from the body.

Chapter XI - General or Special Providence

"Now, if it be taught that there is a providence, and that the world was made by it, other questions meet us which must be discussed.

For it will be asked, In what way providence acts, whether generally towards the whole, or specially towards the parts, or generally also towards the parts, or both generally towards the whole, and specially towards the parts?

But by general providence we mean this:

as if God, at first making the world, has given an order and appointed a course to things, and has ceased to take any further care of what is done.

But special providence towards the parts is of this sort, that He exercises providence over some men or places, but not over others.

But general over all, and at the same time special over the parts, is in this wise:

if God made all things at first, and exercises providence over each individual even to the end, and renders to every one according to his deeds.

Chapter XII - Prayer Inconsistent with Genesis

"Therefore that first proposition, which declares that God made all things in the beginning, and having imposed a course and order upon things, takes no further account of them, affirms that all things are done according to genesis.

To this, therefore, we shall first reply; and especially to those who worship the gods and defend genesis. Assuredly, these men, when they sacrifice to the gods and pray to them, hope that they shall obtain something in opposition to genesis, and so they annul genesis.

But when they laugh at those who incite to virtue and exhort to continence, and say that nobody can do or suffer anything unless what is decreed to him by fate, they assuredly cut up by the roots all worship of the Divinity.

For why should you worship those from whom you can obtain nothing which the method of what is decreed does not allow?

Let this suffice in the meantime, in opposition to these men.

But I say that the world is made by God, and that it is at some time to be destroyed by Him, that that world may appear which is eternal, and which is made for this end, that it may be always, and that it may receive those who, in the judgment of God, are worthy of it.

But that there is another and invisible world, which contains this visible world within itself,--after we have finished our discussion concerning the visible world, we shall come to it also.

Chapter XIII - A Creator Necessary

"Now, in the meantime, that this visible world has been made, very many wise men among the philosophers do testify.

But that we may not seem to make use of assertions as witnesses, as though we needed them, let us inquire, if you please, concerning its principles.

That this visible world is material, is sufficiently evident from the fact that it is visible.

But every body receives one of two Differentiae; for it is either compact and solid, or divided and separate.

And if the body of which the world was made was compact and solid, and that body was parted and divided through diverse species and parts according to its differences, there must necessarily be understood to have been some one to separate the body which was compact and solid, and to draw it into many parts and diverse forms; or if all this mass of the world was compounded and compacted from diverse and dispersed parts of bodies, still there must be understood to have been some one to collect into one the dispersed parts, and to invest these things with their different species.

Chapter XIV - Mode of Creation

"And, indeed, I know that several of the philosophers were rather of this opinion, that God the Creator made divisions and distinctions from one body, which they call Matter, which yet consisted of four elements, mingled into one by a certain tempering of divine providence.

For I think that what some have said is vain, that the body of the world is simple, that is, without any conjunction; since it is evident that what is simple can neither be a body, nor can be mixed, or propagated, or dissolved; all which, we see, happen to the bodies of the world.

For how could it be dissolved if it were simple, and had not within it that from which it might be resolved and divided?

But if bodies seem to be composed of two, or three, or even of four elements,--who that has even a small portion of sense does not perceive that there must have been some one who collected several into one, and preserving the measure of tempering, made a solid body out of diverse parts?

This some one, therefore, we call God, the Creator of the world, and acknowledge Him as the author of the universe.

Chapter XV - Theories of Creation

"For the Greek philosophers, inquiring into the beginnings of the world, have gone, some in one way and some in another.

In short, Pythagoras says that numbers are the elements of its beginnings; Callistratus, that qualities; Alcmaeon, that contrarieties; Anaximander, that immensity; Anaxagoras, that equalities of parts; Epicurus, that atoms; Diodorus, that amere, that is, things in which there are no parts; Asclepius, that onkoi, which we may call tumours or swellings; the geometricians, that ends; Democritus, that ideas; Thales, that water; Heraclitus, that fire; Diogenes, that air; Parmenides, that earth; Zeno, Empedocles, Plato, that fire, water, air, and earth.

Aristotle also introduces a fifth element, which he called akatonomaston; that is, that which cannot be named; without doubt indicating Him who made the world, by joining the four elements into one.

Whether, therefore, there be two, or three, or four, or more, or innumerable elements, of which the world consists, in every supposition there is shown to be a God, who collected many into one, and again drew them, when collected, into diverse species; and by this it is proved that the machine of the world could not have subsisted without a maker and a disposer.

Chapter XVI - The World Made of Nothing by a Creator

"But from this fact also, that in the conjunction of the elements, if one be deficient or in excess, the others are loosened and fall, is shown that they took their beginning from nothing.

For if for example, moisture be wanting in any body, neither will the dry stand; for dry is fed by moisture, as also cold by heat; in which, as we have said, if one be defective, the whole are dissolved.

And in this they give indications of their origin, that they were made out of nothing.

Now if matter itself is proved to have been made, how shall its parts and its species, of which the world consists, be thought to be unmade?

But about matter and its qualities this is not the time to speak:

only let it suffice to have taught this, that God is the Creator of all things, because neither, if the body of which the world consists was solid and united, could it be separated and distinguished without a Creator; nor, if it was collected into one from diverse and separate parts, could it be collected and mixed without a Maker.

Therefore, if God is so clearly shown to be the Creator of the world, what room is there for Epicurus to introduce atoms, and to assert that not only sensible bodies, but even intellectual and rational minds, are made of insensible corpuscles?

Chapter XVII - Doctrine of Atoms Untenable

"But you will say, according to the opinion of Epicurus, that successions of atoms coming in a ceaseless course, and mixing with one another, and conglomerating through unlimited and endless periods of time, are made solid bodies.

I do not treat this opinion as a pure fiction, and that, too, a badly contrived one; but let us examine it, whatever be its character, and see if what is said can stand.

For they say that those corpuscles, which they call atoms, are of different qualities:

that some are moist, and therefore heavy, and tending downwards; others dry and earthy, and therefore still heavy; but others fiery, and therefore always pushing upwards; others cold and inert, and always remaining in the middle.

Since then some, as being fiery, always tend upward, and others, as being moist and dry, always downwards, and others keep a middle and unequal course, how could they meet together and form one body?

For if any one throw down from a height small pieces of straw, for example, and pieces of lead of the same size, will the light straws be able to keep up with the pieces of lead, though they be equal in size?

Nay; the heavier reach the bottom far more quickly.

So also atoms, though they be equal in size, yet, being unequal in weight, the lighter will never be able to keep pace with the heavier; but if they cannot keep pace, certainly neither can they be mixed or form one body.

Chapter XVIII - The Concourse of Atoms Could Not Make the World

"Then, in the next place, if they are ceaselessly borne about, and always coming, and being added to things whose measure is already complete, how can the universe stand, when new weights are always being heaped upon so vast weights?

And this also I ask:

If this expanse of heaven which we see was constructed by the gradual concurrence of atoms, how did it not collapse while it was in construction, if indeed the yawning top of the structure was not propped and bound by any stays?

For as those who build circular domes, unless they bind the fastening of the central top, the whole falls at once; so also the circle of the world, which we see to be brought together in so graceful a form, if it was not made at once, and under the influence of a single forth-putting of divine energy by the power of a Creator, but by atoms gradually concurring and constructing it, not as reason demanded, but as a fortuitous issue befell, how did it not fall down and crumble to pieces before it could be brought together and fastened?

And further, I ask this:

What is the pavement on which the foundations of such an immense mass are laid?

And again, what you call the pavement, on what does it rest?

And again that other, what supports it?

And so I go on asking, until the answer comes to nothing and vacuity!

Chapter XIX - More Difficulties of the Atomic Theory

"But if any one say that atoms of a fiery quality, being joined together, formed a body, and because the quality of fire does not tend downwards, but upwards, that the nature of fire, always pushing upwards, supports the mass of the world placed upon it; to this we answer:

How could atoms of a fiery quality, which always make for the highest place, descend to the lower, and be found in the lowest place of all, so as to form a foundation for all; whereas rather the heavier qualities, that is, the earthy or watery, always come before the lighter, as we have said; hence, also, they assert that the heaven, as the higher structure, is composed of fiery atoms, which are lighter, and always fly upwards?

Therefore the world cannot have foundations of fire, or any other:

nor can there be any association or compacting of the heavier atoms with the lighter, that is, of those which are always borne downwards, with those that always fly upwards.

Thus it is sufficiently shown that the bodies of the world are consolidated by the union of atoms; and that insensible bodies, even if they could by any means concur and be united, could not give forms and measures to bodies, form limbs, or effect qualities, or express quantities; all which, therefore, by their exactness, attest the hand of a Maker, and show the operation of reason, which reason I call the Word, and God.

Chapter XX - Plato's Testimony

"But some one will say that these things are done by nature.

Now, in this, the controversy is about a name.

For while it is evident that it is a work of mind and reason, what you call nature, I call God the Creator.

It is evident that neither the species of bodies, arranged with so necessary distinctions, nor the faculties of minds, could or can be made by irrational and senseless work.

But if you regard the philosophers as fit witnesses, Plato testifies concerning these things in the Timaeus, where, in a discussion on the making of the world, he asks, whether it has existed always, or had a beginning, and decides that it was made.

For,' says he, it is visible and palpable, and corporeal; but it is evident that all things which are of this sort have been made; but what has been made has doubtless an author, by whom it was made. This Maker and Father of all, however, it is difficult to discover; and when discovered, it is impossible to declare Him to the vulgar.'

Such is the declaration of Plato; but though he and the other Greek philosophers had chosen to be silent about the making of the world, would it not be manifest to all who have any understanding?

For what man is there, having even a particle of sense, who, when he sees a house having all things necessary for useful purposes, its roof fashioned into the form of a globe, painted with various splendour and diverse figures, adorned with large and splendid lights; who is there, I say, that, seeing such a structure, would not immediately pronounce that it was constructed by a most wise and powerful artificer?

And so, who can be found so foolish, as, when he gazes upon the fabric of the heaven, perceives the splendour of the sun and moon, sees the courses and beauty of the stars, and their paths assigned to them by fixed laws and periods, will not cry out that these things are made, not so much by a wise and rational artificer, as by wisdom and reason itself?

Chapter XXI - Mechanical Theory

"But if you would rather have the opinions of others of the Greek philosophers,--and you are acquainted with mechanical science,--you are of course familiar with what is their deliverance concerning the heavens.

For they suppose a sphere, equally rounded in every direction, and looking indifferently to all points, and at equal distances in all directions from the centre of the earth, and so stable by its own symmetry, that its perfect equality does not permit it to fall off to any side; and so the sphere is sustained, although supported by no prop.

Now if the fabric of the world really has this form, the divine work is evident in it.

But if, as others think, the sphere is placed upon the waters, and is supported by them, or floating in them, even so the work of a great contriver is shown in it.

Chapter XXII - Motions of the Stars

"But lest the assertion may seem doubtful respecting things which are not manifest to all, let us come to those things of which nobody is ignorant.

Who disposed the courses of the stars with so great reason, ordained their risings and settings, and appointed to each one to accomplish the circuit of the heavens in certain and regular times? Who assigned to some to be always approaching to the setting, and others to be returning to the rising?

Who put a measure upon the courses of the sun, that he might mark out, by his diverse motions, hours, and days, and months, and changes of seasons?--that he might distinguish, by the sure measurement of his course, now winter, then spring, summer, and afterwards autumn, and always, by the same changes of the year, complete the circle with variety, without confusion?

Who, I say, will not pronounce that the director of such order is the very wisdom of God?

And these things we have spoken according to the relations given us by the Greeks respecting the science of the heavenly bodies.

Chapter XXIII - Providence in Earthly Things

"But what of those things also which we see on the earth, or in the sea?
Are we not plainly taught, that not only the work, but also the providence, of God is in them?
For whereas there are on the earth lofty mountains in certain places, the object of this is, that the air, being compressed and confined by them through the appointment of God, may be forced and pressed out into winds, by which fruits may germinate, and the summer heat may be moderated when the Pleiades glow, fired with the blaze of the sun.
But you still say, Why that blaze of the sun, that moderating should be required?
How, then, should fruits be ripened which are necessary for the uses of men?
But observe this also, that at the meridian axis, [10] where the heat is greatest, there is no great collection of clouds, nor an abundant fall of rain, lest disease should be produced among the inhabitants; for watery clouds, if they are acted on by rapid heat, render the air impure and pestilential.
And the earth also, receiving the warm rain, does not afford nourishment to the crops, but destruction.
In this who can doubt that there is the working of divine providence?
In short, Egypt, which is scorched with the heat of AEthiopia, in its neighbourhood, lest its air should be incurably vitiated by the effects of showers, its plains do not receive rain furnished to them from the clouds, but, as it were, an earthly shower from the overflow of the Nile.

Chapter XXIV - Rivers and Seas

"What shall we say of fountains and rivers, which flow with perpetual motion into the sea?
And, by the divine providence, neither does their abundant supply fail, nor does the sea, though it receives so great quantities of water, experience any increase, but both those elements which contribute to it and those which are thus contributed remain in the same proportion.
But you will say to me:
The salt water naturally consumes the fresh water which is poured into it.
Well, in this is manifest the work of providence, that it made that element salt into which it turned the courses of all the waters which it had provided for the use of men.
So that through so great spaces of time the channel of the sea has not been filled, and produced a deluge destructive to the earth and to men.
Nor will any one be so foolish as to think that this so great reason and so great providence has been arranged by irrational nature.

Chapter XXV - Plants and Animals

"But what shall I say of plants, and what of animals?
Is it not providence that has ordained that plants, when they decay by old age, should be reproduced by the suckers or the seeds which they have themselves produced, and animals by propagation?
And by a certain wonderful dispensation of providence, milk is prepared in the udders of the dams for the animals before they are born; and as soon as they are born, with no one to guide them, they seek out the store of nourishment provided for them.
And not only males are produced, but females also, that by means of both the race may be perpetuated.
But lest this should seem, as some think, to be done by a certain order of nature, and not by the appointment of the Creator, He has, as a proof and indication of His providence, ordained a few animals to preserve their stock on the earth in an exceptional way:
for example, the crow conceives through the mouth, and the weasel brings forth through the ear; and some birds, such as hens, sometimes produce eggs conceived of wind or dust; other animals convert the male into the female, and change their sex every year, as hares and hyaenas, which they call monsters; others spring from the earth, and get their bodies from it, as moles; others from ashes, as vipers; others from putrifying flesh, as wasps from horseflesh, bees from ox-flesh; others from cow-dung, as beetles; others from herbs, as the scorpion from the basil; and again, herbs from animals, as parsley and asparagus from the horn of the stag or the she goat.

Chapter XXVI - Germination of Seeds

"And what occasion is there to mention more instances in which divine providence has ordained the production of animals to be effected in various ways, that order being superseded which is thought to be assigned by nature, from which not an irrational course of things, but one arranged by his own reason, might be evinced?

And in this also is there not a full work of providence shown, when seeds sown are prepared by means of earth and water for the sustenance of men?

For when these seeds are committed to the earth, the soil milks upon the seeds, as from its teats, the moisture which it has received into itself by the will of God.

For there is in water a certain power of the spirit given by God from the beginning, by whose operation the structure of the body that is to be begins to be formed in the seed itself, and to be developed by means of the blade and the ear; for the grain of seed being swelled by the moisture, that power of the spirit which has been made to reside in water, running as an incorporeal substance through certain strait passages of veins, excites the seeds to growth, and forms the species of the growing plants.

By means, therefore, of the moist element in which that vital spirit is contained and inborn, it is caused that not only is it revived, but also that an appearance and form in all respects like to the seeds that had been sown is reproduced.

Now, who that has even a particle of sense will think that this method depends upon irrational nature, and not upon divine wisdom?

Lastly, also these things are done in a resemblance of the birth of men; for the earth seems to take the place of the womb, into which the seed being cast, is both formed and nourished by the power of water and spirit, as we have said above.

Chapter XXVII - Power of Water

"But in this also the divine providence is to be admired, that it permits us to see and know the things that are made, but has placed in secrecy and concealment the way and manner in which they are done, that they may not be competent to the knowledge of the unworthy, but may be laid open to the worthy and faithful, when they shall have deserved it.

But to prove by facts and examples that nothing is imparted to seeds of the substance of the earth, but that all depends upon the element of water, and the power of the spirit which is in it,--suppose, for example, that a hundred talents' weight of earth are placed in a very large trough, and that there are sown in it several kinds of seeds, either of herbs or of shrubs, and that water enough is supplied for watering them, and that that care is taken for several years, and that the seeds which are gathered are stored up, for example of corn or barley and other sorts separately from year to year, until the seeds of each sort amount to a hundred talents' weight, then also let the stalks be pulled up by the roots and weighed; and after all these have been taken from the trough, let the earth be weighed, it will still give back its hundred talents' weight undiminished. [11]Whence, then, shall we say that all that weight, and all the quantity of different seeds and stalks, has come?

Does it not appear manifestly that it has come from the water?

For the earth retains entire what is its own, but the water which has been poured in all through is nowhere, on account of the powerful virtue of the divine condition, which by the one species of water both prepares the substances of so many seeds and shrubs, and forms their species, and preserves the kind while multiplying the increase.

Chapter XXVIII - The Human Body

"From all these things I think it is sufficiently and abundantly evident that all things are produced; and the universe consists by a designing sense, and not by the irrational operation of nature.

But let us come now, if you please, to our own substance, that is, the substance of man, who is a small world, a microcosm, in the great world; and let us consider with what reason it is compounded: and from this especially you will understand the wisdom of the Creator.

For although man consists of different substances, one mortal and the other immortal, yet, by the skilful contrivance of the Creator, their diversity does not prevent their union, and that although the substances be diverse and alien the one from the other.

For the one is taken from the earth and formed by the Creator, but the other is given from immortal substances; and yet the honour of its immortality is not violated by this union.

Nor does it, as some think, consist of reason, and concupiscence, and passion, but rather such affections seem to be in it, by which it may be moved in each of these directions.

For the body, which consists of bones and flesh, takes its beginning from the seed of a man, which is extracted from the marrow by warmth, and conveyed into the womb as into a soil, to which it adheres, and is gradually moistened from the fountain of the blood, and so is changed into flesh and bones, and is formed into the likeness of him who injected the seed.

Chapter XXIX - Symmetry of the Body

"And mark in this the work of the Designer, how He has inserted the bones like pillars, on which the flesh might be sustained and carried. Then, again, how an equal measure is preserved on either side, that is, the right and the left, so that foot answers to foot, hand to hand, and even finger to finger, so that each agrees in perfect equality with each; and also eye to eye, and ear to ear, which not only are suitable to and matched with each other, but also are formed fit for necessary uses.

The hands, for instance, are so made as to be fit for work; the feet for walking; the eyes, protected with sentinel eyebrows, to serve the purpose of sight; the ears so formed for hearing, that, like a cymbal, they vibrate the sound of the word that falls upon them, and send it inward, and transmit it even in the understanding of the heart; whereas the tongue, striking against the teeth in speaking, performs the part of a fiddle-bow.

The teeth also are formed, some for cutting and dividing the food, and handing it over to the inner ones; and these, in their turn, bruise and grind it like a mill, that it may be more conveniently digested when it is conveyed into the stomach; whence also they are called grinders.

Chapter XXX - Breath and Blood

"The nostrils also are made for the purpose of collecting, inspiring, and expiring air, that by the renewal of the breath, the natural heat which is in the heart may, by means of the lungs, be either warmed or cooled, as the occasion may require; while the lungs are made to abide in the breast, that by their softness they may soothe and cherish the vigour of the heart, in which the life seems to abide;--the life, I say, not the soul.

And what shall I say of the substance of the blood, which, proceeding as a river from a fountain, and first borne along in one channel, and then spreading through innumerable veins, as through canals, irrigates the whole territory of the human body with vital streams, being supplied by the agency of the liver, which is placed in the right side, for effecting the digestion of food and turning it into blood?

But in the left side is placed the spleen, which draws to itself, and in some way cleanses, the impurities of the blood.

Chapter XXXI - The Intestines

"What reason also is employed in the intestines, which are arranged in long circular windings, that they may gradually carry off the refuse of the food, so as neither to render places suddenly empty, and so as not to be hindered by the food that is taken afterwards!

But they are made like a membrane, that the parts that are outside of them may gradually receive moisture, which if it were poured out suddenly would empty the internal parts; and not hindered by a thick skin, which would render the outside dry, and disturb the whole fabric of man with distressing thirst.

Chapter XXXII - Generation

"Moreover, the female form, and the cavity of the womb, most suitable for receiving, and cherishing, and vivifying the germ, who does not believe that it has been made as it is by reason and foresight?--because in that part alone of her body the female differs from the male, in which the foetus being placed, is kept and cherished.

And again the male differs from the female only in that part of his body in which is the power of injecting seed and propagating mankind.

And in this there is a great proof of providence, from the necessary difference of members; but more in this, where, under a likeness of form there is found to be diversity of use and variety of office.

For males and females equally have teats, but only those of the female are filled with milk; that, as soon as they have brought forth, the infant may find nourishment suited to him.

But if we see the members in man arranged with such method, that in all the rest there is seen to be similarity of form, and a difference only in those in which their use requires a difference, and we neither see anything superfluous nor anything wanting in man, nor in woman anything deficient or in excess, who will not, from all these things, acknowledge the operation of reason, and the wisdom of the Creator?

Chapter XXXIII - Correspondences in Creation

"With this agrees also the reasonable difference of other animals, and each one being suited to its own use and service.

This also is testified by the variety of trees and the diversity of herbs, varying both in form and in juices.

This also is asserted by the change of seasons, distinguished into four periods, and the circle closing the year with certain hours, days, months, and not deviating from the appointed reckoning by a single hour.

Hence, in short, the age of the world itself is reckoned by a certain and fixed account, and a definite number of years.

Chapter XXXIV - Time of Making the World

"But you will say, When was the world made?

And why so late?

This you might have objected, though it had been made sooner.

For you might say, Why not also before this?

And so, going back through unmeasured ages, you might still ask, And why not sooner?

But we are not now discussing this, why it was not made sooner; but whether it was made at all.

For if it is manifest that it was made, it is necessarily the work of a powerful and supreme Artificer; and if this is evident, it must be left to the choice and judgment of the wise Artificer when He should please to make it; unless indeed you think that all this wisdom, which has constructed the immense fabric of the world, and has given to the several objects their forms and kinds, assigning to them a habit not only in accordance with beauty, but also most convenient and necessary for their future uses,--unless, I say, you think that this alone has escaped it, that it should choose a convenient season for so magnificent a work of creation.

He has doubtless a certain reason and evident causes why, and when, and how He made the world; but it were not proper that these should be disclosed to those who are reluctant to inquire into and understand the things which are placed before their eyes, and which testify of His providence.

For those things which are kept in secret, and are hidden within the senses of Wisdom, as in a royal treasury, are laid open to none but those who have learned of Him, with whom these things are sealed and laid up.

It is God, therefore, who made all things, and Himself was made by none.

But those who speak of nature instead of God, and declare that all things were made by nature, do not perceive the mistake of the name which they use.

For if they think that nature is irrational, it is most foolish to suppose that a rational creature can proceed from an irrational creator.

But if it is Reason--that is, Logos [12] --by which it appears that all things were made, they change the name without purpose, when they make statements concerning the reason of the Creator.

If you have anything to say to these things, my father, say on."

Chapter XXXV - A Contest of Hospitality

When Niceta had thus spoken, the old man answered:

"You indeed, my son, have conducted your argument wisely and vigorously; so much so, that I do not think the subject of providence could be better treated. But as it is now late, I wish to say some things to-morrow in answer to what you have argued; and if on these you can satisfy me, I shall confess myself a debtor to your favour."

And when the old man said this, Peter rose up.

Then one of those present, a chief man of the Laodiceans, requested of Peter and us that he might give the old man other clothes instead of the mean and torn ones that he wore. [13] This man Peter and we embraced; and praising him for his honourable and excellent intention, said:

"We are not so foolish and impious as not to bestow the things which are necessary for bodily uses upon him to whom we have committed so precious words; and we hope that he will willingly receive them, as a father from his sons, and also we trust that he will share with us our house and our living."

While we said this, and that chief man of the city strove to take the old man away from us with the greatest urgency and with many blandishments, while we the more eagerly strove to keep him with us, all the people cried out that it should rather be done as the old man himself pleased; and when silence was obtained, the old man, with an oath, said:

"To-day I shall stay with no one, nor take anything from any one, lest the choice of the one should prove the sorrow of the other; afterwards these things may be, if so it seem right."

Chapter XXXVI - Arrangements for To-Morrow

And when the old man had said this, Peter said to the chief man of the city:

"Since you have shown your good-will in our presence, it is not right that you should go away sorrowful; but we will accept from you favour for favour.

Show us your house, and make it ready, so that the discussion which is to be to-morrow may be held there, and that any who wish to be present to hear it may be admitted."

When the chief man of the city heard this, he rejoiced greatly; and all the people also heard it gladly.

And when the crowds had dispersed, he pointed out his house; and the old man also was preparing to depart.

But I commanded one of my attendants to follow the old man secretly, and find out where he stayed.

And when we returned to our lodging, we told our brethren all our dealings with the old man; and so, as usual, we supped and went to sleep.

Chapter XXXVII - "The Form of Sound Words, Which Ye Have Heard of Me."

But on the following day Peter arose early and called us, and we went together to the secret place in which we had been on the previous day, for the purpose of prayer.

And when, after prayer, we were coming thence to the appointed place, he exhorted us by the way, saying: [14]

"Hear me, most beloved fellow-servants:

It is good that every one of you, according to his ability, contribute to the advantage of those who are approaching to the faith of our religion; and therefore do not shrink from instructing the ignorant, and teaching according to the wisdom which has been bestowed upon you by the providence of God, yet so that you only join the eloquence of your discourse with those things which you have heard from me, and which have been committed to you. But do not speak anything which is your own, and which has not been committed to you, though it may seem to yourselves to be true; but hold forth those things, as I have said, which I myself have received from the true Prophet, and have delivered to you, although they may seem to be less full of authority.

For thus it often happens that men turn away from the truth, while they believe that they have found out, by their own thoughts, a form of truth more true and powerful."

Chapter XXXVIII - The Chief Man's House

To these counsels of Peter we willingly assented, saying to him that we should do nothing but what was pleasing to him.

Then said he:

"That you may therefore be exercised without danger, each of you conduct the discussion in my presence, one succeeding another, and each one elucidating his own questions.

Now, then, as Niceta discoursed sufficiently yesterday, let Aquila conduct the discussion to-day; and after Aquila, Clement; and then I, if the case shall require it, will add something."

Meantime, while we were talking in this way, we came to the house; and the master of the house welcomed us, and led us to a certain apartment, arranged after the manner of a theatre, and beautifully built.

There we found great crowds waiting for us, who had come during the night, and amongst them the old man who had argued with us yesterday.

Therefore we entered, having Peter in the midst of us, looking about if we could see the old man anywhere; and when Peter saw him hiding in the midst of the crowd, he called him to him, saying: "Since you possess a soul more enlightened than most, why do you hide yourself, and conceal yourself in modesty?

Rather come hither, and propound your sentiments."

Chapter XXXIX - Recapitulation of Yesterday's Argument

When Peter had thus spoken, immediately the crowd began to make room for the old man.[15] And when he had come forward, he thus began: "Although I do not remember the words of the discourse which the young man delivered yesterday, yet I recollect the purport and the order of it; and therefore I think it necessary, for the sake of those who were not present yesterday, to call up what was said, and to repeat everything shortly, that, although something may have escaped me, I may be reminded of it by him who delivered the discourse, who is now present.

This, then, was the purport of yesterday's discussion:

that all things that we see, inasmuch as they consist in a certain proportion, and art, and form, and species, must be believed to have been made by intelligent power; but if it be mind and reason that has formed them, it follows that the world is governed by the providence of the same reason, although the things which are done in the world may seem to us to be not quite rightly done.

But it follows, that if God and mind is the creator of all things, He must also be just; but if He is just, He necessarily judges.

If He judges, it is of necessity that men be judged with respect to their doings; and if every one is judged in respect of his doings, there shall at some time be a righteous separation between righteous men and sinners.

This, I think, was the substance of the whole discourse.

Chapter XL - Genesis

"If, therefore, it can be shown that mind and reason created all things, it follows that those things which come after are also managed by reason and providence.

But if unintelligent and blind nature produces all things, the reason of judgment is undoubtedly overthrown; and there is no ground to expect either punishment of sin or reward of well-doing where there is no judge.

Since, then, the whole matter depends upon this, and hangs by this head, do not take it amiss, if I wish this to be discussed and handled somewhat more fully.

For in this the first gate, as it were, is shut towards all things which are propounded, and therefore I wish first of all to have it opened to me. Now therefore hear what my doctrine is; and if any one of you pleases, let him reply to me:

for I shall not be ashamed to learn, if I hear that which is true, and to assent to him who speaks rightly.

The discourse, then, which you delivered yesterday, which asserted that all things consist by art, and measure, and reason, does not fully persuade me that it is mind and reason that has made the world; for I have many things which I can show to consist by competent measure, and form, and species, and which yet were not made by mind and reason.

Then, besides, I see that many things are done in the world without arrangement, consequence, or justice, and that nothing can be done without the course of Genesis.

This I shall in the sequel prove most clearly from my own case."

Chapter XLI - The Rainbow

When the old man had thus spoken, Aquila answered:

"As you yourself proposed that any one who pleased should have an opportunity of answering to what you might say, my brother Niceta permits me to conduct the argument today."

Then the old man:

"Go on, my son, as you please."

And Aquila answered:

"You promised that you would show that there are many things in the world which have a form and species arranged by equal reason, which yet it is evident were not effected by God as their Creator.

Now, then, as you have promised, point out these things."

Then said the old man:

"Behold, we see the bow in the heaven assume a circular shape, completed in all proportion, and have an appearance of reality, which perhaps neither mind could have constructed nor reason described; and yet it is not made by any mind. Behold, I have set forth the whole in a word: now answer me."

Chapter XLII - Types and Forms

Then said Aquila:

"If anything is expressed from a type and form, it is at once understood that it is from reason, and that it could not be made without mind; since the type itself, which expresses figures and forms, was not made without mind.

For example, if wax be applied to an engraved ring, it takes the stamp and figure from the ring, which undoubtedly is without sense; but then the ring, which expresses the figure, was engraven by the hand of a workman, and it was mind and reason that gave the type to the ring.

So then the bow also is expressed in the air; for the sun, impressing its rays on the clouds in the process of rarefaction, and affixing the type of its circularity to the cloudy moisture, as it were to soft wax, produces the appearance of a bow; and this, as I have said, is effected by the reflection of the sun's brightness upon the clouds, and reproducing the brightness of its circle from them.

Now this does not always take place, but only when the opportunity is presented by the rarefaction of moistened clouds. And consequently, when the clouds again are condensed and unite, the form of the bow is dissolved and vanishes.

Finally, the bow never is seen without sun and clouds, just as the image is not produced, unless there be the type, and wax, or some other material.

Nor is it wonderful if God the Creator in the beginning made types, from which forms and species may now be expressed.

But this is similar to that, that in the beginning God created insensible elements, which He might use for forming and developing all other things.

But even those who form statues, first make a mould of clay or wax, and from it the figure of the statue is produced.

And then afterwards a shadow is also produced from the statue, which shadow always bears the form and likeness of the statue.

What shall we say then?

That the insensible statue forms a shadow finished with as diligent care as the statue itself?

Or shall the finishing of the shadow be unhesitatingly ascribed to him who has also fashioned the statue?

Chapter XLIII - Things Apparently Useless and Vile Made by God

"If, then, it seems to you that this is so, and what has been said on this subject is enough, let us come to inquire into other matters; or if you think that something is still wanting, let us go over it again."

And the old man said:

"I wish you would go over this again, since there are many other things which I see to be made in like manner:

for both the fruits of trees are produced in like manner, beautifully formed and wonderfully rounded; and the appearance of the leaves is formed with immense gracefulness, and the green membrane is woven with exquisite art:

then, moreover, fleas, mice, lizards, and such like, shall we say that these are made by God?

Hence, from these vile objects a conjecture is derived concerning the superior, that they are by no means formed by the art of mind."

"You infer well," said Aquila, "concerning the texture of leaves, and concerning small animals, that from these belief is withdrawn from the superior creatures; but let not these things deceive you, that you should think that God, working as it were only with two hands, could not complete all things that are made; but remember how my brother Niceta answered you yesterday, and truly disclosed the mystery before the time, as a son speaking with his father, and explained why and how things are made which seem to be useless."

Chapter XLIV - Ordinate and Inordinate

Then the old man:
"I should like to hear from you why those useless things are made by the will of that supreme mind?"

"If," said he, "it is fully manifest to you that there is in them the work of mind and reason, then you will not hesitate to say also why they were made, and to declare that they have been rightly made."

To this the old man answered:
"I am not able, my son, to say that those things which seem formed by art are made by mind, by reason of other things which we see to be done unjustly and disorderly in the world."

"If," says Aquila, "those things which are done disorderly do not allow you say that they are done by the providence of God, why do not those things which are done orderly compel you to say that they are done by God, and that irrational nature cannot produce a rational work?

For it is certain, nor do we at all deny, that in this world some things are done orderly, and some disorderly.

Those things, therefore, that are done rationally, believe that they are done by providence; but those that are done irrationally and inordinately, that they befall naturally, and happen accidentally.

But I wonder that men do not perceive, that where there is sense things may be done ordinately and inordinately, but where there is no sense neither the one nor the other can be done; for reason makes order, and the course of order necessarily produces something inordinate, if anything contrary happen to disturb order." Then the old man:
"This very thing I wish you to show me."

Chapter XLV - Motions of the Sun and Moon

Says Aquila:
"I shall do so without delay.

Two visible signs are shown in heaven--one of the sun, the other of the moon; and these are followed by five other stars, each describing its own separate orbit. These, therefore, God has placed in the heaven, by which the temperature of the air may be regulated according to the seasons, and the order of vicissitudes and alternations may be kept.

But by means of the very same signs, if at any time plague and corruption is sent upon the earth for the sins of men, the air is disturbed, pestilence is brought upon animals, blight upon crops, and a destructive year in every way upon men; and thus it is that by one and the same means order is both kept and destroyed.

For it is manifest even to the unbelieving and unskilful, that the course of the sun, which is useful and necessary to the world, and which is assigned by providence, is always kept orderly; but the courses of the moon, in comparison of the course of the sun, seem to the unskilful to be inordinate and unsettled in her waxings and wanings.

For the sun moves in fixed and orderly periods: for from him are hours, from him the day when he rises, from him also the night when he sets; from him months and years are reckoned, from him the variations of seasons are produced; while, rising to the higher regions, he tempers the spring; but when he reaches the top of the heaven, he kindles the summer's heats:

again, sinking, he produces the temper of autumn; and when he returns to his lowest circle, he bequeaths to us the rigour of winter's cold from the icy binding of heaven.

Chapter XLVI - Sun and Moon Ministers Both of Good and Evil

"But we shall discourse at greater length on these subjects at another time.

Now, meantime, we remark that though he is that good servant for regulating the changes of the seasons, yet, when chastisement is inflicted upon men according to the will of God, he glows more fiercely, and burns up the world with more vehement fires.

In like manner also the course of the moon, and that changing which seems to the unskilful to be disorderly, is adapted to the growth of crops, and cattle, and all living creatures; for by her waxings and wanings, by a certain wonderful contrivance of providence, everything that is born is nourished and grows; concerning which we could speak more at length and unfold the matter in detail, but that the method of the question proposed recalls us.

Yet, by the very same appliances by which they are produced, all things are nourished and increased; but when, from any just cause, the regulation of the appointed order is changed, corruption and distemper arise, so that chastisement may come upon men by the will of God, as we have said above.

Chapter XLVII - Chastisements on the Righteous and the Wicked

"But perhaps you will say, What of the fact that, in that common chastisement, like things befall the pious and the impious?

It is true, and we confess it; but the chastisement turns to the advantage of the pious, that, being afflicted in the present life, they may come more purified to the future, in which perpetual rest is prepared for them, and that at the same time even the impious may somewhat profit from their chastisement, or else that the just sentence of the future judgment may be passed upon them; since in the same chastisements the righteous give thanks to God, while the unrighteous blaspheme. Therefore, since the opinion of things is divided into two parts, that some things are done by order and others against order, it ought, from those things which are done according to order, to be believed that there is a providence; but with respect to those things which are done against order, we should inquire their causes from those who have learned them by prophetic teaching:

for those who have become acquainted with prophetic discourse know when, and for what reason, blight, hail, and pestilence, and such like, have occurred in every generation, and for what sins these have been sent as a punishment; whence causes of sadness, lamentations, and griefs have befallen the human race; whence also trembling sickness has ensued, and that this has been from the beginning the punishment of parricide. [16]

Chapter XLVIII - Chastisements for Sins

"For in the beginning of the world there were none of these evils, but they took their rise from the impiety of men; and thence, with the constant increase of iniquities, the number of evils has also increased.

But for this reason divine providence has decreed a judgment with respect to all men, because the present life was not such that every one could be dealt with according to his deservings.

Those things, therefore, which were well and orderly appointed from the beginning, when no causes of evil existed, are not to be judged of from the evils which have befallen the world by reason of the sins of men. In short, as an indication of the things which were from the beginning, some nations are found which are strangers to these evils.

For the Seres, because they live chastely, are kept free from them all; for with them it is unlawful to come at a woman after she has conceived, or while she is being purified.

No one there eats unclean flesh, no one knows aught of sacrifices; all are judges to themselves according to justice.

For this reason they are not chastened with those plagues which we have spoken of; they live to extreme old age, and die without sickness.

But we, miserable as we are, dwelling as it were with deadly serpents [17] --I mean with wicked men--necessarily suffer with them the plagues of afflictions in this world, but we cherish hope from the comfort of good things to come."

Chapter XLIX - God's Precepts Despised

"If," said the old man, "even the righteous are tormented on account of the iniquities of others, God ought, as foreseeing this, to have commanded men not to do those things from which it should be necessary that the righteous be afflicted with the unrighteous; or if they did them, He ought to have applied some correction or purification to the world." [18]"God," said Aquila, "did so command, and gave precepts by the prophets how men ought to live; but even these precepts they despised:

yea, if any desired to observe them, them they afflicted with various injuries, until they drove them from their purposed observance, and turned them to the rabble of infidelity, and made them like unto themselves.

Chapter L - The Flood

"Wherefore, in short, at the first, when all the earth had been stained with sins, God brought a flood upon the world, which you say happened under Deucalion; and at that time He saved a certain righteous man, with his sons, in an ark, and with him the race of all plants and animals. [19]And yet even those who sprang from them, after a time, again did deeds like to those of their predecessors; for those things that had befallen them were forgotten, so that their descendants did not even believe that the flood had taken place.

Wherefore God also decreed that there should not be another flood in the present world, else there should have been one in every generation, according to the account of their sins by reason of their unbelief; but He rather granted that certain angels who delight in evil should bear sway over the several nations--and to them was given power over individual men, yet only on this condition, if any one first had made himself subject to them by sinning--until He should come who delights in good, and by Him the number of the righteous should be completed, and by the increase of the number of pious men all over the world impiety should be in some measure repressed, and it should be known to all that all that is good is done by God.

Chapter LI - Evils Brought in by Sin

"But by the freedom of the will, every man, while he is unbelieving in regard to things to come, by evil deeds runs into evils.

And these are the things in the world which seem to be done contrary to order, which owe their existence to unbelief.

Therefore the dispensation of divine providence is withal to be admired, which granted to those men in the beginning, walking in the good way of life, to enjoy incorruptible good things; but when they sinned, they gave birth to evil by sin.

And to every good thing evil is joined as by a certain covenant of alliance on the part of sin, since indeed the earth has been polluted with human blood, and altars have been lighted to demons, and they have polluted the very air by the filthy smoke of sacrifices; and so at length the elements, being first corrupted, have handed over to men the fault of their corruption, as roots communicate their qualities to the branches and the fruit.

Chapter LII - "No Rose Without Its Thorn."

"Observe therefore in this, as I have said, how justly divine providence comes to the help of things vitiated; that, inasmuch as evils which had derived their origin from sin were associated with the good things of God, He should assign two chiefs to these two departments. [20]And accordingly, to Him who rejoices in good He has appointed the ordering of good things, that He might bring those who believe in Him to the faith of His providence; but to him who rejoices in evil, He has given over those things which are done without order and uselessly, from which of course the faith of His providence comes into doubt; and thus a just division has been made by a just God.

Hence therefore it is, that whereas the orderly course of the stars produces faith that the world was made by the hand of a designer, on the other hand, the disturbance of the air, the pestilent breeze, the uncontrolled fire of the lightning, cast doubt upon the work of providence.

For, as we have said, every good thing has its corresponding contrary evil thing joined with it; as hail is opposite to the fertilizing showers, the corruption of mildew is associated with the gentle dew, the whirlwinds of storms are joined with the soft winds, unfruitful trees with fruitful, noxious herbs with useful, wild and destructive animals with gentle ones.

But all these things are arranged by God, because that the choice of men's will has departed from the purpose of good, and fallen away to evil.

Chapter LIII - Everything Has Its Corresponding Contrary

"Therefore this division holds in all the things of the world; and as there are pious men, so there are also impious; as there are prophets, so also there are false prophets; and amongst the Gentiles there are philosophers and false philosophers.

Also the Arabian nations, and many others, have imitated the circumcision of the Jews for the service of their impiety.

So also the worship of demons is contrary to the divine worship, baptism to baptism, laws to the law, false apostles to apostles, and false teachers to teachers.

And hence it is that among the philosophers some assert providence, others deny it; some maintain that there is one God, others that there are more than one:

in short, the matter has come to this, that whereas demons are expelled by the word of God, by which it is declared that there is a providence, the magical art, for the confirmation of infidelity, has found out ways of imitating this by contraries.

Thus has been discovered the method of counteracting the poison of serpents by incantations, and the effecting of cures contrary to the word and power of God.

The magic art has also found out ministries contrary to the angels of God, placing the calling up of souls and the figments of demons in opposition to these.

And, not to prolong the discourse by a further enumeration, there is nothing whatever that makes for the belief of providence, which has not something, on the other hand, prepared for unbelief; and therefore they who do not know that division of things, think that there is no providence, by reason of those things in the world which are discordant from themselves.

But do you, my father, as a wise man, choose from that division the part which preserves order and makes for the belief of providence, and do not only follow that part which runs against order and neutralizes the belief of providence."

Chapter LIV - An Illustration

To this the old man answered:

"Show me a way, my son, by which I may establish in my mind one or other of these two orders, the one of which asserts, and the other denies, providence."

"To one having a right judgment," says Aquila, "the decision is easy.

For this very thing that you say, order and disorder, may be produced by a contriver, but not by insensible nature.

For let us suppose, by way of illustration, that a great mass were torn from a high rock, and cast down headlong, and when clashed upon the ground were broken into many pieces, could it in any way happen that, amongst that multitude of fragments, there should be found even one which should have any perfect figure and shape?"

The old man answered:

"It is impossible."

"But," said Aquila, "if there be present a statuary, he can by his skilful hand and reasonable mind form the stone cut from the mountain into whatever figure he pleases."

The old man said:

"That is true."

"Therefore," says Aquila, "when there is not a rational mind, no figure can be formed out of the mass; but when there is a designing mind, there may be both form and deformity:

for example, if a workman cuts from the mountain a block to which he wishes to give a form, he must first cut it out unformed and rough; then, by degrees hammering and hewing it by the rule of his art, he expresses the form which he has conceived in his mind.

Thus, therefore, from informity or deformity, by the hand of the workman form is attained, and both proceed from the workman.

In like manner, therefore, the things which are done in the world are accomplished by the providence of a contriver, although they may seem not quite orderly.

And therefore, because these two ways have been made known to you, and you have heard the divisions of them, flee from the way of unbelief, lest haply it lead you to that prince who delights in evils; but follow the way of faith, that you may come to that King who delighteth in good men."

Chapter LV - The Two Kingdoms

To this the old man answered:
"But why was that prince made who delights in evil? [21] And from what was he made? Or was he not made?"
Aquila said:
"The treatment of that subject belongs to another time; but that you may not go away altogether without an answer to this, I shall give a few hints on this subject also.
God, foreseeing all things before the creation of the world, knowing that the men who were to be would some of them indeed incline to good, but others to the opposite, assigned those who should choose the good to His own government and His own care, and called them His peculiar inheritance;[22] but He gave over the government of those who should turn to evil to those angels who, not by their substance, but by opposition, were unwilling to remain with God, being corrupted by the vice of envy and pride.
Those, therefore, he made worthy princes of worthy subjects; yet he so delivered them over to those angels, that they have not the power of doing what they will against them, unless they transgress the bounds assigned to them from the beginning.
And this is the bound assigned, that unless one first do the will of the demons, the demons have no power over him."

Chapter LVI - Origin of Evil

Then the old man said:
"You have stated it excellently, my son.
It now remains only that you tell me whence is the substance of evil:
for if it was made by God, the evil fruit shows that the root is in fault; for it appears that it also is of an evil nature.
But if this substance was co-eternal with God, how can that which was equally unproduced and co-eternal be subject to the other?"
"It was not always," said Aquila; "but neither does it necessarily follow, if it was made by God, that its Creator should be thought to be such as is that which has been made by Him.
For indeed God made the substance of all things; but if a reasonable mind, which has been made by God, do not acquiesce in the laws of its Creator, and go beyond the bounds of the temperance prescribed to it, how does this reflect on the Creator? Or if there is any reason higher than this, we do not know it; for we cannot know anything perfectly, and especially concerning those things for our ignorance of which we are not to be judged.
But those things for which we are to be judged are most easy to be understood, and are despatched almost in a word.
For almost the whole rule of our actions is summed up in this, that what we are unwilling to suffer we should not do to others.
For as you would not be killed, you must beware of killing another; and as you would not have your own marriage violated, you must not defile another's bed; you would not be stolen from, neither must you steal; and every matter of men's actions is comprehended within this rule."

Chapter LVII - The Old Man Unconvinced

Then the old man:
"Do not take amiss, my son, what I am going to say. Though your words are powerful, yet they cannot lead me to believe that anything can be done apart from Genesis.
For I know that all things have happened to me by the necessity of Genesis, [23] and therefore I cannot be persuaded that either to do well or to do ill is in our power; and if we have not our actions in our power, it cannot be believed that there is a judgment to come, by which either punishments may be inflicted on the evil, or rewards bestowed on the good.
In short, since I see that you are initiated in this sort of learning, I shall lay before you a few things from the art itself."
"If," says Aquila, "you wish to add anything from that science, my brother Clement will answer you with all care, since he has attended more fully to the science of mathematics.
For I can maintain in other ways that our actions are in our own power; but I ought not to presume upon those things which I have not learned."

Chapter LVIII - Sitting in Judgment Upon God

When Aquila had thus spoken, then I Clement said:
"To-morrow, my father, you shall speak as you please, and we will gladly hear you; for I suppose it will also be gratifying to you that you have to do with those who are not ignorant of the science which you profess."

When, therefore, it had been settled between the old man and me, that on the following day we should hold a discussion on the subject of Genesis--whether all things are done under its influence, or there be anything in us which is not done by Genesis, but by the judgment of the mind--Peter rose up, and began to speak to the following effect: [24]

"To me it is exceedingly wonderful, that things which can easily be found out men make difficult by recondite thoughts and words; and those especially who think themselves wise, and who, wishing to comprehend the will of God, treat God as if He were a man, yea, as if He were something less than a man:

for no one can know the purpose or mind of a man unless he himself reveal his thoughts; and neither can any one learn a profession unless he be for a long time instructed by a master.

How much more must it be, that no one can know the mind or the work of the invisible and incomprehensible God, unless He Himself send a prophet to declare His purpose, and expound the way of His creation, so far as it is lawful for men to learn it!

Hence I think it ridiculous when men judge of the power of God in natural ways, and think that this is possible and that impossible to Him, or this greater and that less, while they are ignorant of everything; who, being unrighteous men, judge the righteous God; unskilled, judge the contriver; corrupt, judge the incorruptible; creatures, judge the Creator.

Chapter LIX - The True Prophet

But I would not have you think, that in saying this I take away the power of judging concerning things; but I give counsel that no one walk through devious places, and rush into errors without end.

And therefore I advise not only wise men, but indeed all men who have a desire of knowing what is advantageous to them, that they seek after the true Prophet; for it is He alone who knoweth all things, and who knoweth what and how every man is seeking. [25] For He is within the mind of every one of us, but in those who have no desire of the knowledge of God and His righteousness, He is inoperative; but He works in those who seek after that which is profitable to their souls, and kindles in them the light of knowledge.

Wherefore seek Him first of all; and if you do not find Him, expect not that you shall learn anything from any other.

But He is soon found by those who diligently seek Him through love of the truth, and whose souls are not taken possession of by wickedness.

For He is present with those who desire Him in the innocency of their spirits, who bear patiently, and draw sighs from the bottom of their hearts through love of the truth; but He deserts malevolent minds, [26] because as a prophet He knows the thoughts of every one.

And therefore let no one think that he can find Him by his own wisdom, unless, as we have said, he empty his mind of all wickedness, and conceive a pure and faithful desire to know Him. For when any one has so prepared himself, He Himself as a prophet, seeing a mind prepared for Him, of His own accord offers Himself to his knowledge.

Chapter LX - His Deliverances Not to Be Questioned

"Therefore, if any one wishes to learn all things, he cannot do it by discussing them one by one; for, being mortal, he shall not be able to trace the counsel of God, and to scan immensity itself.

But if, as we have said, he desires to learn all things, let him seek after the true Prophet; and when he has found Him, let him not treat with Him by questions and disputations and arguments; but if He has given any response, or pronounced any judgment, it cannot be doubted that this is certain.

And therefore, before all things, let the true Prophet be sought, and His words be laid hold of.

In respect to these this only should be discussed by every one, that he may satisfy himself if they are truly His prophetic words; that is, if they contain undoubted faith of things to come, if they mark out definite times, if they preserve the order of things, if they do not relate as last those things which are

Chapter LXI - Ignorance of the Philosophers

"For let us consider carefully the work of divine providence. [27] For whereas the philosophers have introduced certain subtile and difficult words, so that not even the terms that they use in their discourses can be known and understood by all, God has shown that those who thought themselves word-framers are altogether unskilful as respects the knowledge of the truth.

For the knowledge of things which is imparted by the true Prophet is simple, and plain, and brief; which those men walking through devious places, and through the stony difficulties of words, are wholly ignorant of.

Therefore, to modest and simple minds, when they see things come to pass which have been foretold, it is enough, and more than enough, that they may receive most certain knowledge from most certain prescience; and for the rest may be at peace, having received evident knowledge of the truth.

For all other things are treated by opinion, in which there can be nothing firm.

For what speech is there which may not be contradicted?

And what argument is there that may not be overthrown by another argument? And hence it is, that by disputation of this sort men can never come to any end of knowledge and learning, but find the end of their life sooner than the end of their questions.

Chapter LXII - End of the Conference

"And, therefore, since amongst these philosophers are things uncertain, we must come to the true Prophet.

Him God the Father wished to be loved by all, and accordingly He has been pleased wholly to extinguish those opinions which have originated with men, and in regard to which there is nothing like certainty--that He the true Prophet might be the more sought after, and that He whom [28] they had obscured should show to men the way of truth.

For on this account also God made the world, and by Him the world is filled; whence also He is everywhere near to them who seek Him, though He be sought in the remotest ends of the earth.

But if any one seek Him not purely, nor holily, nor faithfully, He is indeed within him, because He is everywhere, and is found within the minds of all men; but, as we have said before, He is dormant to the unbelieving, and is held to be absent from those by whom His existence is not believed."

And when Peter had said this, and more to the same effect, concerning the true Prophet, he dismissed the crowds; and when he very earnestly entreated the old man to remain with us, he could prevail nothing; but he also departed, to return next day, as had been agreed upon.

And after this, we also, with Peter, went to our lodging, and enjoyed our accustomed food and rest.

Footnotes:

1. [From this point there are considerable variations in the two narratives.

The old man becomes, in the Recognitions, a prominent participant in the discussions, arguing with Peter, and with Niceta, Aquila, and Clement.

At the close of these discussions he is recognised first by the sons (ix. 35), and then by his wife, as Faustinianus (ix. 37).

In the Homilies Peter tells of an interview with the old man (xiv. 2-8), and the recognition takes place immediately upon his appearance (xiv. 9).

Some discussion with him follows (Homily XV.); but soon the main controversy is with Simon Magus (Homilies XVI.-XIX.), in the presence of the father, who is convinced by Peter.

Book x. contains much matter introduced in Homilies IV.-VII.

The correspondences will be indicated in the footnotes.--R.]

2. [In Homily XIV. 2-5 there is a discussion somewhat similar to the beginning of this one, but reported by the Apostle to the family of Clement.--R.]

3. [There are a number of indications, like this, in the narrative, foreshadowing the recognition of the old man as the father.

In the Homilies nothing similar appears.--R.]

4. Matt. v. 14, 15.

5. [The whole arrangement, introducing the brothers as disputants, is peculiar to the Recognitions. The several discourses are constructed with much skill.

The courtesy of the discussion is in sharp contrast with the tone of those in the Homilies, especially those with Simon Magus.--R.]

6. [Comp. Homily XIII. 7.--R.]

7. Matt. xxiii. 9.

8. [Another foreshadowing of the approaching recognition; peculiar to this narrative.--R.]

9. [The argument of Niceta (chaps. 9-34), while it necessarily includes statements occurring elsewhere in this literature, is, as a whole, peculiar to the Recognitions.

In order of arrangement and logical force it is much superior to most of the discourses.--R.]

10. That is, the equator.

11. [De Maistre, Soirees, vi. 259.]

12. [Comp. John i. 1-3.

The expression seems to be used here with a polemic purpose.--R.]

13. [This incident is peculiar to the Recognitions.

There seems to be a reminiscence of this chief man in Homily IV. 10, where a rich man provides a place for the discussion; comp. chap. 38 here.--R.]

14. [Peculiar to the Recognitions; there is probably here an anti-Pauline purpose.--R.]

15. [The second day's discussion, in which Aquila is the main speaker, is also of a high order.

It is, as already indicated, peculiar to the Recognitions, though with the usual incidental correspondences in the Homilies.--R.]

16. Gen. iv. 12, in LXX.

17. Ezek. ii. 6.

18. This rendering is according to a marginal reading.

19. [Comp. book iv. 12; Homily VIII. 17.--R.]

20. Compare with chaps. 52-54 the doctrine of pairs as stated in book iii. 59-61; Homily II. 15, etc., iii. 23.--R.]

21. [On the creation of the evil one, see book x. 3, etc., and the discussion with Simon in Homily XIX. 2-18.--R.]

22. Deut. xxxii. 8, in LXX.

23. [Comp. Homily XIV. 3, etc.--R.]

24. [This discourse of Peter is peculiar to the Recognitions; it resembles somewhat the earlier discourse to Clement in book i.--R.]

25. [The introduction of these chapters concerning the true Prophet shows a far more orderly method of constructing the entire discussion with the father than that of the Homilies; comp. book xi. 1, 2.--R.]

26. Wisd. i. 4.

27. [Comp. Homily XV. 5.--R.]

28. If we were to read quam instead of quem, the sense would be: that He might lay open to men the way of truth which they had blocked up.

So Whiston.

Book IX

Chapter I - An Explanation

On the following day, Peter, along with us, hastened early to the place in which the discussion had been held the day before; and when he saw that great crowds had assembled there to hear, and saw the old man with them, he said to him: [1]"Old man, it was agreed yesterday that you should confer to-day with Clement; and that you should either show that nothing takes place apart from genesis, or that Clement should prove that there is no such thing as genesis, but that what we do is in our own power."

To this the old man answered:

"I both remember what was agreed upon, and I keep in memory the words which you spoke after the agreement was made, in which you taught that it is impossible for man to know any thing, unless he learn from the true Prophet."

Then Peter said:

"You do not know what I meant; but I shall now explain to you.

I spoke of the will and purpose of God, which He had before the world was, and by which purpose He made the world, appointed times, gave the law, promised a world to come to the righteous for the rewarding of their good deeds, and decreed punishments to the unjust according to a judicial sentence.

I said that this counsel and this will of God cannot be found out by men, because no man can gather the mind of God from conjectures and opinion, unless a prophet sent by Him declare it.

I did not therefore speak of any doctrines or studies, that they cannot be found out or known without a prophet; for I know that both arts and sciences can be known and practised by men, which they have learned, not from the true Prophet, but from human instructors.

Chapter II - Preliminaries

"Since, therefore, you profess to be conversant with the position of the stars and the courses of the heavenly bodies, and that from these you can convince Clement that all things are subject to Genesis, or that you will learn from him that all things are governed by providence, and that we have something in our own power, it is now time for you two to set about this."

To this the old man answered:

"Now indeed it was not necessary to raise questions of this kind, if it were possible for us to learn from the true Prophet, and to hear in a definite proposition, that anything depends on us and on the freedom of our will; for your yesterday's discourse affected me greatly, in which you disputed concerning the prophetic power. [2]Whence also I assent to and confirm your judgment, that nothing can be known by man with certainty, and without doubt, seeing that he has but a short period of life, and a brief and slender breath, by which he seems to be kept in life.

However, since I am understood to have promised to Clement, before I heard anything of the prophetic power, that I should show that all things are subject to Genesis, or that I should learn from him that there is something in ourselves, let him do me this favour, that he first begin, and propound and explain what may be objected:

for I, ever since I heard from you a few words concerning the power of prophecy, have, I confess, been confounded, considering the greatness of prescience; nor do I think that anything ought to be received which is collected from conjectures and opinion."

Chapter III - Beginning of the Discussion

When the old man had said this, I Clement began to speak as follows: "God by His Son created the world as a double house, separated by the interposition of this firmament, which is called heaven; and appointed angelic powers to dwell in the higher, and a multitude of men to be born in this visible world, from amongst whom He might choose friends for His Son, with whom He might rejoice, and who might be prepared for Him as a beloved bride for a bridegroom.

But even till the time of the marriage, which is the manifestation of the world to come, He has appointed a certain power, to choose out and watch over the good ones of those who are born in this world, and to preserve them for His Son, set apart in a certain place of the world, which is without sin; in which there are already some, who are there being prepared, as I said, as a bride adorned for the coming of the bridegroom.

For the prince of this world and of the present age is like an adulterer, who corrupts and violates the minds of men, and, seducing them from the love of the true bridegroom, allures them to strange lovers.

Chapter IV - Why the Evil Prince Was Made

But some one will say, How then was it necessary that that prince should be made, who was to turn away the minds of men from the true prince? [3]Because God, who, as I have said, wished to prepare friends for His Son, did not wish them to be such as by necessity of nature could not be aught else, but such as should desire of their own choice and will to be good; because neither is that praiseworthy which is not desirable, nor is that judged to be good which is not sought for with purpose.

For there is no credit in being that from which the necessity of your nature does not admit of your changing.

Therefore the providence of God has willed that a multitude of men should be born in this world, that those who should choose a good life might be selected from many.

And because He foresaw that the present world could not consist except by variety and inequality, He gave to each mind freedom of motions, [4] according to the diversities of present things, and appointed this prince, through his suggestion of those things which run contrary, that the choice of better things might depend upon the exercise of virtue.

Chapter V - Necessity of Inequality

"But to make our meaning plainer, we shall explain it by particulars. Was it proper, for example, that all men in this world should be kings, or princes, or lords, or teachers, or lawyers, or geometers, or goldsmiths, or bakers, or smiths, or grammarians, or rich men, or farmers, or perfumers, or fishermen, or poor men?

It is certain that all could not be these.

Yet all these professions, and many more, the life of men requires, and without these it cannot be passed; therefore inequality is necessary in this world.

For there cannot be a king, unless he has subjects over whom he may rule and reign; nor can there be a master, unless he has one over whom he may bear sway; and in like manner of the rest.

Chapter VI - Arrangements of the World for the Exercise of Virtue

"Therefore the Creator, knowing that no one would come to the contest of his own accord, while labour is shunned,--that is, to the practice of those professions which we have mentioned, by means of which either the justice or the mercy of every one can be manifested,--made for men a body susceptible of hunger, and thirst, and cold, in order that men, being compelled for the sake of supporting their bodies, might come down to all the professions which we have mentioned, by the necessity of livelihood.

For we are taught to cultivate every one of these arts, for the sake of food, and drink, and clothing.

And in this the purpose of each one's mind is shown, whether he will supply the demands of hunger and cold by means of thefts, and murders, and perjuries, and other crimes of that sort; or whether, keeping justice and mercy and continence, he will fulfil the service of imminent necessity by the practice of a profession and the labour of his hands.

For if he supply his bodily wants with justice, and piety, and mercy, he comes forth as a victor in the contest set before him, and is chosen as a friend of the Son of God.

But if he serve carnal lusts, by frauds, iniquities, and crimes, he becomes a friend of the prince of this world, and of all demons; by whom he is also taught this, to ascribe to the courses of the stars the errors of his own evil doings, although he chose them of purpose, and willingly.

For arts are learned and practised, as we have said, under the compulsion of the desire of food and drink; which desire, when the knowledge of the truth comes to any one, becomes weaker, and frugality takes its place.

For what expense have those who use water and bread, and only expect it from God?

Chapter VII - The Old and the New Birth

"There is therefore, as we have said, a certain necessary inequality in the dispensation of the world.

Since indeed all men cannot know all things, and accomplish all works, yet all need the use and service of almost all.

And on this account it is necessary that one work, and another pay him for his work; that one be servant, and another be master; that one be subject, another be king.

But this inequality, which is a necessary provision for the life of men, divine providence has turned into an occasion of justice, mercy, and humanity:

that while these things are transacted between man and man, every one may have an opportunity of acting justly with him to whom he has to pay wages for his work; and of acting mercifully to him who, perhaps through sickness or poverty, cannot pay his debt; and of acting humanely towards those who by their creation seem to be subject to him; also of maintaining gentleness towards subjects, and of doing all things according to the law of God.

For He has given a law, thereby aiding the minds of men, that they may the more easily perceive how they ought to act with respect to everything, in what way they may escape evil, and in what way tend to future blessings; and how, being regenerate in water, they may by good works extinguish the fire of their old birth.

For our first birth descends through the fire of lust, and therefore, by the divine appointment, this second birth is introduced by water, which may extinguish the nature of fire; [5] and that the soul, enlightened by the heavenly Spirit, may cast away the fear of the first birth:

provided, however, it so live for the time to come, that it do not at all seek after any of the pleasures of this world, but be, as it were, a pilgrim and a stranger, [6] and a citizen of another city.

Chapter VIII - Uses of Evils

"But perhaps you will say, that in those things indeed in which the necessity of nature demands the service of arts and works, any one may have it in his power to maintain justice, and to put what restraint he pleases either upon his desires or his actions; but what shall we say of the sicknesses and infirmities which befall men, and of some being harassed with demons, and fevers, and cold fits, and some being attacked with madness, or losing their reason, and all those things which overwhelm the race of man with innumerable misfortunes?

To this we say, that if any one consider the reason of the whole mystery, he will pronounce these things to be more just than those that we have already explained.

For God has given a nature to men, by which they may be taught concerning what is good, and to resist evil; that is, they may learn arts, and to resist pleasures, and to set the law of God before them in all things.

And for this end He has permitted certain contrary powers to wander up and down in the world, and to strive against us, [7] for the reasons which have been stated before, that by striving with them the palm of victory and the merit of rewards may accrue to the righteous.

The Epistles of Clement
Chapter IX - "Conceived in Sin."

"From this, therefore, it sometimes happens, that if any persons have acted incontinently, and have been willing not so much to resist as to yield, and to give harbour to these demons in themselves, by their noxious breath an intemperate, ill-conditioned, and diseased progeny is begotten.

For while lust is wholly gratified, and no care is taken in the copulation, undoubtedly a weak generation is affected with the defects and frailties of those demons by whose instigation these things are done.

And therefore parents are responsible for their children's defects of this sort, because they have not observed the law of intercourse.

Though there are also more secret causes, by which souls are made subject to these evils, which it is not to our present purpose to state, yet it behoves every one to acknowledge the law of God, that he may learn from it the observance of generation, and avoid causes of impurity, that that which is begotten may be pure.

For it is not right, while in the planting of shrubs and the sowing of crops a suitable season is sought for, and the land is cleaned, and all things are suitably prepared, lest haply the seed which is sown be injured and perish, that in the case of man only, who is over all these things, there should be no attention or caution in sowing his seed.

Chapter X - Tow Smeared with Pitch

"But what, it is said, of the fact that some who in their childhood are free from any bodily defect, yet in process of time fall into those evils, so that some are even violently hurried on to death?

Concerning these also the account is at hand, and is almost the same:

for those powers which we have said to be contrary to the human race, are in some way invited into the heart of every one by many and diverse lusts, and find a way of entrance; and they have in them such influence and power as can only encourage and incite, but cannot compel or accomplish.

If, therefore, any one consents to them, so as to do those things which he wickedly desires, his consent and deed shall find the reward of destruction and the worst kind of death.

But if, thinking of the future judgment, he be checked by fear, and reclaim himself, so that he do not accomplish in action what he has conceived in his evil thought, he shall not only escape present destruction, but also future punishments.

For every cause of sin seems to be like tow smeared over with pitch, which immediately breaks into flame as soon as it receives the heat of fire; and the kindling of this fire is understood to be the work of demons.

If, therefore, any one be found smeared with sins and lusts as with pitch, the fire easily gets the mastery of him.

But if the tow be not steeped in the pitch of sin, but in the water of purification and regeneration, the fire of the demons shall not be able to be kindled in it.

Chapter XI - Fear

"But some one will say, And what shall we do now, whom it has already happened to us to be smeared with sins as with pitch?

I answer: Nothing; but hasten to be washed, that the fuel of the fire may be cleansed out of you by the invocation of the holy name, and that for the future you may bridle your lusts by fear of the judgment to come, and with all constancy beat back the hostile powers whenever they approach your senses.

But you say, If any one fall into love, how shall he be able to contain himself, though he see before his eyes even that river of fire which they call Pyriphlegethon?

This is the excuse of those who will not be converted to repentance.

But now I would not have you talk of Pyriphlegethon.

Place before you human punishments, and see what influence fear has.

When any one is brought to punishment for the crime of love, and is bound to the stake to be burned, can he at that time conceive any desire of her whom he loved, or place her image before his eyes?

By no means, you will say.

You see, then, that present fear cuts off unrighteous desires.

But if those who believe in God, and who confess the judgment to come, and the penalty of eternal fire,--if they do not refrain from sin, it is certain that they do not believe with full faith:

for if faith is certain, fear also becomes certain; but if there be any defect in faith, fear also is weakened, and then the contrary powers find opportunity of entering.

And when they have consented to their persuasions, they necessarily become subject also to their power, and by their instigation are driven to the precipices of sin.

Chapter XII - Astrologers

"Therefore the astrologers, [8] being ignorant of such mysteries, think that these things happen by the courses of the heavenly bodies: hence also, in their answers to those who go to them to consult them as to future things, they are deceived in very many instances.

Nor is it to be wondered at, for they are not prophets; but, by long practice, the authors of errors find a sort of refuge in those things by which they were deceived, and introduce certain Climacteric Periods, that they may pretend a knowledge of uncertain things.

For they represent these Climacterics as times of danger, in which one sometimes is destroyed, sometimes is not destroyed, not knowing that it is not the course of the stars, but the operation of demons, that regulates these things; and those demons, being anxious to confirm the error of astrology, deceive men to sin by mathematical calculations, so that when they suffer the punishment of sin, either by the permission of God or by legal sentence, the astrologer may seem to have spoken truth. And yet they are deceived even in this; for if men be quickly turned to repentance, and remember and fear the future judgment, the punishment of death is remitted to those who are converted to God by the grace of baptism.

Chapter XIII - Retribution Here or Hereafter

"But some one will say, Many have committed even murder, and adultery, and other crimes, and have suffered no evil.

This indeed rarely happens to men, but to those who know not the counsel of God it frequently seems to happen.

But God, who knows all things, knows how and why he who sins does sin, and what cause leads each one to sin. This, however, is in general to be noticed, that if any are evil, not so much in their mind as in their doings, and are not borne to sin under the incitement of purpose, upon them punishment is inflicted more speedily, and more in the present life; for everywhere and always God renders to every one according to his deeds, as He judges to be expedient.

But those who practise wickedness of purpose, so that they sometimes even rage against those from whom they have received benefits, and who take no thought for repentance--their punishment He defers to the future.

For these men do not, like those of whom we spoke before, deserve to end the punishment of their crimes in the present life; but it is allowed them to occupy the present time as they will, because their correction is not such as to need temporal chastisements, but such as to demand the punishment of eternal fire in hell; and there their souls shall seek repentance, where they shall not be able to find it.

Chapter XIV - Knowledge Deadens Lusts

"But if, while in this life, they had placed before their eyes the punishments which they shall then suffer, they would certainly have bridled their lusts, and would in nowise have fallen into sin.

For the understanding in the soul has much power for cutting off all its desires, especially when it has acquired the knowledge of heavenly things, by means of which, having received the light of truth, it will turn away from all darkness of evil actions.

For as the sun obscures and conceals all the stars by the brightness of his shining, so also the mind, by the light of knowledge, renders all the lusts of the soul ineffective and inactive, sending out upon them the thought of the judgment to come as its rays, so that they can no longer appear in the soul.

The Epistles of Clement

Chapter XV - Fear of Men and of God

"But as a proof that the fear of God has much efficacy for the repressing of lusts, take the example of human fear.

Who is there among men that does not covet his neighbour's goods?

And yet they are restrained, and act honestly, through fear of the punishment which is prescribed by the laws.

Through fear, nations are subject to their kings, and armies obey with arms in their hands.

Slaves, although they are stronger than their masters, yet through fear submit to their masters' rule.

Even wild beasts are tamed by fear; the strongest bulls submit their necks to the yoke, and huge elephants obey their masters, through fear.

But why do we use human examples, when even divine are not wanting?

Does not the earth itself remain under the fear of precept, which it testifies by its motion and quaking?

The sea keeps its prescribed bounds; the angels maintain peace; the stars keep their order, and the rivers their channels:

it is certain also that demons are put to flight by fear.

And not to lengthen the discourse by too many particulars, see how the fear of God, restraining everything, keeps all things in proper harmony, and in their fixed order.

How much more, then, may you be sure that the lusts of demons which arise in your hearts may be extinguished and wholly abolished by the admonition of the fear of God, when even the inciters of lust are themselves put to flight by the influence of fear?

You know that these things are so; but if you have anything to answer, proceed."

Chapter XVI - Imperfect Conviction

Then said the old man:

"My son Clement has wisely framed his argument, so that he has left us nothing to say to these things; but all his discourse which he has delivered on the nature of men has this bearing, that along with the fact that freedom of will is in man, there is also some cause of evil without him, whereby men are indeed incited by various lusts, yet are not compelled to sin; and that for this reason, he said, because fear is much more powerful than they, and it resists and checks the violence of desires, so that, although natural emotions may arise, yet sin may not be committed, those demons being put to flight who incite and inflame these emotions.

But these things do not convince me; for I am conscious of certain things from which I know well, that by the arrangement of the heavenly bodies men become murderers or adulterers, and perpetrate other evils; and in like manner honourable and modest women are compelled to act well.

Chapter XVII - Astrological Lore [9]

"In short, when Mars, holding the centre in his house, regards Saturn quarterly, with Mercury towards the centre, the full moon coming upon him, in the daily Genesis, he produces murderers, and those who are to fall by the sword, [10] bloody, drunken, lustful, devilish men, inquirers into secrets,[11] malefactors, sacrilegious persons, and such like; especially when there was no one of the good stars looking on.

But again Mars himself, having a quarterly position with respect to Venus, in a direction toward the centre, while no good star looks on, produces adulterers and incestuous persons.

Venus with the Moon, in the borders and houses of Saturn, if she was with Saturn, and Mars looking on, produces women that are viragos, ready for agriculture, building, and every manly work, to commit adultery with whom they please, and not to be convicted by their husbands, to use no delicacy, no ointments, nor feminine robes and shoes, but to live after the fashion of men.

But the unpropitious Venus makes men to be as women, and not to act in any respect as men, if she is with Mars in Aries; on the contrary, she produces women if she is in Capricorn or Aquarius."

Chapter XVIII - The Reply

And when the old man had pursued this subject at great length, and had enumerated every kind of mathematical figure, and also the position of the heavenly bodies, wishing thereby to show that fear is not sufficient to restrain lusts, I answered again:

"Truly, my father, you have argued most learnedly and skilfully; and reason herself invites me to say something in answer to your discourse, since indeed I am acquainted with the science of mathematics, and gladly hold a conference with so learned a man.

Listen therefore, while I reply to what you have said that you may learn distinctly that Genesis is not at all from the stars, and that it is possible for those to resist the assault of demons who have recourse to God; and, as I said before, that not only by the fear of God can natural lusts be restrained, but even by the fear of men, as we shall now instruct you.

Chapter XIX - Refutation of Astrology

"There are, in every country or kingdom, laws imposed by men, enduring either by writing or simply through custom, which no one easily transgresses.

In short, the first Seres, who dwell at the beginning of the world, [12] have a law not to know murder, nor adultery, nor whoredom, and not to commit theft, and not to worship idols; and in all that country, which is very large, there is neither temple, nor image, nor harlot, nor adulteress, nor is any thief brought to trial.

But neither is any man ever slain there; and no man's liberty of will is compelled, according to your doctrine, by the fiery star of Mars, to use the sword for the murder of man; nor does Venus in conjunction with Mars compel to adultery, although of course with them Mars occupies the middle circle of heaven every day.

But amongst the Seres the fear of laws is more powerful than the configuration of Genesis.

Chapter XX - Brahmans

"There are likewise amongst the Bactrians, in the Indian countries, immense multitudes of Brahmans, who also themselves, from the tradition of their ancestors, and peaceful customs and laws, neither commit murder nor adultery, nor worship idols, nor have the practice of eating animal food, are never drunk, never do anything maliciously, but always fear God.

And these things indeed they do, though the rest of the Indians commit both murders and adulteries, and worship idols, and are drunken, and practise other wickednesses of this sort.

Yea, in the western parts of India itself there is a certain country, where strangers, when they enter it, are taken and slaughtered and eaten; and neither have good stars prevented these men from such wickednesses and from accursed food, nor have malign stars compelled the Brahmans to do any evil.

Again, there is a custom among the Persians to marry mothers, and sisters, and daughters.

In all that district the Persians contract incestuous marriages.

Chapter XXI - Districts of Heaven

"And that those who study mathematics may not have it in their power to use that subterfuge by which they say that there are certain districts of heaven to which it is granted to have some things peculiar to themselves, some of that nation of Persians have gone to foreign countries, who are called Magusaei, of whom there are some to this day in Media, others in Parthia, some also in Egypt, and a considerable number in Galatia and Phrygia, all of whom maintain the form of this incestuous tradition without variation, and hand it down to their posterity to be observed, even although they have changed their district of heaven; nor has Venus with the Moon in the confines and houses of Saturn, with Saturn also and Mars looking on, compelled them to have a Genesis among other men. [13]

Chapter XXII - Customs of the Gelones

"Amongst the Geli also there is a custom, that women cultivate the fields, build, and do every manly work; and they are also allowed to have intercourse with whom they please, and are not found fault with by their husbands, or called adulteresses:

for they have promiscuous intercourse everywhere, and especially with strangers; they do not use ointments; they do not wear dyed garments, nor shoes.

On the other hand, the men of the Gelones are adorned, combed, clothed in soft and various-coloured garments, decked with gold, and besmeared with ointments, and that not through lack of manliness, for they are most warlike, and most keen hunters.

Yet the whole women of the Gelones had not at their birth the unfavourable Venus in Capricornus or Aquarius; nor had all their men Venus placed with Mars in Aries, by which configuration the Chaldean science asserts that men are born effeminate and dissolute.

Chapter XXIII - Manners of the Susidae

"But, further, in Susae the women use ointments, and indeed of the best sort, being decked with ornaments and precious stones; also they go abroad supported by the aid of their maidservants, with much greater ambition than the men.

They do not, however, cultivate modesty, but have intercourse indifferently with whomsoever they please, with slaves and guests, such liberty being allowed them by their husbands; and not only are they not blamed for this, but they also rule over their husbands.

And yet the Genesis of all the Susian women has not Venus, with Jupiter and Mars in the middle of the heaven in the houses of Jupiter.

In the remoter parts of the East, if a boy be treated unnaturally, when it is discovered, he is killed by his brothers, or his parents, or any of his relations, and is left unburied.

And again, among the Gauls, an old law allows boys to be thus treated publicly; and no disgrace is thought to attach to it.

And is it possible, that all those who are so basely treated among the Gauls, have had Lucifer with Mercury in the houses of Saturn and the confines of Mars?

Chapter XXIV - Different Customs of Different Countries

"In the regions of Britain several men have one wife; in Parthia many women have one husband; and each part of the world adheres to its own manners and institutions.

None of the Amazons have husbands, but, like animals, they go out from their own territories once a year about the vernal equinox, and live with the men of the neighbouring nation, observing a sort of solemnity the while, and when they have conceived by them they return; and if they bring forth a male child, they cast him away, and rear only females.

Now, since the birth of all is at one season, it is absurd to suppose that in the case of males Mars is at the time in equal portions with Saturn, but never in the Genesis of females; and that they have not Mercury placed with Venus in his own houses, so as to produce either painters, or sculptors, or money-changers; or in the houses of Venus, so that perfumers, or singers, or poets might be produced.

Among the Saracens, and Upper Libyans, and Moors, and the dwellers about the mouths of the ocean, and also in the remote districts of Germany, and among the Sarmatians and Scythians, and all the nations who dwell in the regions of the Pontic shore, and in the island Chrysea, there is never found a money-changer, nor a sculptor, nor a painter, nor an architect, nor a geometrician, nor a tragedian, nor a poet.

Therefore the influence of Mercury and Venus must be wanting among them.

Chapter XXV - Not Genesis, But Free-Will

"The Medes alone in all the world, with the greatest care, throw men still breathing to be devoured by dogs; yet they have not Mars with the Moon placed in Cancer all through their daily Genesis.

The Indians burn their dead, and the wives of the dead voluntarily offer themselves, and are burned with them.

But all the Indian women who are burned alive have not the Sun under the earth in nightly Genesis, with Mars in the regions of Mars.

Very many of the Germans end their lives by the halter; but all have not therefore the Moon with Hora begirt by Saturn and Mars.

From all this it appears that the fear of the laws bears sway in every country, and the freedom of will which is implanted in man by the Spirit complies with the laws; and Genesis can neither compel the Seres to commit murder, nor the Brahmans to eat flesh, nor the Persians to shun incest, nor the Indians to refrain from burning, nor the Medes from being devoured by dogs, nor the Parthians from having many wives, nor the women of Mesopotamia from preserving their chastity, nor the Greeks from athletic exercises, nor the Gallic boys from being abused; nor can it compel the barbarious nations to be instructed in the studies of the Greeks; but, as we have said, each nation observes its own laws according to free-will, and annuls the decrees of Genesis by the strictness of laws.

Chapter XXVI - Climates

"But some one skilled in the science of mathematics will say that Genesis is divided into seven parts, which they call climates, and that over each climate one of the seven heavenly bodies bears rule; and that those diverse laws to which we have referred are not given by men, but by those dominant stars according to their will, and that that which pleases the star is observed by men as a law.

To this we shall answer, in the first place, that the world is not divided into seven parts; and in the second place, that if it were so, we find many different laws in one part and one country; and therefore there are neither seven laws according to the number of the heavenly bodies, nor twelve according to the number of the signs, nor thirty-six according to that of the divisions of ten degrees; but they are innumerable.

Chapter XXVII - Doctrine of "Climates" Untenable

"Moreover, we ought to remember the things which have been mentioned, that in the one country of India there are both persons who feed on human flesh, and persons who abstain even from the flesh of sheep, and birds, and all living creatures; and that the Magusaei marry their mothers and daughters not only in Persia, but that in every nation where they dwell they keep up their incestuous customs.[14] Then, besides, we have mentioned also innumerable nations, which are wholly ignorant of the studies of literature, and also some wise men have changed the laws themselves in several places; and some laws have been voluntarily abandoned, on account of the impossibility of observing them, or on account of their baseness.

Assuredly we can easily ascertain how many rulers have changed the laws and customs of nations which they have conquered, and subjected them to their own laws.

This is manifestly done by the Romans, who have brought under the Roman law and the civil decrees almost the whole world, and all nations who formerly lived under various laws and customs of their own.

It follows, therefore, that the stars of the nations which have been conquered by the Romans have lost their climates and their portions.

Chapter XXVIII - Jewish Customs

"I shall add another thing which may satisfy even the most incredulous.

All the Jews who live under the law of Moses circumcise their sons on the eighth day without fail, and shed the blood of the tender infant.

But no one of the Gentiles has ever submitted to this on the eighth day; and, on the other hand, no one of the Jews has ever omitted it.

How then shall the account of Genesis stand with this, since Jews live in all parts of the world, mixed with Gentiles, and on the eighth day suffer the cutting of a member?

And no one of the Gentiles, but only they themselves, as I have said, do this, induced to it not by the compulsion of any star, nor by the perfusion [15] of blood, but by the law of their religion; and in whatever part of the world they are, this sign is familiar to them.

But also the fact that one name is among them all, wheresoever they are, does this also come through Genesis?

And also that no child born among them is ever exposed, and that on every seventh day they all rest, wherever they may be, and do not go upon a journey, and do not use fire? [16]Why is it, then, that no one of the Jews is compelled by Genesis to go on a journey, or to build, or to sell or buy anything on that day?

Chapter XXIX - The Gospel More Powerful Than "Genesis."

"But I shall give a still stronger proof of the matters in hand.

For, behold, scarcely seven years have yet passed since the advent of the righteous and true Prophet; and in the course of these, men of all nations coming to Judaea, and moved both by the signs and miracles which they saw, and by the grandeur of His doctrine, received His faith; and then going back to their own countries, they rejected the lawless rites of the Gentiles, and their incestuous marriages.

In short, among the Parthians--as Thomas, who is preaching the Gospel amongst them, has written to us--not many now are addicted to polygamy; nor among the Medes do many throw their dead to dogs; nor are the Persians pleased with intercourse with their mothers, or incestuous marriages with their daughters; nor do the Susian women practise the adulteries that were allowed them; nor has Genesis been able to force those into crimes whom the teaching of religion restrained.

Chapter XXX - "Genesis" Inconsistent with God's Justice

"Behold, from the very matter in which we are now engaged [17] draw an inference, and from the circumstances in which we are now placed deduce a conclusion, how, through a rumour only reaching the ears of men that a Prophet had appeared in Judaea to teach men with signs and miracles to worship one God, all were expecting with prepared and eager minds, even before the coming of my lord Peter, that some one would announce to them what He taught who had appeared.

But lest I should seem to carry the enumeration too far, I shall tell you what conclusion ought to be drawn from the whole.

Since God is righteous, and since He Himself made the nature of men, how could it be that He should place Genesis in opposition to us, which should compel us to sin, and then that He should punish us when we do sin?

Whence it is certain that God punishes no sinner either in the present life or in that to come, except because He knows that he could have conquered, but neglected victory.

For even in the present world He takes vengeance upon men, as He did upon those who perished in the deluge, who were all destroyed in one day, yea, in one hour, although it is certain that they were not all born in one hour according to the order of genesis.

But it is most absurd to say that it befalls us by nature to suffer evils, if sins had not gone before.

Chapter XXXI - Value of Knowledge

"And therefore, if we desire salvation, we ought above all to seek after knowledge, being sure that if our mind remain in ignorance, we shall endure not only the evils of genesis, but also whatever other evils from without the demons may please, unless fear of laws and of the judgment to come resist all our desires, and check the violence of sinning.

For even human fear does much good, and also much evil, unknown to Genesis, as we have shown above.

Therefore our mind is subject to errors in a threefold manner:

from those things which come to us through evil custom; or from those lusts which the body naturally stirs up in us; or from those which hostile powers compel us to.

But the mind has it in its own nature to oppose and fight against these, when the knowledge of truth shines upon it, by which knowledge is imparted fear of the judgment to come, which is a fit governor of the mind, and which can recall it from the precipices of lusts.

That these things, therefore, are in our power, has been sufficiently stated.

Chapter XXXII - Stubborn Facts

"Now, old man, if you have any thing to say in answer to these things, say on."

Then said the old man: [18]"You have most fully argued, my son; but I, as I said at first, am prevented by my own consciousness from according assent to all this incomparable statement of yours.

For I know both my own Genesis and that of my wife, and I know that those things have happened which our Genesis prescribed to each of us; and I cannot now be withdrawn by words from those things which I have ascertained by facts and deeds.

In short, since I perceive that you are excellently skilled in this sort of learning, hear the horoscope of my wife, and you shall find the configuration whose issue has occurred.

For she had Mars with Venus above the centre, and the Moon setting in the houses of Mars and the confines of Saturn.

Now this configuration leads women to be adulteresses, and to love their own slaves, and to end their days in foreign travel and in waters.

And this has so come to pass.

For she fell in love with her slave, and fearing at once danger and reproach, she fled with him, and going abroad, where she satisfied her love, she perished in the sea."

Chapter XXXIII - An Approaching Recognition

Then I answered:
"How know you that she cohabited with her slave abroad, and died in his society?"
Then the old man said:
"I know it with perfect certainty; not indeed that she was married to the slave, as indeed I had not even discovered that she loved him.

But after she was gone, my brother gave me the whole story, telling me that first she had loved himself; but he, being honourable as a brother, would not pollute his brother's bed with the stain of incest.

But she, being both afraid of me, and unable to bear the unhappy reproaches (and yet she should not be blamed for that to which her Genesis compelled her), pretended a dream, and said to me:

Some one stood by me in a vision, who ordered me to leave the city without delay with my two twins.' When I heard this, being anxious for her safety and that of my sons, I immediately sent away her and the children, retaining with myself one who was younger.

For this she said that he had permitted who had given her warning in her sleep."

Chapter XXXIV - The Other Side of the Story

Then I Clement, understanding that he perchance was my father, was drowned in tears, and my brothers also were ready to rush forward and to disclose the matter; but Peter restrained them, saying:

"Be quiet, until I give you permission."
Therefore Peter, answering, said to the old man:
"What was the name of your younger son?"
And he said: "Clement."
Then Peter:
"If I shall this day restore to you your most chaste wife and your three sons, will you believe that a modest mind can overcome unreasonable impulses, and that all things that have been spoken by us are true, and that Genesis is nothing?"

Then said the old man:
"As it is impossible for you to perform what you have promised, so it is impossible that anything can take place apart from Genesis." Then says Peter:

"I wish to have all who are here present as witnesses that I shall this day hand over to you your wife, who is living most chastely, with your three sons.

And now take a token of these things from this, that I know the whole story much more accurately than you do; and I shall relate the whole occurrences in order, both that you may know them, and that those who are present may learn."

Chapter XXXV - Revelations

When he had said this, he turned to the crowds, and thus began:

"This person whom you see, O men, in this poor garb, is a citizen of the city Rome, descended of the stock of Caesar himself.

His name is Faustinianus.

He obtained as his wife a woman of the highest rank, Matthidia by name.

By her he had three sons, two of whom were twins; and the one who was the younger, whose name is Clement, is this man!" When he said this, he pointed to me with his finger.

"And his twin sons are these men, Niceta and Aquila, the one of whom was formerly called Faustinus and the other Faustus." [19]But as soon as Peter pronounced our names, all the old man's limbs were weakened, and he fell down in a swoon.

But we his sons rushed to him, and embraced and kissed him, fearing that we might not be able to recall his spirit. And while these things were going on, the people were confounded with very wonder.

Chapter XXXVI - New Revelations

But Peter ordered us to rise from embracing our father, lest we should kill him; and he himself, laying hold of his hand, and lifting him up as from a deep sleep, and gradually reviving him, began to set forth to him the whole transactions as they had really happened: [20]how his brother had fallen in love with Matthidia, and how she, being very modest, had been unwilling to inform her husband of his brother's lawless love, lest she should stir up hostility between the brothers, and bring disgrace upon the family; and how she had wisely pretended a dream, by which she was ordered to depart from the city with her twin sons, leaving the younger one with his father; and how on their voyage they had suffered shipwreck through the violence of a storm; and how, when they were cast upon an island called Antaradus, Matthidia was thrown by a wave upon a rock, but her twin children were seized by pirates and carried to Caesarea, and there sold to a pious woman, who treated them as sons, and brought them up, and caused them to be educated as gentlemen; and how the pirates had changed their names, and called the one Niceta and the other Aquila; and how afterwards, through common studies and acquaintanceship, they had adhered to Simon; and how they had turned away from him when they saw him to be a magician and a deceiver, and had come to Zacchaeus; and how subsequently they had been associated with himself; and how Clement also, setting out from the city for the sake of learning the truth, had, through his acquaintance with Barnabas, come to Caesarea, and had become known to him, and had adhered to him, and how he had been taught by him the faith of his religion; and also how he had found and recognised his mother begging at Antaradus, and how the whole island rejoiced at his recognition of her; and also concerning her sojourn with her most chaste hostess, and the cure that he had wrought upon her, and concerning the liberality of Clement to those who had been kind to his mother; and how afterwards, when Niceta and Aquila asked who the strange woman was, and had heard the whole story from Clement, they cried out that they were her twin sons Faustinus and Faustus; and how they had unfolded the whole history of what had befallen them; and how afterwards, by the persuasion of Peter himself, they were presented to their mother with caution, lest she should be cut off by the sudden joy.

Chapter XXXVII - Another Recognition

But while Peter was detailing these things in the hearing of the old man, in a narrative which was most pleasing to the crowd, so that the hearers wept through wonder at the events, and through compassion for sufferings incident to humanity, [21] my mother, hearing (I know not how) of the recognition of my father, rushed into the middle of us in breathless haste, crying out, and saying:

"Where is my husband, my lord Faustinianus, who has been so long afflicted, wandering from city to city in search of me?"

While she shouted thus like one demented, and gazed around, the old man, running up, began to embrace and hug her with many tears. [22]And while these things were going on, Peter requested the crowds to disperse, saying that it was unseemly to remain longer; but that opportunity must be afforded them of seeing one another more privately.

"But to-morrow," said he, "if any of you wish it, let them assemble to hear the word."

Chapter XXXVIII - "Angels Unawares."

When Peter had said this, the crowds dispersed; and when we also were intending to go to our lodging, the master of the house said to us: [23]"It is base and wicked that such and so great men should stay in a hostelry, when I have almost my whole house empty, and very many beds spread, and all necessary things provided."

But when Peter refused, the wife of the householder prostrated herself before him with her children, and besought him, saying, "I entreat you, stay with us." But not even so did Peter consent, until the daughter of those people who asked him, who had been for a long time vexed with an unclean spirit, and bound with chains, who had been shut up in a closet, having had the demon expelled from her, and the door of the closet opened, came with her chains and fell down at Peter's feet, saying:

"It is right, my lord, that you keep my deliverance-feast here to-day, and not sadden me or my parents."

But when Peter asked what was the meaning of her chains and of her words, her parents, gladdened beyond hope by the recovery of their daughter, were, as it were, thunderstruck with astonishment, and could not speak; but the servants who were in attendance said:

"This girl has been possessed of a demon from her seventh year, and used to cut, and bite, and even to tear in pieces, all who attempted to approach her, and this she has never ceased to do for twenty years till the present time.

Nor could any one cure her, or even approach her, for she rendered many helpless, and even destroyed some; for she was stronger than any man, being doubtless strengthened by the power of the demon.

But now, as you see, the demon has fled from your presence, and the doors which were shut with the greatest strength have been opened, and she herself stands before you in her sound mind, asking of you to make the day of her recovery gladsome both to herself and her parents, and to remain with them."

When one of the servants had made this statement, and the chains of their own accord were loosened from her hands and feet, Peter, being sure that it was by his means that soundness was restored to the girl, consented to remain with them.

And he ordered those also who had remained in the lodging, with his wife, to come over; and every one of us having got a separate bed-chamber, we remained; and having taken food in the usual manner, and given praises to God, we went to sleep in our several apartments.

Footnotes:

1. [The discourses in book ix. are peculiar to the Recognitions not only in their position in the story, but to a remarkably large extent in the matter.--R.]
2. [Comp. book viii. 58-62.--R.]
3. [Comp. book viii. 55, 56; Homily XIX. 2-18.--R.]
4. [The doctrine of free-will, and the necessity of evil in consequence, appears throughout. Comp. book iii. 21, v. 6.
In the Homilies there is not so much emphasis laid upon this point; but see Homily XI. 8.--R.]
5. [Compare Homily XI. 26 on this view of baptism.--R.]
6. Ps. xxxix. 12.
7. [On the doctrine of demons compare book iv. 14-22; Homily IX. 8-18.--R.]
8. [On the error of astrology compare book x. 7-12.
In Homily XIV. 5 and elsewhere "genesis" and the science of astrology are identified.]--R.
9. Ch. 17 and ch. 19-29 are taken in an altered form from the writing ascribed to Bardesanes, De Fato.
[These chapters have no parallel in the Homilies, but the argument of the old man respecting genesis implies the same position; comp. Homily XIV. 3-7, 11.--R.]
10. Conjectural reading, "to kill with the sword."
11. That is, violators of the sacred mysteries, which was regarded as one of the most horrid of crimes.
12. That is, the farthest east, not, as some of the annotators suppose, from the beginning of the world.
13. This is a literal translation of text.
If we read genesi for genesim, we get:
"nor has Venus, etc., compelled them to keep up this custom in the midst of others through the force of genesis."
Eusebius reads:
"And assuredly Venus, etc., is not found in the genesis of all of them."

The Epistles of Clement

14. The text reads:
"the incestuous customs of their evils, or of their evil persons."
Hilgenfeld (Bardesanes, p. 113) notices that it should be, "of their ancestors."
15. Probably we should read perfusionem instead of perfusione, and then the translation would be: "no star compelling, or even urging on them the shedding of blood."
So Whiston translates.
16. Ex. xxxv. 3.
17. [This conclusion of the argument by a reference to the Prophet is much more dignified than the personal boast of miraculous power which, in the Homilies, is placed in the mouth of the Apostle just before the recognition.--R.]
18. [To chaps. 32-37 a partial parallel is found in Homily XIV. 6-9. The arrangement is quite different, and the details vary.--R.]
19. [Compare the account of the recognition in Homily XIV. 9.--R.]
20. [This recapitulation is peculiar to the Recognitions; in Homily XV. 4 the main facts are cited as a proof of divine providence.--R.]
21. Lit. "through pity of humanity."
22. [Comp. Homily XIV. 9.

The recognition of the mother is represented as occurring first; the variations are quite remarkable.--R.]
23. [This chapter is peculiar to the Recognitions; the detailed description of the exorcism is a curious piece of literature.--R.]

Book X
Chapter I - Probation

But in the morning, after sunrise, I Clement, and Niceta and Aquila, along with Peter, came to the apartment in which my father and mother were sleeping; and finding them still asleep, we sat down before the door, when Peter addressed us in such terms as these: [1]"Listen to me, most beloved fellow-servants:

I know that you have a great affection for your father; therefore I am afraid that you will urge him too soon to take upon himself the yoke of religion, while he is not yet prepared for it; and to this he may perhaps consent, through his affection for you.

But this is not to be depended on; for what is done for the sake of men is not worthy of approbation, and soon falls to pieces.

Therefore it seems to me, that you should permit him to live for a year according to his own judgment; and during that time he may travel with us, and while we are instructing others he may hear with simplicity; and as he hears, if he has any right purpose of acknowledging the truth, he will himself request that he may take up the yoke of religion; or if he do not please to take it, he may remain a friend.

For those who do not take it up heartily, when they begin not to be able to bear it, not only cast off that which they had taken up, but by way of excuse, as it were, for their weakness, they begin to speak evil of the way of religion, and to malign those whom they have not been able to follow or to imitate."

Chapter II - A Difficulty

To this Niceta answered:
"My lord Peter, I say nothing against your right and good counsels; but I wish to say one thing, that thereby I may learn something that I do not know.

What if my father should die within the year during which you recommend that he should be put off? He will go down to hell helpless, and so be tormented for ever."

Then said Peter:
"I embrace your kindly purpose towards your father, and I forgive you in respect of things of which you are ignorant.

For do you suppose that, if any one is thought to have lived righteously, he shall forthwith be saved?

Do you not think that he must be examined by Him who knows the secrets of men, as to how he has lived righteously, whether perchance according to the rule of the Gentiles, obeying their institutions and laws; or for the sake of the friendship of men; or merely from custom, or any other cause; or from necessity, and not on account of righteousness itself, and for the sake of God?

For those who have lived righteously, for the sake of God alone and His righteousness, they shall come to eternal rest, and shall receive the perpetuity of the heavenly kingdom.

For salvation is not attained by force, but by liberty; and not through the favour of men, but by the faith of God.

Then, besides, you ought to consider that God is prescient, and knows whether this man is one of His.

But if He knows that he is not, what shall we do with respect to those things which have been determined by Him from the beginning?

But wherein I can, I give counsel:
when he is awake, and we sit down together, then do you, as if you wished to learn something, ask a question about those matters which it is fitting for him to learn; and while we speak to one another, he will gain instruction.

But yet wait first to see if he himself ask anything; for if he do so, the occasion of discourse will be the fitter.

But if he do not ask anything, let us by turns put questions to one another, wishing to learn something, as I have said. Such is my judgment, state what is yours."

Chapter III - A Suggestion

And when we had commended his right counsel, I Clement said:
"In all things, the end for the most part looks back upon the beginning, and the issue of things is similar to their commencement.

I hope, therefore, with respect to our father also, since God by your means has given a good beginning, that He will bestow also an ending suitable to the beginning, and worthy of Himself.

However, I make this suggestion, that if, as you have said, we begin to speak, in presence of my father, as if for the purpose of discussing some subject, or learning something from one another, you, my lord Peter, ought not to occupy the place of one who has anything to learn; for if he see this, he will rather be offended.

For he is convinced that you fully know all things, as indeed you do.

How then will it be, if he see you pretending ignorance?

This, as I have said, will rather hurt him, being ignorant of your design.

But if we brothers, while we converse among ourselves, are in any doubt, let a fitting solution be given by you to our inquiry.

For if he see even you hesitating and doubting, then truly he will think that no one has knowledge of the truth."

Chapter IV - Free Inquiry

To this Peter answered: "Let us not concern ourselves about this; and if indeed it is fitting that he enter the gate of life, God will afford a fitting opportunity; and there shall be a beginning from God, and not from man.

And therefore, as I have said, let him journey with us, and hear our discussions; but because I saw you in haste, therefore I said that opportunity must be sought; and when God shall give it, do you comply with my advice in what I shall say."

While we were thus talking, a boy came to tell us that our father was now awake; and when we were intending to go in to him, he himself came to us, and saluting us with a kiss, after we had sat down again, he said:

"Is it permitted to one to ask a question, if he wishes it; or is silence enforced, after the manner of the Pythagoreans?"

Then said Peter:

"We do not compel those who come to us either to keep silence continually, or to ask questions; but we leave them free to do as they will knowing that he who is anxious about his salvation, if he feels pain in any part of his soul, does not suffer it to be silent.

But he who neglects his salvation, no advantage is conferred upon him if he is compelled to ask, excepting this only, that he may seem to be earnest and diligent. Wherefore, if you wish to get any information, ask on."

Chapter V - Good and Evil

Then the old man said:

"There is a saying very prevalent among the Greek philosophers, to the effect that there is in reality neither good nor evil in the life of man; but that men call things good or evil as they appear to them, prejudiced by the use and custom of life.

For not even murder is really an evil, because it sets the soul free from the bonds of the flesh.

Further, they say that even just judges put to death those who commit crimes; but if they knew homicide to be an evil, just men would not do that.

Neither do they say that adultery is an evil; for if the husband does not know, or does not care, there is, they say, no evil in it.

But neither, say they is theft an evil; for it takes away what one does not possess from another who has it.

And, indeed, it ought to be taken freely and openly; but in that it is done secretly, that is rather a reproof of his inhumanity from whom it is secretly taken.

For all men ought to have the common use of all things that are in this world; but through injustice one says that this is his, and another that that is his, and so division is caused among men.

In short, a certain man, the wisest among the Greeks, [2] knowing that these things are so, says that friends should have all things common.

Now, in all things unquestionably wives are included. He says also that, as the air and the sunshine cannot be divided, so neither ought other things to be divided, which are given in this world to all to be possessed in common, but should be so possessed.

But I wished to say this, because I am desirous to turn to well-doing, and I cannot act well unless I first learn what is good; and if I can understand that, I shall thereby perceive what is evil, that is, opposite to good.

Chapter VI - Peter's Authority

"But I should like that one of you, and not Peter, should answer what I have said; for it is not fitting to take words and instruction at his hand, with questions; but when he gives a deliverance on any subject, that should be held without answering again.

And therefore let us keep him as an umpire; so that if at any time our discussion does not come to an issue, he may declare what seems good to him, and so give an undoubted end to doubtful matters.

And now therefore I could believe, content with his sole opinion, if he expressed any opinion; and this is what I shall do at last.

Yet I wish first to see if it is possible by discussion to find what is sought.

My wish therefore is, that Clement should begin first, and should show if there is any good or evil in substance or in actions."

Chapter VII - Clement's Argument

To this I answered:
"Since indeed you wish to learn from me if there is any good or evil in nature or in act, or whether it is not rather that men, prejudiced by custom, think some things to be good, and others to be evil, forasmuch as they have made a division among themselves of common things, which ought, as you say, to be as common as the air and the sunshine; I think that I ought not to bring before you any statements from any other quarter than from those studies in which you are well versed, and which you support, so that what I say you will receive without hesitation.

You assign certain boundaries of all the elements and the heavenly bodies, and these, you say, meet in some without hurt, as in marriages; but in others they are hurtfully united, as in adulteries.

And you say that some things are general to all, but other things do not belong to all, and are not general.

But not to make a long discussion, I shall speak briefly of the matter. The earth which is dry is in need of the addition and admixture of water, that it may be able to produce fruits, without which man cannot live:
this is therefore a legitimate conjunction.

On the contrary if the cold of hoar-frost be mixed with the earth, or heat with the water, a conjunction of this sort produces corruption; and this, in such things, is adultery."

Chapter VIII - Admitted Evils

Then my father answered:
"But as the harmfulness of an inharmonious conjunction of elements or stars is immediately betrayed, so ought also adultery to be immediately shown that it is an evil."
Then I:
"First tell me this, whether, as you yourself have confessed, evils are produced from incongruous and inharmonious mixture; and then after that we shall inquire into the other matter."
Then my father said:
"The nature of things is as you say, my son."
Then I answered:
"Since, then, you wish to learn of these things, see how many things there are which no one doubts to be evils.

Do you think that a fever, a fire, sedition, the fall of a house, murder, holds, racks, pains, mournings, and such like, are evils?"
Then said my father:

"It is true, my son, that these things are evil, and very evil; or, at all events, whoever denies that they are evil, let him suffer them!"

Chapter IX - Existence of Evil on Astrological Principles

Then I answered:
"Since, therefore, I have to deal with one who is skilled in astrological science, [3] I shall treat the matter with you according to that science, that, taking my method from those things with which you are familiar, you may the more readily acquiesce. Listen now, therefore:
 you confess that those things which we have mentioned are evils, such as fevers, conflagrations, and such like. Now these, according to you, are said to be produced by malignant stars, such as the humid Saturn and the hot Mars; but things contrary to these are produced by benignant stars, such as the temperate Jupiter and the humid Venus.
Is it not so?"
My father answered:
"It is so, my son; and it cannot be otherwise."
Then said I:
"Since you say, therefore, that good things are produced by good stars--by Jupiter and Venus, for example--let us see what is the product where any one of the evil stars is mixed with the good, and let us understand that that is evil.
For you lay it down that Venus makes marriages, and if she have Jupiter in her configuration she makes the marriages chaste; but if Jupiter be not regarding, and Mars be present, then you pronounce that the marriages are corrupted by adultery."
Then said my father:
"It is even so."
Then I answered:
"Therefore adultery is an evil, seeing that it is committed through the admixture of evil stars; and, to state it in a word, all things that you say that the good stars suffer from the mixture of evil stars, are undoubtedly to be pronounced to be evil.
Those stars, therefore, by whose admixture we have said that fevers, configurations, and other such like evils are produced,--those, according to you, work also murders, adulteries, thefts, and also produce haughty and stolid men."

Chapter X - How to Make Progress

Then my father said:
"Truly you have shown briefly and incomparably that there are evils in actions; but still I should wish to learn this, how God justly judges those who sin, as you say, if Genesis compels them to sin?"
Then I answered:
"I am afraid to speak anything to you, my father, because it becomes me to hold you in all honour, else I have an answer to give you, if it were becoming."
Then says my father: "Speak what occurs to you, my son; for it is not you, but the method of inquiry, that does the wrong, as a modest woman to an incontinent man, if she is indignant for her safety and her honour."
Then I answered: "If we do not hold by the principles that we have acknowledged and confessed, but if those things which have been defined are always loosened by forgetfulness, we shall seem to be weaving Penelope's web, undoing what we have done.
And therefore we ought either not to acquiesce too easily, before we have diligently examined the doctrine propounded; or if we have once acquiesced, and the proposition has been agreed to, then we ought to keep by what has been once determined, that we may go on with our inquiries respecting other matters."
And my father said:
"You say well, my son; and I know why you say this:
 it is because in the discussion yesterday on natural causes, you showed that some malignant power, transferring itself into the order of the stars, excites the lusts of men, provoking them in various ways to sin, yet not compelling or producing sins."
To this I answered:
"It is well that you remember it; and yet, though you do remember it, you have fallen into error."

Then said my father:

"Pardon me, my son; for I have not yet much practice in these things:

for indeed your discourses yesterday, by their truth, shut me up to agree with you; yet in my consciousness there are, as it were, some remains of fevers, which for a little hold me back from faith, as from health.

For I am distracted, because I know that many things, yea, almost all things, have befallen me according to Genesis."

Chapter XI - Test of Astrology

Then I answered:

"I shall therefore tell you, my father, what is the nature of mathematics, and do you act according to what I tell you.

Go to a mathematician, [4] and tell him first that such and such evils have befallen you at such a time, and that you wish to learn of him whence, or how, or through what stars they have befallen you.

He will no doubt answer you that a malignant Mars or Saturn has ruled your times, or that some one of them has been periodic; or that some one has regarded you diametrically, or in conjunction, or centrally; or some such answer will he give, adding that in all these some one was not in harmony with the malignant one, or was invisible, or was in the figure, or was beyond the division, or was eclipsed, or was not in contact, or was among the dark stars; and many other like things will he answer, according to his own reasons, and will condescend upon particulars. After him go to another mathematician, and tell him the opposite, that such and such good happened to you at that time, mentioning to him the same time, and ask him from what parts of your Genesis this good has come to you, and take care, as I said, that the times are the same with those about which you asked concerning evils.

And when you have deceived him concerning the times, see what figures he will invent for you, by which to show that good things ought to have befallen you at those very times.

For it is impossible for those treating of the Genesis of men not to find in every quarter, as they call it, of the heavenly bodies, some stars favourably placed, and some unfavourably; for the circle is equally complete in every part, according to mathematics, admitting of diverse and various causes, from which they can take occasion of saying whatever they please.

Chapter XII - Astrology Baffled by Free-Will

"For, as usually happens when men see unfavourable dreams, and can make nothing certain out of them, when any event occurs, then they adapt what they saw in the dream to what has occurred; so also is mathematics.

For before anything happens, nothing is declared with certainty; but after something has happened, they gather the causes of the event.

And thus often, when they have been at fault, and the thing has fallen out otherwise, they take the blame to themselves, saying that it was such and such a star which opposed, and that they did not see it; not knowing that their error does not proceed from their unskilfulness in their art, but from the inconsistency of the whole system.

For they do not know what those things are which we indeed desire to do, but in regard to which we do not indulge our desires. But we who have learned the reason of this mystery know the cause, since, having freedom of will, we sometimes oppose our desires, and sometimes yield to them. [5]And therefore the issue of human doings is uncertain, because it depends upon freedom of will.

For a mathematician can indeed indicate the desire which a malignant power produces; but whether the acting or the issue of this desire shall be fulfilled or not, no one can know before the accomplishment of the thing, because it depends upon freedom of will.

And this is why ignorant astrologers have invented to themselves the talk about climacterics as their refuge in uncertainties, as we showed fully yesterday.

Chapter XIII - People Admitted

"If you have anything that you wish to say to this, say on."

Then my father:

"Nothing can be more true, my son, than what you have stated."

And while we were thus speaking among ourselves, some one informed us that a great multitude of people were standing outside, having assembled for the purpose of hearing.

Then Peter ordered them to be admitted, for the place was large and convenient.

And when they had come in, Peter said to us:

"If any one of you wishes, let him address the people, and discourse concerning idolatry."

To whom I Clement answered:

"Your great benignity and gentleness and patience towards all encourages us, so that we dare speak in your presence, and ask what we please; and therefore, as I said, the gentleness of your disposition invites and encourages all to undertake the precepts of saving doctrine.

This I never saw before in any one else, but in you only, with whom there is neither envy nor indignation.

Or what do you think?

Chapter XIV - No Man Has Universal Knowledge

Then Peter said:

"These things come not only from envy or indignation; but sometimes there is a bashfulness in some persons, lest haply they may not be able to answer fully the questions that may be proposed, and so they avoid the discovery of their want of skill.

But no one ought to be ashamed of this, because there is no man who ought to profess that he knows all things; for there is only One who knows all things, even He who also made all things.

For if our Master declared that He knew not the day and the hour whose signs even He foretold, and referred the whole to the Father, how shall we account it disgraceful to confess that we are ignorant of some things, since in this we have the example of our Master?

But this only we profess, that we know those things which we have learned from the true Prophet; and that those things have been delivered to us by the true Prophet, which He judged to be sufficient for human knowledge."

Chapter XV - Clement's Disclosure

Then I Clement went on to speak thus:

"At Tripolis, when you were disputing against the Gentiles, my lord Peter, I greatly wondered at you, that although you were instructed by your father according to the fashion of the Hebrews and in observances of your own law, and were never polluted by the studies of Greek learning, you argued so magnificently and so incomparably; and that you even touched upon some things concerning the histories of the gods, which are usually declaimed in the theatres.

But as I perceived that their fables and blasphemies are not so well known to you, I shall discourse upon these in your hearing, repeating them from the very beginning, if it please you."

Then says Peter:

"Say on; you do well to assist my preaching." Then said I:

"I shall speak, therefore, because you order me, not by way of teaching you, but of making public what foolish opinions the Gentiles entertain of the gods."

Chapter XVI - "Would that All God's People Were Prophets."

But when I was about to speak, Niceta, biting his lip, beckoned to me to be silent.

And when Peter saw him, he said:

"Why would you repress his liberal disposition and noble nature, that you would have him be silent for my honour, which is nothing?

Or do you not know, that if all nations, after they have heard from me the preaching of the truth, and have believed, would betake themselves to teaching, they would gain the greater glory for me, if indeed you think me desirous of glory? For what so glorious as to prepare disciples for Christ, not who shall be silent, and shall be saved alone, but who shall speak what they have learned, and shall do good to others?

I wish indeed that both you, Niceta, and you, beloved Aquila, would aid me in preaching the word of God, and the rather because those things in which the Gentiles err are well known to you; and not you only, but all who hear me, I wish, as I have said, so to hear and to learn, that they may be able also to teach:

for the world needs many helpers, by whom men may be recalled from error."

When he had spoken thus, he said to me:
"Go on then, Clement, with what you have begun."

Chapter XVII - Gentile Cosmogony

And I immediately rejoined:
"Seeing that when you were disputing at Tripolis, as I said, you discoursed much concerning the gods of the Gentiles profitably and convincingly, I desire to set forth in your presence the ridiculous legends concerning their origin, both that you may not be unacquainted with the falsehood of this vain superstition, and that the hearers who are present may know the disgraceful character of their error.

The wise men, then, who are among the Gentiles, say that first of all things was chaos; [6] that this, through a long time solidifying its outer parts, made bounds to itself and a sort of foundation, being gathered, as it were, into the manner and form of a huge egg, within which, in the course of a long time, as within the shell of the egg, there was cherished and vivified a certain animal; and that afterwards, that huge globe being broken, there came forth a certain kind of man of double sex, which they call masculo-feminine. This they called Phanetas, from appearing, because when it appeared, they say, then also light shone forth.

And from this, they say that there were produced substance, prudence, motion, and coition, and from these the heavens and the earth were made.

From the heaven they say that six males were produced, whom they call Titans; and in like manner, from the earth six females, whom they called Titanides.

And these are the names of the males who sprang from the heaven:

Oceanus, Coeus, Crios, Hyperion, Iapetus, Chronos, who amongst us is called Saturn.

In like manner, the names of the females who sprang from the earth are these:

Theia, Rhea, Themis, Mnemosyne, Tethys, Hebe. [7]

Chapter XVIII - Family of Saturn

"Of all these, the first-born of the heaven took to wife the first-born of earth; the second second, and in like manner all the rest.

The first male, therefore, who had married the first female, was on her account drawn downwards; but the second female rose upwards, by reason of him to whom she was married; and so each doing in their order, remained in those places which fell to their share by the nuptial lot. From their intercourse they assert that innumerable others sprang.

But of these six males, the one who is called Saturn received in marriage Rhea, and having been warned by a certain oracle that he who should be born of her should be more powerful than himself, and should drive him from his kingdom, he determined to devour all the sons that should be born to him.

First, then, there is born to him a son called Aides, who amongst us is called Orcus; and him, for the reason we have just stated, he took and devoured.

After him he begot a second son, called Neptune; and him he devoured in like manner.

Last of all, he begot him whom they call Jupiter; but him his mother Rhea pitying, by stratagem withdrew from his father when he was about to devour him.

And first, indeed, that the crying of the child might not be noticed, she made certain Corybantes strike cymbals and drums, that by the deafening sound the crying of the infant might not be heard.

Chapter XIX - Their Destinies

"But when he understood from the lessening of her belly that her child was born, he demanded it, that he might devour it; then Rhea presented him with a large stone, and told him that that was what she had brought forth.

And he took it, and swallowed it; and the stone, when it was devoured, pushed and drove forth those sons whom he had formerly swallowed.

Therefore Orcus, coming forth first, descended, and occupies the lower, that is, the infernal regions.

The second, being above him--he whom they call Neptune--is thrust forth upon the waters. The third, who survived by the artifice of his mother Rhea, she put upon a she-goat and sent into heaven.

Chapter XX - Doings of Jupiter

"But enough of the old wife's fables and genealogy of the Gentiles; for it were endless if I should set forth all the generations of those whom they call gods, and their wicked doings.

But by way of example, omitting the rest, I shall detail the wicked deeds of him only whom they hold to be the greatest and the chief, and whom they call Jupiter. [8]For they say that he possesses heaven, as being superior to the rest; and he, as soon as he grew up, married his own sister, whom they call Juno, in which truly he at once becomes like a beast.

Juno bears Vulcan; but, as they relate, Jupiter was not his father.

However, by Jupiter himself she became mother of Medea; and Jupiter having received a response that one who should be born of her should be more powerful than himself, and should expel him from his kingdom, took her and devoured her.

Again Jupiter produced Minerva from his brain, and Bacchus from his thigh.

After this, when he had fallen in love with Thetis, they say that Prometheus informed him that, if he lay with her, he who should be born of her should be more powerful than his father; and for fear of this, he gave her in marriage to one Peleus. Subsequently he had intercourse with Persephone, who was his own daughter by Ceres and by her he begot Dionysius, [9] who was torn in pieces by the Titans.

But calling to mind, it is said, that perhaps his own father Saturn might beget another son, who might be more powerful than himself, and might expel him from the kingdom, he went to war with his father, along with his brothers the Titans; and having beaten them, he at last threw his father into prison, and cut off his genitals, and threw them into the sea.

But the blood which flowed from the wound, being mixed with the waves, and turned into foam by the constant churning, produced her whom they call Aphrodite, and whom with us they call Venus.

From his intercourse with her who was thus his own sister, they say that this same Jupiter begot Cypris, who, they say, was the mother of Cupid.

Chapter XXI - A Black Catalogue

"Thus much of his incests; I shall now speak of his adulteries.

He defiled Europa, the wife of Oceanus, of whom was born Dodonaeus; Helen, the wife of Pandion, of whom Musaeus; Eurynome, the wife of Asopus, of whom Ogygias; Hermione, the wife of Oceanus, of whom the Graces, Thalia, Euphrosyne, Aglaia; Themis, his own sister, of whom the Hours, Eurynomia, Dice, Irene; Themisto, the daughter of Inachus, of whom Arcas; Idaea, the daughter of Minos, of whom Asterion; Phoenissa, the daughter of Alphion, of whom Endymion; Io, the daughter of Inachus, of whom Epaphus; Hippodamia and Isione, daughters of Danaus, of whom Hippodamia was the wife of Olenus, and Isione of Orchomenus or Chryses; Carme, the daughter of Phoenix, of whom was born Britomartis, who was an attendant of Diana; Callisto, the daughter of Lycaon, of whom Orcas; Lybee, the daughter of Munantius, of whom Belus; Latona, of whom Apollo and Diana; Leandia, the daughter of Eurymedon, of whom Coron; Lysithea, the daughter of Evenus, of whom Helenus; Hippodamia, the daughter of Bellerophon, of whom Sarpedon; Megaclite, the daughter of Macarius, of whom Thebe and Locrus; Niobe, the daughter of Phoroneus, of whom Argus and Pelasgus; Olympias, the daughter of Neoptolemus, of whom Alexander; Pyrrha, the daughter of Prometheus, of whom Helmetheus; Protogenia and Pandora, daughters of Deucalion, of whom he begot AEthelius, and Dorus, and Melera, and Pandorus; Thaicrucia, the daughter of Proteus, of whom was born Nympheus; Salamis, the daughter of Asopus, of whom Saracon; Taygete, Electra, Maia, Plutide, daughters of Atlas, of whom respectively he begot Lacedaemon, Dardanus, Mercury, and Tantalus; Phthia, the daughter of Phoroneus, of whom he begot Achaeus; Chonia, the daughter of Aramnus, of whom he begot Lacon; Chalcea, a nymph, of whom was born Olympus; Charidia, a nymph, of whom Alcanus; Chloris, who was the wife of Ampycus, of whom Mopsus was born; Cotonia, the daughter of Lesbus, of whom Polymedes; Hippodamia, the daughter of Anicetus; Chrysogenia, the daughter of Peneus, of whom was born Thissaeus.

Chapter XXII - Vile Transformation of Jupiter

"There are also innumerable adulteries of his, of which no offspring was the result, which it were tedious to enumerate.

But amongst those whom we have mentioned, he violated some being transformed, like a magician.

In short, he seduced Antiope, the daughter of Nycteus, when turned into a satyr, and of her were born Amphion and Zethus; Alcmene, when changed into her husband Amphitryon, and of her was born Hercules; AEgina, the daughter of Asopus, when changed into an eagle, of whom AEacus was born.

So also he defiled Ganymede, the son of Dardanus, being changed into an eagle; Manthea, the daughter of Phocus, when changed into a bear, of whom was born Arctos; Danae, the daughter of Acrisius, being changed into gold, of whom Perseus; Europa, the daughter of Phoenix, changed into a bull, of whom were born Minos, Rhadamanthus, and Sarpedon; Eurymedusa, the daughter of Achelaus, being changed into an ant, of whom Myrmidon; Thalia, the nymph, being changed into a vulture, of whom were born the Palisci, in Sicily; Imandra, the daughter of Geneanus, at Rhodes, being changed into a shower; Cassiopeia, being changed into her husband Phoenix, and of her was born Anchinos; Leda, the daughter of Thestius, being changed into a swan, of whom was born Helen; and again the same, being changed into a star, and of her were born Castor and Pollux; Lamia, being changed into a lapwing; Mnemosyne, being changed into a shepherd, of whom were born the nine Muses; Nemesis, being changed into a goose; the Cadmian Semele, being changed into fire, and of her was born Dionysius.

By his own daughter Ceres he begot Persephone, whom also herself he defiled, being changed into a dragon.

Chapter XXIII - Why a God?

"He also committed adultery with Europa, the wife of his own uncle Oceanus, and with her sister Eurynome, and punished their father; and he committed adultery with Plute, the daughter of his own son Atlas, and condemned Tantalus, whom she bore to him.

Of Larisse, the daughter of Orchomenus, he begot Tityon, whom also he consigned to punishment. He carried off Dia, the wife of his own son Ixion, and subjected him to perpetual punishment; and almost all the sons who sprang from his adulteries he put to violent deaths; and indeed the sepulchres of almost all of them are well known.

Yea, the sepulchre of this parricide himself, who destroyed his uncles and defiled their wives, who committed whoredom with his sisters, this magician of many transformations, is shown among the Cretans, who, although they know and acknowledge his horrid and incestuous deeds, and tell them to all, yet are not ashamed to confess him to be a god.

Whence it seems to me to be wonderful, yea, exceeding wonderful, how he who exceeds all men in wickedness and crimes, has received that holy and good name which is above every name, being called the father of gods and men; unless perhaps he who rejoices in the evils of men has persuaded unhappy souls to confer honour above all others upon him whom he saw to excel all others in crimes, in order that he might allure all to the imitation of his evil deeds.

Chapter XXIV - Folly of Polytheism

"But also the sepulchres of his sons, who are regarded amongst these the Gentiles as gods, are openly pointed out, one in one place, and another in another:

that of Mercury at Hermopolis; that of the Cyprian Venus at Cyprus; that of Mars in Thrace; that of Bacchus at Thebes, where he is said to have been torn in pieces; that of Hercules at Tyre, where he was burnt with fire; that of AEsculapius in Epidaurus.

And all these are spoken of, not only as men who have died, but as wicked men who have been punished for their crimes; and yet they are adored as gods by foolish men. [10]

Chapter XXV - Dead Men Deified

"But if they choose to argue, and affirm that these are rather the places of their birth than of their burial or death, the former and ancient doings shall be convicted from those at hand and still recent, since we have shown that they worship those whom they themselves confess to have been men, and to have died, or rather to have been punished; as the Syrians worship Adonis, and the Egyptians Osiris; the Trojans, Hector; Achilles is worshipped at Leuconesus, Patroclus at Pontus, Alexander the Macedonian at Rhodes; and many others are worshipped, one in one place and another in another, whom they do not doubt to have been dead men.

Whence it follows that their predecessors also, falling into a like error, conferred divine honour upon dead men, who perhaps had had some power or some skill, and especially if they had stupefied stolid men by magical phantasies. [11]

Chapter XXVI - Metamorphoses

"Hence there has now been added, that the poets also adorn the falsehoods of error by elegance of words, and by sweetness of speech persuade that mortals have been made immortal; yea more, they say that men are changed into stars, and trees, and animals, and flowers, and birds, and fountains, and rivers.

And but that it might seem to be a waste of words, I could even enumerate almost all the stars, and trees, and fountains, and rivers, which they assert to have been made of men; yet, by way of example, I shall mention at least one of each class. They say that Andromeda, the daughter of Cepheus, was turned into a star; Daphne, the daughter of the river Lado, into a tree; Hyacinthus, beloved of Apollo, into a flower; Callisto into the constellation which they call Arctos; Progne and Philomela, with Tereus, into birds; that Thysbe in Cilicia was dissolved into a fountain; and Pyramus, at the same place, into a river.

And they assert that almost all the stars, trees, fountains, and rivers, flowers, animals, and birds, were at one time human beings."

Chapter XXVII - Inconsistency of Polytheists

But Peter, when he heard this, said:

"According to them, then, before men were changed into stars, and the other things which you mention, the heaven was without stars, and the earth without trees and animals; and there were neither fountains, nor rivers, nor birds.

And without these, how did those men themselves live, who afterwards were changed into them, since it is evident that, without these things, men could not live upon the earth?"

Then I answered:

"But they are not even able to observe the worship of their own gods consistently; for every one of those whom they worship has something dedicated to himself, from which his worshippers ought to abstain:

as they say the olive is dedicated to Minerva, the she-goat to Jupiter, seeds to Ceres, wine to Bacchus, water to Osiris, the ram to Hammon, the stag to Diana, the fish and the dove to the demon of the Syrians, fire to Vulcan; and to each one, as I have said, is there something specially consecrated, from which the worshippers are bound to abstain, for the honour of those to whom they are consecrated.

But were one abstaining from one thing, and another from another, by doing honor to one of the gods, they incur the anger of all the rest; and therefore, if they would conciliate them all, they must abstain from all things for the honour of all, so that, being self-condemned by a just sentence before the day of judgment, they should perish by a most wretched death through starvation.

Chapter XXVIII - Buttresses of Gentilism

"But let us return to our purpose.

What reason is there, yea, rather, what madness possesses the minds of men, that they worship and adore as a god, a man whom they not only know to be impious, wicked, profane--I mean Jupiter--incestuous, a parricide, an adulterer, but even proclaim him publicly as such in their songs in the theatres?

Or if by means of these deeds he has deserved to be a god, then also, when they hear of any murderers, adulterers, parricides, incestuous persons, they ought to worship them also as gods.

But I cannot understand why they venerate in him what they execrate in others."

Then Peter answered: "Since you say that you cannot understand it, learn of me why they venerate wickedness in him.

In the first place, it is that, when they themselves do like deeds, they may know that they shall be acceptable to him, inasmuch as they have but imitated him in his wickedness.

In the second place, because the ancients have left these things skilfully composed in their writings, and elegantly engrafted in their verses. And now, by the aid of youthful education, since the knowledge of these things adheres to their tender and simple minds, it cannot without difficulty be torn from them and cast away."

Chapter XXIX - Allegories

When Peter had said this, Niceta answered:
"Do not suppose, my lord Peter, but that the learned men of the Gentiles have certain plausible arguments, by which they support those things which seem to be blameworthy and disgraceful.

And this I state, not as wishing to confirm their error (for far be it from me that such a thing should ever come into my thought); but yet I know that there are amongst the more intelligent of them certain defences, by which they are accustomed to support and colour over those things which seem to be absurd.

And if it please you that I should state some of them--for I am to some extent acquainted with them--I shall do as you order me."

And when Peter had given him leave, Niceta proceeded as follows.

Chapter XXX - Cosmogony of Orpheus

"All the literature among the Greeks which is written on the subject of the origin of antiquity, is based upon many authorities, but especially two, Orpheus and Hesiod. [12]Now their writings are divided into two parts, in respect of their meaning,--that is the literal and the allegorical; and the vulgar crowd has flocked to the literal, but all the eloquence of the philosophers and learned men is expended in admiration of the allegorical.

It is Orpheus, then, who says that at first there was chaos, eternal, unbounded, unproduced, and that from it all things were made.

He says that this chaos was neither darkness nor light, neither moist nor dry, neither hot nor cold, but that it was all things mixed together, and was always one unformed mass; yet that at length, as it were after the manner of a huge egg, it brought forth and produced from itself a certain double form, which had been wrought through immense periods of time, and which they call masculo-feminine, a form concrete from the contrary admixture of such diversity; and that this is the principle of all things, which came of pure matter, and which, coming forth, effected a separation of the four elements, and made heaven of the two elements which are first, fire and air, and earth of the others, earth and water; and of these he says that all things now are born and produced by a mutual participation of them.

So far Orpheus.

Chapter XXXI - Hesiod's Cosmogony

"But to this Hesiod adds, that after chaos the heaven and the earth were made immediately, from which he says that those eleven were produced (and sometimes also he speaks of them as twelve) of whom he makes six males and five females.

And these are the names that he gives to the males:
Oceanus, Coeus, Crius, Hyperion, Iapetus, Chronos, who is also called Saturn.
Also the names of the females are:
Theia, Rhea, Themis, Mnemosyne, Tethys. [13]And these names they thus interpret allegorically.
They say that the number is eleven or twelve:
that the first is nature itself, which also they would have to be called Rhea, from Flowing; and they say that the other ten are her accidents, which also they call qualities; yet they add a twelfth, namely Chronos, who with us is called Saturn, and him they take to be time. [14]Therefore they assert that Saturn and Rhea are time and matter; and these, when they are mixed with moisture and dryness, heat and cold, produce all things.

Chapter XXXII - Allegorical Interpretation

"She therefore (Rhea, or nature), it is said, produced, as it were, a certain bubble which had been collecting for a long time; and it being gradually collected from the spirit which was in the waters, swelled, and being for some time driven over the surface of matter, from which it had come forth as from a womb, and being hardened by the rigour of cold, and always increasing by additions of ice, at length was broken off and sunk into the deep, and drawn by its own weight, went down to the infernal regions; and because it became invisible it was called Aides, and is also named Orcus or Pluto. [15]And since it was sunk from the top to the bottom, it gave place to the moist element to flow together; and the grosser part, which is the earth, was laid bare by the retirement of the waters.

They say, therefore, that this freedom of the waters, which was formerly restrained by the presence of the bubble, was called Neptune after the bubble attained the lowest place. After this, when the cold element had been sucked down to the lower regions by the concretion of the icy bubble, and the dry and the moist element had been separated, there being now no hindrance, the warm element rushed by its force and lightness to the upper regions of the air, being borne up by wind and storm.

This storm, therefore, which in Greek is called kataigis, they called aegis--that is, a she-goat; and the fire which ascended to the upper regions they called Jupiter; wherefore they say that he ascended to Olympus riding on a she-goat.

Chapter XXXIII - Allegory of Jupiter, Etc.

"Now this Jupiter the Greeks would have to be called from his living, or giving life, but our people from his giving succour. [16]They say, therefore, that this is the living substance, which, placed in the upper regions, and drawing all things to itself by the influence of heat, as by the convolution of the brain, and arranging them by the moderation of a certain tempering, is said from his head to have produced wisdom, whom they call Minerva, who was called 'Athene by the Greeks on account of her immortality; who, because the father of all created all things by his wisdom, is also said to have been produced from his head, and from the principal place of all, and is represented as having formed and adorned the whole world by the regulated admixture of the elements. [17]Therefore the forms which were impressed upon matter, that the world might be made, because they are constrained by the force of heat, are said to be held together by the energy of Jupiter.

And since there are enough of these, and they do not need anything new to be added to them, but each thing is repaired by the produce of its own seed, the hands of Saturn are said to be bound by Jupiter; because, as I have said, time now produces from matter nothing new:

but the warmth of seeds restores all things according to their kinds; and no birth of Rhea--that is, no increase of flowing matter--ascends further.

And therefore they call that first division of the elements the mutilation of Saturn, because he cannot any more produce a world.

Chapter XXXIV - Other Allegories

"And of Venus they give forth an allegory to this effect.

When, say they, the sea was put under the air, and when the brightness of the heavens shone more pleasantly, being reflected from the waters, the loveliness of things, which appeared fairer from the waters, was called Venus; and she, it, being united with the air as with her, its, own brother, so as to produce beauty, which might be the object of desire, is said to have given birth to Cupid.

In this way, therefore, as we have said, they teach that Chronos, who is Saturn, is allegorically time; Rhea is matter; Aides--that is, Orcus--is the depth of the infernal regions; Neptune is water; Jupiter is air--that is, the element of heat; Venus is the loveliness of things; Cupid is desire, which is in all things, and by which posterity is propagated, or even the reason of things, which gives delight when wisely looked into. Hera--that is, Juno--is said to be that middle air which descends from heaven to earth.

To Diana, whom they call Proserpine, they hand over the air below.

They say that Apollo is the Sun himself, which goes round the heaven; that Mercury is speech, by which a reason is rendered for everything; that Mars is unrestrained fire, which consumes all things.

But not to delay you by enumerating everything, those who have the more abstruse intelligence concerning such things think that they give fair and just reasons, by applying this sort of allegory to every one of their objects of worship."

Chapter XXXV - Uselessness of These Allegories

When Niceta had thus spoken, Aquila answered: [18]"Whoever he was that was the author and inventor of these things, he seems to me to have been very impious, since he covered over those things which seem to be pleasant and seemly, and made the ritual of his superstition to consist in base and shameful observances, since those things which are written according to the letter are manifestly unseemly and base; and the whole observance of their religion consists in these, that by such crimes and impieties they may teach men to imitate their gods whom they worship.

For in these allegories what profit can there be to them? For although they are framed so as to be decent, yet no use is derived from them for worship, nor for amendment of morals.

Chapter XXXVI - The Allegories an Afterthought

"Whence it is the more evident that prudent men, when they saw that the common superstition was so disgraceful, so base, and yet they had not learned any way of correcting it, or any knowledge, endeavoured with what arguments and interpretations they could to veil unseemly things under seemly speech, and not, as they say, to conceal seemly reasons under unseemly fables.

For if this were the case, surely their statues and their pictures would never be made with representations of their vices and crimes.

The swan, which committed adultery with Leda, would not be represented, nor the bull which committed adultery with Europa; nor would they turn into a thousand monstrous shapes, him whom they think better than all.

And assuredly, if the great and wise men who are amongst them knew that all this is fiction and not truth, would not they charge with impiety and sacrilege those who should exhibit a picture or carve an image of this sort, to the injury of the gods?

In short, let them present a king of their own time in the form of an ox, or a goose, or an ant, or a vulture, and let them write the name of their king upon it, and set up such a statue or figure in a public place, and they will soon be made to feel the wrong of their deed, and the greatness of its punishment.

Chapter XXXVII - Like Gods, Like Worshippers

"But since those things rather are true which the public baseness testifies, and concealments have been sought and fabricated by prudent men to excuse them by seemly speeches, therefore are they not only not prohibited, but even in the very mysteries figures are produced of Saturn devouring his sons, and of the boy hidden by the cymbals and drums of the Corybantes; and with respect to the mutilation of Saturn, what better proof of its truth could there be, than that even his worshippers are mutilated, by a like miserable fate, in honour of their god?

Since then these things are manifestly seen, who shall be found of so little sense, yea, of such stolidity, that he does not perceive that those things are true concerning the unfortunate gods, which their more unfortunate worshippers attest by the wounding and mutilation of their bodies?

Chapter XXXVIII - Writings of the Poets

"But if, as they say, these things, so creditably and piously done, are dispensed by so discreditable and impious a ritual, assuredly he is sacrilegious, whoever either gave forth these things at first, or persists in fulfilling them, now that they have unhappily been given forth.

And what shall we say of the books of the poets?

Ought not they, if they have debased the honourable and pious deeds of the gods with base fables, to be forthwith cast away and thrown into the fire, that they may not persuade the still tender age of boys that Jupiter himself, the chief of the gods, was a parricide towards his parents, incestuous towards his sisters and his daughters, and even impure towards boys; that Venus and Mars were adulterers, and all those things which have been spoken of above?

What do you think of this matter, my lord Peter?"

Chapter XXXIX - All for the Best

Then he answered:
"Be sure, beloved Aquila, that all things are done by the good providence of God, that the cause which was to be contrary to the truth should not only be infirm and weak, but also base.

For if the assertion of error had been stronger and more truth-like, any one who had been deceived by it would not easily return to the path of truth.

If even now, when so many wicked and disgraceful things are related concerning the gods of the Gentiles, scarce any one forsakes the base error, how much more if there had been in it anything seemly and truth-like?

For the mind is with difficulty transferred from those things with which it has been imbued in early youth; and on this account, as I said, it has been effected by divine providence, that the substance of error should be both weak and base.

But all other things also divine providence dispenses fitly and advantageously, although the method of the divine dispensation, as good, and the best possible, is not clear to us who are ignorant of the causes of things."

Chapter XL - Further Information Sought

When Peter had thus said, I Clement asked Niceta that he would explain to us, for the sake of instruction, some things concerning the allegories of the Gentiles, which he had carefully studied; "for," said I, "it is useful that when we dispute with the Gentiles, we should not be unacquainted with these things."

Then said Niceta:
"If my lord Peter permits me, I can do as you ask me."
Then said Peter:
"To-day I have given you leave to speak in opposition to the Gentiles, as you know."
And Niceta said:
"Tell me then, Clement, what you would have me speak about."
And I said to him:
"Inform us how the Gentiles represent matters concerning the supper of the gods, which they had at the marriage of Peleus and Thetis. [19]What do they make of the shepherd Paris, and what of less Juno, Minerva, and Venus, between whom he acted as judge?

What of Mercury? and what of the apple, and the other things which follow in order?"

Chapter XLI - Explanation of Mythology

Then Niceta:
"The affair of the supper of the gods stands in this wise.

They say that the banquet is the world, that the order of the gods sitting at table is the position of the heavenly bodies.

Those whom Hesiod calls the first children of heaven and earth, of whom six were males and six females, they refer to the number of the twelve signs, which go round all the world.

They say that the dishes of the banquet are the reasons and causes of things, sweet and desirable, which in the shape of inferences from the positions of the signs and the courses of the stars, explain how the world is ruled and governed. Yet they say these things exist after the free manner of a banquet, inasmuch as the mind of every one has the option whether he shall taste aught of this sort of knowledge, or whether he shall refrain; and as in a banquet no one is compelled, but every one is at liberty to eat, so also the manner of philosophizing depends upon the choice of the will. They say that discord is the lust of the flesh, which rises up against the purpose of the mind, and hinders the desire of philosophizing; and therefore they say that the time was that in which the marriage was celebrated.

Thus they make Peleus and the nymph Thetis to be the dry and the moist element, by the admixture of which the substance of bodies is composed.

They hold that Mercury is speech, by which instruction is conveyed to the mind; that Juno is chastity, Minerva courage, Venus lust, Paris the understanding.

If therefore, say they, it happens that there is in a man a barbarous and uncultivated understanding, and ignorant of right judgment, he will despise chastity and courage, and will give the prize, which is the apple, to lust; and thereby, ruin and destruction will come not only upon himself, but also upon his countrymen and the whole race.

These things, therefore, it is in their power to compose from whatever matter they please; yet they can be adapted to every man; because if any one has a pastoral and rustic and uncultivated understanding, and does not wish to be instructed, when the heat of his body shall make suggestions concerning the pleasure of lust, straightway he despises the virtues of studies and the blessings of knowledge, and turns his mind to bodily pleasures.

And hence it is that implacable wars arise, cities are destroyed, countries fall, even as Paris, by the abduction of Helen, armed the Greeks and the barbarians to their mutual destruction."

Chapter XLII - Interpretation of Scripture

Then Peter, commending his statement, said: [20]"Ingenious men, as I perceive, take many verisimilitudes from the things which they read; and therefore great care is to be taken, that when the law of God is read, it be not read according to the understanding of our own mind. For there are many sayings in the divine Scriptures which can be drawn to that sense which every one has preconceived for himself; and this ought not to be done.

For you ought not to seek a foreign and extraneous sense, which you have brought from without, which you may confirm from the authority of the Scriptures, but to take the sense of truth from the Scriptures themselves; and therefore it behoves you to learn the meaning of the Scriptures from him who keeps it according to the truth handed down to him from his fathers, so that he can authoritatively declare what he has rightly received.

But when one has received an entire and firm rule of truth from the Scriptures, it will not be improper if he contribute to the establishment of true doctrine anything from common education and from liberal studies, which, it may be, he has attached himself to in his boyhood; yet so that, when he has learned the truth, he renounce falsehood and pretence."

Chapter XLIII - A Word of Exhortation

And when he had said this, he looked to our father, and said:
"You therefore, old man, if indeed you care for your soul's safety, that when you desire to be separated from the body, it may, in consequence of this short conversion, find eternal rest, ask about whatever you please, and seek counsel, that you may be able to cast off any doubt that remains in you.

For even to young men the time of life is uncertain; but to old men it is not even uncertain, for there is no doubt that there is but little time remaining to them.

And therefore both young and old ought to be very earnest about their conversion and repentance, and to be taken up with the adornment of their souls for the future with the worthiest ornaments, such as the doctrines of truth, the grace of chastity, the splendour of righteousness, the fairness of piety, and all other things with which it becomes a reasonable mind to be adorned.

Then, besides, they should break off from unseemly and unbelieving companions, and keep company with the faithful, and frequent those assemblies in which subjects are handled relating to chastity, righteousness and piety; to pray to God always heartily, and to ask of Him those things which ought to be asked of God; to give thanks to Him; to repent truly of their past doings; in some measure also, if possible, by deeds of mercy towards the poor, to help their penitence:

for by these means pardon will be more easily bestowed, and mercy will be sooner shown to the merciful.

Chapter XLIV - Earnestness

"But if he who comes to repentance is of more advanced age, he ought the more to give thanks to God, because, having received the knowledge of the truth, after all the violence of carnal lust has been broken, there awaits him no fight of contest, by which to repress the pleasures of the body rising against the mind.

It remains, therefore, that he be exercised in the learning of the truth, and in works of mercy, that he may bring forth fruits worthy of repentance; and that he do not suppose that the proof of conversion is shown by length of time, but by strength of devotion and of purpose.

For minds are manifest to God; and He does not take account of times, but of hearts.

For He approves if any one, on hearing the preaching of the truth, does not delay, nor spend time in negligence, but immediately, and if I may say so, in the same moment, abhorring the past, begins to desire things to come, and burns with love of the heavenly kingdom.

Chapter XLV - All Ought to Repent

"Wherefore, let no one of you longer dissemble nor look backwards, but willingly approach to the Gospel of the kingdom of God.

Let not the poor man say, When I shall become rich, then I shall be converted.

God does not ask money of you, but a merciful heart and a pious mind.

Nor let the rich man delay his conversion by reason of worldly care, while he thinks how he may dispose the abundance of his fruits; nor say within himself, What shall I do? where shall I bestow my fruits?'

Nor say to his soul, Thou hast much goods laid up for many years; feast and rejoice.'

For it shall be said to him, Thou fool, this night thy soul shall be taken from thee, and whose shall those things be which thou hast provided?' [21]Therefore let every age, every sex, every condition, haste to repentance, that they may obtain eternal life.

Let the young be thankful that they put their necks under the yoke of discipline in the very violence of their desires.

The old also are themselves praise-worthy, because they change for the fear of God, the custom of a long time in which they have been unhappily occupied.

Chapter XLVI - The Sure Word of Prophecy

"Let no one therefore put off.

Let no one delay.

For what occasion is there for delaying to do well?

Or are you afraid, lest, when you have done well, you do not find the reward as you supposed?

And what loss will you sustain if you do well without reward?

Would not conscience alone be sufficient in this?

But if you find as you anticipate, shall you not receive great things for small, and eternal for temporal?

But I say this for the sake of the unbelieving.

For the things which we preach are as we preach them; because they cannot be otherwise, since they have been promised by the prophetic word.

Chapter XLVII - "A Faithful Saying, and Worthy of All Acceptation."

"But if any one desires to learn exactly the truth of our preaching, let him come to hear, and let him ascertain what the true Prophet is; and then at length all doubtfulness will cease to him, unless with obstinate mind he resist those things which he finds to be true.

For there are some whose only object it is to gain the victory in any way whatever, and who seek praise for this rather than their salvation. These ought not to have a single word addressed to them, lest both the noble word suffer injury, and condemn to eternal death him who is guilty of the wrong done to it.

For what is there in respect of which any one ought to oppose our preaching? or in respect of which the word of our preaching is found to be contrary to the belief of what is true and honourable?

It says that the God the Father, the Creator of all, is to be honoured, as also His Son, who alone knows Him and His will, and who alone is to be believed concerning all things which He has enjoined.

For He alone is the law and the Lawgiver, and the righteous Judge, whose law decrees that God, the Lord of all, is to be honoured by a sober, chaste, just, and merciful life, and that all hope is to be placed in Him alone.

Chapter XLVIII - Errors of the Philosophers

"But some one will say that precepts of this sort are given by the philosophers also. [22]Nothing of the kind:
for they do indeed give commandments concerning justice and sobriety, but they are ignorant that God is the recompenser of good and evil deeds; and therefore their laws and precepts only shun a public accuser, but cannot purify the conscience.

For why should one fear to sin in secret, who does not know that there is a witness and a judge of secret things?

Besides, the philosophers in their precepts add that even the gods, who are demons, are to be honoured; and this alone, even if in other respects they seemed worthy of approbation, is sufficient to convict them of the most dreadful impiety, and condemn them by their own sentence, since they declare indeed that there is one God, yet command that many be worshipped, by way of humouring human error.

But also the philosophers say that God is not angry, not knowing what they say.

For anger is evil, when it disturbs the mind, so that it loses right counsel.

But that anger which punishes the wicked does not bring disturbance to the mind; but it is one and the same affection, so to speak, which assigned rewards to the good and punishment to the evil; for if He should bestow blessings upon the good and the evil, and confer equal rewards upon the pious and the impious, He would appear to be unjust rather than good.

Chapter XLIX - God's Long-Suffering

"But you say, Neither ought God to do evil.
You say truly; nor does He.
But those who have been created by Him, while they do not believe that they are to be judged, indulging their pleasures, have fallen away from piety and righteousness.

But you will say, If it is right to punish the wicked, they ought to be punished immediately when they do wickedly.

You indeed do well to make haste; but He who is eternal, and from whom nothing is secret, inasmuch as He is without end, in the same proportion is His patience extended, and He regards not the swiftness of vengeance, but the causes of salvation.

For He is not so much pleased with the death as with the conversion of a sinner. [23] Therefore, in short, He has bestowed upon men holy baptism, to which, if any one makes haste to come, and for the future remains without stain, all his sins are thenceforth blotted out, which were committed in the time of his ignorance.

Chapter L - Philosophers Not Benefactors of Men

"For what have the philosophers contributed to the life of man, by saying that God is not angry with men?

Only to teach them to have no fear of any punishment or judgment, and thereby to take away all restraint from sinners.

Or what have they benefited the human race, who have said that there is no God, but that all things happen by chance and accident?

What but that men, hearing this, and thinking that there is no judge, no guardian of things, are driven headlong, without fear of any one, to every deed which either rage, or avarice, or lust may dictate.

For they truly have much benefited the life of man who have said that nothing can be done apart from Genesis; that is, that every one, ascribing the cause of his sin to Genesis, might in the midst of his crimes declare himself innocent, while he does not wash out his guilt by repentance, but doubles it by laying the blame upon fate.

And what shall I say of those philosophers who have maintained that the gods are to be worshipped, and such gods as were described to you a little while ago?

What else was this but to decree that vices, crimes, and base deeds should be worshipped?

I am ashamed of you, and I pity you, if you have not yet discovered that these things were unworthy of belief, and impious, and execrable, or if, having discovered and ascertained them to be evil, ye have nevertheless worshipped them as if they were good, yea, even the best.

Chapter LI - Christ the True Prophet

"Then, besides, of what sort is that which some of the philosophers have presumed to speak even concerning God, though they are mortal, and can only speak by opinion concerning invisible things, or concerning the origin of the world, since they were not present when it was made, or concerning the end of it, or concerning the treatment and judgment of souls in the infernal regions, forgetting that it belongs indeed to a reasonable man to know things present and visible, but that it is the part of prophetic prescience alone to know things past, and things future, and things invisible?

These things, therefore, are not to be gathered from conjectures and opinions, in which men are greatly deceived, but from faith in prophetic truth, as this doctrine of ours is.

For we speak nothing of ourselves, nor announce things gathered by human judgment; for this were to deceive our hearers.

But we preach the things which have been committed and revealed to us by the true Prophet.

And concerning His prophetic prescience and power, if any one, as I have said, wishes to receive clear proofs, let him come instantly and be alert to hear, and we shall give evident proofs by which he shall seem not only to hear the power of prophetic prescience with his ears, but even to see it with his eyes and handle it with his hand; and when he has entertained a sure faith concerning Him, he will without any labour take upon him the yoke of righteousness and piety; [24] and so great sweetness will he perceive in it, that not only will he not find fault with any labour being in it, but will even desire something further to be added and imposed upon him."

Chapter LII - Appion and Anubion

And when he had said this, and more to the same purpose, and had cured some who were present who were infirm and possessed of demons, he dismissed the crowds, while they gave thanks and praised God, charging them to come to the same place on the following days also for the sake of hearing.

And when we were together at home, and were preparing to eat, one entering told us that Appion Pleistonices, [25] with Anubion, were lately come from Antioch, and were lodging with Simon. [26] Then my father, when he heard this, rejoiced, and said to Peter:

"If you permit me, I should like to go and salute Appion and Anubion, for they are great friends of mine; and perhaps I shall be able to persuade Anubion to dispute with Clement on the subject of Genesis."

Then Peter said:

"I consent; and I commend you, because you respect your friends.

But consider how all things occur to you according to your wish by God's providence; for, behold, not only have the objects of proper affection been restored to you by the appointment of God, but also the presence of your friends is arranged for you."

Then said my father:

"Truly I consider that it is so as you say."

And when he had said this, he went away to Anubion.

Chapter LIII - A Transformation

But we, sitting with Peter the whole night, asking questions, and learning of him on many subjects, remained awake through very delight in his teaching and the sweetness of his words; and when it was daybreak, Peter, looking at me and my brothers, said:

"I wonder what has befallen your father."

And while he was speaking my father came in, and found Peter speaking to us about him.

And when he had saluted he began to apologize, and to explain the reason why he had remained abroad.

But we, looking at him, were horrified; for we saw on him the face of Simon, yet we heard the voice of our father.

And when we shrank from him, and cursed him, my father was astonished at our treating him so harshly and barbarously.

Yet Peter was the only one who saw his natural countenance; and he said to us:

"Why do you curse your father?"

And we, along with our mother, answered him:

"He appears to us to be Simon, though he has our father's voice."

Then Peter:

"You indeed know only his voice, which has not been changed by the sorceries; but to me also his face, which to others appears changed by Simon's art, is known to be that of your father Faustinianus."

And looking at my father, he said:

"The cause of the dismay of your wife and your sons is this,--the appearance of your countenance does not seem to be as it was, but the face of the detestable Simon appears in you."

Chapter LIV - Excitement in Antioch

And while he was thus speaking, one of those returned who had gone before to Antioch, and said to Peter:

"I wish you to know, my lord Peter, that Simon at Antioch, doing many signs and prodigies in public, has inculcated upon the people nothing but what tends to excite hatred against you, calling you a magician, a sorcerer, a murderer; and to such an extent has he stirred up hatred against you, that they greatly desire, if they can find you anywhere, even to devour your flesh.

And therefore we who were sent before, seeing the city greatly moved against you, met together in secret, and considered what ought to be done.

Chapter LV - A Stratagem

"And when we saw no way of getting out of the difficulty, there came Cornelius the centurion, being sent by Caesar to the president of Caesarea on public business.

Him we sent for alone, and told him the reason why we were sorrowful, and entreated him that, if he could do anything, he should help us.

Then he most readily promised that he would straightway put him to flight, if only we would aid his plans. And when we promised that we would be active in doing everything, he said, Caesar has ordered sorcerers to be sought out and destroyed in the city of Rome and through the provinces, and a great number of them have been already destroyed.

I shall therefore give out, through my friends, that I am come to apprehend that magician, and that I am sent by Caesar for this purpose, that he may be punished with the rest of his fraternity.

Let your people, therefore, who are with him in disguise, intimate to him, as if they had heard it from some quarter, that I am sent to apprehend him; and when he hears this, he is sure to take to flight.

Or if you think of anything better, tell me.

Why need I say more?'

It was so done by those of ours who were with him, disguised for the purpose of acting as spies on him.

And when Simon learned that this was come upon him, he received the information as a great kindness conferred upon him by them, and took to flight.

He therefore departed from Antioch, and, as we have heard, came hither with Athenodorus.

Chapter LVI - Simon's Design in the Transformation

"All we, therefore, who went before you, considered that in the meantime you should not go up to Antioch, till we see if the hatred of you which he has sown among the people be in any degree lessened by his departure."

When he who had come from Antioch had imparted this information, Peter, looking to our father, said, "Faustinianus, your countenance has been transformed by Simon Magus, as is evident; for he, thinking that he was being sought for by Caesar for punishment, has fled in terror, and has placed his own countenance upon you, if haply you might be apprehended instead of him, and put to death, that so he might cause sorrow to your sons."

But my father, when he heard this, crying out, said with tears:

"You have judged rightly, O Peter:

for Anubion also, who is very friendly with me, began to inform me in a certain mysterious way of his plots; but unhappily I did not believe him, because I had done him no harm."

Chapter LVII - Great Grief

And when all of us, along with my father, were agitated with sorrow and weeping, meantime Anubion came to us, intimating to us that Simon had fled during the night, making for Judaea.

But seeing our father lamenting and bewailing himself, and saying, "Wretch that I am, not to believe when I heard that he is a magician!

What has befallen wretched me, that on one day, being recognised by my wife and my sons, I have not been able to rejoice with them, but have been rolled back to the former miseries which I endured in my wandering!"--but my mother, tearing her dishevelled hair, bewailed much more bitterly,--we also, confounded at the change of our father's countenance, were, as it were, thunderstruck and beside ourselves, and could not understand what was the matter.

But Anubion, seeing us all thus afflicted, stood like one dumb.

Then Peter, looking at us his sons, said:

"Believe me that this is your very father; wherefore also I charge you that you respect him as your father.

For God will afford some opportunity on which he shall be able to put off the countenance of Simon, and to recover the manifest figure of your father--that is, his own."

Chapter LVIII - How It All Happened

Then, turning to my father, he said:

"I gave you leave to salute Appion and Anubion, who, you said, were your friends from boyhood, but not that you should speak with Simon."

Then my father said:

"I confess I have sinned."

Then said Anubion:

"I also with him beg and entreat of you to pardon the old man--good and noble man as he is.

He was unhappily seduced and imposed upon by the magician in question; for I will tell you how the thing was done.

When he came to salute us, it happened that at that very time we were standing around him, hearing him tell that he intended to flee away that night, for that he had heard that some persons had come even to this city of Laodicea to apprehend him by command of the emperor, but that he wished to turn all their rage against this Faustinianus, who has lately come hither.

And he said to us:

Only you make him sup with us, and I shall compound a certain ointment, with which, when he has supped, he shall anoint his face, and from that time he shall seem to all to have my countenance. But you first anoint your faces with the juice of a certain herb, that you may not be deceived as to the change of his countenance, so that to all except you he shall seem to be Simon.'

Chapter LIX - A Scene of Mourning

"And when he said this, I said to him, And what advantage will you gain from this deed?'

Then Simon said:

In the first place, that those who are seeking me may lay hold on him, and so give over the search for me.

But if he be punished by Caesar, that his sons may have much sorrow, who forsook me, and fled to Peter, and are now his assistants.'

Now I confess to you, Peter, what is true.

I did not dare then tell Faustinianus; but neither did Simon give us opportunity of speaking with him in private, and disclosing to him fully Simon's design.

Meantime, about the middle of the night, Simon has fled away, making for Judaea.

And Athenodorus and Appion have gone to convoy him; but I pretended bodily indisposition, that I might remain at home, and make him return quickly to you, if haply he may in any way be concealed with you, lest, being seized by those who are in quest of Simon, he be brought before Caesar, and perish without cause.

And now, in my anxiety about him, I have come to see him, and to return before those who have gone to convoy Simon come back."

And turning to us, Anubion said:

"I, Anubion, indeed see the true countenance of your father, because I was previously anointed by

Simon himself, as I have told you, that the real face of Faustinianus might appear to my eyes; whence I am astonished and wonder at the art of Simon Magus, because you standing here do not recognise your father."

And while my father and mother, and all of us, wept for the things which had befallen, Anubion, moved with compassion, also wept.

Chapter LX - A Counterplot

Then Peter, moved with compassion, promised that he would restore the face of our father, saying to him:

"Listen, Faustinianus:

As soon as the error of your transformed countenance shall have conferred some advantage on us, and shall have subserved the designs which we have in view, then I shall restore to you the true form of your countenance; on condition, however, that you first despatch what I shall command you." And when my father promised that he would with all his might fulfil everything that he might charge him with, provided only that he might recover his own countenance, Peter thus began:

"You have heard with your own ears, that one of those who had been sent before has returned from Antioch, and told us how Simon, while he was there, stirred up the multitudes against me, and inflamed the whole city into hatred of me, declaring that I am a magician, and a murderer, and a deceiver, so that they are eager, if they see me, even to eat my flesh.

Do therefore what I tell you:

leave Clement with me, and go before us to Antioch, with your wife, and your sons Faustus and Faustinus.

And I shall also send others with you, whom I think fit, who shall observe whatsoever I command them.

Chapter LXI - A Mine Dug

"When therefore you come with them to Antioch, as you will be thought to be Simon, stand in a public place, and proclaim your repentance, and say:

I Simon declare to you, and confess that all that I said concerning Peter was false:

for he is neither a seducer, nor a magician, nor a murderer, nor any of the things that I spoke against him; but I said all these things under the instigation of madness.

I therefore entreat you, even I myself, who erewhile gave you causes of hatred against him, that you think no such thing concerning him.

But lay aside your hatred; cease from your indignation; because he is truly sent by God for the salvation of the world--a disciple and apostle of the true Prophet.

Wherefore I advise, exhort, and charge you that you hear him, and believe him when he preaches to you the truth, lest haply, if you despise him, your very city suddenly perish.

But I will tell you why I now make this confession to you.

This night an angel of God rebuked me for my wickedness, and scourged me terribly, because I was an enemy to the herald of the truth.

Therefore I entreat you, that even if I myself should ever again come to you, and attempt to say anything against Peter, you will not receive nor believe me.

For I confess to you, I was a magician, a seducer, a deceiver; but I repent, for it is possible by repentance to blot out former evil deeds.'"

Chapter LXII - A Case of Conscience

When Peter made this intimation to my father, he answered:

"I know what you wish; do not trouble yourself further:

for I understand and know what I am to undertake when I come to the place."

And Peter gave him further instruction, saying:

"When therefore you come to the place, and see the people turned by your discourse, and laying aside their hatred, and returning to their longing for me, send and tell me, and I shall come immediately; and when I come, I shall without delay set you free from this strange countenance, and restore to you your own, which is known to all your friends."

And having said this, he ordered my brothers to go with him, and at the same time our mother Matthidia, and some of our friends.

But my mother refused to go along with him, and said:

"It seems as if I should be an adulteress if I were to associate with the countenance of Simon; but if I be compelled to go along with him, it is at all events impossible that I can lie in the same bed with him; but I do not know if I can consent even to go with him."

And when she stoutly refused, Anubion began to exhort her, saying:

"Believe me and Peter.

But does not even his voice persuade you that he is your husband Faustinianus, whom truly I love not less than you do?

And, in short, I also myself shall come with you."

And when Anubion had said this, my mother promised that she would go with him.

Chapter LXIII - A Pious Fraud

Then said I:

"God arranges our affairs to our liking; for we have with us Anubion an astrologer, with whom, if we come to Antioch, we shall dispute with all earnestness on the subject of Genesis."

And when our father had set out, after the middle of the night, with those whom Peter had ordered to accompany him, and with Anubion; in the morning, before Peter went to the discussion, those men returned who had convoyed Simon, namely Appion and Athenodorus, and came to us inquiring after my father.

But Peter, when he was informed of their coming, ordered them to enter.

And when they were seated, they asked, "Where is Faustinianus?"

Peter answered:

"We do not know; for since the evening that he went to you, no one of his friends has seen him.

But yesterday morning Simon came inquiring for him; and because we gave him no answer, I know not what he meant, but he said that he was Faustinianus.

But when nobody believed him, he went and lamented, and threatened that he would destroy himself; and afterwards he went away towards the sea."

Chapter LXIV - A Competition in Lying

When Appion heard this, and those who were with him, they raised a great howling, saying:

"Why have you done this?

Why did you not receive him?"

And when Athenodorus was going to tell me that it was my father Faustinianus himself, Appion prevented him, and said:

"We have learned from some one that he has gone with Simon, and that at the entreaty of Faustinianus himself, being unwilling to see his sons, because they are Jews.

When therefore we heard this, we came to inquire after him here; but since he is not here, it appears that he must have spoken truly who told us that he has gone with Simon.

This, therefore, we tell you."

But I Clement, when I understood the designs of Peter, that he wished to make them suppose that the old man would be required at their hands, so that they might be afraid and flee away, I began to aid his design, and said to Appion:

"Listen, dear Appion: what we believe to be good, we wish to deliver to our father also; but if he will not receive it, but rather, as you say, flees away through abhorrence of us--it may perhaps be harsh to say so--we care nothing about him."

And when I had said this, they departed, cursing my cruelty, and followed the track of Simon, as we learned on the following day.

Chapter LXV - Success of the Plot

Meantime, while Peter was daily, according to his custom, teaching the people, and working many miracles and cures, after ten days came one of our people from Antioch, sent by my father, informing us how my father stood in public, accusing Simon, whose face indeed he seemed to wear, and extolling Peter with unmeasured praises, and commending him to all the people, and making them long for him, so that all were changed by his speech, and longed to see him; and that many had come to love Peter so much, that they raged against my father in his character of Simon, and thought of laying hands on him, because he had done such wrong to Peter!

"Wherefore," said he, "make haste, lest haply he be murdered; for he sent me with speed to you, being in great fear, to ask you to come without delay, that you may find him alive, and also that you may appear at the favourable moment, when the city is growing in affection towards you." [27]He also told us how, as soon as my father entered the city of Antioch, the whole people were gathered to him, supposing him to be Simon; and he began to make public confession to them all, according to what the restoration of the people demanded:

for all, as many as came, both noble and common, both rich and poor, hoping that some prodigies would be wrought by him in his usual way, he addressed thus:--

Chapter LXVI - Truth Told by Lying Lips

"It is long that the divine patience bears with me, Simon the most unhappy of men; for whatever you have wondered at in me was done, not by means of truth, but by the lies and tricks of demons, that I might subvert your faith and condemn my own soul.

I confess that all things that I said about Peter were lies; for he never was either a magician or a murderer, but has been sent by God for the salvation of you all; and if from this hour you think that he is to be despised, be assured that your very city may suddenly be destroyed.

But, you will ask, what is the reason that I make this confession to you of my own accord?

I was vehemently rebuked by an angel of God this night, and most severely scourged, because I was his enemy.

I therefore entreat you, that if from this hour even I myself shall ever open my mouth against him, you will drive me from your sight; for that foul demon, who is an enemy to the salvation of men, speaks against him through my mouth, that you may not attain to life by his means.

For what miracle could the magic art show you through me?

I made brazen dogs bark, and statues move, men change their appearances, and suddenly vanish from men's sight; and for these things you ought to have cursed the magic art, which bound your souls with devilish fetters, that I might show you a vain miracle, that you might not believe Peter, who cures the sick in the name of Him by whom he is sent, and expels demons, and gives sight to the blind, and restores health to the palsied, and raises the dead."

Chapter LXVII - Faustinianus is Himself Again

Whilst he made these and similar statements, the people began to curse him, and to weep and lament because they had sinned against Peter, believing him to be a magician or wicked man.

But the same day, at evening, Faustinianus had his own face restored to him, and the appearance of Simon Magus left him.

Now Simon, hearing that his face on Faustinianus had contributed to the glory of Peter, came in haste to anticipate Peter, and intending to cause by his art that his likeness should be taken from Faustinianus, when Christ had already accomplished this according to the word of His apostle.

But Niceta and Aquila, seeing their father's face restored after the necessary proclamation, gave thanks to God, and would not suffer him to address the people any more.

Chapter LXVIII - Peter's Entry into Antioch

But Simon began, though secretly, to go amongst his friends and acquaintances, and to malign Peter more than before.

Then all spat in his face, and drove him from the city, saying:

"You will be chargeable with your own death, if you think of coming hither again, speaking against Peter."

These things being known at Laodicea, Peter ordered the people to meet on the following day; and having ordained one of those who followed him as bishop over them, and others as presbyters, and having baptized multitudes, and restored to health all who were troubled with sicknesses or demons, he stayed there three days longer; and all things being properly arranged, he bade them farewell, and set out from Laodicea, being much longed for by the people of Antioch. [28]And the whole city began to hear, through Niceta and Aquila, that Peter was coming.

Then all the people of the city of Antioch, hearing of Peter's arrival, went to meet him, and almost all the old men and the nobles came with ashes sprinkled on their heads, in this way testifying their repentance, because they had listened to the magician Simon, in opposition to his preaching.

Chapter LXIX - Peter's Thanksgiving

Stating these and such like things, they bring to him those distressed with sicknesses, and tormented with demons, paralytics also, and those suffering diverse perils; and there was an infinite number of sick people collected.

And when Peter saw that they not only repented of the evil thoughts they had entertained of him through means of Simon, but also that they showed so entire faith in God, that they believed that all who suffered from every sort of ailment could be healed by him, he spread out his hands towards heaven, pouring out prayers with tears, and gave thanks to God, saying:

"I bless thee, O Father, worthy of all praise, who hast deigned to fulfil every word and promise of Thy Son, that every creature may know that Thou alone art God in heaven and in earth."

Chapter LXX - Miracles

With such sayings, he went up on a height, and ordered all the multitude of sick people to be ranged before him, and addressed them all in these words:

"As you see me to be a man like to yourselves, do not suppose that you can recover your health from me, but through Him who, coming down from heaven, has shown to those who believe in Him a perfect medicine for body and soul.

Hence let all this people be witnesses to your declaration, that with your whole heart you believe in the Lord Jesus Christ, that they may know that themselves also may be saved by Him."

And when all the multitude of the sick with one voice cried out that He is the true God whom Peter preaches, suddenly an overpowering light of the grace of God appeared in the midst of the people; and the paralytics being cured, began to run to Peter's feet, the blind to shout on the recovery of their sight, the lame to give thanks on regaining the power of walking, the sick to rejoice in restored health; some even who were barely alive, being already without consciousness or the power of speech, were raised up; and all the lunatics, and those possessed of demons, were set free.

Chapter LXXI - Success

So great grace of His power did the Holy Spirit show on that day, that all, from the least to the greatest, with one voice confessed the Lord; and not to delay you with many words, within seven days, more than ten thousand men, believing in God, were baptized and consecrated by sanctification:

so that Theophilus, [29] who was more exalted than all the men of power in that city, with all eagerness of desire consecrated the great palace of his house under the name of a church, and a chair was placed in it for the Apostle Peter by all the people; and the whole multitude assembling daily to hear the word, believed in the healthful doctrine which was avouched by the efficacy of cures.

Chapter LXXII - Happy Ending

Then I Clement, with my brothers and our mother, spoke to our father, asking him whether any remnants of unbelief remained in him.

And he said:

"Come, and you shall see, in the presence of Peter, what an increase of faith has grown in me."

Then Faustinianus approached, and fell down at Peter's feet, saying:

"The seeds of your word, which the field of my mind has received, are now sprung up, and have so advanced to fruitful maturity, that nothing is wanting but that you separate me from the chaff by that spiritual reaping-hook of yours, and place me in the garner of the Lord, making me partaker of the divine table."

Then Peter, with all alacrity grasping his hand, presented him to me Clement, and my brothers, saying:

"As God has restored your sons to you, their father, so also your sons restore their father to God."

And he proclaimed a fast to all the people, and on the next Lord's day he baptized him; and in the midst of the people, taking occasion from his conversion, he related all his fortunes, so that the whole city received him as an angel, and paid him no less honour than they did to the apostle. [30] And these things being known, Peter ordered the people to meet on the following day; and having ordained one of his followers as bishop, and others as presbyters, he baptized also a great number of people, and restored to health all who had been distressed with sicknesses. [31]

Footnotes:

1. [In book x. the arrangement, to the close of chap. 51, differs from that of the Homilies.
Here Peter proposes a delay.
In Homily XV. an account is given of the attempt to convert the father immediately; the Apostle arguing with him, and urging the importance of being of the same mind with his family.
Then in Homilies XVI.-XIX. a second discussion with Simon is given, occurring in the presence of the father of Clement.
Here the argument is carried on by Clement (chaps. 7-28), Niceta (chaps. 30-34, 41), Aquila (chaps. 35-38), and concluded by Peter himself (chaps. 42-51).
Much of the mythological matter finds a parallel in the discussion with Appion (Homily IV.-VI.), but there is no direct agreement in the two works from this point to chap. 52. Comp. Homily XX. 11.--R.]
2. Allusion is made to Socrates and community of wives, as stated in the Republic of Plato.
3. [Comp. book ix. 15, 17, etc.
The question of astrology is much more prominent in the Recognitions; but comp. Homily XIV. 5, and elsewhere.--R.]
4. [The connection of mathematics and astrology is indicated also in Homily XIV. 3.--R.]
5. [This argument from human freedom is the favourite one throughout.--R.]
6. [With this cosmogony (chaps. 17-19, 30-34) compare the discourse of Appion, Homily 3-10.--R.]
7. [Comp. chap. 31 and Homily VI. 2.--R.]
8. [Comp. Homily V. 12-15 for a parallel to chaps. 20-23.--R.]
9. Dionysius appears here and subsequently in the text for Dionysus the Greek god corresponding to the Latin Bacchus.
Some of the other names are more or less corrupt forms.
10. [Comp. Homily V. 23, where these details appear in a letter written by Clement as if from a woman; also Homily VI. 21.--R.]
11. [Comp. Homily VI. 22.--R.]
12. [Comp. chaps. 17-19 and Homily VI. 3-10, 12-19.--R.]
13. [Comp. chap. 17 and Homily VI. 2.--R.]
14. [Comp. Homily VI. 5, 12.--R.]
15. [Comp. Homily VI. 6.--R.]
16. [Comp. Homily VI. 7.--R.]
17. [With chaps. 33, 34, compare Homily VI. 8-10.--R.]
18. [With this treatment of the allegories compare Homily VI. 17, 18.--R.]
19. [Comp. Homily VI. 2, 14, 15, on the supper of the gods.--R.]
20. [This discourse of the Apostle (chaps. 42-51) has no exact parallel in the Homilies.
It is a fitting conclusion to the discussion.--R.]
21. Luke xii. 17, 19, 20.
22. [Compare the argument of Clement, as a heathen inquirer, against the philosophers, in Homily VI. 20.--R.]
23. Ezek. xviii. 33.
24. Matt. xi. 30.
25. The name is generally written Apion.
The meaning of Pleistonices is doubtful, some supposing that it indicates his birthplace, some his father; but generally it is taken as an epithet, and it will then refer to his frequent victories in literary contests.
[See Homily IV. 3, and the discussions with Appion which follow in that homily and in V., VI.--R.]
26. [From this point the resemblance to the close of Homily XX. (chaps. 11-22) is quite marked.
But in the Recognitions the conclusion is more detailed and complete; see chap. 65.
This is in accordance with the general design of this narrative, which gives greater prominence to the family of Clement.--R.]
27. [At this point the narrative in the Homilies virtually ends; a sentence follows, resembling a passage in chap. 68.
See note on Homily XX. 23.--R.]
28. [The substance of this sentence forms the somewhat abrupt conclusion of the Homilies; xx. 23.--R.]
29. [It is possible that this character was suggested to the writer by the well-known Theophilus of Antioch.
But, in view of the evident anachronism, it seems more probably that he had in mind the "Theophilus" named in the prologue to the Gospel of Luke (i. 1-4) and in Acts i. 1.--R.]

The Epistles of Clement

30. [The work probably closes with these words; the added sentence is not in harmony with the general plan of the Recognitions, which skilfully treats the material so as to give prominence to the family of Clement.

Some scribe, zealous for the authority of the Apostle Peter, has doubtless contributed the unnecessary sentence which follows.

See next note.

The ordination of a bishop at Antioch by Peter is simply an absurdity.

It is unlikely that even the writer of the Recognitions would venture to ignore the previous existence of a Christian church in that city.--R.]

31. This sentence occurs only in one ms.

Introductory Notice to The Clementine Homilies

[By the Rev. Thomas Smith, D.D.]

We have already given an account of the Clementines in the Introductory Notice to the Recognitions.[1] All that remains for us to do here, is to notice the principal editions of the Homilies.

The first edition was published by Cotelerius in his collection of the Apostolic Fathers, from a manuscript in the Royal Library at Paris, the only manuscript of the work then known to exist.

He derived assistance from an epitome of the work which he found in the same library.

The text of Cotelerius was revised by Clericus in his edition of Cotelerius, but more carefully by Schwegler, Stuttgart, 1847.

The Paris ms. breaks off in the middle of the fourteenth chapter of the nineteenth book.

In 1853 (Goettingen) Dressel published a new recension of the Homilies, having found a complete manuscript of the twenty Homilies in the Ottobonian Library in Rome.

In 1859 (Leipzig) he published an edition of two Epitomes of the Homilies,--the one previously edited by Turnebus and Cotelerius being given more fully, and the other appearing for the first time.

To these Epitomes were appended notes by Frederic Wieseler on the Homilies.

The last edition of the Clementines is by Paul de Lagarde (Leipzig, 1865), which has no new sources, is pretentious, but far from accurate.

Footnote:

1. [The reader is referred to the Introductory Notice prefixed to this edition of the Clementine literature for a brief summary of the views respecting the relations of the two principal works.

The footnotes throughout will aid in making a comparison.

The preparation of these notes has strengthened the conviction of the writer that the Recognitions are not dependent on the Homilies, but that the reverse may be true.--R.]

Epistle of Peter to James

Peter to James, the lord and bishop of the holy Church, under the Father of all, through Jesus Christ, wishes peace always. [1]

Chapter I - Doctrine of Reserve

Knowing, my brother, your eager desire after that which is for the advantage of us all, I beg and beseech you not to communicate to any one of the Gentiles the books of my preachings which I sent to you, nor to any one of our own tribe before trial; but if any one has been proved and found worthy, then to commit them to him, after the manner in which Moses delivered his books to the Seventy who succeeded to his chair.

Wherefore also the fruit of that caution appears even till now.

For his countrymen keep the same rule of monarchy and polity everywhere, being unable in any way to think otherwise, or to be led out of the way of the much-indicating Scriptures.

For, according to the rule delivered to them, they endeavour to correct the discordances of the Scriptures, if any one, haply not knowing the traditions, is confounded at the various utterances of the prophets.

Wherefore they charge no one to teach, unless he has first learned how the Scriptures must be used.

And thus they have amongst them one God, one law, one hope.

Chapter II - Misrepresentation of Peter's Doctrine

In order, therefore, that the like may also happen to those among us as to these Seventy, give the books of my preachings to our brethren, with the like mystery of initiation, that they may indoctrinate those who wish to take part in teaching; for if it be not so done, our word of truth will be rent into many opinions.

And this I know, not as being a prophet, but as already seeing the beginning of this very evil.

For some from among the Gentiles have rejected my legal preaching, attaching themselves to certain lawless and trifling preaching of the man who is my enemy. [2] And these things some have attempted while I am still alive, to transform my words by certain various interpretations, in order to the dissolution of the law; as though I also myself were of such a mind, but did not freely proclaim it, which God forbid!

For such a thing were to act in opposition to the law of God which was spoken by Moses, and was borne witness to by our Lord in respect of its eternal continuance; for thus he spoke:

"The heavens and the earth shall pass away, but one jot or one tittle shall in no wise pass from the law." [3]

And this He has said, that all things might come to pass.

But these men, professing, I know not how, to know my mind, undertake to explain my words, which they have heard of me, more intelligently than I who spoke them, telling their catechumens that this is my meaning, which indeed I never thought of.

But if, while I am still alive, they dare thus to misrepresent me, how much more will those who shall come after me dare to do so!

Chapter III - Initiation

Therefore, that no such thing may happen, for this end I have prayed and besought you not to communicate the books of my preaching which I have sent you to any one, whether of our own nation or of another nation, before trial; but if any one, having been tested, has been found worthy, then to hand them over to him, according to the initiation of Moses, by which he delivered his books to the Seventy who succeeded to his chair; in order that thus they may keep the faith, and everywhere deliver the rule of truth, explaining all things after our tradition; lest being themselves dragged down by ignorance, being drawn into error by conjectures after their mind, they bring others into the like pit of destruction.

Now the things that seemed good to me, I have fairly pointed out to you; and what seems good to you, do you, my lord, becomingly perform.

Farewell.

Chapter IV - An Adjuration Concerning the Receivers of the Book

1.

Therefore James, having read the epistle, sent for the elders; and having read it to them, said:
"Our Peter has strictly and becomingly charged us concerning the establishing of the truth, that we should not communicate the books of his preachings, which have been sent to us, to any one at random, but to one who is good and religious, and who wishes to teach, and who is circumcised, and faithful.

And these are not all to be committed to him at once; that, if he be found injudicious in the first, the others may not be entrusted to him.

Wherefore let him be proved not less than six years.

And then according to the initiation of Moses, he that is to deliver the books should bring him to a river or a fountain, which is living water, where the regeneration of the righteous takes place, and should make him, not swear--for that is not lawful--but to stand by the water and adjure, as we ourselves, when we were re-generated, [4] were made to do for the sake of not sinning.

2.

"And let him say:
I take to witness heaven, earth, water, in which all things are comprehended, and in addition to all these, that air also which pervades all things, and without which I cannot breathe, that I shall always be obedient to him who gives me the books of the preachings; and those same books which he may give me, I shall not communicate to any one in any way, either by writing them, or giving them in writing, or giving them to a writer, either myself or by another, or through any other initiation, or trick, or method, or by keeping them carelessly, or placing them before any one, or granting him permission to see them, or in any way or manner whatsoever communicating them to another; unless I shall ascertain one to be worthy, as I myself have been judged, or even more so, and that after a probation of not less than six years; but to one who is religious and good, chosen to teach, as I have received them, so I will commit them, doing these things also according to the will of my bishop.

3.

"But otherwise, though he were my son or my brother, or my friend, or otherwise in any way pertaining to me by kindred, if he be unworthy, that I will not vouchsafe the favour to him, as is not meet; and I shall neither be terrified by plot nor mollified by gifts.

But if even it should ever seem to me that the books of the preachings given to me are not true, I shall not so communicate them, but shall give them back.

And when I go abroad, I shall carry them with me, whatever of them I happen to possess.

But if I be not minded to carry them about with me, I shall not suffer them to be in my house, but shall deposit them with my bishop, having the same faith, and setting out from the same persons as myself. [5]But if it befall me to be sick, and in expectation of death, and if I be childless, I shall act in the same manner.

But if I die having a son who is not worthy, or not yet capable, I shall act in the same manner.

For I shall deposit them with my bishop, in order that if my son, when he grows up, be worthy of the trust, he may give them to him as his father's bequest, according to the terms of this engagement.

4.

"And that I shall thus do, I again call to witness heaven, earth, water, in which all things are enveloped, and in addition to all these, the all-pervading air, without which I cannot breathe, that I shall always be obedient to him who giveth me these books of the preachings, and shall observe in all things as I have engaged, or even something more.

To me, therefore, keeping this covenant, there shall be a part with the holy ones; but to me doing anything contrary to what I have covenanted, may the universe be hostile to me, and the all-pervading ether, and the God who is over all, to whom none is superior, than whom none is greater.

But if even I should come to the acknowledgment of another God, I now swear by him also, be he or be he not, that I shall not do otherwise.

And in addition to all these things, if I shall lie, I shall be accursed living and dying, and shall be punished with everlasting punishment.

"And after this, let him partake of bread and salt with him who commits them to him."

Chapter V - The Adjuration Accepted

James having thus spoken, the elders were in an agony of terror. Therefore James, perceiving that they were greatly afraid, said:

"Hear me, brethren and fellow-servants.

If we should give the books to all indiscriminately, and they should be corrupted by any daring men, or be perverted by interpretations, as you have heard that some have already done, it will remain even for those who really seek the truth, always to wander in error.

Wherefore it is better that they should be with us, and that we should communicate them with all the fore-mentioned care to those who wish to live piously, and to save others.

But if any one, after taking this adjuration, shall act otherwise, he shall with good reason incur eternal punishment.

For why should not he who is the cause of the destruction of others not be destroyed himself?"

The elders, therefore, being pleased with the sentiments of James exclaimed, "Blessed be He who, as foreseeing all things, has graciously appointed thee as our bishop;" and when they had said this, we all rose up, and prayed to the Father and God of all, to whom be glory for ever.

Amen. [6]

Footnotes:

1. [The object of this apocryphal epistle is to account for the late appearance of the Homilies. It would seem to be the latest portion of the literature.--R.]

2. [This is one of the strongest anti-Pauline insinuations in the entire literature.--R.]

3. Matt. v. 18; comp. Matt. xxiv. 35; Mark xiii. 31; Luke xxii. 33. [This is a fair specimen of the loose method of Scripture citation characteristic of the Clementine literature.

Sometimes the meaning is perverted.--R.]

4. [The form of adjuration has some points of resemblance with the baptismal forms given by Hippolytus, as those of the Elkesaites.

See Introductory Notice to Recognitions, and comp. Recognitions, i. 45-48.--R.]

5. Unless the reading be corrupt here, I suppose the reference must be to episcopal succession.

6. [Rufinus, in his preface to the Recognitions, makes no allusion to this letter.--R.]

Epistle of Clement to James

Clement to James, the lord, [1] and the bishop of bishops, who rules Jerusalem, the holy church of the Hebrews, and the churches everywhere excellently founded by the providence of God, with the elders and deacons, and the rest of the brethren, peace be always.

Chapter I - Peter's Martyrdom

Be it known to you, my lord, that Simon, who, for the sake of the true faith, and the most sure foundation of his doctrine, was set apart to be the foundation of the Church, and for this end was by Jesus Himself, with His truthful mouth, named Peter, the first-fruits of our Lord, the first of the apostles; to whom first the Father revealed the Son; whom the Christ, with good reason, blessed; the called, and elect, and associate at table and in the journeyings of Christ; the excellent and approved disciple, who, as being fittest of all, was commanded to enlighten the darker part of the world, namely the West, and was enabled to accomplish it,--and to what extent do I lengthen my discourse, not wishing to indicate what is sad, which yet of necessity, though reluctantly, I must tell you,--he himself, by reason of his immense love towards men, having come as far as Rome, clearly and publicly testifying, in opposition to the wicked one who withstood him, that there is to be a good King over all the world, while saving men by his God-inspired doctrine, himself, by violence, exchanged this present existence for life.

Chapter II - Ordination of Clement

But about that time, when he was about to die, the brethren being assembled together, he suddenly seized my hand, and rose up, and said in presence of the church:
"Hear me, brethren and fellow-servants. Since, as I have been taught by the Lord and Teacher Jesus Christ, whose apostle I am, the day of my death is approaching, I lay hands upon this Clement as your bishop; and to him I entrust my chair of discourse, even to him who has journeyed with me from the beginning to the end, and thus has heard all my homilies--who, in a word, having had a share in all my trials, has been found stedfast in the faith; whom I have found, above all others, pious, philanthropic, pure, learned, chaste, good, upright, large-hearted, and striving generously to bear the ingratitude of some of the catechumens.
Wherefore I communicate to him the power of binding and loosing, so that with respect to everything which he shall ordain in the earth, it shall be decreed in the heavens.
For he shall bind what ought to be bound, and loose what ought to be loosed, as knowing the role of the Church.
Therefore hear him, as knowing that he who grieves the president of the truth, sins against Christ, and offends the Father of all.
Wherefore he shall not live; and therefore it becomes him who presides to hold the place of a physician, and not to cherish the rage of an irrational beast."

Chapter III - Nolo Episcopari

While he thus spoke, I knelt to him, and entreated him, declining the honour and the authority of the chair.
But he answered:
"Concerning this matter do not ask me; for it has seemed to me to be good that thus it be, and all the more if you decline it.
For this chair has not need of a presumptuous man, ambitious of occupying it, but of one pious in conduct and deeply skilled in the word of God.
But show me a better than yourself, who has travelled more with me, and has heard more of my discourses, and has learned better the regulations of the Church, and I shall not force you to do well

against your will.

But it will not be in your power to show me your superior; for you are the choice first-fruits of the multitudes saved through me.

However, consider this further, that if you do not undertake the administration of the Church, through fear of the danger of sin, you may be sure that you sin more, when you have it in your power to help the godly, who are, as it were, at sea and in danger, and will not do so, providing only for your own interest, and not for the common advantage of all.

But that it behoves you altogether to undertake the danger, while I do not cease to ask it of you for the help of all, you well understand.

The sooner, therefore, you consent, so much the sooner will you relieve me from anxiety.

Chapter IV - The Recompense of the Reward

"But I myself also, O Clement, know the griefs and anxieties, and dangers and reproaches, that are appointed you from the uninstructed multitudes; and these you will be able to bear nobly, looking to the great reward of patience bestowed on you by God.

But also consider this fairly with me:

When has Christ need of your aid?

Now, when the wicked one has sworn war against His bride; or in the time to come, when He shall reign victorious, having no need of further help?

Is it not evident to any one who has even the least understanding, that it is now?

Therefore with all good-will hasten in the time of the present necessity to do battle on the side of this good King, whose character it is to give great rewards after victory.

Therefore take the oversight gladly; and all the more in good time, because you have learned from me the administration of the Church, for the safety of the brethren who have taken refuge with us.

Chapter V - A Charge

"However, I wish, in the presence of all, to remind you, for the sake of all, of the things belonging to the administration.

It becomes you, living without reproach, with the greatest earnestness to shake off all the cares of life, being neither a surety, nor an advocate, nor involved in any other secular business.

For Christ does not wish to appoint you either a judge or an arbitrator in business, or negotiator of the secular affairs of the present life, lest, being confined to the present cares of men, you should not have leisure by the word of truth to separate the good among men from the bad.

But let the disciples perform these offices to one another, and not withdraw you from the discourses which are able to save.

For as it is wicked for you to undertake secular cares, and to omit the doing of what you have been commanded to do, so it is sin for every layman, if they do not stand by one another even in secular necessities.

And if all do not understand to take order that you be without care in respect of the things in which you ought to be, let them learn it from the deacons; that you may have the care of the Church always, in order both to your administering it well, and to your holding forth the words of truth.

Chapter VI - The Duty of a Bishop

"Now, if you were occupied with secular cares, you should deceive both yourself and your hearers.

For not being able, on account of occupation, to point out the things that are advantageous, both you should be punished, as not having taught what was profitable, and they, not having learned, should perish by reason of ignorance.

Wherefore do you indeed preside over them without occupation, so as to send forth seasonably the words that are able to save them; and so let them listen to you, knowing that whatever the ambassador of the truth shall bind upon earth is bound also in heaven, and what he shall loose is loosed. But you shall bind what ought to be bound, and loose what ought to be loosed.

And these, and such like, are the things that relate to you as president.

Chapter VII - Duties of Presbyters

"And with respect to the presbyters, take these instructions.

Above all things, let them join the young betimes in marriage, anticipating the entanglements of youthful lusts.

But neither let them neglect the marriage of those who are already old; for lust is vigorous even in some old men.

Lest, therefore, fornication find a place among you, and bring upon you a very pestilence, take precaution, and search, lest at any time the fire of adultery be secretly kindled among you.

For adultery is a very terrible thing, even such that it holds the second place in respect of punishment, the first being assigned to those who are in error, even although they be chaste.

Wherefore do you, as elders of the Church, exercise the spouse of Christ to chastity (by the spouse I mean the body of the Church); for if she be apprehended to be chaste by her royal Bridegroom, she shall obtain the greatest honour; and you, as wedding guests, shall receive great commendation.

But if she be caught having sinned, she herself indeed shall be cast out; and you shall suffer punishment, if at any time her sin has been through your negligence.

Chapter VIII - "Do Good Unto All?"

"Wherefore above all things be careful about chastity; for fornication has been marked out as a bitter thing in the estimation of God.

But there are many forms of fornication, as also Clement himself will explain to you.

The first is adultery, that a man should not enjoy his own wife alone, or a woman not enjoy her own husband alone.

If any one be chaste, he is able also to be philanthropic, on account of which he shall obtain eternal mercy.

For as adultery is a great evil, so philanthropy is the greatest good.

Wherefore love all your brethren with grave and compassionate eyes, performing to orphans the part of parents, to widows that of husbands, affording them sustenance with all kindliness, arranging marriages for those who are in their prime, and for those who are without a profession, the means of necessary support through employment; giving work to the artificer, and alms to the incapable.

Chapter IX - "Let Brotherly Love Continue."

"But I know that ye will do these things if you fix love into your minds; and for its entrance there is one only fit means, viz., the common partaking of food. [2]Wherefore see to it that ye be frequently one another's guests, as ye are able, that you may not fail of it.

For it is the cause of well-doing, and well-doing of salvation.

Therefore all of you present your provisions in common to all your brethren in God, knowing that, giving temporal things, you shall receive eternal things.

Much more feed the hungry, and give drink to the thirsty, and clothing to the naked; visit the sick; showing yourselves to those who are in prison, help them as ye are able, and receive strangers into your houses with all alacrity. However, not to speak in detail, philanthropy will teach you to do everything that is good, as misanthropy suggests ill-doing to those who will not be saved.

Chapter X - "Whatsoever Things are Honest."

"Let the brethren who have causes to be settled not be judged by the secular authorities; but let them by all means be reconciled by the elders of the church, yielding ready obedience to them.

Moreover, also, flee avarice, inasmuch as it is able, under pretext of temporal gain, to deprive you of eternal blessings.

Carefully keep your balances, your measures, your weights, and the things belonging to your traffic, just.

Be faithful with respect to your trusts.

Moreover, you will persevere in doing these things, and things similar to these, until the end, if you have in your hearts an ineradicable remembrance of the judgment that is from God.

For who would sin, being persuaded that at the end of life there is a judgment appointed of the righteous God, who only now is long-suffering and good, [3] that the good may in future enjoy for ever unspeakable blessings; but the sinners being found as evil, shall obtain an eternity of unspeakable punishment. And, indeed, that these things are so, it would be reasonable to doubt, were it not that the Prophet of the truth has said and sworn that it shall be.

Chapter XI - Doubts to Be Satisfied

"Wherefore, being disciples of the true Prophet, laying aside double-mindedness, from which comes ill-doing, eagerly undertake well-doing.

But if any of you doubt concerning the things which I have said are to be, let him confess it without shame, if he cares for his own soul, and he shall be satisfied by the president.

But if he has believed rightly, let his conversation be with confidence, as fleeing from the great fire of condemnation, and entering into the eternal good kingdom of God.

Chapter XII - Duties of Deacons

"Moreover let the deacons of the church, going about with intelligence, be as eyes to the bishop, carefully inquiring into the doings of each member of the church, ascertaining who is about to sin, in order that, being arrested with admonition by the president, he may haply not accomplish the sin.

Let them check the disorderly, that they may not desist from assembling to hear the discourses, so that they may be able to counteract by the word of truth those anxieties that fall upon the heart from every side, by means of worldly casualties and evil communications; for if they long remain fallow, they become fuel for the fire.

And let them learn who are suffering under bodily disease, and let them bring them to the notice of the multitude who do not know of them, that they may visit them, and supply their wants according to the judgment of the president.

Yea, though they do this without his knowledge, they do nothing amiss.

These things, then, and things like to these, let the deacons attend to.

Chapter XIII - Duties of Catechists

"Let the catechists instruct, being first instructed; for it is a work relating to the souls of men.

For the teacher of the word must accommodate himself to the various judgments of the learners.

The catechists must therefore be learned, and unblameable, of much experience, and approved, as you will know that Clement is, who is to be your instructor after me.

For it were too much for me now to go into details.

However, if ye be of one mind, you shall be able to reach the haven of rest, where is the peaceful city of the great King.

Chapter XIV - The Vessel of the Church

"For the whole business of the Church is like unto a great ship, bearing through a violent storm men who are of many places, and who desire to inhabit the city of the good kingdom.

Let, therefore, God be your shipmaster; and let the pilot be likened to Christ, the mate [4] to the bishop, and the sailors to the deacons, the midshipmen to the catechists, the multitude of the brethren to the passengers, the world to the sea; the foul winds to temptations, persecutions, and dangers; and all manner of afflictions to the waves; the land winds and their squalls to the discourses of deceivers and false prophets; the promontories and rugged rocks to the judges in high places threatening terrible things; the meetings of two seas, and the wild places, to unreasonable men and those who doubt of the promises of truth.

Let hypocrites be regarded as like to pirates.

Moreover, account the strong whirlpool, and the Tartarean Charybdis, and murderous wrecks, and deadly founderings, to be nought but sins.

In order, therefore, that, sailing with a fair wind, you may safely reach the haven of the hoped-for city, pray so as to be heard.

But prayers become audible by good deeds.

Chapter XV - Incidents of the Voyage

"Let therefore the passengers remain quiet, sitting in their own places, lest by disorder they occasion rolling or careening.
Let the midshipmen give heed to the fare.
Let the deacons neglect nothing with which they are entrusted; let the presbyters, like sailors, studiously arrange what is needful for each one.
Let the bishop, as the mate, wakefully ponder the words of the pilot alone.
Let Christ, even the Saviour, be loved as the pilot, and alone believed in the matters of which He speaks; and let all pray to God for a prosperous voyage.
Let those sailing expect every tribulation, as travelling over a great and troubled sea, the world: sometimes, indeed, disheartened, persecuted, dispersed, hungry, thirsty, naked, hemmed in; and, again, sometimes united, congregated, at rest; but also sea-sick, giddy, vomiting, that is, confessing sins, like disease-producing bile,--I mean the sins proceeding from bitterness, and the evils accumulated from disorderly lusts, by the confession of which, as by vomiting, you are relieved of your disease, attaining healthful safety by means of carefulness.

Chapter XVI - The Bishop's Labours and Reward

"But know all of you that the bishop labours more than you all; because each of you suffers his own affliction, but he his own and that of every one.
Wherefore, O Clement, preside as a helper to every one according to your ability, being careful of the cares of all.
Whence I know that in your undertaking the administration, I do not confer, but receive, a favour.
But take courage and bear it generously, as knowing that God will recompense you when you enter the haven of rest, the greatest of blessings, a reward that cannot be taken from you, in proportion as you have undertaken more labour for the safety of all. So that, if many of the brethren should hate you on account of your lofty righteousness, their hatred shall nothing hurt you, but the love of the righteous God shall greatly benefit you.
Therefore endeavour to shake off the praise that arises from injustice, and to attain the profitable praise that is from Christ on account of righteous administration."

Chapter XVII - The People's Duties

Having said this, and more than this, he looked again upon the multitude, and said:
"And you also, my beloved brethren and fellow-servants, be subject to the president of the truth in all things, knowing this, that he who grieves him has not received Christ, with whose chair he has been entrusted; and he who has not received Christ shall be regarded as having despised the Father; wherefore he shall be cast out of the good kingdom.
On this account, endeavour to come to all the assemblies, lest as deserters you incur the charge of sin through the disheartening of your captain.
Wherefore all of you think before all else of the things that relate to him, knowing this, that the wicked one, being the more hostile on account of every one of you, wars against him alone.
Do you therefore strive to live in affection towards him, and in kindliness towards one another, and to obey him, in order that both he may be comforted and you may be saved.

Chapter XVIII - "As a Heathen Man and a Publican."

"But some things also you ought of yourselves to consider, on account of his not being able to speak openly by reason of the plots.
Such as:
if he be hostile to any one, do not wait for his speaking; and do not take part with that man, but prudently follow the bishop's will, being enemies to those to whom he is an enemy, and not conversing with those with whom he does not converse, in order that every one, desiring to have you all as his friends, may be reconciled to him and be saved, listening to his discourse.
But if any one remain a friend of those to whom he is an enemy, and speak to those with whom he

does not converse, he also himself is one of those who would waste the church.

For, being with you in body, but not with you in judgment, he is against you; and is much worse than the open enemies from without, since with seeming friendship he disperses those who are within."

Chapter XIX - Installation of Clement

Having thus spoken, he laid his hands upon me in the presence of all, and compelled me to sit in his own chair.

And when I was seated, he immediately said to me:

"I entreat you, in the presence of all the brethren here, that whensoever I depart from this life, as depart I must, you send to James the brother of the Lord a brief account of your reasonings from your boyhood, and how from the beginning until now you have journeyed with me, hearing the discourses preached by me in every city, and seeing my deeds.

And then at the end you will not fail to inform him of the manner of my death, as I said before.

For that event will not grieve him very much, when he knows that I piously went through what it behoved me to suffer.

And he will get the greatest comfort when he learns, that not an unlearned man, or one ignorant of life-giving words, or not knowing the rule of the Church, shall be entrusted with the chair of the teacher after me.

For the discourse of a deceiver destroys the souls of the multitudes who hear."

Chapter XX - Clement's Obedience

Whence I, my lord James, having promised as I was ordered, have not failed to write in books by chapters the greater part of his discourses in every city, which have been already written to you, and sent by himself, as for a token; and thus I despatched them to you, [5] inscribing them "Clement's Epitome of the Popular Sermons of Peter." However, I shall begin to set them forth, as I was ordered.

Footnotes:

1. More probably "the Lord's brother."

So it must have been in the text from which Rufinus translated.

[That this means "James the Lord's brother" is quite certain, but it is not necessary to adopt this reading here; comp. chap. 20 and the opening sentence of the previous epistle.

In Recognitions, iii. 74, Clement is represented as writing "my lord James."--R.]

2. Literally, "of salt."

3. The common reading would give "who alone is now long-suffering;" but the change of a letter gives the reading which we have adopted.

4. It is impossible to translate these terms very accurately.

I suppose the proreus was rather the "bow-oarsman" in the galley.

5. [Compare with this the remarkable chapter, Recognitions, iii. 75, where a summary is given of previous writings sent to James.

The design of this letter, evidently known to Rufinus, was to authenticate the work which follows.

The language of Rufinus may fairly imply that this letter, known to be of later origin, was sometimes prefixed to the Recognitions also.

This is an evidence of Jewish-Christian origin.--R.]

The Clementine Homilies

Books I. to V. have been translated by Rev. Thomas Smith, D.D.; Books VI.-XII. by Peter Peterson, M.A.; and Books XIII.-XX. by Dr. Donaldson.

Homily I

Chapter I - Boyish Questionings

I Clement, being a Roman citizen, [1] even from my earliest youth was able to live chastely, my mind from my boyhood drawing away the lust that was in me to dejection and distress.

For I had a habit of reasoning--how originating I know not--making frequent cogitations concerning death:

When I die, shall I neither exist, nor shall any one ever have any remembrance of me, while boundless time bears all things of all men into forgetfulness? and shall I then be without being, or acquaintance with those who are; neither knowing nor being known, neither having been nor being?

And has the world ever been made? and was there anything before it was made?

For if it has been always, it shall also continue to be; but if it has been made, it shall also be dissolved.

And after its dissolution, shall there ever be anything again, unless, perhaps, silence and forgetfulness?

Or perhaps something shall be which is not possible now to conceive.

Chapter II - Good Out of Evil

As I pondered without ceasing these and such like questions--I know not whence arising--I had such bitter grief, that, becoming pale, I wasted away; and, what was most terrible, if at any time I wished to drive away this meditation as unprofitable, my suffering became all the more severe; and I grieved over this, not knowing that I had a fair inmate, even my thought, which was to be to me the cause of a blessed immortality, as I afterwards knew by experience, and gave thanks to God, the Lord of all.

For it was by this thought, which at first afflicted me, that I was compelled to come to the search and the finding of things; and then I pitied those whom at first, through ignorance, I ventured to call blessed.

Chapter III - Perplexity

From my boyhood, then, being involved in such reasonings, in order to learn something definite, I used to resort to the schools of the philosophers.

But nought else did I see than the setting up and the knocking down of doctrines, and strifes, and seeking for victory, and the arts of syllogisms, and the skill of assumptions; and sometimes one opinion prevailed,--as, for example, that the soul is immortal, and sometimes that it is mortal.

If, therefore, at any time the doctrine prevailed that it is immortal, I was glad; and when the doctrine prevailed that it is mortal, I was grieved.

And again, I was the more disheartened because I could not establish either doctrine to my satisfaction.

However, I perceived that the opinions on subjects under discussion are taken as true or false, according to their defenders, and do not appear as they really are.

Perceiving, therefore, now that the acceptance does not depend on the real nature of the subjects discussed, but that opinions are proved to be true or false, according to ability of those who defend them, I was still more than ever at a loss in regard of things.

Wherefore I groaned from the depth of my soul.

For neither was I able to establish anything, nor could I shake off the consideration of such things, though, as I said before, I wished it.

For although I frequently charged myself to be at peace, in some way or other thoughts on these subjects, accompanied with a feeling of pleasure, would come into my mind.

Chapter IV - More Perplexity

And again, living in doubt, I said to myself, Why do I labour in vain, when the matter is clear, that if I lose existence when I die, it is not fitting that I should distress myself now while I do exist? Wherefore I shall reserve my grief till that day, when, ceasing to exist, I shall not be affected with grief.

But if I am to exist, what does it profit me now to distress myself gratuitously?

And immediately after this another reasoning assailed me; for I said, Shall I not have something worse to suffer then than that which distresses me now, if I have not lived piously; and shall I not be delivered over, according to the doctrines of some philosophers, to Pyriphlegethon and Tartarus, like Sisyphus, or Tityus, or Ixion, or Tantalus, and be punished for ever in Hades?

But again I replied, saying:

But there are no such things as these.

Yet again I said:

But if there be?

Therefore, said I, since the matter is uncertain, the safer plan is for me rather to live piously.

But how shall I be able, for the sake of righteousness, to subdue bodily pleasures, looking, as I do, to an uncertain hope? But I am neither fully persuaded what is that righteous thing that is pleasing to God, nor do I know whether the soul is immortal or mortal. Neither can I find any well-established doctrine, nor can I abstain from such debatings.

Chapter V - A Resolution

What, then, am I to do, unless this?

I shall go into Egypt, and I shall become friendly with the hierophants of the shrines, and with the prophets; and I shall seek and find a magician, and persuade him with large bribes to effect the calling up of a soul, which is called necromancy, as if I were going to inquire of it concerning some business.

And the inquiry shall be for the purpose of learning whether the soul is immortal.

But the answer of the soul that it is immortal shall not give me the knowledge from its speaking or my hearing, but only from its being seen; so that, seeing it with my very eyes, I may have a self-sufficient and fit assurance, from the very fact of its appearing, that it exists; and never again shall the uncertain words of hearing be able to overturn the things which the eyes have made their own.

However, I submitted this very plan to a certain companion who was a philosopher; and he counselled me not to venture upon it, and that on many accounts.

"For if," said he, "the soul shall not listen to the magician, you will live with an evil conscience, as having acted against the laws which forbid the doing of these things.

But if it shall listen to him, then, besides your living with an evil conscience, I think that matters of piety will not be promoted to you on account of your making this attempt.

For they say that the Deity is angry with those who disturb souls after their release from the body."[2] And I, when I heard this, became indeed more backward to undertake such a thing, but I did not abandon my original plan; but I was distressed, as being hindered in the execution of it.

Chapter VI - Tidings from Judaea

And, not to discuss such matters to you in a long speech, while I was occupied with such reasonings and doings, a certain report, taking its rise in the spring-time, [3] in the reign of Tiberius Caesar, gradually grew everywhere, and ran through the world as truly the good tidings of God, being unable to stifle the counsel of God in silence. Therefore it everywhere became greater and louder, saying that a certain One in Judaea, beginning in the spring season, was preaching to the Jews the kingdom of the invisible God, and saying that whoever of them would reform his manner of living should enjoy it.

And in order that He might be believed that He uttered these things full of the Godhead, He wrought many wonderful miracles and signs by His mere command, as having received power from

God.

For He made the deaf to hear, the blind to see, the lame to walk, raised up the bowed down, drove away every disease, put to flight every demon; and even scabbed lepers, by only looking on Him from a distance, were sent away cured by Him; and the dead being brought to Him, were raised; and there was nothing which He could not do.

And as time advanced, so much the greater, through the arrival of more persons, and the stronger grew--I say not now the report, but--the truth of the thing; for now at length there were meetings in various places for consultation and inquiry as to who He might be that had appeared, and what was His purpose.

Chapter VII - The Gospel in Rome

And then in the same year, in the autumn season, a certain one, standing in a public place, cried and said, "Men of Rome, hearken.

The Son of God is come in Judaea, proclaiming eternal life to all who will, if they shall live according to the counsel of the Father, who hath sent Him.

Wherefore change your manner of life from the worse to the better, from things temporal to things eternal; for know ye that there is one God, who is in heaven, whose world ye unrighteously dwell in before His righteous eyes.

But if ye be changed, and live according to His counsel, then, being born into the other world, and becoming eternal, ye shall enjoy His unspeakable good things.

But if ye be unbelieving, your souls, after the dissolution of the body, shall be thrown into the place of fire, where, being punished eternally, they shall repent of their unprofitable deeds.

For every one, the term of repentance is the present life."

I therefore, when I heard these things, was grieved, because no one among so great multitudes, hearing such an announcement, said:

I shall go into Judaea, that I may know if this man who tells us these things speaks the truth, that the Son of God has come into Judaea, for the sake of a good and eternal hope, revealing the will of the Father who sent Him.

For it is no small matter which they say that He preaches:

for He asserts that the souls of some, being themselves immortal, shall enjoy eternal good things; and that those of others, being thrown into unquenchable fire, shall be punished for ever.

Chapter VIII - Departure from Rome

While I spoke thus concerning others, I also lectured myself, saying, Why do I blame others, being myself guilty of the very same crime of heedlessness?

But I shall hasten into Judaea, having first arranged my affairs. [4]And when I had thus made up my mind, there occurred a long time of delay, my worldly affairs being difficult to arrange. Therefore, meditating further on the nature of life, that by involving [5] men in hope it lays snares for those who are making haste, yea, and how much time I had been robbed of while tossed by hopes, and that we men die while thus occupied, I left all my affairs as they were, and sped to Portus; [6] and coming to the harbour, and being taken on board a ship, I was borne by adverse winds to Alexandria instead of Judaea; and being detained there by stress of weather, I consorted with the philosophers, and told them about the rumour and the sayings of him who had appeared in Rome.

And they answered that indeed they knew nothing of him who had appeared in Rome; but concerning Him who was born in Judaea, and who was said by the report to be the Son of God, they had heard from many who had come from thence, and had learned respecting all the wonderful things that He did with a word.

Chapter IX - Preaching of Barnabas

And when I said that I wished I could meet with some one of those who had seen Him, they immediately brought me to one, saying, "There is one here who not only is acquainted with Him, but is also of that country, a Hebrew, by name Barnabas, who says that he himself is one of His disciples; and hereabouts he resides, and readily announces to those who will the terms of His promise."

Then I went with them; and when I came, I stood listening to his words with the crowd that stood round him; and I perceived that he was speaking the truth not with dialectic art, but was setting forth simply and without preparation what he had heard and seen the manifested Son of God do and say.

And even from the crowd who stood around him he produced many witnesses of the miracles and discourses which he narrated.

Chapter X - Cavils of the Philosophers

But while the multitudes were favourably disposed towards the things that he so artlessly spoke, the philosophers, impelled by their worldly learning, set upon laughing at him and making sport of him, upbraiding and reproaching him with excessive presumption, making use of the great armoury of syllogisms.

But he set aside their babbling, and did not enter into their subtle questioning, but without embarrassment went on with what he was saying.

And then one of them asked, Wherefore it was that a gnat, although it be so small, and has six feet, has wings also; while an elephant, the largest of beasts, is wingless, and has but four feet?

But he, after the question had been put, resuming his discourse, which had been interrupted, as though he had answered the question, resumed his original discourse, only making use of this preface after each interruption:

We have a commission only to tell you the words and the wondrous doings of Him who sent us; and instead of logical demonstration, we present to you many witnesses from amongst yourselves who stand by, whose faces I remember, as living images.

These sufficient testimonies it is left to your choice to submit to, or to disbelieve. [7]But I shall not cease to declare unto you what is for your profit; for to be silent were to me a loss, and to disbelieve is ruin to you.

But indeed I could give answers to your frivolous questions, if you asked them through love of truth.

But the reason of the different structure of the gnat and elephant it is not fitting to tell to those who are ignorant of the God of all."

Chapter XI - Clement's Zeal

When he said this, they all, as in concert, set up a shout of laughter, trying to silence him and put him out, as a barbarous madman.

But I, seeing this, and seized, I know not how, with enthusiasm, could no longer keep silence with righteous indignation, but boldly cried out, saying, "Well has God ordained that His counsel should be incapable of being received by you, foreseeing you to be unworthy, as appears manifestly to such of those who are now present as have minds capable of judging.

For whereas now heralds of His counsel have been sent forth, not making a show of grammatical art, but setting forth His will in simple and in artificial words, so that whosoever hear can understand what is spoken, and not with any invidious feeling, as though unwilling to offer it to all; you come here, and besides your not understanding what is for your advantage, to your own injury you laugh at the truth, which, to your condemnation, consorts with the barbarians, and which you will not entertain when it visits you, by reason of your wickedness and the plainness of its words, lest you be convicted of being merely lovers of words, and not lovers of truth and lovers of wisdom.

How long will you be learning to speak, who have not the power of speech? [8]For many sayings of yours are not worth one word.

What, then, will your Grecian multitude say, being of one mind, if, as he says, there shall be a judgment?

"Why, O God, didst Thou not proclaim to us Thy counsel?"

Shall you not, if you be thought worthy of an answer at all, be told this?

"I, knowing before the foundation of the world all characters that were to be, acted towards each one by anticipation according to his deserts without making it known; [9] but wishing to give full assurance to those who have fled to me that this is so, and to explain why from the beginning, and in the first ages, I did not suffer my counsel to be publicly proclaimed; I now, in the end of the world, [10] have sent heralds to proclaim my will, and they are insulted and flouted by those who will not be benefited, and who wilfully reject my friendship.

Oh, great wrong! The preachers are exposed to danger even to the loss of life, [11] and that by the men who are called to salvation.

Chapter XII - Clement's Rebuke of the People

"And this wrongful treatment of my heralds would have been against all from the beginning, if from the beginning the unworthy had been called to salvation.

For that which is now done wrongfully by these men serves to the vindication of my righteous foreknowledge, that it was well that I did not choose from the beginning to expose uselessly to public contempt the word which is worthy of honour; but determined to suppress it, as being honourable, not indeed from those who were worthy from the beginning--for to them also I imparted it--but from those, and such as those, unworthy, as you see them to be,--those who hate me, and who will not love themselves.

And now, give over laughing at this man, and hear me with respect to his announcement, or let any one of the hearers who pleases answer.

And do not bark like vicious dogs, deafening with disorderly clamour the ears of those who would be saved, ye unrighteous and God-haters, and perverting the saving method to unbelief.

How shall you be able to obtain pardon, who scorn him who is sent to speak to you of the Godhead of God?

And this you do towards a man whom you ought to have received on account of his good-will towards you, even if he did not speak truth."

Chapter XIII - Clement Instructed by Barnabas

While I spake these words, and others to the same effect, there arose a great excitement among the crowd; and some as pitying Barnabas, sympathized with me; but others, being senseless, terribly gnashed their teeth against me.

But, as the evening had already come, I took Barnabas by the hand, and by force conducted him, against his will, to my lodging, and constrained him to remain there, lest some one might lay hands on him.

And having spent several days, and instructed me briefly in the true doctrine, as well as he could in a few days, he said that he should hasten into Judaea for the observance of the festival, and also because he wished for the future to consort with those of his own nation.

Chapter XIV - Departure of Barnabas

But it plainly appeared to me that he was disconcerted.

For when I said to him, "Only set forth to me the words which you have heard of the Man who has appeared, and I will adorn them with my speech, and preach the counsel of God; and if you do so, within a few days I will sail with you, for I greatly desire to go to the land of Judaea, and perhaps I shall dwell with you all my life;"--when he heard this, he answered:

"If you wish to inquire into our affairs, and to learn what is for your advantage, sail with me at once.

But if you will not, I shall now give you directions to my house, and that of those whom you wish to meet, that when you choose to come you may find us.

For I shall set out to-morrow for my home."

And when I saw that he could not be prevailed upon, I went with him as far as the harbour; and having learned of him the directions which he had promised to give me for finding the dwellings, I said to him, "Were it not that to-morrow I am to recover a debt that is due to me, I should straightway set sail with you.

But I shall soon overtake you."

And having said this, and having given him in charge to those who commanded the ship, I returned grieving, remembering him as an excellent and dear friend.

Chapter XV - Introduction to Peter

But having spent some days, and not having been able to recover the whole debt, for the sake of speed I neglected the balance, as being a hindrance, and myself also set sail for Judaea, and in fifteen days arrived at Caesarea Stratonis. [12]And when I had landed, and was seeking for a lodging, I learned that one named Peter, who was the most esteemed disciple of the Man who had appeared in Judaea, and had done signs and wonders, was going to have a verbal controversy next day with Simon, a Samaritan of Gitthi.

When I heard this, I begged to be shown his lodging; and as soon as I learned it, I stood before the door.

And those who were in the house, seeing me, discussed the question who I was, and whence I had come.

And, behold, Barnabas came out; and as soon as he saw me he embraced me, rejoicing greatly, and weeping.

And he took me by the hand, and conducted me to where Peter was, saying to me, "This is Peter, of whom I told you as being the greatest in the wisdom of God, and I have spoken to him of you continually.

Therefore enter freely, [13] for I have told him your excellent qualities, without falsehood; and, at the same time, have disclosed to him your intention, so that he himself also is desirous to see you.

Therefore I offer him a great gift when by my hands I present you to him."

Thus saying, he presented me, and said, "This, O Peter, is Clement."

Chapter XVI - Peter's Salutation

Then the blessed man, springing forward as soon as he heard my name, kissed me; and making me sit down, straightway said, "You acted nobly in entertaining Barnabas, a herald of the truth, to the honour of the living God, being magnanimously not ashamed, nor fearing the resentment of the rude multitude.

Blessed shall you be.

For as you thus with all honour entertained the ambassador of the truth, so also truth herself shall constitute you, who are a stranger, a citizen of her own city. And thus you shall greatly rejoice, because you have now lent a small favour; I mean the kindness of good words.

You shall be heir of blessings which are both eternal and cannot possibly be taken from you.

And do not trouble yourself to detail to me your manner of life; for the veracious Barnabas has detailed to us everything relating to you, making favourable mention of you almost every day.

And in order that I may tell to you briefly, as to a genuine friend, what is in hand, travel with us, unless anything hinders you, partaking of the words of truth which I am going to speak from city to city, as far as Rome itself.

And if you wish to say anything, speak on."

Chapter XVII - Questions Propounded

Then I set forth my purpose from the beginning, and how I had spent myself upon difficult questions, and all the things that I disclosed to you at the outset, so that I need not write the same things again. Then I said, "I hold myself in readiness to journey with you; for this, I know not how, I gladly wish.

However, I wish first to be convinced concerning the truth, that I may know whether the soul is mortal or immortal; and whether, if it is eternal, it is to be judged concerning the things which it hath done here.

Also, whether there is anything that is righteous and well-pleasing to God; and whether the world was made, and for what end it was made; and whether it shall be dissolved; and if it shall be dissolved, whether it shall be made better, or shall not be at all."

And not to mention them in detail, I said that I wished to learn these things, and things consequent upon these.

And to this he answered:

"I shall shortly convey to you, O Clement, the knowledge of the things that are; and even now listen.

Chapter XVIII - Causes of Ignorance

"The will of God has been kept in obscurity in many ways.
In the first place, there is evil instruction, wicked association, terrible society, unseemly discourses, wrongful prejudice.
Thereby is error, then fearlessness, unbelief, fornication, covetousness, vainglory; and ten thousand other such evils, filling the world as a quantity of smoke fills a house, have obscured the sight of the men inhabiting the world, and have not suffered them to look up and become acquainted with God the Creator from the delineation of Himself which He has given, and to know what is pleasing to Him.
Wherefore it behoves the lovers of truth, crying out inwardly from their breasts, to call for aid, with truth-loving reason, that some one living within the house [14] which is filled with smoke may approach and open the door, so that the light of the sun which is without may be admitted into the house, and the smoke of the fire which is within may be driven out.

Chapter XIX - The True Prophet

"Now the Man who is the helper I call the true Prophet; and He alone is able to enlighten the souls of men, so that with our own eyes we may be able to see the way of eternal salvation.
But otherwise it is impossible, as you also know, since you said a little while ago that every doctrine is set up and pulled down, and the same is thought true or false, according to the power of him who advocates it; so that doctrines do not appear as they are, but take the appearance of being or not being truth or falsehood from those who advocate them. [15] On this account the whole business of religion needed a true prophet, that he might tell us things that are, as they are, and how we must believe concerning all things.
So that it is first necessary to test the prophet by every prophetic sign, and having ascertained that he is true, thereafter to believe him in every thing, and not to sit in judgment upon his several sayings, but to receive them as certain, being accepted indeed by seeming faith, yet by sure judgment.
For by our initial proof, and by strict inquiry on every side, all things are received with right reason.
Wherefore before all things it is necessary to seek after the true Prophet, because without Him it is impossible that any certainty can come to men."

Chapter XX - Peter's Satisfaction with Clement

And, at the same time, he satisfied me by expounding to me who He is, and how He is found, and holding Him forth to me as truly to be found, showing that the truth is more manifest to the ear by the discourse of the prophet than things that are seen with the eye; so that I was astonished, and wondered that no one sees those things which are sought after by all, though they lie before him.
However, having written this discourse concerning the Prophet by his order, he caused the volume to be despatched to you from Caesarea Stratonis, saying that he had a charge from you to send his discourses and his acts year by year. [16]
Thus, on the very first day, beginning only concerning the prophet of the truth, he confirmed me in every respect; and then he spoke thus: "Henceforth give heed to the discussions that take place between me and those on the other side; and even if I come off at a disadvantage, I am not afraid of your ever doubting of the truth that has been delivered to you, knowing well that I seem to be beaten, but not the doctrine that has been delivered to us by the Prophet.
However, I hope not to come off in our inquiries at a disadvantage with men who have understanding--I mean lovers of truth, who are able to know what discourses are specious, artificial, and pleasant, and what are unartificial and simple, trusting only to the truth that is conveyed through them."

Chapter XXI - Unalterable Conviction

When he had thus spoken, I answered:

"Now do I thank God; for as I wished to be convinced, so He has vouchsafed to me.

However, so far as concerns me, be you so far without anxiety that I shall never doubt; so much so, that if you yourself should ever wish to remove me from the prophetic doctrine, you should not be able, so well do I know what I have received.

And do not think that it is a great thing that I promise you that I shall never doubt; for neither I myself, nor any man who has heard your discourse concerning the Prophet, can ever doubt of the true doctrine, having first heard and understood what is the truth of the prophetic announcement.

Wherefore have confidence in the God-willed dogma; for every art of wickedness has been conquered.

For against prophecy, neither arts of discourses, nor tricks of sophisms, nor syllogisms, nor any other contrivance, can prevail anything; that is, if he who has heard the true Prophet really is desirous of truth, and does not give heed to aught else under pretext of truth.

So that, my lord Peter, be not disconcerted, as though you had presented the greatest good to a senseless person; for you have presented it to one sensible of the favour, and who cannot be seduced from the truth that has been committed to him.

For I know that it is one of those things which one wishes to receive quickly, and not to attain slowly. Therefore I know that I should not despise, on account of the quickness with which I have got it, what has been committed to me, what is incomparable, and what alone is safe."

Chapter XXII - Thanksgiving

When I had thus spoken, Peter said:

"I give thanks to God, both for your salvation and for my satisfaction.

For I am truly pleased to know that you apprehend what is the greatness of prophecy.

Since, then, as you say, if I myself should ever wish--which God forbid--to transfer you to another doctrine, I shall not be able to persuade you, begin from to-morrow to attend upon me in the discussions with the adversaries.

And to-morrow I have one with Simon Magus."

And having spoken thus, and he himself having partaken of food in private, he ordered me also to partake; [17] and having blessed the food, and having given thanks after being satisfied, and having giving me an account of this matter, he went on to say:

"May God grant you in all things to be made like unto me, and having been baptized, to partake of the same table with me."

And having thus spoken, he enjoined me to go to rest; for now indeed my bodily nature demanded sleep.

Footnotes:

1. [The first six chapters agree closely with the corresponding passage in the Recognitions.--R.]
2. This rendering is from the text in the corresponding passage of the Epitome de gestis S. Petri.
3. [This clause is represented in the Recognitions as follows: "which took its rise in the regions of the East."--R.]
4. [The narrative here varies from that of the Recognitions; comp. book i. chaps. 7-11.--R.]
5. For ekplokon Wieseler proposes ekklepton, "that deceiving by hopes it lays snares," etc.
6. Portus, the port of Rome.
One ms. reads ponton, "the sea."
7. We have here adopted a conjectural reading of Davis.
The common text is thus translated:
"whose faces I remember, and who as being living images are satisfactory testimonies.
These it is left," etc.
8. The Vatican ms. and Epit. have "the power of speaking well."
9. Lit., "I met each one beforehand secretly."
The Latin has, "unicuique praevius occurri."
10. The Greek is biou, "life."
11. The Paris ms. reads phthonou, "envy," instead of phonou, "murder."
12. [Here the two accounts become again closely parallel.--R.]
13. The text is corrupt.
Dressel's reading is adopted in the text, being based on Rufinus's translation.

Some conjecture, "as you will know of your own accord."

14. A conjectural reading, "being without the house," seems preferable.

15. [Comp. Recognitions, i. 16, where the discourse is more fully given.--R.]

16. The text is probably corrupt or defective.

As it stands, grammatically Peter writes the discourse and sends it, and yet "by his order" must also apply to Peter.

The Recognitions make Clement write the book and send it.

The passage is deemed important, and is accordingly discussed in Schliemann, p. 83; Hilgenfeld, p. 37; and Uhlhorn, p. 101.

[See Recognitions, i. 17.

Both passages, despite the variation, may be urged in support of the existence of an earlier document as the common basis of the Clementine literature.--R.]

17. [Comp. Homily XIII. 4. and Recognitions, i. 19.--R.]

Homily II

Chapter I - Peter's Attendants

Therefore the next day, I Clement, awaking from sleep before dawn, and learning that Peter was astir, and was conversing with his attendants concerning the worship of God (there were sixteen of them, [1] and I have thought good to set forth their names, as I subsequently learned them, that you may also know who they were.

The first of them was Zacchaeus, who was once a publican, and Sophonias his brother; Joseph and his foster-brother Michaias; also Thomas and Eliezer the twins; also AEneas and Lazarus the priests; besides also Elisaeus, and Benjamin the son of Saphrus; as also Rubilus and Zacharias the builders; and Ananias and Haggaeus the Jamminians; and Nicetas and Aquila the friends),--accordingly I went in and saluted him, and at his request sat down.

Chapter II - A Sound Mind in a Sound Body

And he, breaking off the discourse in which he was engaged, assured me, by way of apology, why he had not awakened me that I might hear his discourses, assigning as the reason the discomfort of my voyage.

As he wished this to be dispelled, [2] he had suffered me to sleep.

"For," said he, "whenever the soul is distracted concerning some bodily want, it does not properly approach the instructions that are presented to it.

On this account I am not willing to converse, either with those who are greatly grieving through some calamity, or are immoderately angry, or are turned to the frenzy of love, or are suffering under bodily exhaustion, or are distressed with the cares of life, or are harassed with any other sufferings, whose soul, as I said, being downcast, and sympathizing with the suffering body, occupies also its own intelligence therewith.

Chapter III - Forewarned is Forearmed

"And let it not be said, Is it not, then, proper to present comforts and admonitions to those who are in any bad case?

To this I answer, that if, indeed, any one is able, let him present them; but if not, let him bide his time.

For I know [3] that all things have their proper season.

Wherefore it is proper to ply men with words which strengthen the soul in anticipation of evil; so that, if at any time any evil comes upon them, the mind, being forearmed with the right argument, may be able to bear up under that which befalls it:

for then the mind knows in the crisis of the struggle to have recourse to him who succoured it by good counsel.

Chapter IV - A Request

"However, I have learned, O Clement, how that in Alexandria Barnabas perfectly expounded to you the word respecting prophecy.

Was it not so?"

I answered, "Yes, and exceeding well."

Then Peter:

"Therefore it is not necessary now to occupy with the instructions which you know, the time which may serve us for other instructions which you do not know."

Then said I:
"You have rightly said, O Peter.
But vouchsafe this to me, who purpose always to attend upon you, continuously to expound to me, a delighted hearer, the doctrine of the Prophet.
For, apart from Him, as I learned from Barnabas, it is impossible to learn the truth."

Chapter V - Excellence of the Knowledge of the True Prophet

And Peter, being greatly pleased with this, answered:
"Already hath the rectifying process taken its end, as regards you, knowing as you do the greatness of the infallible prophecy, without which it is impossible for any one to receive that which is supremely profitable. For of many and diverse blessings which are in the things which are or which may be, the most blessed of all--whether it be eternal life, or perpetual health, or a perfect understanding, or light, or joy, or immortality, or whatever else there is or that can be supremely good in the nature of things-- cannot be possessed without first knowing things as they are; and this knowledge cannot be otherwise obtained than by first becoming acquainted with the Prophet of the truth.

Chapter VI - The True Prophet

"Now the Prophet of the truth is He who always knows all things--things past as they were, things present as they are, things future as they shall be; sinless, merciful, alone entrusted with the declaration of the truth.
Read, and you shall find that those were deceived [4] who thought that they had found the truth of themselves.
For this is peculiar to the Prophet, to declare the truth, even as it is peculiar to the sun to bring the day.
Wherefore, as many as have even desired to know the truth, but have not had the good fortune to learn it from Him, have not found it, but have died seeking it.
For how can he find the truth who seeks it from his own ignorance?
And even if he find it, he does not know it, and passes it by as if it were not.
Nor yet shall he be able to obtain possession of the truth from another, who, in like manner, promises to him knowledge from ignorance; excepting only the knowledge of morality and things of that sort, which can be known through reason, which affords to every one the knowledge that he ought not to wrong another, through his not wishing himself to be wronged.

Chapter VII - Unaided Quest of Truth Profitless

"All therefore who ever sought the truth, trusting to themselves to be able to find it, fell into a snare.
This is what both the philosophers of the Greeks, and the more intelligent of the barbarians, have suffered.
For, applying themselves to things visible, they have given decisions by conjecture on things not apparent, thinking that that was truth which at any time presented itself to them as such.
For, like persons who know the truth, they, still seeking the truth, reject some of the suppositions that are presented to them, and lay hold of others, as if they knew, while they do not know, what things are true and what are false.
And they dogmatize concerning truth, even those who are seeking after truth, not knowing that he who seeks truth cannot learn it from his own wandering.
For not even, as I said, can he recognise her when she stands by him, since he is unacquainted with her.

Chapter VIII - Test of Truth

"And it is by no means that which is true, but that which is pleasing, which persuades every one who seeks to learn from himself.

Since, therefore, one thing is pleasing to one, and another to another, one thing prevails over one as truth, and another thing over another.

But the truth is that which is approved by the Prophet, not that which is pleasant to each individual.

For that which is one would be many, if the pleasing were the true; which is impossible.

Wherefore also the Grecian philologers--rather than philosophers [5] --going about matters by conjectures, have dogmatized much and diversely, thinking that the apt sequence of hypotheses is truth, not knowing that when they have assigned to themselves false beginnings, their conclusion has corresponded with the beginning.

Chapter IX - "The Weak Things of the World."

"Whence a man ought to pass by all else, and commit himself to the Prophet of the truth alone.

And we are all able to judge of Him, whether he is a prophet, even although we be wholly unlearned, and novices in sophisms, and unskilled in geometry, and uninitiated in music.

For God, as caring for all, has made the discovery concerning Himself easier to all, in order that neither the barbarians might be powerless, nor the Greeks unable to find Him.

Therefore the discovery concerning Him is easy; and thus it is:--

Chapter X - Test of the Prophet

"If he is a Prophet, and is able to know how the world was made, and the things that are in it, and the things that shall be to the end, if He has foretold us anything, and we have ascertained that it has been perfectly accomplished, we easily believe that the things shall be which He says are to be, from the things that have been already; we believe Him, I say, as not only knowing, but foreknowing.

To whom then, however limited an understanding he may have, does it not appear, that it behoves us, with respect to the things that are pleasing to God, to believe beyond all others Him who beyond all men knows, even though He has not learned?

Wherefore, if any one should be unwilling to concede the power of knowing the truth to such an one--I mean to Him who has foreknowledge through the divinity of the Spirit that is in Him--conceding the power of knowing to any one else, is he not void of understanding, in conceding to him who is no prophet, that power of knowing which he would not concede to the Prophet?

Chapter XI - Ignorance, Knowledge, Foreknowledge

"Wherefore, before all things, we must test the Prophet with all judgment by means of the prophetic promise; and having ascertained Him to be the Prophet, we must undoubtedly follow the other words of His teaching; and having confidence concerning things hoped for, we must conduct ourselves according to the first judgment, knowing that He who tells us these things has not a nature to lie.

Wherefore, if any of the things that are afterwards spoken by Him do not appear to us to be well spoken, we must know that it is not that it has been spoken amiss, but that it is that we have not conceived it aright.

For ignorance does not judge knowledge, and so neither is knowledge competent truly to judge foreknowledge; but foreknowledge affords knowledge to the ignorant.

Chapter XII - Doctrine of the True Prophet

"Hence, O beloved Clement, if you would know the things pertaining to God, you have to learn them from Him alone, because He alone knows the truth.

For if any one else knows anything, he has received it from Him or from His disciples.

And this is His doctrine and true proclamation, that there is one God, whose work the world is; who being altogether righteous, shall certainly at some time render to every one according to his deeds.

Chapter XIII - Future Rewards and Punishments

"For there is every necessity, that he who says that God is by His nature righteous, should believe also that the souls of men are immortal:
for where would be His justice, when some, having lived piously, have been evil-treated, and sometimes violently cut off, while others who have been wholly impious, and have indulged in luxurious living, have died the common death of men?
Since therefore, without all contradiction, God who is good is also just, He shall not otherwise be known to be just, unless the soul after its separation from the body be immortal, so that the wicked man, being in hell, [6] as having here received his good things, may there be punished for his sins; and the good man, who has been punished here for his sins, may then, as in the bosom of the righteous, be constituted an heir of good things. Since therefore God is righteous, it is fully evident to us that there is a judgment, and that souls are immortal.

Chapter XIV - Righteousness and Unrighteousness

"But if any one, according to the opinion of this Simon the Samaritan, will not admit that God is just, to whom then can any one ascribe justice, or the possibility of it?
For if the Root of all have it not, there is every necessity to think that it must be impossible to find it in human nature, which, is, as it were, the fruit.
And if it is to be found in man, how much more in God!
But if righteousness can be found nowhere, neither in God nor in man, then neither can unrighteousness. But there is such a thing as righteousness, for unrighteousness takes its name from the existence of righteousness; for it is called unrighteousness, when righteousness is compared with it, and is found to be opposite to it.

Chapter XV - Pairs

"Hence therefore God, teaching men with respect to the truth of existing things, being Himself one, has distinguished all principles into pairs and opposites, [7] Himself being one and sole God from the beginning, having made heaven and earth, day and night, light and fire, sun and moon, life and death.
But man alone amongst these He made self-controlling, having a fitness to be either righteous or unrighteous.
To him also he hath varied the figures of combinations, placing before him small things first, and great ones afterwards, such as the world and eternity.
But the world that now is, is temporary; that which shall be, is eternal.
First is ignorance, then knowledge. So also has He arranged the leaders of prophecy.
For, since the present world is female, as a mother bringing forth the souls of her children, but the world to come is male, as a father receiving his children from their mother, therefore in this world there come a succession of prophets, as being sons of the world to come, and having knowledge of men.
And if pious men had understood this mystery, they would never have gone astray, but even now they should have known that Simon, who now enthralls all men, is a fellow-worker of error and deceit.
Now, the doctrine of the prophetic rule is as follows.

Chapter XVI - Man's Ways Opposite to God's

"As in the beginning God, who is one, like a right hand and a left, made the heavens first and then the earth, so also He constituted all the combinations in order; but upon men He no more does this, but varies all the combinations.
For whereas from Him the greater things come first, and the inferior second, we find the opposite in men--the first worse, and the second superior.
Therefore from Adam, who was made after the image of God, there sprang first the unrighteous Cain, and then the righteous Abel.
Again, from him who amongst you is called Deucalion, [8] two forms of spirits were sent forth, the impure namely, and the pure, first the black raven, and then the white dove. From Abraham also, the patriarchs of our nation, two firsts [9] sprang--Ishmael first, then Isaac, who was blessed of God.
And from Isaac himself, in like manner, there were again two--Esau the profane, and Jacob the pious.

So, first in birth, as the first born in the world, was the high priest Aaron, then the lawgiver Moses.

Chapter XVII - First the Worse, Then the Better

"In like manner, the combination with respect to Elias, which behoved to have come, has been willingly put off to another time, having determined to enjoy it conveniently hereafter. [10]Wherefore, also, he who was among those born of woman came first; then he who was among the sons of men came second.

It were possible, following this order, to perceive to what series Simon belongs, who came before me to the Gentiles, and to which I belong who have come after him, and have come in upon him as light upon darkness, as knowledge upon ignorance, as healing upon disease.

And thus, as the true Prophet has told us, a false prophet must first come from some deceiver; and then, in like manner, after the removal of the holy place, the true Gospel must be secretly sent abroad for the rectification of the heresies that shall be.

After this, also, towards the end, Antichrist must first come, and then our Jesus must be revealed to be indeed the Christ; and after this, the eternal light having sprung up, all the things of darkness must disappear.

Chapter XVIII - Mistake About Simon Magus

"Since, then, as I said, some men do not know the rule of combination, thence they do not know who is my precursor Simon.

For if he were known, he would not be believed; but now, not being known, he is improperly believed; and though his deeds are those of a hater, he is loved; and though an enemy, he is received as a friend; and though he be death, he is desired as a saviour; and though fire, he is esteemed as light; and though a deceiver, he is believed as a speaker of truth."

Then I Clement, when I heard this, said, "Who then, I pray you, is this who is such a deceiver? I should like to be informed."

Then said Peter:

"If you wish to learn, it is in your power to know it from those from whom I also got accurate information on all points respecting him.

Chapter XIX - Justa, a Proselyte

"There is amongst us one Justa, a Syro-Phoenician, by race a Canaanite, whose daughter was oppressed with a grievous disease. [11]And she came to our Lord, crying out, and entreating that He would heal her daughter.

But He, being asked also by us, said, It is not lawful to heal the Gentiles, who are like to dogs on account of their using various [12] meats and practices, while the table in the kingdom has been given to the sons of Israel.'

But she, hearing this, and begging to partake like a dog of the crumbs that fall from this table, having changed what she was, [13] by living like the sons of the kingdom, she obtained healing for her daughter, as she asked.

For she being a Gentile, and remaining in the same course of life, He would not have healed had she remained a Gentile, on account of its not being lawful to heal her as a Gentile. [14]

Chapter XX - Divorced for the Faith

"She, therefore, having taken up a manner of life according to the law, was, with the daughter who had been healed, driven out from her home by her husband, whose sentiments were opposed to ours.

But she, being faithful to her engagements, and being in affluent circumstances, remained a widow herself, but gave her daughter in marriage to a certain man who was attached to the true faith, and who was poor.

And, abstaining from marriage for the sake of her daughter, she bought two boys and educated them, and had them in place of sons.

And they being educated from their boyhood with Simon Magus, have learned all things concerning him.

For such was their friendship, that they were associated with him in all things in which he wished to unite with them.

Chapter XXI - Justa's Adopted Sons, Associates with Simon

"These men having fallen in with Zacchaeus, who sojourned here, and having received the word of truth from him, and having repented of their former innovations, and immediately denouncing Simon as being privy with him in all things, as soon as I came to sojourn here, they came to me with their foster-mother, being presented to me by him, Zacchaeus, and ever since they continue with me, enjoying instructions in the truth."

When Peter had said this, he sent for them, and charged them that they should accurately relate to me all things concerning Simon.

And they, having called God to witness that in nothing they would falsify, proceeded with the relation.

Chapter XXII - Doctrines of Simon

First Aquila began to speak in this wise:

"Listen, O dearest brother, that you may know accurately everything about this man, whose he is, and what, and whence; and what the things are which he does, and how and why he does them.[15]This Simon is the son of Antonius and Rachel, a Samaritan by race, of the village of Gitthae, which is six schoeni distant from the city.

He having disciplined himself greatly in Alexandria,[16] and being very powerful in magic, and being ambitious, wishes to be accounted a certain supreme power, greater even than the God who created the world.

And sometimes intimating that he is Christ, he styles himself the Standing One.[17] And this epithet he employs, as intimating that he shall always stand, and as not having any cause of corruption so that his body should fall.

And he neither says that the God who created the world is the Supreme, nor does he believe that the dead will be raised.

He rejects Jerusalem, and substitutes Mount Gerizzim for it.

Instead of our Christ, he proclaims himself.

The things of the law he explains by his own presumption; and he says, indeed, that there is to be a judgment, but he does not expect it.

For if he were persuaded that he shall be judged by God, he would not dare be impious towards God Himself.

Whence some not knowing that, using religion as a cloak, he spoils the things of the truth, and faithfully believing the hope and the judgment which in some way he says are to be, are ruined.

Chapter XXIII - Simon a Disciple of the Baptist

"But that he came to deal with the doctrines of religion happened on this wise.

There was one John, a day-baptist,[18] who was also, according to the method of combination, the forerunner of our Lord Jesus; and as the Lord had twelve apostles, bearing the number of the twelve months of the sun, so also he, John, had thirty chief men, fulfilling the monthly reckoning of the moon, in which number was a certain woman called Helena,[19] that not even this might be without a dispensational significance.

For a woman, being half a man, made up the imperfect number of the triacontad; as also in the case of the moon, whose revolution does not make the complete course of the month.[20]But of these thirty, the first and the most esteemed by John was Simon; and the reason of his not being chief after the death of John was as follows:--

Chapter XXIV - Electioneering Stratagems

"He being absent in Egypt for the practice of magic, and John being killed, Dositheus desiring the leadership, [21] falsely gave out that Simon was dead, and succeeded to the seat.

But Simon, returning not long after, and strenuously holding by the place as his own, when he met with Dositheus did not demand the place, knowing that a man who has attained power beyond his expectations cannot be removed from it. Wherefore with pretended friendship he gives himself for a while to the second place, under Dositheus.

But taking his place after a few days among the thirty fellow-disciples, he began to malign Dositheus as not delivering the instructions correctly.

And this he said that he did, not through unwillingness to deliver them correctly, but through ignorance.

And on one occasion, Dositheus, perceiving that this artful accusation of Simon was dissipating the opinion of him with respect to many, so that they did not think that he was the Standing One, came in a rage to the usual place of meeting, and finding Simon, struck him with a staff.

But it seemed to pass through the body of Simon as if he had been smoke.

Thereupon Dositheus, being confounded, said to him, If you are the Standing One, I also will worship you.'

Then Simon said that he was; and Dositheus, knowing that he himself was not the Standing One, fell down and worshipped; and associating himself with the twenty-nine chiefs, he raised Simon to his own place of repute; and thus, not many days after, Dositheus himself, while he (Simon) stood, fell down and died.

Chapter XXV - Simon's Deceit

"But Simon is going about in company with Helena, and even till now, as you see, is stirring up the people.

And he says that he has brought down this Helena from the highest heavens to the world; being queen, as the all-bearing being, and wisdom, for whose sake, says he, the Greeks and barbarians fought, having before their eyes but an image of truth; [22] for she, who really is the truth, was then with the chiefest god.

Moreover, by cunningly explaining certain things of this sort, made up from Grecian myths, he deceives many; especially as he performs many signal marvels, so that if we did not know that he does these things by magic, we ourselves should also have been deceived.

But whereas we were his fellow-labourers at the first, so long as he did such things without doing wrong to the interests of religion; now that he has madly begun to attempt to deceive those who are religious, we have withdrawn from him.

Chapter XXVI - His Wickedness

"For he even began to commit murder [23] as himself disclosed to us, as a friend to friends, that, having separated the soul of a child from its own body by horrid incantations, as his assistant for the exhibition of anything that he pleased, and having drawn the likeness of the boy, he has it set up in the inner room where he sleeps, saying that he once formed the boy of air, by divine arts, and having painted his likeness, he gave him back again to the air.

And he explains that he did the deed thus.

He says that the first soul of man, being turned into the nature of heat, drew to itself, and sucked in the surrounding air, after the fashion of a gourd; [24] and then that he changed it into water, when it was within the form of the spirit; and he said that he changed into the nature of blood the air that was in it, which could not be poured out on account of the consistency of the spirit, and that he made the blood solidified into flesh; then, the flesh being thus consolidated, that he exhibited a man not made from earth, but from air.

And thus, having persuaded himself that he was able to make a new sort of man, he said that he reversed the changes, and again restored him to the air.

And when he told this to others, he was believed; but by us who were present at his ceremonies he was religiously disbelieved.

Wherefore we denounced his impieties, and withdrew from him."

Chapter XXVII - His Promises

When Aquila had thus spoken, his brother Nicetas said:

"It is necessary, O Clement our brother, for me to mention what has been left out by Aquila.

For, in the first place, God is witness that we assisted him in no impious work, but that we looked on while he wrought; and as long as he did harmless things, and exhibited them, we were also pleased.

But when, in order to deceive the godly, he said that he did, by means of godhead, the things that were done by magic, we no longer endured him, though he made us many promises, especially that our statues should be thought worthy of a place in the temple, [25] and that we should be thought to be gods, and should be worshipped by the multitude, and should be honoured by kings, and should be thought worthy of public honours, and enriched with boundless wealth.

Chapter XXVIII - Fruitless Counsel

"These things, and things reckoned greater than these, he promised us, on condition only that we should associate with him, and keep silence as to the wickedness of his undertaking, so that the scheme of his deceit might succeed.

But still we would not consent, but even counselled him to desist from such madness, saying to him:

We, O Simon, remembering our friendship towards you from our childhood, and out of affection for you, give you good counsel.

Desist from this attempt.

You cannot be a God.

Fear Him who is really God.

Know that you are a man, and that the time of your life is short; and though you should get great riches, or even become a king, few things accrue to the short time of your life for enjoyment, and things wickedly gotten soon flee away, and procure everlasting punishment for the adventurer. Wherefore we counsel you to fear God, by whom the soul of every one must be judged for the deeds that he hath done here.'

Chapter XXIX - Immortality of the Soul

"When he heard this he laughed; and when we asked him why he laughed at us for giving him good counsel, he answered:

I laugh at your foolish supposition, because you believe that the soul of man is immortal.' Then I said:

We do not wonder, O Simon, at your attempting to deceive us, but we are confounded at the way in which you deceive even yourself.

Tell me, O Simon, even if no one else has been fully convinced that the soul is immortal, at all events you and we ought to be so:

you as having separated one from a human body, and conversed with it, and laid your commands upon it; and we as having been present, and heard your commands, and clearly witnessed the performance of what was ordered.'

Then said Simon:

I know what you mean; but you know nothing of the matters concerning which you reason.'

Then said Nicetas:

If you know, speak; but if you do not know, do not suppose that we can be deceived by your saying that you know, and that we do not.

For we are not so childish, that you can sow in us a shrewd suspicion that we should think that you know some unutterable things, and so that you should take and hold us in subjection, by holding us in restraint through means of desire.'

Chapter XXX - An Argument

"Then Simon said:

I am aware that you know that I separated a soul from a human body; but I know that you are ignorant that it is not the soul of the dead person that ministers to me, for it does not exist; but a certain demon works, pretending to be the soul.'

Then said Nicetas:

Many incredible things we have heard in our lifetime, but aught more senseless than this speech we do not expect ever to hear. For if a demon pretends to be the soul of the dead person, what is the use of the soul at all, that it should be separated from the body? Were not we ourselves present and heard you conjuring the soul from the body?

And how comes it that, when one is conjured, another who is not conjured obeys, as if it were frightened?

And you yourself, when at any time we have asked you why the conferences sometimes cease, did not you say that the soul, having fulfilled the time upon earth which it was to have passed in the body, goes to Hades?

And you added, that the souls of those who commit suicide are not easily permitted to come, because, having gone home into Hades, they are guarded.'"

Chapter XXXI - A Dilemma

Nicetas having thus spoken, Aquila himself in turn said:
"This only should I wish to learn of you, Simon, whether it is the soul or whether it is a demon that is conjured:
what is it afraid of, that it does not despise the conjuration?
Then Simon said:
It knows that it should suffer punishment if it were disobedient.'
Then said Aquila: Therefore, if the soul comes when conjured, there is also a judgment. If, therefore, souls are immortal, assuredly there is also a judgment. As you say, then, that those which are conjured on wicked business are punished if they disobey, how are you not afraid to compel them, when those that are compelled are punished for disobedience?

For it is not wonderful that you do not already suffer for your doings, seeing the judgment has not yet come, when you are to suffer the penalty of those deeds which you have compelled others to do, and when that which has been done under compulsion shall be pardoned, as having been out of respect for the oath which led to the evil action.' [26]And he hearing this was enraged, and threatened death to us if we did not keep silence as to his doings."

Chapter XXXII - Simon's Prodigies

Aquila having thus spoken, I Clement inquired:
"What, then, are the prodigies that he works?"
And they told me that he makes statues walk, and that he rolls himself on the fire, and is not burnt; and sometimes he flies; and he makes loaves of stones; he becomes a serpent; he transforms himself into a goat; he becomes two-faced; he changes himself into gold; he opens lockfast gates; he melts iron; at banquets he produces images of all manner of forms.

In his house he makes dishes be seen as borne of themselves to wait upon him, no bearers being seen.

I wondered when I heard them speak thus; but many bore witness that they had been present, and had seen such things.

Chapter XXXIII - Doctrine of Pairs

These things having been thus spoken, the excellent Peter himself also proceeded to speak:[27]"You must perceive, brethren, the truth of the rule of conjunction, from which he who departs not cannot be misled.

For since, as we have said, we see all things in pairs and contraries, and as the night is first, and then the day; and first ignorance, then knowledge; first disease, then healing, so the things of error come first into our life, then truth supervenes, as the physician upon the disease.

Therefore straightway, when our God-loved nation was about to be ransomed from the oppression of the Egyptians, first diseases were produced by means of the rod turned into a serpent, which was given to Aaron, and then remedies were superinduced by the prayers of Moses.

And now also, when the Gentiles are about to be ransomed from the superstition with respect to idols, wickedness, which reigns over them, has by anticipation sent forth her ally like another serpent, even this Simon whom you see, who works wonders to astonish and deceive, not signs of healing to convert and save.

Wherefore it behoves you also from the miracles that are done to judge the doers, what is the character of the performer, and what that of the deed.

If he do unprofitable miracles, he is the agent of wickedness; but if he do profitable things, he is a leader of goodness.

Chapter XXXIV - Useless and Philanthropic Miracles

"Those, then, are useless signs, which you say that Simon did.

But I say that the making statues walk, and rolling himself on burning coals, and becoming a dragon, and being changed into a goat, and flying in the air, and all such things, not being for the healing of man, are of a nature to deceive many.

But the miracles of compassionate truth are philanthropic, such as you have heard that the Lord did, and that I after Him accomplish by my prayers; at which most of you have been present, some being freed from all kinds of diseases, and some from demons, some having their hands restored, and some their feet, some recovering their eyesight, and some their hearing, and whatever else a man can do, being of a philanthropic spirit."

Chapter XXXV - Discussion Postponed

When Peter had thus spoken, towards dawn Zacchaeus entered and saluted us, and said to Peter: "Simon puts off the inquiry till to-morrow; for to-day is his Sabbath, which occurs at intervals of eleven days."

To him Peter answered:

"Say to Simon, Whenever thou wishest; and know thou that we are always in readiness to meet thee, by divine providence, when thou desirest."

And Zacchaeus hearing this, went out to return the answer.

Chapter XXXVI - All for the Best

But he (Peter) saw me disheartened, and asked the reason; and being told that it proceeded from no cause but the postponement of the inquiry, [28] he said:

"He who has apprehended that the world is regulated by the good providence of God, O beloved Clement, is not vexed by things howsoever occurring, considering that things take their course advantageously under the providence of the Ruler.

Whence, knowing that He is just, and living with a good conscience, he knows how by right reason to shake off from his soul any annoyance that befalls him, because, when complete, it must come to some unknown good.

Now then, let not Simon the magician's postponement of the inquiry grieve you; for perhaps it has happened from the providence of God for your profit.

Wherefore I shall not scruple to speak to you as being my special friend.

Chapter XXXVII - Spies in the Enemy's Camp

"Some [29] of our people attend feignedly upon Simon as companions, as if they were persuaded by his most atheistic error, in order that they may learn his purpose and disclose it to us, so that we may be able to encounter this terrible man on favourable terms.

And now I have learned from them what arguments he is going to employ in the discussion.

And knowing this, I give thanks to God on the one hand, and I congratulate you on the other, on the postponement of the discussion; for you, being instructed by me before the discussion, of the arguments that are to be used by him for the destruction of the ignorant, will be able to listen without danger of falling.

Chapter XXXVIII - Corruption of the Law

"For the Scriptures have had joined to them many falsehoods against God on this account.

The prophet Moses having by the order of God delivered the law, with the explanations, to certain chosen men, some seventy in number, in order that they also might instruct such of the people as chose, after a little the written law had added to it certain falsehoods contrary to the law of God, [30] who made the heaven and the earth, and all things in them; the wicked one having dared to work this for some righteous purpose.

And this took place in reason and judgment, that those might be convicted who should dare to listen to the things written against God, and those who, through love towards Him, should not only disbelieve the things spoken against Him, but should not even endure to hear them at all, even if they should happen to be true, judging it much safer to incur danger with respect to religious faith, than to live with an evil conscience on account of blasphemous words.

Chapter XXXIX - Tactics

"Simon, therefore, as I learn, intends to come into public, and to speak of those chapters against God that are added to the Scriptures, for the sake of temptation, that he may seduce as many wretched ones as he can from the love of God.

For we do not wish to say in public that these chapters are added to the Bible, since we should thereby perplex the unlearned multitudes, and so accomplish the purpose of this wicked Simon.

For they not having yet the power of discerning, would flee from us as impious; or, as if not only the blasphemous chapters were false, they would even withdraw from the word.

Wherefore we are under a necessity of assenting to the false chapters, and putting questions in return to him concerning them, to draw him into a strait, and to give in private an explanation of the chapters that are spoken against God to the well-disposed after a trial of their faith; and of this there is but one way, and that a brief one.

It is this. [31]

Chapter XL - Preliminary Instruction

"Everything that is spoken or written against God is false.

But that we say this truly, not only for the sake of reputation, but for the sake of truth, I shall convince you when my discourse has proceeded a little further.

Whence you, my most beloved Clement, ought not to be sorry at Simon's having interposed a day between this and the discussion.

For to-day, before the discussion, you shall be instructed concerning the chapters added to the Scriptures; and then in the discussion concerning the only one and good God, the Maker also of the world, you ought not to be distracted.

But in the discussion you will even wonder how impious men, overlooking the multitudes of things that are spoken in the Scriptures for God, and looking at those that are spoken against Him, gladly bring these forward; and thus the hearers, by reason of ignorance, believing the things against God, become outcasts from His kingdom.

Wherefore you, by advantage of the postponement, learning the mystery of the Scriptures, and gaining the means of not sinning against God, will incomparably rejoice."

Chapter XLI - Asking for Information, Not Contradiction

Then I Clement, hearing this, said:

"Truly I rejoice, and I give thanks to God, who in all things doeth well.

However, he knows that I shall be able to think nothing other than that all things are for God.

Wherefore do not suppose that I ask questions, as doubting the words concerning God, [32] or those that are to be spoken, but rather that I may learn, and so be able myself to instruct another who is ingenuously willing to learn.

Wherefore tell me what are the falsehoods added to the Scriptures, and how it comes that they are really false."

Then Peter answered:

"Even although you had not asked me, I should have gone on in order, and afforded you the exposition of these matters, as I promised.

Learn, then, how the Scriptures misrepresent Him in many respects, that you may know when you happen upon them.

Chapter XLII - Right Notions of God Essential to Holiness

"But what I am going to tell you will be sufficient by way of example. But I do not think, my dear Clement, that any one who possesses ever so little love to God and ingenuousness, will be able to take in, or even to hear, the things that are spoken against Him.

For how is it that he can have a monarchic [33] soul, and be holy, who supposes that there are many gods, and not one only?

But even if there be but one, who will cherish zeal to be holy, that finds in Him many defects, since he will hope that the Beginning of all things, by reason of the defects of his own nature, will not visit the crimes of others?

Chapter XLIII - A Priori Argument on the Divine Attributes

"Wherefore, far be it from us to believe that the Lord of all, who made the heaven and the earth, and all things that are in them, shares His government with others, or that He lies.

For if He lies, then who speaks truth?

Or that He makes experiments as in ignorance; for then who foreknows?

And if He deliberates, and changes His purpose, who is perfect in understanding and permanent in design?

If He envies, who is above rivalry?

If He hardens hearts, who makes wise?

If He makes blind and deaf, who has given sight and hearing?

If He commits pilfering, who administers justice?

If He mocks, who is sincere?

If He is weak, who is omnipotent?

If He is unjust, who is just?

If He makes evil things, who shall make good things?

If He does evil, who shall do good?

Chapter XLIV - The Same Continued

"But if He desires the fruitful hill, [34] whose then are all things? If He is false, who then is true?

If He dwells in a tabernacle, who is without bounds?

If He is fond of fat, and sacrifices, and offerings, and drink-offerings, who then is without need, and who is holy, and pure, and perfect?

If He is pleased with candles and candlesticks, who then placed the luminaries in heaven?

If He dwells in shadow, and darkness, and storm, and smoke, who is the light that lightens the universe?

If He comes with trumpets, and shoutings, and darts, and arrows, who is the looked-for tranquillity of all?
If He loves war, who then wishes peace?
If He makes evil things, who makes good things?
If He is without affection, who is a lover of men?
If He is not faithful to His promises, who shall be trusted?
If He loves the wicked, and adulterers, and murderers, who shall be a just judge?
If He changes His mind, who is stedfast?
If He chooses evil men, who then takes the part of the good?

Chapter XLV - How God is to Be Thought of

"Wherefore, Clement, my son, beware of thinking otherwise of God, than that He is the only God, and Lord, and Father, good and righteous, the Creator, long-suffering, merciful, the sustainer, the benefactor, ordaining love of men, counselling purity, immortal and making immortal, incomparable, dwelling in the souls of the good, that cannot be contained and yet is contained, [35] who has fixed the great world as a centre in space, who has spread out the heavens and solidified the earth, who has stored up the water, who has disposed the stars in the sky, who has made the fountains flow in the earth, has produced faults, has raised up mountains, hath set bounds to the sea, has ordered winds and blasts, who by the spirit of counsel has kept safely the body comprehended in a boundless sea.

Chapter XLVI - Judgment to Come

"This is our Judge, to whom it behoves us to look. and to regulate our own souls, thinking all things in His favour, speaking well of Him, persuaded that by His long-suffering He brings to light the obstinacy of all, and is alone good.
And He, at the end of all, shall sit as a just Judge upon every one of those who have attempted what they ought not."

Chapter XLVII - A Pertinent Question

When I Clement heard this, I said, "Truly, this is a godliness; truly this is piety."
And again I said:
"I would learn, therefore, why the Bible has written anything of this sort?
For I remember that you said that it was for the conviction of those who should dare to believe anything that was spoken against God.
But since you permit us, we venture to ask, at your command:
If any one, most beloved Peter, should choose to say to us, The Scriptures are true, although to you the things spoken against God seem to be false,' how should we answer him?"

Chapter XLVIII - A Particular Case

Then Peter answered:
"You speak well in your inquiry; for it will be for your safety.
Therefore listen:
Since there are many things that are spoken by the Scriptures against God, as time presses on account of the evening, ask with respect to any one matter that you please, and I will explain it, showing that it is false, not only because it is spoken against God, but because it is really false."
Then I answered: "I wish to learn how, when the Scriptures say that God is ignorant, you can show that He knows?"

Chapter XLIX - Reductio a.d. Absurdum

Then Peter answered:
"You have presented us with a matter that can easily be answered.
However, listen, how God is ignorant of nothing, but even foreknows.
But first answer me what I ask of you.
He who wrote the Bible, and told how the world was made, and said that God does not foreknow, was he a man or not?"
Then I said:
"He was a man."
Then Peter answered:
"How, then, was it possible for him, being a man, to know assuredly how the world was made, and that God does not foreknow?"

Chapter L - A Satisfactory Answer

Then I, already perceiving the explanation, smiled, and said that he was a prophet.
And Peter said:
"If, then, he was a prophet, being a man, he was ignorant of nothing, by reason of his having received foreknowledge from God; how then, should He, who gave to man the gift of foreknowledge, being God, Himself be ignorant?"
And I said:
"You have spoken rightly."
Then Peter said:
"Come with me one step further.
It being acknowledged by us that God foreknows all things, there is every necessity that the scriptures are false which say that He is ignorant, and those are true which say that He knows."
Then said I:
"It must needs be so."

Chapter LI - Weigh in the Balance

Then Peter said:
"If, therefore, some of the Scriptures are true and some false, with good reason said our Master, Be ye good money-changers,' [36] inasmuch as in the Scriptures there are some true sayings and some spurious.
And to those who err by reason of the false scriptures He fitly showed the cause of their error, saying, Ye do therefore err, not knowing the true things of the Scriptures; [37] for this reason ye are ignorant also of the power of God.'"
Then said I:
"You have spoken very excellently."

Chapter LII - Sins of the Saints Denied

Then Peter answered:
"Assuredly, with good reason, I neither believe anything against God, nor against the just men recorded in the law, taking for granted that they are impious imaginations.
For, as I am persuaded, neither was Adam a transgressor, who was fashioned by the hands of God; nor was Noah drunken, who was found righteous above all the world; [38] nor did Abraham live with three wives at once, who, on account of his sobriety, was thought worthy of a numerous posterity; nor did Jacob associate with four--of whom two were sisters--who was the father of the twelve tribes, and who intimated the coming of the presence of our Master; nor was Moses a murderer, nor did he learn to judge from an idolatrous priest--he who set forth the law of God to all the world, and for his right judgment has been testified to as a faithful steward.

The Epistles of Clement

Chapter LIII - Close of the Conference

"But of these and such like things I shall afford you an explanation in due time.

But for the rest, since, as you see, the evening has come upon us, let what has been said be enough for to-day.

But whenever you wish, and about whatever you wish, ask boldly of us, and we shall gladly explain it at once."

Thus having spoken, he rose up.

And then, having partaken of food, we turned to sleep, for the night had come upon us.

Footnotes:

1. [With but two exceptions, these names, or their equivalents, occur in Recognitions, iii. 68, where importance is attached to the number twelve.

Comp. also Recognitions, ii. 1.

A comparison of these lists favors the theory of a common documentary basis.--R.]

2. Literally, "to be boiled out of me."

3. Eccles. iii. 1.

4. "Were deceived" is not in the text, but the sense demands some such expression should be supplied.

5. philologoi, ou philosophoi, "lovers of words, not lovers of wisdom."

6. Lit. Hades.

7. Literally, "twofoldly and oppositely."

[On the doctrine of pairs compare chap. 33, iii. 23, Recognitions, iii. 61.--R.]

8. Noah.

9. For "first" Wieseler conjectures "different,"--two different persons.

10. In this sentence the text is probably corrupted.

The general meaning seems to be, that he does not enter fully at present into the subject of Elias, or John the Baptist, and the Christ, the greatest among the sons of men, coming after, but that he will return to the subject on a fitting occasion.

11. [Chaps. 19-21 are peculiar to the Homilies, though in Recognitions, vii. 32, Justa is named as having purchased and educated Niceta and Aquila.--R.]

12. For diaphorois Duncker proposes adiaphorois, "meats without distinction."

13. That is, having caused to be a Gentile, by abstaining from forbidden foods.

14. There are several various readings in this sentence, and none of them can be strictly construed; but the general sense is obvious.

15. [For the parallel account of Simon, given also by Aquila, see Recognitions, ii. 7-15.--R.]

16. The Vatican ms. adds, "which is in Egypt (or, on the Nile), in Greek culture."

17. [Comp. Recognitions, i. 72--R.]

18. A day-baptist is taken to mean "one who baptizes every day."

19. [Called "Luna" in the Recognitions.--R.]

20. [Peculiar, in this detailed form, to the Homilies.--R.]

21. [Compare the varied account in Recognitions, ii. 8.--R.]

22. We have here an allusion to the tradition that it was only an image of Helen that was taken to Troy, and not the real Helen herself.

23. [With the account of Simon's doings in chaps. 26-32 compare Recognitions, ii. 9, 10, 13-15; iii. 47.--R.]

24. Which was used by the ancients as cupping-glasses are now used.

25. The Vatican ms. and Epitome read, "that a shrine and statues should be erected in honour of us."

26. The Latin translates:

"as having preferred the oath to the evil action."

27. [Chaps. 32, 34, find a parallel in Recognitions, iii. 59, 60, at the close of the discussion with Simon.--R.]

28. [Comp. Recognitions, i. 21.--R.]

29. [From chap. 27 to iii. 28 the matter is peculiar to the Homilies.

The views stated are obviously coloured by the Gnostic Ebionism of the author.--R.]

30. The Vatican ms. reads:

"against the only God."

31. [This view of the Scriptures, as held by Peter, is one of the marked characteristics of the Homilies.--R.]

32. The text has hupo, "by," which has been altered into huper. Davis would read sou, "by you."

33. Cotelerius doubts whether this expression means a soul ruling over his body, or a soul disposed to favor monarchical rule.

The former explanation seems more probable.

34. Wieseler considers this corrupt, and amends:

"if He desires more."

35. The Latin has here, "imperceptus et perceptus;" but Wieseler points out that choroumenos has reference to God's dwelling in the souls of the good, and thus He is contained by them.

36. This is quoted three times in the Homilies as a saying of our Lord, viz., here and in Homily III. chap. 50, and Homily XVIII. chap. 20.

It is probably taken from one of the apocryphal Gospels.

In Homily XVIII. chap. 20 the meaning is shown to be, that as it is the part of a money-changer to distinguish spurious coins from genuine, so it is part of a Christian to distinguish false statements from true.

37. A corruption of the texts, Matt. xxii. 29; Mark xii. 24.

38. Gen. vii. 1.

Homily III

Chapter I - The Morning of the Discussion

Two days, therefore, having elapsed, and while the third was dawning, I Clement, and the rest of our companions, being roused about the second cock-crowing, in order to the discussion with Simon, found the lamp still alight, and Peter kneeling in prayer.

Therefore, having finished his supplication, and turning round, and seeing us in readiness to hear, he said: [1] --

Chapter II - Simon's Design

"I wish you to know that those who, according to our arrangement, associate with Simon that they may learn his intentions, and submit them to us, so that we may be able to cope with his variety of wickedness, these men have sent to me, and informed me that Simon to-day is, as he arranged, prepared to come before all, and show from the Scriptures that He who made the heaven and the earth, and all things in them, is not the Supreme God, but that there is another, unknown and supreme, as being in an unspeakable manner God of gods; and that He sent two gods, one of whom is he who made the world, and the other he who gave the law.

And these things he contrives to say, that he may dissipate the right faith of those who would worship the one and only God who made heaven and earth.

Chapter III - His Object

"When I heard this, how was I not disheartened!

Wherefore I wished you also, my brethren, who associate with me, to know that I am beyond measure grieved in my soul, seeing the wicked one awake for the temptation of men, and men wholly indifferent about their own salvation.

For to those from amongst the Gentiles who were about being persuaded respecting the earthly images that they are no gods, he has contrived to bring in opinions of many other gods, in order that, if they cease from the polytheo-mania, they may be deceived to speak otherwise, and even worse than they now do, against the sole government of God, so that they may not yet value the truths connected with that monarchy, and may never be able to obtain mercy.

And for the sake of this attempt Simon comes to do battle with us, armed with the false chapters of the Scriptures.

And what is more dreadful, he is not afraid to dogmatize thus against the true God from the prophets whom he does not in fact believe.

Chapter IV - Snares Laid for the Gentiles

"And with us, indeed, who have had handed down from our forefathers the worship of the God who made all things, and also the mystery of the books which are able to deceive, he will not prevail; but with those from amongst the Gentiles who have the polytheistic fancy bred in them, and who know not the falsehoods of the Scriptures, he will prevail much.

And not only he; but if any other shall recount to those from among the Gentiles any vain, dreamlike, richly set out story against God, he will be believed, because from their childhood their minds are accustomed to take in things spoken against God.

And few there shall be of them, as a few out of a multitude, who through ingenuousness shall not be willing so much as to hear an evil word against the God who made all things.

And to these alone from amongst the Gentiles it shall be vouchsafed to be saved.

Let not any one of you, therefore, altogether complain of Simon, or of any one else; for nothing happens unjustly, since even the falsehoods of Scripture are with good reason presented for a test."

Chapter V - Use of Errors

Then I Clement, hearing this, said:
"How say you, my lord, that even the falsehoods of the Scriptures are set forth happily for the proof of men?"
And he answered:
"The falsehoods of the Scriptures have been permitted to be written for a certain righteous reason, at the demand of evil.
And when I say happily, I mean this:
In the account of God, the wicked one, not loving God less than the good one, is exceeded by the good in this one thing only, that he, not pardoning those who are impious on account of ignorance, through love towards that which is profound, desires the destruction of the impious; but the good one desires to present them with a remedy.
For the good one desires all to be healed by repentance, but saves those only who know God.
But those who know Him not He does not heal:
not that He does not wish to do so, but because it is not lawful to afford to those who, through want of judgment, are like to irrational animals, the good things which have been prepared for the children of the kingdom.

Chapter VI - Purgatory and Hell

"Such is the nature of the one and only God, who made the world, and who created us, and who has given us all things, that as long as any one is within the limit of piety, and does not blaspheme His Holy Spirit, through His love towards him He brings the soul to Himself by reason of His love towards it.
And although it be sinful, it is His nature to save it, after it has been suitably punished for the deeds it hath done.
But if any one shall deny Him, or in any other way be guilty of impiety against Him, and then shall repent, he shall be punished indeed for the sins he hath committed against Him, but he shall be saved, because he turned and lived.
And perhaps excessive piety and supplication shall even be delivered from punishment, ignorance being admitted as a reason for the pardon of sin after repentance. [2]But those who do not repent shall be destroyed by the punishment of fire, even though in all other things they are most holy.
But, as I said, at an appointed time a fifth [3] part, being punished with eternal fire, shall be consumed.
For they cannot endure for ever who have been impious against the one God.

Chapter VII - What is Impiety?

"But impiety against Him is, in the matter of religion, to die saying there is another God, whether superior or inferior, or in any way saying that there is one besides Him who really is.
For He who truly is, is He whose form the body of man bears; for whose sake the heaven and all the stars, though in their essence superior, submit to serve him who is in essence inferior, on account of the form of the Ruler. So much has God blessed man above all, in order that, loving the Benefactor in proportion to the multitude of His benefits, by means of this love he may be saved for the world to come.

Chapter VIII - Wiles of the Devil

"Therefore the love of men towards God is sufficient for salvation. And this the wicked one knows; and while we are hastening to sow the love towards Him which makes immortal in the souls of those who from among the Gentiles are ready to believe in the one and only God, this wicked one, having sufficient armour against the ignorant for their destruction, hastens to sow the supposition of many gods, or at least of one greater, in order that men, conceiving and being persuaded of what is not wisdom, may die, as in the crime of adultery, and be cast out from His kingdom.

Chapter IX - Uncertainty of the Scriptures

"Worthy, therefore, of rejection is every one who is willing so much as to hear anything against the monarchy of God; but if any one dares to hear anything against God, as trusting in the Scriptures, let him first of all consider with me that if any one, as he pleases, form a dogma agreeable to himself, and then carefully search the Scriptures, he will be able to produce many testimonies from them in favour of the dogma that he has formed.

How, then, can confidence be placed in them against God, when what every man wishes is found in them?

Chapter X - Simon's Intention

"Therefore Simon, who is going to discuss in public with us to-morrow, is bold against the monarchy of God, wishing to produce many statements from these Scriptures, to the effect that there are many gods, and a certain one who is not He who made this world, but who is superior to Him; and, at the same time, he is going to offer many scriptural proofs.

But we also can easily show many passages from them that He who made the world alone is God, and that there is none other besides Him.

But if any one shall wish to speak otherwise, he also shall be able to produce proofs from them at his pleasure.

For the Scriptures say all manner of things, that no one of those who inquire ungratefully may find the truth, but simply what he wishes to find, the truth being reserved for the grateful now gratitude is to preserve our love to Him who is the cause of our being.

Chapter XI - Distinction Between Prediction and Prophecy

"Whence it must before all things be known, that nowhere can truth be found unless from a prophet of truth.

But He is a true Prophet, who always knows all things, and even the thoughts of all men, who is without sin, as being convinced respecting the judgment of God. Wherefore we ought not simply to consider respecting His foreknowledge, but whether His foreknowledge can stand, apart from other cause.

For physicians predict certain things, having the pulse of the patient as matter submitted to them; and some predict by means of having fowls, and some by having sacrifices, and others by having many various matters submitted to them; yet these are not prophets.

Chapter XII - The Same

"But if any one should say that the foreknowledge shown by these predictions is like to that foreknowledge which is really implanted, he were much deceived.

For he only declares such things as being present, and that if he speaks truth.

However, even these things are serviceable to me, for they establish that there is such a thing as foreknowledge.

But the foreknowledge of the one true Prophet does not only know things present, but stretches out prophecy without limit as far as the world to come, and needs nothing for its interpretation, not prophesying darkly and ambiguously, so that the things spoken would need another prophet for the interpretation of them; but clearly and simply, as our Master and Prophet, by the inborn and ever-flowing Spirit, always knew all things.

Chapter XIII - Prophetic Knowledge Constant

"Wherefore He confidently made statements respecting things that are to be--I mean sufferings, places, limits.

For, being a faultless Prophet, and looking upon all things with the boundless eye of His soul, He knows hidden things.

But if we should hold, as many do, that even the true Prophet, not always, but sometimes, when He has the Spirit, and through it, foreknows, but when He has it not is ignorant,--if we should suppose thus, we should deceive ourselves and mislead others. For such a matter belongs to those who are madly inspired by the spirit of disorder--to those who are drunken beside the altars, and are gorged with fat.

Chapter XIV - Prophetic Spirit Constant

"For if it were permitted to any one who will profess prophecy to have it believed in the cases in which he was found false, that then he had not the Holy Spirit of foreknowledge, it will be difficult to convict him of being a false prophet; for among the many things that he speaks, a few come to pass, and then he is believed to have the Spirit, although he speaks the first things last, and the last first; speaks of past events as future, and future as already past; and also without sequence; or things borrowed from others and altered, and some that are lessened, unformed, foolish, ambiguous, unseemly, obscure, proclaiming all unconscientiousness.

Chapter XV - Christ's Prophecies

"But our Master did not prophesy after this fashion; but, as I have already said, being a prophet by an inborn and ever-flowing Spirit, and knowing all things at all times, He confidently set forth, plainly as I said before, sufferings, places, appointed times, manners, limits. Accordingly, therefore, prophesying concerning the temple, He said: See ye these buildings?

Verily I say to you, There shall not be left here one stone upon another which shall not be taken away; and this generation shall not pass until the destruction begin.

For they shall come, and shall sit here, and shall besiege it, and shall slay your children here.' [4]And in like manner He spoke in plain words the things that were straightway to happen, which we can now see with our eyes, in order that the accomplishment might be among those to whom the word was spoken.

For the Prophet of truth utters the word of proof in order to the faith of His hearers.

Chapter XVI - Doctrine of Conjunction

"However, there are many proclaimers of error, having one chief, even the chief of wickedness, just as the Prophet of truth, being one, and being also the chief of piety, shall in His own times have as His prophets all who are found pure.

But the chief cause of men being deceived is this, their not understanding beforehand the doctrine of conjunction, which I shall not fail to expound to you in private every day, summarily; for it were too long to speak in detail.

Be you therefore to me truth-loving judges of the things that are spoken.

Chapter XVII - Whether Adam Had the Spirit

"But I shall begin the statement now.

God having made all things, if any one will not allow to a man, fashioned by His hands, to have possessed His great and Holy Spirit of foreknowledge, how does not he greatly err who attributes it to another born of a spurious stock! [5]And I do not think that he will obtain pardon, though he be misled by spurious scripture to think dreadful things against the Father of all.

For he who insults the image and the things belonging to the eternal King, has the sin reckoned as committed against Him in whose likeness the image was made.

But then, says he, the Divine Spirit left him when he sinned.

In that case the Spirit sinned along with him; and how can he escape peril who says this?

But perhaps he received the Spirit after he sinned.

Then it is given to the unrighteous; and where is justice?
But it was afforded to the just and the unjust.
This were most unrighteous of all.
Thus every falsehood, though it be aided by ten thousand reasonings, must receive its refutation, though after a long time.

Chapter XVIII - Adam Not Ignorant

"Be not deceived.
Our father was ignorant of nothing; since, indeed, even the law publicly current, though charging him with the crime of ignorance for the sake of the unworthy, sends to him those desirous of knowledge, saying, Ask your father, and he will tell you; your elders, and they will declare to you.' [6]This father, these elders ought to be inquired of.

But you have not inquired whose is the time of the kingdom, and whose is the seat of prophecy, though He Himself points out Himself, saying, The scribes and the Pharisees sit in Moses' seat; all things whatsoever they say to you, hear them.' [7]Hear them, He said, as entrusted with the key of the kingdom, which is knowledge, which alone can open the gate of life, through which alone is the entrance to eternal life.

But truly, He says, they possess the key, but those wishing to enter they do not suffer to do so.

Chapter XIX - Reign of Christ

"On this account, I say, He Himself, rising from His seat as a father for his children, proclaiming the things which from the beginning were delivered in secret to the worthy, extending mercy even to the Gentiles, and compassionating the souls of all, neglected His own kindred.

For He, being thought worthy to be King of the world to come, fights against [8] him who, by predestination, has usurped the kingdom that now is.

And the thing which exceedingly grieved Him is this, that by those very persons for whom, as for sons, he did battle, He was assailed, on account of their ignorance.

And yet He loved even those who hated Him, and wept over the unbelieving, and blessed those who slandered Him, and prayed for those who were in enmity against Him. [9]And not only did He do this as a father, but also taught His disciples to do the like, bearing themselves as towards brethren. [10]
This did our Father, this did our Prophet.

This is reasonable, that He should be King over His children; that by the affection of a father towards his children, and the engrafted respect of children towards their father, eternal peace might be produced.

For when the good man reigneth, there is true joy among those who are ruled over, on account of him who rules.

Chapter XX - Christ the Only Prophet Has Appeared in Different Ages

"But give heed to my first discourse of the truth.

If any one do not allow the man fashioned by the hands of God to have had the Holy Spirit of Christ, how is he not guilty of the greatest impiety in allowing another born of an impure stock to have it?

But he would act most piously, if he should not allow to another to have it, but should say that he alone has it, who has changed his forms and his names from the beginning of the world, and so reappeared again and again in the world, until coming upon his own times, and being anointed with mercy for the works of God, he shall enjoy rest for ever.

His honour it is to bear rule and lordship over all things, in air, earth, and waters.

But in addition to these, himself having made man, he had breath, the indescribable garment of the soul, that he might be able to be immortal.

Chapter XXI - The Eating of the Forbidden Fruit Denied

"He himself being the only true prophet, fittingly gave names to each animal, according to the merits of its nature, as having made it.
For if he gave a name to any one, that was also the name of that which was made, being given by him who made it. [11]How, then, had he still need to partake of a tree, that he might know what is good and what is evil, if he was commanded not to eat of it?
But this senseless men believe, who think that a reasonless beast was more powerful than the God who made these things.

Chapter XXII - Male and Female

"But a companion was created along with him, a female nature, much differing from him, as quality from substance, as the moon from the sun, as fire from light.
She, as a female ruling the present world as her like, [12] was entrusted to be the first prophetess, announcing prophecy with all amongst those born of woman. [13]But the other, as the son of man, being a male, prophesies better things to the world to come as a male.

Chapter XXIII - Two Kinds of Prophecy

"Let us then understand that there are two kinds of prophecy: [14] the one male; and let it be defined that the first, being the male, has been ranked after the other in the order of advent; but the second, being female, has been appointed to come first in the advent of the pairs.
This second, therefore, being amongst those born of woman, as the female superintendent of this present world, wishes to be thought masculine. [15]Wherefore, stealing the seeds of the male, and sowing them with her own seeds of the flesh, she brings forth the fruits--that is, words--as wholly her own.
And she promises that she will give the present earthly riches as a dowry, wishing to change the slow for the swift, the small for the greater.

Chapter XXIV - The Prophetess a Misleader

"However, she, not only presuming to say and to hear that there are many gods, but also believing herself to be one, and in hope of being that which she had not a nature to be, and throwing away what she had, and as a female being in her courses at the offering of sacrifices, is stained with blood; and then she pollutes those who touch her.
But when she conceives and brings forth temporary kings, she stirs up wars, shedding much blood; and those who desire to learn truth from her, by telling them all things contrary, and presenting many and various services, she keeps them always seeking and finding nothing, even until death.
For from the beginning a cause of death lies upon blind men; for she, prophesying deceit, and ambiguities, and obliquities, deceives those who believe her.

Chapter XXV - Cain's Name and Nature

"Hence the ambiguous name which she gave to her first-born son, calling him Cain, which has a capability of interpretation in two ways; [16] for it is interpreted both Possession and Envy, as signifying that in the future he was to envy either a woman, or possessions, or the love of the parents towards her. [17]But if it be none of these, then it will befall him to be called the Possession.
For she possessed him first, which also was advantageous to him.
For he was a murderer and a liar, and with his sins was not willing to be at peace with respect to the government.
Moreover, those who came forth by succession from him were the first adulterers.
And there were psalteries, and harps, and forgers of instruments of war.
Wherefore also the prophecy of his descendants being full of adulterers and of psalteries, secretly by means of pleasures excites to wars.

Chapter XXVI - Abel's Name and Nature

"But he who amongst the sons of men had prophecy innate to his soul as belonging to it, expressly, as being a male, indicating the hopes of the world to come, called his own son Abel, which without any ambiguity is translated Grief.

For he assigns to his sons to grieve over their deceived brethren.

He does not deceive them when he promises them comfort in the world to come.

When he says that we must pray to one only God, he neither himself speaks of gods, nor does he believe another who speaks of them.

He keeps the good which he has, and increases more and more.

He hates sacrifices, bloodshed, and libations; he loves the chaste, the pure, the holy.

He quenches the fire of altars, represses wars, teaches pious preachers wisdom, purges sins, sanctions marriage, approves temperance, leads all to chastity, makes men liberal, prescribes justice, seals those of them who are perfect, publishes the word of peace, prophesies explicitly, speaks decidedly, frequently makes mention of the eternal fire of punishment, constantly announces the kingdom of God, indicates heavenly riches, promises unfading glory, shows the remission of sins by works.

Chapter XXVII - The Prophet and the Prophetess

"And what need is there to say more?

The male is wholly truth, the female wholly falsehood.

But he who is born of the male and the female, in some things speaks truth, in some falsehood.

For the female, surrounding the white seed of the male with her own blood, as with red fire, sustains her own weakness with the extraneous supports of bones, and, pleased with the temporary flower of flesh, and spoiling the strength of the judgment by short pleasures, leads the greater part into fornication, and thus deprives them of the coming excellent Bridegroom.

For every person is a bride, whenever, being sown with the true Prophet's whole word of truth, he is enlightened in his understanding.

Chapter XXVIII - Spiritual Adultery

"Wherefore, it is fitting to hear the one only Prophet of the truth, knowing that the word that is sown by another bearing the charge of fornication, is, as it were, cast out by the Bridegroom from His kingdom.

But to those who know the mystery, death is also produced by spiritual adultery.

For whenever the soul is sown by others, then it is forsaken by the Spirit, as guilty of fornication or adultery; and so the living body, the life-giving Spirit being withdrawn, is dissolved into dust, and the rightful punishment of sin is suffered at the time of the judgment by the soul, after the dissolution of the body; even as, among men, she who is caught in adultery is first cast out from the house, and then afterwards is condemned to punishment."

Chapter XXIX - The Signal Given

While Peter was about to explain fully to us this mystic word, Zacchaeus came, saying:

"Now indeed, O Peter, is the time for you to go out and engage in the discussion; for a great crowd awaits you, packed together in the court; and in the midst of them stands Simon, like a war-chieftain attended by his spearmen."

And Peter, hearing this, ordered me to withdraw for prayer, as not yet having received baptism for salvation, and then said to those who were already perfected:

"Let us rise and pray that God, by His unfailing mercies, may help me striving for the salvation of the men whom He has made." And having thus said, and having prayed, he went out into the uncovered portion of the court, which was a large space; and there were many come together for the purpose of seeing him, his pre-eminence having made them more eagerly hasten to hear. [18]

Chapter XXX - Apostolic Salutation

Therefore, standing and seeing all the people gazing upon him in profound silence, and Simon the magician standing in the midst, he began to speak thus:
"Peace be to all you who are in readiness to give your right hands to the truth of God, [19] which, being His great and incomparable gift in the present world, He who sent us, being an infallible Prophet of that which is supremely profitable, gave us in charge, by way of salutation before our words of instruction, to announce to you, in order that if there be any son of peace among you, peace may take hold of him through our teaching; but if any of you will not receive it, then we, shaking off for a testimony the road-dust of our feet, which we have borne through our toils, and brought to you that you may be saved, will go to the abodes and the cities of others. [20]

Chapter XXXI - Faith in God

"And we tell you truly, it shall be more tolerable in the day of judgment to dwell in the land of Sodom and Gomorrah, than in the place of unbelief.
In the first place, because you have not preserved of yourselves what is reasonable; in the second place, because, hearing the things concerning us, you have not come to us; and in the third place, because you have disbelieved us when we have come to you. Wherefore, being concerned for you, we pray of our own accord that our peace may come upon you.
If therefore ye will have it, you must readily promise not to do injustice, and generously to bear wrong; which the nature of man would not sustain, unless it first received the knowledge of that which is supremely profitable, which is to know the righteous nature of Him who is over all, that He defends and avenges those who are wronged, and does good for ever to the pious.

Chapter XXXII - Invitation

"Do you, therefore, as thankful servants of God, perceiving of yourselves what is reasonable, take upon you the manner of life that is pleasing to Him, that so, loving Him, and being loved of Him, you may enjoy good for ever.
For to Him alone is it most possible to bestow it, who gave being to things that were not, who created the heavens, settled the earth, set bounds to the sea, stored up the things that are in Hades, and filled all places with air.

Chapter XXXIII - Works of Creation

"He alone turned into the four contrary elements [21] the one, first, simple substance.
Thus combining them, He made of them myriads of compounds, that, being turned into opposite natures, and mingled, they might effect the pleasure of life from the combination of contraries. In like manner, He alone, having created races of angels and spirits by the Fiat of His will, peopled the heavens; as also He decked the visible firmament with stars, to which also He assigned their paths and arranged their courses.
He compacted the earth for the production of fruits.
He set bounds to the sea, marking out a dwelling-place on the dry land. [22] He stores up the things in Hades, designating it as the place of souls; and He filled all places with air, that all living creatures might be able to breathe safely in order that they might live.

Chapter XXXIV - Extent of Creation

"O the great hand of the wise God, which doeth all in all!
For a countless multitude of birds have been made by Him, and those various, differing in all respects from one another; I mean in respect of their colours, beaks, talons, looks, senses, voices, and all else.
And how many different species of plants, distinguished by boundless variety of colours, qualities, and scents!
And how many animals on the land and in the water, of which it were impossible to tell the figures, forms, habitats, colour, food, senses, natures, multitude!

Then also the multitude and height of mountains, the varieties of stones, awful caverns, fountains, rivers, marshes, seas, harbours, islands, forests, and all the inhabited world, and places uninhabited!

Chapter XXXV - "These are a Part of His Ways."

"And how many things besides are unknown, having eluded the sagacity of men!

And of those that are within our comprehension, who of mankind knows the limit?

I mean, how the heaven rolls, how the stars are borne in their courses, and what forms they have, and the subsistence of their being, [23] and what are their ethereal paths.

And whence the blasts of winds are borne around, and have different energies; whence the fountains ceaselessly spring, and the rivers, being ever flowing, run down into the sea, and neither is that fountain emptied whence they come, nor do they fill that sea whither they come!

How far reaches the unfathomable depth of the boundless Tartarus!

Upon what the heaven is upborne which encircles all!

How the clouds spring from air, and are absorbed into air!

What is the nature of thunder and lightning, snow, hail, mist, ice, storms, showers, hanging clouds!

And how He makes plants and animals!

And these things, with all accuracy, continually perfected in their countless varieties!

Chapter XXXVI - Dominion Over the Creatures

"Therefore, if any one shall accurately scan the whole with reason, he shall find that God has made them for the sake of man.

For showers fall for the sake of fruits, that man may partake of them, and that animals may be fed, that they may be useful to men.

And the sun shines, that he may turn the air into four seasons, and that each time may afford its peculiar service to man.

And the fountains spring, that drink may be given to men.

And, moreover, who is lord over the creatures, so far as is possible?

Is it not man, who has received wisdom to till the earth, to sail the sea: to make fishes, birds, and beasts his prey; to investigate the course of the stars, to mine the earth, to sail the sea; to build cities, to define kingdoms, to ordain laws, to execute justice, to know the invisible God, to be cognizant of the names of angels, to drive away demons, to endeavour to cure diseases by medicines, to find charms against poison-darting serpents, to understand antipathies?

Chapter XXXVII - "Whom to Know is Life Eternal."

But if thou art thankful, O man, understanding that God is thy benefactor in all things, thou mayest even be immortal, the things that are made for thee having continuance through thy gratitude.

And now thou art able to become incorruptible, if thou acknowledge Him whom thou didst not know, if thou love Him whom thou didst forsake, if thou pray to Him alone who is able to punish or to save thy body and soul. Wherefore, before all things, consider that no one shares His rule, no one has a name in common with Him--that is, is called God.

For He alone is both called and is God.

Nor is it lawful to think that there is any other, or to call any other by that name.

And if any one should dare do so, eternal punishment of soul is his."

Chapter XXXVIII - Simon's Challenge

When Peter had thus spoken, Simon, at the outside of the crowd, cried aloud: [24]"Why would you lie, and deceive the unlearned multitude standing around you, persuading them that it is unlawful to think that there are gods, and to call them so, when the books that are current among the Jews say that there are many gods? [25]And now I wish, in the presence of all, to discuss with you from these books on the necessity of thinking that there are gods; first showing respecting him whom you call God, that he is not the supreme and omnipotent Being, inasmuch as he is without foreknowledge, imperfect, needy, not good, and underlying many and innumerable grievous passions.

Wherefore, when this has been shown from the Scriptures, as I say, it follows that there is another, not written of, foreknowing, perfect, without want, good, removed from all grievous passions.

But he whom you call the Creator is subject to the opposite evils.

Chapter XXXIX - Defects Ascribed to God

"Therefore also Adam, being made at first after his likeness, is created blind, and is said not to have knowledge of good or evil, and is found a transgressor, and is driven out of paradise, and is punished with death.

In like manner also, he who made him, because he sees not in all places, says with reference to the overthrow of Sodom, Come, and let us go down, and see whether they do according to their cry which comes to me; or if not, that I may know.' [26]Thus he shows himself ignorant.

And in his saying respecting Adam, Let us drive him out, lest he put forth his hand and touch the tree of life, and eat, and live for ever;' [27] in saying Lest he is ignorant; and in driving him out lest he should eat and live for ever, he is also envious.

And whereas it is written that God repented that he had made man,' [28] this implies both repentance and ignorance.

For this reflection is a view by which one, through ignorance, wishes to inquire into the result of the things which he wills, or it is the act of one repenting on account of the event not being according to his expectation.

And whereas it is written, And the Lord smelled a scent of sweetness,' [29] it is the part of one in need; and his being pleased with the fat of flesh is the part of one who is not good.

But his tempting, as it is written, And God did tempt Abraham,' [30] is the part of one who is wicked, and who is ignorant of the issue of the experiment."

Chapter XL - Peter's Answer

In like manner Simon, by taking many passages from the Scriptures, seemed to show that God is subject to every infirmity.

And to this Peter said:

"Does he who is evil, and wholly wicked, love to accuse himself in the things in which he sins? Answer me this."

Then said Simon:

"He does not."

Then said Peter:

"How, then, can God be evil and wicked, seeing that those evil things which have been commonly written regarding Him, have been added by His own will!"

Then said Simon:

"It may be that the charge against Him is written by another power, and not according to His choice."

Then said Peter:

"Let us then, in the first place, inquire into this.

If, indeed, He has of His own will accused Himself, as you formerly acknowledged, then He is not wicked; but if it is done by another power, it must be inquired and investigated with all energy who hath subjected to all evils Him who alone is good."

Chapter XLI - "Status Quaestionis."

Then said Simon:

"You are manifestly avoiding the hearing of the charge from the Scriptures against your God."

Then Peter:

"You yourself appear to me to be doing this; for he who avoids the order of inquiry, does not wish a true investigation to be made.

Hence I, who proceed in an orderly manner, and wish that the writer should first be considered, am manifestly desirous to walk in a straight path."

Then Simon:

"First confess that if the things written against the Creator are true, he is not above all, since, according to the Scriptures, he is subject to all evil; then afterwards we shall inquire as to the writer."

Then said Peter:

"That I may not seem to speak against your want of order through unwillingness to enter upon the

The Epistles of Clement
investigation. [31] I answer you.

I say that if the things written against God are true, they do not show that God is wicked."

Then said Simon:
"How can you maintain that?"

Chapter XLII - Was Adam Blind?

Then said Peter:
"Because things are written opposite to those sayings which speak evil of him; wherefore neither the one nor the other can be confirmed."

Then Simon:
"How, then, is the truth to be ascertained, of those Scriptures that say he is evil, or of those that say he is good?"

Then Peter:
"Whatever sayings of the Scriptures are in harmony with the creation that was made by Him are true, but whatever are contrary to it are false." [32] Then Simon said:
"How can you show that the Scriptures contradict themselves?"

And Peter said:
"You say that Adam was created blind, which was not so; for He would not have pointed out the tree of the knowledge of good and evil to a blind man, and commanded him not to taste of it."

Then said Simon:
"He meant that his mind was blind."

Then Peter:
"How could he be blind in respect of his mind, who, before tasting of the tree, in harmony with Him who made him, imposed appropriate names on all the animals?"

Then Simon:
"If Adam had foreknowledge, how did he not foreknow that the serpent would deceive his wife?"

Then Peter:
"If Adam had not foreknowledge, how did he give names to the sons of men as they were born with reference to their future doings, calling the first Cain (which is interpreted envy'), who through envy killed his brother Abel (which is interpreted grief'), for his parents grieved over him, the first slain?

Chapter XLIII - God's Foreknowledge

"But if Adam, being the work of God, had foreknowledge, much more the God who created him.

And that is false which is written that God reflected, as if using reasoning on account of ignorance; and that the Lord tempted Abraham, that He might know if he would endure it; and that which is written, Let us go down, and see if they are doing according to the cry of them which cometh to me; and if not, that I may know.'

And, not to extend my discourse too far, whatever sayings ascribe ignorance to Him, or anything else that is evil, being upset by other sayings which affirm the contrary, are proved to be false.

But because He does indeed foreknow, He says to Abraham, Thou shalt assuredly know that thy seed shall be sojourners in a land that is not their own; and they shall enslave them, and shall evil entreat them, and humble them four hundred years.

But the nation to which they shall be in bondage will I judge, and after that they shall come out hither with much property; but thou shalt depart to thy fathers with peace, being nourished in a good old age; and in the fourth generation they shall return hither, for the sins of the Amorites are hitherto not filled up.' [33]

Chapter XLIV - God's Decrees

"But what?
Does not Moses pre-intimate the sins of the people, and predict their dispersion among the nations?

But if He gave foreknowledge to Moses, how can it be that He had it not Himself?
But He has it.

And if He has it, as we have also shown, it is an extravagant saying that He reflected, and that He repented, and that He went down to see, and whatever else of this sort.

Whatsoever things being fore-known before they come to pass as about to befall, take issue by a wise economy, without repentance.

Chapter XLV - Sacrifices

"But that He is not pleased with sacrifices, is shown by this, that those who lusted after flesh were slain as soon as they tasted it, and were consigned to a tomb, so that it was called the grave of lusts.[34]He then who at the first was displeased with the slaughtering of animals, not wishing them to be slain, did not ordain sacrifices as desiring them; nor from the beginning did He require them.

For neither are sacrifices accomplished without the slaughter of animals, nor can the first-fruits be presented.

But how is it possible for Him to abide in darkness, and smoke, and storm (for this also is written), who created a pure heaven, and created the sun to give light to all, and assigned the invariable order of their revolutions to innumerable stars?

Thus, O Simon, the handwriting of God--I mean the heaven--shows the counsels of Him who made it to be pure and stable.

Chapter XLVI - Disparagements of God

"Thus the sayings accusatory of the God who made the heaven are both rendered void by the opposite sayings which are alongside of them, and are refuted by the creation.

For they were not written by a prophetic hand.

Wherefore also they appear opposite to the hand of God, who made all things."

Then said Simon:

"How can you show this?"

Chapter XLVII - Foreknowledge of Moses

Then said Peter:

"The law of God was given by Moses, without writing, to seventy wise men, to be handed down, that the government might be carried on by succession.

But after that Moses was taken up, it was written by some one, but not by Moses.

For in the law itself it is written, And Moses died; and they buried him near the house of Phogor, [35] and no one knows his sepulchre till this day.'

But how could Moses write that Moses died?

And whereas in the time after Moses, about 500 years or thereabouts, it is found lying in the temple which was built, and after about 500 years more it is carried away, and being burnt in the time of Nebuchadnezzar it is destroyed; and thus being written after Moses, and often lost, even this shows the foreknowledge of Moses, because he, foreseeing its disappearance, did not write it; but those who wrote it, being convicted of ignorance through their not foreseeing its disappearance, were not prophets."[36]

Chapter XLVIII - Test of Truth

Then said Simon:

"Since, as you say, we must understand the things concerning God by comparing them with the creation, how is it possible to recognise the other things in the law which are from the tradition of Moses, and are true, and are mixed up with these falsehoods?"

Then Peter said:

"A certain verse has been recorded without controversy in the written law, according to the providence of God, so as to show clearly which of the things written are true and which are false." Then said Simon:

"Which is that?

Show it us."

Chapter XLIX - The True Prophet

Then Peter said:
"I shall tell you forthwith.
It is written in the first book of the law, towards the end:
A ruler shall not fail from Judah, nor a leader from his thighs, until He come whose it is; and He is the expectation of the nations.' [37]If, therefore, any one can apprehend Him who came after the failure of ruler and leader from Judah, and who was to be expected by the nations, he will be able by this verse to recognise Him as truly having come; [38] and believing His teaching, he will know what of the Scriptures are true and what are false."
Then said Simon:
"I understand that you speak of your Jesus as Him who was prophesied of by the scripture.
Therefore let it be granted that it is so.
Tell us, then, how he taught you to discriminate the Scriptures."

Chapter L - His Teaching Concerning the Scriptures

Then Peter:
"As to the mixture of truth with falsehood, [39] I remember that on one occasion He, finding fault with the Sadducees, said, Wherefore ye do err, not knowing the true things of the Scriptures; and on this account ye are ignorant of the power of God.' [40]But if He cast up to them that they knew not the true things of the Scriptures, it is manifest that there are false things in them. And also, inasmuch as He said, Be ye prudent money-changers,' [41] it is because there are genuine and spurious words.
And whereas He said, Wherefore do ye not perceive that which is reasonable in the Scriptures?'
He makes the understanding of him stronger who voluntarily judges soundly.

Chapter LI - His Teaching Concerning the Law

"And His sending to the scribes and teachers of the existing Scriptures, as to those who knew the true things of the law that then was, is well known.
And also that He said, I am not come to destroy the law,' [42] and yet that He appeared to be destroying it, is the part of one intimating that the things which He destroyed did not belong to the law.
And His saying, The heaven and the earth shall pass away, but one jot or one tittle shall not pass from the law,' [43] intimated that the things which pass away before the heaven and the earth do not belong to the law in reality.

Chapter LII - Other Sayings of Christ

"Since, then, while the heaven and the earth still stand, sacrifices have passed away, and kingdoms, and prophecies among those who are born of woman, and such like, as not being ordinances of God; hence therefore He says, Every plant which the heavenly Father has not planted shall be rooted up.' [44]Wherefore He, being the true Prophet, said, I am the gate of life; [45] he who entereth through me entereth into life,' there being no other teaching able to save. Wherefore also He cried, and said, Come unto me, all who labour,' [46] that is, who are seeking the truth, and not finding it; and again, My sheep hear my voice;' [47] and elsewhere, Seek and find,' [48] since the truth does not lie on the surface.

Chapter LIII - Other Sayings of Christ

"But also a witnessing voice was heard from heaven, saying, This is my beloved Son, in whom I am well pleased; hear Him.' [49]And in addition to this, willing to convict more fully of error the prophets from whom they asserted that they had learned, He proclaimed that they died desiring the truth, but not having learned it, saying, Many prophets and kings desired to see what ye see, and to hear what you hear; and verily I say to you, they neither saw nor heard.' [50] Still further He said, I am he concerning whom Moses prophesied, saying, A Prophet shall the Lord our God raise unto you of your brethren, like unto me:

Him hear in all things; and whosoever will not hear that Prophet shall die.' [51]

Chapter LIV - Other Sayings

"Whence it is impossible without His teaching to attain to saving truth, though one seek it for ever where the thing that is sought is not.
But it was, and is, in the word of our Jesus.
Accordingly, He, knowing the true things of the law, said to the Sadducees, asking on what account Moses permitted to marry seven, [52] Moses gave you commandments according to your hardheartedness; for from the beginning it was not so:
for He who created man at first, made him male and female.' [53]

Chapter LV - Teaching of Christ

"But to those who think, as the Scriptures teach, that God swears, He said, Let your yea be yea, and nay, nay; for what is more than these is of the evil one.' [54] And to those who say that Abraham and Isaac and Jacob are dead, He said, God is not of the dead, but of the living.' [55] And to those who suppose that God tempts, as the Scriptures say, He said, The tempter is the wicked one,' [56] who also tempted Himself.
To those who suppose that God does not foreknow, He said, For your heavenly Father knoweth that ye need all these things before ye ask Him.' [57] And to those who believe, as the Scriptures say, that He does not see all things, He said, Pray in secret, and your Father, who seeth secret things, will reward you.' [58]

Chapter LVI - Teaching of Christ

"And to those who think that He is not good, as the Scriptures say, He said, From which of you shall his son ask bread, and he will give him a stone; or shall ask a fish, and he will give him a serpent? If ye then, being evil, know to give good gifts to your children, how much more shall your heavenly Father give good things to those who ask Him, and to those who do His will!' [59] But to those who affirmed that He was in the temple, He said, Swear not by heaven, for it is God's throne; nor by the earth, for it is the footstool of His feet.' [60]
And to those who supposed that God is pleased with sacrifices, He said, God wishes mercy, and not sacrifices' [61] --the knowledge of Himself, and not holocausts.

Chapter LVII - Teaching of Christ

"But to those who are persuaded that He is evil, as the Scriptures say, He said, Call not me good, for One only is good.' [62] And again, Be ye good and merciful, as your Father in the heavens, who makes the sun rise on good and evil men, and brings rain upon just and unjust.' [63] But to those who were misled to imagine many gods, as the Scriptures say, He said, Hear, O Israel; the Lord your God is one Lord.'" [64]

Chapter LVIII - Flight of Simon

Therefore Simon, perceiving that Peter was driving him to use the Scriptures as Jesus taught, was unwilling that the discussion should go into the doctrine concerning God, even although Peter had changed the discussion into question and answer, as Simon himself asked.
However, the discussion occupied three days. [65] And while the fourth was dawning, he set off darkling as far as Tyre of Phoenicia. [66] And not many days after, some of the precursors came and said to Peter: "Simon is doing great miracles in Tyre, and disturbing many of the people there; and by many slanders he has made you to be hated."

Chapter LIX - Peter's Resolution to Follow

Peter, hearing this, on the following night assembled the multitude of hearers; and as soon as they were come together, he said:

"While I am going forth to the nations which say that there are many gods, to teach and to preach that God is one, who made heaven and earth, and all things that are in them, in order that they may love Him and be saved, evil has anticipated me, and by the very law of conjunction has sent Simon before me, in order that these men, if they shall cease to say that there are many gods, disowning those upon earth that are called gods, may think that there are many gods in heaven; so that, not feeling the excellency of the monarchy, they may perish with eternal punishment.

And what is most dreadful, since true doctrine has incomparable power, he forestalls me with slanders, and persuades them to this, not even at first to receive me; lest he who is the slanderer be convicted of being himself in reality a devil, and the true doctrine be received and believed.

Therefore I must quickly catch him up, lest the false accusation, through gaining time, wholly get hold of all men.

Chapter LX - Successor to Be Appointed

"Since, therefore, it is necessary to set apart some one instead of me to fill my place, let us all with one consent pray to God, that He would make manifest who amongst us is the best, that, sitting in the chair of Christ, he may piously rule His Church.

Who, then, shall be set apart?

For by the counsel of God that man is set forth as blessed, whom his Lord shall appoint over the ministry of his fellow-servants, to give them their meat in their season, not thinking and saying in his heart, My Lord delayeth His coming, and who shall not begin to beat his fellow-servants, eating and drinking with harlots and drunkards.

And the Lord of that servant shall come in an hour when he doth not look for Him, and in a day when he is not aware, and shall cut him in sunder, and shall assign his unfaithful part with the hypocrites.' [67]

Chapter LXI - Monarchy

"But if any one of those present, being able to instruct the ignorance of men, shrink from it, thinking only of his own ease, let him expect to hear this sentence:

O wicked and slothful servant, thou oughtest to have given my money to the exchangers, and I at my coming should have got my own.

Cast out the unprofitable servant into the outer darkness.' [68] And with good reason; for,' says He, it is thine, O man, to prove my words, as silver and money are proved among the exchangers.'[69] Therefore the multitude of the faithful ought to obey some one, that they may live in harmony.

For that which tends to the government of one person, in the form of monarchy, enables the subjects to enjoy peace by means of good order; but in case of all, through desire of ruling, being unwilling to submit to one only, they must altogether fall by reason of division.

Chapter LXII - Obedience Leads to Peace

\
"But, further, let the things that are happening before your eyes persuade you; how wars are constantly arising through there being now many kings all over the earth.

For each one holds the government of another as a pretext for war.

But if one were universal superior, he, having no reason why he should make war, would have perpetual peace. In short, therefore, to those who are thought worthy of eternal life, God appoints one universal King in the world that shall then be, that by means of monarchy there may be unfailing peace.

It behoves all, therefore, to follow some one as a leader, honouring him as the image of God; and it behoves the leader to be acquainted with the road that entereth into the holy city.

Chapter LXIII - Zacchaeus Appointed

"But of those who are present, whom shall I choose but Zacchaeus, [70] to whom also the Lord went in [71] and rested, judging him worthy to be saved?"

And having said this, he laid his hand upon Zacchaeus, who stood by, and forced him to sit down in his own chair. But Zacchaeus, falling at his feet, begged that he would permit him to decline the rulership; promising, at the same time, and saying, "Whatever it behoves the ruler to do, I will do; only grant me not to have this name; for I am afraid of assuming the name of the rulership, for it teems with bitter envy and danger."

Chapter LXIV - The Bishopric

Then Peter said:
"If you are afraid of this, do not be called Ruler, but The Appointed One, the Lord having permitted you to be so called, when He said, Blessed is that man whom his Lord shall Appoint to the ministry of his fellow-servants.' [72]But if you wish it to be altogether unknown that you have authority of administration, you seem to me to be ignorant that the acknowledged authority of the president has great influence as regards the respect of the multitude.

For every one obeys him who has received authority, having conscience as a great constraint.

And are you not well aware that you are not to rule as the rulers of the nations, but as a servant ministering to them, as a father to the oppressed, visiting them as a physician, guarding them as a shepherd,--in short, taking all care for their salvation?

And do you think that I am not aware what labours I compel you to undertake, desiring you to be judged by multitudes whom it is impossible for any one to please?

But it is most possible for him who does well to please God.

Wherefore I entreat you to undertake it heartily, by God, by Christ, for the salvation of the brethren, for their ordering, and your own profit.

Chapter LXV - Nolo Episcopar

"And consider this other thing, that in proportion as there is labour and danger in ruling the Church of Christ, so much greater is the reward.

And yet again the greater is also the punishment to him who can, and refuses.

I wish, therefore, knowing that you are the best instructed of my attendants, to turn to account those noble powers of judging with which you have been entrusted by the Lord, in order that you may be saluted with the Well done, good and faithful servant, and not be found fault with, and declared liable to punishment, like him who hid the one talent.

But if you will not be appointed a good guardian of the Church, point out another in your stead, more learned and more faithful than yourself.

But you cannot do this; for you associated with the Lord, and witnessed His marvellous doings, and learned the administration of the Church.

Chapter LXVI - Danger of Disobedience

"And your work is to order what things are proper; and that of the brethren is to submit, and not to disobey.

Therefore submitting they shall be saved, but disobeying they shall be punished by the Lord, because the president is entrusted with the place of Christ. Wherefore, indeed, honour or contempt shown to the president is handed on to Christ, and from Christ to God.

And this I have said, that these brethren may not be ignorant of the danger they incur by disobedience to you, because whosoever disobeys your orders, disobeys Christ; and he who disobeys Christ offends God.

Chapter LXVII - Duties of Church Office-Bearers

"It is necessary, therefore, that the Church, as a city built upon a hill, have an order approved of God, and good government.

In particular, let the bishop, as chief, be heard in the things which he speaks; and let the elders give heed that the things ordered be done. Let the deacons, going about, look after the bodies and the souls of the brethren, and report to the bishop.

Let all the rest of the brethren bear wrong patiently; but if they wish judgment to be given concerning wrongs done to them, let them be reconciled in presence of the elders; and let the elders report the reconciliation to the bishop.

Chapter LXVIII - "Marriage Always Honourable."

"And let them inculcate marriage not only upon the young, but also upon those advanced in years, lest burning lust bring a plague upon the Church by reason of whoredom or adultery.

For, above every other sin, the wickedness of adultery is hated by God, because it not only destroys the person himself who sins, but those also who eat and associate with him.

For it is like the madness of a dog, because it has the nature of communicating its own madness.

For the sake of chastity, therefore, let not only the elders, but even all, hasten to accomplish marriage.

For the sin of him who commits adultery necessarily comes upon all.

Therefore, to urge the brethren to be chaste, this is the first charity.

For it is the healing of the soul. For the nourishment of the body is rest.

Chapter LXIX - "Not Forsaking the Assembling of Yourselves Together."

"But if you love your brethren, take nothing from them, but share with them such things as ye have.

Feed the hungry; give drink to the thirsty; clothe the naked; visit the sick; so far as you can, help those in prison; receive strangers gladly into your own abodes; hate no one.

And how you must be pious, your own mind will teach you, judging rightly.

But before all else, if indeed I need say it to you, come together frequently, if it were every hour, especially on the appointed days of meeting.

For if you do this, you are within a wall of safety. For disorderliness is the beginning of perdition.

Let no one therefore forsake the assembly on the ground of envy towards a brother.

For if any one of you forsake the assembly, he shall be regarded as of those who scatter the Church of Christ, and shall be cast out with adulterers.

For as an adulterer, under the influence of the spirit that is in him, he separates himself on some pretext, and gives place to the wicked one against himself,--a sheep for the stealing, as one found outside the fold. [73]

Chapter LXX - "Hear the Bishop."

"However, hear your bishop, and do not weary of giving all honour to him; knowing that, by showing it to him, it is borne to Christ, and from Christ it is borne to God; and to him who offers it, is requited manifold. [74]Honour, therefore, the throne of Christ.

For you are commanded even to honour the chair of Moses, and that although they who occupy it are accounted sinners. [75]And now I have said enough to you; and I deem it superfluous to say to him how he is to live unblameably, since he is an approved disciple of Him who taught me also.

Chapter LXXI - Various Duties of Christians

"But, brethren, there are some things that you must not wait to hear, but must consider of yourselves what is reasonable.

Zacchaeus alone having given himself up wholly to labour for you, and needing sustenance, and not being able to attend to his own affairs, how can he procure necessary support?

Is it not reasonable that you are to take forethought for his living? not waiting for his asking you, for this is the part of a beggar.

But he will rather die of hunger than submit to do this.

And shall not you incur punishment, not considering that the workman is worthy of his hire?
And let no one say:
Is, then, the word sold which was freely given?
Far be it.
For if any one has the means of living, and takes anything, he sells the word; but if he who has not takes support in order to live--as the Lord also took at supper and among His friends, having nothing, though He alone is the owner of all things--he sins not.

Therefore suitably honour elders, catechists, useful deacons, widows who have lived well, orphans as children of the Church.

But wherever there is need of any provision for an emergency, contribute all together.

Be kind one to another, not shrinking from the endurance of anything whatever for your own salvation."

Chapter LXXII - Ordination

And having thus spoken, he placed his hand upon Zacchaeus, saying, "O Thou Ruler and Lord of all, Father and God, do Thou guard the shepherd with the flock.

Thou art the cause, Thou the power.

We are that which is helped; Thou the helper, the physician, the saviour, the wall, the life, the hope, the refuge, the joy, the expectation, the rest.

In a word, Thou art all things to us.

In order to the eternal attainment of salvation, do Thou co-operate, preserve, protect.

Thou canst do all things.

For Thou art the Ruler of rulers, the Lord of lords, the Governor of kings.

Do Thou give power to the president to loose what ought to be loosed, to bind what ought to be bound.

Do Thou make him wise.

Do Thou, as by His name, protect the Church of Thy Christ as a fair bride.

For Thine is eternal glory.

Praise to the Father and the Son and the Holy Ghost to all ages.

Amen."

Chapter LXXIII - Baptisms

And having thus spoken, he afterwards said:

"Whoever of you wish to be baptized, begin from to-morrow to fast, and have hands laid upon you day by day, and inquire about what matters you please.

For I mean still to remain with you ten days."

And after three days, having begun to baptize, he called me, and Aquila, and Nicetas, and said to us:

"As I am going to set out for Tyre after seven days, I wish you to go away this very day, and to lodge secretly with Bernice the Canaanite, the daughter of Justa, and to learn from her, and write accurately to me what Simon is about.

For this is of great consequence to me, that I may prepare myself accordingly.

Therefore depart straightway in peace."

And leaving him baptizing, as he commanded, we preceded him to Tyre of Phoenicia.

Footnotes:

1. [The first twenty-eight chapters of this homily have no exact parallel in the Recognitions; much of the matter is peculiar to this work.--R.]
2. The text manifestly corrupt.
3. Perhaps, rather, "the greatest part."
4. Matt. xxiv. 2, 34; Luke xix. 43, 44.
5. [Here we find another view, suggesting the speculative opinions for which the author desires the indorsement of Peter.--R.]
6. Deut. xxxii. 7.
7. Matt. xxiii. 2, 3.

8. From a conjectural reading by Neander.

9. Matt. xxiii. 37; Luke xiii. 34; Luke xxiii. 34.

10. Matt. v. 44.

11. Gen. ii. 20.

12. That is, the present world is female, and is under the rule of the female; the world to come is male, and is under the rule of the male.

13. The allusion is to the fact that John the Baptist is called the greatest of those born of woman, while Christ is called the Son of man.

14. Literally, "Let there be to us two genuine prophecies."

15. [The doctrine of these chapters is tinged with Gnostic dualism; much of the matter might, according to tradition, have been equally well put in the mouth of Simon.--R.]

16. [Note the fantastic mysticism of this interpretation here given.--R.]

17. Qu. "towards Abel"?

18. [For a general comparison of the discussions with Simon, see Recognitions, ii. 19. Comp. Homily XVI. 1.--R.]

19. [In Recognitions, ii. 20, this sentence occurs; but the opening discourse of Peter is quite different, far more dignified and consistent with the real character of the Apostle.--R.]

20. Matt. x. 12, etc.; Mark. vi. 11, etc.; Luke. x. 5, etc.

[Comp. Recognitions, ii. 20, where the exordium is quite different, presenting the righteousness of God.--R.]

21. This is rather a paraphrase than a strict translation.

22. Various reading, "assigned it the sea as a habitation for aquatic animals."

23. Literally, "of their life," according to the idea prevalent of old, that the heavenly bodies were living creatures.

24. [The reply of Simon in the Recognitions is quite different, though the substance of this attack is given in the progress of this discussion; see Recognitions, ii. 39.--R.]

25. [The Ebionitic tendency appears in this representation of Simon, as opposing the monotheism of the Old Testament.

Comp. Recognitions, ii. 38.--R.]

26. Gen. xviii. 21.

27. Gen. iii. 22.

28. Gen. vi. 6.

29. Gen. viii. 21.

30. Gen. xxii. 1.

[These objections from the anthropomorphism of the Jewish Scriptures are not found in the Recognitions.--R.]

31. The text of this passage in all the editions is meaningless.

It becomes clear by change of punctuation.

32. [Comp. ii. 38 and many other passages for this view of the errors of Scripture.

The test of truth as here stated is noteworthy.

It suggests some modern affinities.--R.]

33. Gen. xv. 13-16.

34. That is, Kibroth-Hattaavah; Num. xi. 34.

35. Deut. xxxiv. 6, LXX.

36. [It is curious to find the post-exilian theory of the Pentateuch in this place, put in the mouth of the Apostle Peter.--R.]

37. Gen. xlix. 10.

38. From the amended reading of Davis.

39. [Comp. Homily II. 40.

The attitude of Peter, as here represented, disparaging the Old Testament, appearing to exalt the author of Christ's teachings, and yet ignoring the claims of His Person and Work, seeks its justification in rationalistic interpretation.

The attitude is not an uncommon one at present.--R.]

40. Matt. xxii. 29.

[Misquoted and misapplied here, as in Homily II. 51.--R.]

41. This is frequently quoted as a saying of Christ.

It is probably from one of the apocryphal Gospels.

[Comp. Homily II. 51.--R.]

42. Matt. v. 17.

43. Matt. v. 18.

44. Matt. xv. 13.

45. John x. 9.

46. Matt. xi. 28.
47. John x. 3.
48. Matt. vii. 7.
49. Matt. xvii. 5.
50. Matt. xiii. 17; Luke x. 24.
51. Deut. xviii. 15-19; Acts iii. 22; vii. 37.
52. [A curious confusion of two Gospel narratives, mistaking the significance of both.--R.]
53. Matt. xix. 8; Mark x. 5, 6.
54. Matt. v. 37.
55. Matt. xxii. 32; Mark xii. 27; Luke xx. 38.
56. Perhaps Matt. xiii. 39.
57. Matt. vi. 8, 32.
58. Matt. vi. 6.
59. Matt. vii. 9-11.
60. Matt. v. 34, 35.
61. Matt. ix. 13; xii. 7.
[Comp. Hos. vi. 6.--R.]
62. Matt. xix. 17; Mark x. 18; Luke xviii. 19.
63. Matt. v. 44, 45.
64. Mark xii. 29.
[Comp. Deut. vi. 4.--R.]
65. [The three days' discussion is detailed in Recognitions, ii. 20-iii. 48; the account here is confined to the first day.--R.]
66. [Comp. Recognitions, iii. 73.
The historical incidents of the two narratives vary greatly from this point onward.--R.]
67. Matt. xxiv. 45-50.
68. Matt. xxv. 27-30.
69. Probably from an apocryphal Gospel.
70. [Comp. Recognitions, iii. 66.
The account here is much fuller.--R.]
71. Luke xix. 5, etc.
72. Luke xii. 42.
73. There seems to be a corruption of the text here, but the general meaning is evident enough.
74. There are several conjectural readings of this sentence.
We have not exactly followed anyone of them, but have ventured on a conjecture of our own.
75. Matt. xxiii. 2, 3.

Homily IV

Chapter I - Bernice's Hospitality

Thus I Clement, departing from Caesarea Stratonis, together with Nicetas and Aquila, entered into Tyre of Phoenicia; [1] and according to the injunction of Peter, who sent us, we lodged with Bernice, the daughter of Justa the Canaanitess.

She received us most joyfully; and striving with much honour towards me, and with affection towards Aquila and Nicetas, and speaking freely as a friend, through joy she treated us courteously, and hospitably urged us to take bodily refreshment.

Perceiving, therefore, that she was endeavouring to impose a short delay upon us, I said:

"You do well, indeed, to busy yourself in fulfilling the part of love; but the fear of our God must take the precedence of this.

For, having a combat on hand on behalf of many souls, we are afraid of preferring our own ease before their salvation.

Chapter II - Simon's Practices

"For we hear that Simon the magician, being worsted at Caesarea in the discussion with our lord Peter, immediately hastened hither, and is doing much mischief.

For he is slandering Peter, in opposition to truth, to all the adversaries, and stealing away the souls of the multitude.

For he being a magician, calls him a magician; and he being a deceiver, proclaims him as a deceiver.

And although in the discussions he was beaten in all points, and fled, yet he says that he was victorious; and he constantly charges them that they ought not to listen to Peter,--as if, forsooth, he were anxious that they may not be fascinated by a terrible magician.

Chapter III - Object of the Mission

"Therefore our lord Peter, having learned these things, has sent us to be investigators of the things that have been told him; that if they be so, we may write to him and let him know, so that he may come and convict him face to face of the accusations that he has uttered against him.

Since, therefore, danger on the part of many souls lies before us, on this account we must neglect bodily rest for a short time; and we would learn truly from you who live here, whether the things which we have heard be true.

Now tell us particularly."

Chapter IV - Simon's Doings

But Bernice, being asked, said:

"These things are indeed as you have heard; and I will tell you other things respecting this same Simon, which perhaps you do not know.

For he astonishes the whole city every day, by making spectres and ghosts appear in the midst of the market-place; and when he walks abroad, statues move, and many shadows go before him, which, he says, are souls of the dead.

And many who attempted to prove him an impostor he speedily reconciled to him; and afterwards, under pretence of a banquet, having slain an ox, and given them to eat of it, he infected them with various diseases, and subjected them to demons.

And in a word, having injured many, and being supposed to be a god, he is both feared and honoured." [2]

Chapter V - Discretion the Better Part of Valour

"Wherefore I do not think that any one will be able to quench such a fire as has been kindled. For no one doubts his promises; but every one affirms that this is so.

Wherefore, lest you should expose yourselves to danger, I advise you not to attempt anything against him until Peter come, who alone shall be able to resist such a power, being the most esteemed disciple of our Lord Jesus Christ.

For so much do I fear this man, that if he had not elsewhere been vanquished in disputing with my lord Peter, I should counsel you to persuade even Peter himself not to attempt to oppose Simon."

Chapter VI - Simon's Departure

Then I said:

"If our lord Peter did not know that he himself alone can prevail against this power, he would not have sent us before him with orders to get information secretly concerning Simon, and to write to him."

Then, as evening had come on, we took supper, [3] and went to sleep.

But in the morning, one of Bernice's friends came and said that Simon had set sail for Sidon, and that he had left behind him Appion Pleistonices, [4] --a man of Alexandria, a grammarian by profession, whom I knew as being a friend of my father; and a certain astrologer, Annubion the Diospolitan, and Athenodorus the Athenian, attached to the doctrine of Epicurus.

And we, having learned these things concerning Simon, in the morning wrote and despatched a letter to Peter, and went to take a walk.

Chapter VII - Appion's Salutation

And Appion met us, not only with the two companions just named, but with about thirty other men.

And as soon as he saw me, he saluted and kissed me, and said, "This is Clement, of whose noble birth and liberal education I have often told you; for he, being related to the family of Tiberius Caesar, and equipped with all Grecian learning, has been seduced by a certain barbarian called Peter to speak and act after the manner of the Jews.

Wherefore I beg of you to strive together with me for the setting of him right.

And in your presence I now ask him.

Let him tell me, since he thinks that he has devoted himself to piety, whether he is not acting most impiously, in forsaking the customs of his country, and falling away to those of the barbarians."

Chapter VIII - A Challenge

I answered:

"I accept, indeed, your kindly affection towards me, but I take exception to your ignorance.

For your affection is kindly, because you wish to continue in those customs which you consider to be good.

But your inaccurate knowledge strives to lay a snare for me, under the guise of friendship."

Then said Appion:

"Does it seem to you to be ignorance, that one should observe the customs of his fathers, and judge after the manner of the Greeks?"

Then I answered: "It behoves one who desires to be pious not altogether to observe the customs of his fathers; but to observe them if they be pious, and to shake them off if they be impious.

For it is possible that one who is the son of an impious father, if he wishes to be pious, should not desire to follow the religion of his father." [5]Then answered Appion:

"What then?

Do you say that your father was a man of an evil life?"

Then said I:

"He was not of an evil life, but of an evil opinion."

Then Appion:

"I should like to know what was his evil apprehension."

Then said I:
"Because he believed the false and wicked myths of the Greeks."
Then Appion asked:
"What are these false and evil myths of the Greeks?"
Then I said:
"The wrong opinion concerning the gods, which, if you will bear with me, you shall hear, with those who are desirous to learn.

Chapter IX - Unworthy Ends of Philosophers

"Wherefore, before beginning our conversation, let us now withdraw into some quieter place, and there I shall converse with you.

And the reason why I wish to speak privately is this, because neither the multitude, nor even all the philosophers, approach honestly to the judgment of things as they are.

For we know many, even of those who pride themselves on their philosophy, who are vainglorious, or who have put on the philosopher's robe for the sake of gain, and not for the sake of virtue itself; and they, if they do not find that for which they take to philosophy, turn to mockery.

Therefore, on account of such as these, let us choose some place fit for private conference."

Chapter X - A Cool Retreat

And a certain one amongst them--a rich man, and possessing a garden of evergreen plants [6] --said: "Since it is very hot, let us retire for a little from the city to my gardens."

Accordingly they went forth, and sat down in a place where there were pure streams of cool water, and a green shade of all sorts of trees.

There I sat pleasantly, and the others round about me; and they being silent, instead of a verbal request made to me, showed by their eager looks to me that they required the proof of my assertion.

And therefore I proceeded to speak thus:--

Chapter XI - Truth and Custom

"There is a certain great difference, O men of Greece, between truth and custom.

For truth is found when it is honestly sought; but custom, whatsoever be the character of the custom received, whether true or false, is strengthened by itself without the exercise of judgment; and he who has received it is neither pleased with it as being true, nor grieved with it as false.

For such an one has believed not by judgment, but by prejudice, resting his own hope on the opinion of those who have lived before him on a mere peradventure.

And it is not easy to cast off the ancestral garment, though it be shown to himself to be wholly foolish and ridiculous.

Chapter XII - Genesis

"Therefore I say that the whole learning of the Greeks is a most dreadful fabrication of a wicked demon.

For they have introduced many gods of their own, and these wicked, and subject to all kinds of passion; so that he who wishes to do the like things may not be ashamed, which belongs to a man, having as an example the wicked and unquiet lives of the mythological gods.

And through his not being ashamed, such an one affords no hope of his repenting.

And others have introduced fate, which is called genesis, contrary to which no one can suffer or do anything.

This, therefore, also is like to the first. For any one who thinks that no one has aught to do or suffer contrary to genesis easily falls into sin; and having sinned, he does not repent of his impiety, holding it as his apology that he was borne on by genesis to do these things.

And as he cannot rectify genesis, he has no reason to be ashamed of the sins he commits. [7]

Chapter XIII - Destiny

"And others introduce an unforeseeing destiny, as if all things revolved of their own accord, without the superintendence of any master.

But thus to think these things is, as we have said, the most grievous of all opinions.

For, as if there were no one superintending and fore-judging and distributing to every one according to his deserving, they easily do everything as they can through fearlessness. Therefore those who have such opinions do not easily, or perhaps do not at all, live virtuously; for they do not foresee the danger which might have the effect of converting them.

But the doctrine of the barbarous Jews, as you call them, is most pious, introducing One as the Father and Creator of all this world, by nature good and righteous; good, indeed, as pardoning sins to those who repent; but righteous, as visiting to every one after repentance according to the worthiness of his doings.

Chapter XIV - "Doctrine According to Godliness."

"This doctrine, even if it also be mythical, being pious, would not be without advantage for this life.

For every one, in expectation of being judged by the all-seeing God, receives the greater impulse towards virtue.

But if the doctrine be also true, it withdraws him who has lived virtuously from eternal punishment, and endows him with eternal and unspeakable blessings from God.

Chapter XV - Wickedness of the Gods

"But I return to the foremost doctrine of the Greeks, that which states in stories [8] that there are gods many, and subject to all kinds of passions.

And not to spend much time upon things that are clear, referring to the impious deeds of every one of those who are called gods, I could not tell all their amours; those of Zeus and Poseidon, of Pluto and Apollo, of Dionysus and Hercules, and of them all singly. [9]And of these you are yourselves not ignorant, and have been taught their manners of life, being instructed in the Grecian learning, that, as competitors with the gods, you might do like things.

Chapter XVI - Wickedness of Jupiter

"But I shall begin with the most royal Zeus, whose father Kronos, having, as you say, devoured his own children, and having shorn off the members of his father Uranus with a sickle of adamant, showed to those who are zealous for the mysteries of the gods an example of piety towards parents and of love towards children.

And Jupiter himself bound his own father, and imprisoned him in Tartarus; and he also punishes the other gods. [10]And for those who wish to do things not to be spoken of, he begat Metis, and devoured her.

But Metis was seed; for it is impossible to devour a child.

And for an excuse to abusers of themselves with mankind, he carries away Ganymedes.

And as a helper of adulterers in their adultery, he is often found an adulterer.

And to those who wish to commit incest with sisters, he sets the example in his intercourse with his sisters Hera and Demeter, and the heavenly Aphrodite, whom some call Dodona. [11]And to those who wish to commit incest with their daughters, there is a wicked example from his story, in his committing incest with Persephone.

But in myriads of instances he acted impiously, that by reason of his excessive wickedness the fable of his being a god might be received by impious men.

Chapter XVII - "Their Makers are Like Unto Them."

"You will hold it reasonable for ignorant men to be moderately indignant at these fancies.

But what must we say to the learned, some of whom, professing themselves to be grammarians and sophists, affirm that these acts are worthy of gods?

For, being themselves incontinent, they lay hold of this mythical pretext; and as imitators of the gods, [12] they practise unseemly things with freedom.

Chapter XVIII - Second Nature

"On this account, they who live in the country sin much less than they do, not having been indoctrinated in those things in which they have been indoctrinated who dare do these things, having learned from evil instruction to be impious.

For they who from their childhood learn letters by means of such fables, while their soul is yet pliant, engraft the impious deeds of those who are called gods into their own minds; whence, when they are grown up, they ripen fruit, like evil seeds cast into the soul.

And what is worst of all, the rooted impurities cannot be easily cut down, when they are perceived to be bitter by them when they have attained to manhood.

For every one is pleased to remain in those habits which he forms in childhood; and thus, since custom is not much less powerful than nature, they become difficult to be converted to those good things which were not sown in their souls from the beginning.

Chapter XIX - "Where Ignorance is Bliss."

"Wherefore it behoves the young not to be satisfied with those corrupting lessons, and those who are in their prime should carefully avoid listening to the mythologies of the Greeks.

For lessons about their gods are much worse than ignorance, as we have shown from the case of those dwelling in the country, who sin less through their not having been instructed by Greeks.

Truly, such fables of theirs, and spectacles, and books, ought to be shunned, and if it were possible, even their cities.

For those who are full of evil learning, even with their breath infect as with madness those who associate with them, with their own passions.

And what is worst, whoever is most instructed among them, is so much the more turned from the judgment which is according to nature.

Chapter XX - False Theories of Philosophers

"And some of those amongst them who even profess to be philosophers, assert that such sins are indifferent, and say that those who are indignant at such practices are senseless. [13] For they say that such things are not sins by nature, but have been proscribed by laws made by wise men in early times, through their knowing that men, through the instability of their minds, being greatly agitated on these accounts, wage war with one another; for which reason, wise men have made laws to proscribe such things as sins.

But this is a ridiculous supposition.

For how can they be other than sins, which are the cause of tumults, and murders, and every confusion?

For do not shortcomings of life [14] and many more evils proceed from adultery?

Chapter XXI - Evils of Adultery

"But why, it is said, if a man is ignorant of his wife's being an adulteress, is he not indignant, enraged, distracted? why does he not make war?

Thus these things are not evil by nature, but the unreasonable opinion of men make them terrible.

But I say, that even if these dreadful things do not occur, it is usual for a woman, through association with an adulterer, either to forsake her husband, or if she continue to live with him, to plot against him, or to bestow upon the adulterer the goods procured by the labour of her husband; and having conceived by the adulterer while her husband is absent, to attempt the destruction of that which is in her womb, through shame of conviction, and so to become a child-murderer; or even, while destroying it, to be destroyed along with it.

But if while her husband is at home she conceives by the adulterer and bears a child, the child when he grows up does not know his father, and thinks that he is his father who is not; and thus he who is not the father, at his death leaves his substance to the child of another.

And how many other evils naturally spring from adultery!

And the secret evils we do not know.

For as the mad dog destroys all that he touches, infecting them with the unseen madness, so also the hidden evil of adultery, though it be not known, effects the cutting off of posterity.

Chapter XXII - A More Excellent Way

"But let us pass over this now.

But this we all know, that universally men are beyond measure enraged on account of it, that wars have been waged, that there have been overthrows of houses, and captures of cities, and myriads of other evils.

On this account I betook myself to the holy God and law of the Jews, putting my faith in the well-assured conclusion that the law has been assigned by the righteous judgment of God, and that the soul must at some time receive according to the desert of its deeds."

Chapter XXIII - "Whither Shall I Go from Thy Presence?"

When I had thus spoken, Appion broke in upon my discourse.

"What!" said he; "do not the laws of the Greeks also forbid wickedness, and punish adulterers?"

Then said I:

"Then the gods of the Greeks, who acted contrary to the laws, deserve punishment.

But how shall I be able to restrain myself, if I suppose that the gods themselves first practised all wickednesses as well as adultery, and did not suffer punishment; whereas they ought the rather to have suffered, as not being slaves to lust?

But if they were subject to it, how were they gods?"

Then Appion said:

"Let us have in our eye not the gods, but the judges; and looking to them, we shall be afraid to sin."

Then I said:

"This is not fitting, O Appion:

for he who has his eye upon men will dare to sin, in hope of escaping detection; but he who sets before his soul the all-seeing God, knowing that he cannot escape His notice, will refrain from sinning even in secret."

Chapter XXIV - Allegory

When Appion heard this, he said:

"I knew, ever since I heard that you were consorting with Jews, that you had alienated your judgment.

For it has been well said by some one, Evil communications corrupt good manners.'"

Then said I:

"Therefore good communications correct evil manners."

And Appion said:

"Today I am fully satisfied to have learned your position; therefore I permitted you to speak first.

But to-morrow, in this place, if it is agreeable to you, I will show, in the presence of these friends when they meet, that our gods are neither adulterers, nor murderers, nor corrupters of children, nor guilty of incest with sisters or daughters.

But the ancients, wishing that only lovers of learning should know the mysteries, veiled them with those fables of which you have spoken.

For they speak physiologically of boiling substance under the name of Zen, and of time under that of Kronos, and of the ever-flowing nature of water under that of Rhea. However, as I have promised, I shall to-morrow exhibit the truth of things, explaining them one by one to you when you come together in the morning." [15]In reply to this I said:

"To-morrow, as you have promised, so do.

But now hear something in opposition to what you are going to say.

Chapter XXV - An Engagement for To-Morrow

"If the doings of the gods, being good, have been veiled with evil fables, the wickedness of him who wove the veil is shown to have been great, because he concealed noble things with evil narratives, that no one imitate them.

But if they really did things impious, they ought, on the contrary, to have veiled them with good narratives, lest men, regarding them as their superiors, should set about sinning in like manner."

As I spoke thus, those present were evidently beginning to be well-disposed towards the words spoken by me; for they repeatedly and earnestly asked me to come on the following day, and departed.

Footnotes:

1. [In the Recognitions (iv. 1) mention is made of Clement and others accompanying Peter to Dora, Ptolemais, Tyre, Sidon, and Berytus (Beyrout), but no record is made of any discourses.

In Homilies IV.-VII. the details of this journey are given, but with variation in some particulars.

These Homilies are peculiar, in form, to this work; but much of the matter occurs in the Recognitions, in the final discussion with the father of Clement.--R.]

2. [Comp. Acts viii. 9-11.--R.]

3. Literally, "partook of salt."

4. This epithet means, "the conqueror of very many."

Suidas makes Appion the son of Pleistonices.

[Comp. Recognitions, x. 52.

It is evident that the writer has in mind Apion, the opponent of the Jews, against whom Josephus wrote his treatise.

Compare the statement of Homily V. 2.

The entire discussion with Appion, extending over Homilies IV.-VI. is peculiar to this narrative, though much of the argument occurs in the discussion of Clement with his father (Recognitions, x.).

Appion and Annubion are introduced in Recognitions, x. 52, but not as disputants.

The discussion here is constructed with much skill.--R.]

5. We have adopted the emendation of Wieseler, who reads sebasmati for sebasmata.

He also proposes ethei (habit) instead of sebasmati . The readings in the mss. vary.

6. The text here is corrupt.

If we adopt Lobeck's emendation of pammiouson into pamplousion, the literal translation is, "possessing a property around him continually rich in leaves."

[The offer of this man has a partial parallel in Recognitions, viii. 35-38.--R.]

7. [Compare the discussion on Genesis in Homily XIV. 3, etc., but especially the full arguments in Recognitions, viii., ix.--R.]

8. muthologousan.

9. [See Homily V. 11-15, and comp. Recognitions, x. 20.--R.]

10. Wieseler proposes theious instead of theous; and he punishes his uncles also, as in vi. 2, 21.

11. This is properly regarded as a mistake for Dione, or Didone, which is another form of the name Dione.

12. Lit. "of those who are superior or better."

13. [Compare the argument against the philosophers, as put in the mouth of the Apostle, in Recognitions, x. 48-50.--R.]

14. The Vatican ms. inserts here, "upturning of houses, magic practices, deceptions, perplexities."

15. [See Homily VI. 1-10.

Homily V. contains an account of Clement's previous acquaintance with Appion.--R.]

Homily V

Chapter I - Appion Does Not Appear

The next day, therefore, in Tyre, as we had agreed, I came to the quiet place, and there I found the rest, with some others also.

Then I saluted them.

But as I did not see Appion, I asked the reason of his not being present; and some one said that he had been unwell ever since last evening.

Then, when I said that it was reasonable that we should immediately set out to visit him, almost all begged me first to discourse to them, and that then we could go to see him.

Therefore, as all were of one opinion, I proceeded to say: [1] --

Chapter II - Clement's Previous Knowledge of Appion

"Yesterday, when I left this, O friends, I confess that, through much anxiety about the discussion that was to take place with Appion, I was not able to get any sleep.

And while I was unable to sleep, I remembered a trick that I played upon him in Rome. It was this.

From my boyhood I Clement was a lover of truth, and a seeker of the things that are profitable for the soul, and spending my time in raising and refuting theories; but being unable to find anything perfect, through distress of mind I fell sick.

And while I was confined to bed Appion came to Rome, and being my father's friend, he lodged with me; and hearing that I was in bed, he came to me, as being not unacquainted with medicine, and inquired the cause of my being in bed.

But I, being aware that the man exceedingly hated the Jews, as also that he had written many books against them, and that he had formed a friendship with this Simon, not through desire of learning, but because he knew that he was a Samaritan and a hater of the Jews, and that he had come forth in opposition to the Jews, therefore he had formed an alliance with him, that he might learn something from him against the Jews; [2] --

Chapter III - Clement's Trick

"I knowing this before concerning Appion, as soon as he asked me the cause of my sickness, answered feignedly, that I was suffering and distressed in my mind after the manner of young men.

And to this he said, My son, speak freely as to a father:
what is your soul's ailment?'

And when I again groaned feignedly, as being ashamed to speak of love, by means of silence and down-looking I conveyed the impression of what I wished to intimate.

But he, being persuaded that I was in love with a woman, said:
There is nothing in life which does not admit of help.

For indeed I myself, when I was young, being in love with a most accomplished woman, not only thought it impossible to obtain her, but did not even hope ever to address her.

And yet, having fallen in with a certain Egyptian who was exceedingly well versed in magic, and having become his friend, I disclosed to him my love, and not only did he assist me in all that I wished, but, honouring me more bountifully, he hesitated not to teach me an incantation by means of which I obtained her; and as soon as I had obtained her, by means of his secret instruction, being persuaded by the liberality of my teacher, I was cured of love.

Chapter IV - Appion's Undertaking

"Whence, if you also suffer any such thing after the manner of men, use freedom with me with all security; for within seven days I shall put you fully in possession of her.'

When I heard this, looking at the object I had in view, I said:

Pardon me that I do not altogether believe in the existence of magic; for I have already tried many who have made many promises, and have deceived me.

However, your undertaking influences me, and leads me to hope.

But when I think of the matter, I am afraid that the demons are sometimes not subject to the magicians with respect to the things that are commanded them.'

Chapter V - Theory of Magic

"Then Appion said:

Admit that I know more of these things than you do.

However, that you may not think that there is nothing in what you have heard from me in reference to what you have said, I will tell you how the demons are under necessity to obey the magicians in the matters about which they are commanded.

For as it is impossible for a soldier to contradict his general, and impossible for the generals themselves to disobey the king--for if any one oppose those set over him, he is altogether deserving of punishment--so it is impossible for the demons not to serve the angels who are their generals; and when they are adjured by them, they yield trembling, well knowing that if they disobey they shall be fully punished.

But the angels also themselves, being adjured by the magicians in the name of their ruler, obey, lest, being found guilty of disobedience, they be destroyed.

For unless all things that are living and rational foresaw vengeance from the ruler, confusion would ensue, all revolting against one another.'

Chapter VI - Scruples

"Then said I:

Are those things correct, then, which are spoken by poets and philosophers, that in Hades the souls of the wicked are judged and punished for their attempts; such as those of Ixion, and Tantalus, and Tityus, and Sisyphus, and the daughters of Danaus, and as many others as have been impious here?

And how, if these things are not so, is it possible that magic can subsist?'

Then he having told me that these things are so in Hades, I asked him:

Why are not we ourselves afraid of magic, being persuaded of the punishment in Hades for adultery?

For I do not admit that it is a righteous thing to compel to adultery a woman who is unwilling; but if any one will engage to persuade her, I am ready for that, besides confessing my thanks.'

Chapter VII - A Distinction with a Difference

"Then Appion said:

Do you not think it is the same thing, whether you obtain her by magic, or by deceiving her with words?'

Then said I: Not altogether the same; for these differ widely from one another.

For he who constrains an unwilling woman by the force of magic, subjects himself to the most terrible punishment, as having plotted against a chaste woman; but he who persuades her with words, and puts the choice in her own power and will, does not force her.

And I am of opinion, that he who has persuaded a woman will not suffer so great punishment as he who has forced her.

Therefore, if you can persuade her, I shall be thankful to you when I have obtained her; but otherwise, I had rather die than force her against her will.'

Chapter VIII - Flattery or Magic

"Then Appion, being really puzzled, said:
What am I to say to you? For at one time, as one perturbed with love, you pray to obtain her; and anon, as if you loved her not, you make more account of your fear than your desire:
and you think that if you can persuade her you shall be blameless, as without sin; but obtaining her by the power of magic, you will incur punishment.

But do you not know that it is the end of every action that is judged, the fact that it has been committed, and that no account is made of the means by which it has been effected? And if you commit adultery, being enabled by magic, shall you be judged as having done wickedly; and if by persuasion, shall you be absolved from sin in respect of the adultery?'
Then I said:
On account of my love, there is a necessity for me to choose one or other of the means that are available to procure the object of my love; and I shall choose, as far as possible, to cajole her rather than to use magic. But neither is it easy to persuade her by flattery, for the woman is very much of a philosopher.'

Chapter IX - A Love-Letter

"Then Appion said:
I am all the more hopeful to be able to persuade her, as you wish, provided only we be able to converse with her.' That,' said I, is impossible.'
Then Appion asked if it were possible to send a letter to her.
Then I said:
That indeed may be done.'
Then Appion said:
This very night I shall write a paper on encomiums of adultery, which you shall get from me and despatch to her; and I hope that she shall be persuaded, and consent.'
Appion accordingly wrote the paper, and gave it to me; and I thought of it this very night, and I remembered that fortunately I have it by me, along with other papers which I carry about with me."
Having thus spoken, I showed the paper to those who were present, and read it to them as they wished to hear it; and having read it, I said:
"This, O men, is the instruction of the Greeks, affording a bountiful licence to sin without fear.[3] The paper was as follows:--

Chapter X - The Lover to the Beloved One

"Anonymously, on account of the laws of foolish men.
At the bidding of Love, the first-born of all, salutation:
I know that you are devoted to philosophy, and for the sake of virtue you affect the life of the noble.
But who are nobler than the gods among all, and philosophers among men?
For these alone know what works are good or evil by nature, and what, not being so, are accounted so by the imposition of laws. Now, then, some have supposed that the action which is called adultery is evil, although it is in every respect good.
For it is by the appointment of Eros for the increase of life.
And Eros is the eldest of all the gods.
For without Eros there can be no mingling or generation either of elements, or gods, or men, or irrational animals, or aught else.
For we are all instruments of Eros.
He, by means of us, is the fabricator of all that is begotten, the mind inhabiting our souls.
Hence it is not when we ourselves wish it, but when we are ordered by him, that we desire to do his will.
But if, while we desire according to his will, we attempt to restrain the desire for the sake of what is called chastity, what do we do but the greatest impiety, when we oppose the oldest of all gods and men?

Clement of Rome

Chapter XI - "All Uncleanness with Greediness."

"But let all doors be opened to him, and let all baneful and arbitrary laws be set aside, which have been ordained by fanatical men, who, under the power of senselessness, and not willing to understand what is reasonable, and, moreover, suspecting those who are called adulterers, are with good reason mocked with arbitrary laws by Zeus himself, through Minos and Rhadamanthus.

For there is no restraining of Eros dwelling in our souls; for the passion of lovers is not voluntary. Therefore Zeus himself, the giver of these laws, approached myriads of women; and, according to some wise men, he sometimes had intercourse with human beings, as a benefactor for the production of children.

But in the case of those to whom he knew that his being unknown would be a favour, [4] he changed his form, in order that he might neither grieve them, nor seem to act in opposition to the laws given by himself.

It becomes you, therefore, who are debaters of philosophy, for the sake of a good life, to imitate those who are acknowledged to be the nobler, who have had sexual intercourse ten thousand times.

Chapter XII - Jupiter's Amours

"And not to spend the time to no purpose in giving more examples, I shall begin with mentioning some embraces of Zeus himself, the father of gods and men. [5] For it is impossible to mention all, on account of their multitude.

Hear, therefore, the amours of this great Jupiter, which he concealed by changing his form, on account of the fanaticism of senseless men.

For, in the first place, wishing to show to wise men that adultery is no sin, when he was going to marry, being, according to the multitude, knowingly an adulterer, in his first marriage, but not being so in reality, by means, as I said, of a seeming sin be accomplished a sinless marriage. [6] For he married his own sister Hera, assuming the likeness of a cuckoo's wing; and of her were born Hebe and Ilithyia.

For he gave birth to Metis without copulation with any one, as did also Hera to Vulcan.

Chapter XIII - Jupiter's Amours Continued

"Then he committed incest with his sister, who was born of Kronos and Thalasse, after the dismemberment of Kronos, and of whom were born Eros and Cypris, whom they call also Dodone.

Then, in the likeness of a satyr, he had intercourse with Antiope the daughter of Nycteus, of whom were born Amphion and Zethus.

And he embraced Alcmene, the wife of Amphitryon, in the form of her husband Amphitryon, of whom was born Hercules.

And, changed into an eagle, he approached AEgina, the daughter of Asclepius, of whom AEacus was born.

And in the form of a bear he lay with Amalthea the daughter of Phocus; and in a golden shower he fell upon Danae, the daughter of Acrisius, of whom sprang Perseus.

He became wild as a lion to Callisto the daughter of Lycaon and begat Arcus the second.

And with Europa the daughter of Phoenix he had intercourse by means of a bull, of whom sprang Minos, and Rhadamanthus, and Sarpedon; and with Eurymedusa the daughter of Achelous, changing himself into an ant, of whom was born Myrmidon. With a nymph of Hersaeus, in the form of a vulture, from whom sprang the wise men of old in Sicily.

He came to Juno the earth-born in Rhodes, and of her were born Pargaeus, Kronius, Kytis.

And he deflowered Ossia, taking the likeness of her husband Phoenix, of whom Anchinous was born to him.

Of Nemesis the daughter of Thestius, who is also thought to be Leda, he begot Helena, in the form of a swan or goose; and again, in the form of a star, he produced Castor and Polydeuces.

With Lamia he was transformed into a hoopoo.

Chapter XIV - Jupiter's Undisguised Amours

"In the likeness of a shepherd he made Mnemosyne mother of the Muses. Setting himself on fire, he married Semele, the daughter of Cadmus, of whom he begat Dionysus.

In the likeness of a dragon he deflowered his daughter Persephone, thought to be the wife of his brother Pluto.

He had intercourse with many other women without undergoing any change in his form; for the husbands had no ill-will to him as if it were a sin, but knew well that in associating with their wives he bountifully produced children for them, bestowing upon them the Hermeses, the Apollos, the Dionysi, the Endymions, and others whom we have spoken of, most excellent in beauty through his fatherhood.

Chapter XV - Unnatural Lusts

"And not to spend the time in an endless exposition, you will find numerous unions with Jupiter of all the gods.

But senseless men call these doings of the gods adulteries; even of those gods who did not refrain from the abuse of males as disgraceful, but who practised even this as seemly.

For instance, Jupiter himself was in love with Ganymede:

Poseidon with Pelops; Apollo with Cinyras, Zacyinthus, Hyacinthus, Phorbas, Hylas, Admetus, Cyparissius, Amyclas, Troilus, Branchus the Tymnaean, Parus the Potnian, Orpheus; Dionysus with Laonis, Ampelus, Hymenaeus, Hermaphrodites, Achilles; Asclepius with Hippolytus, and Hephaestus with Peleus; Pan with Daphnis; Hermes with Perseus, Chrysas, Theseus, Odrysus; Hercules with Abderus, Dryops, Jocastus, Philoctetes, Hylas, Polyphemus, Haemon, Chonus, Eurystheus.

Chapter XVI - Praise of Unchastity

"Thus have I in part set before you the amours of all the more noted gods, beloved, that you may know that fanaticism respecting this thing is confined to senseless men.

Therefore they are mortal, and spend their lives sadly, because through their zeal they proclaim those things to be evil which the gods esteem as excellent.

Therefore for the future you will be blessed, imitating the gods, and not men.

For men, seeing you preserving that which is thought to be chastity, on account of what they themselves feel, praise you indeed, but do not help you.

But the gods, seeing you like unto themselves, will both praise and help.

Chapter XVII - The Constellations

"For reckon to me how many mistresses they have rewarded, some of whom they have placed among the stars; and of some they have blessed both the children and the associates.

Thus Zeus made Callisto a constellation, called the Little Bear, which some also call the Dog's Tail.

Poseidon also placed the dolphin in the sky for the sake of Amphitrite; and he gave a place among the stars to Orion the son of Euryale, the daughter of Minos, for the sake of his mother Euryale. And Dionysus made a constellation of the crown of Ariadne, and Zeus invested the eagle which assisted him in the rape of Ganymede, and Ganymede himself with the honour of the Water-pourer.

Also he honoured the bull for the sake of Europa; and also having bestowed Castor, and Polydeuces, and Helena upon Leda, he made them stars.

Also Perseus for the sake of Danae; and Arcus for the sake of Callisto.

The virgin who also is Dice, for the sake of Themis; and Heracles for the sake of Alcmene.

But I do not enlarge further; for it were long to tell particularly how many others the gods have blessed for the sake of their many mistresses. in their intercourse with human beings, which senseless men repudiate as evil deeds, not knowing that pleasure is the great advantage among men.

Chapter XVIII - The Philosophers Advocates of Adultery

"But why?
Do not the celebrated philosophers extol pleasure, and have they not had intercourse with what women they would?
Of these the first was that teacher of Greece, of whom Phoebus himself said, "Of all men, Socrates is the wisest."
Does not he teach that in a well-regulated state women should be common? [7] and did he not conceal the fair Alcibiades under his philosopher's gown?
And the Socratic Antisthenes writes of the necessity of not abandoning what is called adultery.
And even his disciple Diogenes, did not he freely associate with Lais, for the hire of carrying her on his shoulders in public?
Does not Epicurus extol pleasure?
Did not Aristippus anoint himself with perfumes, and devote himself wholly to Aphrodite?
Does not Zeno, intimating indifference, say that the deity pervades all things, that it may be known to the intelligent, that with whomsoever a man has intercourse, it is as with himself; and that it is superfluous to forbid what are called adulteries, or intercourse with mother, or daughter, or sister, or children.
And Chrysippus, in his erotic epistles, makes mention of the statue in Argos, representing Hera and Zeus in an obscene position.

Chapter XIX - Close of the Love-Letter

"I know that to those uninitiated in the truth these things seem dreadful and most base; but not so to the gods and the philosophers of the Greeks, nor to those initiated in the mysteries of Dionysus and Demeter.
But above all these, not to waste time in speaking of the lives of all the gods, and all the philosophers, let the two chief be your marks--Zeus the greatest of the gods, and Socrates of philosophic men.
And the other things which I have mentioned in this letter, understand and attend to, that you may not grieve your lover; since, if you act contrarily to gods and heroes, you will be judged wicked, and will subject yourself to fitting punishment.
But if you offer yourself to every lover, then, as an imitator of the gods, you shall receive benefits from them.
For the rest, dearest one, remember what mysteries I have disclosed to you, and inform me by letter of your choice.
Fare thee well.'

Chapter XX - The Use Made of It

"I therefore, having received this billet from Appion, as though I were really going to send it to a beloved one, pretended as if she had written in answer to it; and the next day, when Appion came, I gave him the reply, as if from her, as follows:--

Chapter XXI - Answer to Appion's Letter

"I wonder how, when you commend me for wisdom, you write to me as to a fool.
For, wishing to persuade me to your passion, you make use of examples from the mythologies of the gods, that Eros is the eldest of all, as you say, and above all gods and men, not being afraid to blaspheme, that you might corrupt my soul and insult my body.
For Eros is not the leader of the gods,--he, I mean, who has to do with lusts. For if he lusts willingly, he is himself his own suffering and punishment; and he who should suffer willingly could not be a god.
But if against his will he lust for copulation, and, pervading our souls as through the members of our bodies, is borne into intermeddling with our minds, then he that impels him to love is greater than he.

And again, he who impels him, being himself impelled by another desire, another greater than he is found impelling him.

And thus we come to an endless succession of lovers, [8] which is impossible.

Thus, neither is there an impeller nor an impelled; but it is the lustful passion of the lover himself, which is increased by hope and diminished by despair.

Chapter XXII - Lying Fables

"But those who will not subdue base lusts belie the gods, that, by representing the gods as first doing the things which they do, they may be set free from blame.

For if those who are called gods committed adulteries for the sake of begetting children, and not through lasciviousness, why did they also debauch males?

But it is said they complimented their mistresses by making them stars.

Therefore before this were there no stars, until such time as, by reason of wantonness, the heaven was adorned with stars by adulterers?

And how is it that the children of those who have been made stars are punished in Hades,--Atlas loaded, Tantalus tortured with thirst, Sisyphus pushing a stone, Tityus thrust through the bowels, Ixion continually rolled round a wheel?

How is it that these divine lovers made stars of the women whom they defiled, but gave no such grace to these?

Chapter XXIII - The Gods No Gods

"They were not gods, then, but representations of tyrants.

For a certain tomb is shown among the Caucasian mountains, not in heaven, but in earth, as that of Kronos, a barbarous man and a devourer of children.

Further, the tomb of the lascivious Zeus, so famed in story, who in like manner devoured his own daughter Metis, is to be seen in Crete, and those of Pluto and Poseidon in the Acherusian lake; and that of Helius in Astra, and of Selene in Carrae, of Hermes in Hermopolis, of Ares in Thrace, of Aphrodite in Cyprus, of Dionysus in Thebes, and of the rest in other places.

At all events, the tombs are shown of those that I have named; for they were men, and in respect of these things, wicked men and magicians. [9]For else they should not have become despots--I mean Zeus, renowned in story, and Dionysus--but that by changing their forms they prevailed over whom they pleased, for whatever purpose they designed.

Chapter XXIV - If a Principle Be Good, Carry It Out

"But if we must emulate their lives, let us imitate not only their adulteries, but also their banquets.

For Kronos devoured his own children, and Zeus in like manner his own daughter.

And what must I say?

Pelops served as a supper for all the gods.

Wherefore let us also, before unhallowed marriages, perpetrate a supper like that of the gods; for thus the supper would be worthy of the marriages.

But this you would never consent to; no more will I to adultery.

Besides this, you threaten me with the anger of Eros as of a powerful god.

Eros is not a god, as I conceive him, but a desire occurring from the temperament of the living creature in order to the perpetuation of life, according to the foresight of Him who worketh all things, that the whole race may not fail, but by reason of pleasure another may be produced out of the substance of one who shall die, springing forth by lawful marriage, that he may know to sustain his own father in old age.

And this those born from adultery cannot do, not having the nature of affection towards those who have begotten them.

Chapter XXV - Better to Marry Than to Burn

"Since, therefore, the erotic desire occurs for the sake of continuation and legitimate increasing, as I have said, it behoves parents providing for the chastity of their children to anticipate the desire, by imbuing them with instruction by means of chaste books, and to accustom them beforehand by excellent discourses; for custom is a second nature.

And in addition to this, frequently to remind them of the punishments appointed by the laws, that, using fear as a bridle, they may not run on in wicked pleasures.

And it behoves them also, before the springing of the desire, to satisfy the natural passion of puberty by marriage, first persuading them not to look upon the beauty of another woman.

Chapter XXVI - Close of the Answer

"For our mind, whenever it is impressed delightfully with the image of a beloved one, always seeing the form as in a mirror, is tormented by the recollection; and if it does not obtain its desire, it contrives ways of obtaining it; but if it do obtain it, it is rather increased, like fire having a supply of wood, and especially when there is no fear impressed upon the soul of the lover before the rise of passion.

For as water extinguishes fire, so fear is the extinguisher of unreasonable desire.

Whence I, having learned from a certain Jew both to understand and to do the things that are pleasing to God, am not to be entrapped into adultery by your lying fables.

But may God help you in your wish and efforts to be chaste, and afford a remedy to your soul burning with love.'

Chapter XXVII - A Reason for Hatred

"When Appion heard the pretended answer, he said:
Is it without reason that I hate the Jews?
Here now some Jew has fallen in with her, and has converted her to his religion, and persuaded her to chastity, and it is henceforth impossible that she ever have intercourse with another man; for these fellows, setting God before them as the universal inspector of actions, are extremely persistent in chastity, as being unable to be concealed from Him.'

Chapter XXVIII - The Hoax Confessed

"When I heard this, I said to Appion:
Now I shall confess the truth to you.
I was not enamoured of the woman, or of any one else, my soul being exceedingly spent upon other desires, and upon the investigation of true doctrines.

And till now, although I have examined many doctrines of philosophers, I have inclined to none of them, excepting only that of the Jews,--a certain merchant of theirs having sojourned here in Rome, selling linen clothes, and a fortunate meeting having set simply before me the doctrine of the unity of God.'

Chapter XXIX - Appion's Resentment

"Then Appion, having heard from me the truth, with his unreasonable hatred of the Jews, and neither knowing nor wishing to know what their faith is, being senselessly angry, forthwith quitted Rome in silence. And as this is my first meeting with him since then, I naturally expect his anger in consequence.

However, I shall ask him in your presence what he has to say concerning those who are called gods, whose lives, fabled to be filled with all passions, are constantly celebrated to the people, in order to their imitation; while, besides their human passions as I have said, their graves are also shown in different places."

The Epistles of Clement

Chapter XXX - A Discussion Promised

The others having heard these things from me, and desiring to learn what would ensue, accompanied me to visit Appion.

And we found him bathed, and sitting at a table furnished.

Wherefore we inquired but little into the matter concerning the gods.

But he, understanding, I suppose, our wish, promised that next day he would have something to say about the gods, and appointed to us the same place where he would converse with us.

And we, as soon as he had promised, thanked him, and departed, each one to his home.

Footnotes:

1. [The historical setting of Homily V. is peculiar to this narrative; most of the views appear in a different connection in the Recognitions (mainly book x.).--R.]
2. [See Homily IV. 6, footnote.--R.]
3. [The introduction of the letters is an ingenious literary device.
Much of the mythological matter is given in Recognitions, x.--R.]
4. We have adopted the punctuation of Wieseler.
5. [Comp. Recognitions, x. 20-23, for a parallel to chaps. 12-15.--R.]
6. I have no doubt that this is the general meaning; but the text is hopelessly corrupt.
7. This from a marginal reading.
8. I suspect it should rather be impellers, reading pheronton for eronton.
9. [Compare the different use of these details in Recognitions, x. 24; also in Homily VI. 21.--R.]

Homily VI

Chapter I - Clement Meets Appion

And on the third day, when I came with my friends to the appointed place in Tyre, I found Appion sitting between Anubion and Athenodorus, and waiting for us, along with many other learned men.
But in no wise dismayed, I greeted them, and sat down opposite Appion.
And in a little he began to speak:--
"I wish to start from the following point, and to come with all speed at once to the question.
Before you, my son Clement, joined us, my friend Anubion here, and Athenodorus, who yesterday were among those who heard you discourse, were reporting to me what you said of the numerous false accusations I brought against the gods when I was visiting you in Rome, at the time you were shamming love, how I charged them with paederasty, lasciviousness, and numerous incests of all kinds.
But, my son, you ought to have known that I was not in earnest when I wrote such things about the gods, but was concealing the truth, from my love to you.
That truth, however, if it so please you, you may hear from me now.

Chapter II - The Myths are Not to Be Taken Literally

"The wisest of the ancients, men who had by hard labour learned all truth, kept the path of knowledge hid from those who were unworthy and had no taste for lessons in divine things. [1]For it is not really true that from Ouranos and his mother Ge were born twelve children, as the myth counts them:
six sons, Okeanos, Koios, Krios, Hyperion, Japetos, Kronos; and six daughters, Thea, Themis, Mnemosyne, Demeter, Tethys, and Rhea. [2]Nor that Kronos, with the knife of adamant, mutilated his father Ouranos, as you say, and threw the part into the sea; nor that Aphrodite sprang from the drops of blood which flowed from it; nor that Kronos associated with Rhea, and devoured his first-begotten son Pluto, because a certain saying of Prometheus led him to fear that a child born from him would wax stronger than himself, and spoil him of his kingdom; nor that he devoured in the same way Poseidon, his second child; nor that, when Zeus was born next, his mother Rhea concealed him, and when Kronos asked for him that he might devour him, gave him a stone instead; nor that this, when it was devoured, pressed those who had been previously devoured, and forced them out, so that Pluto, who was devoured first, came out first, and after him Poseidon, and then Zeus; [3] nor that Zeus, as the story goes, preserved by the wit of his mother, ascended into heaven, and spoiled his father of the kingdom; nor that he punished his father's brothers; nor that he came down to lust after mortal women; nor that he associated with his sisters, and daughters, and sisters-in-law, and was guilty of shameful paederasty; nor that he devoured his daughter Metis, in order that from her he might make Athene be born out of his own brain (and from his thigh might bear Dionysos, who is said to have been rent in pieces by the Titans) [4] ; nor that he held a feast at the marriage of Peleus and Thetis; [5] nor that he excluded Eris (discord) from the marriage; nor that Eris on her part, thus dishonoured, contrived an occasion of quarrelling and discord among the feasters; nor that she took a golden apple from the gardens of the Hesperides, and wrote on it For the fair.'
And then they fable how Hera, and Athena, and Aphrodite, found the apple, and quarrelling about it, came to Zeus; and he did not decide it for them, but sent them by Hermes to the shepherd Paris, to be judged of their beauty.
But there was no such judging of the goddesses; nor did Paris give the apple to Aphrodite; nor did Aphrodite, being thus honoured, honour him in return, by giving him Helen to wife.
For the honour bestowed by the goddess could never have furnished a pretext for a universal war, and that to the ruin of him who was honoured, himself nearly related to the race of Aphrodite.
But, my son, as I said, such stories have a peculiar and philosophical meaning, which can be

allegorically set forth in such a way that you yourself would listen with wonder."

And I said, "I beseech you not to torment me with delay."

And he said, "Do not be afraid; for I shall lose no time, but commence at once.

Chapter III - Appion Proceeds to Interpret the Myths

"There was once a time when nothing existed but chaos and a confused mixture of orderless elements, which were as yet simply heaped together. [6]This nature testifies, and great men have been of opinion that it was so.

Of these great men I shall bring forward to you him who excelled them all in wisdom, Homer, where he says, with a reference to the original confused mass, But may you all become water and earth;'[7] implying that from these all things had their origin, and that all things return to their first state, which is chaos, when the watery and earthy substances are separated.

And Hesiod in the Theogony says, Assuredly chaos was the very first to come into being.'[8]Now, by come into being,' he evidently means that chaos came into being, as having a beginning, and did not always exist, without beginning.

And Orpheus likens chaos to an egg, in which was the confused mixture of the primordial elements.

This chaos, which Orpheus calls an egg, is taken for granted by Hesiod, having a beginning, produced from infinite matter, and originated in the following way.

Chapter IV - Origin of Chaos

"This matter, of four kinds, and endowed with life, was an entire infinite abyss, so to speak, in eternal stream, borne about without order, and forming every now and then countless but ineffectual combinations (which therefore it dissolved again from want of order); ripe indeed, but not able to be bound so as to generate a living creature.

And once it chanced that this infinite sea, which was thus by its own nature driven about with a natural motion, flowed in an orderly manner from the same to the same (back on itself), like a whirlpool, mixing the substances in such a way that from each [9] there flowed down the middle of the universe (as in the funnel of a mould) precisely that which was most useful and suitable for the generation of a living creature.

This was carried down by the all-carrying whirlpool, drew to itself the surrounding spirit, and having been so conceived that it was very fertile, formed a separate substance.

For just as a bubble is usually formed in water, so everything round about contributed to the conception of this ball-like globe.

Then there came forth to the light, after it had been conceived in itself, and was borne upwards by the divine spirit which surrounded it, [10] perhaps the greatest thing ever born; a piece of workmanship, so to speak, having life in it which had been conceived from that entire infinite abyss, in shape like an egg, and as swift as a bird.

Chapter V - Kronos and Rhea Explained

"Now you must think of Kronos as time (chronos), and Rhea as the flowing (rheon) of the watery substance. [11]For the whole body of matter was borne about for some Time, before it brought forth, like an egg, the sphere-like, all-embracing heaven (ouranos), which at first was full of productive marrow, so that it was able to produce out of itself elements and colours of all sorts, while from the one substance and the one colour it produced all kinds of forms.

For as a peacock's egg seems to have only one colour, while potentially it has in it all the colours of the animal that is to be, so this living egg, conceived out of infinite matter, when set in motion by the underlying and ever-flowing matter, produces many different forms.

For within the circumference a certain living creature, which is both male and female, is formed by the skill of the indwelling divine spirit.

This Orpheus calls Phanes, because when it appeared (phaneis) the universe shone forth from it, with the lustre of that most glorious of the elements, fire, perfected in moisture.

Nor is this incredible, since in glowworms nature gives us to see a moist light.

Chapter VI - Phanes and Pluto

"This egg, then, which was the first substance, growing somewhat hot, was broken by the living creature within, and then there took shape and came forth something; [12] such as Orpheus also speaks of, where he says, when the capacious egg was broken,' [13] etc.

And so by the mighty power of that which appeared (phaneis) and came forth, the globe attained coherency, and maintained order, while it itself took its seat, as it were, on the summit of heaven, there in ineffable mystery diffusing light through endless ages.

But the productive matter left inside the globe, separated the substances of all things.

For first its lower part, just like the dregs, sank downwards of its own weight; and this they called Pluto from its gravity, and weight, and great quantity (polu) of underlying matter, styling it the king of Hades and the dead. [14]

Chapter VII - Poseidon, Zeus, and Metis

"When, then, they say that this primordial substance, although most filthy and rough, was devoured by Kronos, that is, time, this is to be understood in a physical sense, as meaning that it sank downwards.

And the water which flowed together after this first sediment, and floated on the surface of the first substance, they called Poseidon.

And then what remained, the purest and noblest of all, for it was translucent fire, they called Zeus, from its glowing (zeousa) nature.

Now since fire ascends, this was not swallowed, and made to descend by time or Kronos; but, as I said, the fiery substance, since it has life in it, and naturally ascends, flew right up into the air, which from its purity is very intelligent.

By his own proper heat, then, Zeus--that is, the glowing substance--draws up what is left in the underlying moisture, to wit, that very strong [15] and divine spirit which they called Metis.

Chapter VIII - Pallas and Hera

"And this, when it had reached the summit of the aether, was devoured by it (moisture being mixed with heat, so to say); and causing in it that ceaseless palpitation, it begat intelligence, which they call Pallas from this palpitating (pallesthai). [16] And this is artistic wisdom, by which the aetherial artificer wrought out the whole world.

And from all-pervading Zeus, that is, from this very hot aether, air (aer) extends all the way to our earth; and this they call Hera.

Wherefore, because it has come below the aether, which is the purest substance (just as a woman, as regards purity, is inferior), when the two were compared to see which was the better, she was rightly regarded as the sister of Zeus, in respect of her origin from the same substance, but as his spouse, as being inferior like a wife.

Chapter IX - Artemis

"And Hera we understand to be a happy tempering of the atmosphere, and therefore she is very fruitful; but Athena, as they call Pallas, was reckoned a virgin, because on account of the intense heat she could produce nothing.

And in a similar fashion Artemis is explained:

for her they take as the lowest depth of air, and so they called her a virgin, because she could not bear anything on account of the extreme cold.

And that troubled and drunken composition which arises from the upper and lower vapours they called Dionysus, as troubling the intellect.

And the water under the earth, which is in nature indeed one, but which flows through all the paths of earth, and is divided into many parts, they called Osiris, as being cut in pieces.

And they understand Adonis as favourable seasons, Aphrodite as coition and generation, Demeter as the earth, the Girl (Proserpine) as seeds; and Dionysus some understand as the vine.

Chapter X - All Such Stories are Allegorical

"And I must ask you to think of all such stories as embodying some such allegory.

Look on Apollo as the wandering Sun (peri-polon), a son of Zeus, who was also called Mithras, as completing the period of a year. And these said transformations of the all-pervading Zeus must be regarded as the numerous changes of the seasons, while his numberless wives you must understand to be years, or generations.

For the power which proceeds from the aether and passes through the air unites with all the years and generations in turn, and continually varies them, and so produces or destroys the crops.

And ripe fruits are called his children, the barrenness of some seasons being referred to unlawful unions."

Chapter XI - Clement Has Heard All This Before

While Appion was allegorizing in this way, I became plunged in thought, and seemed not to be following what he was saying.

So he interrupted his discourse, and said to me, "If you do not follow what I am saying, why should I speak at all?"

And I answered, "Do not suppose that I do not understand what you say.

I understand it thoroughly; and that the more that this is not the first time I have heard it.

And that you may know that I am not ignorant of these things, I shall epitomize what you have said, and supply in their order, as I have heard them from others, the allegorical interpretations of those stories you have omitted." And Appion said:

"Do so."

Chapter XII - Epitome of Appion's Explanation

And I answered: [17]"I shall not at present speak particularly of that living egg, which was conceived by a happy combination out of infinite matter, and from which, when it was broken, the masculo-feminine Phanes leaped forth, as some say.

I say little about all that, up to the point when this broken globe attained coherency, there being left in it some of its marrow-like matter; and I shall briefly run over the description of what took place in it by the agency of this matter, with all that followed.

For from Kronos and Rhea were born, as you say--that is, by time and matter--first Pluto, who represents the sediment which settled down; and then Poseidon, the liquid substance in the middle,[18] which floated over the heavier body below; and the third child--that is, Zeus--is the aether, and is highest of all.

It was not devoured; but as it is a fiery power, and naturally ascends, it flew up as with a bound to the very highest aether.

Chapter XIII - Kronos and Aphrodite

"And the bonds of Kronos are the binding together of heaven and earth, as I have heard others allegorizing; and his mutilation is the separation and parting of the elements; for they all were severed and separated, according to their respective natures, that each kind might be arranged by itself.

And time no longer begets anything; but the things which have been begotten of it, by a law of nature, produce their successors.

And the Aphrodite who emerged from the sea is the fruitful substance which arises out of moisture, with which the warm spirit mixing, causes that sexual desire, and perfects the beauty of the world.

Chapter XIV - Peleus and Thetis, Prometheus, Achilles, and Polyxena

"And the marriage banquet, at which Zeus held the feast on the occasion of the marriage of the Nereid Thetis and the beautiful Peleus, has in it this allegory, [19] --that you may know, Appion, that you are not the only one from whom I have heard this sort of thing.

The banquet, then, is the world, and the twelve are these heavenly props of the Fates, [20] called the Zodiac.

Prometheus is foresight (prometheia), by which all things arose; Peleus is clay (pelos), namely, that which was collected [21] from the earth and mixed with Nereis, or water, to produce man; and from the mixing of the two, i.e., water and earth, the first offspring was not begotten, but fashioned complete, and called Achilles, because he never put his lips (cheile) to the breast. [22]

Still in the bloom of life, he is slain by an arrow while desiring to have Polyxena, that is, something other than the truth, and foreign (xene) to it, death stealing on him through a wound in his foot.

Chapter XV - The Judgment of Paris

"Then Hera, and Athena, and Aphrodite, and Eris, and the apple, and Hermes, and the judgment, and the shepherd, have some such hidden meaning as the following:--Hera is dignity; Athena, manliness; Aphrodite, pleasure; Hermes, language, which interprets (hermeneutikos) thought; the shepherd Paris, unreasoned and brutish passion.

Now if, in the prime of life, reason, that shepherd of the soul, is brutish, does not regard its own advantage, will have nothing to do with manliness and temperance, chooses only pleasure, and gives the prize to lust alone, bargaining that it is to receive in return from lust what may delight it,--he who thus judges incorrectly will choose pleasure to his own destruction and that of his friends.

And Eris is jealous spite; and the golden apples of the Hesperides are perhaps riches, by which occasionally even temperate persons like Hera are seduced, and manly ones like Athena are made jealous, so that they do things which do not become them, and the soul's beauty like Aphrodite is destroyed under the guise of refinement.

To speak briefly, in all men riches provoke evil discord.

Chapter XVI - Hercules

"And Hercules, who slew the serpent which led and guarded riches, is the true philosophical reason which, free from all wickedness, wanders all over the world, visiting the souls of men, and chastising all it meets,--namely, men like fierce lions, or timid stags, or savage boars, or multiform hydras; and so with all the other fabled labours of Hercules, they all have a hidden reference to moral valour.

But these instances must suffice, for all our time would be insufficient if we were to go over each one.

Chapter XVII - They are Blameworthy Who Invented Such Stories

"Now, [23] since these things can be clearly, profitably, and without prejudice to piety, set forth in an open and straightforward manner, I wonder you call those men sensible and wise who concealed them under crooked riddles, and overlaid them with filthy stories, and thus, as if impelled by an evil spirit, deceived almost all men.

For either these things are not riddles, but real crimes of the gods, in which case they should not have been exposed to contempt, nor should these their needs have been set before men at all as models; or things falsely attributed to the gods were set forth in an allegory, and then, Appion, they whom you call wise erred, in that, by concealing under unworthy stories things in themselves worthy, they led men to sin, and that not without dishonouring those whom they believed to be gods.

Chapter XVIII - The Same

"Wherefore do not suppose that they were wise men, but rather evil spirits, who could cover honourable actions with wicked stories, in order that they who wish to imitate their betters may emulate these deeds of so-called gods, which yesterday in my discourse I spoke so freely of,--namely, their parricides, their murders of their children, their incests of all kinds, their shameless adulteries and countless impurities.

The most impious of them are those who wish these stories to be believed, in order that they may not be ashamed when they do the like.

If they had been disposed to act reverently, they ought, as I said a little ago, even if the gods really did the things which are sung of them, to have veiled their indecencies under more seemly stories, and not, on the contrary, as you say they did, when the deeds of the gods were honourable, clothed them in wicked and indecent forms, which, even when interpreted, can only be understood by much labour; and when they were understood by some, they indeed got for their much toil the privilege of not being deceived, which they might have had without the toil, while they who were deceived were utterly ruined. (Those, however, who trace the allegories to a more honourable source I do not object to; as, for instance, those who explain one allegory by saying that it was wisdom which sprang from the head of Zeus.)

On the whole, it seems to me more probable that wicked men, robbing the gods of their honour, ventured to promulgate these insulting stories.

Chapter XIX - None of These Allegories are Consistent

"Nor do we find the poetical allegory about any of the gods consistent with itself.

To go no further than the fashioning of the universe, the poets now say that nature was the first cause of the whole creation, now that it was mind.

For, say they, the first moving and mixture of the elements came from nature, but it was the foresight of mind which arranged them in order.

Even when they assert that it was nature which fashioned the universe, being unable absolutely to demonstrate this on account of the traces of design in the work, they in weave the foresight of mind in such a way that they are able to entrap even the wisest.

But we say to them:

If the world arose from self-moved nature, how did it ever take proportion and shape, which cannot come but from a superintending wisdom, and can be comprehended only by knowledge, which alone can trace such things?

If, on the other hand, it is by wisdom that all things subsist and maintain order, how can it be that those things arose from self-moved chance?

Chapter XX - These Gods Were Really Wicked Magicians

"Then those who chose to make dishonourable allegories of divine things--as, for instance, that Metis was devoured by Zeus--have fallen into a dilemma, because they did not see that they who in these stories about the gods indirectly taught physics, denied the very existence of the gods, revolving all kinds of gods into mere allegorical representations of the various substances of the universe.

And so it is more likely that the gods these persons celebrate were some sort of wicked magicians, who were in reality wicked men, but by magic assumed different shapes, committed adulteries, and took away life, and thus to the men of old who did not understand magic seemed to be gods by the things they did; and the bodies and tombs of these men are to be seen in many towns.

Chapter XXI - Their Graves are Still to Be Seen

"For instance, as I have mentioned already, in the Caucasian mountains there is shown the tomb of a certain Kronos, a man, and a fierce monarch who slew his children.

And the son of this man, called Zeus, became worse than his father; and having by the power of magic been declared ruler of the universe, he committed many adulteries, and inflicted punishment on his father and uncles, and so died; and the Cretans show his tomb.

And in Mesopotamia there lie buried a certain Helios at Atir, and a certain Selene at Carrhae.

A certain Hermes, a man, lies buried in Egypt; Ares in Thrace; Aphrodite in Cyprus; AEsculapius in Epidaurus; and the tombs of many other such persons are to be seen. [24]

Chapter XXII - Their Contemporaries, Therefore, Did Not Look on Them as Gods

"Thus, to right-thinking men, it is clear that they were admitted to be mortals.

And their contemporaries, knowing that they were mortal, when they died paid them no more heed; and it was length of time which clothed them with the glory of gods.

Nor need you wonder that they who lived in the times of AEsculapius and Hercules were deceived, or the contemporaries of Dionysus or any other of the men of that time, when even Hector in Ilium, and Achilles in the island of Leuce, are worshipped by the inhabitants of those places; and the Opuntines worship Patroclus, and the Rhodians Alexander of Macedon. [25]

Chapter XXIII - The Egyptians Pay Divine Honours to a Man

"Moreover, among the Egyptians even to the present day, a man is worshipped as a god before his death.

And this truly is a small impiety, that the Egyptians give divine honours to a man in his lifetime; but what is of all things most absurd is, that they worship birds and creeping things, and all kinds of beasts.

For the mass of men neither think nor do anything with discretion.

But look, I pray you, at what is most disgraceful of all:

he who is with them the father of gods and men is said by them to have had intercourse with Leda; and many of them set up in public a painting of this, writing above it the name Zeus.

To punish this insult, I could wish that they would paint their own present king in such base embraces as they have dared to do with Zeus, and set it up in public, that from the anger of a temporary monarch, and him a mortal, they might learn to render honour where it is due.

This I say to you, not as myself already knowing the true God; but I am happy to say that even if I do not know who is God, I think I at least know clearly what God is.

Chapter XXIV - What is Not God

"And first, then, the four original elements cannot be God, because they have a cause.

Nor can that mixing be God, nor that compounding, nor that generating, nor that globe which surrounds the visible universe; nor the dregs which flow together in Hades, nor the water which floats over them; nor the fiery substance, nor the air which extends from it to our earth.

For the four elements, if they lay outside one another, could not have been mixed together so as to generate animal life without some great artificer.

If they have always been united, even in this case they are fitted together by an artistic mind to what is requisite for the limbs and parts of animals, that they may be able to preserve their respective proportions, may have a clearly defined shape, and that all the inward parts may attain the fitting coherency.

In the same way also the positions suitable for each are determined, and that very beautifully, by the artificer mind. To be brief, in all other things which a living creature must have, this great being of the world is in no respect wanting.

Chapter XXV - The Universe is the Product of Mind

"Thus we are shut up to the supposition that there is an unbegotten artificer, who brought the elements together, if they were separate; or, if they were together, artistically blended them so as to generate life, and perfected from all one work.

For it cannot be that a work which is completely wise can be made without a mind which is greater than it.

Nor will it do to say that love is the artificer of all things, or desire, or power, or any such thing. All these are liable to change, and transient in their very nature.

Nor can that be God which is moved by another, much less what is altered by time and nature, and can be annihilated." [26]

Chapter XXVI - Peter Arrives from Caesarea

While I was saying these things to Appion, Peter drew near from Caesarea, and in Tyre the people were flocking together, hurrying to meet him and unite in an expression of gratification at his visit.

And Appion withdrew, accompanied by Anubion and Athenodorus only; but the rest of us hurried to meet Peter, and I was the first to greet him at the gate, and I led him towards the inn.

When we arrived, we dismissed the people; and when he deigned to ask what had taken place, I concealed nothing, but told him of Simon's slanders, and the monstrous shapes he had taken, and all the diseases he had sent after the sacrificial feast, and that some of the sick persons were still there in Tyre, while others had gone on with Simon to Sidon just as I arrived, hoping to be cured by him, but that I had heard that none of them had been cured by him.

I also told Peter of the controversy I had with Appion; and he, from his love to me, and desiring to encourage me, praised and blessed me.

Then, having supped, he betook himself to the rest the fatigues of his journey rendered so necessary.

Footnotes:

1. [Compare in general, with chaps. 2-22, the mythological statements in Recognitions, x. 17-41.--R.]
2. [Compare Recognitions, x. 17, 31.--R.]
3. The passage seems to be corrupt.
4. The common story about Dionysus is, that he was the unborn son, not of Metis, but of Semele.
Wieseler supposes that some words have fallen out, or that the latter part of the sentence is a careless interpolation.
5. [Compare, on "the supper of the gods," chap. 15, and Recognitions, x. 41.--R.]
6. [With this discourse and its cosmogony compare the discourse of Clement and his brothers in Recognitions, x. 17-19, 30-34.--R.]
7. Iliad, vii. 99.
8. L. 116.
9. This is the emendation of Davisius.
The Greek has ex akoustou; the Latin, "mirum in modum."
Wieseler suggests exakontiston.
10. This is Wieseler's emendation for "received."
11. [Comp. Recognitions, x. 17, 31, 32.--R.]
12. Wieseler corrects to "some such being," etc.; and below, "of him who appeared," etc.; and "he took his seat."
13. The first word of this quotation gives no sense, and has been omitted in the translation.
Lobeck suggests "at its prime;" Hermann, "Heracapeian;" Duentzer, "ancient;" and Wieseler, "white."
14. [Comp. Recognitions, x. 32.--R.]
15. The Paris ms. has "very fine."
16. [With chaps. 8-10 compare Recognitions, x. 32, 34.--R.]
17. [Comp. Recognitions, x. 17-19, 29-36, 41, for statements similar to those in chaps. 12-19.--R.]
18. This is Wiesler's conjecture.
19. [Comp. chap. 2, and Recognitions, 40, 41.--R.]
20. The Latin takes "moira" in the sense of "district," and translates, "these props of the districts of

the sky."

21. This is Wieseler's conjecture for reading of the mss., "contrived."
22. This is Schwegler's restoration of the passage.
Davisius proposes, "He is in the bloom of life, at which time if any one desires," etc.
23. [Compare with the arguments here, Recognitions, x. 35-38.--R.]
24. [Comp. v. 23, and Recognitions, x. 24.--R.]
25. [Comp. Recognitions, x. 25, where these facts are also used.--R.]
26. [The conclusion of the discussion is noteworthy, not only from the fairness of the argument, but from the skill with which the position of Clement, as a heathen inquirer, is maintained.--R.]

Homily VII

Chapter I - Peter Addresses the People

And on the fourth day of our stay in Tyre, [1] Peter went out about daybreak, and there met him not a few of the dwellers round about, with very many of the inhabitants of Tyre itself, who cried out, and said, "God through you have mercy upon us, God through you heal us!"

And Peter stood on a high stone, that all might see him; and having greeted them in a godly manner, thus began:--

Chapter II - Reason of Simon's Power

"God, who created the heavens and the whole universe, does not want occasion for the salvation of those who would be saved.

Wherefore let no one, in seeming evils, rashly charge Him with unkindness to man. For men do not know the issue of those things which happen to them, nay, suspect that the result will be evil; but God knows that they will turn out well.

So is it in the case of Simon.

He is a power of the left hand of God, and has authority to do harm to those who know not God, so that he has been able to involve you in diseases; but by these very diseases, which have been permitted to come upon you by the good providence of God, you, seeking and finding him who is able to cure, have been compelled to submit to the will of God on the occasion of the cure of the body, and to think of believing, in order that in this way you may have your souls as well as your bodies in a healthy state.

Chapter III - The Remedy

"Now I have been told, that after he had sacrificed an ox he feasted you in the middle of the forum, and that you, being carried away with much wine, made friends with not only the evil demons, but their prince also, and that in this way the most of you were seized by these sicknesses, unwittingly drawing upon yourselves with your own hands the sword of destruction.

For the demons would never have had power over you, had not you first supped with their prince.

For thus from the beginning was a law laid by God, the Creator of all things, on each of the two princes, him of the right hand and him of the left, that neither should have power over any one whom they might wish to benefit or to hurt, unless first he had sat down at the same table with them. As, then, when you partook of meat offered to idols, you became servants to the prince of evil, in like manner, if you cease from these things, and flee for refuge to God through the good Prince of His right hand, honouring Him without sacrifices, by doing whatsoever He wills, know of a truth that not only will your bodies be healed, but your souls also will become healthy.

For He only, destroying with His left hand, can quicken with His right; He only can both smite and raise the fallen.

Chapter IV - The Golden Rule

"Wherefore, as then ye were deceived by the forerunner Simon, and so became dead in your souls to God, and were smitten in your bodies; so now, if you repent, as I said, and submit to those things which are well-pleasing to God, you may get new strength to your bodies, and recover your soul's health.

And the things which are well-pleasing to God are these:

to pray to Him, to ask from Him, recognising that He is the giver of all things, and gives with discriminating law; to abstain from the table of devils, not to taste dead flesh, not to touch blood; to be washed from all pollution; and the rest in one word,--as the God-fearing Jews have heard, do you also hear, and be of one mind in many bodies; let each man be minded to do to his neighbour those good things he wishes for himself.

And you may all find out what is good, by holding some such conversation as the following with yourselves: You would not like to be murdered; do not murder another man:

you would not like your wife to be seduced by another; do not you commit adultery:

you would not like any of your things to be stolen from you; steal nothing from another.

And so understanding by yourselves what is reasonable, and doing it, you will become dear to God, and will obtain healing; otherwise in the life which now is your bodies will be tormented, and in that which is to come your souls will be punished." [2]

Chapter V - Peter Departs for Sidon

After Peter had spent a few days in teaching them in this way, and in healing them, they were baptized.

And after that, [3] all sat down together in the market-places in sackcloth and ashes, grieving because of his other wondrous works, and repenting their former sins.

And when they of Sidon heard it, they did likewise, and sent to beseech Peter, since they could not come themselves for their diseases.

And Peter did not spend many days in Tyre; but when he had instructed all its inhabitants, and freed them from all manners of diseases and had founded a church, and set over it as bishop one of the elders who were with him, he departed for Sidon.

But when Simon heard that Peter was coming, he straightway fled to Beyrout with Appion and his friends.

Chapter VI - Peter in Sidon

And as Peter entered Sidon, they brought many in couches, and laid them before him.

And he said to them:

"Think not, I pray you, that I can do anything to heal you, who am a mortal man, myself subject to many evils.

But I shall not refuse to show you the way in which you must be saved.

For I have learned from the Prophet of truth the conditions fore-ordained of God before the foundation of the world; that is to say, the evil deeds which if men do He has ordained that they shall be injured by the prince of evil, and in like manner the good deeds for which He has decreed that they who have believed in Him as their Physician shall have their bodies made whole, and their souls established in safety.

Chapter VII - The Two Paths

"Knowing, then, these good and evil deeds, I make known unto you as it were two paths, [4] and I shall show you by which travellers are lost and by which they are saved, being guided of God.

The path of the lost, then, is broad and very smooth--it ruins them without troubling them; but the path of the saved is narrow, rugged, and in the end it saves, not without much toil, those who have journeyed through it.

And these two paths are presided over by unbelief and faith; and these journey through the path of unbelief, those who have preferred pleasure, on account of which they have forgotten the day of judgment, doing that which is not pleasing to God, and not caring to save their souls by the word, and have not anxiously sought their own good.

Truly they know not that the counsels of God are not like men's counsels; for, in the first place, He knows the thoughts of all men, and all must give an account not only of their actions, but also of their thoughts. And their sin is much less who strive to understand well and fall, than that of those who do not at all strive after good things.

Because it has pleased God that he who errs in his knowledge of good, as men count errors, should be saved after being slightly punished.

But they who have taken no care at all to know the better way, even though they may have done countless other good deeds, if they have not stood in the service He has Himself appointed, come under the charge of indifference, and are severely punished, and utterly destroyed.

Chapter VIII - The Service of God's Appointment

"And this is the service He has appointed:

To worship Him only, and trust only in the Prophet of truth, and to be baptized for the remission of sins, and thus by this pure baptism to be born again unto God by saving water; to abstain from the table of devils, that is, from food offered to idols, from dead carcases, from animals which have been suffocated or caught by wild beasts, and from blood; [5] not to live any longer impurely; to wash after intercourse; that the women on their part should keep the law of purification; that all should be sober-minded, given to good works, refraining from wrongdoing, looking for eternal life from the all-powerful God, and asking with prayer and continual supplication that they may win it."

Such was Peter's counsel to the men of Sidon also.

And in few days many repented and believed, and were healed.

And Peter having founded a church, and set over it as bishop one of the elders who were with him, left Sidon.

Chapter IX - Simon Attacks Peter

No sooner had he reached Beyrout than an earthquake took place; and the multitude, running to Peter, said, "Help us, for we are afraid we shall all utterly perish."

Then Simon ventured, along with Appion and Anubion and Athenodorus, and the rest of his companions, to cry out to the people against Peter in public:

"Flee, friends, from this man! he is a magician; trust us, he it was who caused this earthquake: he sent us these diseases to terrify us, as if he were God Himself."

And many such false charges did Simon and his friends bring against Peter, as one who could do things above human power.

But as soon as the people gave him a moment's quiet, Peter with surprising boldness gave a little laugh, and said, "Friends, I admit that I can do, God willing, what these men say; and more than that, I am ready, if you do not believe what I say, to overturn your city from top to bottom."

Chapter X - Simon is Driven Away

And the people were afraid, and promised to do whatever he should command.

"Let none of you, then," said Peter, "either hold conversation with these sorcerers, or have any thing to do with them." And as soon as the people heard this concise command, they took up sticks, and pursued them till they had driven them wholly out of the town.

And they who were sick and possessed with devils came and cast themselves at Peter's feet.

And he seeing all this, and anxious to free them from their terror, said to them:--

Chapter XI - The Way of Salvation

"Were I able to cause earthquakes, and do all that I wish, I assure you I would not destroy Simon and his friends (for not to destroy men am I sent), but would make him my friend, that he might no longer, by his slanders against my preaching the truth, hinder the salvation of many. But if you believe me, he himself is a magician; he is a slanderer; he is a minister of evil to them who know not the truth.

Therefore he has power to bring diseases on sinners, having the sinners themselves to help him in his power over them.

But I am a servant of God the Creator of all things, and a disciple of His Prophet who is at His right hand. Wherefore I, being His apostle, preach the truth:

to serve a good man I drive away diseases, for I am His second messenger, since first the disease comes, but after that the healing.

By that evil-working magician, then, you were stricken with disease because you revolted from God.

By me, if you believe on Him ye shall be cured:

and so having had experience that He is able, you may turn to good works, and have your souls saved."

Chapter XII - Peter Goes to Byblus and Tripolis

As he said these things, all fell on their knees before his feet.

And he, lifting up his hands to heaven, prayed to God, and healed them all by his simple prayer alone.

And he remained not many days in Beyrout; but after he had accustomed many to the service of the one God, and had baptized them, and had set over them a bishop from the elders who were with him, he went to Byblus.

And when he came there, and learned that Simon had not waited for them for a day, but had gone straightway to Tripolis, he remained there only a few days; and after that he had healed not a few, and exercised them in the Scriptures, he followed in Simon's track to Tripolis, preferring to pursue him rather than flee from him.

Footnotes:

1. [The historical details of this Homily also have no parallel in the Recognitions.--R.]
2. [With this discourse respecting Simon, compare Recognitions, ii. 6-18.

But the statements respecting Simon's power and the design of it are much stronger than here.--R.]
3. We have adopted Wieseler's emendation.

The text may be translated thus:

"And after that, among his other wondrous deeds, all the rest (who had not been baptized) sat down," etc.

4. [Compare with this chapter the recently discovered "Teaching" and Apostolic Constitutions, book vii. chap. 1, in vol. vii. pp. 377, 465.--R.]
5. [Comp. Recognitions, iv. 36.

The language recalls Acts xv. 20 and 1 Cor. x. 21.--R.]

Homily VIII

Chapter I - Peter's Arrival at Tripolis

Now, as Peter was entering Tripolis, [1] the people from Tyre and Sidon, Berytus and Byblus, who were eager [2] to get instruction, and many from the neighbourhood, entered along with him; and not least were there gatherings of the multitudes from the city itself wishing to see him.

Therefore there met with us in the suburbs the brethren who had been sent forth by him to ascertain as well other particulars respecting the city, as the proceedings of Simon, and to come and explain them.

They received him, and conducted him to the house of Maroones. [3]

Chapter II - Peter's Thoughtfulness

But he, when he was at the very gate of his lodging, turned round, and promised to the multitudes that after the next day he would converse with them on the subject of religion.

And when he had gone in, the forerunners assigned lodgings to those who had come with him.

And the hosts and the entertainers did not fall short of the desire of those who sought hospitality.

But Peter, knowing nothing of this, being asked by us to partake of food, said that he would not himself partake until those who had come with him were settled.

And on our assuring him that this was already done, all having received them eagerly by reason of their affection towards him, so that those were grieved beyond measure who had no guests to entertain,--Peter hearing this, and being pleased with their eager philanthropy, blessed them and went out, and having bathed in the sea, partook of food with the forerunners; and then, the evening having come, he slept.

Chapter III - A Conversation Interrupted

But awaking about the second cock-crowing, he found us astir.

We were in all sixteen, viz., Peter himself, and I Clement, Nicetas and Aquila, and the twelve who had preceded us. [4]Having therefore saluted us, he said, "To-day, not being occupied with those without, we are free to be occupied with one another.

Wherefore I shall tell you the things that happened after your departure from Tyre; and do you minutely relate to me what have been the doings of Simon here."

While, therefore, we were answering one another by narratives on either side, one of our friends entered, and announced to Peter that Simon, learning of his arrival, had set off for Syria, and that the multitudes, thinking this one night to be like a year's time, and not able to wait for the appointment which he had made, were standing before the doors conversing with one another in knots and circles about the accusation brought by Simon, and how that, having raised their expectations, and promised that he would charge Peter when he came with many evils, he had fled by night when he knew of his arrival.

"However," said he, "they are eager to hear you; and I know not whence some rumour has reached them to the effect that you are going to address them to-day. In order, therefore, that they may not when they are very tired be dismissed without reason, you yourself know what it is proper for you to do."

Chapter IV - Many Called

Then Peter, wondering at the eagerness of the multitudes, answered, [5] "You see, brethren, how the words of our Lord are manifestly fulfilled.

For I remember His saying, Many shall come from the east and from the west, the north and the south, and shall recline on the bosoms of Abraham, and Isaac, and Jacob.' [6]But many,' said He also, are called, but few chosen.' [7]The coming, therefore, of these called ones is fulfilled.

But inasmuch as it is not of themselves, but of God who has called them and caused them to come, on this account alone they have no reward, since it is not of themselves but of Him who has wrought in them.

But if, after being called, they do things that are excellent, for this is of themselves, then for this they shall have a reward.

Chapter V - Faith the Gift of God

"For even the Hebrews who believe Moses, and do not observe the things spoken by him, are not saved, unless they observe the things that were spoken to them.

For their believing Moses was not of their own will, but of God, who said to Moses, Behold, I come to thee in a pillar of cloud, that the people may hear me speaking to thee, and may believe thee for ever.' [8]Since, therefore, both to the Hebrews and to those who are called from the Gentiles, believing in the teachers of truth is of God, while excellent actions are left to every one to do by his own judgment, the reward is righteously bestowed upon those who do well.

For there would have been no need of Moses, or of the coming of Jesus, if of themselves they would have understood what is reasonable. Neither is there salvation in believing in teachers and calling them lords.

Chapter VI - Concealment and Revelation

"For on this account Jesus is concealed from the Jews, who have taken Moses as their teacher, and Moses is hidden from those who have believed Jesus.

For, there being one teaching by both, God accepts him who has believed either of these.

But believing a teacher is for the sake of doing the things spoken by God.

And that this is so our Lord Himself says, I thank thee, Father of heaven and earth, because Thou hast concealed these things from the wise and elder, and hast revealed them to sucking babes.' [9]Thus God Himself has concealed a teacher from some, as foreknowing what they ought to do, and has revealed him to others, who are ignorant what they ought to do.

Chapter VII - Moses and Christ

"Neither, therefore, are the Hebrews condemned on account of their ignorance of Jesus, by reason of Him who has concealed Him, if, doing the things commanded by Moses, they do not hate Him whom they do not know.

Neither are those from among the Gentiles condemned, who know not Moses on account of Him who hath concealed him, provided that these also, doing the things spoken by Jesus, do not hate Him whom they do not know.

And some will not be profited by calling the teachers lords, but not doing the works of servants.

For on this account our Jesus Himself said to one who often called Him Lord, but did none of the things which He prescribed, Why call ye me Lord, Lord, and do not the things which I say?' [10]For it is not saying that will profit any one, but doing.

By all means, therefore, is there need of good works. Moreover, if any one has been thought worthy to recognise both as preaching one doctrine, that man has been counted rich in God, understanding both the old things as new in time, and the new things as old."

Chapter VIII - A Large Congregation

While Peter was thus speaking, the multitudes, as if they had been called by some one, entered into the place where Peter was.

Then he, seeing a great multitude, like the smooth current of a river gently flowing towards him, said to Maroones, "Have you any place here that is better able to contain the crowd?"

Then Maroones conducted him to a garden-plot in the open air, and the multitudes followed.

But Peter, standing upon a base of a statue which was not very high, as soon as he had saluted the multitude in pious fashion, knowing that many of the crowd that stood by were tormented with demons and many sufferings of long standing, and hearing them shrieking with lamentation, and falling down before him in supplication, rebuked them, and commanded them to hold their peace; and promising healing to them after the discourse, [11] began to speak on this wise:--

Chapter IX - "Vindicate the Ways of God to Men."

"While beginning to discourse on the worship of God to those who are altogether ignorant of everything, and whose minds have been corrupted by the accusations of our adversary Simon, I have thought it necessary first of all to speak of the blamelessness of the God who hath made all things, starting from the occasion seasonably afforded by Him according to His providence, that it may be known how with good reason many are held by many demons, and subjected to strange sufferings, that in this the justice of God may appear; and that those who through ignorance blame Him, now may learn by good speaking and well-doing what sentiments they ought to hold, and recall themselves from their previous accusation, assigning ignorance as the cause of their evil presumption, in order that they may be pardoned.

Chapter X - The Original Law

"But thus the matter stands.

The only good God having made all things well, and having handed them over to man, who was made after His image, he who had been made breathing of the divinity of Him who made him, being a true prophet and knowing all things, for the honour of the Father who had given all things to him, and for the salvation of the sons born of him, as a genuine father preserving his affection towards the children born of him, and wishing them, for their advantage, to love God and be loved of Him, showed them the way which leads to His friendship, teaching them by what deeds of men the one God and Lord of all is pleased; and having exhibited to them the things that are pleasing to Him, appointed a perpetual law to all, which neither can be abrogated by enemies, nor is vitiated by any impious one, nor is concealed in any place, but which can be read by all.

To them, therefore, by obedience to the law, all things were in abundance,--the fairest of fruits, fulness of years, freedom from grief and from disease, bestowed upon them without fear, with all salubrity of the air.

Chapter XI - Cause of the Fall of Man

"But they, because they had at first no experience of evils, being insensible to the gift of good things, were turned to ingratitude by abundance of food and luxuries, so that they even thought that there is no Providence, since they had not by previous labour got good things as the reward of righteousness, inasmuch as no one of them had fallen into any suffering or disease, or any other necessity; so that, as is usual for men afflicted on account of wicked transgression, they should look about for the God who is able to heal them. [12]But immediately after their despite, which proceeded from fearlessness and secure luxury, a certain just punishment met them, as following from a certain arranged harmony, removing from them good things as having hurt them, and introducing evil things instead, as advantageous.

Chapter XII - Metamorphoses of the Angels

"For of the spirits who inhabit the heaven, [13] the angels who dwell in the lowest region, being grieved at the ingratitude of men to God, asked that they might come into the life of men, that, really becoming men, by more intercourse they might convict those who had acted ungratefully towards Him, and might subject every one to adequate punishment.

When, therefore, their petition was granted, they metamorphosed themselves into every nature; for, being of a more godlike substance, they are able easily to assume any form.

So they became precious stones, and goodly pearl, and the most beauteous purple, and choice gold, and all matter that is held in most esteem. And they fell into the hands of some, and into the bosoms of others, and suffered themselves to be stolen by them.

They also changed themselves into beasts and reptiles, and fishes and birds, and into whatsoever they pleased.

These things also the poets among yourselves, by reason of fearlessness, sing, as they befell, attributing to one the many and diverse doings of all.

Chapter XIII - The Fall of the Angels

"But when, having assumed these forms, they convicted as covetous those who stole them, and changed themselves into the nature of men, in order that, living holily, and showing the possibility of so living, they might subject the ungrateful to punishment, yet having become in all respects men, they also partook of human lust, and being brought under its subjection they fell into cohabitation with women; [14] and being involved with them, and sunk in defilement and altogether emptied of their first power, were unable to turn back to the first purity of their proper nature, their members turned away from their fiery substance: [15] for the fire itself, being extinguished by the weight of lust, and changed into flesh, they trode the impious path downward.

For they themselves, being fettered with the bonds of flesh, were constrained and strongly bound; wherefore they have no more been able to ascend into the heavens.

Chapter XIV - Their Discoveries

"For after the intercourse, being asked to show what they were before, and being no longer able to do so, on account of their being unable to do aught else after their defilement, yet wishing to please their mistresses, instead of themselves, they showed the bowels [16] of the earth; I mean, the choice metals, [17] gold, brass, silver, iron, and the like, with all the most precious stones.

And along with these charmed stones, they delivered the arts of the things pertaining to each, and imparted the discovery of magic, and taught astronomy, and the powers of roots, and whatever was impossible to be found out by the human mind; also the melting of gold and silver, and the like, and the various dyeing of garments.

And all things, in short, which are for the adornment and delight of women, are the discoveries of these demons bound in flesh.

Chapter XV - The Giants

"But from their unhallowed intercourse spurious men sprang, much greater in stature than ordinary men, whom they afterwards called giants; not those dragon-footed giants who waged war against God, as those blasphemous myths of the Greeks do sing, but wild in manners, and greater than men in size, inasmuch as they were sprung of angels; yet less than angels, as they were born of women.

Therefore God, knowing that they were barbarized to brutality, and that the world was not sufficient to satisfy them (for it was created according to the proportion of men and human use), that they might not through want of food turn, contrary to nature, to the eating of animals, and yet seem to be blameless, as having ventured upon this through necessity, the Almighty God rained manna upon them, suited to their various tastes; and they enjoyed all that they would.

But they, on account of their bastard nature, not being pleased with purity of food, longed only after the taste of blood.

Wherefore they first tasted flesh.

Chapter XVI - Cannibalism

"And the men who were with them there for the first time were eager to do the like.

Thus, although we are born neither good nor bad, we become one or the other; and having formed habits, we are with difficulty drawn from them.

But when irrational animals fell short, these bastard men tasted also human flesh.

For it was not a long step to the consumption of flesh like their own, having first tasted it in other forms.

Chapter XVII - The Flood

"But by the shedding of much blood, the pure air being defiled with impure vapour, and sickening those who breathed it, rendered them liable to diseases, so that thenceforth men died prematurely.

But the earth being by these means greatly defiled, these first teemed with poison-darting and deadly creatures.

All things, therefore, going from bad to worse, on account of these brutal demons, God wished to cast them away like an evil leaven, lest each generation from a wicked seed, being like to that before it, and equally impious, should empty the world to come of saved men.

And for this purpose, having warned a certain righteous man, [18] with his three sons, together with their wives and their children, to save themselves in an ark, He sent a deluge of water, that all being destroyed, the purified world might be handed over to him who was saved in the ark, in order to a second beginning of life.

And thus it came to pass.

Chapter XVIII - The Law to the Survivors

"Since, therefore, the souls of the deceased giants were greater than human souls, inasmuch as they also excelled their bodies, they, as being a new race, were called also by a new name.

And to those who survived in the world a law was prescribed of God through an angel, how they should live.

For being bastards in race, of the fire of angels and the blood of women, and therefore liable to desire a certain race of their own, they were anticipated by a certain righteous law.

For a certain angel was sent to them by God, declaring to them His will, and saying:--

Chapter XIX - The Law to the Giants or Demons

"These things seem good to the all-seeing God, that you lord it over no man; that you trouble no one, unless any one of his own accord subject himself to you, worshipping you, and sacrificing and pouring libations, and partaking of your table, or accomplishing aught else that they ought not, or shedding blood, or tasting dead flesh, or filling themselves with that which is torn of beasts, or that which is cut, or that which is strangled, or aught else that is unclean.

But those who betake themselves to my law, you not only shall not touch, but shall also do honour to, and shall flee from, their presence.

For whatsoever shall please them, being just, respecting you, that you shall be constrained to suffer.

But if any of those who worship me go astray, either committing adultery, or practising magic, or living impurely, or doing any other of the things which are not well-pleasing to me, then they will have to suffer something at your hands or those of others, according to my order.

But upon them, when they repent, I, judging of their repentance, whether it be worthy of pardon or not, shall give sentence.

These things, therefore, ye ought to remember and to do, well knowing that not even your thoughts shall be able to be concealed from Him.'

Chapter XX - Willing Captives

"Having charged them to this effect, the angel departed.

But you are still ignorant of this law, that every one who worships demons, or sacrifices to them, or partakes with them of their table, shall become subject to them and receive all punishment from them, as being under wicked lords.

And you who, on account of ignorance of this law, have been corrupted beside their altars, [19] and have been satiated with food offered to them, have come under their power, and do not know how you have been in every way injured in respect of your bodies.

But you ought to know that the demons have no power over any one, unless first he be their table-companion; since not even their chief can do anything contrary to the law imposed upon them by God, wherefore he has no power over any one who does not worship him; but neither can any one receive from them any of the things that he wishes, nor in anything be hurt by them, as you may learn from the following statement.

Chapter XXI - Temptation of Christ

"For once the king of the present time came to our King of righteousness, using no violence, for this was not in his power, but inducing and persuading, because the being persuaded lies in the power of every one. [20] Approaching Him, therefore, as being king of things present, he said to the King of things future, All the kingdoms of the present world are subject to me; also the gold and the silver and all the luxury of this world are under my power.

Wherefore fall down and worship me, and I will give you all these things.'

And this he said, knowing that after He worshipped him he would have power also over Him, and thus would rob Him of the future glory and kingdom.

But He, knowing all things, not only did not worship him, but would not receive aught of the things that were offered by him.

For He pledged Himself with those that are His, to the effect that it is not lawful henceforth even to touch the things that are given over to him. Therefore He answered and said, Thou shalt fear the Lord thy God, and Him only shalt thou serve.' [21]

Chapter XXII - The Marriage Supper

"However, the king of the impious, striving to bring over to his own counsel the King of the pious, and not being able, ceased his efforts, undertaking to persecute Him for the remainder of His life.

But you, being ignorant of the fore-ordained law, are under his power through evil deeds.

Wherefore you are polluted in body and soul, and in the present life you are tyrannized over by sufferings and demons, but in that which is to come you shall have your souls to be punished.

And this not you alone suffer through ignorance, but also some of our nation, who by evil deeds having been brought under the power of the prince of wickedness, like persons invited to a supper by a father celebrating the marriage of his son, have not obeyed. [22] But instead of those who through preoccupation disobeyed, the Father celebrating the marriage of his Son, has ordered us, through the Prophet of the truth, to come into the partings of the ways, that is, to you, and to invest you with the clean wedding-garment, which is baptism, which is for the remission of the sins done by you, and to bring the good to the supper of God by repentance, although at the first they were left out of the banquet.

Chapter XXIII - The Assembly Dismissed

"If, therefore, ye wish to be the vesture of the Divine Spirit, hasten first to put off your base presumption, which is an unclean spirit and a foul garment.

And this you cannot otherwise put off, than by being first baptized in good works.

And thus being pure in body and in soul, you shall enjoy the future eternal kingdom.

Therefore neither believe in idols, nor partake with them of the impure table, nor commit murder, nor adultery, nor hate those whom it is not right to hate, nor steal, nor set upon any evil deeds; since, being deprived of the hope of future blessings in the present life, you shall be subjected to evil demons and terrible sufferings, and in the world to come you shall be punished with eternal fire.

Now, then, what has been said is enough for to-day.

For the rest, those of you who are afflicted with ailments remain for healing; and of the others, you who please go in peace."

Chapter XXIV - The Sick Healed

When he had thus spoken, all of them remained, some in order to be healed, and others to see those who obtained cures.

But Peter, only laying his hands upon them, and praying, healed them; [23] so that those who were straightway cured were exceeding glad, and those who looked on exceedingly wondered, and blessed God, and believed with a firm hope, and with those who had been healed departed to their own homes, having received a charge to meet early on the following day. And when they had gone, Peter remained there with his associates, and partook of food, and refreshed himself with sleep.

Footnotes:

1. [For the general parallelism of Homilies VIII.-XI. with Recognitions, iv.-vi., see the footnote on Recognitions, iv. 1. Homilies VIII., IX., contain matter included in the single discourse of Recognitions, book iv.--R.]
   2. Lit.:
More willing to learn than the others.
   3. ["Maro" in Recognitions, iv.
The resemblance between that book and this Homily is quite marked.--R.]
   4. [Comp. Recognitions, iv. 3.--R.]
   5. [With chaps. 4-11 compare the closely resembling passage, Recognitions, iv. 4-11.--R.]
   6. Matt. viii. 11; Luke xiii. 29.
   7. Matt. xx. 16.
   8. Ex. xix. 9.
   9. Matt. xi. 25.
[Luke x. 21.--R.]
   10. Luke vi. 46.
   11. [In Recognitions, iv. 7, the healing is represented as occurring at once.--R.]
   12. The general meaning seems to be as given; but the text is undoubtedly corrupt, and scarcely intelligible.
   13. [Chaps. 12-16 have no parallel in the corresponding discourse in the Recognitions.
The doctrine here is peculiar.
But compare Recognitions, iv. 26.--R.]
   14. [Comp. Recognitions, i. 30.
The details here are not only fuller, but apparently represent a more developed speculation.--R.]
   15. The text is somewhat obscure; but the following sentence shows this to be the meaning of it.
   16. Literally, "the marrow."
   17. Literally, "the flowers of metals."
   18. [Comp. Recognitions, v. 12.--R.]
   19. tois auton bomois prosphtharentes kai auton ekplerothentes.
   20. [The conclusion of this Homily resembles Recognitions, iv. 34-37, but much of the matter of that book is contained in Homily IX.; see footnotes.--R.]
   21. Matt. iv.; Luke iv.
   22. Matt. xxii.
   23. [Comp. Recognitions, iv. 7.--R.]

Homily IX

Chapter I - Peter's Discourse Resumed

Therefore on the next day, Peter going out with his companions, and coming to the former place, and taking his stand, proceeded to say: [1]"God having cut off by water all the impious men of old, having found one alone amongst them all that was pious, caused him to be saved in an ark, with his three sons and their wives.

Whence may be perceived that it is His nature not to care for a multitude of wicked, nor to be indifferent to the salvation of one pious.

Therefore the greatest impiety of all is forsaking the sole Lord of all, and worshipping many, who are no gods, as if they were gods.

Chapter II - Monarchy and Polyarchy

"If, therefore, while I expound and show you that this is the greatest sin, which is able to destroy you all, it occur to your mind that you are not destroyed, being great multitudes, you are deceived.

For you have the example of the old world deluged.

And yet their sin was much less than that which is chargeable against you.

For they were wicked with respect to their equals, murdering or committing adultery.

But you are wicked against the God of all, worshipping lifeless images instead of Him or along with Him, and attributing His divine name to every kind of senseless matter.

In the first place, therefore, you are unfortunate in not knowing the difference between monarchy and polyarchy--that monarchy, on the one hand, is productive of concord, but polyarchy is effective of wars.

For unity does not fight with itself, but multitude has occasion of undertaking battle one against another.

Chapter III - Family of Noe

"Therefore straightway after the flood, [2] Noe continued to live three hundred and fifty years with the multitude of his descendants in concord, being a king according to the image of the one God.

But after his death many of his descendants were ambitious of the kingdom, and being eager to reign, each one considered how it might be effected; and one attempted it by war, another by deceit, another by persuasion, and one in one way and another in another; one of whom was of the family of Ham, whose descendant was Mestren, from whom the tribes of the Egyptians and Babylonians and Persians were multiplied.

Chapter IV - Zoroaster

"Of this family there was born in due time a certain one, who took up with magical practices, by name Nebrod, who chose, giant-like, to devise things in opposition to God.

Him the Greeks have called Zoroaster.

He, after the deluge, being ambitious of sovereignty, and being a great magician, by magical arts compelled the world-guiding star of the wicked one who now rules, to the bestowal of the sovereignty as a gift from him.

But he, [3] being a prince, and having authority over him who compelled him, [4] wrathfully poured out the fire of the kingdom, that he might both bring to allegiance, and might punish him who at first constrained him.

Chapter V - Hero-Worship

"Therefore the magician Nebrod, being destroyed by this lightning falling on earth from heaven, for this circumstance had his name changed to Zoroaster, on account of the living (zosan) stream of the star (asteros) being poured upon him.

But the unintelligent amongst the men who then were, thinking that through the love of God his soul had been sent for by lightning, buried the remains of his body, and honoured his burial-place with a temple among the Persians, where the descent of the fire occurred, and worshipped him as a god.

By this example also, others there bury those who die by lightning as beloved of God, and honour them with temples, and erect statues of the dead in their own forms.

Thence, in like manner, the rulers in different places were emulous of like honour, and very many of them honoured the tombs of those who were beloved of them, though not dying by lightning, with temples and statues, and lighted up altars, and ordered them to be adored as gods.

And long after, by the lapse of time, they were thought by posterity to be really gods.

Chapter VI - Fire-Worship

"Thus, in this fashion, there ensued many partitions of the one original kingdom.

The Persians, first taking coals from the lightning which fell from heaven, preserved them by ordinary fuel, and honouring the heavenly fire as a god, were honoured by the fire itself with the first kingdom, as its first worshippers.

After them the Babylonians, stealing coals from the fire that was there, and conveying it safely to their own home, and worshipping it, they themselves also reigned in order.

And the Egyptians, acting in like manner, and calling the fire in their own dialect Phthae, which is translated Hephaistus or Osiris, he who first reigned amongst them is called by its name.

Those also who reigned in different places, acting in this fashion, and making an image, and kindling altars in honour of fire, most of them were excluded from the kingdom.

Chapter VII - Sacrificial Orgies

"But they did not cease to worship images, [5] by reason of the evil intelligence of the magicians, who found excuses for them, which had power to constrain them to the foolish worship.

For, establishing this things by magical ceremonies, they assigned them feasts from sacrifices, libations, flutes, and shoutings, by means of which senseless men, being deceived, and their kingdom being taken from them, yet did not desist from the worship that they had taken up with.

To such an extent did they prefer error, on account of its pleasantness, before truth.

They also howl after their sacrificial surfeit, their soul from the depth, as it were by dreams, forewarning them of the punishment that is to befall such deeds of theirs.

Chapter VIII - The Best Merchandise

"Many forms of worship, [6] then, having passed away in the world, we come, bringing to you, as good merchantmen, the worship that has been handed down to us from our fathers, and preserved; showing you, as it were, the seeds of plants, and placing them under your judgment and in your power.

Choose that which seems good unto you.

If, therefore, ye choose our wares, not only shall ye be able to escape demons, and the sufferings which are inflicted by demons, but yourselves also putting them to flight, and having them reduced to make supplication to you, shall for ever enjoy future blessings.

Chapter IX - How Demons Get Power Over Men

"Since, on the other hand, you are oppressed by strange sufferings inflicted by demons, on your removal from the body you shall have your souls also punished for ever; not indeed by God's inflicting vengeance, but because such is the judgment of evil deeds.

For the demons, having power by means of the food given to them, are admitted into your bodies by your own hands; and lying hid there for a long time, they become blended with your souls.

And through the carelessness of those who think not, or even wish not, to help themselves, upon the dissolution of their bodies, their souls being united to the demon, are of necessity borne by it into whatever places it pleases.

And what is most terrible of all, when at the end of all things the demon is first consigned to the purifying fire, the soul which is mixed with it is under the necessity of being horribly punished, and the demon of being pleased.

For the soul, being made of light, and not capable of bearing the heterogeneous flame of fire, is tortured; but the demon, being in the substance of his own kind, is greatly pleased, becoming the strong chain of the soul that he has swallowed up.

Chapter X - How They are to Be Expelled

"But the reason why the demons delight in entering into men's bodies is this.

Being spirits, and having desires after meats and drinks, and sexual pleasures, but not being able to partake of these by reason of their being spirits, and wanting organs fitted for their enjoyment, they enter into the bodies of men, in order that, getting organs to minister to them, they may obtain the things that they wish, whether it be meat, by means of men's teeth, or sexual pleasure, by means of men's members.

Hence, in order to the putting of demons to flight, the most useful help is abstinence, and fasting, and suffering of affliction. For if they enter into men's bodies for the sake of sharing pleasures, it is manifest that they are put to flight by suffering.

But inasmuch as some, [7] being of a more malignant kind, remain by the body that is undergoing punishment, though they are punished with it, therefore it is needful to have recourse to God by prayers and petitions, refraining from every occasion of impurity, that the hand of God may touch him for his cure, as being pure and faithful.

Chapter XI - Unbelief the Demon's Stronghold

"But it is necessary in our prayers to acknowledge that we have had recourse to God, and to bear witness, not to the apathy, but to the slowness of the demon.

For all things are done to the believer, nothing to the unbeliever.

Therefore the demons themselves, knowing the amount of faith of those of whom they take possession, measure their stay proportionately.

Wherefore they stay permanently with the unbelieving, tarry for a while with the weak in faith; but with those who thoroughly believe, and who do good, they cannot remain even for a moment.

For the soul being turned by faith, as it were, into the nature of water, quenches the demon as a spark of fire.

The labour, therefore, of every one is to be solicitous about the putting to flight of his own demon.

For, being mixed up with men's souls, they suggest to every one's mind desires after what things they please, in order that he may neglect his salvation.

Chapter XII - Theory of Disease

"Whence many, not knowing how they are influenced, consent to the evil thoughts suggested by the demons, as if they were the reasoning of their own souls.

Wherefore they become less active to come to those who are able to save them, and do not know that they themselves are held captive by the deceiving demons.

Therefore the demons who lurk in their souls induce them to think that it is not a demon that is distressing them, but a bodily disease, such as some acrid matter, or bile, or phlegm, or excess of blood, or inflammation of a membrane, or something else.

But even if this were so, the case would not be altered of its being a kind of demon.

For the universal and earthly soul, which enters on account of all kinds of food, being taken to excess by over-much food, is itself united to the spirit, as being cognate, which is the soul of man; and the material part of the food being united to the body, is left as a dreadful poison to it. Wherefore in all respects moderation is excellent.

Chapter XIII - Deceits of the Demons

"But some of the maleficent demons deceive in another way.

For at first they do not even show their existence, in order that care may not be taken against them; but in due time, by means of anger, love, or some other affection, they suddenly injure the body, by sword, or halter, or precipice, or something else, and at last bring to punishment the deceived souls of those who have been mixed up with them, as we said, withdrawing into the purifying fire.

But others, who are deceived in another way, do not approach us, being seduced by the instigations of maleficent demons, as if they suffered these things at the hands of the gods themselves, on account of their neglect of them, and were able to reconcile them by sacrifices, and that it is not needful to come to us, but rather to flee from and hate us.

And at the same time [8] they hate and flee from those who have greater compassion for them, and who follow after them in order to do good to them.

Chapter XIV - More Tricks

"Therefore shunning and hating us they are deceived, not knowing how it happens that they devise things opposed to their health.

For neither can we compel them against their will to incline towards health, since now we have no such power over them, nor are they able of themselves to understand the evil instigation of the demon; for they know not whence these evil instigations are suggested to them.

And these are they whom the demons affright, appearing in such forms as they please.

And sometimes they prescribe remedies for those who are diseased, and thus they receive divine honours from those who have previously been deceived.

And they conceal from many that they are demons, but not from us, who know their mystery, and why they do these things, changing themselves in dreams against those over whom they have power; and why they terrify some, and give oracular responses to others, and demand sacrifices from them, and command them to eat with them, that they may swallow up their souls.

Chapter XV - Test of Idols

"For as dire serpents draw sparrows to them by their breath, so also these draw to their own will those who partake of their table, being mixed up with their understanding by means of food and drink, changing themselves in dreams according to the forms of the images, that they may increase error.

For the image is neither a living creature, nor has it a divine spirit, but the demon that appeared abused the form. [9] How many, in like manner, have been seen by others in dreams; and when they have met one another when awake, and compared them with what they saw in their dream, they have not accorded:

so that the dream is not a manifestation, but is either the production of a demon or of the soul, giving forms to present fears and desire.

For the soul, being struck with fear, conceives forms in dreams.

But if you think that images, as being alive, can accomplish such things, place them on a beam accurately balanced, and place an equipoise in the other scale, then ask them to become either heavier or lighter:

and if this be done, then they are alive.

But it does not so happen.

But if it were so, this would not prove them to be gods.

For this might be accomplished by the finger of the demon.

Even maggots move, yet they are not called gods.

Chapter XVI - Powers of the Demons

"But that the soul of each man embodies the forms of demons after his own preconceptions, and that those who are called gods do not appear, is manifest from the fact that they do not appear to the Jews.

But some one will say, How then do they give oracular responses, forecasting future things? This also is false.

But suppose it were true, this does not prove them to be gods; for it does not follow, if anything prophesies, that it is a god.

For pythons prophesy, yet they are cast out by us as demons, and put to flight.

But some one will say, They work cures for some persons.

It is false.

But suppose it were true, this is no proof of Godhead; for physicians also heal many, yet are not gods.

But, says one, physicians do not completely heal those of whom they take charge, but these heal oracularly.

But the demons know the remedies that are suited to each disease.

Wherefore, being skilful physicians, and able to cure those diseases which can be cured by men, and also being prophets, and knowing when each disease is healed of itself, they so arrange their remedies that they may gain the credit of producing the cure.

Chapter XVII - Reasons Why Their Deceits are Not Detected

"For why do they oracularly foretell cures after a long time?

And why, if they are almighty, do they not effect cures without administering any medicine?

And for what reason do they prescribe remedies to some of those who pray to them, while to some, and it may be more suitable cases, they give no response?

Thus, whenever a cure is going to take place spontaneously, they promise, in order that they may get the credit of the cure; and others, having been sick, and having prayed, and having recovered spontaneously, attributed the cure to those whom they had invoked, and make offerings to them.

Those, however, who, after praying, have failed, are not able to offer their sacrifices. But if the relatives of the dead, or any of their children, inquired into the losses, you would find the failures to be more than the successes.

But no one who has been taken in by them is willing to exhibit an accusation against them, through shame or fear; but, on the other hand, they conceal the crimes which they believe them to be guilty of.

Chapter XVIII - Props of the System

"And how many also falsify the responses given and the cures effected by them, and confirm them with an oath!

And how many give themselves up to them for hire, undertaking falsely to suffer certain things, and thus proclaiming their suffering, and being restored by remedial means, they say that they oracularly promised them healing, in order that they may assign as the cause the senseless worship!

And how many of these things were formerly done by magical art, in the way of interpreting dreams, and divining!

Yet in course of time these things have disappeared.

And how many are there now, who, wishing to obtain such things, make use of charms!

However, though a thing be prophetical or healing, it is not divine.

Chapter XIX - Privileges of the Baptized

"For God is almighty.

For He is good and righteous, now long-suffering to all, that those who will, repenting of the evils which they have done, and living well, may receive a worthy reward in the day in which all things are judged.

Wherefore now begin to obey God by reason of good knowledge, [10] and to oppose your evil lusts and thoughts, that you may be able to recover the original saving worship which was committed to humanity.

For thus shall blessings straightway spring up to you, which, when you receive, you will thenceforth quit the trial of evils.

But give thanks to the Giver; being kings for ever of unspeakable good things, with the King of peace.

But in the present life, washing in a flowing river, or fountain, or even in the sea, with the thrice-blessed invocation, you shall not only be able to drive away the spirits which lurk in you; but yourselves no longer sinning, and undoubtingly believing God, you shall drive out evil spirits and dire demons, with terrible diseases, from others.

And sometimes they shall flee when you but look on them.

For they know those who have given themselves up to God.

Wherefore, honouring them, they flee affrighted, as you saw yesterday, how, when after the address I delayed praying for those who were suffering these maladies, through respect towards the worship they cried out, not being able to endure it for a short hour.

Chapter XX - "Not Almost, But Altogether Such as I Am."

"Do not then suppose that we do not fear demons on this account, that we are of a different nature from you.

For we are of the same nature, but not of the same worship.

Wherefore, being not only much but altogether superior to you, we do not grudge you becoming such as we are; but, on the other hand, counsel you, knowing that all these demons beyond measure honour and fear those who are reconciled to God."

Chapter XXI - The Demons Subject to the Believer

"For, in like manner as the soldiers who are put under one of Caesar's captains know to honour him who has received authority on account of him who gave it, so that the commanders say to this one, Come, and he comes, and to another, Go, and he goes; so also he who has given himself to God, being faithful, is heard when he only speaks to demons and diseases; and the demons give place, though they be much stronger than they who command them.

For with unspeakable power God subjects the mind of every one to whom He pleases.

For as many captains, with whole camps and cities, fear Caesar, who is but a man, every one's heart being eager to honour the image of all [11] for the will of God, all things being enslaved by fear, do not know the cause; so also all disease-producing spirits, being awed in some natural way, honour and flee from him who has had recourse to God, and who carries right faith as His image in his heart.

Chapter XXII - "Rather Rejoice."

"But still, though all demons, with all diseases, flee before you, you are not to rejoice in this only, but in that, through grace, your names, as of the ever-living, are written in heaven.

Thus also the Divine Holy Spirit rejoices because man hath overcome death; for the putting of the demons to flight makes for the safety of another.

But this we say, not as denying that we ought to help others, but that we ought not to be inflated by this and neglect ourselves.

It happens, also, that the demons flee before some wicked men by reason of the honoured name, and both he who expels the demon and he who witnesses it are deceived:

he who expels him, as if he were honoured on account of righteousness, not knowing the wickedness of the demon.

For he has at once honoured the name, and by his flight has brought the wicked man into a thought of his righteousness, and so deceived him away from repentance.

But the looker-on, associating with the expeller as a pious man, hastens to a like manner of life, and is ruined.

Sometimes also they pretend to flee before adjurations not made in the name of God, that they may deceive men, and destroy them whom they will.

Chapter XXIII - The Sick Healed

"This then we would have you know, that unless any one of his own accord give himself over as a slave to demons, as I said before, the demon has no power against him.

Choosing, therefore, to worship one God, and refraining from the table of demons, and undertaking chastity with philanthropy and righteousness, and being baptized with the thrice-blessed invocation for the remission of sins, and devoting yourselves as much as you can to the perfection of purity, you can escape everlasting punishment, and be constituted heirs of eternal blessings."

Having thus spoken, he ordered those to approach who were distressed with diseases;[12] and thus many approached, having come together through the experience of those who had been healed yesterday.

And he having laid his hands upon them and prayed, and immediately healed them, and having charged them and the others to come earlier, he bathed and partook of food, and went to sleep.

Footnotes:

1. [Much of the matter in this Homily is to be found in Recognitions, iv.--R.]

2. [With this and the succeeding chapters compare Recognitions, i. 30, 31, but more particularly iv. 27-31, which furnish a close parallel.--R.]

3. That is, I suppose, the wicked one.

4. I suppose Nimrod, or Zoroaster.

5. [Comp. Recognitions, iv. 13.--R.]

6. [Compare with chapters 8-18 the parallel passage in Recognitions, iv. 14-22.
The resemblances are quite close.--R.]

7. The gender is here changed, but the sense shows that the reference is still to the demons.
I suppose the author forgot that in the preceding sentences he had written daimones (masc.) and not daimonia (neut.).

8. Some read houtos, thus.

9. The meaning is:
"the idols or images of the heathen deities are not living, but the demons adopt the forms of these images when they appear to men in dreams."

10. [With chaps. 19-21 compare Recognitions, iv. 32, 35, which closely resemble them.--R.]

11. I prefer here the common text to any of the proposed emendations, and suppose that the author represents Caesar, though but one man, as the image or personification of the whole empire.

12. [Comp. Recognitions, iv. 7.--R.]

Homily X

Chapter I - The Third Day in Tripolis

Therefore on the third day in Tripolis, [1] Peter rose early and went into the garden, where there was a great water-reservoir, into which a full stream of water constantly flowed.

There having bathed, and then having prayed, he sat down; and perceiving us sitting around and eagerly observing him, as wishing to hear something from him, he said:--

Chapter II - Ignorance and Error

"There seems to me to be a great difference between the ignorant and the erring.

For the ignorant man seems to me to be like a man who does not wish to set out for a richly stored city, through his not knowing the excellent things that are there; but the erring man to be like one who has learned indeed the good things that are in the city, but who has forsaken the highway in proceeding towards it, and so has wandered.

Thus, therefore, it seems to me that there is a great difference between those who worship idols and those who are faulty in the worship of God.

For they who worship idols are ignorant of eternal life, and therefore they do not desire it; for what they do not know, they cannot love.

But those who have chosen to worship one God, and who have learned of the eternal life given to the good, if they either believe or do anything different from what is pleasing to God, are like to those who have gone out from the city of punishment, and are desirous to come to the well-stored city, and on the road have strayed from the right path."

Chapter III - Man the Lord of All

While he was thus discoursing to us, there entered one of our people, who had been appointed to make the following announcement to him, and said:

"My lord Peter, there are great multitudes standing before the doors."

With his consent, therefore, a great multitude entered.

Then he rose up, and stood on the basis, as he had done the day before; and having saluted them in religious fashion, he said:

"God having formed the heaven and the earth, and having made all things in them, as the true Prophet has said to us, man, being made after the image and likeness of God, was appointed to be ruler and lord of things, I say, in air and earth and water, as may be known from the very fact that by his intelligence he brings down the creatures that are in the air, and brings up those that are in the deep, hunts those that are on the earth, and that although they are much greater in strength than he; I mean elephants, and lions, and such like.

Chapter IV - Faith and Duty

"While, therefore, he was righteous, he was also superior to all sufferings, as being unable by his immortal body to have any experience of pain; but when he sinned, as I showed you yesterday and the day before, becoming as it were the servant of sin, he became subject to all sufferings, being by a righteous judgment deprived of all excellent things.

For it was not reasonable, the Giver having been forsaken, that the gifts should remain with the ungrateful.

Whence, of His abundant mercy, in order to our receiving, with the first, also future blessings, He sent His Prophet.

And the Prophet has given in charge to us to tell you what you ought to think, and what to do. Choose, therefore; and this is in your power.

What, therefore, you ought to think is this, to worship the God who made all things; whom if you receive in your minds, you shall receive from Him, along with the first excellent things, also the future eternal blessings.

Chapter V - The Fear of God

"Therefore you shall be able to persuade yourselves with respect to the things that are profitable, if, like charmers, you say to the horrible serpent which lurks in your heart, The Lord God thou shalt fear, and Him alone thou shalt serve.' [2]On every account it is advantageous to fear Him alone, not as an unjust, but as a righteous God.

For one fears an unjust being, lest he be wrongfully destroyed, but a righteous one, lest he be caught in sin and punished.

You can therefore, by fear towards Him, be freed from many hurtful fears.

For if you do not fear the one Lord and Maker of all, you shall be the slaves of all evils to your own hurt, I mean of demons and diseases, and of everything that can in any way hurt you.

Chapter VI - Restoration of the Divine Image

"Therefore approach with confidence to God, you who at first were made to be rulers and lords of all things:

ye who have His image in your bodies, have in like manner the likeness of His judgment in your minds.

Since, then, by acting like irrational animals, you have lost the soul of man from your soul, becoming like swine, you are the prey of demons.

If, therefore, you receive the law of God, you become men. For it cannot be said to irrational animals, Thou shalt not kill, thou shalt not commit adultery, thou shalt not steal,' and so forth. Therefore do not refuse, when invited, to return to your first nobility; for it is possible, if ye be conformed to God by good works. And being accounted to be sons by reason of your likeness to Him, you shall be reinstated as lords of all.

Chapter VII - Unprofitableness of Idols

"Begin, [3] then, to divest yourselves of the injurious fear of vain idols, that you may escape unrighteous bondage.

For they have become your masters, who even as servants are unprofitable to you.

I speak of the material of the lifeless images, which are of no use to you as far as service is concerned.

For they neither hear nor see nor feel, nor can they be moved.

For is there any one of you who would like to see as they see, and to hear as they hear, and to feel as they feel, and to be moved as they are?

God forbid that such a wrong should be done to any man bearing the image of God, though he have lost His likeness.

Chapter VIII - No Gods Which are Made with Hands

"Therefore reduce your gods of gold and silver, or any other material, to their original nature; I mean into cups and basins and all other utensils, such as may be useful to you for service; and those good things which were given you at first shall be able to be restored.

But perhaps you will say, The laws of the emperors do not permit us to do this. [4]You say well that it is the law, and not the power of the vain idols themselves, which is nothing.

How, then, have ye regarded them as gods, who are avenged by human laws, guarded by dogs, kept by multitudes?--and that if they are of gold, or silver, or brass.

For those of wood or earthenware are preserved by their worthlessness, because no man desires to steal a wooden or earthenware god!

So that your gods are exposed to danger in proportion to the value of the material of which they are made.

How, then, can they be gods, which are stolen, molten, weighed, guarded?

Chapter IX - "Eyes Have They, But They See Not."

"Oh the minds of wretched men, who fear things deader than dead men! For I cannot call them even dead, which have never lived, unless they are the tombs of ancient men.

For sometimes a person, visiting unknown places, does not know whether the temples which he sees are monuments of dead men, or whether they belong to the so-called gods; but on inquiring and hearing that they belong to the gods, he worships, without being ashamed that if he had not learned on inquiring, he would have passed them by as the monuments of a dead man, on account of the strictness of the resemblance.

However, it is not necessary that I should adduce much proof in regard to such superstition.

For it is easy for any one who pleases to understand that it, an idol, is nothing, unless there be any one who does not see.

However, now at least hear that it does not hear, and understand that it does not understand.

For the hands of a man who is dead made it.

If, then, the maker is dead, how can it be that which was made by him shall not be dissolved?

Why, then, do you worship the work of a mortal which is altogether senseless? whereas those who have reason do not worship animals, nor do they seek to propitiate the elements which have been made by God,--I mean the heaven, the sun, the moon, lightning, the sea, and all things in them,--rightly judging not to worship the things that He has made, but to reverence the Maker and Sustainer of them.

For in this they themselves also rejoice, that no one ascribes to them the honour that belongs to their Maker.

Chapter X - Idolatry a Delusion of the Serpent

"For His alone is the excellent glory of being alone uncreated, while all else is created.

As, therefore, it is the prerogative of the uncreated to be God, so whatever is created is not God indeed.

Before all things, therefore, you ought to consider the evil-working suggestion of the deceiving serpent that is in you, which seduces you by the promise of better reason, creeping from your brain to your spinal marrow, and setting great value upon deceiving you. [5]

Chapter XI - Why the Serpent Tempts to Sin

"For he knows the original law, that if he bring you to the persuasion of the so-called gods, so that you sin against the one good of monarchy, your overthrow becomes a gain to him.

And that for this reason, because he being condemned eats earth, he has power to eat him who through sin being dissolved into earth, has become earth, your souls going into his belly of fire.

In order, therefore, that you may suffer these things, he suggests every thought to your hurt.

Chapter XII - Ignorantia Neminem Excusa

"For all the deceitful conceptions against the monarchy are sown in your mind by him to your hurt.

First, that you may not hear the discourses of piety, and so drive away ignorance, which is the occasion of evils, he ensnares you by a pretence of knowledge, giving in the first instance, and using throughout this presumption, which is to think and to be unhappily advised, that if any one do not hear the word of piety, he is not subject to judgments.

Wherefore also some, being thus deceived, are not willing to hear, that they may be ignorant, not knowing that ignorance is of itself a sufficient deadly drug.

For if any one should take a deadly drug in ignorance, does he not die?

So naturally sins destroy the sinner, though he commit them in ignorance of what is right.

Chapter XIII - Condemnation of the Ignorant

"But if judgment follows upon disobedience to instruction, much more shall God destroy those who will not undertake His worship.

For he who will not learn, lest that should make him subject to judgment, is already judged as knowing, for he knew what he will not hear; so that imagination avails nothing as an apology in presence of the heart-knowing God.

Wherefore avoid that cunning thought suggested by the serpent to your minds.

But if any one end this life in real ignorance, this charge will lie against him, that, having lived so long, he did not know who was the bestower of the food supplied to him:

and as a senseless, and ungrateful, and very unworthy servant, he is rejected from the kingdom of God.

Chapter XIV - Polytheistic Illustration

"Again, the terrible serpent suggests this supposition to you, to think and to say that very thing which most of you do say; viz., We know that there is one Lord of all, but there also are gods.

For in like manner as there is one Caesar, but he has under him procurators, proconsuls, prefects, commanders of thousands, and of hundreds, and of tens; in the same way, there being one great God, as there is one Caesar, there also, after the manner of inferior powers, are gods, inferior indeed to Him, but ruling over us.

Hear, therefore, ye who have been led away by this conception as by a terrible poison--I mean the evil conception of this illustration--that you may know what is good and what is evil. For you do not yet see it, nor do you look into the things that you utter.

Chapter XV - Its Inconclusiveness

"For if you say that, after the manner of Caesar, God has subordinate powers--those, namely, which are called gods--you do not thus go by your illustration.

For if you went by it, you must of necessity know that it is not lawful to give the name of Caesar to another, whether he be consul, or prefect, or captain, or any one else, and that he who gives such a name shall not live, and he who takes it shall be cut off.

Thus, according to your own illustration, the name of God must not be given to another; and he who is tempted either to take or give it is destroyed.

Now, if this insult of a man induces punishment, much more they who call others gods shall be subject to eternal punishment, as insulting God.

And with good reason; because you subject to all the insult that you can the name which it was committed to you to honour, in order to His monarchy.

For God is not properly His name; but you having in the meantime received it, insult what has been given you, that it may be accounted as done against the real name, according as you use that.

But you subject it to every kind of insult.

Chapter XVI - Gods of the Egyptians

"Therefore you ringleaders among the Egyptians, boasting of meteorology, and promising to judge the natures of the stars, by reason of the evil opinion lurking in them, subjected that name to all manner of dishonour as far as in them lay.

For some of them taught the worship of an ox called Apis, some that of a he-goat, some of a cat, some of a serpent; yea, even of a fish, and of onions, and rumblings in the stomach, [6] and common sewers, and members of irrational animals, and to myriads of other base abominations they gave the name of god."

Chapter XVII - The Egyptians' Defence of Their System

On Peter's saying this, the surrounding multitude laughed.

Then Peter said to the laughing multitude:

"You laugh at their proceedings, not knowing that you are yourselves much more objects of ridicule to them. But you laugh at one another's proceedings; for, being led by evil custom into deceit, you do not see your own.

But I admit that you have reason to laugh at the idols of the Egyptians, since they, being rational, worship irrational animals, and these altogether dying.

But listen to what they say when they deride you.

We, they say, though we worship dying creatures, yet still such as have once had life: but you reverence things that never lived.

And in addition to this, they say, We wish to honour the form of the one God, but we cannot find out what it is, and so we choose to give honour to every form.

And so, making some such statements as these, they think that they judge more rightly than you do.

Chapter XVIII - Answer to the Egyptians

"Wherefore answer them thus:

You lie, for you do not worship these things in honour of the true God, for then all of you would worship every form; not as ye do.

For those of you who suppose the onion to be the divinity, and those who worship rumblings in the stomach, contend with one another; and thus all in like manner preferring some one thing, revile those that are preferred by others.

And with diverse judgments, one reverences one and another of the limbs of the same animal.

Moreover, those of them who still have a breath of right reason, being ashamed of the manifest baseness, attempt to drive these things into allegories, wishing by another vagary to establish their deadly error.

But we should confute the allegories, if we were there, the foolish passion for which has prevailed to such an extent as to constitute a great disease of the understanding.

For it is not necessary to apply a plaster to a whole part of the body, but to a diseased part.

Since then, you, by your laughing at the Egyptians, show that you are not affected with their disease, with respect to your own disease it were reasonable I should afford to you a present cure of your own malady.

Chapter XIX - God's Peculiar Attribute

"He who would worship God ought before all things to know what alone is peculiar to the nature of God, which cannot pertain to another, that, looking at His peculiarity, and not finding it in any other, he may not be seduced into ascribing godhead to another.

But this is peculiar to God, that He alone is, as the Maker of all, so also the best of all. That which makes is indeed superior in power to that which is made; that which is boundless is superior in magnitude to that which is bounded:

in respect of beauty, that which is comeliest; in respect of happiness, that which is most blessed; in respect of understanding, that which is most perfect.

And in like manner, in other respects, He has incomparably the pre-eminence.

Since then, as I said, this very thing, viz., to be the best of all, is peculiar to God, and the all-comprehending world was made by Him, none of the things made by Him can come into equal comparison with Him.

Chapter XX - Neither the World Nor Any of Its Parts Can Be God

"But the world, not being incomparable and unsurpassable, and altogether in all respects without defect, cannot be God.

But if the whole world cannot be God, in respect of its having been made, how much more should not its parts be reasonably called God; I mean the parts that are by you called gods, being made of gold and silver, brass and stone, or of any other material whatsoever; and they constructed by mortal hand.

However, let us further see how the terrible serpent through man's mouth poisons those who are seduced by his solicitations.

Chapter XXI - Idols Not Animated by the Divine Spirit

"For many say, We do not worship the gold or the silver, the wood or the stone, of the objects of our worship.

For we also know that these are nothing but lifeless matter, and the art of mortal man.

But the spirit that dwells in them, that we call God.

Behold the immorality of those who speak thus!

For when that which appears is easily proved to be nothing, they have recourse to the invisible, as not being able to be convicted in respect of what is non-apparent.

However, they agree with us in part, that one half of their images is not God, but senseless matter.

It remains for them to show how we are to believe that these images have a divine spirit.

But they cannot prove to us that it is so, for it is not so; and we do not believe them when they say that they have seen it.

We shall afford them proofs that they have not a divine spirit, that lovers of truth, hearing the refutation of the thought that they are animated, may turn away from the hurtful delusion.

Chapter XXII - Confutation of Idol-Worship

"In the first place, indeed, if you worship them as being animated, why do you also worship the sepulchres of memorable men of old, who confessedly had no divine spirit?

Thus you do not at all speak truth respecting this.

But if your objects of worship were really animated, they would move of themselves; they would have a voice; they would shake off the spiders that are on them; they would thrust forth those that wish to surprise and to steal them; they would easily capture those who pilfer the offerings.

But now they do none of these things, but are guarded, like culprits, and especially the more costly of them, as we have already said.

But what?

Is it not so, that the rulers demand of you imposts and taxes on their account, as if you were greatly benefited by them?

But what?

Have they not often been taken as plunder by enemies, and been broken and scattered?

And do not the priests, more than the outside worshippers, carry off many of the offerings, thus acknowledging the uselessness of their worship?

Chapter XXIII - Folly of Idolatry

"Nay, it will be said; but they are detected by their foresight.

It is false; for how many of them have not been detected?

And if on account of the capture of some it be said that they have power, it is a mistake.

For of those who rob tombs, some are found out and some escape; but it is not by the power of the dead that those who are apprehended are detected.

And such ought to be our conclusion with respect to those who steal and pilfer the gods.

But it will be said, The gods that are in them take no care of their images.

Why, then, do you tend them, wiping them, and washing them, and scouring them, crowning

them, and sacrificing to them?
Wherefore agree with me that you act altogether without right reason.
For as you lament over the dead, so you sacrifice and make libations to your gods.

Chapter XXIV - Impotence of Idols

"Nor yet is that in harmony with the illustration of Caesar, and of the powers under him, to call them administrators; whereas you take all care of them, as I said, tending your images in every respect.

For they, having no power, do nothing.

Wherefore tell us what do they administer? what do they of that sort which rulers in different places do? and what influence do they exert, as the stars of God?

Do they show anything like the sun, or do you light lamps before them?

Are they able to bring showers, as the clouds bring rain,--they which cannot even move themselves, unless men carry them?

Do they make the earth fruitful to your labours, these to whom you supply sacrifices? Thus they can do nothing.

Chapter XXV - Servants Become Masters

"But if they were able to do something, you should not be right in calling them gods:

for it is not right to call the elements gods, by which good things are supplied; but only Him who ordereth them, to accomplish all things for our use, and who commandeth them to be serviceable to man,--Him alone we call God in propriety of speech, whose beneficence you do not perceive, but permit those elements to rule over you which have been assigned to you as your servants.

And why should I speak of the elements, when you not only have made and do worship lifeless images, but deign to be subject to them in all respects as servants?

Wherefore, by reason of your erroneous judgments, you have become subject to demons.

However, by acknowledgment of God Himself, by good deeds you can again become masters, and command the demons as slaves, and as sons of God be constituted heirs of the eternal kingdom."

Chapter XXVI - The Sick Healed

Having said this, he ordered the demoniacs, and those taken with diseases, to be brought to him; and when they were brought, he laid his hands on them, and prayed, and dismissed them healed, reminding them and the rest of the multitude to attend upon him there every day that he should discourse.

Then, when the others had withdrawn, Peter bathed in the reservoir that was there, with those who pleased; and then ordering a table to be spread on the ground under the thick foliage of the trees, for the sake of shade, he ordered us each to recline, according to our worth; and thus we partook of food.

Therefore having blessed and having given thanks to God for the enjoyment, according to the accustomed faith of the Hebrews; and there being still a long time before us, he permitted us to ask him questions about whatever we pleased; and thus, though there were twenty of us putting questions to him all round, he satisfied every one.

And now evening having descended, we all went with him into the largest apartment of the lodging, and there we all slept.

Footnotes:

1. [Book v. of the Recognitions, assigned to the second day at Tripolis, contains most of the matter in this Homily, but has many passages without a parallel here.--R.]

2. Matt. iv. 10; [Luke iv. 8; Deut. vi. 13.--R.].

3. [Recognitions, v. 14, is parallel to this chapter, and the resemblance is close throughout some of the succeeding chapters.--R.]

4. [This, with the corresponding passage in Recognitions, v. 15, points to an early origin of the literature, under the heathen emperors.--R.]

5. [Comp. Recognitions, ii. 45, and especially the full discussion about the serpent in Recognitions, v. 17-26.--R.]

6. gastron pneumata.

Homily XI

Chapter I - Morning Exercises

Therefore on the fourth day at Tripolis, Peter rising and finding us awake, saluted us and went out to the reservoir, that he might bathe and pray; and we also did so after him.

To us, therefore, when we had prayed together, and were set down before him, he gave a discourse touching the necessity of purity.

And when thereafter it was day, he permitted the multitudes to enter.

Then, when a great crowd had entered, he saluted them according to custom, and began to speak.

Chapter II - "Giving All Diligence."

"Inasmuch as, by long-continued neglect on your part, to your own injury, your mind has caused to sprout many hurtful conceptions about religion, and ye have become like land fallow by the carelessness of the husbandman, you need a long time for your purification, that your mind, receiving like good seed the true word that is imparted to you, may not choke it with evil cares, and render it unfruitful with respect to works that are able to save you.

Wherefore it behoves those who are careful of their own salvation to hear more constantly, that their sins which have been long multiplying may, in the short time that remains, be matched with constant care for their purification.

Since, therefore, no one knows the time of his end, hasten to pluck out the many thorns of your hearts; but not by little and little, for then you cannot be purified, for you have been long fallow. [1]

Chapter III - "Behold What Indignation."

"But not otherwise will you endure to undertake much care for your purification unless you be angry with yourselves, and chastise yourselves for those things with which, as unprofitable servants, you have been ensnared, consenting to your evil lusts, that you may be able to let in your righteous indignation upon your mind, as fire upon a fallow field.

If, therefore, ye have not righteous fire, I mean indignation, against evil lusts, learn from what good things ye have been seduced, and by whom ye have been deceived, and for what punishment ye are prepared; and thus, your mind being sober, and kindled into indignation like fire by the teaching of Him who sent us, may be able to consume the evil things of lust.

Believe me, that if you will, you can rectify all things.

Chapter IV - The Golden Rule

"Ye are the image of the invisible God. [2] Whence let not those who would be pious say that idols are images of God, and therefore that it is right to worship them.

For the image of God is man.

He who wishes to be pious towards God does good to man, because the body of man bears the image of God.

But all do not as yet bear His likeness, but the pure mind of the good soul does.

However, as we know that man was made after the image and after the likeness of God, we tell you to be pious towards him, that the favour may be accounted as done to God, whose image he is.

Therefore it behoves you to give honour to the image of God, which is man--in this wise:

food to the hungry, drink to the thirsty, clothing to the naked, care to the sick, shelter to the stranger, and visiting him who is in prison, to help him as you can. And not to speak at length, whatever good things any one wishes for himself, so let him afford to another in need, and then a good reward can be reckoned to him as being pious towards the image of God.

And by like reason, if he will not undertake to do these things, he shall be punished as neglecting the image.

Chapter V - Forasmuch as Ye Did It Unto One of These

"Can it therefore be said that, for the sake of piety towards God, ye worship every form, while in all things ye injure man who is really the image of God, committing murder, adultery, stealing, and dishonouring him in many other respects?

But you ought not to do even one evil thing on account of which man is grieved.

But now you do all things on account of which man is disheartened, for wrong is also distress. Wherefore you murder and spoil his goods, and whatever else you know which you would not receive from another.

But you, being seduced by some malignant reptile to malice, by the suggestion of polytheistic doctrine, are impious towards the real image, which is man, and think that ye are pious towards senseless things.

Chapter VI - Why God Suffers Objects of Idolatry to Subsist

"But some say, Unless He wished these things to be, they should not be, but He would take them away.

But I say this shall assuredly be the case, when all shall show their preference for Him, and thus there shall be a change of the present world.

However, if you wished Him to act thus, so that none of the things that are worshipped should subsist, tell me what of existing things you have not worshipped.

Do not some of you worship the sun, and some the moon, and some water, and some the earth, and some the mountains, and some plants, and some seeds, and some also man, as in Egypt?

Therefore God must have suffered nothing, not even you, so that there should have been neither worshipped nor worshipper.

Truly this is what the terrible serpent which lurks in you would have, and spares you not.

But so it shall not be.

For it is not the thing that is worshipped that sins; for it suffers violence at the hands of him who will worship it.

For though unjust judgment is passed by all men, yet not by God.

For it is not just that the sufferer and the disposer receive the same punishment, unless he willingly receive the honour which belongs only to the Most Honourable.

Chapter VII - "Let Both Grow Together Till the Harvest."

"But it will be said that the worshippers themselves ought to be taken away by the true God, that others may not do it.

But you are not wiser than God, that you should give Him counsel as one more prudent than He.

He knows what He does; for He is long-suffering to all who are in impiety, as a merciful and philanthropic father, knowing that impious men become pious.

And of those very worshippers of base and senseless things, many becoming sober have ceased to worship these things and to sin, and many Greeks have been saved so as to pray to the true God.

Chapter VIII - Liberty and Necessity

"But, you say, God ought to have made us at first so that we should not have thought at all of such things.

You who say this do not know what is free-will, and how it is possible to be really good; that he who is good by his own choice is really good; but he who is made good by another under necessity is not really good, because he is not what he is by his own choice. ³Since therefore every one's freedom constitutes the true good, and shows the true evil, God has contrived that friendship or hostility should be in each man by occasions.

But no, it is said:

everything that we think He makes us to think.

Stop! Why do you blaspheme more and more, in saying this?

For if we are under His influence in all that we think, you say that He is the cause of fornications, lusts, avarice, and all blasphemy.

Cease your evil-speaking, ye who ought to speak well of Him, and to bestow all honour upon Him.

And do not say that God does not claim any honour; for if He Himself claims nothing, you ought to look to what is right, and to answer with thankful voice Him who does you good in all things.

Chapter IX - God a Jealous God

"But, you say, we do better when we are thankful at once to Him and to all others.

Now, when you say this, you do not know the plot that is formed against you.

For as, when many physicians of no power promise to cure one patient, one who is really able to cure him does not apply his remedy, considering that, if he should cure him, the others would get the credit; so also God does not do you good, when He is asked along with many who can do nothing.

What! it will be said, is God enraged at this, if, when He cures, another gets the credit?

I answer:

Although He be not indignant, at all events He will not be an accomplice in deceit; for when He has conferred a benefit, the idol, which has done nothing, is credited with the power.

But also I say to you, if he who crouches in adoration before senseless idols had not been injured naturally, perhaps He (God) would have endured even this. Wherefore watch ye that you may attain to a reasonable understanding on the matter of salvation. ⁴For God being without want, neither Himself needs anything, nor receives hurt; for it belongs to us to be profited or injured.

For in like manner as Caesar is neither hurt when he is evil spoken of, nor profited when he is thanked, but safety accrues to the renderer of thanks, and ruin to the evil-speaker, so they who speak well of God indeed profit Him nothing, but save themselves; and in like manner, those who blaspheme Him do not indeed injure Him, but themselves perish.

Chapter X - The Creatures Avenge God's Cause

"But it will be said that the cases are not parallel between God and man; and I admit that they are not parallel:

for the punishment is greater to him who is guilty of impiety against the greater, and less to him who sins against the less.

As, therefore, God is greatest of all, so he who is impious against Him shall endure greater punishment, as sinning against the greater; not through His defending Himself with His own hand, but the whole creation being indignant at him, and naturally taking vengeance on him.

For to the blasphemer the sun will not give his light, nor the earth her fruits, nor the fountain its water, nor in Hades shall he who is there constituted prince give rest to the soul; since even now, while the constitution of the world subsists, the whole creation is indignant at him.

Wherefore neither do the clouds afford sufficient rains, nor the earth fruits, whereby many perish; yea, even the air itself, inflamed with anger, is turned to pestilential courses.

However, whatsoever good things we enjoy, He of His mercy compels the creature to our benefits.

Still, against you who dishonour the Maker of all, the whole creation is hostile.

Chapter XI - Immortality of the Soul

"And though by the dissolution of the body you should escape punishment, how shall you be able by corruption to flee from your soul, which is incorruptible?

For the soul even of the wicked is immortal, for whom it were better not to have it incorruptible.

For, being punished with endless torture under unquenchable fire, and never dying, it can receive no end of its misery.

But perhaps some one of you will say, You terrify us, O Peter.'

Teach us then how we can be silent about these things, and yet tell you things as they are, for not otherwise can we tell you them.

But if we should be silent, you should be ensnared by evils through ignorance.

But if we speak, we are suspected of terrifying you with a false theory.

How then shall we charm that wicked serpent that lurks in your soul, and subtilely insinuates suspicions hostile to God, under the guise of love of God? Be reconciled with yourselves; for in order to your salvation recourse is to Him with well-doing.

Unreasonable lust in you is hostile to God, for by conceit of wisdom it strengthens ignorance.

Chapter XII - Idols Unprofitable

"But others say, God does not care for us.

This also is false.

For if really He did not care, He would neither cause His sun to rise on the good and the evil, nor send His rain on the just and the unjust.

But others say, We are more pious than you, since we worship both him and images.

I do not think, if one were to say to a king, I give you an equal share of honour with that which I give to corpses and to worthless dung,'--I do not think that he would profit by it.

But some one will say, Do you call our objects of worship dung?

I say Yes, for you have made them useless to yourselves by setting them aside for worship, whereas their substance might perhaps have been serviceable for some other purpose, or for the purpose of manure.

But now it is not useful even for this purpose, since you have changed its shape and worship it.

And how do you say that you are more pious, you who are the most wicked of all, who deserve destruction of your souls by this very one incomparable sin, at the hands of Him who is true, if you abide in it?

For as if any son having received many benefits from his father, give to another, who is not his father, the honour that is due to his father, he is certainly disinherited; but if he live according to the judgment of his father, and so thanks him for his kindnesses, he is with good reason made the heir.

Chapter XIII - Arguments in Favour of Idolatry Answered

"But others say, We shall act impiously if we forsake the objects of worship handed down to us by our fathers; for it is like the guarding of a deposit.

But on this principle the son of a robber or a debauchee ought not to be sober and to choose the better part, lest he should act impiously, and sin by doing differently from his parents!

How foolish, then, are they who say, We worship these things that we may not be troublesome to Him; as if God were troubled by those who bless Him, and not troubled by those who ungratefully blaspheme Him.

Why is it, then, that when there is a withholding of rain, you look only to heaven and pour out prayers and supplications; and when you obtain it, you quickly forget?

For when you have reaped your harvest or gathered your vintage, you distribute your first-fruits among those idols which are nothing, quickly forgetting God your benefactor; and thus you go into groves and temples, and offer sacrifices and feasts.

Wherefore some of you say, These things have been excellently devised for the sake of good cheer and feasting.

Chapter XIV - Heathen Orgies

"Oh men without understanding!
Judge ye rightly of what is said.
For if it were necessary to give one's self to some pleasure for the refreshment of the body, whether were it better to do so among the rivers and woods and groves, where there are entertainments and convivialities and shady places, or where there is the madness of demons, and cuttings of hands, and emasculations, and fury and mania, and dishevelling of hair, and shoutings and enthusiasms and howlings, and all those things which are done with hypocrisy for the confounding of the unthinking, when you offer your prescribed prayers and thanksgivings even to those who are deader than the dead?

Chapter XV - Heathen Worshippers Under the Power of the Demon

"And why do ye take pleasure in these doings?
Since the serpent which lurks in you, which has sown in you fruitless lust, will not tell you, I shall speak and put it on record.
Thus the case stands.
According to the worship of God, the proclamation is made to be sober, to be chaste, to restrain passion, not to pilfer other men's goods, to live uprightly, moderately, fearlessly, gently; rather to restrain one's self in necessities, than to supply his wants by wrongfully taking away the property of another.
But with the so-called gods the reverse is done.
And ye renounce some things as done by you, in order to the admiration of your righteousness; whereas, although you did all that you are commanded, ignorance with respect to God is alone sufficient for your condemnation.
But meeting together in the places which you have dedicated to them, you delight in making yourselves drunk, and you kindle your altars, of which the diffused odour through its influence attracts the blind and deaf spirits to the place of their fumigation. And thus, of those who are present, some are filled with inspirations, and some with strange fiends, and some betake themselves to lasciviousness, and some to theft and murder.
For the exhalation of blood, and the libation of wine, satisfies even these unclean spirits, which lurk within you and cause you to take pleasure in the things that are transacted there, and in dreams surround you with false phantasies, and punish you with myriads of diseases.
For under the show of the so-called sacred victims you are filled with dire demons, which, cunningly concealing themselves, destroy you, so that you should not understand the plot that is laid for you.
For, under the guise of some injury, or love, or anger, or grief, or strangling you with a rope, or drowning you, or throwing you from a precipice, or by suicide, or apoplexy, or some other disease, they deprive you of life.

Chapter XVI - All Things Work for Good to Them that Love God

"But no one of us can suffer such a thing; but they themselves are punished by us, when, having entered into any one, they entreat us that they may go out slowly.
But some one will say perhaps, Even some of the worshippers of God fall under such sufferings.
I say that is impossible.
For he is a worshipper of God, of whom I speak, who is truly pious, not one who is such only in name, but who really performs the deeds of the law that has been given him.
If any one acts impiously, he is not pious; in like manner as, if he who is of another tribe keeps the law, he is a Jew; but he who does not keep it is a Greek.
For the Jew believes God and keeps the law, by which faith he removes also other sufferings, though like mountains and heavy. [5]
But he who keeps not the law is manifestly a deserter through not believing God; and thus as no Jew, but a sinner, he is on account of his sin brought into subjection to those sufferings which are ordained for the punishment of sinners.

For, by the will of God prescribed at the beginning, punishment righteously follows those who worship Him on account of transgressions; and this is so, in order that having reckoned with them by punishment for sin as for a debt, he may set forth those who have turned to Him pure in the universal judgment.

For as the wicked here enjoy luxury to the loss of eternal blessings, so punishments are sent upon the Jews who transgress for a settlement of accounts, that, expiating their transgression here, they may there be set free from eternal punishments.

Chapter XVII - Speaking the Truth in Love

"But you cannot speak thus; for you do not believe that things are then as we say; I mean, when there is a recompense for all.

And on this account, you being ignorant of what is advantageous, are seduced by temporal pleasures from taking hold of eternal things.

Wherefore we attempt to make to you exhibitions of what is profitable, that, being convinced of the promises that belong to piety, you may by good deeds inherit with us the griefless world.

Until then you know us, do not be angry with us, as if we spoke falsely of the good things which we desire for you.

For the things which are regarded by us as true and good, these we have not scrupled to bring to you, but, on the contrary, have hastened to make you fellow-heirs of good things, which we have considered to be such.

For thus it is necessary to speak to the unbelievers.

But that we really speak the truth in what we say, you cannot know otherwise than by first listening with love of the truth.

Chapter XVIII - Charming of the Serpent

"Wherefore, as to the matter in hand, although in ten thousand ways the serpent that lurks in you suggesting evil reasonings and hindrances, wishes to ensnare you, therefore so much the more ought ye to resist him, and to listen to us assiduously.

For it behoves you, consulting, as having been grievously deceived, to know how he must be charmed. But in no other way is it possible.

But by charming I mean the setting yourselves by reason in opposition to their evil counsels, remembering that by promise of knowledge he brought death into the world at the first. [6]

Chapter XIX - Not Peace, But a Sword

"Whence the Prophet of the truth, knowing that the world was much in error, and seeing it ranged on the side of evil, did not choose that there should be peace to it while it stood in error.

So that till the end he sets himself against all those who are in concord with wickedness, setting truth over against error, sending as it were fire upon those who are sober, namely wrath against the seducer, which is likened to a sword, [7] and by holding forth the word he destroys ignorance by knowledge, cutting, as it were, and separating the living from the dead.

Therefore, while wickedness is being conquered by lawful knowledge, war has taken hold of all.

For the submissive son is, for the sake of salvation, separated from the unbelieving father, or the father from the son, or the mother from the daughter, or the daughter from the mother, and relatives from relatives, and friends from associates.

Chapter XX - What If It Be Already Kindled?

"And let not any one say, How is this just, that parents should be separated from their children, and children from their parents?

It is just, even entirely.

For if they remained with them, and, after profiting them nothing, were also destroyed along with them, how is it not just that he who wishes to be saved should be separated from him who will not, but who wishes to destroy him along with himself. Moreover, it is not those who judge better that wish to be separated, but they wish to stay with them, and to profit them by the exposition of better things; and therefore the unbelievers, not wishing to hearken to them, make war against them, banishing, persecuting, hating them. But those who suffer these things, pitying those who are ensnared by ignorance, by the teaching of wisdom pray for those who contrive evil against them, having learned that ignorance is the cause of their sin. For the Teacher Himself, being nailed to the cross, prayed to the Father that the sin of those who slew Him might be forgiven, saying, Father, forgive them their sins, for they know not what they do.' [8]They also therefore, being imitators of the Teacher in their sufferings, pray for those who contrive them, as they have been taught.

Therefore they are not separated as hating their parents, since they make constant prayers even for those who are neither parents nor relatives, but enemies, and strive to love them, as they have been commanded.

Chapter XXI - "If I Be a Father, Where is My Fear?"

"But tell me, how do you love your parents?

If, indeed, you do it as always regarding what is right, I congratulate you; but if you love them as it happens, then not so, for then you may on a small occasion become their enemies.

But if you love them intelligently, tell me, what are parents?

You will say they are the sources of our being. Why, then, do ye not love the source of the being of all things, if indeed you have with right understanding elected to do this?

But you will now say again, we have not seen Him.

Why, then, do ye not seek for Him, but worship senseless things?

But what?

If it were even difficult for you to know what God is, you cannot fail to know what is not God, so as to reason that God is not wood, nor stone, nor brass, nor anything else made of corruptible matter.

Chapter XXII - "The Gods that Have Not Made the Heavens."

"For are not they graven with iron?

And has not the graying iron been softened by fire?

And is not the fire itself extinguished with water? And has not the water its motion from the spirit?

And has not the spirit the beginning of its course from the God who hath made all things?

For thus said the prophet Moses:

In the beginning God made the heaven and the earth.

And the earth was unsightly, and unadorned; and darkness was over the deep:

and the Spirit of God was borne above the waters.'

Which Spirit, at the bidding of God, as it were His hand, makes all things, dividing light from darkness, and after the invisible heaven spreading out the visible, that the places above might be inhabited by the angels of light, and those below by man, and all the creatures that were made for his use.

Chapter XXIII - "To Whom Much is Given."

"For on thy account, O man, God commanded the water to retire upon the face of the earth, that the earth might be able to bring forth fruits for thee.

And He made water-courses, that He might provide for thee fountains, and that river-beds might be disclosed, that animals might teem forth; in a word, that He might furnish thee with all things.

For is it not for thee that the winds blow, and the rains fall, and the seasons change for the production of fruits?

Moreover, it is for thee that the sun and moon, with the other heavenly bodies, accomplish their risings and settings; and rivers and pools, with all fountains, serve thee.

Whence to thee, O senseless one, as the greater honour has been given, so for thee, ungrateful, the greater punishment by fire has been prepared, because thou wouldest not know Him whom it behoved thee before all things to know.

Chapter XXIV - "Born of Water."

"And now from inferior things learn the cause of all, reasoning that water makes all things, and water receives the production of its movement from spirit, and the spirit has its beginning from the God of all.

And thus you ought to have reasoned, in order that by reason you might attain to God, that, knowing your origin, and being born again by the first-born water, you may be constituted heir of the parents who have begotten you to incorruption.

Chapter XXV - Good Works to Be Well Done

"Wherefore come readily, as a son to a father, that God may assign ignorance as the cause of your sins.

But if after being called you will not, or delay, you shall be destroyed by the just judgment of God, not being willed, through your not willing.

And do not think, though you were more pious than all the pious that ever were, but if you be unbaptized, that you shall ever obtain hope.

For all the more, on this account, you shall endure the greater punishment, because you have done excellent works not excellently.

For well-doing is excellent when it is done as God has commanded.

But if you will not be baptized according to His pleasure, you serve your own will and oppose His counsel.

Chapter XXVI - Baptism

"But perhaps some one will say, What does it contribute to piety to be baptized with water?

In the first place, because you do that which is pleasing to God; and in the second place, being born again to God of water, by reason of fear you change your first generation, which is of lust, and thus you are able to obtain salvation.

But otherwise it is impossible.

For thus the prophet has sworn to us, saying, "Verily I say to you, Unless ye be regenerated by living water into the name of Father, Son, and Holy Spirit, you shall not enter the kingdom of heaven."[9] Wherefore approach.

For there is there something that is merciful from the beginning, borne upon the water, and rescues from the future punishment those who are baptized with the thrice blessed invocation, offering as gifts to God the good deeds of the baptized whenever they are done after their baptism.

Wherefore flee to the waters, for this alone can quench the violence of fires. [10] He who will not now come to it still bears the spirit of strife, on account of which he will not approach the living water for his own salvation.

Chapter XXVII - All Need Baptism

"Therefore approach, be ye righteous or unrighteous.

For if you are righteous, baptism alone is lacking in order to salvation.

But if you are unrighteous, come to be baptized for the remission of the sins formerly committed in ignorance.

And to the unrighteous man it remains that his well-doing after baptism be according to the proportion of his previous impiety.

Wherefore, be ye righteous or unrighteous, hasten to be born to God, because delay brings danger, on account of the fore-appointment of death being unrevealed; and show by well-doing your likeness to the Father, who begetteth you of water.

As a lover of truth, honour the true God as your Father.

But His honour is that you live as He, being righteous, would have you live.

And the will of the righteous One is that you do no wrong.

But wrong is murder, hatred, envy, and such like; and of these there are many forms.

Chapter XXVIII - Purification

"However, it is necessary to add something to these things which has not community with man, but is peculiar to the worship of God.

I mean purification, not approaching to a man's own wife when she is in separation, for so the law of God commands.

But what?

If purity be not added to the service of God, you would roll pleasantly like the dung-flies.

Wherefore as man, having something more than the irrational animals, namely, rationality, purify your hearts from evil by heavenly reasoning, and wash your bodies in the bath.

For purification according to the truth is not that the purity of the body precedes purification after the heart, but that purity follows goodness.

For our Teacher also, dealing with certain of the Pharisees and Scribes among us, who are separated, and as Scribes know the matters of the law more than others, still He reproved them as hypocrites, because they cleansed only the things that appear to men, but omitted purity of heart and the things seen by God alone.

Chapter XXIX - Outward and Inward Purity

"Therefore He made use of this memorable expression, speaking the truth with respect to the hypocrites of them, not with respect to all.

For to some He said that obedience was to be rendered, because they were entrusted with the chair of Moses.

However, to the hypocrites he said, Woe to you, Scribes and Pharisees, hypocrites, for ye make clean the outside of the cup and the platter, but the inside is full of filth. Thou blind Pharisee, cleanse first the inside of the cup and the platter, that their outsides may be clean also.'

And truly:

for when the mind is enlightened by knowledge, the disciple is able to be good, and thereupon purity follows; for from the understanding within a good care of the body without is produced.

As from negligence with respect to the body, care of the understanding cannot be produced, so the pure man can purify both that which is without and that which is within. And he who, purifying the things without, does it looking to the praise of men, and by the praise of those who look on, he has nothing from God.

Chapter XXX - "Whatsoever Things are Pure."

"But who is there to whom it is not manifest that it is better not to have intercourse with a woman in her separation, but purified and washed.

And also after copulation it is proper to wash.

But if you grudge to do this, recall to mind how you followed after the parts of purity when you served senseless idols; and be ashamed that now, when it is necessary to attain, I say not more, but to attain the one and whole of purity, you are more slothful.

Consider, therefore, Him who made you, and you will understand who He is that casts upon you this sluggishness with respect to purity.

Chapter XXXI - "What Do Ye More Than Others?"

"But some one of you will say, Must we then do whatsoever things we did while we were idolaters?

I say to you, Not all things; but whatsoever you did well, you must do now, and more:

for whatsoever is well done in error hangs upon truth, as if anything be ill done in the truth it is from error.

Receive, therefore, from all quarters the things that are your own, and not those that are another's, and do not say, If those who are in error do anything well we are not bound to do it. For, on this principle, if any one who worships idols do not commit murder, we ought to commit murder, because he who is in error does not commit it.

Chapter XXXII - "To Whom Much is Given."

"No; but rather, if those who are in error do not kill, let us not be angry; if he who is in error do not commit adultery, let us not lust even in the smallest degree; if he who is in error loves him who loves him, let us love even those who hate us; if he who is in error lends to those who have, let us give to those who have not.

Unquestionably we ought--we who hope to inherit eternal life--to do better things than the good things that are done by those who know only the present life, knowing that if their works, being judged with ours in the day of judgment, be found equal in goodness, we shall have shame, and they perdition, having acted against themselves through error.

And I say that we shall be put to shame on this account, because we have not done more than they, though we have known more than they.

And if we shall be put to shame if we show well-doing equal to theirs, and no more, how much more if we show less than their well-doing?

Chapter XXXIII - The Queen of the South and the Men of Nineveh

"But that indeed in the day of judgment the doings of those who have known the truth are compared with the good deeds of those who have been in error, the unlying One Himself has taught us, saying to those who neglected to come and listen to Him, The queen of the south shall rise up with this generation, and shall condemn it; because she came from the extremities of the earth to hear the wisdom of Solomon:

and behold, a greater than Solomon is here,' [11] and ye do not believe Him.

And to those amongst the people who would not repent at His preaching He said, The men of Nineveh shall rise up with this generation and shall condemn it, for they heard and repented on the preaching of Jonas:

and behold, a greater is here, and no one believes.' [12] And thus, setting over against all their impiety those from among the Gentiles who have done well, in order to condemn those who, possessing the true religion, had not acted so well as those who were in error, he exhorted those having reason not only to do equally with the Gentiles whatsoever things are excellent, but more than they.

And this speech has been suggested to me, taking occasion from the necessity of respecting the separation, and of washing after copulation, and of not denying such purity, though those who are in error do the same, since those who in error do well, without being saved, are for the condemnation of those who are in the worship of God, and do ill; because their respect for purity is through error, and not through the worship of the true Father and God of all."

Chapter XXXIV - Peter's Daily Work

Having said this, he dismissed the multitudes; and according to his custom, having partaken of food with those dearest to him, he went to rest.

And thus doing and discoursing day by day, he strongly buttressed the law of God, challenging the reputed gods with the reputed Genesis, [13] and arguing that there is no automatism, but that the world is governed according to providence.

Chapter XXXV - "Beware of False Prophets."

Then after three months were fulfilled, he ordered me to fast for several days, and then brought me to the fountains that are near to the sea, and baptized me as in ever-flowing water.

Thus, therefore, when our brethren rejoiced at my God-gifted regeneration, not many days after he turned to the elders in presence of all the church, and charged them, saying:

"Our Lord and Prophet, who hath sent us, declared to us that the wicked one, having disputed with Him forty days, and having prevailed nothing against Him, promised that he would send apostles from amongst his subjects, to deceive.

Wherefore, above all, remember to shun apostle or teacher or prophet who does not first accurately compare his preaching with that of James, who was called the brother of my Lord, and to whom was entrusted to administer the church of the Hebrews in Jerusalem,--and that even though he come to you with witnesses: [14]lest the wickedness which disputed forty days with the Lord, and prevailed nothing, should afterwards, like lightning falling from heaven upon the earth, send a preacher to your injury, as now he has sent Simon upon us, preaching, under pretence of the truth, in the name of the Lord, and sowing error.

Wherefore He who hath sent us, said, Many shall come to me in sheep's clothing, but inwardly they are ravening wolves.

By their fruits ye shall know them.'"

Chapter XXXVI - Farewell to Tripolis

Having spoken thus, he sent the harbingers into Antioch of Syria, bidding them expect him there forthwith.

Then when they had gone, Peter having driven away diseases, sufferings, and demons from great multitudes who were persuaded, and having baptized them in the fountains which are near to the sea, and having celebrated [15] the Eucharist, and having appointed Maroones, who had received him into his house, and was now perfected, as their bishop, and having set apart twelve elders, and having designated deacons, and arranged matters relating to widows, and having discoursed on the common good what was profitable for the ordering of the church, and having counselled them to obey the bishop Maroones, three months being now fulfilled; he bade those in Tripolis of Phoenicia farewell, and took his journey to Antioch of Syria, all the people accompanying us with due honour.

Footnotes:

1. [With chaps. 2, 3, the corresponding chapters in Recognitions, vi., agree.
The parallel is resumed in chap. 19.--R.]
2. [Most of the matter in chaps. 4-18 is found in Recognitions, v. 23-36.--R.]
3. [Comp. Recognitions, iii. 21, etc.
In that work the freedom of the will, as necessary to goodness, is more frequently affirmed.--R.]
4. We have adopted the reading of Codex O.
The reading in the others is corrupt.
5. Matt. xvii. 20.
6. [At this point the first discourse in the Recognitions (v. 36) ends; the following chapters (19-33) agrees with the discourse in Recognitions, vi. 4-14.--R.]
7. Matt. x. 34.
8. Luke xxiii. 34.
9. Altered from John iii. 5.
10. [Comp. Recognitions, ix. 7.--R.]
11. Matt. xii. 42; [Luke xi. 31.--R.]
12. [Matt. xii. 41]; Luke xi. 32.
[The order of the two citations suggests that they were taken from Luke.--R.]
13. [Comp. Homily IV. 12 and the full discussion in XIV. 3-11.
In the Recognitions there is no reference to "genesis" before book viii. 2, etc., which is parallel with the passage just referred to.--R.]
14. A conjectural reading, which seems probable, is, Unless he come to you with credentials, viz., from James.
[The whole charge is peculiar to the Homilies.--R.].
15. Literally, "having broken."

Homily XII

Chapter I - Two Bands

Therefore starting from Tripolis of Phoenicia to go to Antioch of Syria, on the same day we came to Orthasia, and there stayed. ¹ And on account of its being near the city which we had left, almost all having heard the preaching before, we stopped there only one day, and set out to Antaradus.

And as there were many who journeyed with us, Peter, addressing Nicetus and Aquila, said, "Inasmuch as the great crowd of those who journey with us draws upon us no little envy as we enter city after city, I have thought that we must of necessity arrange, so that neither, on the one hand, these may be grieved at being prevented from accompanying us, nor, on the other hand, we, by being so conspicuous, may fall under the envy of the wicked. ² Wherefore I wish you, Nicetus and Aquila, to go before me in two separate bodies, and enter secretly into the Gentile cities.

Chapter II - Love of Preachers and Their Converts

"I know, indeed, that you are distressed at being told to do this, being separated from me by a space of two days.

I would have you know, therefore, that we the persuaders love you the persuaded much more than you love us who have persuaded you.

Therefore loving one another as we do by not unreasonably doing what we wish, let us provide, as much as in us lies, for safety.

For I prefer, as you also know, to go into the more notable cities of the provinces, and to remain some days, and discourse.

And for the present lead the way into the neighbouring Laodicea, and, after two or three days, so far as it depends upon my choice, I shall overtake you.

And do you alone receive me at the gates, on account of the confusion, that thus we may enter along with you without tumult.

And thence, in like manner, after some days' stay, others in your stead will go forward by turns to the places beyond, preparing lodgings for us."

Chapter III - Submission

When Peter had thus spoken they were compelled to acquiesce, saying, "It does not altogether grieve us, my lord, to do this on account of its being your command; in the first place, indeed, because you have been chosen by the providence of God, as being worthy to think and counsel well in all things; and in addition to this, for the most part we shall be separated from you only for two days by the necessity of preceding you.

And that were indeed a long time to be without sight of thee, O Peter, did we not consider that they will be more grieved who are sent much farther forward, being ordered to wait for thee longer in every city, distressed that they are longer deprived of the sight of thy longed-for countenance.

And we, though not less distressed than they, make no opposition, because you order us to do it for profit." Thus, having spoken, they went forward, having it in charge that at the first stage they should address the accompanying multitude that they should enter the cities apart from one another.

Chapter IV - Clement's Joy

When, therefore, they had gone, I, Clement, rejoiced greatly that he had ordered me to remain with himself.

Then I answered and said, "I thank God that you have not sent me away as you have done the others, as I should have died of grief."

But he said, "But what?

If there shall ever be any necessity that you be sent away for the sake of teaching, would you, on account of being separated for a little while from me, and that for an advantageous purpose, would you die for that? Would you not rather impress upon yourself the duty of bearing the things that are arranged for you through necessity, and cheerfully submit?

And do you not know that friends are present with one another in their memories, although they are separated bodily; whereas some, being bodily present, wander from their friends in their souls, by reason of want of memory?"

Chapter V - Clement's Office of Service

Then I answered, "Do not think, my lord, that I should endure that grief foolishly, but with some good reason.

For since I hold you, my lord, in place of all, father, mother, brothers, relatives, you who are the means through God of my having the saving truth, holding you in place of all, I have the greatest consolation.

And in addition to this, being afraid of my natural youthful lust, I was concerned lest, being left by you (being but a young man, and having now such a resolution that it would be impossible to desert you without incurring the anger of God,) [3] I should be overcome by lust.

But since it is much better and safer for me to remain with you, when my mind is with good reason set upon venerating, therefore I pray that I may always remain with you.

Moreover, I remember you saying in Caesarea, If any one wishes to journey with me, let him piously journey.'

And by piously you meant, that those who are devoted to the worship of God should grieve no one in respect of God, such as by leaving parents, an attached wife, or any others. [4]Whence I am in all respects a fitting fellow-traveller for you, to whom, if you would confer the greatest favour, you would allow to perform the functions of a servant."

Chapter VI - Peter's Frugality

Then Peter, hearing, smiled and said, "What think you, then, O Clement?

Do you not think that you are placed by very necessity in the position of my servant?

For who else shall take care of those many splendid tunics, with all my changes of rings and sandals?

And who shall make ready those pleasant and artistic dainties, which, being so various, need many skilful cooks, and all those things which are procured with great eagerness, and are prepared for the appetite of effeminate men as for some great wild beast?

However, such a choice has occurred to you, perhaps, without you understanding or knowing my manner of life, that I use only bread and olives, and rarely pot-herbs; and that this is my only coat and cloak which I wear; and I have no need of any of them, nor of aught else:

for even in these I abound. For my mind, seeing all the eternal good things that are there, regards none of the things that are here.

However, I accept of your good will; and I admire and commend you, for that you, a man of refined habits, have so easily submitted your manner of living to your necessities. For we, from our childhood, both I and Andrew, my brother, who is also my brother as respects God, not only being brought up in the condition of orphans, but also accustomed to labour through poverty and misfortune, easily bear the discomforts of our present journeys. Whence, if you would obey me, you would allow me, a working man, to fulfil the part of a servant to you."

The Epistles of Clement

Chapter VII - "Not to Be Ministered Unto, But to Minister."

But I, when I heard this, fell a-trembling and weeping, that such a word should be spoken by a man to whom all the men of this generation are inferior in point of knowledge and piety.

But he, seeing me weeping, asked the cause of my tears.

Then I said, "In what have I sinned so that you have spoken to me such a word?"

Then Peter answered, "If it were wrong of me to speak of being your servant, you were first in fault in asking to be mine."

Then I said, "The cases are not parallel; for to do this indeed becomes me well; but it is terrible for you, the herald of God, and who savest our souls, to do this to me."

Then Peter answered, "I should agree with you, but that [5] our Lord, who came for the salvation of all the world, being alone noble above all, submitted to the condition of a servant, that He might persuade us not to be ashamed to perform the ministrations of servants to our brethren, however well-born we may be."

Then I said, "If I think to overcome you in argument, I am foolish.

However, I thank the providence of God, that I have been thought worthy to have you instead of parents."

Chapter VIII - Family History

Then Peter inquired, "Are you really, then, alone in your family?" Then I answered, "There are indeed many and great men, being of the kindred of Caesar.

Wherefore Caesar himself gave a wife of his own family to my father, who was his foster-brother; and of her three sons of us were born, two before me, who were twins and very like each other, as my father told me.

But I scarcely know either them or our mother, but bear about with me an obscure image of them, as through dreams.

My mother's name was Mattidia, and my father's, Faustus; and of my brothers one was called Faustinus, and the other Faustinianus. [6]Then after I, their third son, was born, my mother saw a vision-- so my father told me--which told her, that unless she immediately took away her twin sons, and left the city of Rome for exile for twelve years, she and they must die by an all-destructive fate.

Chapter IX - The Lost Ones

"Therefore my father, being fond of his children, supplying them suitably for the journey with male and female servants, put them on board ship, and sent them to Athens with her to be educated, and kept me alone of his sons with him for his comfort; and for this I am very thankful, that the vision had not ordered me also to depart with my mother from the city of Rome.

Then, after the lapse of a year, my father sent money to them to Athens, and at the same time to learn how they did.

But those who went on this errand did not return.

And in the third year, my father being distressed, sent others in like manner with supplies, and they returned in the fourth year with the tidings that they had seen neither my mother nor my brothers, nor had they ever arrived at Athens, nor had they found any trace of any one of those who set out with them.

Chapter X - The Seeker Lost

"Then my father, hearing this, and being stupefied with excessive grief, and not knowing where to go in quest of them, used to take me with him and go down to the harbour, and inquire of many where any one of them had seen or heard of a shipwreck four years ago.

And one turned one place, and another another.

Then he inquired whether they had seen the body of a woman with two children cast ashore.

And when they told him they had seen many corpses. in many places, my father groaned at the information.

But, with his bowels yearning, he asked unreasonable questions, that he might try to search so great an extent of sea.

However, he was pardonable, because, through affection towards those whom he was seeking for, he fed on vain hopes.

And at last, placing me under guardians, and leaving me at Rome when I was twelve years old, he himself, weeping, went down to the harbour, and went on board ship, and set out upon the search.

And from that day till this I have neither received a letter from him, nor do I know whether he be alive or dead.

But I rather suspect that he is dead somewhere, either overcome by grief, or perished by shipwreck.

And the proof of that is that it is now the twentieth year that I have heard no true intelligence concerning him."

Chapter XI - The Afflictions of the Righteous

But Peter, hearing this, wept through sympathy, and immediately said to the gentlemen who were present:

"If any worshipper of God had suffered these things, such as this man's father hath suffered, he would immediately have assigned the cause of it to be his worship of God, ascribing it to the wicked one.

Thus also it is the lot of the wretched Gentiles to suffer; and we worshippers of God know it not. But with good reason I call them wretched, because here they are ensnared, and the hope that is thine they obtain not.

For those who in the worship of God suffer afflictions, suffer them for the expiation of their transgressions."

Chapter XII - A Pleasure Trip

When Peter had spoken thus, a certain one amongst us ventured to invite him, in the name of all, that next day, early in the morning, he should sail to Aradus, an island opposite, distant, I suppose, not quite thirty stadia, for the purpose of seeing two pillars of vine-wood that were there, and that were of very great girth.

Therefore the indulgent Peter consented, saying, "When you leave the boat, do not go many of you together to see the things that you desire to see; for I do not wish that the attention of the inhabitants should be turned to you." And so we sailed, and in short time arrived at the island.

Then landing from the boat, we went to the place where the vine-wood pillars were, and along with them we looked at several of the works of Phidias.

Chapter XIII - A Woman of a Sorrowful Spirit

But Peter alone did not think it worth while to look at the sights that were there; but noticing a certain woman sitting outside before the doors, begging constantly for her support, he said to her, "O woman, is any of your limbs defective, that you submit to such disgrace--I mean that of begging,--and do not rather work with the hands which God has given you, and procure your daily food?"

But she, groaning, answered, "Would that I had hands able to work!

But now they retain only the form of hands, being dead and rendered useless by my gnawing of them." Then Peter asked her, "What is the cause of your suffering so terribly?"

And she answered, "Weakness of soul; and nought else.

For if I had the mind of a man, there was a precipice or a pool whence I should have thrown myself, and have been able to rest from my tormenting misfortunes."

Chapter XIV - Balm in Gilead

Then said Peter, "What then?

Do you suppose, O woman, that those who destroy themselves are freed from punishment?

Are not the souls of those who thus die punished with a worse punishment in Hades for their suicide?"

But she said, "Would that I were persuaded that souls are really found alive in Hades; then I should love death, making light of the punishment, that I might see, were it but for an hour, my longed for sons!"

Then said Peter, "What is it that grieves you?
I should like to know, O woman.
For if you inform me, in return for this favour, I shall satisfy you that souls live in Hades; and instead of precipice or pool, I shall give you a drug, that you may live and die without torment."

Chapter XV - The Woman's Story

Then the woman, not understanding what was spoken ambiguously, being pleased with the promise, began to speak thus:--"Were I to speak of my family and my country, I do not suppose that I should be able to persuade any one.

But of what consequence is it to you to learn this, excepting only the reason why in my anguish I have deadened my hands by gnawing them?

Yet I shall give you an account of myself, so far as it is in your power to hear it.

I, being very nobly born, by the arrangement of a certain man in authority, became the wife of a man who was related to him.

And first I had twins sons, and afterwards another son.

But my husband's brother, being thoroughly mad, was enamoured of wretched me, who exceedingly affected chastity.

And I, wishing neither to consent to my lover nor to expose to my husband his brother's love of me, reasoned thus:

that I may neither defile myself by the commission of adultery nor disgrace my husband's bed, nor set brother at war with brother, nor subject the whole family, which is a great one, to the reproach of all, as I said.

I reasoned that it was best for me to leave the city for some time with my twin children, until the impure love should cease of him who flattered me to my disgrace.

The other son, however, I left with his father, to remain for a comfort to him.

Chapter XVI - The Shipwreck

"However, that matters might be thus arranged, I resolved to fabricate a dream, to the effect that some one stood by me by night, and thus spoke:

O woman, straightway leave the city with your twin children for some time, until I shall charge you to return hither again; otherwise you forthwith shall die miserably, with your husband and all your children.'

And so I did.

For as soon as I told the false dream to my husband, he being alarmed, sent me off by ship to Athens with my two sons, and with slaves, maids, and abundance of money, to educate the boys, until, said he, it shall please the giver of the oracle that you return to me.

But, wretch that I am, while sailing with my children, I was driven by the fury of the winds into these regions, and the ship having gone to pieces in the night, I was wrecked.

And all the rest having died, my unfortunate self alone was tossed by a great wave and cast upon a rock; and while I sat upon it in my misery, I was prevented, by the hope of finding my children alive, from throwing myself into the deep then, when I could easily have done it, having my soul made drunk by the waves.

Chapter XVII - The Fruitless Search

"But when the day dawned, I shouted aloud, and howled miserably, and looked around, seeking for the dead bodies of my hapless children. Therefore the inhabitants took pity on me, and seeing me naked, they first clothed me and then sounded the deep, seeking for my children. And when they found nothing of what they sought, some of the hospitable women came to me to comfort me, and every one told her own misfortunes, that I might obtain comfort from the occurrences of similar misfortunes.

But this only grieved me the more for I said that I was not so wicked that I could take comfort from the misfortunes of others.

And so, when many of them asked me to accept their hospitality, a certain poor woman with much urgency constrained me to come into her cottage, saying to me, Take courage, woman, for my husband, who was a sailor, also died at sea, while he was still in the bloom of his youth; and ever since, though many have asked me in marriage, I have preferred living as a widow, regretting the loss of my husband.

But we shall have in common whatever we can both earn with our hands.'

Chapter XVIII - Trouble Upon Trouble

"And not to lengthen out unnecessary details, I went to live with her, on account of her love to her husband.

And not long after, my hands were debilitated by my gnawing of them; and the woman who had taken me in, being wholly seized by some malady, is confined in the house. Since then the former compassion of the women has declined, and I and the woman of the house are both of us helpless.

For a long time I have sat here, as you see, begging; and whatever I get I convey to my fellow-sufferer for our support.

Let this suffice about my affairs. For the rest, what hinders your fulfilling of your promise to give me the drug, that I may give it to her also, who desires to die; and thus I also, as you said, shall be able to escape from life?"

Chapter XIX - Evasions

While the woman thus spoke, Peter seemed to be in suspense on account of many reasonings.

But I came up and said, "I have been going about seeking you for a long time.

And now, what is in hand?"

But Peter ordered me to lead the way, and wait for him at the boat; and because there was no gainsaying when he commanded, I did as I was ordered.

But Peter, as he afterwards related the whole matter to me, being struck in his heart with some slight suspicion, inquired of the woman, saying, "Tell me, O woman, your family, and your city, and the names of your children, and presently I shall give you the drug."

But she, being put under constraint, and not wishing to speak, yet being eager to obtain the drug, cunningly said one thing for another.

And so she said that she was an Ephesian and her husband a Sicilian; and in like manner she changed the names of the three children.

Then Peter, supposing that she spoke the truth, said, "Alas! O woman, I thought that this day was to bring you great joy, suspecting that you are a certain person of whom I was thinking, and whose affairs I have heard and accurately know."

But she adjured him, saying, "Tell me, I entreat of you, that I may know if there is among women any one more wretched than myself."

Chapter XX - Peter's Account of the Matter

Then Peter, not knowing that she had spoken falsely, through pity towards her, began to tell her the truth:

"There is a certain young man in attendance upon me, thirsting after the discourses on religion, a Roman citizen, who told me how that, having a father and two twin brothers, he has lost sight of them all.

For," says he, "my mother, as my father related to me, having seen a vision, left the city Rome for a time with her twin children, lest she should perish by an evil fate, and having gone away with them, she cannot be found; and her husband, the young man's father, having gone in search of her, he also cannot be found."

Chapter XXI - A Disclosure

While Peter thus spoke, the woman, who had listened attentively, swooned away as if in stupor.

But Peter approached her, and caught hold of her, and exhorted her to restrain herself, persuading her to confess what was the matter with her.

But she, being powerless in the rest of her body, as through intoxication, turned her head round, being able to sustain the greatness of the hoped for joy, and rubbing her face:

"Where," said she, "is this youth?"

And he, now seeing through the whole affair, said, "Tell me first; for otherwise you cannot see him."

Then she earnestly said, "I am that youth's mother."

The Epistles of Clement

Then said Peter, "What is his name?"

And she said, "Clement."

Then Peter said, "It is the same, and he it was that spoke to me a little while ago, whom I ordered to wait for me in the boat."

And she, falling at Peter's feet, entreated him to make haste to come to the boat.

Then Peter, "If you will keep terms with me, I shall do so."

Then she said, "I will do anything; only show me my only child.

For I shall seem to see in him my two children who died here."

Then Peter said, "When ye see him, be quiet, until we depart from the island."

And she said, "I will."

Chapter XXII - The Lost Found

Peter, therefore, took her by the hand, and led her to the boat.

But I, when I saw him leading the woman by the hand, laughed, and approaching, offered to lead her instead of him, to his honour.

But as soon as I touched her hand, she gave a motherly shout, and embraced me violently, and eagerly kissed me as her son.

But I, being ignorant of the whole affair, shook her off as a madwoman.

But, through my respect for Peter, I checked myself.

Chapter XXIII - Reward of Hospitality

But Peter said, "Alas!

What are you doing, my son Clement, shaking off your real mother?"

But I, when I heard this, wept, and falling down by my mother, who had fallen, I kissed her.

For as soon as this was told me, I in some way recalled her appearance indistinctly.

Then great crowds ran together to see the beggar woman, telling one another that her son had recognised her, and that he was a man of consideration. Then, when we would have straightway left the island with my mother, she said to us, "My much longed-for son, it is right that I should bid farewell to the woman who entertained me, who, being poor and wholly debilitated, lies in the house."

And Peter hearing this, and all the multitude who stood by, admired the good disposition of the woman.

And immediately Peter ordered some persons to go and bring the woman on her couch.

And as soon as the couch was brought and set down, Peter said, in the hearing of the whole multitude, "If I be a herald of the truth, in order to the faith of the bystanders, that they may know that there is one God, who made the world, let her straightway rise whole."

And while Peter was still speaking, the woman arose healed, and fell down before Peter, and kissed her dear associate, and asked her what it all meant.

Then she briefly detailed to her the whole business of the recognition, [7] to the astonishment of the hearers.

Then also my mother, seeing her hostess cured, entreated that she herself also might obtain healing.

And his placing his hand upon her, cured her also.

Chapter XXIV - All Well Arranged

And then Peter having discoursed concerning God and the service accorded to Him, he concluded as follows:

"If any one wishes to learn these things accurately, let him come to Antioch, where I have resolved to remain some length of time, and learn the things that pertain to his salvation.

For if you are familiar with leaving your country for the sake of trading or of warfare, and coming to far-off places, you should not be unwilling to go three days' journey for the sake of eternal salvation."

Then, after the address of Peter, I presented the woman who had been healed, in the presence of all the multitude, with a thousand drachmas, for her support, giving her in charge to a certain good man, who was the chief man of the city, and who of his own accord joyfully undertook the charge.

Further, having distributed money amongst many other women, and thanked those who at any time had comforted my mother, I sailed away to Antaradus, along with my mother, and Peter, and the rest of our companions; and thus we proceeded to our lodging.

Chapter XXV - Philanthropy and Friendship

And when we were arrived and had partaken of food, and given thanks according to our custom, there being still time, [8] I said to Peter:

"My lord Peter, my mother has done a work of philanthropy in remembering the woman her hostess."

And Peter answered, "Have you indeed, O Clement, thought truly that your mother did a work of philanthropy in respect of her treatment of the woman who took her in after her shipwreck, or have you spoken this word by way of greatly complimenting your mother?

But if you spoke truly, and not by way of compliment, you seem to me not to know what the greatness of philanthropy is, which is affection towards any one whatever in respect of his being a man, apart from physical persuasion.

But not even do I venture to call the hostess who received your mother after her shipwreck, philanthropic; for she was impelled by pity, and persuaded to become the benefactress of a woman who had been shipwrecked, who was grieving for her children,--a stranger, naked, destitute, and greatly deploring her misfortunes.

When, therefore, she was in such circumstances, who that saw her, though he were impious, could but pity her?

So that it does not seem to me that even the stranger-receiving woman did a work of philanthropy, but to have been moved to assist her by pity for her innumerable misfortunes.

And how much more is it true of your mother, than when she was in prosperous circumstances and requited her hostess, she did a deed, not of philanthropy, but of friendship! for there is much difference between friendship and philanthropy, because friendship springs from requital.

But philanthropy, apart from physical persuasion, loves and benefits every man as he is a man.

If, therefore, while she pitied her hostess, she also pitied and did good to her enemies who have wronged her, she would be philanthropic; but if, on one account she is friendly or hostile, and on another account is hostile or friendly, such an one is the friend or enemy of some quality, not of man as man."

Chapter XXVI - What is Philanthropy

Then I answered, "Do you not think, then, that even the stranger-receiver was philanthropic, who did good to a stranger whom she did not know?"

Then Peter said, "Compassionate, indeed, I can call her, but I dare not call her philanthropic, just as I cannot call a mother philoteknic, for she is prevailed on to have an affection for them by her pangs, and by her rearing of them.

As the lover also is gratified by the company and enjoyment of his mistress, and the friend by return of friendship, so also the compassionate man by misfortune. However the compassionate man is near to the philanthropic, in that he is impelled, apart from hunting after the receipt of anything, to do the kindness.

But he is not yet philanthropic."

Then I said, "By what deeds, then, can any one be philanthropic?"

And Peter answered, "Since I see that you are eager to hear what is the work of philanthropy, I shall not object to telling you.

He is the philanthropic man who does good even to his enemies.

And that it is so, listen:

Philanthropy is masculo-feminine; and the feminine part of it is called compassion, and the male part is named love to our neighbour.

But every man is neighbour to every man, and not merely this man or that; for the good and the bad, the friend and the enemy, are alike men.

It behoves, therefore, him who practises philanthropy to be an imitator of God, doing good to the righteous and the unrighteous, as God Himself vouchsafes His sun and His heavens to all in the present world.

But if you will do good to the good, but not to the evil, or even will punish them, you undertake to do the work of a judge, you do not strive to hold by philanthropy."

Chapter XXVII - Who Can Judge

Then I said, "Then even God, who, as you teach us, is at some time to judge, is not philanthropic."

Then said Peter, "You assert a contradiction; for because He shall judge, on that very account He is philanthropic.

For he who loves and compassionates those who have been wronged, avenges those who have wronged them."

Then I said, "If, then, I also do good to the good, and punish the wrong-doers in respect of their injuring men, am I not philanthropic?"

And Peter answered, "If along with knowledge [9] you had also authority to judge, you would do this rightly on account of your having received authority to judge those whom God made, and on account of your knowledge infallibly justifying some as the righteous, and condemning some as unrighteous." Then I said, "You have spoken rightly and truly; for it is impossible for any one who has not knowledge to judge rightly.

For sometimes some persons seem good, though they perpetrate wickedness in secret, and some good persons are conceived to be bad through the accusation of their enemies.

But even if one judges, having the power of torturing and examining, not even so should he altogether judge righteously.

For some persons, being murderers, have sustained the tortures, and have come off as innocent; while others, being innocent, have not been able to sustain the tortures, but have confessed falsely against themselves, and have been punished as guilty."

Chapter XXVIII - Difficulty of Judging

Then said Peter, "These things are ordinary:
now hear what is greater.

There are some men whose sins or good deeds are partly their own, and partly those of others; but it is right that each one be punished for his own sins, and rewarded for his own merits.

But it is impossible for any one except a prophet, who alone has omniscience, to know with respect to the things that are done by any one, which are his own, and which are not; for all are seen as done by him."

Then I said, "I would learn how some of men's wrong-doings or right-doings are their own, and some belong to others."

Chapter XXIX - Sufferings of the Good

Then Peter answered, "The prophet of the truth has said, Good things must needs come, and blessed, said he, is he by whom they come; in like manner evil things must needs come, but woe to him through whom they come.' [10] But if evil things come by means of evil men, and good things are brought by good men, it must needs be in each man as his own to be either good or bad, and proceeding from what he has proposed, in order to the coming of the subsequent good or evil, [11] which, being of his own choice, are not arranged by the providence of God to come from him.

This being so, this is the judgment of God, that he who, as by a combat, comes through all misfortune and is found blameless, he is deemed worthy of eternal life; for those who by their own will continue in goodness, are tempted by those who continue in evil by their own will, being persecuted, hated, slandered, plotted against, struck, cheated, accused, tortured, disgraced,--suffering all these things by which it seems reasonable that they should be enraged and stirred up to vengeance.

Chapter XXX - Offences Must Come

"But the Master knowing that those who wrongfully do these things are guilty by means of their former sins, and that the spirit of wickedness works these things by means of the guilty, has counselled to compassionate men, as they are men, and as being the instruments of wickedness through sin; and this counsel He has given to His disciples as claiming philanthropy, and, as much as in us lies, to absolve the wrong-doers from condemnation, that, as it were, the temperate may help the drunken, by prayers, fastings, and benedictions, not resisting, not avenging, lest they should compel them to sin more.

For when a person is condemned by any one to suffer, it is not reasonable for him to be angry with him by whose means the suffering comes; for he ought to reason, that if he had not ill-used him, yet because he was to be ill-used, he must have suffered it by means of another.

Why, then, should I be angry with the dispenser, when I was condemned at all events to suffer? But yet, further:

if we do these same things to the evil on pretence of revenge, we who are good do the very things which the evil do, excepting that they do them first, and we second; and, as I said, we ought not to be angry, as knowing that in the providence of God, the evil punish the good.

Those, therefore, who are bitter against their punishers, sin, as disdaining the messengers of God; but those who honour them, and set themselves in opposition to those who think to injure them, [12] are pious towards God who has thus decreed."

Chapter XXXI - "Howbeit, They Meant It Not."

To this I answered, "Those, therefore, who do wrong are not guilty, because they wrong the just by the judgment of God."

Then Peter said, "They indeed sin greatly, for they have given themselves to sin. Wherefore knowing this, God chooses from among them some to punish those who righteously repented of their former sins, that the evil things done by the just before their repentance may be remitted through this punishment.

But to the wicked who punish and desire to ill-use them, and will not repent, it is permitted to ill-use the righteous for the filling up of their own punishment.

For without the will of God, not even a sparrow can fall into a girn. [13] Thus even the hairs of the righteous are numbered by God.

Chapter XXXII - The Golden Rule

"But he is righteous who for the sake of what is reasonable fights with nature.

For example, it is natural to all to love those who love them.

But the righteous man tries also to love his enemies and to bless those who slander him, and even to pray for his enemies, and to compassionate those who do him wrong.

Wherefore also he refrains from doing wrong, and blesses those who curse him, pardons those who strike him, and submits to those who persecute him, and salutes those who do not salute him, shares such things as he has with those who have not, persuades him that is angry with him, conciliates his enemy, exhorts the disobedient, instructs the unbelieving, comforts the mourner; being distressed, he endures; being ungratefully treated, he is not angry. But having devoted himself to love his neighbour as himself, he is not afraid of poverty, but becomes poor by sharing his possessions with those who have none.

But neither does he punish the sinner.

For he who loves his neighbour as himself, as he knows that when he has sinned he does not wish to be punished, so neither does he punish those who sin.

And as he wishes to be praised, and blessed, and honoured, and to have all his sins forgiven, thus he does to his neighbour, loving him as himself. [14] In one word, what he wishes for himself, he wishes also for his neighbour.

For this is the law of God and of the prophets [15] this is the doctrine of truth.

And this perfect love towards every man is the male part of philanthropy, but the female part of it is compassion; that is, to feed the hungry, to give drink to the thirsty, to clothe the naked, to visit the sick, to take in the stranger, to show herself to, and help to the utmost of her power, him who is in prison, [16] and, in short, to have compassion on him who is in misfortune."

Chapter XXXIII - Fear and Love

But I, hearing this, said:

"These things, indeed, it is impossible to do; but to do good to enemies, bearing all their insolences, I do not think can possibly be in human nature."

Then Peter answered:

"You have said truly; for philanthropy, being the cause of immortality, is given for much."

Then I said, "How then is it possible to get it in the mind?"

Then Peter answered:

"O beloved Clement, the way to get it is this:

if any one be persuaded that enemies, ill-using for a time those whom they hate, become the cause to them of deliverances from eternal punishment; and forthwith he will ardently love them as benefactors.

But the way to get it, O dear Clement, is but one, which is the fear of God.

For he who fears God cannot indeed from the first love his neighbour as himself; for such an order does not occur to the soul.

But by the fear of God he is able to do the things of those who love; and thus, while he does the deeds of love, the bride Love is, as it were, brought to the bridegroom Fear.

And thus this bride, bringing forth philanthropic thoughts, makes her possessor immortal, as an accurate image of God, which cannot be subject in its nature to corruption."

Thus while he expounded to us the doctrine of philanthropy, the evening having set in, we turned to sleep.

Footnotes:

1. [On the correspondence of Homilies XII., XIII., with Recognitions, vii., see note on vii. 1. Chaps. 1-24 here agree quite closely, even in the divisions of chapters, with Recognitions, vii. 1-24.--R.]
2. Literally, "of wickedness."
3. Here the text is hopelessly corrupt, and the meaning can only be guessed at.
4. I have ventured to make a very slight change on the reading here, so as to bring out what I suppose to be the sense.
5. A negative particle seems to be dropped from the text.
6. [The family names as given in the Recognitions are: Matthidia; Faustinianus (the father); Faustinus and Faustus, the twin sons.--Comp. Recognitions, viii. 8, and passim.--R.]
7. [Comp. Recognitions, vii. 23, where the translator prints the word in italics.--R.]
8. [The remainder of this Homily has no parallel in the Recognitions. The views presented are peculiar, and indicate a speculative tendency, less marked in the Recognitions.--R.]
9. The word repeatedly rendered knowledge and once omniscience in this passage, properly signifies foreknowledge.

The argument shows clearly that it means omniscience, of which foreknowledge is the most signal manifestation.

10. An incorrect quotation from Matt. xviii. 7; Luke xvii. 1.
11. This from a various reading.
12. That is, I suppose, who render good for evil.
13. See Luke xii. 6, 7; [Matt. x. 29, 30.--R.].
14. Matt. xxii. 39.
15. Matt. vii. 12.
16. Matt. xxv. 35, 36.

Homily XIII

Chapter I - Journey to Laodicea

Now at break of day Peter entered, and said: [1]"Clement, and his mother Mattidia, and my wife, must take their seats immediately on the waggon."

And so they did straightway.

And as we were hastening along the road to Balanaeae, my mother asked me how my father was; and I said:

"My father went in search of you, and of my twin brothers Faustinus and Faustinianus, and is now nowhere to be found.

But I fancy he must have died long ago, either perishing by shipwreck, or losing his way, [2] or wasted away by grief."

When she heard this, she burst into tears, and groaned through grief; but the joy which she felt at finding me, mitigated in some degree the painfulness of her recollections.

And so we all went down together to Balanaeae.

And on the following day we went to Paltus, and from that to Gabala; and on the next day we reached Laodicea.

And, lo! before the gates of the city Nicetas and Aquila met us, and embracing us, brought us to our lodging.

Now Peter, seeing that the city was beautiful and great, said:

"It is worth our while to stay here for some days; for, generally speaking, a populous place is most capable of yielding us those whom we seek." [3]Nicetas and Aquila asked me who that strange woman was; and I said:

"My mother, whom God, through my lord Peter, has granted me to recognise."

Chapter II - Peter Relates to Nicetas and Aquila the History of Clement and His Family

On my saying this, Peter gave them a summary account [4] of all the incidents,--how, when they had gone on before, I Clement had explained to him my descent, the journey undertaken by my mother with her twin children on the false pretext of the dream; and furthermore, the journey undertaken by my father in search of her; and then how Peter himself, after hearing this, went into the island, met with the woman, saw her begging, and asked the reason of her so doing; and then ascertained who she was, and her mode of life, and the feigned dream, and the names of her children--that is, the name borne by me, who was left with my father, and the names of the twin children who travelled along with her, and who, she supposed, had perished in the deep.

Chapter III - Recognition of Nicetas and Aquila

Now when this summary narrative had been given by Peter, Nicetas and Aquila in amazement said:

"Is this indeed true, O Ruler and Lord of the universe, or is it a dream?"

And Peter said:

"Unless we are asleep, it certainly is true."

On this they waited for a little in deep meditation, and then said:

"We are Faustinus and Faustinianus. From the commencement of your conversation we looked at each other, and conjectured much with regard to ourselves, whether what was said had reference to us or not; for we reflected that many coincidences take place in life.

Wherefore we remained silent while our hearts beat fast.

But when you came to the end of your narrative, we saw clearly [5] that your statements referred to us, and then we avowed who we were."

And on saying this, bathed in tears, they rushed in to see their mother; and although they found her asleep, they were yet anxious to embrace her.

But Peter forbade them, saying:

"Let me bring you and present you to your mother, lest she should, in consequence of her great and sudden joy, lose her reason, as she is slumbering, and her spirit is held fast by sleep."

Chapter IV - The Mother Must Not Take Food with Her Son

The Reason Stated.

As soon as my mother had enough of sleep, she awoke, and Peter at once began first to talk to her of true piety, saying:

"I wish you to know, O woman, the course of life involved in our religion. [6]We worship one God, who made the world which you see; and we keep His law, which has for its chief injunctions to worship Him alone, and to hallow His name, and to honour our parents, and to be chaste, and to live piously.

In addition to this, we do not live with all indiscriminately; nor do we take our food from the same table as Gentiles, inasmuch as we cannot eat along with them, because they live impurely.

But when we have persuaded them to have true thoughts, and to follow a right course of action, and have baptized them with a thrice blessed invocation, then we dwell with them.

For not even if it were our father, or mother, or wife, or child, or brother, or any other one having a claim by nature on our affection, can we venture to take our meals with him; for our religion compels us to make a distinction. Do not, therefore, regard it as an insult if your son does not take his food along with you, until you come to have the same opinions and adopt the same course of conduct as he follows."

Chapter V - Mattidia Wishes to Be Baptized

When she heard this, she said:

"What, then, prevents me from being baptized this day? for before I saw you I turned away from the so-called gods, induced by the thought that, though I sacrificed much to them almost every day, they did not aid me in my necessities.

And with regard to adultery, what need I say? for not even when I was rich was I betrayed into this sin by luxury, and the poverty which succeeded has been unable to force me into it, since I cling to my chastity as constituting the greatest beauty, [7] on account of which I fell into so great distress.

But I do not at all imagine that you, my lord Peter, are ignorant that the greatest temptation [8] arises when everything looks bright.

And therefore, if I was chaste in my prosperity, I do not in my despondency give myself up to pleasures. Yea, indeed, you are not to suppose that my soul has now been freed from distress, although it has received some measure of consolation by the recognition of Clement.

For the gloom which I feel in consequence of the loss of my two children rushes in upon me, and throws its shadow to some extent over my joy; for I am grieved, not so much because they perished in the sea, but because they were destroyed, both soul and body, without possessing true [9] piety towards God.

Moreover, my husband, their father, as I have learned from Clement, went away in search of me and his sons, and for so many years has not been heard of; and, without doubt, he must have died.

For the miserable man, loving me as he did in chastity, was fond of his children; and therefore the old man, deprived of all of us who were dear to him above everything else, died utterly broken-hearted."

Chapter VI - The Sons Reveal Themselves to the Mother

The sons, on hearing their mother thus speak, could no longer, in obedience to the exhortation of Peter, restrain themselves, but rising up, they clasped her in their arms, showering down upon her tears and kisses.

But she said:

"What is the meaning of this?"

And Peter answered:

"Courageously summon up your spirits, O woman, that you may enjoy your children; for these are Faustinus and Faustinianus, your sons, who, you said, had perished in the deep.

For how they are alive, after they had in your opinion died on that most disastrous night, and how one of them now bears the name of Nicetas, and the other that of Aquila, they will themselves be able to tell you; for we, as well as you, have yet to learn this."

When Peter thus spoke, my mother fainted away through her excessive joy, and was like to die.

But when we had revived her she sat up, and coming to herself, she said:

"Be so good, my darling children, as tell us what happened to you after that disastrous night."

Chapter VII - Nicetas Tells What Befell Him

And Nicetas, who in future is to be called Faustinus, began to speak. "On that very night when, as you know, the ship went to pieces, we were taken up by some men, who did not fear to follow the profession of robbers on the deep.

They placed us in a boat, and brought us along the coast, sometimes rowing and sometimes sending for provisions, and at length took us to Caesarea Stratonis, [10] and there tormented us by hunger, fear, and blows, that we might not recklessly disclose anything which they did not wish us to tell; and, moreover, changing our names, they succeeded in selling us.

Now the woman who bought us was a proselyte of the Jews, an altogether worthy person, of the name of Justa.

She adopted us as her own children, and zealously brought us up in all the learning of the Greeks.

But we, becoming discreet with our years, were strongly attached to her religion, and we paid good heed to our culture, in order that, disputing with the other nations, we might be able to convince them of their error.

We also made an accurate study of the doctrines of the philosophers, especially the most atheistic,--I mean those of Epicurus and Pyrrho,--in order that we might be the better able to refute them. [11]

Chapter VIII - Nicetas Like to Be Deceived by Simon Magus

"We were brought up along with one Simon, a magician; and in consequence of our friendly intercourse with him, we were in danger of being led astray.

Now there is a report in regard to some man, that, when he appears, the mass of those who have been pious are to live free from death and pain in his kingdom.

This matter, however, mother, will be explained more fully at the proper time.

But when we were going to be led astray by Simon, a friend of our lord Peter, by name Zacchaeus, came to us and warned us not to be led astray by the magician; and when Peter came, he brought us to him that he might give us full information, and convince us in regard to those matters that related to piety.

Wherefore we beseech you, mother, to partake of those blessings which have been vouchsafed to us, that we may unite around the same table! [12]This, then, is the reason, mother, why you thought we were dead.

On that disastrous night we had been taken up in the sea by pirates, but you supposed that we had perished."

Chapter IX - The Mother Begs Baptism for Herself and Her Hostess

When Faustinus had said this, our mother fell down at Peter's feet, begging and entreating him to send for her and her hostess, and baptize them immediately, in order that, says she, not a single day may pass after the recovery of my children, without my taking food with them. When we united with our mother in making the same request, Peter said: "What can you imagine?

Am I alone heartless, so as not to wish that you should take your meals with your mother, baptizing her this very day?

But yet it is incumbent on her to fast one day before she be baptized.

And it is only one day, because, in her simplicity, she said something in her own behalf, which I looked on as a sufficient indication of her faith; otherwise, her purification must have lasted many days."

Chapter X - Mattidia Values Baptism Aright

And I said:

"Tell us what it was that she said which made her faith manifest."

And Peter, said:

"Her request that her hostess and benefactress should be baptized along with her.

For she would not have besought this to be granted to her whom she loves, had she not herself first felt that baptism was a great gift.

And for this reason I condemn many that, after being baptized, and asserting that they have faith, they yet do nothing worthy of faith; nor do they urge those whom they love--I mean their wives, or sons, or friends--to be baptized. [13]For if they had believed that God grants eternal life with good works on the acceptance of baptism, [14] they without delay would urge those whom they loved to be baptized.

But some one of you will say, They do love them, and care for them.'

That is nonsense. For do they not, most assuredly, when they see them sick, or led away along the road that ends in death, or enduring any other trial, lament over them and pity them?

So, if they believed that eternal fire awaits those who worship not God, they would not cease admonishing them, or being in deep distress for them as unbelievers, if they saw them disobedient, being fully assured that punishment awaits them.

But now I shall send for the hostess, and question her as to whether she deliberately accepts the law which is proclaimed through us; [15] and so, according to her state of mind, shall we do what ought to be done.

Chapter XI - Mattidia Has Unintentionally Fasted One Day

"But since your mother has real confidence in the efficacy of baptism, [16] let her fast at least one day before her baptism."

But she swore:

"During the two past days, while I related to the woman [17] all the events connected with the recognition, I could not, in consequence of my excessive joy, partake of food:

only yesterday I took a little water."

Peter's wife bore testimony to her statement with an oath, saying:

"In truth she did not taste anything."

And Aquila, who must rather be called Faustinianus [18] in future, said: "There is nothing, therefore, to prevent her being baptized."

And Peter, smiling, replied:

"But that is not a baptismal fast which has not taken place on account of the baptism itself."

And Faustinus answered:

"Perhaps God, not wishing to separate our mother a single day after our recognition from our table, has arranged beforehand the fast.

For as she was chaste in the times of her ignorance, doing what the true religion inculcated, [19] so even now perhaps God has arranged that she should fast one day before for the sake of the true baptism, that, from the first day of her recognising us, she might take her meals along with us."

Chapter XII - The Difficulty Solved

And Peter said:

"Let not wickedness have dominion over us, finding a pretext in Providence and your affection for your mother; but rather abide this day in your fast, and I shall join you in it, and tomorrow she will be baptized.

And, besides, this hour of the day is not suitable for baptism."

Then we all agreed that it should be so.

Chapter XIII - Peter on Chastity

That same evening we all enjoyed the benefit of Peter's instruction. Taking occasion by what had happened to our mother, he showed us how the results of chastity are good, while those of adultery are disastrous, and naturally bring destruction on the whole race, if not speedily, at all events slowly.[20] "And to such an extent," he says, "do deeds of chastity please God, that in this life He bestows some small favour on account of it, even on those who are in error; for salvation in the other world is granted only to those who have been baptized on account of their trust [21] in Him, and who act chastely and righteously.

This ye yourselves have seen in the case of your mother, that the results of chastity are in the end good.

For perhaps she would have been cut off if she had committed adultery; but God took pity on her for having behaved chastely, rescued her from the death that threatened her, and restored to her her lost children.

Chapter XIV - Peter's Speech Continued

"But some one will say, How many have perished on account of chastity!'

Yes; but it was because they did not perceive the danger. For the woman who perceives that she is in love with any one, or is beloved by any one, should immediately shun all association with him as she would shun a blazing fire or a mad dog.

And this is exactly what your mother did, for she really loved chastity as a blessing: wherefore she was preserved, and, along with you, obtained the full knowledge of the everlasting kingdom.

The woman who wishes to be chaste, ought to know that she is envied by wickedness, and that because of love many lie in wait for her.

If, then, she remain holy through a stedfast persistence in chastity, she will gain the victory over all temptations, and be saved; whereas, even if she were to do all that is right, and yet should once commit the sin of adultery, she must be punished, as said the prophet.

Chapter XV - Peter's Speech Continued

"The chaste wife doing the will of God, is a good reminiscence of His first creation; for God, being one, created one woman for one man.

She is also still more chaste if she does not forget her own creation, and has future punishment before her eyes, and is not ignorant of the loss of eternal blessings.

The chaste woman takes pleasure in those who wish to be saved, and is a pious example to the pious, for she is the model of a good life.

She who wishes to be chaste, cuts off all occasions for slander; but if she be slandered as by an enemy, though affording him no pretext, she is blessed and avenged by God.

The chaste woman longs for God, loves God, pleases God, glorifies God; and to men she affords no occasion for slander.

The chaste woman perfumes the Church with her good reputation, and glorifies it by her piety.

She is, moreover, the praise of her teachers, and a helper to them in their chastity. [22]

Chapter XVI - Peter's Speech Continued

"The chaste woman is adorned with the Son of God as with a bridegroom. She is clothed with holy light.

Her beauty lies in a well-regulated soul; and she is fragrant with ointment, even with a good reputation. She is arrayed in beautiful vesture, even in modesty.

She wears about her precious pearls, even chaste words.

And she is radiant, for [23] her mind has been brilliantly lighted up.

Onto a beautiful mirror does she look, for she looks into God.

Beautiful cosmetics [24] does she use, namely, the fear of God, with which she admonishes her soul. Beautiful is the woman not because she has chains of gold on her, [25] but because she has been set free from transient lusts.

The chaste woman is greatly desired by the great King; [26] she has been wooed, watched, and loved by Him.

The chaste woman does not furnish occasions for being desired, except by her own husband.

The chaste woman is grieved when she is desired by another.

The chaste woman loves her husband from the heart, embraces, soothes, and pleases him, acts the slave to him, and is obedient to him in all things, except when she would be disobedient to God.

For she who obeys God is without the aid of watchmen chaste in soul and pure in body.

Chapter XVII - Peter's Speech Continued

"Foolish, therefore, is every husband who separates his wife from the fear of God; for she who does not fear God is not afraid of her husband.

If she fear not God, who sees what is invisible, how will she be chaste in her unseen choice? [27] And how will she be chaste, who does not come to the assembly to hear chaste-making words?

And how could she obtain admonition?

And how will she be chaste without watchmen, if she be not informed in regard to the coming judgement of God, and if she be not fully assured that eternal punishment is the penalty for the slight pleasure?

Wherefore, on the other hand, compel her even against her will always to come to hear the chaste-making word, yea, coax her to do so.

Chapter XVIII - Peter's Speech Continued

"Much better is it if you will take her by the hand and come, in order that you yourself may become chaste; for you will desire to become chaste, that you may experience the full fruition of a holy marriage, and you will not scruple, if you desire it, to become a father, [28] to love your own children, and to be loved by your own children.

He who wishes to have a chaste wife is also himself chaste, gives her what is due to a wife, takes his meals with her, keeps company with her, goes with her to the word that makes chaste, does not grieve her, does not rashly quarrel with her, does not make himself hateful to her, furnishes her with all the good things he can, and when he has them not, he makes up the deficiency by caresses.

The chaste wife does not expect to be caressed, recognises her husband as her lord, bears his poverty when he is poor, is hungry with him when he is hungry, travels with him when he travels, consoles him when he is grieved, and if she have a large [29] dowry, is subject to him as if she had nothing at all.

But if the husband have a poor wife, let him reckon her chastity a great dowry.

The chaste wife is temperate in her eating and drinking, in order that the weariness of the body, thus pampered, may not drag the soul down to unlawful desires.

Moreover, she never assuredly remains alone with young men, and she suspects [30] the old; she turns away from disorderly laughter, gives herself up to God alone; she is not led astray; she delights in listening to holy words, but turns away from those which are not spoken to produce chastity.

Chapter XIX - Peter's Speech Ended

"God is my witness:
one adultery is as bad as many murders; and what is terrible in it is this, that the fearfulness and impiety of its murders are not seen.

For, when blood is shed, the dead body remains lying, and all are struck by the terrible nature of the occurrence. But the murders of the soul caused by adultery, though they are more frightful, yet, since they are not seen by men, do not make the daring a whit less eager in their impulse.

Know, O man, whose breath it is that thou hast to keep thee in life, and thou shalt not wish that it be polluted.

By adultery alone is the breath of God polluted.
And therefore it drags him who has polluted it into the fire; for it hastens to deliver up its insulter to everlasting punishment."

Chapter XX - Peter Addresses Mattidia

While Peter was saying this, he saw the good and chaste Mattidia weeping for joy; but thinking that she was grieved at having suffered so much in past times, he said: [31]"Take courage, O woman; for while many have suffered many evils on account of adultery, you have suffered on account of chastity, and therefore you did not die.

But if you had died, your soul would have been saved.

You left your native city of Rome on account of chastity, but through it you found the truth, the diadem of the eternal kingdom.

You underwent danger in the deep, but you did not die; and even if you had died, the deep itself would have proved to you, dying on account of chastity, a baptism for the salvation of your soul.

You were deprived of your children for a little; but these, the true offspring of your husband, have been found in better circumstances.

When starving, you begged for food, but you did not defile your body by fornication.

You exposed your body to torture, but you saved your soul; you fled from the adulterer, that you might not defile the couch of your husband:

but, on account of your chastity, God, who knows your flight, will fill up the place of your husband.

Grieved and left desolate, you were for a short time deprived of husband and children, but all these you must have been deprived of, some time or other, by death, the preordained lot of man.

But better is it that you were willingly deprived of them on account of chastity, than that you should have perished unwillingly after a time, simply on account of sins.

Chapter XXI - The Same Subject Continued

"Much better is it, then, that your first circumstances should be distressing.

For when this is the case, they do not so deeply grieve you, because you hope that they will pass away, and they yield joy though the expectation of better circumstances.

But, above all, I wish you to know how much chastity is pleasing to God.

The chaste woman is God's choice, God's good pleasure, God's glory, God's child.

So great a blessing is chastity, [32] that if there had not been a law that not even a righteous person should enter into the kingdom of God unbaptized, perhaps even the erring Gentiles might have been saved solely on account of chastity.

Wherefore I am exceedingly sorry for those erring ones who are chaste because they shrink from baptism--thus choosing to be chaste without good hope.

Wherefore they are not saved; for the decree of God is clearly set down, that an unbaptized person cannot enter into His kingdom."

When he said this, and much more, we turned to sleep.

Footnotes:

1. [Comp. Recognitions, vii. 25.
Here the narrative is somewhat fuller in detail.--R.]
2. Cotelerius conjectured sphagenta for sphalenta--"being slain on our journey."
3. The first Epitome explains "those whom we seek" as those who are worthy to share in Christ or in Christ's Gospel.
4. [In Recognitions, vii. 26, 27, the recapitulation is more extended.--R.]
5. The text is somewhat doubtful.
We have given the meaning contained in the first Epitome.
6. threskeia.
7. One ms. and the first Epitome read, "as being the greatest blessing."
8. Lit., "desire."

The Epistles of Clement

9. The Greek has, "apart from divine piety towards God."

As Wieseler remarks, the epithet "divine" is corrupt.

The meaning may be, "without having known the proper mode of worshipping God."

10. This clause, literally translated, is, "and sometimes impelling it with oars, they brought us along the land; and sometimes sending for provisions, they conveyed us to Caesarea Stratonis."

The Latin translator renders "to land," not "along the land."

The passage assumes a different form in the Recognitions, the first Epitome, and the second Epitome; and there is, no doubt, some corruption in the text.

The text has dakruontas, which makes no sense.

We have adopted the rendering given in the Recognitions.

Various attempts have been made to amend the word.

11. [Comp. Recognitions, viii. 7, where the studies of the brothers are more fully indicated, as a preface to the discussions in which they appear as disputants.--R.]

12. Lit., "that we may be able to partake of common salt and table."

13. Lit., "to this."

14. epi to baptismati; lit., "on the condition of baptism."

15. Lit., "the law which is by means of us."

But the Epitomes, and a various reading in Cotelerius, give "our law."

16. Lit., "since your mother is faithfully disposed in regard to baptism."

17. The second Epitome makes her the wife of Peter:

a various reading mentions also her hostess.

18. Dressel strangely prefers the reading "Faustinus."

19. Lit., "doing what was becoming to the truth."

20. [This detailed discourse is peculiar to the Homilies.

In Recognitions, vii. 37, 38, there is, however, a briefer statement on the same topic.--R.]

21. Lit., "hope."

22. The Greek is autois sophronousi.

The Latin translator and Lehmann (Die Clementinischen Schriften, Gotha, 1869) render, "to those who are chaste, i.e., love or practice chastity," as if the reading were tois sophronousi.

23. Lit., "when."

24. kosmo--properly ornaments; but here a peculiar meaning is evidently required.

25. Lit., "as being chained with gold."

26. Ps. xlv. 11.

27. "In her unseen choice" means, in what course of conduct she really prefers in her heart.

This reading occurs in one ms.; in the other ms. it is corrupt.

Schwegler amended it into, How shall she be chaste towards him who does not see what is invisible?" and the emendation is adopted by Dressel.

28. There seems to be some corruption in this clause.

Literally, it is, "and you will not scruple, if you love, I mean, to become a father."

29. Lit., "larger" than usual.

30. hupopteuei.

The Latin translator and Lehmann render "respects" or "reveres."

31. [Something similar to chaps. 20, 21, occurs in Recognitions, vii. 38, addressed to the sons of Mattidia after her baptism.

But this is so much fuller.--R.]

32. We have adopted an emendation of Wieseler's.

The emendation is questionable; but the sense is the best that can be got out of the words.

Homily XIV

Chapter I - Mattidia is Baptized in the Sea

Much earlier than usual Peter awoke, and came to us, and awaking us, said: "Let Faustinus and Faustinianus, along with Clement and the household, accompany me, that we may go to some sheltered spot by the sea, and there be able to baptize her without attracting observation." Accordingly, when we had come to the sea-shore, he baptized her between some rocks, which supplied a place at once free from wind and dust. [1]But we brothers, along with our brother and some others, retired because of the women and bathed, and coming again to the women, we took them along with us, and thus we went to a secret place and prayed.

Then Peter, on account of the multitude, sent the women on before, ordering them to go to their lodging by another way, and he permitted us alone of the men to accompany our mother and the rest of the women. [2]We went then to our lodging, and while waiting for Peter's arrival, we conversed with each other.

Peter came several hours after, and breaking the bread for the Eucharist, [3] and putting salt upon it, he gave it first to our mother, and, after her, to us her sons.

And thus we took food along with her and blessed God.

Chapter II - The Reason of Peter's Lateness

Then, [4] at length, Peter seeing that the multitude had entered, sat down, and bidding us sit down beside him, he related first of all why he had sent us on before him after the baptism, and why he himself had been late in returning. [5]He said that the following was the reason:

"At the time that you came up," [6] he says, "an old man, a workman, entered along with you, concealing himself out of curiosity. He had watched us before, as he himself afterwards confessed, in order to see what we were doing when we entered into the sheltered place, and then he came out secretly and followed us.

And coming up to me at a convenient place, and addressing me, he said, For a long time I have been following you and wishing to talk with you, but I was afraid that you might be angry with me, as if I were instigated by curiosity; but now I shall tell you, if you please, what I think is the truth.'

And I replied, Tell us what you think is good, and we shall approve your conduct, even should what you say not be really good, since with a good purpose you have been anxious to state what you deem to be good.'

Chapter III - The Old Man Does Not Believe in God or Providence

"The old man began to speak as follows:

When I saw you after you had bathed in the sea retire into the secret place, I went up and secretly watched what might be your object in entering into a secret place, and when I saw you pray, I retired;[7] but taking pity on you, I waited that I might speak with you when you came out, and prevail on you not to be led astray.

For there is neither God nor providence; but all things are subject to Genesis. [8]Of this I am fully assured in consequence of what I have myself endured, having for a long time made a careful study of the science. [9]Do not therefore be deceived, my child.

For whether you pray or not, you must endure what is assigned to you by Genesis.

For if prayers could have done anything or any good, I myself should now be in better circumstances.

And now, unless my needy garments mislead you, you will not refuse to believe what I say.

I was once in affluent circumstances; I sacrificed much to the gods, I gave liberally to the needy; and yet, though I prayed and acted piously, I was not able to escape my destiny.'

And I said:

What are the calamities you have endured?'

And he answered:

I need not tell you now; perhaps at the end you shall learn who I am, and who are my parents, and into what straitened circumstances I have fallen.

But at present I wish you to become fully assured that everything is subject to Genesis.'

Chapter IV - Peter's Arguments Against Genesis

"And I said:

If all things are subject to Genesis, and you are fully convinced that this is the case, your thoughts and advice are contrary to your own opinion. [10]For if it is impossible even to think in opposition to Genesis, why do you toil in vain, advising me to do what cannot be done?

Yea, moreover, even if Genesis subsists, do not make haste to prevail on me not to worship Him who is also Lord of the stars, by whose wish that a thing should not take place, that thing becomes an impossibility.

For always that which is subject must obey that which rules.

As far, however, as the worship of the common gods is concerned, that is superfluous, if Genesis has sway.

For neither does anything happen contrary to what seems good to fate, nor are they themselves able to do anything, since they are subject to their own universal Genesis.

If Genesis exists, there is this objection to it, that that which is not first has the rule; or, in other words, the uncreated cannot be subject, for the uncreated, as being uncreated, has nothing that is older than itself.' [11]

Chapter V - Practical Refutation of Genesis

"While we were thus talking, a great multitude gathered round us.

And then I looked to the multitude, and said:

I and my tribe have had handed down to us from our ancestors the worship of God, and we have a commandment to give no heed to Genesis, I mean to the science of astrology; [12] and therefore I gave no attention to it.

For this reason I have no skill in astrology, but I shall state that in which I have skill.

Since I am unable to refute Genesis by an appeal to the science which relates to Genesis, I wish to prove in another way that the affairs of this world are managed by a providence, and that each one will receive reward or punishment according to his actions. Whether he shall do so now or hereafter, is a matter of no consequence to me; all I affirm is, that each one without doubt will reap the fruit of his deeds.

The proof that there is no Genesis is this.

If any one of you present has been deprived of eyes, or has his hand maimed, or his foot lame, or some other part of the body wrong, and if it is utterly incurable, and entirely beyond the range of the medical profession,--a case, indeed, which not even the astrologers profess to cure, for no such cure has taken place within the lapse of a vast period,--yet I praying to God will cure it, [13] although [14] it could never have been set right by Genesis. [15]Since this is so, do not they sin who blaspheme the God that fashioned all things?'

And the old man answered:

Is it then blasphemy to say that all things are subject to Genesis?'

And I replied:

Most certainly it is.

For if all the sins of men, and all their acts of impiety and licentiousness, owe their origin to the stars, and if the stars have been appointed by God to do this work, so as to be the efficient causes of all evils, then the sins of all are traced up to Him who placed Genesis [16] in the stars.'

Chapter VI - The Old Man Opposes His Personal Experience to the Argument of Peter

"And the old man answered: [17]You have spoken truly, [18] and yet, notwithstanding all your incomparable demonstration, I am prevented from yielding assent by my own personal knowledge. For I was an astrologer, and dwelt first at Rome; and then forming a friendship with one who was of the family of Caesar, I ascertained accurately the genesis of himself and his wife.

And tracing their history, I find all the deeds actually accomplished in exact accordance with their genesis, and therefore I cannot yield to your argument.

For the arrangement [19] of her genesis was that which makes women commit adultery, fall in love with their own slaves, and perish abroad in the water.

And this actually took place; for she fell in love with her own slave, and not being able to bear the reproach, she fled with him, hurried to a foreign land, shared his bed, and perished in the sea.'

Chapter VII - The Old Man Tells His Story

"And I answered:
How then do you know that she who fled and took up her residence in a foreign land married the slave, and marrying him died?'
And the old man said:
I am quite sure that this is true, not indeed that she married him, for I did not know even that she fell in love with him; but after her departure, a brother of her husband's told me the whole story of her passion, and how he acted as an honourable man, and did not, as being his brother, wish to pollute his couch, and how she the wretched woman (for she is not blameable, inasmuch as she was compelled to do and suffer all this in consequence of Genesis) longed for him, and yet stood in awe of him and his reproaches, and how she devised a dream, whether true or false I cannot tell; for he stated that she said, "Some one in a vision stood by me, and ordered me to leave the city of the Romans immediately with my children."

But her husband being anxious that she should be saved with his sons, sent them immediately to Athens for their education, accompanied by their mother and slaves, while he kept the third and youngest son with himself, for he who gave the warning in the dream permitted this son to remain with his father.

And when a long time had elapsed, during which [20] he received no letters from her, he himself sent frequently to Athens, and at length took me, as the truest of all his friends, and went in search of her.

And much did I exert myself along with him in the course of our travels with all eagerness; for I remembered that, in the old times of his prosperity, he had given me a share of all he had and loved me above all his friends.

At length we set sail from Rome itself, and so we arrived in these parts of Syria, and we landed at Seleucia, and not many days after we had landed he died of a broken heart.

But I came here, and have procured my livelihood from that day till this by the work of my hands.'

Chapter VIII - The Old Man Gives Information in Regard to Faustus the Father of Clement

"When the old man had thus spoken, I knew from what he said that the old man who he stated had died, was no other than your father.
I did not wish, however, to communicate your circumstances to him until I should confer with you.

But I ascertained where his lodging was, and I pointed out mine to him; and to make sure that my conjecture was right, I put this one question to him:
What was the name of the old man?' And he said, Faustus.'
And what were the names of his twin sons?'
And he answered, Faustinus and Faustinianus.'
What was the name of the third son?'
He said, Clement.'
What was their mother's name?'
He said, Mattidia.'

Accordingly, from compassion, I shed tears along with him, and, dismissing the multitudes, I came to you, in order that I might take counsel with you after we had partaken of food [21] together.

But I did not wish to disclose the matter to you before we had partaken of food, lest perchance you should be overcome by sorrow, and continue sad on the day of baptism, when even angels rejoice."

At these statements of Peter we all fell a weeping along with our mother. But he beholding us in tears, said:

"Now let each one of you, through fear of God, bear bravely what has been said:

for certainly it was not to-day that your father died, but long ago, as you conjecturing said."

Chapter IX - Faustus Himself Appears

When Peter said this, our mother could no longer endure it, but cried out, "Alas! my husband! loving us, you died by your own decision, [22] while we are still alive, see the light, and have just partaken of food."

This one scream had not yet ceased, when, lo! the old man came in, and at the same time wishing to inquire into the cause of the cry, he looked on the woman and said, "What does this mean?

Whom do I see?"

And going up to her, and looking at her, and being looked at more carefully, he embraced her.

But they were like to die through the sudden joy, and wishing to speak to each other, they could not get the power in consequence of their unsatisfied joy, for they were seized with speechlessness.

But not long after, our mother said to him:

"I now have you, Faustus, in every way the dearest being to me.

How then are you alive, when we heard a short time ago that you were dead?

But these are our sons, Faustinus, Faustinianus, and Clement."

And when she said this, we all three fell on him, and kissed him, and in rather an indistinct way we recalled his form to our memory. [23]

Chapter X - Faustus Explains His Narrative to Peter

Peter seeing this, said:

"Are you Faustus, the husband of this woman, and the father of her children?"

And he said:

"I am."

And Peter said:

"How, then, did you relate to me your own history as if it were another's; telling me of your toils, and sorrow, and burial?"

And our father answered:

"Being of the family of Caesar, and not wishing to be discovered, I devised the narrative in another's name, in order that it might not be perceived who I was.

For I knew that, if I were recognised, the governors in the place would learn this, and recall me to gratify Caesar, and would bestow upon me that former prosperity to which I had formerly bidden adieu with all the resolution I could summon.

For I could not give myself up to a luxurious life when I had pronounced the strongest condemnation on myself, because I believed that I had been the cause of death to those who were loved by me." [24]

Chapter XI - Discussion on Genesis

And Peter said:

"You did this according to your resolution.

But in regard to Genesis, were you merely playing a part when you affirmed it, or were you in earnest in asserting that it existed?"

Our father said:

"I will not speak falsely to you.

I was in earnest when I maintained that Genesis existed.

For I am not uninitiated in the science; on the contrary, I associated with one who is the best of the astrologers, an Egyptian of the name of Annubion, who became my friend in the commencement of my

travels, and disclosed to me the death of my wife and children." [25]And Peter said:
"Are you not now convinced by facts, that the doctrine of Genesis has no firm foundation?"
And my father answered:
"I must lay before you all the ideas that occur to my mind, that listening to them I may understand your refutation of them. [26]I know, indeed, that astrologers both make many mistakes, and frequently speak the truth.
I suspect, therefore, that they speak the truth so far as they are accurately acquainted with the science, and that their mistakes are the result of ignorance; so that I conjecture that the science has a firm foundation, but that the astrologers themselves speak what is false solely on account of ignorance, because they cannot know all things with absolute [27] accuracy."
And Peter answered:
"Consider [28] whether their speaking of the truth is not accidental, and whether they do not make their declarations without knowing the matters accurately.
For it must by all means happen that, when many prophecies are uttered, some of them should come true."
And the old man said:
"How, then, is it possible to be fully convinced of this, whether the science of Genesis has a sure foundation or not?"

Chapter XII - Clement Undertakes the Discussion

When both were silent, I said:
"Since I know accurately the science, but our lord and our father are not in this condition, I should like if Annubion himself were here, to have a discussion with him in the presence of my father.
For thus would the matter be able to become public, when one practically acquainted with the subject has held the discussion with one equally informed." [29]And our father answered:
"Where, then, is it possible to fall in with Annubion?"
And Peter said:
"In Antioch, for I learn that Simon Magus is there, whose inseparable companion Annubion is.
When, then, we go there, if we come upon them, the discussion can take place."
And so, when we had discussed many subjects, and rejoiced at the recognition and given thanks to God, evening came down upon us, and we turned to sleep.

Footnotes:

1. Lit., "tranquil and clean."
[The baptism is narrated in Recognitions, vii. 38.--R.]
2. We have adopted an emendation of Schwegler's.
The mss. read either "these" or "the same" for "the rest of."
3. The words "for the Eucharist" might be translated "after thanksgiving."
But it is much the same which, for the Eucharist is plainly meant.
The Epitomes have it:
"taking the bread, giving thanks, blessing, and consecrating it, he gave it; " but no mention is made of salt.
[The details here are more specific than in Recognitions, vii. 38.
[The mention of "salt" is peculiar.
Compare "the salt" named as one of the "seven witnesses" in the baptismal form of the Elkesaites, Hippolytus, Ante-Nicene Fathers, v. pp. 132, 133.--R.]
4. [For the extensive variations in the plan of the two narratives from this point to the end, see footnote on Recognitions, viii. 1.
In the Recognitions the family of Clement are brought into greater prominence as disputants; in the Homilies Simon Magus, and Peter's discourses against him, are the main features; both, however, preserve the dramatic element of the re-united family, though the details are given differently in the two narratives.--R.]
5. [The old man is introduced at once in Recognitions, viii. 1, and the subsequent discussion takes place in the presence of Clement and many others.--R.]
6. We have adopted an emendation of Wieseler's.
The text has, "at the time that you went away."
7. Wieseler thinks that the reading should be:
"I did not retire."
8. Genesis is destiny determined by the stars which rule at each man's birth.
[Comp. iv. 12.

In Recognitions, viii. 2, the long discussion with the old man begins in the same way.--R.]

9. mathema, mathematical science specially, which was closely connected with astrology. [Comp. Recognitions, x. 11-12.--R.]

10. Lit., "thinking you counsel what is contrary to yourself."

11. The argument here is obscure.
Probably what is intended is as follows:
Genesis means origination, coming into being.
Origination cannot be the ruling power, for there must be something unoriginated which has given rise to the origination.
The origination, therefore, as not being first, cannot have sway, and it must itself be subject to that which is unoriginated.

12. [On the error of astrology compare the full discussion in Recognitions, ix. 12, x. 7-12.--R.]

13. We have adopted the reading given in the two Epitomes.

14. Lit., "when."

15. [This method of proof, by appeal to the supernatural power of the Apostle, is peculiar to the Homilies.
In the Recognitions, ix. 30, an argument is made by Clement, who appeals to the power of the true Prophet.--R.]

16. That is, the power of origination.

17. [With chaps. 6-9, there is a general correspondence in Recognitions, ix. 32-37.
The arrangement is quite different.
The old man's representation, that the story he tells is that of a friend, is peculiar to the Homilies.--R.]

18. One ms. adds "greatly," and an Epitome "great things."

19. That is, the position of the stars at her birth.

20. We have inserted hos from the Epitomes.

21. Lit., "of salt."

22. Lit., "you died by a judgment;" but it is thought that krisei is corrupt.

23. [In the Recognitions the old man is not recognised until long discussions have been held; see book ix. 35, 37.
Hints of the relationship are, however, given in advance.--R.]

24. Lit., "Having judged the greatest things in regard to those who were loved by me, as having died."
The text is doubtful; for the first Epitome has something quite different.

25. [Comp. Homily IV. 6.
Annubion and Appion are not introduced in the Recognitions until book x. 52.--R.]

[26. Here mss. and Epitomes differ in their readings.
The text adopted seems a combination of two ideas:
"that you may listen and refute them, and that I may thus learn the truth."

27. We have adopted the reading of Codex O, pantos.
The other ms. reads, "that all cannot know all things accurately."

28. The mss. read apeche, "hold back."
The reading of the text is in an Epitome.

29. Lit., "when artist has had discussion with fellow-artist."

Homily XV

Chapter I - Peter Wishes to Convert Faustus

At break of day our father, with our mother and his three sons, entered the place where Peter was, and accosting him, sat down.

Then we also did the same at his request; and Peter looking at our father, said: [1]"I am anxious that you should become of the same mind as your wife and children, in order that here you may live along with them, and in the other world, [2] after the separation of the soul from the body, you will continue to be with them free from sorrow.

For does it not grieve you exceedingly that you should not associate with each other?"

And my father said:

"Most assuredly."

And Peter said:

"If, then, separation from each other here gives you pain, and if without doubt the penalty awaits you that after death you should not be with each other, how much greater will your grief be that you, a wise man, should be separated from your own family on account of your opinions? They too, must[3] feel the more distressed from the consciousness that eternal punishment awaits you because you entertain different opinions from theirs, and deny the established truth." [4]

Chapter II - Reason for Listening to Peter's Arguments

Our father said:

"But it is not the case, my very dear friend, that souls are punished in Hades, for the soul is dissolved into air as soon as it leaves the body."

And Peter said:

"Until we convince you in regard to this point, answer me, does it not appear to you that you are not grieved as having no faith in a future punishment, but they who have full faith in it must be vexed in regard to you?"

And our father said:

"You speak sense."

And Peter said:

"Why, then, will you not free them from the greatest grief they can have in regard to you by agreeing to their religion, not, I mean, through dread, but through kindly feeling, listening and judging about what is said by me, whether it be so or not? and if the truth is as we state it, then here you will enjoy life with those who are dearest to you, and in the other world you will have rest with them; but if, in examining the arguments, you show that what is stated by us is a fictitious story, [5] you will thus be doing good service, for you will have your friends on your side, and you will put an end to their leaning upon false hopes, and you will free them from false fears."

Chapter III - Obstacles to Faith

And our father said:

"There is evidently much reason in what you say."

And Peter said:

"What is it, then, that prevents you from coming to our faith?

Tell me, that we may begin our discussion with it.

For many are the hindrances.

The faithful are hindered by occupation with merchandise, or public business, or the cultivation of the soil, or cares, and such like; the unbelievers, of whom you also are one, are hindered by ideas such as that the gods, which do not exist, really exist, or that all things are subject to Genesis, or chance,[6] or that souls are mortal, or that our doctrines are false because there is no providence.

Chapter IV - Providence Seen in the Events of the Life of Faustus and His Family

"But I maintain, from what has happened to you,[7] that all things are managed by the providence of God, and that your separation from your family for so many years was providential;[8] for since, if they had been with you, they perhaps would not have listened to the doctrines of the true religion, it was arranged that your children should travel with their mother, should be shipwrecked, should be supposed to have perished, and should be sold;[9] moreover, that they should be educated in the learning of the Greeks, especially in the atheistic doctrines, in order that, as being acquainted with them, they might be the better able to refute them; and in addition to this, that they should become attached to the true religion, and be enabled to be united with me, so as to help me in my preaching; furthermore, that their brother Clement should meet in the same place, and that thus his mother should be recognised, and through her cure[10] should be fully convinced of the right worship of God;[11] that after no long interval the twins should recognise and be recognised, and the other day should fall in with you, and that you should receive back your own.

I do not think, then, that such a speedy filling in of circumstances, coming as it were from all quarters, so as to accomplish one design, could have happened without the direction of Providence."

Chapter V - Difference Between the True Religion and Philosophy

And our father began to say:
"Do not suppose, my dearest Peter, that I am not thinking of the doctrines preached by you. I was thinking of them.

But during the past night, when Clement urged me earnestly to give in my adhesion to the truth preached by you, I at last answered, Why should I? for what new commandment can any one give more than what the ancients urged us to obey?'

And he, with a gentle smile, said, There is a great difference, father, between the doctrines of the true religion and those of philosophy;[12] for the true religion receives its proof from prophecy, while philosophy, furnishing us with beautiful sentences, seems to present its proofs from conjecture.'

On saying this, he took an instance, and set before us the doctrine of philanthropy,[13] which you had explained to him,[14] which rather appeared to me to be very unjust, and I shall tell you how.

He alleged that it was right to present to him who strikes you on the one cheek the other[15] also, and to give to him who takes away your cloak your tunic also, and to go two miles with him who compels you to go one, and such like."[16]

Chapter VI - The Love of Man

And Peter answered:
"You have deemed unjust what is most just.
If you are inclined, will you listen to me?"
And my father said:
"With all my heart."
And Peter said:
"What is your opinion?
Suppose that there were two kings, enemies to each other, and having their countries cut off from each other; and suppose that some one of the subjects of one of them were to be caught in the country of the other, and to incur the penalty of death on this account;
now if he were let off from the punishment by receiving a blow instead of death, is it not plain that he who let him off is a lover of man?"
And our father said:
"Most certainly."
And Peter said:

"Now suppose that this same person were to steal from some one something belonging to him or to another; and if when caught he were to pay double, instead of suffering the punishment that was due to him, namely, paying four times the amount, and being also put to death, as having been caught in the territories of the enemy; is it not your opinion that he who accepts double, and lets him off from the penalty of death, is a lover of man?"

And our father said:

"He certainly seems so."

And Peter said:

"Why then?

Is it not the duty of him who is in the kingdom of another, and that, too, a hostile and wicked monarch, to be pleasing to all [17] for the sake of life, and when force is applied to him, to yield still more, to accost those who do not accost him, to reconcile enemies, not to quarrel with those who are angry, to give his own property freely to all who ask, and such like?"

And our father said:

"He should with reason endure all things rather, if he prefers life to them."

Chapter VII - The Explanation of a Parable; The Present and the Future Life

And Peter [18] said:

"Are not those, then, who you said received injustice, themselves transgressors, inasmuch as they are in the kingdom of the other, and is it not by overreaching that they have obtained all they possess? while those who are thought to act unjustly are conferring a favour on each subject of the hostile kingdom, so far as they permit him to have property.

For these possessions belong to those who have chosen the present. [19] And they are so far kind as to permit the others to live.

This, then, is the parable; now listen to the actual truth.

The prophet of the truth who appeared on earth taught us that the Maker and God of all gave two kingdoms to two, [20] good and evil; granting to the evil the sovereignty over the present world along with law, so that he, it, should have the right to punish those who act unjustly; but to the good He gave the eternal [21] to come.

But He made each man free with the power to give himself up to whatsoever he prefers, either to the present evil or the future good.

Those men who choose the present have power to be rich, to revel in luxury, to indulge in pleasures, and to do whatever they can.

For they will possess none of the future goods.

But those who have determined to accept the blessings of the future reign have no right to regard as their own the things that are here, since they belong to a foreign king, with the exception only of water and bread, and those things procured with sweat to maintain life (for it is not lawful for them to commit suicide), [22] and also one garment, for they are not permitted to go naked on account of the all-seeing [23] Heaven.

Chapter VIII - The Present and the Future

"If, then, you wish to have an accurate account of the matter, listen. Those of whom you said a little before that they receive injustice, rather act unjustly themselves; for they who have chosen the future blessings, live along with the bad in the present world, having many enjoyments the same as the bad,--such as life itself, light, bread, water, clothing, and others of a like nature.

But they who are thought by you to act unjustly, shall not live with the good men in [24] the coming age."

And our father replied to this:

"Now when you have convinced me that those who act unjustly suffer injustice themselves, while those who suffer injustice have by far the advantage, the whole affair seems to me still more the most unjust of transactions; for those who seem to act unjustly grant many things to those who have chosen the future blessings, but those who seem to receive injustice do themselves commit injustice, because they do not give in the other world, to those who have given them blessings here, the same advantages which these gave to them."

And Peter said:

"This is not unjust at all, because each one has the power to choose the present or the future goods, whether they be small or great.

He who chooses by his own individual judgment and wish, receives no injustice,--I mean, not even should his choice rest on what is small, since the great lay within his choice, as in fact did also the small."

And our father said:

"You are right; for it has been said by one of the wise men of the Greeks, The blame rests with those who chose--God is blameless.' [25]

Chapter IX - Possessions are Transgressions

"Will you be so good as to explain this matter also?

I remember Clement saying to me, that we suffer injuries and afflictions for the forgiveness of our sins."

Peter said:

"This is quite correct.

For we, who have chosen the future things, in so far as we possess more goods than these, whether they be clothing, or food or drink, or any other thing, possess sins, because we ought not to have anything, as I explained to you a little ago.

To all of us possessions are sins. [26] The deprivation of these, in whatever way it may take place, is the removal of sins."

And our father said:

"That seems reasonable, as you explained that these were the two boundary lines of the two kings, and [27] that it was in the power of each to choose whatever he wished of what was under their authority.

But why are the afflictions sent, or [28] do we suffer them justly?"

And Peter said:

"Most justly; for since the boundary line of the saved is, as I said, that no one should possess anything, but since many have many possessions, or in other words sins, for this reason the exceeding love of God sends afflictions on those who do not act in purity of heart, that on account of their having some measure of the love of God, they might, by temporary inflictions, be saved from eternal punishments."

Chapter X - Poverty Not Necessarily Righteous

And our father said:

"How then is this?

Do we not see many impious men poor?

Then do these belong to the saved on this account?"

And Peter said:

"Not at all; for that poverty is not acceptable which longs for what it ought not.

So that some are rich as far as their choice goes, though poor in actual wealth, and they are punished because they desire to have more.

But one is not unquestionably righteous because he happens to be poor.

For he can be a beggar as far as actual wealth is concerned, but he may desire and even do what above everything he ought not to do. Thus he may worship idols, or be a blasphemer or fornicator, or he may live indiscriminately, or perjure himself, or lie, or live the life of an unbeliever. But our teacher pronounced the faithful poor blessed; [29] and he did so, not because they had given anything, for they had nothing, but because they were not to be condemned, as having done no sin, simply because they gave no alms, because they had nothing to give."

And our father said:

"In good truth all seems to go right as far as the subject of discussion is concerned; wherefore I have resolved to listen to the whole of your argument in regular order."

Chapter XI - Exposition of the True Religion Promised

And Peter said:

"Since, then, you are eager henceforth to learn what relates to our religion, I ought to explain it in order, beginning with God Himself, and showing that we ought to call Him alone God, and that we neither ought to speak of the others as gods nor deem them such, and that he who acts contrary to this will be punished eternally, as having shown the greatest impiety to Him who is the Lord of all."

And saying this, he laid his hands on those who were vexed by afflictions, and were diseased, and possessed by demons; and, praying, he healed them, and dismissed the multitudes.

And then entering in this way, he partook of his usual food, and went to sleep.

Footnotes:

1. [In Recognitions, x. 1, after the father becomes known, the Apostle is represented as proposing delay in the attempt to convert him.--R.]
2. Lit., "there."
3. We have inserted a dei, probably omitted on account of the previous de.
4. The words are peculiar.
Lit., "eternal punishment awaits you thinking other things, through denial of the fixed dogma" (rhetou dogmatos).
The Latin translator gives:
"ob veri dogmatis negationem."
5. muthon tina pseude.
6. Properly, self-action.
7. [The recapitulation of Peter in Recognitions, ix. 26, is in explanation to the sons, and not for a doctrinal purpose.--R.]
8. We have adopted a reading suggested by the second Epitome.
9. The word aprasiai is corrupt.
We have adopted the emendation prasis.
The word is not given in the ms. O, nor in the Epitomes.
10. hupo therapeias, which Cotelerius translates recuperata sanitate.
11. Lit., "convinced of the Godhead."
"Godhead" is omitted in the Epitomes.
12. [Compare the fuller statement in Recognitions, viii. 61; also Recognitions, x. 48-51.--R.]
13. Or "love of man" in all its phases--kindliness, gentleness, humanity, etc.
14. Hom. XII. 25 ff.
15. Matt. v. 39-41; Luke vi. 29.
The writer of the Homilies changes the word chitona, "tunic," of the New Testament into maphorion, which Suicer describes "a covering for the head, neck, and shoulders, used by women."
Wieseler is in doubt whether the writer of the Homilies uses maphorion as equivalent to chitona, or whether he intentionally changed the word, for the person who lost both cloak and tunic would be naked altogether; and this, the writer may have imagined, Christ would not have commanded.
16. [The larger part of the discussion in chaps. 5-11 is peculiar to the Homilies.
There is little matter in it found in the longer arguments of Recognitions.--R.]
17. Lit., "to flatter."
18. The following words would be more appropriately put in the mouth of the father, as is done in fact by the Epitomes.
Peter's address would commence, "And the parable is."
The Epitomes differ much from each other and the text, and there seems to be confusion in the text.
19. This sentence would be more appropriate in the explanation of the parable.
20. The Greek leaves it uncertain whether it is two persons or two things,--whether it is a good being and an evil being, or good and evil.
Afterwards, a good being and an evil are distinctly introduced.
21. The word aidios, properly and strictly "eternal," is used.
22. Lit., "to die willingly."
23. We have adopted an obvious emendation, panta for pantos.
24. We have translated Schwegler's emendation.
He inserted en.
25. Plato, Rep., x. 617 E.

26. One ms. inserts before the sentence:
"For if in all of us possessions are wont to occasion sins in those who have them."
27. We have adopted Wieseler's emendation of ta into kai.
28. We have changed ei into e.
29. Matt. v. 3.
The Epitomes run thus:
"Our Lord Jesus Christ, the Son of the living God, said."
And then they quote the words of our Gospel.

Homily XVI

Chapter I - Simon Wishes to Discuss with Peter the Unity of God

At break of day Peter went out, and reaching the place where he was wont to discourse, he saw a great multitude assembled.

At the very time when he was going to discourse, one of his deacons entered, and said:

"Simon has come from Antioch, [1] starting as soon as it was evening, having learned that you promised to speak on the unity [2] of God; and he is ready, along with Athenodorus the Epicurean, to come to hear your speech, in order that he may publicly oppose all the arguments ever adduced by you for the unity of God."

Just as the deacon said this, lo! Simon himself entered, accompanied by Athenodorus and some other friends.

And before Peter spoke at all, he took the first word, and said:--

Chapter II - The Same Subject Continued

"I heard that you promised yesterday to Faustus to prove this day, giving out your arguments in regular order, and beginning with Him who is Lord of the universe, that we ought to say that He alone is God, and that we ought neither to say nor to think that there are other gods, because he that acts contrary to this will be punished eternally.

But, above all, I am truly amazed at your madness in hoping to convert a wise man, and one far advanced in years, to your state of mind.

But you will not succeed in your designs; and all the more that I am present, and can thoroughly refute your false arguments.

For perhaps, if I had not been present, the wise old man might have been led astray, because he has no critical acquaintance [3] with the books publicly believed in amongst the Jews. [4] At present I shall omit much, in order that I may the more speedily refute that which you have promised to prove.

Wherefore begin to speak what you promised to say before us, who know the Scriptures.

But if, fearing our refutation, you are unwilling to fulfil your promise in our presence, this of itself will be sufficient proof that you are wrong, because you did venture to speak in the presence of those who know the Scriptures.

And now, why should I wait till you tell me, when I have a most satisfactory witness of your promise in the old man who is present?"

And, saying this, he looked to my father, and said:

"Tell me, most excellent of all men, is not this the man who promised to prove to you to-day that God is one, and that we ought not to say or think that there is any other god, and that he who acts contrary to this will be punished eternally, as committing the most heinous sin?

Do you, then, refuse to reply to me?"

Chapter III - The Mode of the Discussion

And our father said:

"Well might you have demanded testimony from me, Simon, if Peter had first denied that he had made the promise.

But now I shall feel no shame in saying what I am bound to say.

I think that you wish to enter on the discussion inflamed with anger.

Now this is a state of mind in which it is improper for you to speak and for us to listen to you; for we are no longer being helped on to the truth, but we are watching the progress of a contest.

And now, having learned from Hellenic culture how those who seek the truth ought to act, I shall remind you.

Let each of you give an exposition of his own opinion, [5] and let the right of speech pass from the one to the other. [6]For if Peter alone should wish to expound his thought, but you should be silent as to yours, it is possible that some argument adduced by you might crush both your and his opinion; and both of you, though defeated by this argument, would not appear defeated, but only the one who expounded his opinion; while he who did not expound his, though equally defeated, would not appear defeated, but would even be thought to have conquered."

And Simon answered:

"I will do as you say; but I am afraid lest you do not turn out a truth-loving judge, as you have been already prejudiced by his arguments."

Chapter IV - The Prejudices of Faustus Rather on the Side of Simon Than on that of Peter

Our father answered:

"Do not compel me to agree with you without any exercise of my judgment in order that I may seem to be a truth-loving judge; but if you wish me to tell you the truth, my prepossessions are rather the side of your opinions."

And Simon said:

"How is this the case, when you do not know what my opinions are?"

And our father said:

"It is easy to know this, and I will tell you how.

You promised that you would convict Peter of error in maintaining the unity of God; but if one undertakes to convict of error him who maintains the unity of God. it is perfectly plain that he, as being in the right, [7] does not hold the same opinion.

For if he holds the same opinion as the man who is thoroughly in error, then he himself is in error; but if he gives his proofs holding opposite opinions, then he is in the right.

Not well [8] then do you assert that he who maintains the unity of God is wrong, unless you believe that there are many gods.

Now I maintain that there are many gods.

Holding, therefore, the same opinion as you before the discussion, I am prepossessed rather in your favour.

For this reason you ought to have no anxiety in regard to me, but Peter ought, for I still hold opinions contrary to his.

And so after your discussion I hope that, as a truth-loving judge, who has stripped himself of his prepossessions, I shall agree to that doctrine which gains the victor."

When my father said this, a murmur of applause burst insensibly from the multitudes because my father had thus spoken.

Chapter V - Peter Commences the Discussion

Peter then said:

"I am ready to do as the umpire of our discussion has said; and straight-way without any delay I shall set forth my opinion in regard to God.

I then assert that there is one God who made the heavens and the earth, and all things that are in them.

And it is not right to say or to think that there is any other."

And Simon said: "But I maintain that the Scriptures believed in amongst the Jews say that there are many gods, and that God is not angry at this, because He has Himself spoken of many gods in His Scriptures.

Chapter VI - Simon Appeals to the Old Testament to Prove that There are Many Gods

"For instance, in the very first words of the law, He evidently speaks of them as being like even unto Himself.

For thus it is written, that, when the first man received a commandment from God to eat of every tree that was in the garden, [9] but not to eat of the tree of the knowledge of good and evil, the serpent having persuaded them by means of the woman, through the promise that they would become gods, made them look up; [10] and then, when they had thus looked up, God said, [11] Behold, Adam is become as one of us.'

When, then, the serpent said, [12] Ye shall be as gods,' he plainly speaks in the belief that gods exist; all the more as God also added His testimony, saying, Behold, Adam is become as one of us.'

The serpent, then, who said that there are many gods, did not speak falsely.

Again, the scripture, [13] Thou shalt not revile the gods, nor curse the rulers of thy people,' points out many gods whom it does not wish even to be cursed. But it is also somewhere else written,[14] Did another god dare to enter and take him a nation from the midst of another nation, as did I the Lord God?'

When He says, Did another God dare?' He speaks on the supposition that other gods exist.

And elsewhere: [15]Let the gods that have not made the heavens and the earth perish;' as if those who had made them were not to perish.

And in another place, when it says, [16] Take heed to thyself lest thou go and serve other gods whom thy fathers knew not,' it speaks as if other gods existed whom they were not to follow.

And again: [17]The names of other gods shall not ascend upon thy lips.'

Here it mentions many gods whose names it does not wish to be uttered.

And again it is written, [18] Thy God is the Lord, He is God of gods.'

And again: [19]Who is like unto Thee, O Lord, among the Gods?'

And again: [20]God is Lord of gods.'

And again: [21]God stood in the assembly of gods: He judgeth among the gods.'

Wherefore I wonder how, when there are so many passages in writing which testify that there are many gods, you have asserted that we ought neither to say nor to think that there are many. [22]Finally, if you have anything to say against what has been spoken so distinctly, say it in the presence of all."

Chapter VII - Peter Appeals to the Old Testament to Prove the Unity of God

And Peter said:

"I shall reply briefly to what you have said.

The law, which frequently speaks of gods, itself says to the Jewish multitude, [23] Behold, the heaven of heavens is the Lord's thy God, with all that therein is;' implying that, even if there are gods, they are under Him, that is, under the God of the Jews.

And again: [24] The Lord thy God, He is God in heaven above, and upon the earth beneath, and there is none other except Him.'

And somewhere else the Scripture says to the Jewish multitude, [25] The Lord your God is God of gods;' so that, even if there are gods, they are under the God of the Jews.

And somewhere else the Scripture says in regard to Him, [26] God, the great and true, who regardeth not persons, nor taketh reward, He doth execute the judgment of the fatherless and widow.'

The Scripture, in calling the God of the Jews great and true, and executing judgment, marked out the others as small, and not true.

But also somewhere else the Scripture says, [27] As I live, saith the Lord, there is no other God but me.

I am the first, I am after this; except me there is no God.'

And again: [28]Thou shalt fear the Lord thy God, and Him only shalt thou serve.'

And again: [29]Hear, O Israel, the Lord your God is one Lord.'

And many passages besides seal with an oath that God is one, and except Him there is no God.

Whence I wonder how, when so many passages testify that there is one God, you say that there are many."

Chapter VIII - Simon and Peter Continue the Discussion

And Simon said:

"My original stipulation with you was that I should prove from the Scriptures that you were wrong in maintaining that we ought not to speak of many gods."

Accordingly I adduced many written passages to show that the divine Scriptures themselves speak of many gods."

And Peter said:

"Those very Scriptures which speak of many gods, also exhorted us, saying, The names of other gods shall not ascend upon thy lips.' [30]Thus, Simon, I did not speak contrary to what was written."

And Simon said:

"Do you, Peter, listen to what I have to say.

You seem to me to sin in speaking against them, [31] when the Scripture says, [32] Thou shalt not revile the gods, nor curse the rulers of thy people.'"

And Peter said:

"I am not sinning, Simon, in pointing out their destruction according to the Scriptures; for thus it is written: [33]Let the gods who did not make the heavens and the earth perish.'

And He said thus, not as though some had made the heavens and were not to perish, as you interpreted the passage.

For it is plainly declared that He who made them is one in the very first part of Scripture: [34]In the beginning God created the heaven and the earth.

And it did not say, the gods.'

And somewhere else it says, [35] And the firmament showeth His handiwork.'

And in another place it is written, [36] The heavens themselves shall perish, but Thou shalt remain for ever.'"

Chapter IX - Simon Tries to Show that the Scriptures Contradict Themselves

And Simon said:

"I adduced clear passages from the Scriptures to prove that there are many gods; and you, in reply, brought forward as many or more from the same Scriptures, showing that God is one, and He the God of the Jews.

And when I said that we ought not to revile gods, you proceeded to show that He who created is one, because those who did not create will perish.

And in reply to my assertion that we ought to maintain that there are gods, because the Scriptures also say so, you showed that we ought not to utter their names, because the same Scripture tells us not to utter the names of other gods.

Since, then, these very Scriptures say at one time that there are many gods, and at another that there is only one; and sometimes that they ought not to be reviled, and at other times that they ought; what conclusion ought we to come to in consequence of this, but that the Scriptures themselves lead us astray?"

Chapter X - Peter's Explanation of the Apparent Contradictions of Scripture

And Peter said: "They do not lead astray, but convict and bring to light the evil disposition against God which lurks like a serpent in each one.

For the Scriptures lie before each one like many divers types.

Each one, then, has his own disposition like wax, and examining the Scriptures and finding everything in them, he moulds his idea of God according to his wish, laying upon them, as I said, his own disposition, which is like wax. [37]Since, then, each one finds in the Scriptures whatever opinion he wishes to have in regard to God, for this reason he, Simon, moulds from them the forms [38] of many gods, while we moulded the form of Him who truly exists, coming to the knowledge of the true type from our own shape. [39]For assuredly the soul within us is clothed with His image for immortality.

If I abandon the parent of this soul, it also will abandon me to just judgment, making known the injustice by the very act of daring; [40] and as coming from one who is just, it will justly abandon me; and so, as far as the soul is concerned, I shall, after punishment, be destroyed, having abandoned the help that comes from it.

But if there is another god, first let him put on another form, another shape, in order that by the new shape of the body I may recognise the new god. But if he should change the shape, does he thereby change the substance of the soul?

But if he should change it also, then I am no longer myself, having become another both in shape and in substance.

Let him, therefore, create others, if there is another.

But there is not.

For if there had been, he would have created.

But since he has not created, then let him, as nonexistent, leave him who is really existent.[41] For he is nobody, [42] except only in the opinion of Simon.

I do not accept of any other god but Him alone who created me."

Chapter XI - Gen. I. 26 Appealed to by Simon

And Simon said:

"Since I see that you frequently speak of the God who created you, learn from me how you are impious even to him.

For there are evidently two who created, as the Scripture says: [43] And God said, Let us make man in our image, after our likeness.'

Now let us make,' implies two or more; certainly not one only."

Chapter XII - Peter's Explanation of the Passage

And Peter answered:

"One is He who said to His Wisdom, Let us make a man.'

But His Wisdom [44] was that with which He Himself always rejoiced [45] as with His own spirit.

It is united as soul to God, but it is extended by Him, as hand, fashioning the universe.

On this account, also, one man was made, and from him went forth also the female.

And being a unity generically, it is yet a duality, for by expansion and contraction the unity is thought to be a duality.

So that I act rightly in offering up all the honour to one God as to parents."

And Simon said:

"What then?

Even if the Scriptures say that there are other gods, will you not accept the opinion?"

Chapter XIII - The Contradictions of the Scriptures Intended to Try Those Who Read Them

And Peter answered: [46] "If the Scriptures or prophets speak of gods, they do so to try those who hear.

For thus it is written: [47]

If there arise among you a prophet, giving signs and wonders, and that sign and wonder shall then come to pass, and he say to thee, Let us go after and worship other gods which thy fathers have not known, ye [48] shall not hearken to the words of that prophet; let thy hands be among the first to stone him.

For he hath tried to turn thee from the Lord thy God.

But if thou say in thy heart, How did he do that sign or wonder? thou shalt surely know that he who tried thee, tried thee to see if thou dost fear the Lord thy God.'

The words he who tried thee, tried thee,' have reference to the earliest times; [49] but it appears to be otherwise after the removal to Babylon.

For God, who knows all things, would not, as can be proved by many arguments, try in order that He Himself might know, for He fore-knows all things.

But, if you like, let us discuss this point, and I shall show that God foreknows.

But it has been proved that the opinion is false that He does not know, and that this was written to try us.

Thus we, Simon, can be led astray [50] neither by the Scriptures nor by any one else; nor are we deceived into the admission of many gods, nor do we agree to any statement that is made against God.

Chapter XIV - Other Beings Called Gods

"For we ourselves also know that angels are called gods by the Scriptures,--as, for instance, He who spake at the bush, and wrestled with Jacob,--and the name is likewise applied to Him who is born Emmanuel, and who is called the mighty God. [51] Yea, even Moses became a god to Pharaoh, though in reality he was a man.

The same is the case also with the idols of the Gentiles.

But we have but one God, one who made creation and arranged the universe, whose Son is the Christ.

Obeying Christ, [52] we learn to know what is false from the Scriptures.

Moreover, being furnished by our ancestors with the truths of the Scriptures, we know that there is only one who has made the heavens and the earth, the God of the Jews, and of all who choose to worship Him.

Our fathers, with pious thought, setting down a fixed belief in Him as the true God, handed down this belief to us, that we may know that if any thing is said against God, it is a falsehood.

I shall add this remark over and above what I need say:

If the case be not as I have said, then may I, and all who love the truth, incur danger in regard to the praise of the God who made us."

Chapter XV - Christ Not God, But the Son of God

When Simon heard this, he said:

"Since you say that we ought not to believe even the prophet that gives signs and wonders if he say that there is another god, and that you know that he even incurs the penalty of death, therefore your teacher also was with reason cut off for having given signs and wonders."

And Peter answered:

"Our Lord neither asserted that there were gods except the Creator of all, nor did He proclaim Himself to be God, but He with reason pronounced blessed him who called Him the Son of that God who has arranged the universe."

And Simon answered:

"Does it not seem to you, then, that he who comes from God is God?" [53] And Peter said:

"Tell us how this is possible; for we cannot affirm this, because we did not hear it from Him.

Chapter XVI - The Unbegotten and the Begotten Necessarily Different from Each Other

"In addition to this, it is the peculiarity of the Father not to have been begotten, but of the Son to have been begotten; but what is begotten cannot be compared with that which is unbegotten or self-begotten."

And Simon said:

"Is it not the same on account of its origin?" [54] And Peter said:

"He who is not the same in all respects as some one, cannot have all the same appellations applied to him as that person."

And Simon said:

"This is to assert, not to prove."

And Peter said:

"Why, do you not see that if [55] the one happens to be self-begotten or unbegotten, they cannot be called the same; nor can it be asserted of him who has been begotten that he is of the same substance as he is who has begotten him? [56] Learn this also:

The bodies of men have immortal souls, which have been clothed with the breath of God; and having come forth from God, they are of the same substance, but they are not gods.

But if they are gods, then in this way the souls of all men, both those who have died, and those who are alive, and those who shall come into being, are gods.

But if in a spirit of controversy you maintain that these also are gods, what great matter is it, then, for Christ to be called God? for He has only what all have.

Chapter XVII - The Nature of God

"We call Him God whose peculiar attributes cannot belong to the nature of any other; for, as He is called the Unbounded because He is boundless on every side, it must of necessity be the case that it is no other one's peculiar attribute to be called unbounded, as another cannot in like manner be boundless.

But if any one says that it is possible, he is wrong; for two things boundless on every side cannot co-exist, for the one is bounded by the other.

Thus it is in the nature [57] of things that the unbegotten is one.

But if he possesses a figure, even in this case the figure is one and incomparable. [58]Wherefore He is called the Most High, because, being higher than all, He has the universe subject to Him."

Chapter XVIII - The Name of God

And Simon said:

"Is this word God' His ineffable name, which all use, because you maintain so strongly in regard to a name that it cannot be given to another?"

And Peter said:

"I know that this is not His ineffable name, but one which is given by agreement among men; but if you give it to another, you will also assign to this other that which is not used; and that, too, deliberately. [59]The name which is used is the forerunner of that which is not used.

In this way insolence is attributed even to that which has not yet been spoken, just as honour paid to that which is known is handed on to that which has not yet been known."

Chapter XIX - The Shape of God in Man

And Simon said:

"I should like to know, Peter, if you really believe that the shape of man has been moulded after the shape of God." [60]

And Peter said:

"I am really quite certain, Simon, that this is the case."

And Simon said:

"How can death dissolve the body, impressed as it has thus been with the greatest seal?"

And Peter said:

"It is the shape of the just God.

When, then, the body begins to act unjustly, the form which is in it takes to flight, and thus the body is dissolved, by the shape disappearing, in order that an unjust body may not have the shape of the just God.

The dissolution, however, does not take place in regard to the seal, but in regard to the sealed body. But that which is sealed is not dissolved without Him who sealed it. And thus it is not permitted to die without judgment."

And Simon said:

"What necessity was there to give the shape of such a being to man, who was raised from the earth?"

And Peter said:

"This was done because of the love of God, who made man.

For while, as far as substance is concerned, all things are superior to the flesh of man,--I mean the ether, the sun, the moon, the stars, the air, the water, the fire--in a word, all the other things which have been made for the service of man,--yet, though superior in substance, they willingly endure to serve the inferior in substance, because of the shape of the superior.

For as they who honour the clay image of a king have paid honour to the king himself, whose shape the clay happens to have, so the whole creation with joy serves man, who is made from earth, looking to the honour thus paid to God.

Chapter XX - The Character of God

The Epistles of Clement

"Behold, then, the character of that God to whom you, Simon, wish to persuade us to be ungrateful, and the earth continues to bear you, perhaps wishing to see who will venture to entertain similar opinions to yours.

For you were the first to dare what no other dared:
you were the first to utter what we first heard.

We first and alone have seen the boundless long-suffering of God in bearing with such great impiety as yours, and that God no other than the Creator of the world, against whom you have dared to act impiously.

And yet openings of the earth took not place, and fire was not sent down from heaven and went not forth to burn up men, and rain was not poured out, [61] and a multitude of beasts was not sent from the thickets, and upon us ourselves the destructive wrath of God did not begin to show itself, on account of one who sinned the sin, as it were, of spiritual adultery, which is worse than the carnal.

For it is not God the Creator of heaven and earth that in former times punished sins, since now, when He is blasphemed in the highest degree, He would inflict the severest punishment. [62]But, on the contrary, He is long-suffering, calls to repentance, having the arrows which end in the destruction of the impious laid up in His treasures, which He will discharge like living animals when He shall sit down to give judgment to those that are His. [63]Wherefore let us fear the just God, whose shape the body of man bears for honour."

Chapter XXI - Simon Promises to Appeal to the Teaching of Christ. Peter Dismisses the Multitudes

When Peter said this, Simon answered:

"Since I see you skilfully hinting that what is written in the books [64] against the framer [65] of the world does not happen to be true, to-morrow I shall show, from the discourses of your teacher, that he asserted that the framer of the world was not the highest God."

And when Simon said this, he went out.

But Peter said to the assembled multitudes:

"If Simon can do no other injury to us in regard to God, he at least prevents you from listening to the words that can purify the soul."

On Peter saying this, much whispering arose amongst the crowds, saying, "What necessity is there for permitting him to come in here, and utter his blasphemies against God?"

And Peter heard, and said, "Would that the doctrines against God which are intended to try men[66] went no further than Simon!

For there will be, as the Lord said, false apostles, false prophets, [67] heresies, desires for supremacy, who, as I conjecture, finding their beginning in Simon, who blasphemes God, will work together in the assertion of the same opinions against God as those of Simon."

And saying this with tears, he summoned the multitudes to him by his hand; and when they came, he laid his hands upon them and prayed, and then dismissed them, telling them to come at an earlier hour next day.

Saying this, and groaning, he entered and went to sleep, without taking food.

Footnotes:

1. [Homilies XVI.-XIX., giving the details of a second discussion with Simon at Laodicea, are peculiar to this narrative.

Much of the matter finds a parallel in the longer account of the previous discussion at Caesarea in Recognitions, ii. iii. (comp. Homily III.), but all the circumstances are different.

Uhlhorn formerly regarded this portion of the Homilies as the nucleus of the entire literature. He has modified his view.

An analysis of the discussion cannot be attempted; but in the footnote to Recognitions, ii. 19, a general comparison is given of the three accounts of discussions with Simon Magus.--R.]

2. The word properly signifies the "sole government or monarchy of God."
It means that God alone is ruler.

3. idiotes.

4. ton para 'Ioudaiois demosia pepisteumenon biblon.

The literal translation, given in the text, means that the Jews as a community believed in these books as speaking the truth.

Cotelerius translates: "the books which were publically entrusted to the Jews."

One ms. reads, pepistomenon, which might mean, "deemed trustworthy among the Jews."

5. dogma.

6. One ms. and an Epitome have:
"And you must address your arguments to another who acts as judge."
7. The words translated "error," pseusma, and "to be in the right," aletheuein, are, properly rendered, "falsehood," and "to speak the truth."
8. The mss. read:
"not otherwise."
The reading of the text is found in an Epitome.
9. paradeiso, "paradise."
Gen. ii. 16, 17.
10. anablepsai.
It signifies either to look up, or to recover one's sight.
Possibly the second meaning is the one intended here, corresponding to the words of our version: "Then your eyes shall be opened."
11. Gen. iii. 22.
12. Gen. iii. 5.
13. Ex. xxii. 28.
14. Deut. iv. 34.
15. Jer. x. 11.
16. Deut. xiii. 6.
17. Josh. xxiii. 7, LXX.
18. Deut. x. 17.
19. Ps. xxxv. 10, lxxxvi. 8.
20. Ps. l. 1.
21. Ps. lxxxii. 1.
22. [Comp. Recognitions, ii. 39.--R.]
23. Deut. x. 14.
24. Deut. iv. 39.
25. Deut. x. 17.
26. Deut. x. 17.
27. Isa. xlix. 18, xlv. 21, xliv. 6.
28. Deut. vi. 13.
29. Deut. vi. 4.
30. Josh. xxiii. 7, LXX.
31. Namely, the gods.
32. Ex. xxii. 28.
The mss. omit theous, though they insert it in the passage as quoted a little before this.
One ms. reads "the ruler" with our version.
33. Jer. x. 11.
34. Gen. i. 1.
35. Ps. xix. 1.
36. Ps. cii. 26, 27.
37. [This statement of the subjective method of interpretation is in curious harmony with the prevalent theory of this work respecting the mixture of error and truth in the Scriptures.--R.]
38. ideas.
39. morphes.
40. Probably tolmemati should be changed into hormemati, or some such word:
making known that an act of injustice has been committed by taking its departure.
41. This might possibly be translated, "let him leave him who exists to him who exists;" i.e., let him leave the real God to man, who really exists.
42. Wieseler proposes, "for he exists to no one."
43. Gen. i. 26.
44. This is the only passage in the Homilies relating to the sophia.
The text is in some parts corrupt.
It is critically discussed by Uhlhorn, some of whose emendations are adopted by Dressel and translated here.
45. Prov. viii. 30.
46. [On the theory of the Scriptures which is here set forth, compare ii. 38, etc., iii. 42, etc.--R.]
47. Deut. xiii. 1 ff.
48. The change from the singular to the plural is in the Greek.
49. Lit., "But it had been said that he who tried, tried."
The idea seems to be, Before the removal to Babylon true prophets tested the people by urging them to worship these gods; but after that event false prophets arose who really wished to seduce the

The Epistles of Clement
Jews from the worship of the true God.

50. Lit., "nor can we be made to stumble from the Scriptures nor by any one or anything else."
51. Isa. ix. 6.
52. Lit., "whom obeying:"
the "whom" might refer to God.
53. [Here we encounter marked evidence of Ebionism. Compare with these chapters the letter of Rufinus prefixed to the Recognitions.--R.]
54. The word genesis, "arising, coming into being," is here used, not gennesis, "begetting." The idea fully expressed is:
"Is not that which is begotten identical in essence with that which begets it?"
55. We have inserted ei.
The passage is amended in various ways; this seems to be the simplest.
56. [The very ancient variant in John i. 18, "God only begotten," indicates the distinction between the Unbegotten God and the Son.
Even the Arians use the phrase, "Only-begotten God."--R.]
57. Lit., "thus it is nature."
58. We have adopted an emendation here.
The text has:
"Even thus the incomparable is one."
59. Wieseler proposes to join this clause with the following:
"And in point of choice the name which."
60. Lit., "of that one, of Him."
[The chapter is peculiar to the Homilies; comp. xvii. 7, 8.--R.]
61. One ms. reads, "was not restrained."
62. We have inserted an, and suppose the sentence to be ironical. The meaning might be the same without an.
The text of Dressel is as follows:
"For is not He who then punished the sins God, Creator of heaven and earth; since even now, being blasphemed in the highest degree, He punished it in the highest degree?"
63. Cotelerius translates:
"to His enemies."
64. i.e., the Scriptures.
65. A distinction has to be made between the Creator, or maker out of nothing, and the framer, or fashioner, or Demiurge, who puts the matter into shape.
66. Lit., "the word against God for the trial of men."
67. Comp. Matt. xxiv. 24.

Homily XVII

Chapter I - Simon Comes to Peter

The next day, therefore, as Peter was to hold a discussion with Simon, he rose earlier than usual and prayed.
On ceasing to pray, Zacchaeus came in, and said:
"Simon is seated without, discoursing with about thirty of his own special followers."
And Peter said:
"Let him talk until the multitude assemble, and then let us begin the discussion in the following way.
We shall hear all that has been said by him, and having fitted our reply to this, we shall go out and discourse."
And assuredly so it happened.
Zacchaeus, therefore, went out, and not long after entered again, and communicated to Peter the discourse delivered by Simon against him. [1]

Chapter II - Simon's Speech Against Peter

Now he said:
"He accuses you, Peter, of being the servant of wickedness, of having great power in magic, and as charming the souls of men in a way worse than idolatry. [2]To prove that you are a magician, he seemed to me to adduce the following evidence, saying:
I am conscious of this, that when I come to hold a discussion with him, I do not remember a single word of what I have been meditating on by myself.
For while he is discoursing, and my mind is engaged in recollecting what it is that I thought of saying on coming to a conference with him, I do not hear anything whatsoever of what he is saying.
Now, since I do not experience this in the presence of any other than in his alone, is it not plain that I am under the influence of his magic?
And as to his doctrines being worse than those of idolatry, I can make that quite clear to any one who has understanding.
For there is no other benefit than this, that the soul should be freed from images [3] of every kind.
For when the soul brings an image before its eye, it is bound by fear, and it pines away through anxiety lest it should suffer some calamity; and being altered, it falls under the influence of a demon; and being under his influence, it seems to the mass to be wise.

Chapter III - Simon's Accusation of Peter

"Peter does this to you while promising to make you wise.
For, under the pretext of proclaiming one God, he seems to free you from many lifeless images, which do not at all injure those who worship them, because they are seen by the eyes themselves to be made of stone, or brass, or gold, or of some other lifeless material.
Wherefore the soul, because it knows that what is seen is nothing, cannot be spell-bound by fear in an equal degree by means of what is visible. But looking to a terrible God through the influence of deceptive teaching, it has all its natural foundations overturned.
And I say this, not because I exhort you to worship images, but because Peter, seeming to free your souls from terrible images, [4] drives mad the mind of each one of you by a more terrible image, introducing God in a shape, and that, too, a God extremely just,--an image which is accompanied by what is terrible and awful to the contemplative soul, by that which can entirely destroy the energy of a sound mind.
For the mind, when in the midst of such a storm, is like the depth stirred by a violent wind,

perturbed and darkened.

Wherefore, if he comes to benefit you, let him not, while seeming to dissolve your fears which gently proceed from lifeless shapes, introduce in their stead the terrible shape of God.

But has God a shape?

If He has, He possesses a figure.

And if He has a figure, how is He not limited?

And if limited, He is in space.

But if He is in space, He is less than the space which encloses Him.

And if less than anything, how is He greater than all, or superior to all, or the highest of all?

This, then, is the state of the case.

Chapter IV - It is Asserted that Christ's Teaching is Different from Peter's

"And that he does not really believe even the doctrines proclaimed by his teacher is evident, for he proclaims doctrines opposite to his. [5]For he said to some one, as I learn, [6] "Call me not good, for the good is one."

Now in speaking of the good one, he no longer speaks of that just one, [7] whom the Scriptures proclaim, who kills and makes alive,--kills those who sin, and makes alive those who live according to His will.

But that he did not really call Him who is the framer of the world good, is plain to any one who can reflect.

For the framer of the world was known to Adam whom He had made, and to Enoch who pleased Him, and to Noah who was seen to be just by Him; likewise to Abraham, and Isaac, and Jacob; also to Moses, and the people, and the whole world.

But Jesus, the teacher of Peter himself, came and said, [8] "No one knew the Father except the Son, as no one knoweth [9] even the Son except the Father, and those to whom the Son may wish to reveal Him."

If, then, it was the Son himself who was present, it was from the time of his appearance that he began to reveal to those to whom he wished, Him who was unknown to all.

And thus the Father was unknown to all who lived before him, and could not thus be He who was known to all.

Chapter V - Jesus Inconsistent in His Teaching

"In saying this, Jesus is consistent not even with himself.

For sometimes by other utterances, taken from the Scriptures, he presents God as being terrible and just, saying, [10] "Fear not him who killeth the body, but can do nothing to the soul; but fear Him who is able to cast both body and soul into the Gehenna of fire.

Yea, I say unto you, fear Him."

But that he asserted that He is really to be feared as being a just God, to whom he says those who receive injustice cry, is shown in a parable of which he gives the interpretation, saying: [11]"If, then, the unjust judge did so, because he was continually entreated, how much more will the Father avenge those who cry to Him day and night?

Or do you think that, because He bears long with them, He will not do it?

Yea, I say to you, He will do it, and that speedily."

Now he who speaks of God as an avenging and rewarding God, presents Him as naturally just, and not as good.

Moreover he gives thanks to the Lord of heaven and earth. [12]But if He is Lord of heaven and earth, He is acknowledged to be the framer of the world, and if framer, then He is just.

When, therefore, he sometimes calls Him good and sometimes just, he is not consistent with himself in this point. [13]But his wise disciple maintained yesterday a third point, that real sight[14] is more satisfactory than vision, not knowing that real sight can be human, but that vision confessedly proceeds from divinity.

Chapter VI - Peter Goes Out to Answer Simon

"These and such like were the statements, Peter, which Simon addressed to the multitudes while he stood outside; and he seems to me to be disturbing the minds of the greater number.

Wherefore go forth immediately, and by the power of truth break down his false statements."

When Zacchaeus said this, Peter prayed after his usual manner and went out, and standing in the place where he spoke the day before, and saluting the multitudes according to the custom enjoined by his religion, he began to speak as follows:

"Our Lord Jesus Christ, who is the true prophet (as I shall prove conclusively at the proper time), made concise declarations in regard to those matters that relate to the truth, for these two reasons:

first, because He was in the habit of addressing the pious, who had knowledge enough to enable them to believe the opinions uttered by Him by way of declaration; for His statements were not strange to their usual mode of thought; and in the second place, because, having a limited time assigned Him for preaching, He did not employ the method of demonstration in order that He might not spend all His limited time in arguments, for in this way it might happen that He would be fully occupied in giving the solutions of a few problems which might be understood by mental exertion, while He would not have given us to any great extent [15] those statements which relate to the truth.

Accordingly He stated any opinions He wished, as to a people who were able to understand Him, to whom we also belong, who, whenever we did not understand anything of what had been said by Him,--a thing which rarely happened,--inquired of Him privately, that nothing said by Him might be unintelligible to us.

Chapter VII - Man in the Shape of God

"Knowing therefore that we knew all that was spoken by Him, and that we could supply the proofs, He sent us to the ignorant Gentiles to baptize them for remission of sins, and commanded us to teach them first. [16]Of His commandments this is the first and great one, to fear the Lord God, and to serve Him only.

But He meant us to fear that God whose angels they are who are the angels of the least of the faithful amongst us, and who stand in heaven continually beholding the face of the Father. [17]For He has shape, and He has every limb primarily and solely for beauty's sake, and not for use. [18]For He has not eyes that He may see with them; for He sees on every side, since He is incomparably more brilliant in His body than the visual spirit which is in us, and He is more splendid than everything, so that in comparison with Him the light of the sun may be reckoned as darkness.

Nor has He ears that He may hear; for He hears, perceives, moves, energizes, acts on every side.

But He has the most beautiful shape on account of man, that the pure in heart [19] may be able to see Him, that they may rejoice because they suffered.

For He moulded man in His own shape as in the grandest seal, in order that he may be the ruler and lord of all, and that all may be subject to him.

Wherefore, judging that He is the universe, and that man is His image (for He is Himself invisible, but His image man is visible), the man who wishes to worship Him honours His visible image, which is man.

Whatsoever therefore any one does to man, be it good or bad, is regarded as being done to Him. Wherefore the judgment which proceeds from Him shall go before, giving to every one according to his merits.

For He avenges His own shape.

Chapter VIII - God's Figure

Simon's Objection Therefrom Refuted.

"But someone will say, If He has shape, then He has figure also, and is in space; but if He is in space, and is, as being less, enclosed by it, how is He great above everything?

How can He be everywhere if He has figure?

The first remark I have to make to him who urges these objections is this:

The Scriptures persuade us to have such sentiments and to believe such statements in regard to Him; and we know that their declarations are true, for witness is borne to them by our Lord Jesus Christ, by whose orders we are bound to afford proofs to you that such is the case.

But first I shall speak of space.

The space of God is the non-existent, but God is that which exists.

But that which is non-existent cannot be compared with that which is existent.

For how can space be existent? unless it be a second space, such as heaven, earth, water, air, and if there is any other body that fills up the vacuity, which is called vacuity on this account, that it is nothing. For nothing' is its more appropriate name.

For what is that which is called vacuity but as it were a vessel which contains nothing, except the vessel itself?

But being vacuity, it is not itself space; but space is that in which vacuity itself is, if indeed it is the vessel. For it must be the case that that which exists is in that which does not exist.

But by this which is non-existent I mean that which is called by some, space, which is nothing.

But being nothing, how can it be compared with that which is, except by expressing the contrary, and saying that it is that which does not exist, and that that which does not exist is called space?

But even if it were something, there are many examples which I have at hand, but I shall content myself with one only, to show that that which encloses is not unquestionably superior to that which is enclosed.

The sun is a circular figure, and is entirely enclosed by air, yet it lightens up the air, it warms it, it divides it; and if the sun be away from it, it is enveloped in darkness; and from whatsoever part of it the sun is removed, it becomes cold as if it were dead; but again it is illuminated by its rising, and when it has been warmed up by it, it is adorned with still greater beauty.

And it does this by giving a share of itself, though it has its substance limited.

What, then, is there to prevent God, as being the Framer and Lord of this and everything else, from possessing figure and shape and beauty, and having the communication of these qualities proceeding from Himself extended infinitely?

Chapter IX - God the Centre or Heart of the Universe

"One, then, is the God who truly exists, who presides in a superior shape, being the heart of that which is above and that which is below twice, [20] which sends forth from Him as from a centre the life-giving and incorporeal power; the whole universe with the stars and regions [21] of the heaven, the air, the fire, and if anything else exists, is proved to be a substance infinite in height, boundless in depth, immeasurable in breadth, extending the life-giving and wise nature from Him over three infinites. [22]It must be, therefore, that this infinite which proceeds from Him on every side exists, [23] having as its heart Him who is above all, and who thus possesses figure; for wherever He be, He is as it were in the centre of the infinite, being the limit of the universe.

And the extensions taking their rise with Him, possess the nature of six infinites; of whom the one taking its rise with Him penetrates [24] into the height above, another into the depth below, another to the right hand, another to the left, another in front, and another behind; to whom He Himself, looking as to a number that is equal on every side, [25] completes the world in six temporal intervals, [26] Himself being the rest, [27] and having the infinite age to come as His image, being the beginning and the end.

For in Him the six infinites end, and from Him they receive their extension to infinity.

Chapter X - The Nature and Shape of God

"This is the mystery of the hebdomad.

For He Himself is the rest of the whole who grants Himself as a rest to those who imitate His greatness within their little measure.

For He is alone, sometimes comprehensible, sometimes incomprehensible, sometimes limitable,[28] sometimes illimitable, having extensions which proceed from Him into infinity.

For thus He is comprehensible and incomprehensible, near and far, being here and there, as being the only existent one, and as giving a share of that mind which is infinite on every hand, in consequence of which souls breathe and possess life; [29] and if they be separated from the body and be found with a longing for Him, they are borne along into His bosom, as in the winter time the mists of the mountains, attracted by the rays of the sun, are borne along immortal [30] to it.

What affection ought therefore to arise within us if we gaze with our mind on His beautiful shape!

But otherwise it is absurd to speak of beauty.

For beauty cannot exist apart from shape; nor can one be attracted to the love of God, nor even deem that he can see Him, if God has no form.

Chapter XI - The Fear of God

"But some who are strangers to the truth, and who give their energies to the service of evil, on pretext of glorifying God, say that He has no figure, in order that, being shapeless and formless, He may be visible to no one, so as not to be longed for.

For the mind, not seeing the form of God, is empty of Him.

But how can any one pray if he has no one to whom he may flee for refuge, on whom he may lean?

For if he meets with no resistance, he falls out into vacuity.

Yea, says he, we ought not to fear God, but to love Him.

I agree; but the consciousness of having done well in each good act will accomplish this.

Now well-doing proceeds from fearing.

But fear, says he, strikes death into the soul.

Nay, but I affirm that it does not strike death, but awakens the soul, and converts it.

And perhaps the injunction not to fear God might be right, if we men did not fear many other things; such, for instance, as plots against us by those who are like us, and wild beasts, serpents, diseases, sufferings, demons, and a thousand other ills.

Let him, then, who asks us not to fear God, rescue us from these, that we may not fear them; but if he cannot, why should he grudge that we should be delivered from a thousand fears by one fear, the fear of the Just One, and that it should be possible by a slight [31] faith in Him to remove a thousand afflictions from ourselves and others, and receive instead an exchange of blessings, and that, doing no ill in consequence of fear of the God who sees everything, we should continue in peace even in the present life.

Chapter XII - The Fear and Love of God

"Thus, then, grateful service to Him who is truly Lord, renders us free from service to all other masters. [32] If, then, it is possible for any one to be free from sin without fearing God, let him not fear; for under the influence of love to Him one cannot do what is displeasing to Him.

For, on the one hand, it is written that we are to fear Him, and we have been commanded to love Him, in order that each of us may use that prescription which is suitable to his constitution. Fear Him, therefore, because He is just; but whether you fear Him or love Him, sin not.

And may it be the case that any one who fears Him shall be able to gain the victory over unlawful desires, shall not lust after what belongs to others, shall practise kindness, shall be sober, and act justly!

For I see some who are imperfect in their fear of Him sinning very much.

Let us therefore fear God, not only because He is just; for it is through pity for those who have received injustice that He inflicts punishment on those who have done the injustice.

As water therefore quenches fire, so does fear extinguish the desire for evil practices.

He who teaches fearlessness does not himself fear; but he who does not fear, does not believe that there will be a judgment, strengthens his lusts, acts as a magician, and accuses others of the deeds which he himself does."

Chapter XIII - The Evidence of the Senses Contrasted with that from Supernatural Vision

Simon, on hearing this, interrupted him, and said:

"I know against whom you are making these remarks; but in order that I may not spend any time in discussing subjects which I do not wish to discuss, repeating the same statements to refute you, reply to that which is concisely stated by us.

You professed that you had well understood the doctrines and deeds [33] of your teacher because you saw them before you with your own eyes, [34] and heard them with your own ears, and that it is not possible for any other to have anything similar by vision or apparition.

But I shall show that this is false.

He who hears any one with his own ears, is not altogether fully assured of the truth of what is said; for his mind has to consider whether he is wrong or not, inasmuch as he is a man as far as appearance goes.

But apparition not merely presents an object to view, but inspires him who sees it with confidence, for it comes from God.

Now reply first to this." [35]

Chapter XIV - The Evidence of the Senses More Trustworthy Than that of Supernatural Vision

And Peter said:

"You proposed to speak to one point, you replied to another. [36]For your proposition was, that one is better able to know more fully, and to attain confidence, [37] when he hears in consequence of an apparition, than when he hears with his own ears; but when you set about the matter, you were for persuading us that he who hears through an apparition is surer than he who hears with his own ears.

Finally, you alleged that, on this account, you knew more satisfactorily the doctrines of Jesus than I do, because you heard His words through an apparition.

But I shall reply to the proposition you made at the beginning.

The prophet, because he is a prophet, having first given certain information with regard to what is objectively [38] said by him, is believed with confidence; and being known beforehand to be a true prophet, and being examined and questioned as the disciple wishes, he replies:

But he who trusts to apparition or vision and dream is insecure.

For he does not know to whom he is trusting.

For it is possible either that he may be an evil demon or a deceptive spirit, pretending in his speeches to be what he is not.

But if any one should wish to inquire of him who he is who has appeared, he can say to himself whatever he likes.

And thus, gleaming forth like a wicked one, and remaining as long as he likes, he is at length extinguished, not remaining with the questioner so long as he wished him to do for the purpose of consulting him.

For any one that sees by means of dreams cannot inquire about whatever he may wish.

For reflection is not in the special power of one who is asleep.

Hence we, desiring to have information in regard to something in our waking hours, inquire about something else in our dreams; or without inquiring, we hear about matters that do not concern us, and awaking from sleep we are dispirited because we have neither heard nor inquired about those matters which we were eager to know."

Chapter XV - The Evidence from Dreams Discussed

And Simon said:

"If you maintain that apparitions do not always reveal the truth, yet for all that, visions and dreams, being God-sent, do not speak falsely in regard to those matters which they wish to tell."

And Peter said:

"You were right in saying that, being God-sent, they do not speak falsely.

But it is uncertain if he who sees has seen a God-sent dream."

And Simon said:

"If he who has had the vision is just, he has seen a true vision."

And Peter said:

"You were right. But who is just, if he stands in need of a vision that he may learn what he ought to learn, and do what he ought to do?"

And Simon said: "Grant me this, that the just man alone can see a true vision, and I shall then reply to that other point.

For I have come to the conclusion that an impious man does not see a true dream."

And Peter said:

"This is false; and I can prove it both apart from Scripture and by Scripture; but I do not undertake to persuade you.

For the man who is inclined to fall in love with a bad woman, does not change his mind so as to care for a lawful union with another woman in every respect good; but sometimes they love the worse woman through prepossessions, though they are conscious that there is another who is more excellent. And you are ignorant, in consequence of some such state of mind."

And Simon said:

"Dismiss this subject, and discuss the matter on which you promised to speak.

For it seems to me impossible that impious men should receive dreams from God in any way whatever."

Chapter XVI - None But Evil Demons Appear to the Impious

And Peter said:
"I remember that I promised to prove this point, and to give my proofs in regard to it from Scripture and apart from Scripture.

And now listen to what I say.

We know that there are many (if you will pardon me the statement; and if you don't, I can appeal to those who are present as judges) who worship idols, commit adultery, and sin in every way, and yet they see true visions and dreams, and some of them have also apparitions of demons.

For I maintain that the eyes of mortals cannot see the incorporeal form of the Father or Son, because it is illumined by exceeding great light.

Wherefore it is not because God envies, but because He pities, that He cannot be seen by man who has been turned into flesh.

For he who sees God cannot live. For the excess of light dissolves the flesh of him who sees; unless by the secret power of God the flesh be changed into the nature of light, so that it can see light, or the substance of light be changed into flesh, so that it can be seen by flesh.

For the power to see the Father, without undergoing any change, belongs to the Son alone.

But the just shall also in like manner behold God; [39] for in the resurrection of the dead, when they have been changed, as far as their bodies are concerned, into light, and become like the angels, they shall be able to see Him.

Finally, then, if any angel be sent that he may he seen by a man, he is changed into flesh, that he may be able to be seen by flesh.

For no one can see the incorporeal power not only of the Son, but not even of an angel.

But if one sees an apparition, he should know that this is the apparition of an evil demon.

Chapter XVII - The Impious See True Dreams and Visions

"But it is manifest that the impious see true visions and dreams, and I can prove it from Scripture.

Finally, then, it is written in the law, how Abimelech, who was impious, wished to defile the wife of just Abraham by intercourse, and how he heard the commandment from God in his sleep, as the Scripture saith, not to touch her, [40] because she was dwelling with her husband.

Pharaoh, also an impious man, saw a dream in regard to the fulness and thinness of the ears of corn, [41] to whom Joseph said, when he gave the interpretation, that the dream had come from God.[42] Nebuchadnezzar, who worshipped images, and ordered those who worshipped God to be cast into fire, saw a dream [43] extending over the whole age of the world. [44] And let no one say, No one who is impious sees a vision when awake.'

That is false.

Nebuchadnezzar himself, having ordered three men to be cast into fire, saw a fourth when he looked into the furnace, and said, I see the fourth as the Son of God.' [45] And nevertheless, though they saw apparitions, visions, and dreams, they were impious.

Thus, we cannot infer with absolute certainty that the man who has seen visions, and dreams, and apparitions, is undoubtedly pious.

For in the case of the pious man, the truth gushes up natural and pure [46] in his mind, not worked up through dreams, but granted to the good through intelligence.

Chapter XVIII - The Nature of Revelation

"Thus to me also was the Son revealed by the Father.

Wherefore I know what is the meaning of revelation, having learned it in my own case. For at the very time when the Lord said, Who do they say that I am?' [47] and when I heard one saying one thing of Him, and another another, it came into my heart to say (and I know not, therefore, how I said it), Thou art the Son of the living God.' [48] But He, pronouncing me blessed, pointed out to me that it was the

Father who had revealed it to me; and from this time I learned that revelation is knowledge gained without instruction, and without apparition and dreams.

And this is indeed the case.

For in the soul [49] which has been placed in us by [50] God, there is all the truth; but it is covered and revealed by the hand of God, who works so far as each one through his knowledge deserves. [51]But the declaration of anything by means of apparitions and dreams from without is a proof, not that it comes from revelation, but from wrath.

Finally, then, it is written in the law, that God, being angry, said to Aaron and Miriam, [52] If a prophet arise from amongst you, I shall make myself known to him through visions and dreams, but not so as to my servant Moses; because I shall speak to him in an outward appearance, and not through dreams, just as one will speak to his own friend.'

You see how the statements of wrath are made through visions and dreams, but the statements to a friend are made face to face, in outward appearance, and not through riddles and visions and dreams, as to an enemy.

Chapter XIX - Opposition to Peter Unreasonable

"If, then, our Jesus appeared to you in a vision, made Himself known to you, and spoke to you, it was as one who is enraged with an adversary; and this is the reason why it was through visions and dreams, or through revelations that were from without, that He spoke to you.

But can any one be rendered fit for instruction through apparitions?

And if you will say, It is possible,' then I ask, Why did our teacher abide and discourse a whole year to those who were awake?'

And how are we to believe your word, when you tell us that He appeared to you?

And how did He appear to you, when you entertain opinions contrary to His teaching?

But if you were seen and taught by Him, and became His apostle for a single hour, proclaim His utterances, interpret His sayings, love His apostles, contend not with me who companied with Him.

For in direct opposition to me, who am a firm rock, the foundation of the Church, [53] you now stand.

If you were not opposed to me, you would not accuse me, and revile the truth proclaimed by me, in order that I may not be believed when I state what I myself have heard with my own ears from the Lord, as if I were evidently a person that was condemned and in bad repute. [54]But if you say that I am condemned, you bring an accusation against God, who revealed the Christ to me, and you inveigh against Him who pronounced me blessed on account of the revelation.

But if, indeed, you really wish to work in the cause of truth, learn first of all from us what we have learned from Him, and, becoming a disciple of the truth, become a fellow-worker with us."

Chapter XX - Another Subject for Discussion Proposed

When Simon heard this, he said:

"Far be it from me to become his or your disciple.

For I am not ignorant of what I ought to know; but the inquiries which I made as a learner were made that I may see if you can prove that actual sight is more distinct than apparition. [55]But you spoke according to your own pleasure; you did not prove.

And now, to-morrow I shall come to your opinions in regard to God, whom you affirmed to be the framer of the world; and in my discussion with you, I shall show that he is not the highest, nor good, and that your teacher made the same statements as I now do; and I shall prove that you have not understood him."

On saying this he went away, not wishing to listen to what might be said to the propositions which he had laid down.

Footnotes:

1. The text has: "against Peter."
2. [Comp. Recognitions, iii. 12, for a similar accusation made by Simon, at the beginning of the second day's discussion.--R.]
3. eidolon, idols.
4. ideon.
5. [These chapters are peculiar to the Homilies.--R.]
6. Matt. xix. 17.
7. The Gnostic distinction between the God who is just and the God who is good, is here insisted on.
8. Matt. xi. 27; [Luke x. 22. Comp. Recognitions, ii. 47.--R.]
9. One ms. reads, "saw."
10. Matt. x. 28.
11. Luke xviii. 6-8.
12. Matt. xi. 25; [Luke x. 21.]
13. [Comp. xviii. 1, etc.; also Recognitions, iii. 37, 38.--R.]
14. The mss. read energeian, "activity."
Clericus amended it into enargeian, which means vision or sight in plain open day with one's own eyes, in opposition to the other word optasia, vision in sleep, or ecstasy, or some similar unusual state.
15. Lit. "to a greater extent."
16. Matt. xxviii. 19, 20.
17. Matt. xviii. 10.
18. [Comp. xvi. 19.
The theosophical views here presented are peculiar to the Homilies, though some traces of them appear in the Recognitions.--R.]
19. Matt. v. 8.
20. The whole of this chapter is full of corruption; "twice" occurs in one ms.
Various attempts have been made to amend the passage.
21. An emendation.
22. The text is corrupt.
We have translated ep' apeirous treis. Some think "three" should be omitted.
The three infinites are in respect of height, depth, and breadth.
23. As punctuated in Dressel, this reads, "that the infinite is the heart."
24. The emendation of the transcriber of one of the mss.
25. This refers to the following mode of exhibiting the number:
*** where each side presents the number three.
26. The creation of the world in six days.
27. The seventh day on which God rested, the type of the rest of the future age.
See Epistle of Barnabas, c. xv.
28. The words in italics are inserted by conjecture.
"Sometimes incomprehensible, sometimes illimitable," occur only in onems.
29. We have adopted Wieseler's suggestions.
30. This word is justly suspected.
The passage is in other respects corrupt.
31. The word "slight" is not used in reference to the character of the faith, but to indicate that the act of faith is a small act compared with the results that flow from it.
32. We have adopted an emendation of a passage which is plainly corrupt.
33. Doctrines and deeds; lit., the things of your teacher.
34. The mss. have here energeia, "activity."
This has been amended into enargeia, "with plainness, with distinctness."
'Enargeia is used throughout in opposition to optasia, horama, and enupnion, and means the act of seeing and hearing by our own senses in plain daylight, when to doubt the fact observed is to doubt the senses; optasia is apparition or vision in ecstasy, or some extraordinary way but that of sleep; horama and enupnion are restricted to visions in sleep.
The last term implies this.
The first means simply "a thing seen."
35. [Comp. Recognitions, ii. 50, 51, 61-65.
The emphasis laid upon supernatural visions in the remainder of the Homily has been supposed to convey an insinuation against the revelations to the Apostle Paul.--R.]
36. Probably it should be apeklino instead of apekrino, "you turned aside to another."

37. The words in italics are inserted conjecturally, to fill up a lacuna in the best ms.
38. enargos, "with reference to things palpable to our senses."
39. We have translated a bold conjecture.
The text has, "The just not in like manner," without any verb, which Schwegler amended: "To the just this power does not belong in like manner."
40. Gen. xx. 3.
41. Gen. xli. 5, ff.
42. Gen. xli. 25.
43. Dan. ii. 31.
44. Lit., of the whole length of the age.
45. Dan. iii. 25.
46. We have amended this passage.
The text applies the words "natural or innate and pure" to the mind.
47. Matt. xvi. 13.
48. Matt. xvi. 16.
49. This word is not in the text.
Schliemann proposed the word "heart."
Possibly "breath" or "spirit" may be the lost word.
See above.
50. "By" should properly be "from."
51. Lit., "who produces according to the merit of each one knowing."
Cotelerius translated, "who, knowing the merit of each man, does to him according to it."
The idea seems to be, that God uncovers the truth hidden in the soul to each man according to his deserts.
52. Num. xii. 6, 7; Ex. xxxiii. 11.
53. Matt. xvi. 18.
54. We have adopted an emendation of Schwegler's.
The text reads, "in good repute."
[The word "condemned" is supposed to be borrowed from the account of the contest at Antioch in Gal. ii. 11, where it is applied to the Apostle Peter.
This passage has therefore been regarded as a covert attack upon the Apostle Paul.--R.]
55. This passage is corrupt in the text.
Dressel reads, "that activity is more distinct than apparition."
By activity would be meant, "acting while one is awake, and in full possession of his sense;" and thus the meaning would be nearly the same as in our translation.

Homily XVIII

Chapter I - Simon Maintains that the Framer of the World is Not the Highest God

At break of day, when Peter went forth to discourse, Simon anticipated him, and said:

"When I went away yesterday, I promised to you to return to-day, and in a discussion show that he who framed the world is not the highest God, but that the highest God is another who alone is good, and who has remained unknown up to this time.

At once, then, state to me whether you maintain that the framer of the world is the same as the lawgiver or not?

If, then, he is the lawgiver, he is just; but if he is just, he is not good.

But if he is not good, then it was another that Jesus proclaimed, when he said, [1] Do not call me good; for one is good, the Father who is in the heavens.'

Now a lawgiver cannot be both just and good, for these qualities do not harmonize." [2] And Peter said:

"First tell us what are the actions which in your opinion constitute a person good, and what are those which constitute him just, in order that thus we may address our words to the same mark."

And Simon said:

"Do you state first what in your opinion is goodness, and what justice."

Chapter II - Definition of Goodness and Justice

And Peter said:

"That I may not waste my time in contentious discussions, while I make the fair demand that you should give answers to my propositions, I shall myself answer those questions which I put, as is your wish.

I then affirm that the man who bestows [3] goods is good, just as I see the Framer of the world doing when He gives the sun to the good, and the rain to the just and unjust."

And Simon said:

"It is most unjust that he should give the same things to the just and the unjust."

And Peter said:

"Do you, then, in your turn state to us what course of conduct would constitute Him good."

And Simon said:

"It is you that must state this."

And Peter said:

"I will.

He who gives the same things to the good and just, and also to the evil and unjust, is not even just according to you; but you would with reason call Him just if He gave goods to the good and evils to the evil.

What course of conduct, then, would He adopt, if He does not adopt the plan of giving things temporal to the evil, if perchance they should be converted, and things eternal to the good, if at least they remain good?

And thus by giving to all, but by gratifying the more excellent, [4] His justice is good; and all the more long-suffering in this, that to sinners who repent He freely grants forgiveness of their sins, and to those who have acted well He assigns even eternal life.

But judging at last, and giving to each one what he deserves, He is just.

If, then, this is right, confess it; but if it appears to you not to be right, refute it."

The Epistles of Clement

Chapter III - God Both Good and Just

And Simon said:
"I said once for all, Every lawgiver, looking to justice, is just.'"
And Peter said:
"If it is the part of him who is good not to lay down a law, but of him who is just to lay down a law, in this way the Framer of the world is both good and just.

He is good, inasmuch as it is plain that He did not lay down a law in writing from the times of Adam to Moses; but inasmuch as He had a written law from Moses to the present times, [5] He is just also."

And Simon said: "Prove to me from the utterances of your teacher that it is within the power of the same man to be good and just; for to me it seems impossible that the lawgiver who is good should also be just."

And Peter said:
"I shall explain to you how goodness itself is just.

Our teacher Himself first said to the Pharisee who asked Him, [6] What shall I do to inherit eternal life?'

Do not call me good; for one is good, even the Father who is in the heavens;' and straightway He introduced these words, But if thou shalt wish to enter into life, keep the commandments.'

And when he said, What commandments?' He pointed him to those of the law.

Now He would not, if He were indicating some other good being, have referred him to the commandments of the Just One.

That indeed justice and goodness are different I allow, but you do not know that it is within the power of the same being to be good and just.

For He is good, in that He is now long-suffering with the penitent, and welcomes them; but just, when acting as judge He will give to every one according to his deserts."

Chapter IV - The Unrevealed God

And Simon said:
"How, then, if the framer of the world, who also fashioned Adam, was known, and known too by those who were just according to the law, and moreover by the just and unjust, and the whole world, does your teacher, coming after all these, say, [7] No one has known the Father but the Son, even as no one knoweth the Son but the Father, and those to whom the Son may wish to reveal Him?'

But he would not have made this statement, had he not proclaimed a Father who was still unrevealed, whom the law speaks of as the highest, and who has not given any utterance either good or bad (as Jeremiah testifies in the Lamentations [8]); who also, limiting the nations to seventy languages, according to the number of the sons of Israel who entered Egypt, and according to the boundaries of these nations, gave to his own Son, who is also called Lord, and who brought into order the heaven and the earth, the Hebrews as his portion, and defined him to be God of gods, that is, of the gods who received the other nations as their portions.

Laws, therefore, proceeded from all the so-called gods to their own divisions, which consist of the other nations.

In like manner also from the Son of the Lord of all came forth the law which is established among the Hebrews.

And this state of matters was determined on, that if any one should seek refuge in the law of any one, he should belong to the division of him whose law he undertook to obey.

No one knew the highest Father, who was unrevealed, just as they did not know that his Son was his Son.

Accordingly at this moment you yourself, in assigning the special attributes of the unrevealed Most High to the Son, do not know that he is the Son, being the Father of Jesus, who with you is called the Christ."

Chapter V - Peter Doubts Simon's Honesty

When Simon had made these statements, Peter said to him:
"Can you call to witness that these are your beliefs that being Himself,--I do not mean Him whom you speak of now as being unrevealed, but Him in whom you believe, though you do not confess Him? For you are talking nonsense when you define one thing in stead of another.
Wherefore, if you call Him to witness that you believe what you say, I shall answer you.
But if you continue discussing with me what you do not believe, you compel me to strike the empty air."
And Simon said:
"It is from some of your own disciples that I have heard that this is the truth." [9]And Peter said:
"Do not bear false witness?"
And Simon said:
"Do not rebuke me, most insolent man."
And Peter said:
"So long as you do not tell who it was who said so, I affirm that you are a liar."
And Simon said:
"Suppose that I myself have got up these doctrines, or that I heard them from some other, give me your answer to them.
For if they cannot be overturned, then I have learned that this is the truth."
And Peter said:
"If it is a human invention, I will not reply to it; but if you are held fast by the supposition that it is the truth, acknowledge to me that this is the case, and I can then myself say something in regard to the matter."
And Simon said:
"Once for all, then, these doctrines seem to me to be true.
Give me your reply, if you have aught to say against them."

Chapter VI - The Nature of Revelation

And Peter said:
"If this is the case, you are acting most impiously. For if it belongs to the Son, who arranged heaven and earth, to reveal His unrevealed Father to whomsoever He wishes, you are, as I said, acting most impiously in revealing Him to those to whom He has not revealed Him."
And Simon said:
"But he himself wishes me to reveal him."
And Peter said:
"You do not understand what I mean, Simon.
But listen and understand.
When it is said that the Son will reveal Him to whom He wishes, it is meant that such an one is to learn of Him not by instruction, but by revelation only.
For it is revelation when that which lies secretly veiled in all the hearts of men is revealed unveiled by His God's own will without any utterance.
And thus knowledge comes to one, not because he has been instructed, but because he has understood.
And yet the person who understands it cannot demonstrate it to another, since he did not himself receive it by instruction; nor can he reveal it, since he is not himself the Son, unless he maintains that he is himself the Son.
But you are not the standing Son.
For if you were the Son, assuredly you would know those who are worthy of such a revelation.
But you do not know them.
For if you knew them, you would do as they do who know."

Chapter VII - Simon Confesses His Ignorance

And Simon said:
"I confess I have not understood what you mean by the expression, You would do as they do who know.'"

And Peter said:
"If you have not understood it, then you cannot know the mind of every one; and if you are ignorant of this, then you do not know those who are worthy of the revelation.

You are not the Son, for [10] the Son knows.

Wherefore He reveals Him to whomsoever He wishes, because they are worthy."

And Simon said:
"Be not deceived.

I know those who are worthy, and I am not the Son.

And yet I have not understood what meaning you attach to the words, He reveals Him to whomsoever He wishes.'

But I said that I did not understand it, not because I did not know it, but because I knew that those who were present did not understand it, in order that you may state it more distinctly, so that they may perceive what are the reasons why we are carrying on this discussion."

And Peter said:
"I cannot state the matter more clearly:
explain what meaning you have attached to the words."

And Simon said:
"There is no necessity why I should state your opinions." And Peter said:
"You evidently, Simon, do not understand it, and yet you do not wish to confess, that you may not be detected in your ignorance, and thus be proved not to be the standing Son.

For you hint this, though you do not wish to state it plainly; and, indeed, I who am not a prophet, but a disciple of the true Prophet, know well from the hints you have given what your wishes are.

For you, though you do not understand even what is distinctly said, wish to call yourself son in opposition to us."

And Simon said:
"I will remove every pretext from you.

I confess I do not understand what can be the meaning of the statement, The Son reveals Him to whomsoever He wishes.'

State therefore what is its meaning more distinctly."

Chapter VIII - The Work of Revelation Belongs to the Son Alone

And Peter said:
"Since, at least in appearance, you have confessed that you do not understand it, reply to the question I put to you, and you will learn the meaning of the statement.

Tell me, do you maintain that the Son, whoever he be, is just, or that he is not just?"

And Simon said:
"I maintain that he is most just."

And Peter said: "Seeing He is just, why does He not make the revelation to all, but only to those to whom He wishes?"

And Simon said:
"Because, being just, he wishes to make the revelation only to the worthy."

And Peter said:
"Must He not therefore know the mind of each one, in order that He may make the revelation to the worthy?"

And Simon said:
"Of course he must."

And Peter said:
"With reason, therefore, has the work of giving the revelation been confined to Him alone, for He alone knows the mind of every one; and it has not been given to you, who are not able to understand even that which is stated by us."

Chapter IX - How Simon Bears His Exposure

When Peter said this, the multitudes applauded. [11]But Simon, being thus exposed, [12] blushed through shame, and rubbing his forehead, said:

"Well, then, do they declare that I, a magician, yea, even I who syllogize, am conquered by Peter? It is not so.

But if one should syllogize, though carried away and conquered, he still retains the truth that is in him.

For the weakness in the defender is not identical with the truth in the conquered man. [13]But I assure you that I have judged all those who are bystanders worthy to know the unrevealed Father.

Wherefore, because I publicly reveal him to them, you yourself, through envy, are angry with me who wish to confer a benefit on them."

Chapter X - Peter's Reply to Simon

And Peter said:

"Since you have thus spoken to please the multitudes who are present, I shall speak to them, not to please them, but to tell them the truth.

Tell me how you know all those who are present to be worthy, when not even one of them agreed with your exposition of the subject; for the giving of applause to me in opposition to you is not the act of those who agree with you, but of those who agree with me, to whom they gave the applause for having spoken the truth.

But since God, who is just, judges the mind of each one--a doctrine which you affirm to be true-- He would not have wished this to be given through the left hand to those on the right hand, exactly as the man who receives anything from a robber is himself guilty.

So that, on this account, He did not wish them to receive what is brought by you; but they are to receive the revelation through the Son, who has been set apart for this work.

For to whom is it reasonable that the Father should give a revelation, but to His only Son, because He knows Him to be worthy of such a revelation?

And so this is a matter which one cannot teach or be taught, but it must be revealed by the ineffable hand to him who is worthy to know it."

Chapter XI - Simon Professes to Utter His Real Sentiments

And Simon said:

It contributes much to victory, if the man who wars uses his own weapons; for what one loves he can in real earnest defend, and that which is defended with genuine earnestness has no ordinary power in it.

Wherefore in future I shall lay before you my real opinions.

I maintain that there is some unrevealed power, unknown to all, even to the Creator himself, as Jesus himself has also declared, though he did not know what he said.

For when one talks a great deal he sometimes hits the truth, not knowing what he is saying.

I am referring to the statement which he uttered, No one knows the Father.'"

And Peter said:

"Do not any longer profess that you know His doctrines."

And Simon said:

"I do not profess to believe his doctrines; but I am discussing points in which he was by accident right."

And Peter said:

"Not to give you any pretext for escape, I shall carry on the discussion with you in the way you wish.

At the same time, I call all to witness that you do not yet believe the statement which you just now made.

For I know your opinions.

And in order that you may not imagine that I am not speaking the truth, I shall expound your opinions, that you may know that you are discussing with one who is well acquainted with them.

The Epistles of Clement

Chapter XII - Simon's Opinions Expounded by Peter

"We, Simon, do not assert that from the great power, which is also called the dominant [14] power, two angels were sent forth, the one to create the world, the other to give the law; nor that each one when he came proclaimed himself, on account of what he had done, as the sole creator; nor that there is one who stands, will stand, and is opposed. [15] Learn how you disbelieve even in respect to this subject.

If you say that there is an unrevealed power, that power is full of ignorance.

For it did not foreknow the ingratitude of the angels who were sent by it."

And Simon became exceedingly angry with Peter for saying this, and interrupted his discourse, saying:

"What nonsense is this you speak, you daring and most impudent of men, revealing plainly before the multitudes the secret doctrines, so that they can be easily learned?"

And Peter said:

"Why do you grudge that the present audience should receive benefit?"

And Simon said:

"Do you then allow that such knowledge is a benefit?"

And Peter said:

"I allow it:

for the knowledge of a false doctrine is beneficial, inasmuch as you do not fall into it because of ignorance."

And Simon said:

"You are evidently not able to reply to the propositions I laid before you.

I maintain that even your teacher affirms that there is some Father unrevealed."

Chapter XIII - Peter's Explanation of the Passage

And Peter said:

"I shall reply to that which you wish me to speak of,--namely, the passage, No one knows the Father but the Son, nor does any one know the Son but the Father, and they to whom the Son may wish to reveal Him.'

First, then, I am astonished that, while this statement admits of countless interpretations, you should have chosen the very dangerous position of maintaining that the statement is made in reference to the ignorance of the Creator (Demiurge), and all who are under him.

For, first, the statement can apply to all the Jews who think that David is the father of Christ, and that Christ himself is his son, and do not know that He is the Son of God.

Wherefore it is appropriately said, No one knows the Father,' since, instead of God, they affirmed David to be his father; and the additional remark, that no one knows even the Son, is quite correct, since they did not know that He was the Son.

The statement also, to whomsoever the Son may wish to reveal Him,' is also correct; for He being the Son from the beginning, was alone appointed to give the revelation to those to whom He wishes to give it.

And thus the first man (protoplast) Adam must have heard of Him; and Enoch, who pleased God, must have known Him; and Noah, the righteous one, must have become acquainted with Him; and Abraam His friend must have understood Him; and Isaac must have perceived Him; and Jacob, who wrestled with Him, must have believed in Him; and the revelation must have been given to all among the people who were worthy.

Chapter XIV - Simon Refuted

"But if, as you say, it will be possible to know Him, because He is now revealed to all through Jesus, [16] are you not stating what is most unjust, when you say that these men did not know Him, who were the seven pillars of the world, and who were able to please the most just God, and that so many now from all nations who were impious know Him in every respect?

Were not those who were superior to every one not deemed worthy to know Him? [17] And how can that be good which is not just? unless you wish to give the name of good,' not to him who does good to those who act justly, but to him who loves the unjust, even though they do not believe, and reveals to them the secrets which he would not reveal to the just.

But such conduct is befitting neither in one who is good nor just, but in one who has come to hate the pious.

Are not you, Simon, the standing one, who have the boldness to make these statements which never have been so made before?"

Chapter XV - Matthew XI. 25 Discussed

And Simon, being vexed at this, said:
"Blame your own teacher, who said, I thank Thee, Lord of heaven and earth, that what was concealed from the wise, Thou hast revealed to suckling babes.'" [18] And Peter said:
"This is not the way in which the statement was made; but I shall speak of it as if it had been made in the way that has seemed good to you.

Our Lord, even if He had made this statement, What was concealed from the wise, the Father revealed to babes,' could not even thus be thought to point out another God and Father in addition to Him who created the world.

For it is possible that the concealed things of which He spoke may be those of the Creator (Demiurge) himself; because Isaiah [19] says, I will open my mouth in parables, and I will belch forth things concealed from the foundation of the world.'

Do you allow, then, that the prophet was not ignorant of the things concealed, which Jesus says were concealed from the wise, but revealed to babes? And how was the Creator (Demiurge) ignorant of them, if his prophet Isaiah was not ignorant of them?

But our Jesus did not in reality say what was concealed,' but He said what seems a harsher statement; for He said, Thou hast concealed these things from the wise, and [20] hast revealed them to sucking babes.'

Now the word Thou hast concealed' implies that they had once been known to them; for the key of the kingdom of heaven, that is, the knowledge of the secrets, lay with them.

Chapter XVI - These Things Hidden Justly from the Wise

"And do not say He acted impiously towards the wise in hiding these things from them.
Far be such a supposition from us.

For He did not act impiously; but since they hid the knowledge of the kingdom, [21] and neither themselves entered nor allowed those who wished to enter, on this account, and justly, inasmuch as they hid the ways from those who wished, were in like manner the secrets hidden from them, in order that they themselves might experience what they had done to others, and with what measure they had measured, an equal measure might be meted out to them. [22] For to him who is worthy to know, is due that which he does not know; but from him who is not worthy, even should he seem to have any thing it is taken away, [23] even if he be wise in other matters; and it is given to the worthy, even should they be babes as far as the times of their discipleship are concerned.

Chapter XVII - The Way to the Kingdom Not Concealed from the Israelites

"But if one shall say nothing was concealed from the sons of Israel, because it is written, [24] Nothing escaped thy notice, O Israel (for do not say, O Jacob, The way is hid from me),' he ought to understand that the things that belong to the kingdom had been hid from them, but that the way that leads to the kingdom, that is, the mode of life, had not been hid from them.

Wherefore it is that He says, For say not that the way has been hid from me.'

But by the way is meant the mode of life; for Moses says, [25] Behold, I have set before thy face the way of life and the way of death.'

And the Teacher spoke in harmony with this: [26] Enter ye through the strait and narrow way, through which ye shall enter into life.'

And somewhere else, when one asked Him, [27] What shall I do to inherit eternal life?' He pointed out to him the commandments of the law.

Chapter XVIII - Isaiah I. 3 Explained

"From the circumstance that Isaiah said, in the person of God, [28] But Israel hath not known me, and the people hath not understood me,' it is not to be inferred that Isaiah indicated another God besides Him who is known; [29] but he meant that the known God was in another sense unknown, because the people sinned, being ignorant of the just character of the known God, and imagined that they would not be punished by the good God.

Wherefore, after he said, But Israel hath not known me, and the people hath not understood me,' he adds, Alas! a sinful nation, a people laden with sins.'

For, not being afraid, in consequence of their ignorance of His justice, as I said, they became laden with sins, supposing that He was merely good, and would not therefore punish them for their sins.

Chapter XIX - Misconception of God in the Old Testament

"And some sinned thus, on account of imagining that there would be no judgment [30] because of His goodness.

But others took an opposite course.

For, supposing the expressions of the Scriptures which are against God, and are unjust and false, to be true, they did not know His real divinity and power.

Therefore, in the belief that He was ignorant and rejoiced in murder, and let off the wicked in consequence of the gifts of sacrifices; yea, moreover, that He deceived and spake falsely, and did every thing that is unjust, they themselves did things like to what their God did, and thus sinning, asserted that they were acting piously.

Wherefore it was impossible for them to change to the better, and when warned they took no heed.

For they were not afraid, since they became like their God through such actions.

Chapter XX - Some Parts of the Old Testament Written to Try Us

"But one might with good reason maintain that it was with reference to those who thought Him to be such that the statement was made, No one knoweth the Father but the Son, as no one knoweth even the Son, but the Father.'

And reasonably.

For if they had known, they would not have sinned, by trusting to the books written against God, really for the purpose of trying.

But somewhere also He says, wishing to exhibit the cause of their error more distinctly to them, On this account ye do err, not knowing the true things of the Scriptures, on which account ye are ignorant also of the power of God.' [31] Wherefore every man who wishes to be saved must become, as the Teacher said, a judge of the books written to try us.

For thus He spake:

Become experienced bankers.'

Now the need of bankers arises from the circumstance that the spurious is mixed up with the genuine."

Chapter XXI - Simon's Astonishment at Peter's Treatment of the Scriptures

When Peter said this, Simon pretended to be utterly astonished at what was said in regard to the Scriptures; and as if in great agitation, he said:

"Far be it from me, and those who love me, to listen to your discourses.

And, indeed, as long as I did not know that you held these opinions in regard to the Scriptures, I endured you, and discussed with you; but now I retire.

Indeed, I ought at the first to have withdrawn, because I heard you say, I, for my part, believe no one who says anything against Him who created the world, neither angels, nor prophets, nor Scriptures, nor priests, nor teachers, nor any one else, even though one should work signs and miracles, even though he should lighten brilliantly in the air, or should make a revelation through visions or through dreams.'

Who, then, can succeed in changing your mind, whether well or ill, so as that you should hold opinions different from what you have determined on, seeing that you abide so persistently and immoveably in your own decision?"

Chapter XXII - Peter Worships One God

When Simon said this, and was going to depart, Peter said:
"Listen to this one other remark, and then go where you like."
Whereupon Simon turned back and remained, and Peter said:
"I know how you were then astonished when you heard me say, Whosoever says anything whatever against God who created the world, I do not believe him.'
But listen now to something additional, and greater than this.
If God who created the world has in reality such a character as the Scriptures assign Him, and if somehow or other He is incomparably wicked, more wicked [32] than either the Scriptures were able to represent Him, or any other can even conceive Him to be, nevertheless [33] I shall not give up worshipping Him alone, and doing His will.
For I wish you to know and to be convinced, that he who has not affection for his own Creator, can never have it towards another.
And if he has it towards another, he has it contrary to nature, and he is ignorant that he has this passion for the unjust from the evil one.
Nor will he be able to retain even it stedfastly.
And, indeed, if there is another above the Creator (Demiurge), he will welcome me, since he is good, all the more that I love my own Father; and he will not welcome you, as he knows that you have abandoned your own natural Creator:
for I do not call Him Father, influenced by a greater hope, and not caring for what is reasonable.
Thus, even if you find one who is superior to Him, he knows that you will one day abandon him; and the more so that he has not been your father, since you have abandoned Him who was really your Father.

Chapter XXIII - Simon Retires

"But you will say, He knows that there is no other above him, and on this account he cannot be abandoned.'
Thanks, then, to there being no other; but He knows that the state of your mind is one inclined to ingratitude.
But if, knowing you to be ungrateful, He welcomes you, and knowing me to be grateful, He does not receive me, He is inconsiderate, according to your own assertion, and does not act reasonably.
And thus, Simon, you are not aware that you are the servant of wickedness."
And Simon answered:
"Whence, then, has evil arisen? tell us."
And Peter said:
"Since to-day you were the first to go out, and you declared that you would not in future listen to me as being a blasphemer, come to-morrow, if indeed you wish to learn, and I shall explain the matter to you, and I will permit you to ask me any questions you like, without any dispute."
And Simon said:
"I shall do as shall seem good to me."
And saying this, he went away.
Now, none of those who entered along with him went out along with him; but, falling at Peter's feet, they begged that they might be pardoned for having been carried away with Simon, and on repenting, to be welcomed. But Peter, admitting those persons who repented, and the rest of the multitudes, laid his hands upon them, praying, and healing those who were sick amongst them; and thus dismissing them, he urged them to return early about dawn.
And saying this, and going in with his intimate friends, he made the usual preparations for immediate repose, for it was now evening.

The Epistles of Clement
Footnotes:
1. Matt. xix. 17.
2. [Comp. xvii. 5, and Recognitions, iii. 37, 38.--R.]
3. There is a lacuna in one of the mss. here, which is supplied in various ways.
We have inserted the word "goods."
4. This translation of Cotelerius is doubtful.
More correctly it would be, "by gratifying different people," which does not make sense. Wieseler proposes, "by gratifying in different ways."
5. The text seems corrupt here.
Literally it is, "from Moses to the present times, as has been written, He is just also."
6. Luke xviii. 18, ff.; Matt. xix. 16, ff.
7. Matt. xi. 27; [Luke x. 22.
Comp. Homily XVII. 4; Recognitions, ii. 47, 48.
The discussion here is much fuller.--R.].
8. Lam. iii. 38.
9. The words in italics are inserted to fill up a lacuna which occurs here in the Vaticanms.
10. The Greek has "but."
11. [The remainder of the Homily is without a close parallel in the Recognitions.--R.]
12. Lit., "caught in the act."
13. This passage is deemed corrupt by commentators.
We have made no change in the reading of the mss., except that of nenikemenen into nenikemenos, and perhaps even this is unnecessary.
The last sentence means:
"A man may overcome the weakness of his adversary:
but he does not therefore strip him of the truth, which he possesses even when he is conquered."
The Latin translation of Cotelerius, with some emendations from later editors, yields this:
"But they say that I, a magician, am not merely conquered by Peter, but reduced to straits by his reasonings.
But not even though one be reduced to straits by reasonings, has he the truth which is in him conquered.
For the weakness of the defender is not the truth of the conqueror."
14. Kuria.
15. The text is corrupt.
Various emendations have been proposed, none of which are satisfactory.
Uhlhorn proposes, "That there is a standing one, one who will stand.
You who are opposed, learn how you disbelieve, and that this subject which you say is the power unrevealed is full of ignorance."
P. 328, note 1.
16. The text is corrupt.
We have placed dia to after eidenai.
17. Another reading is:
"Were not those deemed better worthy than any one else to know Him?"
18. Matt. xi. 25; [Luke x. 21; comp. Recognitions, iv. 5].
19. The passage does not occur in Isaiah, but in Ps. lxxviii. 2. The words are quoted not from the LXX., but from the Gospel of Matthew (xiii. 35), where in somemss. they are attributed to Isaiah.
See Uhlhorn, p. 119.
20. The words in italics are omitted in the mss.; but the context leaves no doubt that they were once in the text.
21. Luke xi. 52.
22. Matt. vii. 2; [Luke vi. 38].
23. Luke viii. 18.
24. Isa. xl. 26, 27.
25. Deut. xxx. 15.
26. Matt. vii. 13, 14.
27. Luke xviii. 18, ff.; Matt. xix. 16, ff.
28. Isa. i. 3.
29. Cotelerius'ms. inserts "the Creator" (Demiurge).
30. We have adopted the Latin translation here, as giving the meaning which was intended by the writer:
but the Greek will scarcely admit of such a translation.
Probably the text is corrupt, or something is omitted.
The literal translation is, "in consequence of the unjudging supposition on account of the

goodness."
31. Mark xii. 24.
32. "Incomparably wicked, more wicked than;" literally, "incomparably wicked as."
33. The Greek has homoios, "in like manner."
We have translated homos.

Homily XIX

Chapter I - Simon Undertakes to Prove that the Creator of the World is Not Blameless

The next day Peter came forth earlier than usual; and seeing Simon with many others waiting for him, he saluted the multitude, and began to discourse.

But no sooner did he begin than Simon interrupted him, and said:

"Pass by these long introductions of yours, and answer directly the questions I put to you.

Since I perceive that you [1] (as I know from what I heard at the beginning, that you have no other purpose, than by every contrivance to show that the Creator himself is alone the blameless God),--since, as I said, I perceive that you have such a decided desire to maintain this, that you venture to declare to be false some portions of the Scriptures that clearly speak against him, for this reason I have determined to-day to prove that it is impossible that he, being the Creator of all, should be blameless.

But thus proof I can now begin, if you reply to the questions which I put to you.

Chapter II - The Existence of the Devil Affirmed

"Do you maintain that there is any prince of evil or not? [2] For if you say that there is not, I can prove to you from many statements, and those too of your teacher, that there is; but if you honestly allow that the evil one exists, then I shall speak in accordance with this belief."

And Peter said:

"It is impossible for me to deny the assertion of my Teacher.

Wherefore I allow that the evil one exists, because my Teacher, who spoke the truth in all things, has frequently asserted that he exists.

For instance, then, he acknowledges that he conversed with Him, and tempted Him for forty days. [3]

And I know that He has said somewhere else, If Satan casts out Satan, he is divided against himself:

how then is his kingdom to stand?' [4] And He pointed out that He saw the evil one like lightning falling down from heaven. [5] And elsewhere He said, He who sowed the bad seed is the devil.' [6] And again, Give no pretext to the evil one.' [7] Moreover, in giving advice, He said, Let your yea be yea, and your nay nay; for what is more than these is of the evil one.' [8] Also, in the prayer which He delivered to us, we have it said, Deliver us from the evil one.' [9] And in another place, He promised that He would say to those who are impious, Go ye into outer darkness, which the Father prepared for the devil and his angels.' [10] And not to prolong this statement further, I know that my Teacher often said that there is an evil one.

Wherefore I also agree in thinking that he exists.

If, then, in future you have anything to say in accordance with this belief, say it, as you promised."

Chapter III - Peter Refuses to Discuss Certain Questions in Regard to the Devil

And Simon said:
"Since, then, you have honestly confessed, on the testimony of the Scriptures, that the evil one exists, state to us how he has come into existence, if indeed he has come into existence, and by whom, and why." [11]And Peter said:
"Pardon me, Simon, if I do not dare to affirm what has not been written.
But if you say that it has been written, prove it.
But if, since it has not been written, you cannot prove it, why should we run risk in stating our opinions in regard to what has not been written?
For if we discourse too daringly in regard to God, it is either because we do not believe that we shall be judged, or that we shall be judged only in respect to that which we do, but not also in regard to what we believe and speak." [12]But Simon, understanding that Peter referred to his own madness, said: "Permit me to run the risk; but do not you make what you assert to be blasphemy a pretext for retiring.
For I perceive that you wish to withdraw, in order that you may escape refutation before the masses, sometimes as if you were afraid to listen to blasphemies, and at other times by maintaining that, as nothing has been written as to how, and by whom, and why the evil one came into existence, we ought not to dare to assert more than the Scripture.
Wherefore also as a pious man you affirm this only, that he exists.
But by these contrivances you deceive yourself, not knowing that, if it is blasphemy to inquire accurately regarding the evil one, the blame rests with me, the accuser, and not with you, the defender of God.
And if the subject inquired into is not in Scripture, [13] and on this account you do not wish to inquire into it, there are some satisfactory methods which can prove to you what is sought not less effectively than the Scriptures.
For instance, must it not be the case that the evil one, who you assert exists, is either originated or unoriginated?" [14]

Chapter IV - Suppositions in Regard to the Devil's Origin

And Peter said:
"It must be so."
And Simon:
"Therefore, if he is originated, he has been made by that very God who made all things, being either born as an animal, or sent forth substantially, and resulting from an external mixture of elements.
For either [15] the matter, being living or lifeless, from which he was made was outside of Him, [16] or he came into being through God Himself, or through his own self, or he resulted from things non-existent, or he is a mere relative thing, or he always existed.
Having thus, as I think, clearly, pointed out all the possible ways by which we may find him, in going along some one of these we must find him.
We must therefore go along each one of these in search of his origin; and when we find him who is his author, we must perceive that he is to blame.
Or how does the matter seem to you?"

Chapter V - God Not Deserving of Blame in Permitting the Existence of the Devil

And Peter said:
"It is my opinion that, even if it be evident that he was made by God, the Creator who made him should not be blamed; for it might perchance be found that the service he performs [17] was an absolute necessity.

But if, on the other hand, it should be proved that he was not created, inasmuch as he existed for ever, not even is the Creator to be blamed in this respect, since He is better than all others, even if He has not been able to put an end to a being who had no beginning, because his nature did not admit of it; or if, being able, He does not make away with him, deeming it unjust to put an end to that which did not receive a beginning, and pardoning that which was by nature wicked, because he could not have become anything else, even if he were to wish to do so. [18]But if, wishing to do good, He is not able, even in this case He is good in that He has the will, though He has not the power; and while He has not the power, He is yet the most powerful of all, in that the power is not left to another.

But if there is some other that is able, and yet does not accomplish it, it must be allowed that, in so far as, being able, he does not accomplish it, he is wicked in not putting an end to him, as if he took pleasure in the deeds done by him.

But if not even he is able, then he is better who, though unable, is yet not unwilling to benefit us according to his ability."

Chapter VI - Peter Accuses Simon of Being Worse Than the Devil

And Simon said:
"When you have discussed all the subjects which I have laid before you, I shall show you the cause of evil.

Then I shall also reply to what you have now said, and prove that that God whom you affirm to be blameless is blameable."

And Peter said:
"Since I perceive from what you say at the commencement that you are striving after nothing else than to subject God, as being the author of evil, to blame, I have resolved to go along with you all the ways you like, and to prove that God is entirely free from blame."

And Simon said:
"You say this as loving God, whom you suppose you know; but you are not right."

And Peter said:
"But you, as being wicked, and hating God whom you have not known, utter blasphemous words."

And Simon said: "Remember that you have likened me to the author of evil."

And Peter said:
"I confess it, I was wrong in comparing you to the evil one; for I was compelled to do so, because I have not found one who is your equal, or worse than you.

For this reason I likened you to the evil one; for you happen to be much more wicked than the author of evil. For no one can prove that the evil one spoke against God; but all of us who are present see you speaking daringly against Him."

And Simon said:
"He who seeks the truth ought not to gratify any one in any respect contrary to what is really true. For why does he make the inquiry at all?

Why, I ask? for I am not also able, laying aside the accurate investigation of things, to spend all my time in the praise of that God whom I do not know." [19]

Chapter VII - Peter Suspects Simon of Not Believing Even in a God

And Peter said:

"You are not so blessed as to praise Him, nor indeed can you do such a good deed as this; for then you would be full of Him.

For thus said our Teacher, who always spoke the truth:

Out of the abundance of the heart the mouth speaketh.' [20]Whence you, abounding in evil purposes, through ignorance speak against the only good God.

And not yet suffering what you deserve to suffer for the words which you have dared to utter,[21] you either imagine that there will be no judgment, or perchance you think that there is not even a God.

Whence, not comprehending such long-suffering as His, you are moving on to still greater madness."

And Simon said:

"Do not imagine that you will frighten me into not investigating the truth of your examples.

For I am so eager for the truth, that for its sake I will not shrink from undergoing danger.

If, then, you have anything to say in regard to the propositions made by me at the commencement, say it now."

Chapter VIII - Peter Undertakes to Discuss the Devil's Origin

And Peter said:

"Since you compel us, after we have made accurate investigations into the contrivances of God, to venture to state them, and that, too, to men who are not able to comprehend thoroughly the contrivances of their fellow-men, for the sake at least of those who are present, I, instead of remaining silent--a course which would be most pious--shall discuss the subjects of which you wish me to speak. I agree with you in believing that there is a prince of evil, of whose origin the Scripture has ventured to say nothing either true or false. But let us follow out the inquiry in many ways, as to how he has come into existence, if it is the fact that he has come into existence; and of the opinions which present themselves, let us select that which is most reverential, since in the case of probable opinions, that one is assumed with confidence which is based on the principle that we ought to attribute to God that which is more reverential; and all the more so, if, when all other suppositions are removed, there still remains one which is adequate and involves less danger. [22]But I promise you, before I proceed with the investigation, that every method in the investigation can show that God alone is blameless.

Chapter IX - Theories in Regard to the Origin of the Devil

"But, as you said, if the evil one is created either he has been begotten as an animal, or he has been sent forth substantially by Him, [23] or he has been compounded externally, or his will has arisen through composition; or it happened that he came into existence from things non-existent, without composition and the will of God; or he has been made by God from that which in no manner and nowhere exists; or the matter, being lifeless or living, from which he has arisen was outside of God; or he fashioned himself, or he was made by God, or he is a relative thing, or he ever existed:

for we cannot say that he does not exist, since we have agreed in thinking that he does exist." And Simon said:

"Well have you distinguished all the methods of accounting for his existence in a summary manner.

Now it is my part to examine these various ideas, and to show that the Creator is blameable.

But it is your business to prove, as you promised, that he is free from all blame.

But I wonder if you will be able.

For, first, if the devil has been begotten from God as an animal, the vice which is his is accordingly the same as that of him who sends him forth."

And Peter said:

"Not at all.

For we see many men who are good the fathers of wicked children, and others who are wicked the fathers of good children, and others again who are wicked producing both good and wicked [24] children, and others who are good having both wicked and good children.

For instance, the first man who was created produced the unrighteous Cain and the righteous Abel."

To this Simon said: "You are acting foolishly, in using human examples when discoursing about God."

And Peter said:

"Speak you, then, to us about God without using human examples, and yet so that what you say can be understood; but you are not able to do so.

Chapter X - The Absolute God Entirely Incomprehensible by Man

"For instance, then, what did you say in the beginning?

If the wicked one has been begotten of God, being of the same substance as He, then God is wicked.

But when I showed you, from the example which you yourself adduced, that wicked beings come from good, and good from wicked, you did not admit the argument, for you said that the example was a human one.

Wherefore I now do not admit that the term being begotten' [25] can be used with reference to God; for it is characteristic of man, and not of God, to beget.

Not only so; but God cannot be good or evil, just or unjust.

Nor indeed can He have intelligence, or life, or any of the other attributes which can exist in man; for all these are peculiar to man.

And if we must not, in our investigations in regard to God, give Him the good attributes which belong to man, it is not possible for us to have any thought or make any statement in regard to God; but all we can do is to investigate One point alone,--namely, what is His will which He has Himself allowed us to apprehend, in order that, being judged, we might be without excuse in regard to those laws which we have not observed, though we knew them."

Chapter XI - The Application of the Attributes of Man to God

And Simon, hearing this, said:

"You will not force me through shame to remain silent in regard to His substance, and to inquire into His will alone.

For it is possible both to think and to speak of His substance.

I mean from the good attributes that belong to man.

For instance, life and death are attributes of man; but death is not an attribute of God, but life, and eternal life.

Furthermore, men may be both evil and good; but God can be only incomparably good.

And, not to prolong the subject too much, the better attributes of man are eternal attributes of God."

And Peter said:

"Tell me, Simon, is it an attribute of man to beget evil and good, and to do evil and good?"

And Simon said:

"It is."

And Peter said:

"Since you made this assertion, we must assign the better attributes of man to God; and so, while men beget evil and good, God can beget good only; and while men do evil and good, God rejoices only in doing good.

Thus, with regard to God, we must either not predicate any of the attributes of man and be silent, or it is reasonable that we should assign the best of the good attributes to Him.

And thus He alone is the cause of all good things."

Chapter XII - God Produced the Wicked One, But Not Evil

And Simon said:
"If, then, God is the cause only of what is good, what else can we think than that some other principle begot the evil one; [26] or is evil unbegotten?"

And Peter said:
"No other power begot the wicked one, nor is evil unbegotten, as I shall show in the conclusion; for now my object is to prove, as I promised in the commencement, that God is blameless in every[27] respect.

We have granted, then, that God possesses in an incomparable way the better attributes that belong to men.

Wherefore also it is possible for Him to have been the producer of the four substances,--heat, I mean, and cold, moist and dry.

These, as being at first simple and unmixed, were naturally indifferent in their desire; [28] but being produced by God, and mixed externally, they would naturally become a living being, possessing the free choice to destroy those who are evil.

And thus, since all things have been begotten from Him, the wicked one is from no other source.

Nor has he derived his evil from the God who has created all things (with whom it is impossible that evil should exist), because the substances were produced by Him in a state of indifference, and carefully separated from each other; and when they were externally blended through his art, there arose through volition the desire for the destruction of the evil ones.

But the good cannot be destroyed by the evil that arose, even though it should wish to do so:

for it exercises its power only [29] against those who sin.

Ignorant, then, of the character of each, [30] he makes his attempt against him, and convicting him, he punishes him."

And Simon said:
"God being able to mingle the elements, and to make His mixtures so as to produce any dispositions that He may wish, why did He not make the composition of each such as that it would prefer what is good?"

Chapter XIII - God the Maker of the Devil

And Peter said:
"Now indeed our object is to show how and by whom the evil one came into being, since he did come into being; but we shall show if he came into being blamelessly, when we have finished the subject now in hand.

Then I shall show how and on account of what he came into being, and I shall fully convince you that his Creator is blameless. [31] We said, then, that the four substances were produced by God.

And thus, through the volition of Him who mingled them, arose, as He wished, the choice of evils.

For if it had arisen contrary to His determination, or from some other substance or cause, then God would not have had firmness of will:

for perchance, even though He should not wish it, leaders of evil might continually arise, who would war against His wishes.

But it is impossible that this should be the case.

For no living being, and especially one capable of giving guidance, can arise from accident:

for everything that is produced must be produced by some one."

Chapter XIV - Is Matter Eternal?

And Simon said:
"But what if matter, being coeval with Him, and possessing equal power, produces as His foe leaders who hinder His wishes?"

And Peter said:
"If matter is eternal, then it is the foe of no one:

for that which exists for ever is impassible, and what is impassible is blessed; but what is blessed cannot be receptive of hatred, since, on account of its eternal creation, [32] it does not fear that it will be deprived of anything.

But how does not matter rather love the Creator, when [33] it evidently sends forth its fruits to nourish all who are made by Him?

And how does it not fear Him as superior, as trembling through earthquakes it confesses, and as, though its billows ran high, yet, when the Teacher was sailing on it and commanded a calm, it immediately obeyed and became still? [34] What! did not the demons go out through fear and respect for Him, and others of them desired to enter into swine; but they first entreated Him before going, plainly because they had no power to enter even into swine without His permission?" [35]

Chapter XV - Sin the Cause of Evil

And Simon said:
"But what if, being lifeless, it possesses a nature capable of producing what is evil and what is good?"

And Peter said: "According to this statement, it is neither good nor evil, because it does not act by free choice, being lifeless and insensible.

Wherefore it is possible to perceive distinctly in this matter, how, being lifeless, it produces as if it were living; [36] and being insensible, it yet plainly fashions artistic shapes both in animals and plants."

And Simon said:
"What! if God Himself gave it life, is not He, then, the cause of the evils which it produces?"

And Peter said: "If God gave it life according to His own will, then it is His Spirit that produces it, and no longer is it anything hostile to God, or of equal power with Him; or it is impossible that everything made by Him is made according as He wishes.

But you will say, He Himself is the cause of evil, since He Himself produces the evils through it. What sort, then, are the evils of which you speak?

Poisonous serpents and deadly plants, or demons, or any other of those things that can disturb men?--which things would not have been injurious had not man sinned, for which reason [37] death came in.

For if man were sinless, the poison of serpents would have no effect, nor the activities of injurious plants, nor would there be the disturbances of demons, nor would man naturally have any other suffering; but losing his immortality on account of his sin, he has become, as I said, capable of every suffering.

But if you say, Why, then, was the nature of man made at the beginning capable of death? I tell you, because of free-will; for if we were not capable of death, we could not, as being immortal, be punished on account of our voluntary sin. [38] And thus, on account of our freedom from suffering, righteousness would be still more weakened if we were wicked by choice; for those who should have evil purposes could not be punished, on account of their being incapable of suffering. [39]

Chapter XVI - Why the Wicked One is Entrusted with Power

And Simon said to this:
"I have one thing more to say in regard to the wicked one.

Assuredly, since God made him out of nothing, he is in this respect wicked, [40] especially since he was able to make him good, by giving him at his creation a nature in no way capable of selecting wickedness."

And Peter said:
"The statement that He created him out of nothing, with a power of choice, is like the statement we have made above, that, having made such a constitution as can rejoice in evils, He Himself appears to be the cause of what took place.

But since there is one explanation of both statements, we shall show afterwards why it was that He made him rejoice in the destruction of the wicked."

And Simon said:
"If he made the angels also voluntary agents, and the wicked one departed from a state of righteousness, why has he been honoured with a post of command?

Is it not plain that he who thus honoured him takes pleasure in the wicked, in that he has thus honoured him?" [41] And Peter said:

"If God set him by law, when he rebelled, to rule over those who were like him, ordering him to inflict punishment on those who sin, He is not unjust.

But if it be the case that He has honoured him even after his revolt, He who honoured him saw beforehand his usefulness; for the honour is temporary, and it is right that the wicked should be ruled by the wicked one, and that sinners should be punished by him."

Chapter XVII - The Devil Has Not Equal Power with God

And Simon said:
"If, then, he exists for ever, is not the fact of the sole government of God thus destroyed, since there is another power, namely, that concerned with matter, which rules along with Him?"
And Peter said:
"If they are different in their substances, they are different also in their powers, and the superior rules the inferior. But if they are of the same substance, then they are equal in power, and they are in like manner good or bad.
But it is plain that they are not equal in power; for the Creator put matter into that shape of a world into which He willed to put it.
Is it then at all possible to maintain that it always existed, being a substance; and is not matter, as it were, the storehouse of God?
For it is not possible to maintain that there was a time [42] when God possessed nothing, but He always was the only ruler of it.
Wherefore also He is an eternal sole ruler; [43] and on this account it would justly be said to belong to Him who exists, and rules, and is eternal." [44] And Simon said:
"What then?
Did the wicked one make himself?
And was God good in such a way, that, knowing he would be the cause of evil, he yet did not destroy him at his origination, when he could have been destroyed, as not yet being perfectly made?
For if he came into being suddenly and complete, then on that account [45] he is at war with the Creator, as having come suddenly into being, possessed of equal power with him."

Chapter XVIII - Is the Devil a Relation?

And Peter said:
"What you state is impossible; for if he came into existence by degrees, He could have cut him off as a foe by His own free choice.
And knowing beforehand that he was coming into existence, He would not have allowed him as a good, had He not known that by reason of him what was useful was being brought into existence. [46]
And he could not have come into existence suddenly, complete, of his own power.
For he who did not exist could not fashion himself; and he neither could become complete out of nothing, nor could any one justly say that he had substance, [47] so as always to be equal in power if he were begotten."
And Simon said:
"Is he then a mere relation, and in this way wicked? [48] --being injurious, as water is injurious to fire, but good for the seasonably thirsty land; as iron is good for the cultivation of the land, but bad for murders; and lust is not evil in respect of marriage, but bad in respect of adultery; as murder is an evil, but good for the murderer so far as his purpose is concerned; and cheating is an evil, but pleasant to the man who cheats; and other things of a like character are good and bad in like manner.
In this way, neither is evil, nor good; for the one produces the other.
For does not that which seems to be done injuriously rejoice the doer, but punish the sufferer?
And though it seems unjust that a man should, out of self-love, gratify himself by every means in his power, to whom, on the other hand, does it not seem unjust that a man should suffer severe punishments at the hand of a just judge for having loved himself?"

The Epistles of Clement

Chapter XIX - Some Actions Really Wicked

And Peter said:
"A man ought to punish himself through self-restraint, [49] when his lust wishes to hurry on to the injury of another, knowing that [50] the wicked one can destroy the wicked, for he has received power over them from the beginning.

And not yet is this an evil to those who have done evil; but that their souls should remain punished after the destruction, you are right in thinking to be really harsh, though the man who has been fore-ordained for evil should say that it is right. [51] Wherefore, as I said, we ought to avoid doing injury[52] to another for the sake of a short lived pleasure, that we may not involve ourselves in eternal punishment for the sake of a little pleasure."

And Simon said:
"Is it the case, then, that there is nothing either bad or good by nature, but the difference arises through law and custom?

For is it not [53] the habit of the Persians to marry their own mothers, sisters and daughters, while marriage with other women is prohibited [54] as most barbarous?

Wherefore, if it is not settled what things are evil, it is not possible for all to look forward to the judgment of God."

And Peter said:
"This cannot hold; for it is plain to all that cohabitation with mothers is abominable, even though the Persians, who are a mere fraction of the whole, should under the effects of a bad custom fail to see the iniquity of their abominable conduct.

Thus also the Britons publicly cohabit in the sight of all, and are not ashamed; and some men eat the flesh of others, and feel no disgust; and others eat the flesh of dogs; and others practice other unmentionable deeds.

Thus, then we ought not to form our judgments with a perception which through habit has been perverted from its natural action.

For to be murdered is an evil, even if all were to deny it; for no one wishes to suffer it himself, and in the case of theft [55] no one rejoices at his own punishment.

If, then, no one [56] were at all ever to confess that these are sins, it is right even then to look forward of necessity to a judgment in regard to sins."

When Peter said this, Simon answered:
"Does this, then, seem to you to be the truth in regard to the wicked one? Tell me."

Chapter XX - Pain and Death the Result of Sin

And Peter said:
"We remember that our Lord and Teacher, commanding us, said, Keep the mysteries for me and the sons of my house.'

Wherefore also He explained to His disciples privately the mysteries of the kingdom of heaven.
[57] But to you who do battle with us, and examine into nothing else but our statements, whether they be true or false, it would be impious to state the hidden truths.

But that none of the bystanders may imagine that I am contriving excuses, [58] because I am unable to reply to the assertions made by you, I shall answer you by first putting the question, If there had been a state of painlessness, what is the meaning of the statement, The evil one was?'"

And Simon said:
"The words have no meaning."

And Peter:
"Is then evil the same as pain and death?"

And Simon:
"It seems so."

And Peter said:
"Evil, then, does not exist always, yea, it cannot even exist at all substantially; for pain and death belong to the class of accidents, neither of which can co-exist with abiding strength.

For what is pain but the interruption of harmony?

And what is death but the separation of soul from body?

There is therefore no pain when there is harmony.

For death does not even at all belong to those things which substantially exist:

for death is nothing, as I said, but the separation of soul from body; and when this takes place, the body, which is by nature incapable of sensation, is dissolved; but the soul, being capable of sensation, remains in life and exists substantially. Hence, when there is harmony there is no pain, no death, no, not even deadly plants nor poisonous reptiles, nor anything of such a nature that its end is death.

And hence, where immortality reigns, all things will appear to have been made with reason.

And this will be the case when, on account of righteousness, man becomes immortal through the prevalence of the peaceful reign of Christ, when his composition will be so well arranged as not to give rise [59] to sharp impulses; and his knowledge, moreover, will be unerring, so as that he shall not mistake [60] evil for good; and he will suffer no pain, so that he will not be mortal." [61]

Chapter XXI - The Uses of Lust, Anger, Grief

And Simon said: [62]"You were right in saying this; but in the present world does not man seem to you to be capable of every kind of affection,--as, for instance, of lust, anger, grief, and the like?" And Peter said:

"Yes, these belong to the things that are accidental, not to those that always exist, and it will be found that they now occur with advantage to the soul.

For lust has, by the will of Him who created all things well, been made to arise within the living being, that, led by it to intercourse, he may increase humanity, from a selection of which a multitude of superior beings arise who are fit for eternal life.

But if it were not for lust, no one would trouble himself with intercourse with his wife; but now, for the sake of pleasure, and, as it were, gratifying himself, man carries out His will.

Now, if a man uses lust for lawful marriage, he does not act impiously; but if he rushes to adultery, he acts impiously, and he is punished because he makes a bad use of a good ordinance.

And in the same way, anger has been made by God to be lighted up naturally within us, in order that we may be induced by it to ward off injuries.

Yet if any one indulges it without restraint, he acts unjustly; but if he uses it within due bounds, he does what is right.

Moreover, we are capable of grief, that we may be moved with sympathy at the death of relatives, of a wife, or children, or brothers, or parents, or friends, or some others, since, if we were not capable of sympathy, we should be inhuman.

In like manner, all the other affections will be found to be adapted for us, if at least the reason for their existence [63] be considered."

Chapter XXII - Sins of Ignorance

And Simon:

"Why is it, then, that some die prematurely, and periodical diseases arise; and that there are, moreover, attacks of demons, and of madness, and all other kinds of afflictions which can greatly punish?" And Peter said:

"Because men, following their own pleasure in all things, cohabit without observing the proper times; and thus the deposition of seed, taking place unseasonably, naturally produces a multitude of evils.

For they ought to reflect, that as a season has been fixed suitable for planting and sowing, [64] so days have been appointed as appropriate for cohabitation, which are carefully to be observed.

Accordingly some one well instructed in the doctrines taught by Moses, finding fault with the people for their sins, called them sons of the new moons and the sabbaths. [65]Yet in the beginning of the world men lived long, and had no diseases.

But when through carelessness they neglected the observation of the proper times, then the sons in succession cohabiting through ignorance at times when [66] they ought not, place their children under innumerable afflictions.

Whence our Teacher, when we inquired of Him [67] in regard to the man who was blind from his birth, and recovered his sight, if this man sinned, or his parents, that he should be born blind, answered, Neither did he sin at all, nor his parents, but that the power of God might be made manifest through him in healing the sins of ignorance.' [68]And, in truth, such afflictions arise because of ignorance; as, for instance, by not knowing when one ought to cohabit with his wife, as if she be pure from her discharge.

Now the afflictions which you mentioned before are the result of ignorance, and not, assuredly, of any wickedness that has been perpetrated.

Moreover, give me the man who sins not, and I will show you the man who suffers not; and you will find that he not only does not suffer himself, but that he is able [69] to heal others.

For instance, Moses, on account of his piety, continued free from suffering all his life, and by his prayers he healed the Egyptians when they suffered on account of their sins."

Chapter XXIII - The Inequalities of Lot in Human Life

And Simon said:
"Let me grant that this is the case:
does not the inequality of lot amongst men seem to you most unjust?
For one is in penury, another is rich; one is sick, another is in good health:
and there are innumerable differences of a like character in human life." [70] And Peter said:
"Do you not perceive, Simon, that you are again shooting your observations beyond the mark?
For while we were discussing evil, you have made a digression, and introduced the question of the anomalies that appear in this world.
But I shall speak even to this point.
The world is an instrument artistically contrived, that for the male who is to exist eternally, the female may bear eternal righteous sons.
Now they could not have been rendered perfectly pious here, had there been no needy ones for them to help. In like manner there are the sick, that they may have objects for their care.
And the other afflictions admit of a like explanation."
And Simon said:
"Are not those in humble circumstances unfortunate? for they are subjected to distress, that others may be made righteous." And Peter said:
"If their humiliation were eternal, their misfortune would be very great.
But the humiliations and exaltations of men take place according to lot; and he who is not pleased with his lot can appeal, [71] and by trying his case according to law, he can exchange his mode of life for another."
And Simon said:
"What do you mean by this lot and this appeal?"
And Peter said:
"You are now demanding the exposition of another topic; but if you permit me, we can show you how, being born again, and changing your origin, and living according to law, you will obtain eternal salvation."

Chapter XXIV - Simon Rebuked by Faustus

And Simon hearing this, said:
"Do not imagine that, when I, while questioning you, agreed with you in each topic, I went to the next, as being fully assured of the truth of the previous; but I appeared to yield to your ignorance, that you might go on to the next topic, in order that, becoming acquainted with the whole range of your ignorance, I might condemn you, not through mere conjecture, but from full knowledge. [72] Allow me now to retire for three days, and I shall come back and show that you know nothing."
When Simon said this, and was on the point of going out, my father said:
"Listen to me, Simon, for a moment, and then go wherever you like.
I remember that in the beginning, before the discussion, you accused me of being prejudiced, though as yet you had no experience of me.
But now, having heard you discuss in turn, and judging that Peter has the advantage, and now assigning to him the merit of speaking the truth, do I appear to you to judge correctly, and with knowledge; [73] or is it not so?
For if you should say that I have judged correctly, but do not agree, then you are plainly prejudiced, inasmuch as you do not wish to agree, after confessing your defeat.
But if I was not correct in maintaining that Peter has the advantage in the discussion, do you convince us how we have not judged correctly, or you will cease [74] to discuss with him before all, since you will always be defeated and agree, and in consequence your own soul will suffer pain, condemned as you will be, and in disgrace, through your own conscience, even if you do not feel shame before all the listeners as the greatest torture; for we have seen you conquered, in fact, and we have heard your own lips confess it.

Finally, therefore, I am of opinion that you will not return to the discussion, as you promised; but that you may seem not to have been defeated, [75] you have promised, when going away, that you will return."

Chapter XXV - Simon Retires

Sophonias Asks Peter to State His Real Opinions in Regard to Evil.

And Simon hearing this, gnashed his teeth for rage, and went away in silence.

But Peter (for a considerable portion of the day still remained) laid his hands on the large multitude to heal them; and having dismissed them, went into the house with his more intimate friends, and sat down.

And one of his attendants, of the name of Sophonias, said:

"Blessed is God, O Peter, who selected you and instructed [76] you for the comfort of the good.

For, in truth, you discussed with Simon with dignity and great patience.

But we beg of you to discourse to us of evil; for we expect that you will state to us your own genuine belief in regard to it,--not, however at the present moment, but to-morrow, if it seems good to you:

for we spare you, because of the fatigue you feel on account of your discussion."

And Peter said:

"I wish you to know, that he who does anything with pleasure, finds rest in the very toils themselves; but he who does not do what he wishes, is rendered exceedingly weary by the very rest he takes.

Wherefore you confer on me a great rest when you make me discourse on topics which please me."

Content, then, with his disposition, and sparing him on account of his fatigue, we requested him to put the discussion off till the night, when it was his custom to discourse to his genuine friends.

And partaking of salt, we turned to sleep.

Footnotes:

1. This passage is corrupt.
Wieseler has proposed to amend it by bold transposition of the clauses.
We make one slight alteration in the text.
2. [Compare with this discussion respecting the origin of the evil one, Recognitions, ix. 55, 56; x. 3, etc.
In Recognitions, iii. 15-23, the existence of evil is discussed.--R.]
3. Mark i. 13.
4. Matt. xii. 26.
5. Luke x. 18.
6. Matt. xiii. 39.
7. This passage is not found in the New Testament.
It resembles Eph. iv. 27.
8. Matt. v. 37; Jas. v. 12.
9. Matt. vi. 13.
10. Matt. xxv. 41.
11. [Comp. Homily XX. 8, 9.--R.]
12. This passage is probably corrupt.
We have adopted the readings of Cotelerius--e, e, instead of ei and me.
13. Lit., "unwritten."
14. The words genetos and agenetos are difficult to translate.
The first means one who has somehow or other come into being; the second, one who has never come into being; but has always been.
The mss. confound genetos with gennetos, begotten, and agenetos with agennetos, unbegotten.
15. We have changed ei into e.
16. By "Him" is understood God, though it may mean the devil.
17. Lit., "his usefulness was most necessary of all."
18. This sentence is obscure in the original.
We have, with Wieseler, read epei, omitting arche.
Instead of supplying me, we have turned sungnonai into the participle.
19. We have adopted the pointing of Wieseler.
20. Matt. xii. 34.
21. We have altered the punctuation.

Editors connect this clause with the previous sentence, and change e of the ms. into ei.

22. This sentence is regarded as corrupt by Wieseler.

We have retained the reading of the Paris ms., ho, and understand lambanetai after it.

De would naturally be inserted after taute, but it is not necessary.

Kathartheison is translated in the Latin purgatis, which may mean the same as in our translation if we take it in the sense of "washed away;" but kathairetheison would be a better reading.

The translation of Cotelerius gives, "Since this is reasonably assumed with firmness,--namely, that it is right to give to God," etc.

23. The text here is evidently corrupt in many places.

If the reading "by him" is to be retained, we must suppose, with Wieseler, that "by God" is omitted in the previous clause.

Probably it should be, "by himself."

24. "And bad" is not in the mss., but is required by the context.

25. The text is corrupt here.

Literally it is, "I do not admit that God had been begotten."

26. "Evil" is not in the mss.

It is inserted from the next sentence.

27. "Every" is inserted by a conjecture of Schwegler's.

28. Lit., "naturally had their desire towards neither."

29. The mss. have "by law."

We have changed nomo into monon.

30. The devil is plainly meant by the "he."

31. This passage is evidently corrupt.

But it is not easy to amend it.

32. Probably "eternity" should be read, instead of "eternal creation."

33. At this word thems. of Cotelerius breaks off; and we have the rest only in the Ottobonian ms., first edited by Dressel.

34. Matt. xxvii. 51, viii. 24-26.

35. Matt. viii. 31.

36. Possibly the right reading is empsuchous, "it produces living beings."

37. Or, "on whose account."

38. [Comp. xi. 8; Recognitions, iii. 21, 26, etc.--R.]

39. The text is corrupt.

40. The ms. reads:

"In this respect he who made him is wicked, who gave existence to what was non-existent."

41. The Greek is either ungrammatical or corrupt, but the sense is evident.

42. This passage is supposed by most to be defective, and various words have been suggested to supply the lacuna.

43. Or, "monarch."

But only two letters of the word are in the ms.; the rest is filled in by conjecture.

44. Supplied by conjecture.

45. Three words are struck out of the text of the ms. by all editors, as being a repetition.

46. The editors punctuate differently, thus:

"And knowing beforehand that he was becoming not good, He would not have allowed him, unless He knew that he would be useful to Himself."

We suppose the reference in the text to be to Gen. i. 31.

47. Or, "self-subsistence."

We have supposed a transposition of the words in the text.

The text is without doubt corrupt.

48. We have adopted an emendation of Lagarde's.

49. Dressel translates viriliter, "manfully."

50. This word is supplied by conjecture.

51. This passage is hopelessly corrupt.

We have changed dikaios into dikaiois, the verb, and ton prodiorismenon into tou prodiorismenou.

52. We have adopted Wieseler's emendation of adikon into adikein.

53. This is a conjectural filling up of a blank.

54. This is partly conjecture, to fill up a blank.

55. The text is likely corrupt.

56. Uhlhorn changed oun henos into oudenos.

We have changed kai triten into kai tote ten.

Various emendations have been proposed.

57. Mark iv. 34.

[More probably, Matt. xiii. 11.--R.]
58. We have adopted an emendation of Wieseler's.
59. The words in italics supplied by conjecture.
60. The words in italics supplied by conjecture.
61. This last sentence has two blanks, which are filled up by conjectures: and one emendation has been adopted.
62. [With chaps. 21, 22, compare Homily XX. 4.--R.]
63. We have adopted an emendation of Lagarde's.
64. Eccles. iii. 2.
65. Lit., "new moons that are according to the moon."
Gal. iv. 10.
66. "At times when" is supplied by conjecture.
67. We have followed an emendation of Wieseler's.
68. John ix. 2, 3.
[This clear instance of citation from the Gospel of John is found in that portion of the text recovered by Dressel.
It is of importance, since writers of the Tuebingen school previously denied that this author uses the fourth Gospel.--R.]
69. We have adopted an obvious emendation of Wieseler's.
70. [Comp. Recognitions, iii. 40, 41.--R.]
71. An emendation of Wieseler's.
72. The whole of this sentence is corrupt.
We have adopted the conjectures of Wieseler, though they are not entirely satisfactory.
73. Possibly something is corrupt here.
The words may be translated:
"Is it not plain that I know how to judge correctly?"
74. The ms. has, "do not cease."
We have omitted me, and changed pause into pausei.
We have inserted the me after e, changed into ei before aideisthai.
75. We have adopted an emendation of Wieseler's.
76. An emendation of Wieseler's.

Homily XX

Chapter I - Peter is Willing to Gratify Sophonias

In the night-time Peter rose up and wakened us, and then sat down in his usual way, and said: "Ask me questions about anything you like." [1] And Sophonias was the first to begin to speak to him:

"Will you explain to us who are eager to learn what is the real truth in regard to evil?"

And Peter said:

"I have already explained it in the course of my discussion with Simon; but because I stated the truth in regard to it in combination with other topics, it was not altogether clearly put; for many topics that seem to be of equal weight with the truth afford some kind of knowledge of the truth to the masses.

So that, if now I state what I formerly stated to Simon along with many topics, do not imagine that you are not [2] honoured with honour equal to his."

And Sophonias said:

"You are right; for if you now separate it for us from many of the topics that were then discussed, you will make the truth more evident."

Chapter II - The Two Ages

And Peter said:

"Listen, therefore, to the truth of the harmony in regard to the evil one.

God appointed two kingdoms, and established two ages, determining that the present world should be given to the evil one, because it is small, and passes quickly away; but He promised to preserve for the good one the age to come, as it will be great and eternal.

Man, therefore, He created with free-will, and possessing the capability of inclining to whatever actions he wishes.

And his body consists of three parts, deriving its origin from the female; for it has lust, anger, and grief, and what is consequent on these.

But the spirit not being uniform, [3] but consisting of three parts, derives its origin from the male; and it is capable of reasoning, knowledge, and fear, and what is consequent on these.

And each of these triads has one root, so that man is a compound of two mixtures, the female and the male.

Wherefore also two ways have been laid before him--those of obedience and disobedience to law; and two kingdoms, have been established,--the one called [4] the kingdom of heaven, and the other the kingdom of those who are now kings upon earth.

Also two kings have been appointed, of whom the one is selected to rule by law over the present and transitory world, and his composition is such that he rejoices in the destruction of the wicked.

But the other and good [5] one, who is the King of the age to come, loves the whole nature of man; but not being able to have boldness in the present world, he counsels what is advantageous, like one who tries to conceal who he really is. [6]

Chapter III - The Work of the Good One and of the Evil One

"But of these two, the one [7] acts violently towards the other by the command of God.

Moreover, each man has power to obey whichever of them he pleases for the doing of good or evil.

But if any one chooses to do what is good, he becomes the possession of the future good king; but if any one should do evil, he becomes the servant of the present evil one, who, having received power over him by just judgment on account of his sins, and wishing to use it [8] before the coming age, rejoices in punishing him in the present life, and thus by gratifying, as it were, his own private passion, he accomplishes the will of God.

But the other, being made to rejoice in power over the righteous, when he finds a righteous man, is exceedingly glad, and saves him with eternal life; and he also, as if gratifying himself, traces the gratification which he feels on account of these to God. Now it is within the power of every unrighteous man to repent and be saved; and every righteous man may have to undergo punishment for sins committed at the end of his career.

Moreover, these two leaders are the swift hands of God, eager to anticipate Him so as to accomplish His will.

But that this is so, has been said even by the law in the person of God:

I will kill, and I will make alive; I will strike, and I will heal.' [9]For, in truth, He kills and makes alive.

He kills through the left hand, that is, through the evil one, who has been so composed as to rejoice in afflicting the impious.

And he saves and benefits through the right hand, that is, through the good one, who has been made to rejoice in the good deeds and salvation of the righteous. Now these have not their substances outside of God:

for there is no other primal source.

Nor, indeed, have they been sent forth as animals from God, for they were of the same mind with Him; nor are they accidental, [10] arising spontaneously in opposition to His will, since thus the greatest exercise of His power would have been destroyed.

But from God have been sent forth the four first elements--heat and cold, moist and dry.

In consequence of this, He is the father of every substance, but not of the disposition [11] which may arise from the combination of the elements; for when these were combined from without, disposition was begotten in them as a child. The wicked one, then, having served God blamelessly to the end of the present world, can become good by a change in his composition, [12] since he assuredly is not of one uniform substance whose sole bent is towards sin.

For not even more does he do evil, although he is evil, since he has received power to afflict lawfully."

Chapter IV - Men Sin Through Ignorance

When Peter said this, Micah, who was himself one of his followers, asked:
"What, then, is the reason why men sin?"
And Peter said:
"It is because they are ignorant that they will without doubt be punished for their evil deeds when judgment takes place. [13]For this reason they, having lust, as I elsewhere said, for the continuance of life, gratify it in any accidental way, it may be by the vitiation of boys, [14] or by some other flattering sin.

For in consequence of their ignorance, as I said before, they are urged on through fearlessness to satisfy their lust in an unlawful manner.

Wherefore God is not evil, who has rightly placed lust within man, that there may be a continuance of life, but they are most impious who have used the good of lust badly.

The same considerations apply to anger also, that if one uses it righteously, as is within his power, he is pious; but going beyond measure, and taking judgment to himself, [15] he is impious."

Chapter V - Sophonias Maintains that God Cannot Produce What is Unlike Himself

And Sophonias said again:
"Your great patience, my lord Peter, gives us boldness to ask you many questions for the sake of accuracy. Wherefore we make our inquiries with confidence in every direction.

I remember, then, that Simon said yesterday, in his discussion with you, that the evil one, if he was born of God, possesses in consequence the same substance as He does who sent him forth, and he ought to have been good, and not wicked.

But you answered that this was not always the case, since many wicked sons are born of good parents, as from Adam two unlike [16] sons were begotten, one of whom was bad and the other good.

And when Simon found fault with you for having used human examples, you answered that in this way we ought not to admit that God begets at all; for this also is a human example.

The Epistles of Clement

And I, Sophonias, admit that God begets; but I do not allow that He begets what is bad, even though the good among men beget bad children.

And do not imagine [17] that I am without reason attributing to God some of the qualities that distinguish men, and refusing to attribute others, when I grant that He begets, but do not allow that He begets what is unlike Himself.

For men, as you might expect, beget sons who are unlike them in their dispositions for the following reason.

Being composed of four parts, they change their bodies variously, according to the various changes of the year; and thus, the appropriate change either of increase or decrease taking place in the human body, each season destroys the harmonious combination.

Now, when the combinations do not always remain exactly in the same position, the seeds, having sometimes one combination, sometimes another, are sent off; and these are followed, according to the combination belonging to the season, by dispositions either good or bad.

But in the case of God we cannot suppose any such thing; for, being unchangeable and always existing, whenever He wishes to send forth, there is an absolute necessity that what is sent forth should be in all respects in the same position as that which has begotten, I mean in regard to substance and disposition.

But if any one should wish to maintain that He is changeable, I do not know how it is possible for him to maintain that He is immortal."

Chapter VI - God's Power of Changing Himself

When Peter heard this, he thought for a little, and said:

"I do not think that any one can converse about evil without doing the will of the evil one.

Therefore knowing this, I do not know what I shall do, whether I shall be silent or speak.

For if I be silent, I should incur the laughter of the multitude, because, professing to proclaim the truth, I am ignorant of the explanation of vice.

But if I should state my opinion, I am afraid lest it be not at all pleasing to God that we should seek after evil, for only seeking after good is pleasing to Him.

However, in my reply to the statements of Sophonias, I shall make my ideas more plain.

I then agree with him in thinking that we ought not to attribute to God all the qualities of men.

For instance, men not having bodies that are convertible are not converted; but they have a nature that admits of alteration by the lapse of time through the seasons of the year.

But this is not the case with God; for through His inborn [18] Spirit He becomes, by a power which cannot be described, whatever body He likes.

And one can the more easily believe this, as the air, which has received such a nature from Him, is converted into dew by the incorporeal mind permeating it, and being thickened becomes water, and water being compacted becomes stone and earth, and stones through collision light up fire.

According to such [19] a change and conversion, air becomes first water, and ends in being fire through conversions, and the moist is converted into its natural opposite.

Why?

Did not God convert the rod of Moses into an animal, making it a serpent, [20] which He reconverted into a rod? And by means of this very converted rod he converted the water of the Nile [21] into blood, which again he reconverted into water.

Yea, even man, who is dust, He changed by the inbreathing of His breath [22] into flesh, and changed him back again into dust. [23] And was not Moses, [24] who himself was flesh, converted into the grandest light, so that the sons of Israel could not look him in the face?

Much more, then, is God completely able to convert Himself into whatsoever He wishes.

Chapter VII - The Objection Answered, that One Cannot Change Himself

"But perhaps some one of you thinks that one may become something under the influence of one, and another under the influence of another, but no one can change himself into whatever he wishes, and that it is the characteristic of one who grows old, and who must die according to his nature, [25] to change, but we ought not to entertain such thoughts of immortal beings.

For were not angels, who are free from old age, and of a fiery substance, [26] changed into flesh,-- those, for instance, who received the hospitality of Abraham, [27] whose feet men washed, as if they were the feet of men of like substance? [28] Yea, moreover, with Jacob, [29] who was a man, there wrestled an angel, converted into flesh that he might be able to come to close quarters with him.

And, in like manner, after he had wrestled by his own will, he was converted into his own natural form; and now, when he was changed into fire, he did not burn up the broad sinew of Jacob, but he inflamed it, and made him lame.

Now, that which cannot become anything else, whatever it may wish, is mortal, inasmuch as it is subject to its own nature; but he who can become whatever he wishes, whenever he wishes, is immortal, returning to a new condition, inasmuch as he has control over his own nature.

Wherefore much more does the power of God change the substance of the body into whatever He wishes and whenever He wishes; and by the change that takes place [30] He sends forth what, on the one hand, is of similar substance, but, on the other, is not of equal power.

Whatever, then, he who sends forth turns into a different substance, that he can again turn back into his own; [31] but he who is sent forth, arising in consequence of the change which proceeds from him, and being his child, cannot become anything else without the will of him who sent him forth, unless he wills it."

Chapter VIII - The Origin of the Good One Different from that of the Evil One

When Peter said this, Micah, [32] who was himself also one of the companions that attended on him, said:

"I also should like to learn from you if the good one has been produced in the same way that the evil one came into being.

But if they came into being in a similar manner, then they are brothers in my opinion."

And Peter said:

"They have not come into being in a similar way:

for no doubt you remember what I said in the beginning, that the substance of the body of the wicked one, being fourfold in origin, was carefully selected and sent forth by God; but when it was combined externally, according to the will of Him who sent it forth, there arose, in consequence of the combination, the disposition which rejoices in evils: [33] so that you may see that the substance, fourfold in origin, which was sent forth by Him, and which also always exists, is the child of God; but that the accidentally arising disposition which rejoices in evils has supervened when the substance [34] was combined externally by him. And thus disposition has not been begotten by God, nor by any one else, nor indeed has it been sent forth by Him, nor has it come forth spontaneously, [35] nor did it always exist, like the substance before the combination; but it has come on as an accident by external combination, according to the will of God.

And we have often said that it must be so.

But the good one having been begotten from the most beautiful change of God, and not having arisen accidentally through an external combination, is really His Son.

Yet, since these doctrines are unwritten, and are confirmed to us only by conjecture, let us by no means deem it as absolutely certain that this is the true state of the case.

For if we act otherwise, our mind will cease from investigating the truth, in the belief that it has already fully comprehended it. Remember these things, therefore; for I must not state such things to all, but only to those who are found after trial most trustworthy.

Nor ought we rashly to maintain such assertions towards each other, nor ought ye to dare to speak as if you were accurately acquainted with the discovery of secret truths, but you ought simply to reflect over them in silence; for in stating, perchance, that a matter is so, [36] he who says it will err, and he will suffer punishment for having dared to speak even to himself what has been honoured with silence."

Chapter IX - Why the Wicked One is Appointed Over the Wicked by the Righteous God

When Peter said this, Lazarus, who also was one of his followers, said:

"Explain to us the harmony, how it can be reasonable that the wicked one should be appointed by the righteous God to be the punisher of the impious, and yet should himself afterwards be sent into lower darkness along with his angels and with sinners;

for I remember that the Teacher Himself said this." [37] And Peter said:

"I indeed allow that the evil one does no evil, inasmuch as he is accomplishing the law given to him.

And although he has an evil disposition, yet through fear of God he does nothing unjustly; but, accusing the teachers of truth so as to entrap the unwary, he is himself named the accuser (the devil).

But the statement of our unerring Teacher, that he and his angels, along with the deluded sinners, shall go into lower darkness, admits of the following explanation.

The evil one, having obtained the lot [38] of rejoicing in darkness according to his composition, delights to go down to the darkness of Tartarus along with angels who are his fellow-slaves; for darkness is dear to fire.

But the souls of men, being drops of pure light, are absorbed by the substance fire, which is of a different class; and not possessing a nature capable of dying, they are punished according to their deserts. But if he who is the leader of men [39] into vice is not sent into darkness, as not rejoicing in it, then his composition, which rejoices in evils, cannot be changed by another combination into the disposition for good.

And thus he will be adjudged to be with the good, [40] all the more because, having obtained a composition which rejoices in evils, through fear of God he has done nothing contrary to the decrees of the law of God.

And did not the Scripture by a mysterious hint [41] point out by the statement [42] that the rod of the high priest Aaron became a serpent, and was again converted into a rod, that a change in the composition of the wicked one would afterwards take place?"

Chapter X - Why Some Believe, and Others Do Not

And after Lazarus, Joseph, who also was one of his followers, said: "You have spoken all things rightly.

Teach me also this, as I am eager to know it, why, when you give the same discourses to all, some believe and others disbelieve?"

And Peter said:

"It is because my discourses are not charms, so that every one that hears them must without hesitation believe them.

The fact that some believe, and others do not, points out to the intelligent the freedom of the will."

And when he said this, we all blessed him.

Chapter XI - Arrival of Appion and Annubion

And as we were going to take our meals, [43] some one ran in and said:

"Appion Pleistonices has just come with Annubion from Antioch, and he is lodging with Simon."

And my father hearing this, and rejoicing, said to Peter:

"If you permit me, I shall go to salute Appion and Annubion, who have been my friends from childhood.

For perchance I shall persuade Annubion to discuss genesis with Clement." And Peter said:

"I permit you, and I praise you for fulfilling the duties of a friend.

But now consider how in the providence of God there come together from all quarters considerations which contribute to your full assurance, rendering the harmony complete.

But I say this because the arrival of Annubion happens advantageously for you."

And my father:

"In truth, I see that this is the case."

And saying this, he went to Simon.

Chapter XII - Faustus Appears to His Friends with the Face of Simon

Now all of us who were with Peter asked each other questions the whole of the night, and continued awake, because of the pleasure and joy we derived from what was said.

But when at length the dawn began to break, Peter, looking at me and my brothers, said:

"I am puzzled to think what your father has been about."

And just as he was saying this, our father came in and caught Peter talking to us of him; and seeing him displeased, he accosted him, and rendered an apology for having slept outside.

But we were amazed when we looked at him:

for we saw the form of Simon, but heard the voice of our father Faustus. And when we were fleeing from him, and abhorring him, our father was astonished at receiving such harsh and hostile treatment from us.

But Peter alone saw his natural shape, and said to us:

"Why do you in horror turn away from your own father?"

But we and our mother said: "It is Simon that we see before us, with the voice of our father."

And Peter said:

"You recognise only his voice, which is unaffected by magic; but as my eyes also are unaffected by magic, I can see his form as it really is, that he is not Simon, but your father Faustus."

Then, looking to my father, he said:

"It is not your own true form that is seen by them, but that of Simon, our deadliest foe, and a most impious man." [44]

Chapter XIII - The Flight of Simon

While Peter was thus talking, there entered one of those who had gone before to Antioch, and who, coming back from Antioch, said to Peter: "I wish you to know, my lord, that Simon, by doing many miracles publicly in Antioch, and calling you a magician and a juggler and a murderer, [45] has worked them up to such hatred against you, that every man is eager to taste your very flesh if you should sojourn there. [46] Wherefore we who went before, along with our brethren who were in pretence attached by you to Simon, seeing the city raging wildly against you, met secretly and considered what we ought to do. And assuredly, while we were in great perplexity, Cornelius the centurion arrived, who had been sent by the emperor to the governor of the province.

He was the person whom our Lord cured when he was possessed of a demon in Caesarea.

This man we sent for secretly; and informing him of the cause of our despondency, we begged his help.

He promised most readily that he would alarm Simon, and make him take to flight, if we should assist him in his effort.

And when we all promised that we should readily do everything, he said, I shall spread abroad the news [47] through many friends that I have secretly come to apprehend him; and I shall pretend that I am in search of him, because the emperor, having put to death many magicians, and having received information in regard to him, has sent me to search him out, that he may punish him as he punished the magicians before him; while those of your party who are with him must report to him, as if they had heard it from a secret source, that I have been sent to apprehend him. And perchance when he hears it from them, he will be alarmed and take to flight.'

When, therefore, we had intended to do something else, nevertheless the affair turned out in the following way.

For when he heard the news from many strangers who gratified him greatly by secretly informing him, and also from our brethren who pretended to be attached to him, and took it as the opinion of his own followers, he resolved on retiring.

And hastening away from Antioch, he has come here with Athenodorus, as we have heard.

Wherefore we advise you not yet to enter that city, until we ascertain whether they can forget in his absence the accusations which he brought against you."

Chapter XIV - The Change in the Form of Faustus Caused by Simon

When the person who had gone before gave this report, Peter looked to my father, and said:

"You hear, Faustus; the change in your form has been caused by Simon the magician, as is now evident.

For, thinking that a servant [48] of the emperor was seeking him to punish him, he became afraid and fled, putting you into his own shape, that if you were put to death, your children might have sorrow."

When my father heard this, he wept and lamented, and said:

"You have conjectured rightly, Peter.

For Annubion, who is my dear friend, [49] hinted his design to me; but I did not believe him, miserable man that I am, [50] since I deserved to suffer."

Chapter XV - The Repentance of Faustus

When my father said this, after no long time Annubion came [51] to us to announce to us the flight of Simon, and how that very night he had hurried to Judaea.

And he found our father wailing, and with lamentations saying:

"Alas, alas! unhappy man!

I did not believe when I was told that he was a magician.

Miserable man that I am!

I have been recognised for one day by my wife and children, and have speedily gone back to my previous sad condition when I was still ignorant."

And my mother lamenting, plucked her hair; and we groaned in distress on account of the transformation of our father, and could not comprehend what in the world it could be.

But Annubion stood speechless, seeing and hearing these things; while Peter said to us, his children, in the presence of all:

"Believe me, this is Faustus your father.

Wherefore I urge you to attend to him as being your father.

For God will vouchsafe some occasion for his putting off the shape of Simon, and exhibiting again distinctly that of your father."

And saying this, and looking to my father, he said:

"I permitted you to salute Appion and Annubion, since you asserted that they were your friends from childhood, but I did not permit you to associate with the magician Simon."

Chapter XVI - Why Simon Gave to Faustus His Own Shape

And my father said:

"I have sinned; I confess it."

And Annubion said:

"I also along with him beg you to forgive the noble and good old man who has been deceived: for the unfortunate man has been the sport of that notorious fellow.

But I shall tell you how it took place. [52] The good old man came to salute us.

But at that very hour we who were there happened to be listening to Simon, who wished to run away that night, for he had heard that some people had come to Laodicea in search of him by the command of the emperor.

But as Faustus was entering, he turned [53] his own rage on him, and thus addressed us: Make him, when he comes, share your meals; and I will prepare an ointment, so that, when he has supped, he may take some of it, and anoint his face with it, and then he will appear to all to have my shape.

But I will anoint you with the juice [54] of some plant, and then you will not be deceived by his new [55] shape; but to all others Faustus will seem to be Simon.'

Chapter XVII - Annubion's Services to Faustus

"And while he stated this beforehand, I said, What, then, is the advantage you now expect to get from such a contrivance?'

And Simon said, First, those who seek me, when they apprehend him, will give up the search after me.

But if he be executed by the hand of the emperor, very great sorrow will fall upon his children, who left me, and fleeing to Peter, now aid him in his work.'

And now, Peter, I confess the truth to you:

I was prevented by fear of Simon from informing Faustus of this.

But Simon did not give us an opportunity for private conversation, lest some one of us might reveal [56] to him the wicked design of Simon.

Simon then rose up in the middle of the night and fled to Judaea, convoyed by Appion and Athenodorus.

Then I pretended that I was sick, in order that, remaining after they had gone, I might make Faustus go back immediately to his own people, if by any chance he might be able, by being concealed with you, to escape observation, lest, being caught as Simon by those who were in search of Simon, he might be put to death through the wrath of the emperor.

At the dead of night, therefore, I sent him away to you; and in my anxiety for him I came by night to see him, with the intention of returning before those who convoyed Simon should return."

And looking to us, he said:

"I, Annubion, see the true shape of your father; for I was anointed, as I related to you before, by Simon himself, that the true shape of Faustus might be seen by my eyes.

Astonished, therefore, I exceedingly wonder at the magic power of Simon, in that standing [57] you do not recognise your own father."

And while our father and our mother and we ourselves wept on account of the calamity common to all of us, Annubion also through sympathy wept with us.

Chapter XVIII - Peter Promises to Restore to Faustus His Own Shape

Then Peter promised to us to restore the shape of our father, and he said to him:

"Faustus, you heard how matters stand with us.

When, therefore, the deceptive shape which invests you has been useful to us, and you have assisted us in doing what I shall tell you to do, then I shall restore to you your true form, when you have first performed my commands."

And when my father said, "I shall do everything that is in my power most willingly; only restore to my own people my own form;" Peter answered, "You yourself heard with your own ears how those who went before me came back from Antioch, and said that Simon had been there, and had strongly excited the multitudes against me by calling me a magician and a murderer, a deceiver and a juggler, to such an extent that all the people there were eager to taste my flesh.

You will do, then, as I tell you.

You will leave Clement with me, and you will go before us into Antioch with your wife, and your sons Faustinus and Faustinianus.

And some others will accompany you whom I deem capable of helping forward my design.

Chapter XIX - Peter's Instructions to Faustus

"When you are with these in Antioch, while you look like Simon, proclaim publicly your repentance, saying, I Simon proclaim this to you:

I confess [58] that all my statements in regard to Peter are utterly false; [59] for he is not a deceiver, nor a murderer, nor a juggler; nor are any of the evil things true which I, urged on by wrath, said previously in regard to him.

I myself therefore beg of you, I who have been the cause of your hatred to him, cease from hating him; for he is the true apostle of the true Prophet that was sent by God for the salvation of the world.

Wherefore also I counsel you to believe what he preaches; [60] for if you do not, your whole city will be utterly destroyed.

Now I wish you to know for what reason I have made this confession to you.

This night angels of God scourged me, the impious one, terribly, as being an enemy to the herald of the truth.

I beseech you, therefore, do not listen to me, even if I myself should come at another time and attempt to say anything against Peter. For I confess to you I am a magician, I am a deceiver, I am a juggler. Yet perhaps it is possible for me by repentance to wipe out the sins which were formerly committed by me.'"

Chapter XX - Faustus, His Wife, and Sons, Prepare to Go to Antioch

When Peter suggested this, my father said:

"I know what you want; wherefore take no trouble.

For assuredly I shall take good care, when I reach that place, to make such statements in regard to you as I ought to make."

And Peter again suggested:

"When, then, you perceive the city changing from its hatred of me, and longing to see me, send information to me of this, and I shall come to you immediately.

And when I arrive there, that same day I shall remove the strange shape which now invests you, and I shall make your own unmistakeably visible to your own people and to all others."

Saying this, he made his sons, my brothers, and our mother Mattidia to go along with him; and he also commanded some of his more intimate acquaintances to accompany him. But my mother was [61] unwilling to go with him, and said:

"I seem to be an adulteress if I associate with the shape of Simon; but if I shall be compelled to go along with him, [62] it is impossible for me to recline on the same couch with him!

But I do not know if I shall be persuaded to go along with him."

And while she was very unwilling to go, Annubion urged her, saying:

"Believe me and Peter, and the very voice itself, that this is Faustus your husband, whom I love not less than you.

And I myself will go [63] along with him."

When Annubion said this, our mother promised to go with him.

Chapter XXI - Appion and Athenodorus Return in Quest of Faustus

But Peter said:

"God arranges our affairs in a most satisfactory manner; [64] for we have with us Annubion the astrologer. [65] For when we arrive at Antioch, he will in future discourse regarding genesis, giving us his genuine opinions as a friend."

Now when, after midnight, our father hurried with those whom Peter had ordered to go along with him and with Annubion to Antioch, which was near, early next day, before Peter went forth to discourse, Appion and Athenodorus, who had convoyed Simon, returned to Laodicea in search of our father.

But Peter, ascertaining the fact, urged them to enter.

And when they came in and sat down, and said, "Where is Faustus?" Peter answered:

"We know not; for since the evening, when he went to you, he has not been seen by his kinsmen.

But yesterday morning Simon came in search of him; and when we made no reply to him, something seemed to come over him, [66] for he called himself Faustus; but not being believed, he wept and lamented, and threatened to kill himself, and then rushed out in the direction of the sea."

Chapter XXII - Appion and Athenodorus Return to Simon

When Appion and those who were with him heard this, they howled and lamented, saying: "Why did you not receive him?"

And when at the same time Athenodorus wished to say to me, "It was Faustus, your father;" Appion anticipated him, and said, "We learned from some one that Simon, finding him, urged him to go along with him, [67] Faustus himself entreating him, since he did not wish to see his sons after they had become Jews.

And hearing this, we came, for his own sake, in search of him.

But since he is not here, it is plain that he spake the truth who gave us the information which we, hearing it from him, have given to you."

And I Clement, perceiving the design of Peter, that he wished to beget a suspicion in them that he intended to look out among them for the old man, that they might be afraid and take to flight, assisted in his design, and said to Appion:

"Listen to me, my dearest Appion.

We were eager to give to him, as being our father, what we ourselves deemed to be good.

But if he himself did not wish to receive it, but, on the contrary, fled from us in horror, I shall make a somewhat harsh remark, Nor do we care for him.'"

And when I said this, they went away, as if irritated by my savageness; and, as we learn next day, they went to Judaea in the track of Simon.

Chapter XXIII - Peter Goes to Antioch

Now, when ten days had passed away, there came one of our people [68] from our father to announce to us how our father stood forward publicly in the shape of Simon, accusing him; [69] and how by praising Peter he had made the whole city of Antioch long for him:

and in consequence of this, all said that they were eager to see him, and that there were some who were angry with him as being Simon, on account of their surpassing affection for Peter, and wished to lay hands on Faustus, believing he was Simon.

Wherefore he, fearing that he might be put to death, had sent to request Peter to come immediately if he wished to meet him alive, and to appear at the proper time to the city, when it was at the height of its longing for him. [70] Peter, hearing this, called the multitude together to deliberate, and appointed one of his attendants bishop; and having remained three days in Laodicea baptizing and healing, he hastened to the neighboring city of Antioch.

Amen.

Footnotes:

1. [Chaps. 1-10 are also peculiar to the Homilies, though there are incidental resemblances to passages in the Recognitions, particularly in the presentation of free-will.--R.]
2. "Not" is supplied by conjecture.
3. A doubtful emendation of Wieseler's for the senseless tritogenes.
Possibly it may be for protogenes, original, and is underived.
4. An obvious correction of the ms. is adopted.
5. We have changed autos into agathos.
6. [With these views compare the doctrine of pairs, as repeatedly set forth; Homily II. 33, 34; Recognitions, iii. 59, 60, etc.--R.]
7. "One" is supplied by Dressel's conjecture.
8. The words in italics are supplied by Dressel's conjecture.
9. Deut. xxxii. 39.
10. We have adopted an obvious emendation of Wieseler's.
11. We have changed ouses into ou tes.
12. We have given a meaning to metasunkritheis not found in dictionaries, but warranted by etymology, and demanded by the sense.
13. Part of this is supplied by Dressel's conjecture.
14. There is a lacuna, which has been filled up in various ways.
We have supposed hem to be for e m., possibly meteron e.
Wieseler supposes "immature boys."
15. Dressel translates, "drawing judgment on himself."
16. An emendation of Wieseler's.
17. An emendation of Wieseler's.
18. emphutou.
19. We have changed toiouton into toiauten.
20. Ex. iv. 3, 4.
21. Ex. vii. 19, 20.
22. Gen. ii. 7.
23. Eccles. iii. 20.
24. Ex. xxxiv. 29.
25. One word of this is supplied conjecturally by Dressel.
26. Gen. vi. 2.
[Comp. Ps. civ. 4.]
27. Part of this is conjectural.
28. Gen. xviii. 4.
29. Gen. xxxii. 24.

30. We have adopted Wieseler's emendation of me into men.
31. This passage is corrupt.
We have changed hoti into ho, ti, and supplied trepei.
32. Dressel remarks that this cannot be the true reading.
Some other name mentioned in Hom. II. c. 1 must be substituted here or in c. 4.
33. This passage is corrupt.
We have adopted Wieseler's emendations for the most part.
34. We have read tes with Wieseler for tis.
35. Wieseler translates "accidentally."
36. We have changed ouch hos echon into houtos echein.
37. Matt. xxv. 41.
38. We have adopted an emendation of Wieseler's.
39. Wieseler's emendation.
40. We have changed agathos into agathois.
41. An emendation of Weiseler's.
42. Ex. vii. 9.
43. [Chaps. 11-22 are almost identical with Recognitions, x. 52-64. But the conclusion of that narrative is fuller, giving prominence to the re-united family; comp. also chap. 23 here.--R.]
44. There are some blanks here, supplied from the Epitome.
45. Supplied from Epitome.
The passage in Epitome Second renders it likely that the sentence ran:
"But Simon, while doing many miracles publicly in Antioch, did nothing else by his discourses than excite hatred amongst them against you, and by calling you," etc.
46. This passage is amended principally according to Wieseler and the Recognitions.
47. An emendation of Wieseler's.
48. Inserted by conjecture.
49. Part of this is supplied from the Recognitions.
50. Inserted from the Recognitions.
51. These words are taken from the Recognitions.
52. An emendation of Dressel's.
53. Supplied by Dressel from the Recognitions.
54. An emendation of Wieseler's.
55. ms. reads "empty."
Wieseler proposed "new" or "assumed."
56. An emendation of Wieseler's.
The parts in italics are supplied by conjecture.
57. We should have expected "standing near" or something similar, as Weiseler remarks; but the Latin of the Recognitions agrees with the Greek in having the simple "standing."
58. Amended according to Epitome.
59. Partly filled up from Epitome and Recognitions.
60. ms. reads, "I preach."
61. We have changed eide into eike, and added kai eipe, according to the Recognitions.
62. One word, tuches, is superfluous.
63. Supplied from the Recognitions.
64. We read epitedeiotata, in harmony with the Recognitions.
65. Part in italics supplied from Recognitions.
66. The Greek is probably corrupt here; but there can scarcely be a doubt about the meaning.
67. This is supplied purely by conjecture.
68. Supplied from the Recognitions.
69. This part is restored by means of the Recognitions.
70. [The narrative in the Recognitions (x. 65) is the same up to this point.

But, instead of this somewhat abrupt conclusion of this chapter, we find there several chapters (from the close of chap. 65 to the end, chap. 72), which round out the story:

the confession of the father in his metamorphosis, his restoration, the Apostle's entry into Antioch, his miracles there, with the happy re-union of the entire family of Clement as believers.

It should be added, as indicating the close relation of the two narratives, that the closing sentence of the Homilies is found, with slight variations, in Recognitions, x. 18.--R.]

www.ingramcontent.com/pod-product-compliance
Lightning Source LLC
Chambersburg PA
CBHW020118240426
43673CB00038B/519